# About This Book

## Why is this topic important?

Organization development (OD) is about planned change. As change has turned into the only constant, many managers and other people are pursuing change strategies with vigor. OD is a major strategy with a process for leading and managing change at the individual, group, intergroup, organizational, inter-organizational, and large systems levels. This book is about what it takes to be an effective change manager, change leader, and OD practitioner.

## What can you achieve with this book?

Simply stated, this book provides everything you need to think through on how to function as a competent OD professional.

## How is this book organized?

The book is organized into five parts. Part One consists of Chapters One through Seven and is entitled "Foundations." It includes information on key terms and definitions, models, origins of OD, practitioner competencies, mindful leadership, and post-modern OD: Appreciative Inquiry. Part Two consists of Chapters Eight through Twelve and is entitled "OD Process to Guide Change." This section covers marketing, pre-launch, launch, implementation, evaluation, and separation. Part Three consists of Chapters Thirteen through Eighteen and is entitled "Levels and Types of Change." In it we discuss the issue of organization culture and interventions across various levels: individual, team, large systems, whole system, and inter-level. Part Four addresses "Special Issues in OD": global OD, positive states of organizing, sustainability, organization design, mergers and acquisitions, values, ethics, human systems dynamics, technology, transformational learning journeys, strategic change and fitness, HR-OD audits, Gestalt theory and approach, whole system transformation, and other issues.

The book concludes with Part Five: "The Future of Organization Development," with insights from our contributors, the movement toward dialogic OD, and the role of the OD practitioner. The book's website offers a variety of supplementary information, including a self-assessment tool for OD competencies, reproducible slides, podcasts, articles to support chapters, syllabi, and resource lists.

# About Pfeiffer

Pfeiffer serves the professional development and hands-on resource needs of training and human resource practitioners and gives them products to do their jobs better. We deliver proven ideas and solutions from experts in HR development and HR management, and we offer effective and customizable tools to improve workplace performance. From novice to seasoned professional, Pfeiffer is the source you can trust to make yourself and your organization more successful.

**Essential Knowledge** Pfeiffer produces insightful, practical, and comprehensive materials on topics that matter the most to training and HR professionals. Our Essential Knowledge resources translate the expertise of seasoned professionals into practical, how-to guidance on critical workplace issues and problems. These resources are supported by case studies, worksheets, and job aids and are frequently supplemented with CD-ROMs, websites, and other means of making the content easier to read, understand, and use.

**Essential Tools** Pfeiffer's Essential Tools resources save time and expense by offering proven, ready-to-use materials—including exercises, activities, games, instruments, and assessments—for use during a training or team-learning event. These resources are frequently offered in looseleaf or CD-ROM format to facilitate copying and customization of the material.

Pfeiffer also recognizes the remarkable power of new technologies in expanding the reach and effectiveness of training. While e-hype has often created whizbang solutions in search of a problem, we are dedicated to bringing convenience and enhancements to proven training solutions. All our e-tools comply with rigorous functionality standards. The most appropriate technology wrapped around essential content yields the perfect solution for today's on-the-go trainers and human resource professionals.

**Pfeiffer**
www.pfeiffer.com

*Essential resources for training and HR professionals*

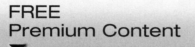

**FREE**
Premium Content

Pfeiffer®
An Imprint of
 **WILEY**

This book includes premium content that can be accessed from our Web site when you register at **www.pfeiffer.com/go/practiceod** using the password *professional*.

# Practicing Organization Development

## A Guide for Leading Change

*A Third Edition*

Edited by
William J. Rothwell
Jacqueline M. Stavros
Roland L. Sullivan
Arielle Sullivan

**Pfeiffer**

A Wiley Imprint
www.pfeiffer.com

Published by Pfeiffer
An Imprint of Wiley
989 Market Street, San Francisco, CA 94103-1741
www.pfeiffer.com

For additional copies/bulk purchases of this book in the U.S. please contact 800-274-4434.

Pfeiffer books and products are available through most bookstores.To contact Pfeiffer directly call our Customer Care Department within the U.S. at 800-274-4434, outside the U.S. at 317-572-3985, fax 317-572-4002, or visit www.pfeiffer.com.

Pfeiffer also publishes its books in a variety of electronic formats. Some content that appears in print may not be available in electronic books.

**Library of Congress Cataloging-in-Publication Data**
Practicing organization development: a guide for leading change / edited by
William J. Rothwell ... [et al.]. — 3rd ed.
p.   cm.
Includes bibliographical references and index.
Summary: "Completely revised, this new edition of the classic book offers contributions from experts in the field (Warner Burke, Chris Worley, David Jamieson, Kim Cameron, Michael Beer, Edgar Schein, Gibb Dyer, and) and provides a road map through each episode of change facilitation. This updated edition features new chapters on positive change, leadership transformation, sustainability, and globalization. In addition, it includes exhibits, activities, instruments, and case studies, as well as an instructor's guide and supplemental materials on accompanying Website. This resource is written for OD practitioners, consultants, and scholars"—Provided by publisher.
ISBN 978-0-470-40544-4 (hardback)
1. Organizational change—Management.   2. Business consultants—Handbooks, manuals, etc.
I. Rothwell, William J.
HD58.8.P7 2010
658.4'063—dc22
2009027721

Acquiring Editor: Matthew Davis
Director of Development: Kathleen Dolan Davies
Production Editor: Dawn Kilgore
Editor: Rebecca Taff

Editorial Assistant: Lindsay Morton
Manufacturing Supervisor: Becky Morgan

Printed in the United States of America
Printing    10 9 8 7 6 5 4 3 2

# CONTENTS

# LIST OF FIGURES, TABLES,
# AND EXHIBITS

**Figures**

# ACKNOWLEDGMENTS

No book is the product of its author(s) or editor(s) alone. This book is no different. Creating a Third Edition takes a great deal of time, effort, and depth of conversations with many people. Accordingly, we would especially like to thank the editorial, design, and production team at Pfeiffer for their support of this project, especially Matt Davis and Lindsay Morton, who are always available to provide direction and answer our questions. We also enjoyed working again with Dawn Kilgore, our stalwart production editor, on this edition, and Rebecca Taff.

We are tremendously grateful and want to thank the participating authors for their willingness to write their chapters and respond to our repeated demands for revisions, proper citations, and references. The array of authors provides a wealth of history, present moments, and future possibilities of OD since the 1950s. It has been a privilege to work with them! Thank you to Lou Carter, who has made many contributions to the field of OD and took the time to write the Foreword for the Third Edition, capturing the growth, success, and challenges of the field. However, we must accept ultimate responsibility for any mistakes or misstatements made in this edition because we read all the chapters and revised them so as to maintain consistent writing styles.

We acknowledge the helpful insights and feedback from the DBA students at Lawrence Technological University's College of Management. A special thank you to family and friends who provided back-up reviews and edits to our chapter reviews as the deadline came to a close. These include Stan Baran, Marji

Czajka, Ed Kimball, Jane Seiling, and Paul Stavros. We would also like to give special thanks to Ally Stavros, who provided devoted assistance to double-checking citations and references for each chapter.

And we thank our families and friends for their support and patience during the long writing and editing hours.

William J. Rothwell
Jacqueline M. Stavros
Roland L. Sullivan
Arielle Sullivan

# FOREWORD

## OD: CREATING A CULTURE OF "BELONGING" TO DRIVE BUSINESS RESULTS

Since 1998, Best Practice Institute has released its best practice organization development (OD) programs highlighting the most admired and innovative companies around the world. Topping the 2009 best practice leaders are the global brands, Microsoft, Starbucks, Corning, all globally recognized leaders in their respective industries. These titans of the workplace represent organizations whose employees report high levels of job satisfaction, are convinced of their management's credibility, and enjoy strong ties to their companies' culture, vision, and operating philosophy. Prominent OD theorist and author Edgar Schein describes organization culture, such as that exemplified by HP, as:

> "A pattern of shared basic assumptions that the group learned as it solved its problems of external adaptation and internal integration that has worked well enough to be considered valid and therefore, to be taught to new members as the correct way to perceive, think, and feel in relation to those problems." (Schein, *Organizational Culture and Leadership*, pp. 373–374)

What is clear upon creating these books from any given year is that the companies profiled have demonstrated their ability to attract, motivate, engage, and retain high-quality employees, not only by offering many sought-after benefits such as complete healthcare packages or child care services, but also by developing and sustaining a corporate culture of "belonging." In other words, these companies have created a strong sense of community and loyalty among their workforce that extends to their business and community partners, their customers, and their shareholders. Employees are partners with their companies, are invested in their companies' ongoing success, and are empowered to be innovative and forward-thinking. Furthermore, the companies' enthusiasm and dedication are recognized by potential stakeholders who desire to partner with thriving companies.

Today's business leaders who seek to advance their own corporations, business divisions, or individual teams can take a page from the business initiatives of the world's pioneering companies. A defining factor in the accomplishments of these companies is the focus on *development*, the ongoing process of innovation and improvement whether it be a product, a process, a policy, or a person. Today's business strategists must be mindful not just of product growth, but of the importance of planned, careful organization development (OD) and change. While the concept of OD is not new, it has become even more important in today's globalized, competitive environment as organizations must adapt quickly to evolving marketplace pressures, streamline global supply chain processes, adopt technological advances, and compete for the best and brightest talent. Yet, many business executives still do not take full advantage of OD in meeting these business demands. By understanding the foundation, theories, and practices of successful OD, internal and external business consultants can help their companies identify avenues for organizational culture transformation; this planned process ultimately results in the very successes identified by the employees, partners, and customers of Best Practice Institute's best practice organizations.

In exploring various models of OD and frameworks for effecting improved organizational performance, *Practicing Organization Development: A Guide for Leading Change* has been a strategic resource for business leaders, HR professionals, process consultants, trainers, and researchers since the first edition was first published in 1995. The new, third edition of the book continues in this tradition and also provides insight into exciting new voices and research within the field of OD and change including:

- Creating an organizational culture of "belonging,"
- Leadership development and transformation,
- Competency work and individual development, and
- Multi-level and global strategic change.

Similarly, the third edition includes a comprehensive consideration of practical applications and special issues such as:

- Culture change that drives business change,
- Triple bottom-line sustainability (as it relates to people, planet, and profits),
- Globalization,
- Technological innovation and OD,
- Positive states of organizing, and
- Building an inclusive mindset.

The enduring popularity of *Practicing Organization Development* among OD practitioners and scholars is owing to its reach beyond the typical business casebook; it is designed from proven OD theories and practical application as well as focused on current and future challenges and implications of the OD field. Over sixty internationally recognized OD professionals and scholars have contributed their knowledge and expertise to the third edition. The third edition signals a period of tremendous growth in the theories, applications, and disseminations of OD throughout the world from critical research and action research to positive change theory and Appreciative Inquiry.

I would like to take this opportunity to recognize the editors' visionary contributions to amass in one book the best and most complete and practical set of materials for anyone wanting to learn more about OD and how to lead change. The book remains the basic primer for OD, "what is it," "how to do it," "what to do," and "why to do it" and for using OD theories and methods. This edition contains more contributions and applications with meaningful and measurable impacts, more evidence of positive impacts of transformational change, and new insights. The resources brought forth in this book is a rich companion to anyone engaged or wanting to become engaged in OD. I expect that, no matter what your experience in OD, you will want to reference this book again and again.

Today, the success of these organizations is not simply measured by profits and stock prices, but also by company culture, employee satisfaction and retention, employee empowerment, systems productivity, sustainability, and social responsibility. OD plays a critical role in this success by bringing companies forward and effecting positive change from the single individual to whole-systems transformation. The inclusion of case studies from for-profit, non-profit, and government cases to medium-sized organizations to Best Practice Institute's fifty companies demonstrates a whole system organizational culture transformation in *Practicing Organization Development* that further demonstrates the editors' and contributors' pragmatic approaches to effective, *authentic* OD.

As the praxis of OD matures, so does our understanding of the theoretical underpinnings that remain valid and the new ones that provide change for the field itself. In return, this book provides confidence for the OD practitioners to work in organizations to make them healthy and effective. The editors have assembled a wide range of views for you. They bring their wisdom, contacts, and extensive experience of the first, second, third, and emerging fourth generation of OD. They have carefully selected contributors to bring historical, current, and future perspectives on the state of OD.

The array of contributors provides a dialogue over the past sixty-five years through the multiple generations of OD. With this resource, you can work with your organizations to create systemic approaches to whole system planned change that truly leave the organization stronger and healthier to embrace and anticipate the future. As the future unfolds in our global complex environment, the focus of OD is on human values and potential in organizational life.

I wish you great health, strength, and courage as you continue your practice in organization development.

Louis Carter
Founder and CEO
Best Practice Institute
North Palm Beach, Florida
September 2009

# Introduction

*Getting the Most from This Resource*

William J. Rothwell, Jacqueline M. Stavros, and Roland L. Sullivan

The organizational mantra over the last decade has been change. Change will continue to be a major dynamic in organization life. Changes occur in our lives and organizations every day. Organizations are started, and some evolve while others dissolve. Some undergo mergers, takeovers, or buyouts; some thrive while others go bankrupt. Changes in the economy or corporate ownership may result in corporate rightsizing, downsizing, early retirement offers, or various other staffing alterations. Corporations that were traditionally considered dominant within their industry have shrunk or disappeared. The march toward globalization, innovation, ethics, and sustainability has accelerated.

Given the challenges that organizations are now facing, what are they doing to ensure success? Some organizations are ignoring the change and are facing extinction. Some organizations are imposing more controls and are becoming more bureaucratic while others are becoming more entrepreneurial. Many organizations are responding to the change in only operational or tactical ways. These organizations are answering the "call of the changing world" with such approaches as new and streamlined processes, new procedures, reducing headcount, virtual integration, and other new ways of running their business. Some methods have been shown to produce short-term results. However, the theme that runs through all of these responses is their focus on new ways of performing the organization's daily operations—a new twist on an old way of doing things.

To cope with change, organizations and their leaders need to take innovative strategic paths by applying organization development (OD) and change efforts. Results can be more healthy, vibrant, productive, and high performance workplaces. New theories, methods, technologies, and approaches must be designed specifically to prepare for the changing future, ranging from engaging multiple classes of stakeholders to strengths-based, whole system approaches to OD. To make the leap, we need to change the way we think, plan, implement, and evaluate OD.

*Practicing Organization Development: A Guide for Leading Change* (3rd ed.) is about facilitating these and other organizational changes. This book is not about just any type of organizational change; rather, it focuses on planned, systemic, and educationally oriented change that is carried out for organization improvement. The book is about the power and possibilities of OD. Organization development is defined as "a process that applies a broad range of behavioral science knowledge and practices to help organizations build their capacity to change and to achieve greater effectiveness, including increased financial performance, customer satisfaction, and organization member engagement" (Cummings & Worley, 2009, p. 1).

Although the book addresses organizational change, many principles described also apply to change efforts with individuals, with teams, or across organizations and industries.

## THE AUDIENCE FOR THE BOOK

*Practicing Organization Development: A Guide for Leading Change* (3rd ed.) was written for existing and new OD practitioners and scholars and line managers who wish to broaden their understanding of OD and stay current with leading knowledge of the profession. Those who are new to the field will find the entire book useful from the foundations to the applications. Those experienced business leaders, practitioners, and scholars will find the book as a most comprehensive organization change resource compendium.

At the broadest level, this book is designed for those interested in planned change and unplanned change. This is evidenced by the increase in memberships by national and local OD networks, the expansion of the Appreciative Inquiry and positive organizational scholarship communities, the Academy of Management divisions on OD and Change, Strategy, and Social Issues in Management, and the expanding Asian OD networks. This book has several intended audiences: internal and external OD consultants, workplace learning and performance professionals, human resource generalists, and managers and executives.

The primary audience is OD professionals. OD professionals usually work as consultants, either external or internal within organizations to guide, facilitate, and support change. OD consultants come in two levels of skill and experience:

*practitioners* and *master practitioners*. This book is geared to practitioners, those who are already carrying out the role of change agent but need more formal grounding in OD theory and practice. They include students enrolled in courses on OD, organizational behavior, or organization change courses and programs. Master practitioners will also find this book valuable as a guide to OD literature, new theories and applications, and as a resource to help them orient, train, and mentor other OD consultants.

Our second audience includes human resource (HR) generalists and work-place learning and performance (WLP) practitioners, previously called human resource development (HRD) practitioners. Some WLP practitioners specifically train employees. They devote their attention largely to increasing employees' job knowledge and to improving individual performance in organizational settings. But many WLP practitioners go beyond training to ensure that identified training needs take organization and work-group cultures into account. In addition, results-oriented WLP practitioners are aware that individual performance improvement can only occur when the surrounding work environment supports it. The theory and practice of changing organization and work-group cultures are OD topics. To do their jobs and achieve results, WLP practitioners often apply competencies associated with OD.

Our third audience consists of managers, executives, management consultants, social entrepreneurs, and leaders who are looking for ways to transform whole organizations and communities to thrive in the 21st Century. In today's dynamic business environment, they must know how to introduce and consolidate change successfully if they are to realize their visions for organizational improvement. Executives or managers who lack competence in change theory will have trouble seeing their visions realized.

## THE PURPOSE AND OBJECTIVES OF THE BOOK

The purpose of *Practicing Organization Development: A Guide for Leading Change* (3rd ed.) is to build the readers' competencies in assessing the need for change, managing change, and facilitating the implementation of change in organization settings. After finishing this book, the reader should be able to do the following:

1. Define OD and how to do it;
2. Define a model of planned change, its key steps, and explain how it is related to OD;
3. Describe and apply the competencies needed to conduct planned change;
4. Understand the levels of change and various approaches to change at each level;

5. Facilitate the contracting of an external OD consultant/practitioner and work successfully with that person—if the need exists;

6. Define intervention as it is used in the OD field and describe typical OD interventions; and

7. Understand the impact of special issues to OD like globalization, technology, sustainability, whole system approaches, transformation, complex adaptive systems, mergers and acquisitions, values, ethics, and human systems dynamics.

This handbook supports the ongoing development of practitioners and consultants with its coverage of the foundations, key theories, concepts, methodologies, models, and applications as they apply to individuals, teams, organizations, and industries. The book has been designed so that each major section and chapter can stand alone and can also serve as a reference to other chapters.

# WHAT'S NEW IN THE THIRD EDITION

The convergence of OD and change is more prevalent today than it ever has been before given the changes in our global world. The *Practicing Organization Development: A Guide for Leading Change* (3rd ed.) expands and dramatically updates the second edition to reflect the current and future states of the field of OD and change. The third edition is the most comprehensive OD and change roadmap. It provides the essentials: foundations and principles, OD phases, current state and future challenges and implications of the OD field with the latest and most widely used models, frameworks, strategies, and methods to improve human and organization health and performance.

Readers will note unique similarities and differences between the second and third editions of this book. The editions are similar in that both share the foundations and phases of planned change in OD. The third edition is different in that it has been wholly rewritten and updated from the previous authors from the second edition—to the extent that the first and second editions may be properly regarded as entirely separate books.

The third edition includes twenty-four *new* chapters and thirty-eight *new* contributors who share their theory and practices of OD as it relates to whole system, strengths-based and positive change methods, sustainability, and the importance of practicing OD at five levels: individual, organizational, inter-organizational, trans-organizational, and global. For example, our returning contributors were asked for updated chapters, and all of our contributors were asked to consider how human, economic, and environmental capital impacts OD theory and practice.

These new chapters demonstrate and document the versatility and extension of the latest contributions to the field on how OD connects to other areas such as human resource development, mergers and acquisitions, organization design, globalization, technology, and strategic change. For OD to stay current and relevant, this growth and development must continue and that is why there will be an accompanying website to support the book.

The book's website (www.pfeiffer.com/go/williamrothwell) contains the following:

- PowerPoint and media presentations;
- Sample syllabi for an introduction to OD course;
- Supplemental materials from authors that can be used in preparing lectures and workshops;
- Various OD competency lists;
- Podcasts and videos supporting the materials in the book;
- Interviews from the founders and elders of the OD field;
- Additional papers, articles, and cutting-edge OD presentations;
- OD and change websites;
- Poetry and creative media supporting change efforts; and
- Archives of significant chapters and studies from the earlier editions of *Practicing Organization Development.*

This website will be updated periodically. We invite your submission to be included. Please send to Arielle@sullivantransformationagents.com.

Based on the contributions in this third edition, we have come to realize that OD has been transitioning from being primarily focused on "organizations" to more inclusive of how the "human systems" impact the organization as a whole. Over the last several years, communication on OD and change-related listservs and articles in leading OD journals are moving in this direction. One of our contributors, Bill Gellerman, sees another focus that "Our OD profession has the potential to leverage change in our more inclusive systems on such issues as coping with climate change crisis, the financial crisis, and the contracting global economy" (personal communication, June 6, 2008).

## THEORETICAL FOUNDATION OF THE BOOK

This book is based on OD practitioners' and scholars' research activities, including those consultants functioning as internal or external OD change agents or organizational leaders applying OD theories, methods, and tools. The current research results appear on the Organization Development Network (ODN) website. Earlier drafts of this research study on the competencies of OD consultants appeared as early as 1990 in *OD Practitioner* (McLean & Sullivan, 1990) and, even before that, in an earlier draft of "Essential Competencies of Internal and External OD Consultants."

"The Essential Competencies" were developed from an attempt to combine previous efforts to describe what change agents do as they diagnose the need for change and participate in planned-change efforts. A *competency* is defined as any "personal quality" that contributes to the successful practice of OD. As such it includes who one is (*being*), from what theory one acts (*knowing*), and how one performs (*doing*). The concept of Be-Know-Do is further explored in Chapter Thirty-Seven. In this new edition, in Chapter Six, there is a process of how to self-assess one's leadership style and competencies to effectively plan and lead change.

Roland Sullivan started the study in the mid-1970s with a review of OD literature. It has been updated annually, based on continuing literature reviews. It has been repeatedly scrutinized in feedback sessions held at Pepperdine University, Malibu, California; the Southern Minnesota Chapter and Region 6 Conference of the American Society for Training and Development (ASTD); the Minnesota OD Network; the OD Interorganization Group Worldwide in Austria; the Asian OD Network; and annual Organization Development Institute (ODI) conferences. In 1988 a committee of twenty top OD consultants examined the study under the auspices of ODI. Since then, it has been revisited countless times and in settings all over the world.

*Practicing Organization Development: A Guide for Leading Change* (3rd ed.) takes up where competency studies on OD leave off. The book emphasizes practice in several senses. As Kinnunen (1992, p. 6) points out, *to practice* can mean any or all of the following:

- To do frequently or by force of habit;
- To use knowledge and skill in a profession or occupation;
- To adhere to a set of beliefs or ideals;
- To do repeatedly to become proficient; and
- To drill in order to give proficiency.

The various meanings of practice listed above apply to the editors' intentions in assembling this book: to emphasize the need for development as a practitioner through a focus on the knowledge and skills—and the beliefs and ideals—that are important to be proficient in the practice of OD. This book explains the competencies described, in abbreviated form, in OD competency studies in Chapter Five. As you will see, "competence" in this book is imbued with a deep connection to the human endeavor involved in both personal and organization change. Thus, we must first understand what we mean by *competency* with respect to the effectiveness of OD practitioners. As noted by Worley, Rothwell, and Sullivan in Chapter Five:

> "A competency refers to—according to an often-cited definition—'an underlying characteristic of an employee (that is, motive, trait, skill, aspects of one's self-image, social role, or a body of knowledge) which results in effective and/or superior performance in a job' (Boyatzis, 1982, pp. 20–21). A competency is thus associated with an individual's characteristics in performing work and includes *anything* that leads to successful performance and results.... In short, *competencies of people doing certain kind of work*" (p. 136; italics in text).

All five sections of this book emphasize competence and the development of your own competencies and the characteristics that define successful performance of the practitioner: "who one needs to be, what one needs to know, and what one must be capable of doing." Your devotion to reading the following chapters will be rewarded with this information.

# THE STRUCTURE OF THE BOOK

*Practicing Organization Development: A Guide for Leading Change* (3rd ed.) brings together a rich collection of theories, concepts, models, case applications, innovations, and historical and post-modern expansions in OD and change. This book is structured in five parts:

- Part One (Chapters One through Seven), "Foundations," provides essential background information about OD, planned change, convergence of HR and OD, OD competencies, mindful leadership development, and Appreciative Inquiry (post-modern OD).
- Part Two (Chapters Eight through Twelve), "OD Process to Guide Change," includes five chapters that focus on the OD process. Chapters in Part Two address marketing, contracting, pre-launch (front-end work), assessment, planning, launch, implementation, evaluation, and separation (closure).
- Part Three (Chapters Thirteen through Eighteen), "Levels and Types of Change," starts with culture of change and covers different levels of change interventions from individual, team, and organization to whole system and strengths-based interventions in large-scale and strategic change.
- Part Four (Chapters Nineteen through Thirty-Nine), "Special Issues in OD," has been dramatically expanded in this edition on issues directly related to OD such as positive states of organizing, sustainability, global OD, employee engagement and retention, organization design, mergers

and acquisitions, culture, human systems dynamics, complexity science, complex adaptive systems, technology, personal and organization transformation, Gestalt theory and approach, values and ethics, technology and virtual connectivity, transformational change and learning, strategic fit, HR-OD audit, success rates, and the unique challenges facing internal OD practitioners. This section ends with a whole system transformation case study and a thoughtful interview with OD founder Edith Seashore on how to build a transformative OD practice. In this chapter, Ms. Seashore reflects on the times in which we have practiced and lived OD.

- Part Five, "The Future of Organization Development," explores future perspectives in the field and includes a survey completed by our contributors. The results represent an excellent cross-section of scholars and practitioners in the field. This part addresses three critical questions: How relevant is OD for today's organizations? What is the purpose of OD? What are the major challenges facing OD?

Change is constant and fundamental to human systems at all levels from cellular to global. By learning to anticipate and plan for change, you can strategically build strong, flexible, capable, and healthy people and organizations that perform in humane, sustainable, and profitable ways to achieve ethical, moral, value-laden success, both from a financial standpoint and other standpoints. More than any other time in history, our organizations must be able to have the capability to master enterprise-wide ongoing change. Indeed, this book provides the conceptual frameworks and approaches to help our organization leaders and members become agents of change.

# References

Boyatzis, A.R. (1982). *The competent manager: A model for effective performance.* Hoboken, NJ: John Wiley & Sons.

Cummings, T.G., & Worley, C.G. (2009). *Organization development and change* (9th ed.). Cincinnati, OH: South-Western.

Kinnunen, G. (1992, November). The practice of practice. *NSPI Insight,* p. 6.

McLean, G., & Sullivan, R. (1990). OD skills: An ongoing competency list. *OD Practitioner, 22*(2), 11–12.

# PART ONE

# FOUNDATIONS

# CHAPTER ONE

# Organization Development and Change

William J. Rothwell, Jacqueline M. Stavros, and Roland L. Sullivan

What are organization development (OD) and change management (CM)? Why should you care about them? What are some key terms used in OD and CM? What is systems thinking and why is it important to OD practitioners? How is OD related to other HR fields? How does OD relate to globalization? What is global OD? This first chapter addresses these and related questions.

## WHAT ARE ORGANIZATION DEVELOPMENT AND CHANGE MANAGEMENT?

Organization development (OD) and change management (CM) help people in organizations identify and plan how to deal with changes—intentional and unintentional—in their environment. Before we define them more precisely, try the following exercise. Get some paper and record your answers to the following questions. Write down the first thing that comes to your mind in response to each question:

1. *Who* should be involved in an organization change effort, and how should they be involved?

2. *Who* should make decisions about the way in which a change effort of any kind is launched? Implemented on a continual basis? Evaluated?

3. *What* do you believe about change in the world generally?

4. *What* do you believe about change in today's organizations?

5. *What* do you believe are the biggest challenges facing decision-makers in organization change efforts?

6. *What* do you believe are your strengths and developmental needs in enacting the role of "helper to others" in a change effort? What do you do especially well? What do you wish to personally develop to become a more effective change agent? On what basis do you believe as you do?

7. *When* do you believe that a group of people might need an external facilitator in a change effort?

8. *Where* do you believe are the most profound changes occurring in the world, and why do you think as you do?

9. *Why* should OD and change be a focus for managers? Other groups?

10. *How* should change be defined? Marketed? Launched? Implemented? Evaluated?

11. *How* have you reacted in the past to change in an organization in which you have been employed or to which you have been a consultant? Think about what you did and how you felt as the change occurred.

12. *What* are some common examples of organization change in organizations? Reflect on what they are. Consider such interventions as team building, implementing technological change, succession planning, culture development, aligning management, enterprise-wide change, mergers and acquisitions, and structural reorganizations.

Now identify a few professional peers or colleagues—or find some mentors whom you believe to be more experienced than you are—and pose these questions to them. Use this activity as a "warm-up exercise" to focus your thinking about OD and change. When you finish, continue reading because many of your answers will most likely *change*.

## Organization Development Defined

According to Clardy (2003, p. 785):

"The field of planned organization change was long equated with organization development (OD). OD proponents were up-front with the bona fides of their approach: full disclosure, informed consent, inclusive participation, and so on. These canons of OD provided the principles and practices that could be applied to any organizational change project. Yet, for a number of years, standing alongside the OD literature were smaller volumes (Zaltman & Duncan, 1977) that did not so neatly fit the OD mold. By these accounts, the geography of organizational change management was bigger than that encompassed by OD."

While some might disagree with the assertions in the preceding paragraph, those assertions are effective in helping readers to clarify their beliefs about the field of OD and to recognize that there are multiple ways of defining the field.

Over the years, OD has been defined and redefined by just about every author who has written about it. Here are a few definitions, organized chronologically, that represent a range of ways to understand OD:

- Organization development is "an effort (1) planned, (2) organization-wide, and (3) managed from the top, to (4) increase organization effectiveness and health through (5) planned interventions in the organization's "processes," using behavioral-science knowledge" (Beckhard, 1969, p. 9).

- Organization development is "a response to change, a complex educational strategy intended to change the beliefs, attitudes, values, and structure of organizations so that they can better adapt to new technologies, markets, and challenges, and the dizzying rate of change itself" (Bennis, 1969, p. 2).

- Most people in the field agree that "OD involves consultants who work to help clients improve their organizations by applying knowledge from the behavioral sciences—psychology, sociology, cultural anthropology, and other related disciplines. Most would also agree that OD implies change and, if we accept that shifts in the way an organization functions suggests that change has occurred, then, broadly defined, OD is analogous to organizational change" (Burke, 1982, p. 3).

- Organization development is "a systemic and systematic change effort, using behavioral science knowledge and skill, to change or transform the organization to a new state" (Beckhard, 1999, personal communication).

- Organization development is "a process that applied a broad range of behavioral science knowledge and practices to help organizations build their capacity to change and to achieve greater effectiveness, including increased financial performance, customer satisfaction, and organization member engagement" (Cummings & Worley, 2009, p. 1).

These definitions imply several key points:

First, *OD is long-range in perspective.* It is not a "quick-fix" strategy for solving short-term performance issues, as employee training is often inappropriately perceived to be. Many managers are becoming acutely aware of the need to move beyond quick and often unworkable solutions for complex organizational problems. Organization development is a means to bring about complex, deep, and lasting change. This may include *any* domain in the organization that is in need of discovering ways to improve performance. Traditional OD asserts a need for patience and a long-term effort in order to achieve deep and significant change. In many organizations OD is coupled with strategic business planning, a natural fit because both can be long-range in scope. For more information on OD and strategy, see Chapters Sixteen and Eighteen.

Second, *OD works best when it is supported by top managers.* They are traditionally the chief power brokers and change agents in any organization; top managers often control an organization's resources and reward systems. Although OD efforts can be undertaken at any organizational level without direct top-management participation, OD is more likely to succeed if it has at least tacit approval from top management.

Third, *OD effects change primarily, although not exclusively, through education.* Organization development expands people's ideas, beliefs, and behaviors so that they can apply new approaches to old states of existence. Even more important, OD change efforts go beyond employee-training efforts and concentrate on the work group or organization in which new ideas, beliefs, or behaviors are to be applied. Organization development has often been synonymous with organization learning (Argyris, 1993, 2004; Bennis, 1969; Kanter, 1995; Lippitt, 1958; Senge, 1990; Vail, 1996). Peter Senge (1990, p. 13) says, "A learning organization is a place where people are continually discovering how they create reality and how they can change it. Organization-wide learning involves change in culture and change in the most basic managerial practices, not just within a company, but within a whole system's management.... I guarantee that when you start to create a learning environment, people will not feel as though they are in control."

The words *change* and *learning* are often used to mean the same thing. Consider, for example, the title of a classic book, *The Laboratory Method of Learning and Changing,* by OD founders Benne, Bradford, Gibb, and Lippitt (1975). Many of these early leaders of the field were innovative educators. Many OD founders were leading educators. They saw that one of OD's major goals was to innovate and re-invent education. It is important to remember that learning is broader than education, and learning occurs outside classroom settings. For instance, how a manager or consultant models behavior provides an important learning lesson for others, who may be inclined to imitate how their leaders behave.

Fourth, another OD effort that is interrelated to organization learning is *knowledge management* (KM). KM focuses on organization learning as it transforms to elicit tacit knowledge and new knowledge that can be organized and used to improve performance (Cummings & Worley, 2009). Many case studies on KM as it relates to OD are available in *Harvard Business Review* and the Society for Organizational Learning (SOL: www.solonline.org).

Fifth, *OD emphasizes employee participation in assessing the current state and in planning for a positive future state; making free and collaborative choices on how implementation should proceed; and, empowering the system to take responsibility for creating and evaluating results.* In this sense, OD differs from other methods that hold managers or consultants responsible for the success or failure of a change effort. In OD, at its best, the entire system is accountable rather than just management. Further, in OD, everyone in an organization who is affected by change should have an opportunity to contribute to—and accept responsibility for—the change. Organizational effectiveness and humanistic values meet as employee ownership of processes and outcomes increases. Although early OD contributors did not focus on business effectiveness, it has become equally important in OD ideology over the past decade (Gottlieb, 1998).

## What Organization Development Is Not

OD is not a toolkit filled with canned tricks, piecemeal programs, gimmicks, and techniques. Rosabeth Moss Kanter said, "Piecemeal programs are not enough. Only total transformation will help companies and people master change" (1995, p. 83).

Consultants reduce their chances for success if they rely on cookbook approaches to change. One size does not fit all. One approach to change, as listed in a step-by-step model, does not work with all groups, corporate cultures, national cultures, or people, unless the "approach" is designed for guidance, is understood to be flexible, and is subject to adaptation to the needs of the group and the culture in which the intervention is being used.

OD is not a mechanical rote application of someone else's best practice. On the contrary, it uses one's whole self, encountering the full and quantum living system. Living systems are made up of vibrant communities and changing networks (formal and informal) that practice feedback, self-organization, continuous change, and learning. Such systems need helping processes that are organic and emerging. Rote mechanisms and un-integrated change processes are less effective and usually short-lived.

OD is not about short-term manipulation to achieve immediate financial gains. Using OD in such a way ensures failure. Instead, OD provides an adaptable and real-time discipline for living systems that require information sharing to govern next moves and adjustments. It is interactive, relational, participative, and engaging. Rigid tools most often prevent the use of living robust processes and can actually keep high-performing culture from emerging.

Effective trainers are often understood to be in control of a management development effort. But facilitators of organization change are not in control of the change effort. Instead, they facilitate collaboration with internal partners. Facilitators learn, personally shift, and change with the organization. Successful change efforts require an ebb and flow. If an inappropriate approach is chosen, it quite likely will not relate to the living and constantly changing "realities" of the system.

Edgar Schein sent us the following comment via email this past June. It is in regard to his well-known contribution to the OD field, *Process Consultation*: "What gets me is that people still see it as a technique to be chosen among other techniques rather than as a core philosophy of how to establish a relationship with a human system. Oh well."

In his classic book, *Process Consultation Revisited*, Schein (1999, p. 245) wrote:

"In previous versions of this book, I attempted to categorize interventions...I have concluded that such categories are not really useful because they divert one from the more fundamental question of figuring out what will be helpful at any given moment in the evolving relationship. I prefer a general concept of 'Facilitative Intervention' that implies that a consultant should always select whatever intervention will be most helpful at any given moment, given all one knows about the situation."

Schein's statement suggests that "facilitation intervention" requires judgment calls on the part of the OD practitioner and leader. According to Tichy and Bennis (2007), judgment always includes the suggestion of high stakes or "something big at risk," (p. 78), yet not making the choice for intervention, when needed, is a risk of lack of facilitative intervention.

## Change Management Defined

"Defining change management is tough under any circumstances," write Holland and Skarke (2003, p. 24), "especially in the context of a new technology being implemented in an existing organization." Mention the issue of change management and a typical response is the question "Does it really matter in the real world?" The answer to that question is "Of course." After all, definitions are important because they can provide clarity.

In the simplest sense, *change management* means the process of helping a person, group, or organization change. The word "management" implies an effort to plan the change and exert influence over other people in the process. Change management thus implies a purposeful effort to bring about change. Kudray and Kleiner (1997, p. 18) define change management as "the continuous process of aligning an organization with its marketplace—and doing it more responsively and effectively than competitors." Anderson and Anderson (2001, p. xxviii) define change management as "a set of principles, techniques, and prescriptions applied to the human aspects of executing major change initiatives in organizational settings. Its focus is not on 'what' is driving change (technology, reorganization plans, mergers/acquisitions, globalization, etc.), but on 'how' to orchestrate the human infrastructure that surrounds key projects so that people are better prepared to absorb the implications affecting them."

In discussing OD, Warner Burke (2008) states, "The change that occurs in organizations is, for the most part, unplanned and gradual. Planned organization change, especially on a large scale, affecting the entire system, is unusual; not exactly an everyday occurrence" (p. 1). "Planned change" has always been a key ingredient in any definition and application of OD. Planned change results from an extensive assessment of the situation and then plans for customized interventions that are created to increase organizational excellence. Change management is the management of the planned changes.

Given the situation that we have described—that change is continuous and that the rate of that continuous change is speeding up—the field of OD today is shifting from focus on "assessment" and "planned change" and driven instead by the knowledge that, in order to keep up with this current reality of continuous and rapid change, the focus of both OD and CM must shift to processes that help organizations identify and plan for ways to move toward their "desired future state." Change management as a methodology has always been "more mechanistic" than traditional OD. As the future is emerging, both CM and OD are discovering that regardless of the "model" one uses, it is the perspective of continuous and relentless change that must guide the process.

## WHY CARE ABOUT OD AND CHANGE?

According to the Greek philosopher Heraclitus, "There is nothing permanent but change." By that he meant that everything is always in flux. As the Chinese suggest, no one can step in the same river twice, because the river is always in motion and is therefore always changing. What is new since the last edition of this book is that the pace of change has accelerated and the theories, approaches, and techniques have multiplied.

The year 2009 has seen radical change in global markets and national economies. Our world is getting more interconnected and our economies and industries are global. There are crises in financial institutions, the housing market, automotive production and sales, education, healthcare, and energy markets, to name only a few major issues. We will likely experience more change during the next few decades than has been experienced since the beginning of civilization. We can expect more confusion in our organizations attempting to cope with change than at any other time in history.

On the positive side, nano-technology, green technology, unified communications technology, virtualization technologies, social software, and information systems—the whole technology world—will bring advances beyond our imagination. These technologies will inevitably impact the way we "do" OD.

The field of OD has a history of over fifty years during which time the rate of change has sped up exponentially. OD practitioners have been thinking about, and actively intervening to help, organizations cope with this changing reality. It is worth reflecting on what changes are occurring, why they are occurring so fast, and what effects those changes are having on the world around us and on the field of organization change—in particular on the practice of OD.

# What Changes Are Occurring?

As cited in the second edition of *Practicing Organization Development*, Rothwell, Prescott, and Taylor (1998; 2008) identified six key changes that would have the greatest impact in the workplace and workforce over the next ten years. The study began with an analysis of published accounts of workplace trends. Only trends mentioned three or more times were included on the initial list, resulting in a total of 158 trends. Then a handpicked group of HR experts rated the trends for their relative importance to the present and future workplace and workforce. The result was a narrowed-down list of six key trends:

- Changing technology;
- Increasing globalization;
- Continuing cost containment;
- Increasing speed in market change;
- Growing importance of knowledge capital; and
- Increasing rate and magnitude of change.

*Changing technology* refers to rapid advances in human know-how. *Increasing globalization* refers to the impact that rapid transportation and global communication have on how organizations conduct business. *Continuing cost containment* refers to efforts undertaken by organizations to address declining profit margins, wrought by the ease of price comparisons through web-based technology. To maintain a profitable business, organizations are making major efforts to improve profits by reducing the costs of business operations. *Increasing speed in market change* refers to the continuing importance of beating competitors to the punch by meeting the rapidly changing tastes of consumers. *The growing importance of knowledge capital* refers to the key value-added capabilities of human creativity and innovation to identify new businesses, new products, new services, and new markets. Finally, *the increasing rate and magnitude of change* refers to the increasing speed and scope of changes that are occurring. In short, change itself is changing—and posing ever-more-daunting challenges for business leaders who need to respond in real time to breaking events.

Each trend influences the others. The definition of each trend may vary by organizational context and even by functional area. The trends are related in that many are root causes of other trends or consequences of other trends. And each trend requires new competencies from leaders to respond to, or even anticipate, the changes brought by each trend.

Today, these changes can be seen everywhere, in all types of organizations. They continue with organizational downsizing; continuous implementation and updating of technologies to enhance performance; mergers and acquisitions; globalization of industries like automotive and aerospace; mandated governmental or community action group pressures; and communications (Palmer, Dunford, & Akin, 2009). Organizations are experiencing a multitude of forces for change, both external and internal.

## Why Is Change Occurring So Fast?

Time has become a key strategic resource largely because of the unprecedented development of ways to communicate, from computers and cell phones to airplanes. The challenge of the future is to help people learn to ride the waves of change in real time and as events unfold. Time has become important precisely because changing technology provides strategic advantages to organizations that understand the importance of time and timely action. Today the organization that makes it to market first often seizes the lion's share of the market and is likely to keep it. And organizations that miss technological innovations that increase production speed or improve quality lose out to global competitors who function in a world where differences in labor costs can easily be taken advantage of because of the relative ease of international travel and communication.

Changing technology is also a driver for the information explosion—and vice versa. Consider the sheer magnitude and pace of the information explosion:

- The sheer quantity of information is increasing so fast that no one can keep pace with it. The amount of information created over the last thirty years is greater than what was produced over the previous five thousand years. "Researchers from the University of California estimate that 800MB of new information is produced and stored each year for every member of the human race" (see "Reclaim Your Brain," 2003, downloaded on 19 January, 2009 from http://news.bbc.co.uk/1/hi/magazine/3230665.stm).

- According to one source (see www.softpanorama.org/Social/overload.html), more than 100,000 new book titles are published in the United States every year—and the total number of books published worldwide may exceed one million.

- The "millions of data" that are on the Internet are not stored on a single computer, but rather on a network of millions of independently owned and located computers. No one, not even Google or MSN, has successfully indexed or cataloged the entire Internet because it is so vast (see www.barbarafeldman, *Where is all the data stored?*).

- We all are experiencing an invasion of our time with a tremendous number of phone calls, emails, voice mails, and text messages. Many people carry cell phones twenty-four hours a day, seven days a week.

People have different ways of responding to information overload and change. One approach is to give up. Another approach, widely used, is to try to master clever ways to do more than one thing at a time—that is, multi-tasking. But efforts to cope with the effects of change by trying to do more than one thing at a time are causing additional problems. Multi-tasking can actually reduce productivity because it may take as much as 50 percent longer to process two tasks performed simultaneously than it takes to do them one after the other (Meyer & Evans, 2001).

## What Effects Are Those Changes Having?

There are many effects of change.

One effect is that change begets more change. As organization leaders struggle to meet competitive challenges, they search for ways to slash cycle times for product development, chase fads to discover new ways to gain advantage, and struggle with efforts to manage a burgeoning number of initiatives and improvement efforts.

A second effect is that the turbulent changes in the environment (political, economic, technological, and social) have prompted increasing cynicism about change, an emerging theme in the literature about change management (Bruhn, Zajac, & Al-Kazemi, 2001; Stanley, Meyer, & Topolnytsky, 2005). Cynicism about change means that workers and managers increasingly question the motives of those who sponsor, champion, or drive change. Cynicism about the motives of other people erodes trust and confidence in organizational leaders. A growing number of scandals in business, government, education, the media, and the church only reinforce that cynicism.

A third effect is growing stress on individuals and their families. As the rate and magnitude of change increase, individuals struggle to keep up emotionally as well as cognitively. Their stressed-out feelings about change, if expressed, occasionally erupt in workplace violence, as found from studies of over 300,000 instances of workplace violence annually in the United States (Magyar, 2003). Stress may also prompt increasing instances of "desk rage" (Wulfhorst, 2008), create pushback through growing interest in work/life balance programs (The 24/7 Work Life Balance Survey, 2008), and encourage some people to seek innovative ways to work through telecommuting or other efforts that distance them from others.

## So Why Should Anyone Care?

The field of OD can help an organization anticipate, adapt, and respond to change. According to Cummings and Worley (2009), "OD is both a professional field of social action and an area of scientific inquiry into the organization" (p. 1) that we feel can positively impact human and organizational effectiveness and performance. So people should care about OD because it is rapidly emerging as the leading business topic—if not *the* key business topic—on how to handle change and lead effectively.

The ability to lead and manage change successfully sets leaders apart from followers. A study by Rosen and Digh (2001) identified "guiding people successfully through change" as one of twenty key competencies for global managers. According to a second study by the Center for Creative Leadership on "Essential Leadership Skills for Leading Change" (2006) in today's marketplace, the ability to lead employees is number 1, and the ability to manage change is number 2 (compared to 1 and 7, respectively, in the 2002 study) as requirements for continued success and competent change leadership. As the pace increases, the field of OD is beginning to experiment with the idea that "leadership" skills will be essential at every level of the organization. New experimental OD type processes are already creating ways to empower all levels and categories of workers to become leaders and innovators within their own spheres of influence. This topic is further discussed in Chapter Six on leadership and OD.

There is clearly a need for improvements in demonstrating these and other OD competencies presented in Chapter Five. After all, the track record of change efforts is not so good. Consider: success rates for reengineering efforts in Fortune 1000 companies range from 20 to 50 percent (Strebel, 1996). A study of corporate mergers revealed approximately 50 to 75 percent of mergers and acquisitions fail to meet the expectations that were initially projected (Schraeder & Self, 2003). Furthermore, even five years after a completed merger or acquisition, 70 percent of the surviving organizations are continual underperformers in their respective industries (Perry & Herd, 2004). Finally, only 15 percent of information technology projects are commonly cited as successful (Amber, 2007), and 50 percent of firms that downsized actually experienced a decrease—not an increase—in productivity (Applebaum, Everard, & Hung, 1999).

Smith (2002) reaches several conclusions about failed change efforts based on a survey of 210 managers. His survey results reveal that 75 percent of change efforts fail to make dramatic improvements, that top and middle management support for change is essential to success in change efforts, that about 50 percent of all change efforts emanate from the top while 47 percent come from division or department heads, and that most change efforts occur as a reaction to a combination of organizational and environmental factors. Further, the survey results reveal that most organizations rely on financial, operational, and customer service metrics to evaluate the success of change efforts, that success is highly correlated with visible support from a change sponsor, that failure is associated with missing or conflicted leadership, and that managers agree much more clearly on why change succeeds than on why it fails.

To summarize, then, organization change presents one of the greatest challenges in modern organizational life. All managers and employees will have to deal with it. If they cannot, they are not likely to be successful in what they do in the future—no matter what their specialty areas might be.

As the field of OD begins to cope with these disappointing outcomes, innovation in the field itself is emerging. The rapid rate of change makes it obvious that new and innovative processes must be agile, situational, and involving of all levels of the organization. While it has become common knowledge that traditional change processes are not as successful as one would hope, the OD innovations of whole system transformation, solution-focused practices, and system-wide invitation to experiment with and create innovative ways of planning and implementing change are emerging. These experiments are proving to be ways to re-energize the practice of OD with new and innovative applications that are more aligned with the changing rate of change. (See Parts Three and Four in this book for examples of these new OD practices.)

# WHAT SPECIAL TERMS ARE USED IN ORGANIZATION DEVELOPMENT?

Like every other field of endeavor, OD has its own nomenclature or special terms. Although these terms can create barriers to understanding and may be sources of suspicion for those not versed in them, they are useful when consultants and customers communicate with one another.

## Organization Change

Roland Sullivan invited the professional OD community, which often dialogues at www.odnetwork.org/listsinfo, to respond to a concern he heard often from the late Bob Tannenbaum. Bob felt that OD needed a fresh definition of "change." He wished for a common definition that those who initiate change would find useful in helping the larger world better understand who we are and what we do.

Matt Minahan summarized the dialogue:

"We put this question to our 1500+ members, and found, to no one's real surprise, that there isn't one agreed-upon definition among our members. There were discussions of many factors in our field, change for what reasons, with which values, at the service of whom, at what scale; whether it has to be proactive or could be reactive; whether it should be led or managed; and, even, whether our field should just use the existing definitions for simplicity and clarity.

"Integrating the best of everything that was offered, we could say that: 'Organization change is the process of learning and behaving differently, in order to achieve new and better outcomes, by reordering the system structures that drive behavior.'

"Of course, 'new' and 'better' are loaded with implicit values, but a values basis for the definition seemed to be important to our members."

Other variables that came up in the list discussion included:

- The beliefs that we, and our client organizations, hold about the world and change and how we organize those beliefs;
- The fit between our capability/willingness to change and the challenge, danger, or opportunity that confronts us;
- The alignment between the organization and its environment and the likelihood of suboptimization at some point;
- The ability to deeply influence the organization, down to the pattern, or second loop, level;
- The patterns of relationships resulting in and arising from different conversations; and
- Finally, there was an interesting conversation about the difference between managing change as reacting to the environment, versus leading change as anticipating and influencing the environment.

Change is a departure from the status quo. It implies movement toward a goal, an idealized state, or a vision of what should be, and movement away from present conditions, beliefs, or attitudes.

Different degrees of change exist. In a classic discussion on that topic, Golembiewski (1990) distinguished among three levels of change:

- *Alpha change* implies constant progress, a shift from a pre-change state to a post-change state in which variables and measurement remain constant. It is sometimes associated with incremental change.
- *Beta change* implies variable progress, a shift from a pre-change state to a post-change state in which variables and measurement methods themselves change. For example, as members of an organization participate in a change effort, they become aware of emerging issues that were unknown to them at the outset. The members change their vision of what should be and thereby alter the course of the change effort itself.
- *Gamma change* implies, in addition to beta change, a radical shift from what was originally defined as a pre-change state and a post-change state. It is sometimes called transformational change, a radical alteration from the status quo, a quantum leap or paradigm shift. It involves a complete revolution in "how we do things" or "what results we strive to achieve."

Anderson and Anderson (2001) provide another classic perspective on levels or types of change. They distinguish among:

- *Developmental change*: "[It] represents the improvement of an existing skill, method, performance standard, or condition that for some reason does not measure up to current or future needs." (p. 34)

- *Transitional change*: "Rather than simply improve what is, transitional change replaces what is with something entirely different." (p. 35)

- *Transformational change*: It is the "most complex type of change facing organizations today. Simply said, transformation is the radical shift from one state of being to another, so significant that it requires a shift of culture, behavior, and mindset to implement successfully and sustain over time." (p. 39)

Finally, there is a common distinction of levels of change that combine the first two above: first-order, incremental change and second-order, transformational change.

- *First-order, incremental*: This is "evolutionary"—the kind of change that moves strategically, slowly, and purposefully, bringing a "learning perspective" into an organization. First-order change often occurs without disruption of routine work. Change feels like an adjustment that supports organizational effectiveness (Palmer, Dunford, & Akin, 2009).

- *Second-order, discontinuous change* "is transformational, radical, and fundamentally alters the organization at its core" (Newman, 2000, p. 604).

Although categorizing change can be misleading, disruption is often present in gamma type, transformational, and second-order change. It is this kind of change that disrupts past assumptions, encouraging leaders to look to others to fill gaps of need and to support the identification of new ways of doing things. This type of change transforms the structure and disrupts the comfort zones of the organizational members (Beer, 2008; Burke, 2008; Palmer, Dunford, & Akin, 2009), often causing confusion, loss, separation, and frustration. However, if there is an awareness of each other's role and it is handled right, it can be very effective. .

## Change Agent

In the 1950s the National Training Laboratories (NTL) founders were in Europe collaborating with the Tavistock Institute. Someone from Tavistock used the phrase "change agent" to describe a person who facilitates change by intervening in groups and organizations. The NTL group started using it, and now it has become a common phrase among change makers and leaders. So when you hear the phrase "change agent," recognize that it is a key OD phrase that has become popularized over the years. It says what we do. We are agents who facilitate positive learning, change, and development.

A change agent is a person who attempts to change some aspect of an organization or an environment. Change agents "are often OD practitioners who assist through their process and OD expertise" (Jones & Brazzel, 2006, p. 117). These practitioners may be internal or external to the organization. A major impact of this new age of continuous change on the field of OD is on the role and tasks of the "change agents" themselves. While OD consultants have most often been defined as "facilitators" of change (rather than "leaders"), the complexity of every individual environment in which OD practitioners work demands a more "facilitative" and even "educational" approach to helping the system identify and plan for new ways of functioning and relating. The major reason for this shift is that people internal to any organization must learn how to cope with the changing rate of change. Without this approach of imbedding OD competencies in the system itself, we see the high rates of "failure" reported earlier in this chapter.

In response to this reality, it is interesting to note that Drucker took the term "change agent" to a new level. As the classic definition above states, the phrase traditionally refers to a person. But management pundit Drucker challenges us now to see the *organization* as change agent. Writing in *Executive Excellence*, Drucker (2004, p. 3) says:

> "We can already see the future taking shape. But I believe that the future will turn in unexpected ways. The greatest changes are still ahead of us. The society of 2030 will be very different from today's society and bear little resemblance to that predicted by today's futurists. The next society is close enough for action to be considered in five areas. [The fourth area is] change agents. To survive and succeed, organizations will have to become change agents. The most effective way to manage change successfully is to create it."

In his conscious shifting of meaning that we attach to the work "change," Drucker tapped into the emerging idea in the field of OD that "change" is not an event, but rather the constant state in which we live. While the rate of change may vary, in fact, as in any living system from the human body to the universe, once change ends, the living system is dead! Change is the water we swim in. OD is a process for enabling human systems to embrace and continuously build upon the changes that are an inevitable part of a living system.

## Client

The *client* is the organization, group, or individuals whose interests the change agent primarily serves.

Although consultants often think of the client as the one who authorized the change effort and pays their bills, they are not always certain whose purposes are to be served. For this reason, a key question for any OD consultant to consider is "Who is the client?" (Varney, 1977). On occasion, the "client" may not be the one who originally sponsored or participated in the change effort.

Again, in this new era, the potential exists for the whole system to be the client.

# Culture

One focal point of OD is making changes in an organization's *culture*. Prior to the early 1980s, the issue of culture was restricted to anthropology and OD circles, but culture became a popular buzzword after the publication of *Corporate Cultures: The Rites and Rituals of Corporate Life* by Deal and Kennedy (1982) and *In Search of Excellence: Lessons from America's Best-Run Companies* by Peters and Waterman (1982). Peters and Waterman provided numerous examples demonstrating the importance of culture in many of the best-known and best-run companies in the United States at that time. Generally, corporate culture means:

> "Basic assumptions and beliefs that are shared by members of an organization, that operate unconsciously, and that define in a basic 'taken-for-granted' fashion an organization's view of itself and its environment. These assumptions and beliefs are learned responses to a group's problems. They come to be taken for granted because they solve those problems repeatedly and reliably." (Schein, 1985, pp. 6–7)

# Intervention

An *intervention* is a change effort or a change process. It implies an intentional entry into an ongoing system. Cummings and Worley (2009, p.750) define intervention as "any action on the part of a change agent. [An] intervention carries the implication that the action is planned, deliberate, and presumably functional."

Many people suggest that an OD intervention requires valid information, free choice, and a high degree of ownership in the course of action by the client system. Argyris defined an intervention with the following classic statement: "To intervene is to enter into an ongoing system of relationships, to come between or among persons, groups or objects for the purpose of helping them. The intervener exists independently of the system" (1970, p. 15). Once again in this emerging environment where systems are seen as whole organisms, the field is examining assumptions about the viability of seeing any person working within that system as "independent." Many of the emerging processes in the field of OD are focused on the "wholeness" of any human system.

# Sponsor

A *sponsor* is one who underwrites, legitimizes, and champions a change effort or OD intervention. Sponsor tactics can include listening, supporting, developing, empowering, or promoting a person or group as capable. It can include verbalizing positive impressions and images regarding performance, expression of feelings of goodwill, or promoting acceptance, or making statements of capability, or the likeability of a person or group.

Of necessity, sponsorship is not a one-time gesture. Just doing it once won't work. Sponsorship gestures performed over time can create assumptions of capability and appropriateness.

A person can also be a negative sponsor. A skeptical or cynical comment shared with the right person, or expression of "concerns" regarding intervention needs with a targeted person or group, whether valid or not, can lower or eliminate positive assumptions held by listener(s). The potential for an intervention to succeed can be lowered by comments made by a negative sponsor.

## Stakeholder

A *stakeholder* is anyone who has a stake in an OD intervention. Stakeholders are the people who maintain an interest in the organization's success or failure. Stakeholders may be employees, board members, customers, suppliers, distributors, and government regulators. Many of the OD interventions presented in the upcoming chapters are from a stakeholder's perspective. The role of stakeholders is growing more important to organizational success. The goal is to establish what some have called a "boundaryless organization" (Ashkenas, Ulrich, Jick, & Kerr, 2002), which has permeable boundaries.

# WHAT IS SYSTEMS THINKING AND WHY IS IT IMPORTANT?

In the simplest sense, a *system* is a series of interdependent components (Burke, 1980). For example, organizations may be viewed as social systems because they depend on interactions among people (Katz & Kahn, 1978). In addition, any organization that gives and takes information from the environment is an *open system*. Organizations take in *inputs* (customer requirements, raw materials, capital, information, or people), appreciate value through the input of a *transformation process* (production or service-delivery methods), and release them into the environment as *outputs* (finished goods, services, information, or people) (see Figure 1.1). This transformation cycle must continue to add value in the process of producing desired results if an organization is to survive.

A *subsystem* is a system that is part of a larger system. In one sense, subsystems of an organization (a system) may include work units, departments, or divisions. In another sense, subsystems may cut across an organization and encompass activities, processes, or structures. It is thus possible to focus on an organization's maintenance, adaptive, or managerial subsystems (Katz & Kahn, 1978).

Facilitating collaboration with our clients is a key competency for OD practitioners. The identity of a system shifts when it creates a new collective and common understanding. The shift creates a culture where many ideas for action will bubble up. Helping the system distill "B" (suboptimal) ideas from

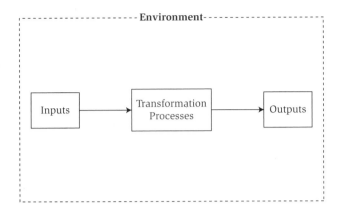

**Figure 1.1.** A Model of a System

"A" (best) ideas is a role very much needed today. And as OD practitioners experiment with whole system processes, the trend is toward "trying out" ideas in multiple experimental processes rather than trying to sort ideas with pre-experimental judgments. In other words, it is sometimes the idea that we might label "sub-optimal" that turns out to be the solution!

Interdependence comes from a trusting, open, self-realizing process. It is the opposite of a culture that is hindered by fear, closed behavior, and imposition. Such fearful cultures create dependence on autocratic leaders. Today we need the collaborative spirit of an engaged system to meet customer requirements and create success both for the system and for their customers. Systems thinking and acting can hurl an organization into higher levels of performance.

Systems thinking is also important to OD for the simple reason that a change in any part of a system inevitably changes other parts of the system. The implications of this simple statement are, in fact, profound. The change process in any part of a system creates change in all parts of the system. Any change in a system will have both predictable and unpredictable consequences. Mitigating the unpredictable consequences best occurs if all parts of the system are in collaboration throughout the change effort. The book's website has an exhibit that compares and contrasts systems and non-systems behavior.

# WHAT ARE THE PHILSOPHICAL FOUNDATIONS OF OD, AND WHY ARE THEY IMPORTANT?

One way to view the history of OD stresses its emergence from four separate but related behavioral-science applications: (1) laboratory training, (2) survey research and feedback, (3) Tavistock sociotechnical systems, and (4) process consultation. While Chapter Three will provide a different, and more comprehensive, perspective on the origins of OD, it is worthwhile here to offer a brief view of historical influences to provide readers with essential background information right at the start of the book.

## Laboratory Training

An early precursor of thinking about OD and change, laboratory training is associated with unstructured, small-group sessions in which participants share their experiences and learn from their interactions. Bradford, Gibb, and Benne (1964) explain this application in the following way:

> "The term 'laboratory' was not idly chosen. A training laboratory is a community dedicated to the stimulation and support of experimental learning and change. New patterns of behavior are invented and tested in a climate supporting change and protected for the time from the full practical consequences of innovative action in ongoing associations." (p. 3)

Unlike employee-training sessions, which focus on increasing individual knowledge or skill in conformance with the participant's job requirements, laboratory-training sessions focus on group processes and group dynamics. The first laboratory-training sessions were carried out in the 1940s. In particular, the work of the New Britain Workshop in 1946, under the direction of such major social scientists as Kurt Lewin, Kenneth Benne, Leland Bradford, and Ronald Lippitt, stimulated much interest in laboratory training. The leaders and members of the workshop accidentally discovered that providing feedback to groups and to individuals at the *end of each day* produced more real learning about group dynamics than did lectures. The groundbreaking work of the New Britain Workshop led to the founding of the National Training Laboratories (NTL Institute for Applied Behavioral Science).

Early laboratory-training sessions were usually composed of participants from different organizations, a fact that led such groups to be called "stranger T-groups." (The term *T-group* is an abbreviation of "training group.") Bradford, Gibb, and Benne (1964) define a T-group as relatively unstructured where individuals participate as learners. The data for learning are not outside these individuals or removed from their immediate experience within the T-group. The data are transactions among members' behaviors in the group, as they work to create a productive and viable organization and support one another's learning within that society.

Behavioral scientists later discovered that the participants had difficulty transferring insights and behavioral changes to their work lives. This transfer-of-learning problem increased interest in conducting such sessions in a single organization, a technique that has evolved into what is now called *team building*.

Laboratory training was an important forerunner of OD because it focused attention on the dynamics of group or team interaction. In addition, it provided a basis for team building, which is still an important OD intervention, as discussed in Chapter Fifteen.

## Survey Research and Feedback

Survey research and feedback also made an important contribution to the evolution of OD. This approach to change was developed and refined by the Survey Research Center at the University of Michigan under the direction of Rensis Likert. Likert directed the Survey Research Center from 1950 to 1970. He became widely recognized for his innovative use of written survey questionnaires to collect information about an organization and its problems, provide feedback to survey respondents, and stimulate joint planning for improvement. This technique is called *survey research and feedback* or *survey-guided development*.

Likert's method began evolving when he observed that many organizations seldom used the results from attitude surveys to guide their change efforts. Managers authorized the surveys but did not always act on the results. This "ask-but-don't-act" approach produced greater frustration among employees than not asking for their opinions in the first place.

The centerpiece of Likert's approach was a technique called the *interlocking conference*. Survey results were given to top managers during the first conference, and then other conferences were held to inform the organization's successively lower levels. In each conference, group members worked together to establish an action plan to address problems or weaknesses revealed by the survey. This top-down strategy of feedback and performance planning ensured that the action plan devised by each group was tied to those at higher levels.

A philosophy about organizational systems governed much of Likert's work. He believed that any system—that is, an organization or a component part of an organization—can be categorized into one of four types based on eight key characteristics. The four organizational types are shown in Exhibit 1.1.

Likert's System 4 type of organization suggests the "ideal" organization. In Likert's System 4 organization, leadership is based on influence, not authority or power. Employees are motivated through the intrinsic rewards stemming from the work itself. Communication is balanced, with a great deal of two-way interaction between managers and employees. Likert (1961) justified System 4 as a norm or ideal because he found that "supervisors with the best records of performance focus their primary attention on the human aspects of their subordinates' problems and on endeavoring to build effective work groups with high performance goals" (p. 7).

Likert's views, described in his two major books, *New Patterns of Management* (1961) and *The Human Organization* (1967), had a profound influence on OD. He demonstrated how information can be collected from members of

Exhibit 1.1. Characteristics of Likert's Four Types of Organizations

| **System 1** | **System 2** |
|---|---|
| *Exploitive-Authoritarian* | *Benevolent-Authoritative* |
| • Dogmatic leadership | • Parental approach to management |
| • Manipulative use of rewards | • Supervisors expect subservience lower down |
| • Top-down communication | |
| **System 3** | **System 4** |
| *Consultative* | *Participative* |
| • Management listens to employees, but reserves the right to make decision | • Leadership based on influence |
| | • Authentic and trusting relations |
| • Some reliance on intrinsic rewards; most rewards are based on extrinsic (money) rewards | • Intrinsic rewards predominate |
| | • Two-way communication |

an organization and used as the basis for participative problem solving and action planning. In addition, he advocated pursuit of a norm for organizational functioning (System 4) that has since prompted others to pursue similar norms for organizations. In some respects, Likert's views about the System 4 organization are important precursors to the modern-day interest in self-directed work teams and high-performance work environments.

Likert, along with the other experimenters in the OD field, were men and women of vision who helped move our image of the ideal organization from mechanistic model of "organization as machine" to the reality of "organization as human system." In this decade, the shift has to incorporate the idea of "organization as continuous change."

Much of the experience and methodologies of traditional OD practice still inform the work of OD practitioners. But the field is expanding rapidly, not so much toward new "models" for change, but rather toward an understanding of the compelling need to be agile and innovative as we work to include the complexity of the rapid and continuous change that can make our traditional "data-gathering" obsolete as we realize that "data" in human systems can become irrelevant in a nano-second!

## Tavistock Sociotechnical Systems

Another major contributor to the evolution of OD is Tavistock Sociotechnical Systems. Tavistock, founded in 1920, is a clinic in England. Its earliest work was devoted to family therapy in which both child and parents received simultaneous treatment.

A team of Tavistock researchers conducted an important experiment in work redesign for coal miners at about the same time that laboratory training was introduced in the United States. Before the experiment, coal miners worked closely in teams of six. They maintained control over who was placed on a team and were rewarded for team, not individual, production. New technology was introduced to the mine, changing work methods from a team to an individual orientation. The result was a decrease in productivity and an increase in absenteeism. The Tavistock researchers recommended that the new technology could be used by miners grouped into teams. The researchers' advice, when implemented, improved productivity and restored absenteeism rates to historically low levels in the organization.

Tavistock sociotechnical systems' key contribution to OD was an emphasis on both the social and the technical subsystems. Tavistock researchers believed that organizations are systems composed of key subsystems. One such subsystem is the people in an organization. The other is the non-human subsystem. Both must be taken into account if a change is to be successful.

## Process Consultation

Another influence on our field has been Schein's process consultation. *Process consultation* can be defined as the creation of a relationship that permits both the consultant and the client to perceive, understand, and act on the process events that occur in the client's internal and external environment in order to improve the situation as defined by the client.

Schein writes:

> "In reflecting on process consultation and the building of a 'helping relationship,' the question arises: where is the emphasis or the essence that makes this philosophy of helping 'different'? In my reflections on some forty years of practicing 'this stuff,' I have concluded that the essence is in the word relationship. To put it bluntly, I have come to believe that the *decisive factor as to whether or not help will occur in human situations involving personality, group dynamics, and culture is the relationship between the helper and the person, group, or organization that needs help.* From that point of view, every action I take, from the beginning contact with a client, should be an intervention that simultaneously allows both the client and me to diagnose what is going on and that builds a relationship between us. When all is said and done, I measure success in every contact by whether or not I feel the relationship has been helpful and whether or not the client feels helped.

> "Furthermore, from that point of view, the principles, guidelines, practical tips, call them what you like, fall out as the kinds of things I have to constantly remind myself of in my efforts to build that kind of helping relationship. Let us review the principles from that point of view.

1. Always try to be helpful.
2. Always stay in touch with current reality.
3. Access your ignorance.
4. Everything you do is an intervention.
5. It is the client who owns the problem and the solution.
6. Go with the flow.
7. Timing is crucial.
8. Be constructively opportunistic with confrontive interventions.
9. Everything is a source of data; errors are inevitable—learn from them.
10. When in doubt share the problem.

"These principles do not tell me what to do. Rather, they are reminders of how to think about the situation I am in. They offer guidelines when the situation is a bit ambiguous." (1999, pp. 243–245)

So there you have it! Remember always that OD is more than just applying techniques, tools, and methods. Good OD is built on having a clear understanding of its theory base and terminology. Effective OD involves building effective relationships that are trusting, open, self-discovering, and interdependent. We best serve by staying in the here and now and innovating responses and interactions that facilitate movement to a client-desired state that helps the clients discover with us action that will bring them success and unprecedented results. It is about adding both meaningful and measurable value to any encounter. This is a world of work that is most personal, challenging, and meaningful.

## HOW OD IS RELATED TO THE HR FIELD

Organization development (OD) may be regarded as part of a larger human resource (HR) field that is unified in its focus on people—primarily people in organizational settings. However, OD's central focus differs from that of other HR fields. Yet, it is worth considering the relationship between OD and this field, because OD activities are affected by—and, in turn, affect—other HR activities.

Leonard Nadler (1980, 1989) is one prominent authority who made an early attempt to explain these relationships. He distinguished between human resource development (HRD), human resource management (HRM), and human resource environment (HRE) activities. Taken together, they encompass all HR fields. In Chapter Four, Rothwell shares how the fields have converged.

# Human Resource Development

*Human resource development*, according to Nadler (1989), consists of training, education, and development. It is defined as "organized learning experiences provided by employers within a specified period of time to bring about the possibility of performance improvement and/or personal growth" (p. 6). *Training* is a short-term change effort intended to equip individuals with the knowledge, skills, and attitudes they need to perform their jobs better. *Education* is an intermediate-term change effort intended to prepare individuals for promotions (vertical career progression) or for enhanced technical abilities in their current jobs (horizontal career progression). *Development* is a long-term change effort intended to broaden individuals through experience and to give them new insights about themselves and their organizations. All HRD efforts share a common goal of bringing about "the possibility of performance improvement and/or personal growth" (p. 6).

# Human Resource Management

Nadler believes that HRM includes all activities traditionally linked with the personnel function except training. *Human resource management* (HRM) is thus associated with recruitment, selection, placement, compensation, benefits, appraisal, and HR information systems. According to Nadler, all HRM efforts share one common goal: to increase organizational productivity by using the talents of its current employees.

# Human Resource Environment

*Human resource environment* includes OD and job—or work-redesign—efforts. According to Nadler, HRE activities focus on changing working conditions and interpersonal relationships that interfere with performance or impede employee creativity. Unlike other HR fields, HRE activities share one goal: to improve the work environment through planned, long-term, and group-oriented change in organizational structures or interpersonal relations.

# More Recent Thinking About HR, OD, Training, and HRD

The HR, OD, training, and HRD fields have not remained static. Thinking about all these fields has been changing in recent years. A major change has been a movement away from activities or techniques and toward a greater focus on results and on demonstrated, measurable achievements. The HR and OD fields are converging—a topic treated at greater length in a later chapter of this book. The training field has been changing, with increased recognition of the importance of obtaining results rather than just the activity of training people. While systematically designed training has remained important, even as e-learning methods have come into vogue and then faded in the face of the growing importance of blended learning (Rothwell & Kazanas, 2008), greater focus has turned to what learners must do to take responsibility for their own learning process (Rothwell, 2002).

*Human resource development* (HRD), now an outdated term that reflects outdated thinking, has evolved into a new generation called *workplace learning and performance* (WLP). WLP is defined as "the integrated use of learning and other interventions for the purpose of improving individual and organizational performance. It uses a systematic process of analyzing performance and responding to individual, group, and organizational needs. WLP creates positive, progressive change within organizations by balancing human, ethical, technological, and operational considerations" (Rothwell, Sanders, & Soper, 1999, p. 121). Unlike HRD, which was operationally defined in terms of such activities as training, OD, and career development (McLagan, 1989), WLP focuses on results, performance, outputs, and productivity through learning. It is thus goal-oriented (Rothwell & Sredl, 2000). The most recent research after Nadler, and others, in the field of HRD has broadened the definition of what the field is, pushing the boundaries to include anything that uses learning as the means to the end of improving human performance and innovation (Bernthal, Colteryahn, Davis, Naughton, Rothwell, & Wellins, 2004; Salopek, 2008).

# GLOBAL OD

As the world "shrinks," the practice of OD has spread across the globe. Global OD begins with the same definition of OD that has to do with the application of behavioral science knowledge yet makes it explicit that there are additional cultures beyond those where the roots of OD have been located (USA and Great Britain). Therefore, Global OD faces the challenge of changing individual, group, and organizational behavior without having the usual and anticipated "rate of predictability." According to Eric Gaynor (personal communication), "the challenge has to do with the fact that—at present—there is an incomplete and insufficient body of knowledge in behavioral science for the diversity of existing cultures and sub-cultures, and we are in the first stages of learning."

Global organization development is a process for changing an organization to improve its effectiveness. The *global* reference refers to being cognizant that there are, in addition to factors that are political, economical, and technological, cultural factors that may influence your change initiative or may alter your approach.

For certain, global means we are in a period of unprecedented change that is affecting all of us and will continue to do so as we become more globally integrated. In comparison, Yaeger, Head, and Sorensen (2006) stated a similar premise of producing change to improve effectiveness in an increasingly interdependent world. But their book also points out that OD is founded on optimistic and democratic values and the concern for basic human principles, and that it must be considered that these principles may not be accepted globally. As a global OD practitioner, you must be aware of culture values and understand economic, political, and social factors. Chapter Twenty-One discusses the meaning, application, and implications of global OD.

OD, as supported by Blake, Carlson, McKee, Sorensen, and Yaeger (2000), is applicable across diverse cultures, environments, and boundaries, which is critical in this era of globalization. Whether OD is local or global, it is primarily concerned with a thoughtful understanding of the changes in the cultural, economic, political, and humanistic perspectives of people in different places around the world. These considerations must be made as you plan and implement change.

OD is faced with a globe that is getting smaller with markets that are getting more demanding every day. Customers and competition are no longer in this city, this state, this region, or in this country or on this continent. As noted in *BusinessWeek* (1994), "Not only is work becoming seamless as it moves between home, office, and phone, but it also is becoming endless as it rolls through a twenty-four-hour day" (pp. 24–26). This is partly caused by the "continental time divide" that exists as OD working partners and clients exist across the world instead of in the next conference room. Reflecting these issues, OD is far from understanding the dynamics and effects of the issues caused by the practice of OD in a globalized world.

# SUMMARY

In this first chapter and the literature of recent years, the labels of "organization development" and "change management" have been, in many cases, intermingled. Marshak (2005) suggests that the difference between the two is ideological and methodological. We suggest a difference just might be that OD works from a set of human values and base of valid information coming from assessment, along with making free choices with the client system regarding what tools or interventions to enact the change as you will learn from this book.

In change management, managers and executives, using OD practitioners as agents and resources, identify, plan, direct, and steer change. Changes are made with the participation of the members in order to secure buy-in and support for the changes. The changes are, for the most part, meant to advance the competitive and economic well-being of the organization and its stakeholders. Marshak states:

> "In organization development, in contrast, the assumption is that changes cannot be successfully identified, let alone implemented without the true involvement of those responsible for doing the actual work. The purpose of involvement is to secure the best ideas and information to address the situation, with buy-in a side benefit. It is also usually assumed that there will be interdependencies and dynamics that cannot be fully anticipated or planned for, requiring an interactive process open to new developments and outcomes." (2005, p. 22)

In this chapter we also addressed many important questions. The questions and brief answers as a starting point to them supplied in the chapter follow:

*Question:* What do you believe about change?

*Answer:* Clarify your beliefs about people, change, organizations, and other issues relevant to organization change and development.

*Question:* What are change management (CM) and organization development (OD)?

*Answer:* Change management implies "a purposeful effort to bring about change. Organization development is a system-wide application of behavioral science knowledge to the planned development, improvement, and reinforcement of the strategies, structures, and processes that lead to organization effectiveness" (Cummings & Worley, 2009, p. 1). Another key difference between OD and other change management strategies may be OD's important focus on values and ethics, both key issues to business in the wake of a continuing spate of ethical scandals affecting previously respected organizations.

*Question:* Why should you care about organization development (OD)?

*Answer:* People should care about organization development because it is rapidly emerging as a key business topic—if not the key business topic in the change global environment and economy.

*Question:* What special terms of importance are used in organization change and development?

*Answer:* Key terms include change; change agent; client; culture; intervention; sponsor; and stakeholder.

*Question:* What is systems thinking, and why is it important to OD practitioners?

*Answer:* Systems thinking is important to OD for the simple reason that any change in any part of a system changes other parts of a system.

*Question:* How is OD related to other HR fields?

*Answer:* A simple way to distinguish OD from WLP is to think in terms of what is to be changed and how it is to be changed. OD focuses on changing an organization and the modes of behavior demonstrated in the corporate culture. WLP focuses on getting results in organizational settings, using any and all methods appropriate to do that—but with a heavy emphasis on learning-oriented efforts for individuals and groups.

*Question:* What is global OD?

*Answer:* Global OD is, as noted above, a planned process for changing an organization to improve its effectiveness while being cognizant that there are, in addition to factors that are political, economical, and technological, cultural factors that may alter the humanistic perspectives of people in different places around the world, ultimately altering your approach from the OD perspective.

In this chapter we have discussed and answered questions pertaining to OD and change management, with a focus on OD. We discussed what OD is and what it is not and defined terms that are curious to OD. With these topics and others, it has been our goal to give you a glance at history (which will be discussed in more depth in Chapter Three) and to prepare you for what is to come. OD is an exciting and ever-changing field—after all, change is our working and learning topic and our vocation. To follow, you are offered the opportunity to read the thoughts of leaders in the field...and to reflect on and digest their experiences of the past and anticipations of the future of OD. We think you will find the contributions in this book exciting and beneficial to your practice of organization development.

# References

Amber, S. (2007). Defining success: There are lessons to be learned when defining IT project successes. [www.ddj.com].

Anderson, L.A., & Anderson, D. (2001). *The change leader's roadmap: How to navigate your organization's transformation.* San Francisco: Pfeiffer.

Appelbaum, S.H., Everard, A., & Hung, L.T.S. (1999). Strategic downsizing: Critical success factors. *Management Decision, 37*(7), 535–552.

Argyris, C. (1970). *Intervention theory and method: A behavioral science view.* Reading, MA: Addison-Wesley.

Argyris, C. (1993) *Knowledge for action: A guide to overcoming barriers to organizational change.* San Francisco: Jossey-Bass.

Argyris, C. (2004) *Reasons and rationalizations: The limits to organizational knowledge.* Oxford: Oxford University Press.

Ashkenas, R., Ulrich, D., Jick, T., & Kerr, S. (2002). *The boundaryless organization: Breaking the chains of organization structure* (rev. ed.). San Francisco: Jossey-Bass.

Beckhard, R. (1969). *Organization development: Strategies and models*. Reading, MA: Addison-Wesley.

Beer, M. (2008). Transforming organizations: Embracing the paradox of E and O. In T.G. Cummings (Ed.), *Handbook of organization development*, pp. 405–429. Thousand Oaks, CA: Sage.

Benne, K., Bradford, K., Gibb, J., & Lippitt, R. (1975). *The laboratory method of learning and changing*. Palo Alto, CA: Science and Behavior Books.

Bennis, W. (1969). *Organization development: Its nature, origin and prospects*. Reading, MA: Addison-Wesley.

Bernthal, P., Colteryahn, K., Davis, P., Naughton, J., Rothwell, W., & Wellins, R. (2004). *Mapping the future: Shaping new workplace learning and performance competencies*. Alexandria, VA: The American Society for Training and Development.

Blake, R., Carlson, B., McKee, R., Sorensen, P., & Yaeger, T.F. (2000). Contemporary issues of grid international: Sustaining and extending the core values of OD. *Organizational Development Journal*, *18*(2), 54–61.

Bradford, D., Burke, W., Seashore, E., Worley, C., & Tannenbaum, B. (2001). Statement of the board. In L. Ackerman Anderson & D. Anderson, *The change leader's roadmap*. San Francisco: Pfeiffer.

Bradford, L., Gibb, J., & Benne, K. (1964). *T-group theory and laboratory method: Innovation in re-education*. Hoboken, NJ: John Wiley & Sons.

Bruhn, J.G., Zajac, G., & Al-Kazemi, A.A. (2001). Ethical perspectives on employee participation in planned organizational change: A survey of two state public welfare agencies. *Public Performance & Management Review*, *25*(2), 208.

Burke, W.W. (1980). Systems theory, gestalt therapy, and organization development. In T. Cummings (Ed.), *Systems theory for organization development* (pp. 209–222). Chichester, UK: John Wiley & Sons.

Burke, W.W. (1982). *Organization development: Principles and practices*. New York: Little, Brown & Company.

Burke, W.W. (2008). *Organization change theory and practice*. Thousand Oaks, CA: Sage.

Burke, W.W., Spencer, J.L., Clark, L.P., & Corruzzi, C. (1991). Managers get a "C" in managing change. *Training & Development*, *45*(5), 87–92.

*BusinessWeek* (1994, May 23). Borderless management: Companies strive to become truly stateless. *BusinessWeek*, pp. 24–26.

Clardy, A. (2003). Learning to change: A guide for organization change agents. *Personnel Psychology*, *56*(3), 785.

Cummings T.G., & Worley, C.G. (2009). *Organization development and change* (9th ed). Cincinnati, OH: South-Western College Publishing.

Deal, T., & Kennedy, A. (1982). *Corporate cultures: The rites and rituals of corporate life*. Reading, MA: Addison-Wesley.

Drucker, P. (2004, May). The way ahead: Get ready for what is next. *Executive Excellence, 21*(5), 3.

Essential Leadership Skills for Leading Change. (2006, January). *Leading effectively.* e-newsletter by Center for Creative Leadership. [www.ccl.org].

Golembiewski, R. (1990). *Ironies in organization development.* New Brunswick, NJ: Transaction Publishers.

Gottlieb, J.Z. (1998). Understanding the role of organization development practitioners. In R.W. Woodman & W.A. Passmore (Eds.), *Research in organizational change and development*, Vol. 11, pp. 117–158. Stanford, CT: JAI Press.

Holland, D., & Skarke, G. (2003). Change management for big systems. *Industrial Management, 45*(4), 24.

Jones, B.B., & Brazzel, M. (2006). *The NTL handbook of OD and change: Principles, practices, and perspectives.* San Francisco: Pfeiffer.

Kanter, R.M. (1995). Mastering change. In S. Chawla & J. Renesch (Eds.), *Learning organizations: Developing cultures for tomorrow's workplace.* Portland, OR: Productivity Press.

Katz, D., & Kahn, R. (1978). *The social psychology of organizations* (2nd ed.). Hoboken, NJ: John Wiley & Sons.

Kudray, L., & Kleiner, B.H. (1997). Global trends in managing change. *Industrial Management, 39*(3), 18–20.

Lippitt, R. (1958). *The dynamics of planned change.* New York: Harcourt, Brace, and World.

Likert, R. (1961). *New patterns of management.* New York: McGraw-Hill.

Likert, R. (1967). *The human organization: Its management and value.* New York: McGraw-Hill.

Magyar, S.V. (2003). Preventing workplace violence. *Occupational Health and Safety, 72*(6), 64.

Marshak, R.J. (2005). Contemporary challenges to the philosophy and practice of organization development. In D.L. Bradford & W.W. Burke (Eds.), *Reinventing organization development: New approaches to change in organizations*, pp. 19–42. San Francisco: Pfeiffer.

McLagan, P. (1989). *Models for HRD practice.* Alexandria, VA: American Society for Training and Development.

Meyer D., & Evans, J.E. (2001). Executive control of cognitive processes in task switching. *Journal of Experimental Psychology—Human Perception and Performance, 27*(4).

Nadler, L. (1980). *Corporate human resources development.* New York: Van Nostrand Reinhold.

Nadler, L. (1989). *Developing human resources* (3rd ed.). New York: Van Nostrand Reinhold.

Newman, K.L.(2000). Organizational transformation during institutional upheaval. *Academy of Management Review, 25*(3), 602–619.

Palmer, I., Dunford, R., & Akin, G. (2009). *Managing organizational change: A multiple perspectives approach* (2nd ed.). New York: McGraw-Hill/Irwin.

Perry, J.S., & Herd, T.J. (2004). Mergers and acquisitions: Reducing M&A risk through improved due diligence. *Strategy & Leadership, 32*(2), 12–19.

Peters, T., & Waterman, R. (1982). *In search of excellence: Lessons from America's best-run companies*. New York: Harper & Row.

Rosen, R., & Digh, P. (2001). Developing globally literate leaders. *Training & Development, 55*(5), 70–81.

Rothwell, W. (2002). *The workplace learner: How to align training initiatives with individual learning competencies*. New York: AMACOM.

Rothwell, W., & Kazanas, H. (2008). *Mastering the instructional design process: A systematic approach* (5th ed.). San Francisco: Pfeiffer.

Rothwell, W., Prescott, R., & Taylor, M. (1998). *Strategic human resource leader: How to prepare your organization for the six key trends shaping the future*. Palo Alto, CA: Davies-Black.

Rothwell, W., Prescott, R., & Taylor, M. (2008). *Human resource transformation: Demonstrating strategic leadership in the face of future trends*. Palo Alto, CA: Davies-Black.

Rothwell, W., Sanders, E., & Soper, J. (1999). *ASTD models for workplace learning and performance*. Alexandria, VA: The American Society for Training and Development.

Rothwell, W., & Sredl, H. (2000). *The ASTD reference guide to workplace learning and performance* (3rd ed., 2 vols.). Amherst, MA: Human Resource Development Press.

Salopek, J. (2008, August). Keeping it real. *Training & Development*, pp. 42–45.

Schein, E. (1985). *Organizational culture and leadership*. San Francisco: Jossey-Bass.

Schein, E. (1999). *Process consultation revisited: Building the helping relationship*. Reading, MA: Addison-Wesley.

Schraeder, M., & Self, D.R. (2003). Enhancing the success of mergers and acquisitions: An organizational cultural perspective. *Management Decision, 41*(5), 511–522.

Senge, P. (1990). *The fifth discipline: The art and practice of the learning organization*. New York: Doubleday Currency.

Smith, M.E. (2002). Implementing organizational change: Correlates of success and failure. *Performance Improvement Quarterly, 15*(1), 67–83.

Stanley, D.J., Meyer, J.P., & Topolnytsky, L. (2005). Employee cynicism and resistance to organizational change. *Journal of Business and Psychology, 19*(4), 429–459.

Strebel, P. (1996, May/June). Why do employees resist change? Reprinted in *Harvard Business Review* on change in 1998. Boston: Harvard Business School Publishing, pp. 139–157.

The 24/7 Work Life Balance Survey Report (2008, March). [www.worklifebalance centre.org].

Tichy, N.O., & Bennis, W.G. (2007). *Judgment: How winning leaders make great calls*. New York: Portfolio, Penguin Group.

Vail, P. (1996). *Learning as a way of being*. San Francisco: Jossey-Bass.

Varney, G. (1977). *Organization development for managers*. Reading, MA: Addison-Wesley.

Wulfhorst, E. (2008, July 11). Do you suffer from desk rage? *The Huffington Post*.

Yaeger, T., Head, G., & Sorensen, P. (2006). *Global organization development: Managing unprecedented change*. Greenwich, CT: Information Age Publishing.

Zaltman, G., & Duncan, R. (1977). *Strategies for planned change*. Hoboken, NJ: John Wiley & Sons.

# CHAPTER TWO

# Change Process and Models

William J. Rothwell and Roland L. Sullivan

A model for change is a simplified representation of the general steps in initiating and carrying out a change process. It is rooted in solid research and theory. Managers and consultants, when demonstrating the competencies of an OD practitioner, are well-advised to rely on a model for change as a compass to show them the direction in which to lead the change effort and change process. But, as Stewart and Kringas (2003, p. 675) note, "The change-management literature contains a bewildering variety of understandings of, and approaches to, change." Collins's (1998) work usefully contrasts two basic types of models. The first, which might loosely be called the rational model, emphasizes the importance of planning, problem solving, and execution. The second approach, more sociological in orientation, explores changing rather than change and emphasizes the uniqueness and contextual richness of each situation.

In this chapter we review numerous models for changing rather than change—essentially, the change process. Finally, in the last section of the chapter, we point readers to other change models found in the literature and distill some key issues associated with change.

## AN OVERVIEW OF KEY MODELS
## FOR ORGANIZATIONAL CHANGE

The change models that we share rely primarily on a normative, re-educative, and innovative approach to behavioral change. They are (1) the critical research model; (2) the traditional action research model; (3) Appreciative Inquiry; and (4) an evolving view of the action research model.

While mainstream OD practitioners have long relied on action research as the change model underpinning their efforts, recent research and practice underscore the need to modify the model and provide guidance for doing so (Burke, 2002). At the same time, much work has focused on analyzing common characteristics of successful change efforts so as to derive a change model from them.

## The Critical Research Model

Critical research (CR) stems ultimately from Marxist practices. The key idea underlying CR is similar to a dialectic approach to change in which opposing positions are used to power change. Critical research assumes that every organization or group has an *ideology*, a more or less consistent rationale about how decisions should be made, how resources should be used, how people should be managed, and how the organization should respond to the environment in which it functions. In a classic definition, Katz and Kahn (1978) describe ideology as "generated to provide justification for the organization's existence and functions" (p. 101). In one sense, an ideology is a step above culture, and "culture is the manifestation of ideology, giving `life' to ideology" (Lang, 1992, p. 191).

A natural tension develops between what people believe should be happening and what they believe is actually happening. The basic thrust of CR is to identify this discrepancy and use it to power change. Because individual perceptions differ within groups, CR builds an impetus for change by dramatizing these differences between the organization's ideology about what should be and actual situations contradicting its ideology that thereby underscore the need for change. Critical research heightens the tension by pointing out inconsistency.

Although critical research has not been widely used in mainstream OD, interventions such as Beckhard's (1997) confrontation meetings can lend themselves to it. (A confrontation meeting brings together two conflicting groups to discuss their differences and to arrive at ways of working together more effectively.) Critical research views conflict between ideology and actual practices as constructive, leading to self-examination and eventually to change. The steps in applying critical research (CR) to a change effort are listed in Exhibit 2.1.

Perhaps a simple example will underscore how the model works. Suppose the leaders of an organization have long underscored their commitment to strong customer service. In annual reports, executive speeches, and company advertising, the company's leaders pledge that they are willing to do anything to satisfy a customer. The ideology of the company is thus centered on customer service as the most important single commitment of the organization.

But then suppose that employees in the company's call center are well aware that the company is not honoring warranties on a defective product. They have been told to "find others ways to satisfy customers than by honoring the warranties."

Exhibit 2.1. The Critical Research Model

1. Describe the ideology. (How do people believe the organization or group should be functioning?)

2. Identify situations, events, or conditions that conflict with the ideology. (What is actually happening?)

3. Identify individuals or groups desiring progressive change. (Who wants to challenge the ideology and/or actual situations to create an impetus for progressive change?)

4. Confront proponents of the ideology with conflicting situations, events, or conditions.

5. Devise a new ideology or action steps to correct inconsistency.

6. Help the client establish a timetable for change.

7. Implement the change.

8. Ask the client to monitor the change, identifying opportunities for continuous improvement as necessary.

In this simplistic example, the difference between the company's ideology (a strong commitment to customer service) and actual practices (refusal to honor warranties) provides the basis for an obvious, and troubling, difference between "what the organization's leaders say they want" and "what the organization's leaders actually do." That difference, if used to best effect, can provide an impetus for change.

Critical research has captured a large following among educators, and particularly adult educators, in recent years. It lends itself well to considering the political issues involved in change and relies on the differences of opinions among groups of people as a way of leveraging change.

## The Traditional Action Research Model

Action research has long been the foundation for many change efforts. It is properly regarded as a philosophy, a model, and a process. Like any change model, action research is a simplified representation of the complex activities that should occur in a change effort if it is to be participative, engaging, and empowering for those affected by it. The model serves as a compass to consultants facilitating change. While it does not tell consultants, managers, or workers exactly what to do in paint-by-the-numbers fashion, it does provide a process whereby the consultant and client can jointly inquire and decide what change is required. It helps consultants track where they are and where they are going. While the action research model has been depicted in different ways, the depictions of it share common characteristics. Figure 2.1 illustrates a general model of action research.

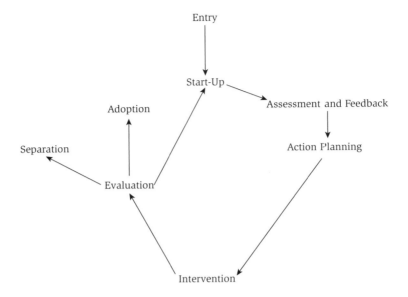

**Figure 2.1.** The Traditional Action Research Model

From G. McLean & R. Sullivan (1989). Essential Competencies of Internal and External OD Consultants (p. 14). Unpublished manuscript. All rights reserved. Used by permission.

Action research may also be understood as a process, a continuing series of events and actions. In a classic description, French and Bell (1990, p. 99) defined this interpretation of action research in this way:

> "[It is] the process of systematically collecting research data about an ongoing system relative to some objective, goal, or need of that system; feeding these data back into the system; taking actions by altering selected variables within the system based both on the data and on hypotheses; and evaluating the results of actions by collecting more data."

As a process, action research is thus a cycle in which research is followed by change activities, the results of which are fed into further research. In that respect, action research (as used in OD) is sometimes confused with the related notion of action research (as used in education), where experience with classroom-based activities becomes the foundation for continuous improvement in delivering education.

One way to think about the traditional action research model depicts it as eight steps in any change effort. This traditional depiction is based on the steps originally presented in Burke (1982) and in *Essential Competencies of Internal and External OD Consultants* (McLean & Sullivan, 1989). The steps are as follows:

| *Step* | *Brief Description* |
|---|---|
| 1. Entry | The need for change in an organization becomes apparent. A dream is articulated. Someone or a group of people in the organization look for help in facilitating change toward the realization of the dream. |
| 2. Start-Up | The change agent (consultant) enters the picture, working to discover what might be done, contracts with the client, and gains commitment to proceed. |
| 3. Assessment and Feedback | Information is gathered and validated about a desired positive future and gives decision-makers and those having a stake in the change process feedback that can be used to design change action. |
| 4. Action Planning | The change agent collaborates with decision-makers and stakeholders to muster all their creativity to agree on a preferred future state along with innovative first steps. |
| 5. Intervention | The action plan is implemented, monitored, and continually adjusted and embellished as the situation warrants. |
| 6. Evaluation | The change agent helps decision-makers and stakeholders assess the change effort's progress and organizational learnings to illuminate next steps as the previous phases are repeated. |
| 7. Adoption | Members of the organization maintain the new state as resulting changes are integrated into daily work life. |
| 8. Separation | The change agent prepares for closure and departure. She or he works to disengage while ensuring that improvement or transformation will continue after her or his departure. This step is possible because the knowledge and skills of the change agent have been transferred to the organization. |

Although the length and depth of each step may vary across change efforts, the steps are usually present in one form or another. In long-term change efforts—as many are—each step in the model may actually turn into the whole model in miniature. For example, when it is time for action planning, the consultant may use all or some of the generic action research model phases. In other words, that step alone may call for a start-up phase, followed by assessment, action planning, and an evaluation component once or several times during the action planning process. The steps will be discussed in Part Two of the book.

## Appreciative Inquiry (AI)

Appreciative Inquiry (AI) is the most exciting development in thinking about change in recent years. In one of the last conversations with the authors, Dick Beckhard, the person who coined the phrase "managing change" in the 1950s, told the authors of this chapter that he believed that AI held within it the most promising future for OD. Like the action research model, AI is a way of being, a model, a conceptual framework, and a process to guide change. Originally conceptualized by Case Western Reserve professor David Cooperrider (see Cooperrider & Srivastva, 1987), it has captured much attention in recent years (see, for instance, Cooperrider, 1990; Cooperrider, 1995; Cooperrider, Barrett, & Srivastva, 1995; Cooperrider & Passmore, 1991; Cooperrider, Sorensen, Whitney, & Yaeger, 1999; Cooperrider, Whitney, & Stavros, 2008; Watkins & Mohr, 2001). If the action research model can be regarded as comparable to the chip inside the computer that drives change efforts, then the Appreciative Inquiry model can be regarded as a different—but complementary—chip.

Appreciative Inquiry (AI) is an OD approach and process to change management that grows out of social constructionist thought. AI is the "cooperative co-evolutionary search for the best in people, their organizations, and the world around them" (Cooperrider, Whitney, & Stavros, 2008, p. 3). Instead of starting out to solve problems—a typical focus of traditionally trained managers, steeped in a philosophy of management by exception—AI focuses on what is going right, what is motivating, what is energizing, and what are the key strengths of a setting. Instead of asking the question, "What is going wrong and how do we solve that problem?" AI begins by asking, "What is going right and how do we leverage that strength to achieve quantum leaps in productivity improvement?"

Applying AI thus requires a paradigm shift from focusing on what is going wrong to what is going right and then trying to leverage what is going right into new, higher-level visions of a positive future. AI is both a philosophy and has a 4-D method that can be applied: Discovery, Dream, Design, and Destiny. See the AI 4-D Cycle in Figure 2.2. To learn more about AI, see Chapter Seven.

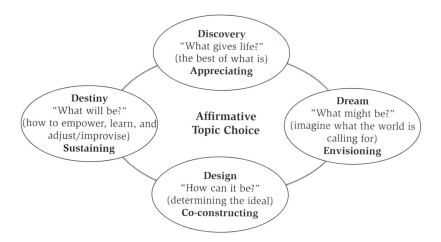

**Figure 2.2.** AI 4-D Model

# THE EVOLVING VIEW OF THE ACTION RESEARCH MODEL

## Burke's Change Model for Leaders of Change

Burke (2002) reviewed the change process. In doing so, he posited what might be regarded as the seeds for evolving the action research model. What is exciting about this new view is that it gets away from the traditional action research model, which implicitly describes any change process as functioning as a drawn out and somewhat simplistic process.

Unfortunately, recent experience suggests that so many change efforts are going on at the same time in many organizations that a linear change approach no longer works. One reason is that so many concurrent change efforts lead to a crowding out effect. They burn people out and drive people crazy because it is not possible to remember everything going on at once.

One of the author's clients stated the case well. His organization was installing self-directed work teams, a customer service improvement effort, a Baldrige Award effort, a continuous improvement effort, a business process reengineering effort, a process improvement effort, and a statistical process control (SPC) improvement effort. He remarked, "If we have just one more change effort in this plant, the whole place is going to sink into the ground." Against that backdrop of too many simultaneous change "projects" going on, a project-based approach to change is no longer workable. What is needed is a new model to guide change that does not assume a beginning, middle, and end to a change effort. Instead, change efforts are regarded as continuing and are regarded from a whole systems standpoint.

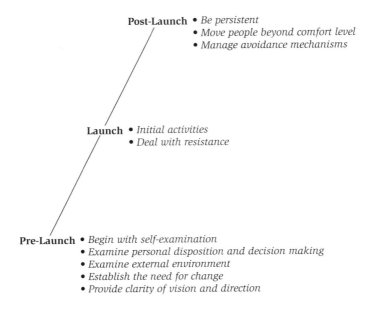

**Figure 2.3.** A New View of the Action Research Model

Burke (2002) describes the phases of change as pre-launch, launch, and post-launch. The model is written as a guide for change leaders. Change efforts are regarded as proceeding like spirals rather than circles to depict their ongoing chaotic nature—and the view that what is learned from each phase of a change effort can be rolled into subsequent phases. In this way, organizations are transformed into learning organizations that "learn" from experience. The new view of the action research model is depicted in Figure 2.3. It is briefly summarized below. "An interesting paradox about organization change," notes Burke (2002, pp. 246–247), "is that we plan as if the process is linear when in reality, it is anything but linear."

**Pre-Launch.** The pre-launch phase occurs before the change effort begins. It establishes the foundation for a successful change effort. Without it, a change effort is likely to fail—or be short-lived—as other, more pressing daily crises demand attention. Pre-launch begins effectively when leaders follow the famous advice of Socrates to "know thyself" and start with self-examination. As Burke points out, leaders should be aware of their own tolerance for ambiguity, their need for control, and their understanding of how feelings affect behavior. They should reflect on their personal dispositions and the decision-making processes they generally use—as well as their own values and motives for change.

Burke (2002, pp. 252–257) suggests considering several additional issues during the pre-launch phase:

- *The external environment*: Leaders should gather information about the environment that necessitates change. What is the business case for change? Why is change warranted to address current crises or seize future opportunities?

- *Establishing the need for change*: When leaders communicate the compelling case for change to others in the organization, they build a sense of urgency and reduce resistance to change.

- *Providing clarity of vision and direction*: The direction of the effort must be clear. What objectives are to be met by the change and what will success look like? A clear vision must be established and communicated so it is embraced by key stakeholders and others in the organization.

**Launch.** The launch phase is the beginning of the change effort. It begins with communication to key stakeholders inside and outside the organization about the need. This is what some leaders call "making the business case," and the case for change must be made by credible people who will be believed. Communication must be provided in many channels, since people are so bombarded with messages that they are unlikely to pick up on one short message provided in a single medium.

According to Burke (2002, pp. 258–260), the key issues to address in the launch phase are

- *Initial activities*: An event that will seize attention helps to fire imagination and enthusiasm.

- *Dealing with resistance*: Identify likely sources of resistance and try to address them before they can arise and destroy the impetus for change.

A major challenge in a long-term intervention is to maintain communication about the change effort. Stakeholders must be reminded what is being changed, why it is being changed, how the change effort is proceeding, and what benefits are being realized from the change effort (Rothwell, 2001).

**Post-Launch.** Post-launch involves sustaining a change effort over time. That can be particularly frustrating. The reason is that events in a change effort, even when successful, may appear to be spiraling out of control.

Burke (2002) recommends that CEOs follow the advice of Heifetz (1994). He has three suggestions. First, be persistent. Second, help people in the organization move beyond their comfort levels while keeping stress to a minimum. And third, be prepared to manage the predictable "avoidance mechanisms" that can surface during a change effort. These include "blaming other people, scapegoating, and appealing to authority figures for answers" (Burke, 2002, p. 261).

## NEW ACTION RESEARCH CHANGE MODEL: PERPETUAL AND INSTANTANEOUS POSITIVE CHANGE

Change consulting in the 21st Century requires a new model—a model that works in an environment of rapid, chaotic change. Many consultants today are frustrated by the time required for the traditional action research model, but it should not be abandoned. The response in our practice has been to create a model that responds more adroitly to the growing complexity of the consulting world, but is based on the founding principles of the field.

Edgar Schein (1999) writes:

"Consultation projects evolve in complex ways. One cannot really identify simple sequential patterns, such as 'scouting,' 'entry,' 'contracting,' 'diagnosis,' and 'intervention.' Instead what happens is that one finds oneself intervening initially with contact clients, then with intermediate clients, then with primary clients who may engage one in a project that involves a whole new set of contact and primary clients, all the while thinking about ultimate and unwitting clients to ensure that their needs and issues are not ignored or marginalized. In each relationship, consultants must perpetually diagnose and gear their interventions carefully to build and maintain helpful relationships." (p. 219)

We reviewed hundreds of models that are being used in the field today. One we particularly liked was Warner Burke's. It seemed to supply a foundational framework to integrate into our traditional eight-phase model. We feel a high level of confidence that what he was learning was on target for the burst of change happening in a typical organization's life. Using his framework of pre-launch, launch, and post-launch, we came up with the model shown in Figure 2.4.

The model reflects the most current research around change agent competencies. It provides architecture to frame what we do as change technologists. The model is not a technique to be followed but a change framework that drives what we do. This framework becomes a philosophical foundation that comes alive only with your personal and creative application.

Each phase of our new change model is discussed in depth by well-known experts in Part Two of this book. Here we will provide a brief overview of each phase. We call them phases because, unlike steps, different elements blend with others in myriad ways. As we have noted above, change efforts are seldom sequential, so keeping the overall framework in mind is important.

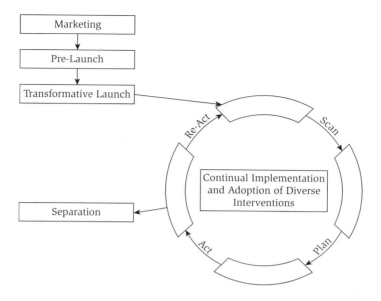

**Figure 2.4.** Sullivan/Rothwell Change Process Model

# Marketing

In our competency research, only the category of self-awareness ranked more important than marketing. Yet OD practitioners often stumble over themselves when it comes to marketing and selling. Marketing competencies may include being:

- Aware of systems wanting to change;
- Known to those needing you;
- Able to match one's competence with a potential client's profile;
- Credible in conveying one's qualifications;
- Fast in grasping the nature of the system;
- Perceptive in identifying appropriate decision-makers;
- Able to form connective interpersonal relationships instantly; and
- Able to understand customer requirements and sell results that will meet those requirements, rather than a process such as team building or whole system transformation.

We believe that internal change agents must also attend to marketing. Often they do not publicize their successes in their own enterprises and are thereby robbed of the credit they richly deserve. All organizations want a present better than the past and a future better than the present. OD is all about doing just that. So the need for OD services exists. It's up to the OD consultants to identify the need and help those in decision-making positions to see the benefits of an OD solution.

One good way is to help decision-makers become aware of the kinds of competencies you possess and have demonstrated. Selling after the sale is a useful strategy. One can schedule periodic sessions with current clients to assess results, and at the same time suggest ways one can provide help in the next iteration of the change process. Dr. Alan Weiss's chapter on marketing will open a window to countless useful resources. Your challenge will be to spend the time and discipline to learn how to be a competent marketer of your professional services. Change facilitation is needed today more than ever and will be needed tomorrow even more.

## Pre-Launch

Pre-launch begins when consultants clearly have clients committed to work with them. The marketing, selling, and entry issues are complete. It ends when the psychological and non-psychological contract, relationship connecting, and clarification of expectations are completed. There is an old adage in the field that says that if anything goes awry in the change effort, it can usually be traced back to this phase.

Peter Block has had much to say about the importance of relationships in the early phases of a change effort. He says that the core competency in consulting is how to contract with clients. This is the heart of his most popular book, *Flawless Consulting* (Block, 2000). For Block, contracting is about treating the relationship as significant and central. He believes one must continually process and re-set the relationship. Modeling competency in relationship development will also go a long way toward helping the client deal with key relationships. After all, it is our intention to transfer our competence to the client system.

Our research over the years has led us to believe that the ability to initiate and maintain excellent interpersonal relationships is paramount to success in the pre-launch phase and is essential to a successful engagement. The consultant and the client must like each other and must be able to continually and honestly clarify expectations.

An indication of a solid relationship is this: When the consultant has been away from the organization for awhile and returns, he or she is greeted with warmth and smiles by all. This is unlike the story that we heard about an internal consultant: When people saw him coming down the hall, they would slip into the first open office to avoid him. In summary, a strong measure of an effective consultant is the quality of the relationships that remain at the end of engagements.

# Transformative Launch

This phase starts the change process by assessing the situation and planning for action in order to launch a long-term and ongoing effort. In some cases, it's a good idea to start with a bang—a striking catharsis or a euphoric liftoff! In other cases a quiet start can be more effective as a team searches for early wins in a sensitive situation. Ideally, the top team starts with itself. In either case, a flawless beginning can do much to commit the entire top team to supporting engagement and involvement of all parts of the organization.

Some situations require *transformative change*, that dramatic shift in focus and priorities that can occur when conditions are just right. Transformative change is more than step improvement or incremental change. Freeing a caterpillar from an enclosed jar improves its situation, but doesn't change its nature. In transformation, the caterpillar becomes a butterfly. For transformative changes, the launch phase should be a striking and dramatically positive jump into a brilliant future. Exhibit 2.2 outlines some of the distinctions between change and transformation.

The launch phase is time to set a norm regarding the importance of informal channels of communication. This is not the time to change participants' basic learning modalities, and indeed the chances are they could not be changed if we wanted to. The gossip chain, the water cooler bulletin board, and the lunchroom conversations are parts of the informal networks, often where the real conversations are. It is the role of the change agent to bring the informal talk to the OD table. Participants need help trusting a process where truth prevails and they are ready to have a natural and authentic experience with valid data.

We expect a launch to move the organization to a point of no return. The system moves itself to a new state in which it encompasses the essential core competencies of being and becoming a change agent enterprise.

The launch (or implementation) phase we present here is distinctly different from our change model in the previous edition. In the 21st Century, change happens so fast that it seems it is at the speed of imagination. There is seldom time for a long assessment with a change plan.

Today, we see the change cycle requiring a process and philosophy built in for constant reaction and continual planning efforts. It is not a phase of a long-term effort, but rather an ongoing implementation of a myriad of interventions, an endless loop (some would say a spiral) of short-cycle change.

In fact, these days, the traditional assessment and action planning can all happen in three or four days if key stakeholders are in the room. The resistance that took years to unfreeze in the traditional action research model can now be broken in an afternoon if all the right people and information are present.

Exhibit 2.2. Distinctions Between Organization Change and Transformation

| *Change* | *Transformation* |
|---|---|
| • Single-loop learning (adaptive; errors are corrected without altering the fundamental nature of the system | • Double-loop learning (inquires into and changes existing norms and deeper value foundations; generative learning or learning how to learn) |
| • Status quo facilitated toward betterment | • Major disruption of the what is and was going to be |
| • Change in one or a few dimensions, variables, or parts | • Multidimensional, multi-component change and aspects |
| • Change in one or a few levels (maybe the individual and/or group level) | • Multilevel change (individuals, groups, or whole system) |
| • Change in one or two behavioral aspects (attitudes, values) | • Changes in all the behavioral aspects (attitude, norms, values, perceptions, beliefs, world view, and behaviors) |
| • Quantitative change—move the chairs on the deck | • Qualitative change—new ideology or shift in philosophy |
| • Change in content | • Change in context and underlying structure |
| • Identity stays the same | • Re-imagined and reformulated identity |
| • Corrective action | • Destruction of the old way |
| • Continuous improvement | • Discontinuous change |
| • Development in the same direction | • Exciting, explosive, fiery, disruptive, dramatic jumps in different directions |
| • Incremental changes and change that reverts back to the old state | • Irreversible change with arrival of a new state of being |
| • Change that does not alter the world view, the paradigm | • Change that results in a new world view, new paradigm (The system sees itself through a new window.) |
| • Micro results and improvement in performance | • Macro results and performance levels never reached before |

In Figure 2.4, you can see the launch phase broken out into a sub-model, which we call SPAR: Scan, Plan, Act, and Re-Act. This simple model is universal in application. This kind of change model is not just useful for one's work life but may be used in one's personal and recreational life as well. Client system, family, or little league team—the principles are the same. It can be used in a

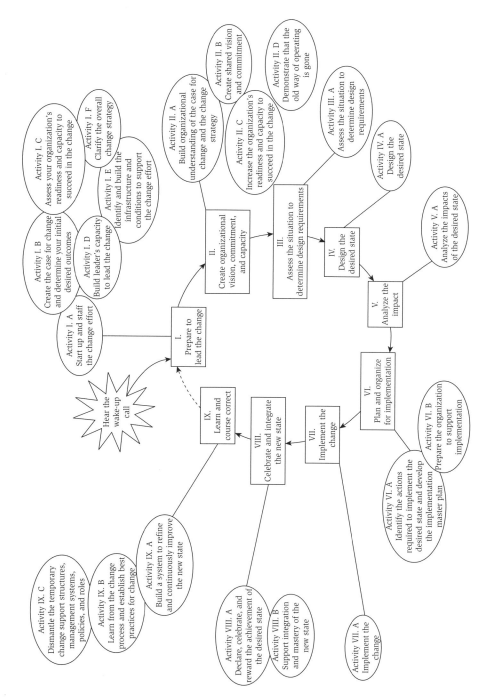

**Figure 2.5.** Three Models of the Change Process

From A.J. Mento, R.M. Jones, and W. Dirndorfer (2002). A Change Management Process: Grounded in Both Theory and Practice. *Journal of Change Management*, 3(1), 45–59.

long-term effort or in an intervention as short as a ten-minute phone call. It can be used as an intervention at any level of change. For example:

- An individual can use it to make changes in his or her own life;
- A coach or mentor can use it to work with a client;
- Two members of an executive team can use it to find new ways to collaborate;
- A team can use it to learn how to be more effective;
- Multiple teams can use it in the application of system theory and practice;
- Institution or enterprise-wide change efforts can use it—especially in ongoing, engaging change; and/or
- Network, community, or trans-organization development efforts can employ it.

Each phase or each session within a phase may include all four elements of SPAR. That is the Chinese box phenomenon—the famous puzzle consisting of a series of progressively smaller boxes inside a large box—which may typify many change efforts. In other words, when a change effort is big enough and long-term enough, the assessment and feedback moment or experience (for instance) may itself have an entry component, a start-up component, and so forth.

**Scan.** Diagnosis traditionally is the phrase that has been used to describe the major function of the scan phase. Our quantitative research over the years involving almost four thousand change agents has produced many heated arguments over whether to use assessment or diagnosis. We have been won over to the assessment side of the street because diagnosis comes more from a disease and medical model looking for something that is sick or problem-related. We prefer to look on the bright side of life. The glass is half full. Like the Appreciative Inquiry change agents, we strongly believe in the new positive psychology movement. Assessment is typically known as a classification of someone or something with respect to its worth. When a change process is positive, conversations are energizing. The process entropies when conversations are about problems, negativity, and the blues.

This is the phase where valid information is central. Common sense and classic research agree. Too often we see people in organizations jump right into the end-state planning without generating an accurate picture of where they are now and a clear view of a desired destiny.

It's important for the client to feel ownership of the assessment information. The more we can involve the client in jointly bringing forth valid information, the better. A key competency to be utilized here is the ability to create a trusting climate so the client feels safe to reveal disturbing, grandiose, or thought-provoking information and feelings. Gathering stories of best practices from within or from without the system is often exhilarating. A positive spirit of inquiry melts resistance.

Active and non-judgmental listening is paramount at this phase. When the client senses that the consultant is being judgmental, the consultant's ability to facilitate is impaired, and his or her influence is lessened. Trust is reduced because the common ground that is facilitated toward is colored with the consultant's own bias. Of course, there are exceptions. Sometimes a consultant will have one gigantic idea, and all will say, "YES! YES!" and welcome the contribution because the people in the system as a whole will benefit. Living systems move in the direction of what is assessed as being worthy.

Asking the right questions is key. David Cooperrider (founder of Appreciative Inquiry, which depends heavily on crafting the right questions) says that he spent days of intense concentration determining the exact questions he would use in breakout groups while he facilitated leaders of all the major world religions in a summit. Asking the right questions has much to do with where the client system lands in the next phase of planning.

Questions might include:

- What's up?
- What is working?
- What is our purpose?
- What outcomes do we wish to reach?
- What are your wishes and dreams?
- What do we want to change?
- What is a focus that you could really become passionate about?
- What best practices do we wish to enhance?
- What changes can we make to augment communication?
- Describe an ideal organization structure.
- Give me one strategy that, if implemented, would make a huge difference.

Usually we like to co-create scanning questions with the client. They know better than we do what is important. Often they need help rephrasing questions that could elicit negative, and perhaps unhelpful, responses. For example, "What is the problem with quality?" could become "What can you do to ensure superior quality?" or "The best example of high quality I have experienced around here is...."

In sum, the scan phase is about helping the client system get a comprehensive view from individuals or small groups about where they are and wish to be. Creating a system-wide synthesis and common-ground intelligence base comes in the next phase.

**Plan.** There is a wide assortment of techniques and methods that can be used to plan what you will act on. What approach should you use? It all depends. It may depend on the scope of the effort, the style of leadership, or the nature of the data-collection methodology. One idea is to have a change team representative of the larger system help design a planning process that fits the situation.

Here are some practical tips for the plan phase:

- *Feed back the data in a distilled manner.* Normally, one has more data than can be used. A process needs to be invented that will funnel all the accumulated ideas into common themes. Go for ideas that can easily turn into new attitude and behavioral commitments and action items. Involve participants in organizing the ideas. We do not encourage prepared recommendation reports assembled in the closet of the consultant's office and then presented and sold to the clients. Always prepare the data for planning with clients.

- *Spend some time validating the data that was collected.* Clients need help seeing collectively the state they are in. Rarely will they deny what has surfaced. Validating accommodates ownership and ultimate commitment.

- *Do allow the system to disturb itself.* Do facilitate so clients are able to confront themselves. Do allow them to self-realize what they will do with the dissatisfaction. Facilitate a wake-up call. Get their attention. The value of a consultant is to help the system face itself as it is and to realize what it wishes to become.

- *Be sensitive in confrontation.* Clients want to get rid of a past that is not working, but need help to destroy a past that is nonetheless theirs. Know how much disturbance they can handle. Realize that more change will happen if feelings are evoked and worked through. Authentic feelings in a room set the stage for serious and concentrated conversations. So it's important to intervene only as deeply as you know the client can handle. Expert and masterful facilitation is required, especially if there are five hundred people in the room.

- *Together create compelling propositions.* Establish a realistic preferred future that grows out of all the work that has been done up to this point. Unleash the creativity. Blend in the weird. Develop a bold plan that matches the audacious and enterprising times of today. Challenge clients to make a dramatic difference, a difference that will have a huge impact on the success of the system. Help them create a future that will give them a real reason to believe in themselves. They have it in them. The answers are in the system. Surface them. Bring them to life. Just pull the right cords to unleash the extraordinary mind power that all systems have. Let the compelling possibility give them hope.

- *Ensure that clients are able to freely choose their plan*. This concept is paramount. Remember the financial case above where the executive team did not buy the strategic plan until they felt they freely chose it. People follow through and own the plan when they have choices.

- *Anticipate and name the resistance that may arise.* You considered all possible sources of resistance in your planning and engaged people in the project insofar as possible. Still, additional resistance may arise now that implementation is inevitable. Rehearse how the different choices may play out, and consider ways to involve people even at this point, giving them options in implementation that will help them feel a measure of control over their destinies.

- *Create a simple, elegant master plan format*. The plan should go after specific actions that can make the biggest splash with the least amount of resources and effort. Surface the priority focus. Establish long-term goals, but only specify activity for shorter periods, certainly not more than 120 days. Most organizations are moving too fast to plan in detail much further out. Ideally you will be able to publish the plan on a website. One of our clients used a technology where an automatic email was sent to the person responsible to alert him or her before an action was due.

Here's an example of the potential power of such a process. We had a three-day whole system transformation summit with the top 350 people of a Fortune 250 organization. During one module of the design, the issue for interaction was the executive team's relationship with the remaining 340 leaders. A design team created an activity so the room could react to the behavioral commitments that the executive team made in the previous year's summit. After a very honest and open reaction from the first table's report-out, the second person reporting started by acknowledging his pleasure with the directness that had been heard and said, "I think we must hear a detailed assessment of the executive team from every table in the room." Applause and a standing ovation occurred.

On the spot we changed the design so all were heard. The rapt attention of the participants was stunning. The executive team spent from 8:00 p.m. to 1:00 a.m. crafting their response. When they presented it the next morning, they received a standing ovation. The people had been heard! In fact, this group decided not to have any structured follow-up or reaction phase. They did not need it. They just went and performed.

Six months later when the board was challenging the executive team about flying three hundred people to Minneapolis for the session, the second person in charge said, "Remember how you have been challenging us for the last five years to increase our profit in one of the financial variables? Well, look at the numbers. Note the five-million-dollar difference. We know that was the result of our organization change summit."

**Act.** Acting the plan is the heart and soul of what we do in OD, where the interventions we have planned with clients are carried out. The Act phase is where we get the results, where we add value. When we do it well, performance increases. If we have done all previous phases and sub-phases competently, success should spontaneously and authentically occur.

Chris Argyris offers a clear, simple, and profound statement around "Act." He writes, "In order to act, human beings diagnose problems, invent solutions, and evaluate the effectiveness of what they have produced" (2004, p. 2). These are indeed the same steps we are describing in SPAR. A key competency of an OD practitioner is to facilitate client conversation to help these effective change actions happen.

Argyris continues by saying, "Productive reasoning (1) produces valid knowledge, (2) creates informed choices, and (3) makes personal reasoning transparent in order for the claims to be tested robustly. The core of productive reasoning is that the parties involved are vigilant about striving to avoid unknowingly deceiving themselves and others" (2004, p. 3).

The following are some practical tips for the Act phase:

- *Increase the quality of the conversation.* Being transparent includes fishing for doubts and reservations so the concerns of all parties can be on the table. Name the resistance and honor it. Part of our role is to surface the "undiscussables," to surface the below-the-table thinking, to shed light on the shadow of the system. To get a view of the "whole," representing all parts of the system is required. (Of course, we must do so without getting ourselves fired by leadership that is not yet prepared for truth. And we must protect the truth tellers so they will continue to feel safe in speaking their view of the truth.)

- *Facilitate high-performing relationships.* Let us share an example. We had an executive team come to a four-day residential retreat prepared to light the fire in their team. The first day they were overwhelmed by the challenges before them. The team went into a funk. We anticipated such a state from our scan. We knew that there were serious relationship issues in the team so we spent a couple of days in deep dialogue around specific relationships and the climate of the team as a whole. By noon of the third day, there was a dramatic shift. They began to feel a confidence that they could handle the challenges before them better than any other team in the world. Why? We believe that the time they spent in effective dialogue (and our masterful facilitation, of course) moved them to a place where they deepened the genuine connection to all others in the team. Deep relationships generate confidence to act on significant challenges.

- *Establish a climate of trust and openness.* Our experience indicates that participants become very excited and engaged while they are working with the reality of their system. Without doubt, if they have been in honest dialogue, they will be likely to generate effective solutions. Expectations increase. An increase in results often does not happen until an expectation is declared.

- *Empower all to "act" through engagement*. Peter Block acknowledges that he learned much about engagement from Kathie Dannemiller. Kathie is known for her co-invention of whole-scale-change methodologies and especially for her belief in empowerment. Peter says:

"A core strategy for building emotional commitment to implementation is to design new ways for people to engage each other. This may be more critical than the clarity or rightness of a decision. Results are achieved when members of a system collectively choose to move in a certain direction. It is this act of choice that is critical.... We tenaciously hold onto the belief that leaders can induce others to act. Leaders can no more induce action on the part of their followers than consultants can induce action on the part of their clients." (2000, p. 265)

- *Ensure that the people in the organization are prepared to support the action*. We have found that it is best if the entire system is engaged in helping leadership define high-performance behavior. If it happens, the payoff is remarkable. If the participants have been genuinely connected to the change process up to this point, support, ownership, and commitment will prevail. Also structures, high-level systems, policies, and procedures must be adapted to help the system conduct the "Act" phase successfully.

- *Engage the leaders*. Leaders must visibly support the action. If in the past they were among those leaders who do not walk their talk, a change process is a great opportunity for them to now have a breakthrough. Anyone can change behavior. The desired behaviors just need to be clarified and committed to. Leaders need to model the changed or transformed mindset. How the organization views the congruency of leadership cannot be underestimated.

- *Help internal change agents*. They can prepare to and be available to move the action plan forward. If the SPAR model is effective, the client group's resolute spirit reaches out to internals to receive support and assistance in realizing their dreams. Perhaps they can be of assistance in areas that may be "stuck." In other instances, internal practitioners can offer themselves as coaches. Essentially, this is the time for them to initiate their own "SPAR" process. They will best serve the system if they are continually scanning, planning, acting, and re-acting to what is occurring.

**Re-Act.** The "Re-Act" phase occurs in more than one way. Planning renewal is a must. Re-action is necessary as the organization responds to the implementation of the plan. The action plan always evolves differently than you might have expected, so your plan must be updated and adjusted. Reaction feeds corrective action. Now is also the time to extract the learning from the previous three phases, and to be prepared for the next cycle of SPAR.

The following section highlights some issues related to this phase:

- *Obtain information on which to base re-action.* One of the best ways to get reaction is to have informal and frequent sessions where participants can converse. That will allow unforeseen obstacles and developing resistance to be identified. This is the time to monitor what has taken place. Monitoring may include scientific or non-scientific measured reactions to what has happened and is taking place. Monitoring is the reflective process to discern what we have learned from what has just happened in the previous three steps to guide us as we repeat SPAR.

     It may be done with periodic online surveys. One company had all computers set so they would not fire up until the person signing on completed a brief survey on the status of the department action plan. For example, people were asked:

  - What they had accomplished the previous week
  - What they would accomplish the upcoming week
  - What the best change practice they had observed in the organization the past week was
  - What one wish they had for the larger system to change in the immediate future to increase results

- *Deal with challenges.* It's important that challenges that arise be dealt with quickly and effectively. Challenges are not always bad news. One manufacturing client in the midst of dramatically transforming the entire enterprise just to survive struck gold with an unprecedented amount of new work. For the first time in their almost 100-year history, they were getting and turning away new work from the prestigious automotive industry. Thirty percent of the industry had just gone kaput the previous twenty months. Work was going to China in waves. But not for them; they could select high-quality customers who were willing to pay a premium for their products. An entire new focus for the change plan was required. They knew that not handling the opportunity wisely could take the company under. They had to quickly scale up for the increased business.

- *Avoid slippage.* It happens that organizations revert to previous behavior. Very often systems in place for years—systems that supported the old behavior—will become apparent now and provide pressure to do things the old way. The reaction phase is the time for the organization to invent ways to get back on track. If resistance persists after offering people chances to learn and use the new ways, leadership may have to say, "The boat to the new land has just left. If we are going to survive and you believe in what we are doing here, then we need your best.

If you are not willing to give us 100 percent, we have some rowboats that you can use to make your exit." Most importantly, people must be encouraged, supported, and cheered on in the efforts they are making toward change or transformation.

- *Celebrate success*. This is the time to celebrate. Tell stories of success. Seek out and share best practices and examples of progress of new work process or team behaviors. One of our clients collected hundreds of success stories and made them available on the web. Leaders of the organization might give their reactions to the change action commencing. A vote of confidence from them can go a long way. Such reaction activities can be fantastic momentum boosters.

- *Apply lessons learned*. A very important aspect of the SPAR cycle is to glean the best of the change practices and institutionalize them. A learning organization recognizes what has worked and adopts it into the ongoing process of doing business, so the best new practices become standard operating procedures, culture, or policies. Once they are accepted and working smoothly, resources can be again freed up to find the next new improvements.

Every year or so, depending on how much people in an organization thirst for positive change, the change effort may start back at the launch phase when a deep dive transformation lift is needed. For one of our clients, the largest financial system in South Africa, launching transformative change has become a way of life. They are known to do a dozen summits per year. The summits are designed where the system boundaries are open to customers and events in the larger culture. That keeps them close to their customers and has made them one of the most loved brands in Africa.

**Competencies for SPAR.** We have selected a few of the many competencies required in the SPAR approach to list here, as we feel they are the most critical to remember. Here they are

- Keeping the client focused on the stated purpose yet allowing flexibility to flow with the river of change rather than against it;

- Being perceptive and hearing what really is happening and facilitating a response that moves the system forward;

- Ability to quickly and accurately adapt to unexpected forces;

- Knowing how to help set parallel interventions amidst a chaotic and complex environment;

- Joining with participants as the implementation unfolds in a collaborative manner to better learn to interact around how the work can achieve more results;

- Building and mobilizing commitment to the change process;
- Generalizing learnings and making new knowledge explicit so others can utilize it;
- Helping the client apply systems theory to include expansionist thinking and the establishment of connectivity;
- Looking for the positive and bringing out success stories;
- Building interdependency within the client system rather than fostering dependency on the change agent;
- Ensuring that feedback loops are functioning effectively so specific data are flowing in a timely manner;
- Setting up a monitored accountability process to surface success and new challenges; and
- Helping the client see when a change is ready for adoption and when a change needs to be maintained.

So we see that the SPAR model can be a cycle within a cycle—a Chinese box within a box—an endless loop of response to the ongoing change in today's organizations. Leaving the SPAR model, we come back to our larger change frame and conclude.

## Separation

When we search the literature, we find little on consultant separation or closure. Yet we know from our learning on the dynamics of small groups that saying good-bye and endings are very important. Recall the organization change and transformation that grew out of the group development era of the 1950s through the 1980s. The best source of wisdom on this phase has come from our competency research.

Separation is already treated in this book, so we only wish to add one story. We know of a well-known and respected OD consultant who establishes up-front ground rules for separation. One key ground rule is this: Either the consultant or the client can call a separation meeting at any time. The clients and the consultant commit to a full-day session offsite in an environment free from distractions. At that time they can process the engagement with honesty and openness, trusting that a mutual decision about how and when to separate will evolve. Such a contractual arrangement gave the consultant an opportunity to give the client system a wake-up call regarding what was being stirred in the system because of the intervention, while providing an opportunity to adjust the change process so breakthrough progress could be made. If the client was having issues with the change process or the consultant behavior, an opportunity was provided to work through the issues. Sometimes clients do not understand the consultant's approach. They have a natural tendency to become resistant and defensive. A heart-to-heart conversation will start movement for additional external help or a termination that can be settled on in a manner that is agreeable to both the client and the consultant.

# OTHER CHANGE MODELS

Writings about organizational change are replete with a dizzying array of different change models to guide change leaders and change facilitators. Three of the best-known to corporate managers are Kotter's eight-step model for strategic change, Jick's ten-step model, and General Electric's seven-step model.

## Common Elements

Kotter's (1995) model is based on a study of change in over one hundred organizations of different sizes and industry categories. Kotter's model is intended to help change leaders avoid common errors. It might be regarded as a vision of what the change process should be and how it should be carried out.

Jick's (1991a; 1991b) model is focused on the tactical level of change. It is really a blueprint for a change process. The model serves a dual purpose. It can be useful in evaluating and reacting to the progress of change efforts that have already been launched. It can also serve as a roadmap for the issues to consider when launching a change effort. He labels it tactical because of his belief that most change efforts fail in execution.

Garvin (2000) published a version of General Electric's change model. GE's model is based on Kurt Lewin's (1947) model for change, which emphasizes the importance of unfreezing, movement, and refreezing. The model stresses what leaders need to do to make change happen.

The three models are summarized in Figure 2.5. According to Mento, Jones, and Dirndorfer (2002), the models share some elements in common and can be distilled to identify specific steps to be taken during a change effort:

Step 1: Discover the idea and its context.

Step 2: Assess to define the change initiative.

Step 3: Evaluate the climate for change.

Step 4: Develop a change plan.

Step 5: Find and cultivate a sponsor.

Step 6: Prepare your target audience, the recipients of change.

Step 7: Create the cultural fit making the change last.

Step 8: Develop and choose a change leader team.

Step 9: Create small wins for motivation.

Step 10: Constantly and strategically communicate the change.

Step 11: Measure the progress of the change effort.

Step 12: Integrate the lessons learned in the change process.

## Critiques of Existing Change Models

Existing change models have not been immune from criticism. As Schaafsma (1997, p. 41) has written, "Middle managers who search the current literature for successful models and case studies of change may have difficulty finding something that meets their needs." In short, the issues involving middle managers in change efforts are too often forgotten in existing change models.

Existing change models can be criticized for focusing too much attention on top-down change (Whiteley, 1995), leaving vague the details on how to establish vision, mission, and strategy, providing too much emphasis on the corporate hierarchy as a tool for the change process, directing too much attention to short-term and bottom-line measures of success, and playing too much to the "old boy network" as an instrument for change.

There is no "one best way" to manage change, when (in reality) organizational transformation may require a range of models to be used selectively. Models must be attuned to the corporate cultures and group norms of the settings in which they are applied, and so improvisation is essential (Orlikowski & Hofman, 1997).

*The Change Handbook* (Holman, Devane, & Cady, 2007) describes over sixty methods and models from founders and leaders in the OD. change, and management field based on engaging whole systems. Please visit the book's website for a more expansive list of change models.

# SUMMARY

A model for change serves as a compass to guide managers and consultants as they lead or facilitate change efforts. These models are best understood as a simplified representation of the general steps in initiating and carrying out a change process. This chapter reviewed numerous models for change…some old, some evolving.

Critical research was the first model. Stemming ultimately from Marxist practices, CR is similar to a dialectic approach to change in which opposing positions are used to power change. Critical research drives change from the natural tension that develops between what people believe should be happening and what they believe is actually happening. The basic thrust of CR is to identify this discrepancy and use it to power change. Although critical research has not been widely used in mainstream OD, interventions such as confrontation meetings can lend themselves to it.

Traditional action research was the second model examined in this chapter. Long the foundation for many change efforts, it is properly regarded as both a model and a process. A typical way to view it is that change is managed as a project and encompasses eight key steps.

A third model examined in this chapter was Appreciative Inquiry. Appreciative Inquiry is a philosophy. It "invites us to choose consciously to seek out and inquire into that which is generative and life-enriching, both in our own lives and in the lives of others, and to explore our hopes and dreams for the future" (Watkins & Mohr, 2001, p. 58).

A new view of action research was the fourth and final model examined in this chapter. Its creation is in response to recent research that indicates that the old linear models are not working. It reinvents the traditional action research model based on the assumption that change efforts should not be managed as projects but instead as a process.

The final section of the chapter reviewed some other change models that have been described in the literature. A large section of this book is based on the new view of action research. The reader will therefore find chapters in the rest of the book that address these methods in more detail.

# References

Argyris, C. (2004). *Reasons and rationalizations: The limits to organizational knowledge*. New York: Oxford University Press.

Beckhard, R. (1997). *Agents of change: My life, my practice*. San Francisco: Jossey-Bass.

Block, P. (2000). *Flawless consulting* (2nd ed.). San Francisco: Pfeiffer.

Burke, W.W. (1982). *Organization development: Principles and practices*. Boston, MA: Little, Brown.

Burke, W.W. (2002). *Organization change: Theory and practice*. Thousand Oaks, CA: Sage.

Collins, D. (1998). *Organizational change: Sociological perspectives*. New York: Routledge.

Cooperrider, D.L. (1990). Positive image; positive action: The affirmative basis of organizing. In S. Srivastva & D.L. Cooperrider (Eds.), *Appreciative management and leadership* (pp. 91–125). San Francisco: Jossey-Bass.

Cooperrider, D.L. (1995). *Introduction to appreciative inquiry: Organization development* (5th ed.). Upper Saddle River, NJ: Prentice-Hall.

Cooperrider, D.L., Barrett, F.J., & Srivastva, S. (1995). Social construction and appreciative inquiry: A journey in organizational theory. In D. Hosking, P. Dachler, & K. Gergen (Eds.), *Management and organization: Relational alternatives to individualism* (pp. 157–200). Aldershot, UK: Avebury Press.

Cooperrider, D.L., & Passmore, W.A. (1991). The organization dimension of global change. *Human Relations, 44*(8), 763–787.

Cooperrider, D.L., Sorensen, P., Whitney, D., & Yaeger, T. (Eds.). (1999). *Appreciative inquiry: Rethinking human organization toward a positive theory of change*. Champaign, IL: Stipes.

Cooperrider, D., & Srivastva, S. (1987). Appreciative inquiry in organizational life. In W. Pasmore & R. Woodman (Eds.), *Research in organizational change and development* (Vol. 1). Greenwich, CT: JAI Press.

Cooperrider, D., Whitney, D., & Stavros, J. (2008). *Appreciative inquiry handbook: For leaders of change* (2nd ed.). Brunswick, OH: Crown Custom Publishing.

French, W., & Bell, C., Jr. (1990). *Organization development: Behavioral science interventions for organization improvement* (4th ed.). Englewood Cliffs, NJ: Prentice-Hall.

Garvin, D. (2000). *Learning in action: A guide to putting the learning organization to work*. Boston, MA: Harvard Business School Press.

Heifetz, R.A. (1994). *Leadership without easy answers*. Cambridge, MA: Belknap Press.

Holman, P., Devane, T., & Cady, S. (2007). *The change handbook*. San Francisco: Berrett-Koehler Publishers.

Jick, T. (1991a). *Implementing change*. [Note 9–191–114.] Boston, MA: Harvard Business School Press.

Jick, T. (1991b). *Note on the recipients of change*. [Note 9–491–039.] Boston, MA: Harvard Business School Press.

Katz, D., & Kahn, R. (1978). *The social psychology of organizations* (2nd ed.). Hoboken, NJ: John Wiley & Sons.

Kotter, J.P. (1995). Why transformation efforts fail. *Harvard Business Review, 74*(2) (Reprint No. 95204).

Lang, D. (1992). Organizational culture and commitment. *Human Resource Development Quarterly, 3*(2), 191–196.

Lewin, K. (1947). Group decision and social change. In E.E. Maccoby, T. Newcomb, & E. Hartley (Eds.), *Readings in social psychology*. New York: Holt, Rinehart and Winston.

McLean, G., & Sullivan, R. (1989). Essential competencies of internal and external OD consultants. Unpublished manuscript.

Mento, A.J., Jones, R.M., & Dirndorfer, W. (2002). A change management process: Grounded in both theory and practice. *Journal of Change Management, 3*(1), 45–59.

Orlikowski, W.J., & Hofman, J.D. (1997). An improvisational model for change management: The case of groupware technologies. *Sloan Management Review, 38*(2), 11–21.

Rothwell, W. (2001). *The manager and change leader*. Alexandria, VA: American Society for Training and Development.

Schaafsma, H. (1997). A networking model of change for middle managers. *Leadership and Organization Development Journal, 18*(1), 41.

Schein, E.H. (1999). *Process consultation revisited*. Englewood Cliffs, NJ: Prentice-Hall.

Stewart, J., & Kringas, P. (2003). Change management—strategy and values in six agencies from the Australian Public Service. *Public Administration Review, 63*(6), 675.

Watkins, J.M., & Mohr, B.J. (2001). *Appreciative inquiry: Change at the speed of imagination*. San Francisco: Pfeiffer.

Whiteley, A. (1995). *Managing change: A core values approach*. Melbourne: Macmillan Education.

CHAPTER THREE

# On the Shoulders of Giants

*The Origins of OD\**

John J. Scherer and Billie T. Alban

In our work as OD practitioners, whose shoulders are we standing on? Whose "conceptual DNA" runs in our veins? What are our operating assumptions and where did they come from?

More often than not, we do our OD work inside a culture of practice whose principles are simply taken for granted—things like involving people in planning and taking action, group decision making, action research, "feedback," high-performance/high-satisfaction team development, leadership and management coaching, the stages in the consulting process. These methods and principles have not always been around. Who figured them out—and passed them on to us?

You may know some of the people on whose shoulders you are standing; certainly you have read the works of earlier "elders" who have shaped your work, but many of those who attempted to improve their social systems are lost in the mists of time…

---

\*Many colleagues contributed to this chapter, among them Warner Burke, John Adams, Saul Eisen, Edie Seashore, Denny Gallagher, Marvin Weisbord, and others. We have drawn heavily from Weisbord's wonderfully rich, easy-to-read, and well-documented description of the origins of our field in *Productive Workplaces* (1987).

# OD'S ANCIENT ROOTS

We will get to the more recent aspects of the origin of our field, but first, it is important to acknowledge that people have been attempting to create more effective organizations since the dawn of time.

- No doubt small groups of Neanderthal cave-dwellers discussed ways to kill the mastodon more effectively—and without losing so many hunters.
- The early Egyptians had what could best be described as "consulting engineers" who made sure the many communities up and down the Nile practiced proper flood control so everyone would survive another year with an irrigated harvest.
- The biblical story of Moses and his father-in-law Jethro tells of what could be called the first recorded consultation for large-scale change.
- We know that kings and religious leaders across the centuries and around the world had advisors they would turn to when facing difficult decisions.
- There was also the court jester, who played a major if undefined role as an executive development coach, holding up a (hopefully) humorous mirror so the ruler could see the potential folly in a particular path of action.

These historical attempts to have more effective organizations were missing several important ingredients, however, especially the distinction between *content* (where most of the above "consulting" almost certainly focused) and *process* (something yet to be discovered). It was up to the unique exploration of more recent minds and hearts to discover and apply the principles that launched what we would recognize today as organization development.

# BIG BRANCHES IN OUR OD FAMILY TREE

Since 1900, there have been major contributors to the shaping of our discipline:

- Sigmund Freud was one of the first to postulate the existence of an inner world that drives what human beings do—something we hold today as obvious as gravity.
- Carl Jung postulated the power of archetypes operating in the human psyche and emphasized the role of the Shadow, those aspects of who we are that have not yet been integrated. He also legitimated the world of dreams and intuition and suggested that we were much more than rational beings living in a Cartesian/Newtonian world.
- B.F. Skinner took Pavlov's salivating dogs to the next (human) level, theorizing that we are not making free-will decisions at all, but are

products of stimulus/response-driven operant conditioning: what gets rewarded gets repeated. (Today's field of Performance Management comes directly from this school of thought.)

- Erik Erikson saw the human being's life as a developmental journey with predictable stages or phases that must be successfully traversed. All the life cycle and developmental models of today owe a debt to his thinking.

- Abraham Maslow showed that what motivates people varies, depending on where they are in their hierarchy of needs, and that we should be investigating not just "sick" people, but those who are doing "well," to discover what makes us tick. (Appreciative Inquiry, one of the more recent innovations in OD, is a direct descendant of Maslow in this regard.)

- Carl Rogers, along with Maslow, initiated what came to be called Third Force (or Humanistic) Psychology, an alternative to the operant conditioning of Skinner and the psychoanalytic model of Freud. Rogers also showed that increasing people's effectiveness happened within a relationship between the helper and the helpee, and that the movement toward wholeness was accelerated by empathy rather than advice-giving.

- Eric Berne, creator of Transactional Analysis, pioneered the current self-help movement by simplifying the principles of personal effectiveness and making them available to lay people. He saw the role of an internal adult mediating between the internal child and parent, and showed people the "games" they were playing inside their "life script."

But none of these extraordinary people has had more direct impact on the conception, birth, and early growth of OD than the next four. Frederick Taylor, the first in chronological order, set the stage; the second and third (Kurt Lewin and Wilfred Bion) developed and applied the principles; and the last (Douglas McGregor) made them available to managers of organizations and the general public. They are also among the first names on the Origins of OD Time-Line (see Figure 3.1). Hundreds of people have contributed to this field. Regrettably, space does not permit all the contributors to be mentioned. We have had to make choices and apologize to those who do not find their names listed.

## Frederick Taylor—Scientific Management (ca. 1893)

Following the Civil War, industrialization in America went rampant. Large factories began dotting the landscape where farms had once stood. Machines, the exciting new technology, were promising to make business owners wealthier than ever. If only they could get those lazy and greedy front-line workers to use the machines to their maximum potential. This ever-widening gulf between wealthy business owners and disgruntled and exhausted workers led to the growth of unions, providing at least some leverage for protecting employees

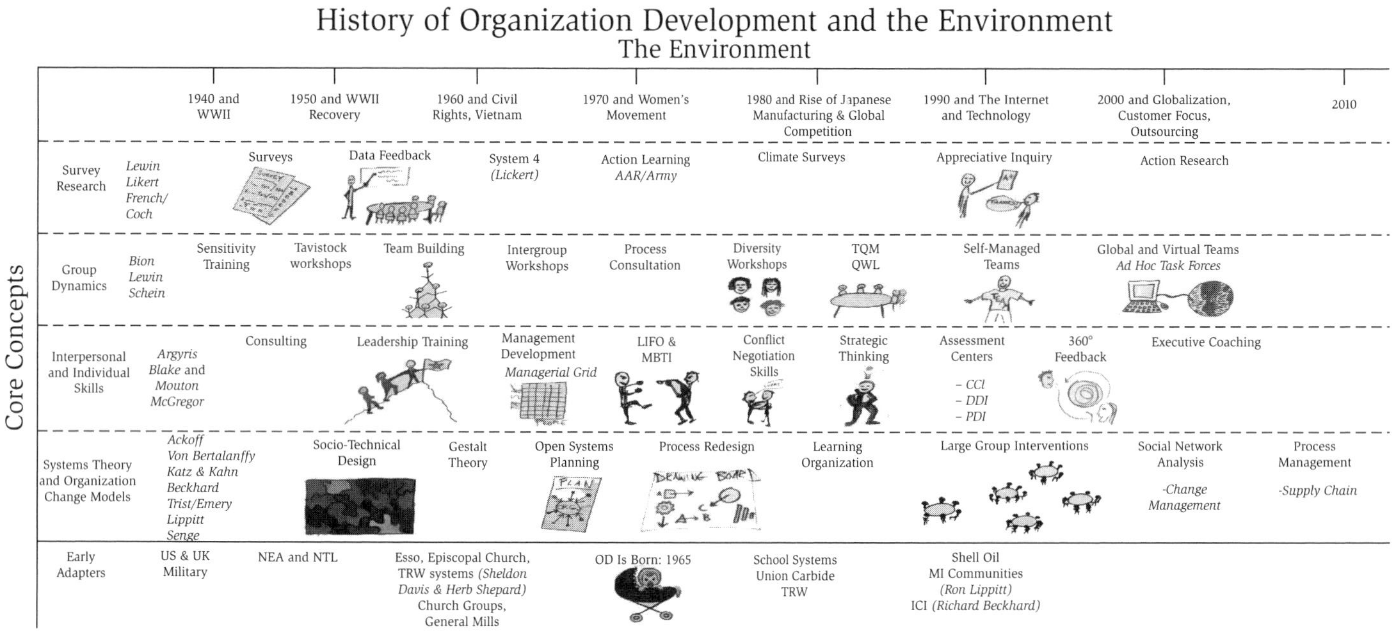

# History of Organization Development and the Environment

## The Environment

| Core Concepts | 1940 and WWII | 1950 and WWII Recovery | 1960 and Civil Rights, Vietnam | 1970 and Women's Movement | 1980 and Rise of Japanese Manufacturing & Global Competition | 1990 and The Internet and Technology | 2000 and Globalization, Customer Focus, Outsourcing | 2010 |
|---|---|---|---|---|---|---|---|---|
| Survey Research | *Lewin* *Likert* *French/Coch* | Surveys / Data Feedback | System 4 (*Lickert*) | Action Learning *AAR/Army* | Climate Surveys | Appreciative Inquiry | Action Research | |
| Group Dynamics | Sensitivity Training / *Bion* *Lewin* *Schein* | Tavistock workshops / Team Building | Intergroup Workshops | Process Consultation | Diversity Workshops / TQM QWL | Self-Managed Teams | Global and Virtual Teams *Ad Hoc Task Forces* | |
| Interpersonal and Individual Skills | Consulting / *Argyris* *Blake and Mouton* *McGregor* | Leadership Training | Management Development *Managerial Grid* | LIFO & MBTI | Conflict Negotiation Skills / Strategic Thinking | Assessment Centers – CCI – DDI – PDI / 360° Feedback | Executive Coaching | |
| Systems Theory and Organization Change Models | *Ackoff* *Von Bertalanffy* *Katz & Kahn* *Beckhard* *Trist/Emery* *Lippitt* *Senge* | Socio-Technical Design | Gestalt Theory / Open Systems Planning | Process Redesign | Learning Organization | Large Group Interventions | Social Network Analysis / -Change Management | Process Management -Supply Chain |
| Early Adapters | US & UK Military | NEA and NTL | Esso, Episcopal Church, TRW systems (*Sheldon Davis & Herb Shepard*) Church Groups, General Mills | OD Is Born: 1965 | School Systems Union Carbide TRW | Shell Oil MI Communities (*Ron Lippitt*) ICI (*Richard Beckhard*) | | |

**Figure 3.1.** Origins of OD Time-Line

Source: Alban, Bunker, and Axelrod, 2007; Design by Bridgecase, LLC.

from becoming essentially slaves-with-a-paycheck. It was inside this social cauldron that Frederick Taylor developed and implemented the first truly systematic and scientific approach to resolving workplace production problems.

No one in our long chain of OD ancestors is as controversial as Taylor, founder of what he called "scientific management" (Taylor, 1915). You might think of him as a hard-hearted efficiency expert with a stopwatch who tried to remake each worker into the exact image of the one who could do a specific task the best. Taylor studied "Schmidt," the now-famous pig iron loader, who was shoveling more pig iron than anyone else. The popular image is of Taylor using Schmidt like a hamster in a wheel, driving him to accomplish even more to see what human beings were capable of. However, according to one Taylor biographer, Schmidt jogged to and from work each day for two months and built a house in his spare time! Taylor's great discovery was that to load as much pig iron as Schmidt (and others) could do, the arms had to be free of load 57 percent of the day. Taylor was focused on making work easier, not harder.

Along the same vein, few people know Taylor as the father of matrix management, the incentive wage system, the champion of the front-line worker, labor-management cooperation, and paying the person, not the job. He was a man who believed that respect in the workplace should be based on knowledge and performance, not position. Taylor was the one who championed "servant leadership" among supervisors. As Weisbord (1987) points out, Taylor's overriding objective was productive labor-management cooperation, not just time-and-motion efficiency.

Taylor's thinking dramatically shaped the world's workplace and its leaders and continues to shape them—and our OD work today. Taylor's insistence on (a) maintaining tight control of his interventions to ensure implementation of changes and (b) piecework—breaking down tasks into their simplest "chunks" and requiring a single person to do a single task—became his undoing. It was left to our next progenitor, Kurt Lewin, to discover an even better way to (a) get good ideas for work improvement and (b) get people to actually follow through. Lewin's approach meant, however, letting go of control and trusting the people themselves to figure out—with some support and guidance—what to do.

## Kurt Lewin—The Grandfather of OD (ca. 1946)

Anyone who has ever uttered the words "feedback" or "action research" or "group dynamics" or "self-managed work teams" or "force field" has been impacted by Kurt Lewin (Marrow, 1969). Known today as "the grandfather of applied behavioral science," Lewin, a Berlin-educated Polish Jew majoring in psychology, left Nazi-dominated Germany for the United States in 1933, saying, "I will not teach in a country where my daughter cannot be a student." This practical way of thinking about real-world situations led him to create his revolutionary conceptual models for human behavior. As he was so fond of saying,

"There is nothing so useful as a good theory." This is because a theory (from the Greek *theorein*, to see) allows one to see what is happening in new ways.

Many of his new ways of seeing things were put to work in a single, well-documented project that began in 1939. In response to an urgent request from the manager at The Harwood Manufacturing Company in rural Virginia for help in raising production levels, John R.P. French (an external consultant from the University of Michigan and dyed-in-the-wool Lewinian) went to see what could be done. Working with an internal personnel manager, Lester Coch, they designed and carried out what was probably the very first "action research process." Harwood, a pajama-making facility, was losing money rapidly, with very high turnover and absenteeism, in spite of wages and other benefits greater than workers could make elsewhere. Supervisors had tried every carrot-and-stick motivation and reward system they knew, all with little or no effect.

When the consultants arrived, they initiated what was then a radically different process, one that you will recognize as standard practice for consultants today. First they interviewed the plant manager, then the other managers and supervisors, and a representative group of front-line employees. After observing the system in action for a while, they made recommendations to the management team. The gist of their proposal: begin an experiment with the front-line people, to learn what might make a difference in their productivity. It is hard for us to understand how revolutionary this was in 1939! One can imagine some managers and supervisors thinking, "Oh, great…we're going to let the inmates run the prison…."

In support of this process, they also recommended:

- That supervisors stop trying to raise production levels by addressing the work of individuals, and work instead on a system emphasizing and involving entire work teams; and

- That management set production goals that are clearly attainable by workers (when they appear impossible, there is no sense of failure when they are not reached).

**Self-Managed Work Teams (ca 1939).** When production increased slightly, French and Coch began to hold informal weekly meetings with a cross-functional collection of high-producing workers to discuss what difficulties they encountered and how they might be overcome. Management agreed to try whatever this group suggested (they had nothing to lose).

After getting management's permission, the high-performing group was invited to vote on what the production goal for individual workers should be. They raised the existing piecework targets from 75 to 87, a level never attained before, and said they would get there in five days—which they did, much to the astonishment of everyone involved. Meanwhile, other groups in the plant doing the same work had no appreciable increase in productivity.

The Lewin-oriented consultants hypothesized that motivation alone does not suffice to lead to change. This link is provided by *people making decisions that affect them*. His conclusion: a simple process like decision making, which takes only a few moments, is able to affect workers' conduct for a long time. The making of a decision seems to have a "freezing" effect, which is partly due to the individual's tendency to "stick to his decisions" and partly due to his wanting to be a part of "the commitment of the group."

**Force Field Analysis.**  The consultants then had a small group of workers plan their own hourly production rates by using "pacing cards." This group hit and maintained an amazing pace, going from 67 units prior to the experiment to 82 and stabilizing there. The other groups stayed where they were. Why?

Lewin had observed that the output of a worker was "quasi-stationary" and existed not in a vacuum, but in a constantly shifting "field of forces," some helping and some hindering the desired increase. Changes in performance could be achieved by either (a) strengthening a "driving" force or (b) weakening a "restraining" force. The increases created at Harwood were not achieved by increasing driving forces, like more pressure to produce, or management-driven motivational methods, or even paying for performance. This is because such a top-down approach usually creates its own backlash of worker fatigue, nervousness, and roller-coaster productivity. The results at Harwood, the consultants believed, came from involving the people themselves in discovering and then reducing selected restraining forces holding production back.

**B = f(p, e).**  Perhaps the single most significant conceptual input to OD is this one: individual behavior (B) is a function (f) of personal factors (p), plus the impact of the current social environment (e). This model explains why some training-oriented change efforts aimed at the individual often fail. Like the alcoholic treated alone and then sent back to an unchanged family system, change efforts that do not take into account making changes in the (social) environment will not sustain themselves. This is because personal factors are multiplied by environmental factors. As Lewin said, "I have found it easier to change the group than to change one individual in the group" (personal communication between John Scherer and Ron Lippitt). Training conducted with intact work groups can reduce this problem, since both the individual (p) and the group (e) are being impacted.

**The Birth of the T-Group.**  In the summer of 1946, Lewin was invited by the Connecticut State Inter-Racial Commission to conduct a training program in race relations for local community leaders. In typical Lewinian "elegance," he suggested that they design a program that would allow them to train the participants and conduct an experiment in "change" at the same time. Working with a team of colleagues, including two young graduate students, Ron Lippitt and

Lee Bradford, the researchers led discussions during the day about the roots of inter-ethnic prejudice (primarily among Polish, Irish, and Italian immigrants) and its impact on communities.

The first evening the staff met alone in a basement room at the training site (The Teacher's College in New Britain, Connecticut) to discuss what had happened during the day. Several participants wandered by looking for a lost jacket and, when they heard a snatch of the facilitators' conversation, asked if they could sit in. Some staffers said, "No, this is a staff meeting." But Lewin said, "Ya, ya, come in!" During a report by one of the researchers, a participant disagreed with the "feedback," and a heated debate began. The discussion excited Lewin ("like an electric shock," said Bradford later) because it took the whole room out of a conversation about prejudice and plunged them into an experience of prejudice in action. He saw that in this real-time group discussion, they had created a microcosm of "community" within which the forces that create prejudice were happening in front of their eyes, triggered by "feedback." The next evening, more participants attended the evening debriefing session, which, because of its less-structured, free-for-all nature, became the most energized session of the program!

Lewin saw immediately the power of what he dubbed the "here-and-now" sessions, and suggested that the next year's program be planned to feature such conversations. The small group trainings were initially called "sensitivity training sessions," since they were designed to sensitize participants to the forces of group dynamics (things like decision making and conflict resolution) in exploring attitude formation and other forms of prejudice in community life. (The use of the term "sensitivity training" as a vehicle for personal growth was a later offshoot, led by a group called the Western Behavioral Science Institute.)

**The Housewives Experiment.** Another important Lewin experiment was with the U.S. military during WW II, a result of Ron Lippitt and his colleague Margaret Mead's connections with the Department of the Navy. The government was interested in trying to get housewives to use what were euphemistically called "variety meats" (basically Spam), rather than the prime cuts, since there was a meat shortage and the best meat was needed for soldiers overseas. In this research project, there were two groups made up of housewives. One heard lectures on the nutritional value of variety meats and why they should try the recipes that were given out. The second group, while they attended a preliminary lecture on the topic, attended a group discussion on the topic, where they could share their thoughts, concerns, and reasons for resisting the idea and discuss recipes. At the end of the day, they were asked who would be willing to try some of the recipes, using variety meats instead of better cuts. Many of the women in both groups made a public commitment to trying the recipes. The follow-up research, however, found that the discussion method—which allowed people to voice their resistance—had actually lowered their resistance and been far more effective than the simple "telling" approach in generating long-term change in the housewives' attitude and behavior. Lewin's notion of the field of forces and how to reduce resistance by surfacing and accepting it was proven once again.

**The Story of the Small Group and OD.** Lewin died suddenly at age 57 in February 1947, but his followers continued his work. Some of the more individually focused practitioners, like Carl Rogers, Jack Gibb, Will Schutz, and Matt Miles, realized the impact the small-group sessions had on participants' personal development. They began to use the powerful unstructured training group format (referred to almost immediately as the "T [for Training] group") both in work settings and in "stranger laboratories" for the general public. Soon it became obvious that the person-centered T-group triggered so much inner change and so many new behaviors, accompanied by potential embarrassment on re-entry, that its use inside organizations all but halted. OD consultants, however, like Herb Shepard, Tony Petrella, Peter Block, Bob Golembiewski, Stuart Atkins, and Allen Catcher, in true Lewinian fashion, tinkered with the format and created many variations that retained the power of the small group while reducing unnecessary personal exposure and risk. As Weisbord points out, Roger Harrison's "role negotiation" was a major programmatic step in reducing the threat of team building. John and Joyce Weir got rid of interpersonal feedback entirely in their self-differentiation labs. Their invention of "percept language" made it possible for people to provide feedback to themselves while using others as projection screens.

In this way, the small-group training experience took its central place in the practice of "planned change" and, as you will see, led directly to the "discovery" of our field of organization development. We would like to settle two unsettling questions that have been dogging our field for years:

Q. Who named OD, Herb Shepard or Dick Beckhard?

Q. What does "OD" actually stand for?

The friendly debates have "raged" for years, but we are hereby putting it to rest. In 1974, Larry Porter, long-time editor of *The OD Practitioner*, sat down and conducted an interview with both of them, during which he raised the question (Porter, 1974). As Larry reported it in a tongue-in-cheek footnote:

"They created this response 'for the record'—prompted by Herb's sense of humor: Both Herb Shepard and Dick Beckhard are OD consultants of the external persuasion. After some discussion among the three of us as to who did what, we agreed that I (Larry) would identify them as follows in the article: Dick Beckhard, while consulting at General Electric in 1957, invented the term organization development. Herb Shepard, while consulting at Esso in 1957, invented the term organization development."

The proper full name for OD—at least insofar as the original co-namers intended—is "*Organization* Development" and not "*Organizational* Development." The incorrect linguistic version probably came out of the early emphasis on personal development described above.

## Wilfred Bion—The Tavistock Method (1948)

While Lewin was working in America, on the other side of the Atlantic a British psychiatrist named Wilfred Bion was responding to the fallout of World War II. Bion (1940) was asked by London's Tavistock Institute to work with traumatized and shell-shocked soldiers from the battlefield. There were too many to treat individually, so Bion brought them together into groups. His intention was to move around the group working with one veteran at a time while the group basically observed and supported nonverbally. In the process, he, like Lewin, discovered the power of the group. The soldiers couldn't sit still while Bion worked with someone else, and they spontaneously began to share their experiences, reaching out to their buddies. As they helped each other, they were also learning from each other—not just from Bion, the psychiatrist and authority figure. Bion came to see that the way leaders conduct themselves creates predictable responses from those they are leading. When the leader takes responsibility for the group's output, participants will predictably react to the authority figure with one of these three behavioral options:

- Fight—resisting or doing the opposite of whatever the leader suggests;
- Flight—finding a way to leave, physically or emotionally, or going along with whatever the authority suggests in a subservient way; or
- Pairing—forming coalitions with one or two others in the group as a safe haven.

When the leader takes responsibility for simply raising awareness of the group's process to the group, participants are more likely to respond with what Bion called "Work," the fourth option. A participant who is engaged in Work is authentically staying in touch with what is happening and working through whatever conflicts emerge to the learning that exists on the other side. Bion discovered how to empower a group to take responsibility for its own work and learning.

**The Origin of Socio-Technical Consulting and Self-Managed Work Teams.** Marvin Weisbord (1987) recounts a marvelous anecdote, told to him by his dear friend and mentor, Eric Trist, about something that has had a quantum impact on our field. It happened immediately after WW II in the coal mines of England, as they tried desperately to recover economically and socially from the devastation of the war. Kenneth Bamforth, a long-time unionized coal miner and then a Tavistock student of Trist's, went back to visit the South Yorkshire mine where he had worked for many years.

What he saw stunned him. His former colleagues had been experimenting with new ways to make extracting the ore continuous, having thrown out the older, traditional "long wall" approach in which groups of miners were organized into teams that performed a single task (think Taylorism). Instead, the union miners and general manager had gotten together with union support and planned the new system. The new technology of roof control enabled the miners to go back to an earlier social system—in which miners were multi-skilled and performed all jobs—an old way of doing things that had died under the influence of the Industrial Revolution. The result was that they could now mine coal twenty-four hours a day, not having to wait for an earlier shift to complete a task. Bamforth went back to Tavistock and invited his favorite professor, Eric Trist, to come down into the mine with him to see if this might not be useful to the country's business recovery. As Trist reported to friends later, he came up a different man.

This combination of a technical innovation, coupled with a social innovation, made "short wall" mining possible, significantly increasing both hard output and morale. Trist realized immediately the connection between England's business recovery and what he had just seen, putting together the therapeutic work Bion had done with leaderless groups and Lewin's work in small group dynamics. Teams, it appeared, if given the proper support and resources, could manage their own work—and produce at high levels.

You can see the similarity between Trist's insights and the ones Lewin and his successors were having as the T-group evolved. It was inevitable that cross-pollination would occur, and it did, as members of the U.S.-based A.K. Rice Institute, trained in Bion's "Group Relations" work, connected with people trained in the emerging "applied behavioral science" work of Lewin and his successors, Ken Benne, Ron Lippitt, Warren Bennis, Jack Gibb, Ed Schein, and others.

The Tavistock coal mine study had an impact on several European and Scandinavian companies that began to experiment with self-managed teams, including Volvo of Sweden, Shell Oil in Canada, and Esso in Norway. A few U.S. companies, such as Scott Paper and Procter & Gamble, also applied Bion's approach to self-managed work teams, with mixed results.

Bion and The Tavistock Institute recognized in the late 1940s and early 1950s the relationship of the larger social network to the work structure and the technical system, setting the stage for the naming and exploration of the systems thinking we know today. Their finding: It was not enough to focus on individuals or groups internally; you had to look at the structures and systems that surrounded them. Work redesign and job enrichment were also systems approaches to worker motivation, with Frederick Herzberg (1959) being the foremost explorer of applying the insights from Bion to motivating employees. These approaches recognized that an employee's productivity and creativity have more to do with the way the job is designed and the system around that employee than with the characteristics of the person. The Tavistock Institute had seen and highlighted this truth in the earlier coal mine studies.

# Douglas McGregor—Theory X and Theory Y (1954)

It was Douglas McGregor, a young faculty member in psychology, who enticed Lewin to come to MIT in 1946 to create the Research Center for Group Dynamics. McGregor, an industrial relations manager during WW II, found in Lewin the theoretical base for his own work in solving labor-management problems. Like Lewin, McGregor liked the real, rough-and-tumble world of the workplace and, by attaching the Center to the School of Engineering, the two of them were able to avoid many of the constrictions and traditional paradigms they would have faced had they joined the school of academic psychology. (Because of little turns in the road like this, OD's birth took place in the laboratory of work—money, machines, information, and people—and not in the laboratory of pigeons or rats.)

McGregor is best known for his Theory X and Theory Y management model, which asserts that there are two diametrically opposed world views available to managers, and they result in completely different workplace results. You may know the essence of his theory; you may not know the source. Just as Lewin's lifelong fascination with democratic processes grew out of his early experiences in and around Hitler's top-down, elitist Nazism, McGregor's model had its roots in his family of origin. His father was a second-generation lay minister, running a shelter for men who had lost their jobs—and some their souls—a man who carried the pain of his "clients" heavily in his heart. His Theory X manager has an uncanny resemblance to his father and grandfather's "hard" and largely negative view of human nature as dominated by sin and "fallenness" (Bennis, 1966). Young Doug, it could be asserted, tried his whole life to choose another path, one with a more "positive" view of human nature, his Theory Y.

Theory X managers hold the assumption about human nature that people are, by nature, lazy, greedy, and self-centered and must be tightly watched and managed (controlled) from the outside in order to get the best work out of them. Theory Y managers believe that people are, by nature, predisposed to want to do well, to make a contribution, and to learn and grow and only need a sense of direction and support in the form of feedback and coaching to manage themselves to do their best.

McGregor's book, *The Human Side of Enterprise* (1960), took the workplace world by storm. It seemed to encapsulate two well-known sides of human nature and offered a rational explanation, with supporting evidence, for what could be counted on from each approach when it came to motivating people. The book is still in print, attesting to its staying power. OD owes a great deal of its positive stance regarding human beings and the potential of teams and organizations to Douglas McGregor. People like Frederick Herzberg (1959) took McGregor's theories to the next level and made the distinction between "satisfiers" (pay, benefits, working conditions), which can never motivate—only dissatisfy if they are not sufficiently present—and true "motivators" (recognition, achievement, responsibility, learning)—from Maslow's hierarchy of needs.

Barry Johnson (1996) sees this as a clear polarity-to-be-managed, not an either/or. Both Theory X and Y assumptions are present in most of us, often in conflict. It is now widely believed that there is a time for telling people what to do, temporarily accepting dependency, and a time for supporting independence and self-motivation. The trick is learning as much as we can about both polarities in ourselves if we want to work effectively with a wide range of others. McGregor receives our deepest appreciation for making the "other" pole of the polarity (Theory Y) so clear and defensible.

## WHAT IS DIFFERENT ABOUT OD

Our OD "grandparents"—Taylor, Lewin, Bion, and McGregor—handed this fundamental truth down to us, each in his own way:

> **Finding out what is actually happening (research)—and why it
> is happening (diagnosis)—and getting all that data "on the table"
> where it is seen and discussed by stakeholders in a safe environ-
> ment, has the power to change people and systems (action).**

It is this principle that differentiates the field of OD from other efforts to help or fix social systems. Every subsequent OD theoretical model, exercise, and/or practice engages clients in participative reflection on the process(es) governing what is happening. The next section describes what OD's subsequent generations—now "elders" themselves—have done with what they received.

## THE ORIGINS OF OD TIME-LINE

Co-author Billie Alban has done a huge service for everyone who ever practices OD by creating what we are calling "The Origins of OD Time-Line" (presented earlier in Figure 3.1). Developed using a process she and her colleagues pioneered in the now well-established practice of Large Scale Change (Bunker & Alban, 1997; Weisbord & Janoff, 2000), the time-line shows us clearly:

- What was happening as OD came into being—and evolved;
- The core OD concepts and when they emerged;
- The major contributors—theorists, researchers, writers, practitioners;
- The significant external forces and events that paralleled—and impacted—the birth and early years of our field; and

- The institutions that were first to adapt OD as part of their workplace culture.

As you can see in the figure, the horizontal axis is time, with the decades rolling from left to right. Along the side, vertically, are Core Concepts. (Even though, for graphic reasons, they are shown to run across the page as discrete elements, they often merge and blend with other elements. For instance, data feedback is also used in team building, and systems theory is applied in many of the core concepts.) The following material describes the core concepts and related elements.

## Action Research

Lewin's now-classic postulate—"No research without action; no action without research"—defines this element on the chart. One of OD's fundamental principles is the use of data-gathering as the basis for planning subsequent interventions. Rensis Likert developed a widely used approach to action research using a scale of responses, allowing people to indicate how strongly they held a particular position on some item of organizational concern. The survey-feedback process was pioneered by Ron Lippitt and is a staple in every OD consultant's repertoire today. Ron Lippitt and his brother, Gordon Lippitt, pioneered methods for feeding back the data and for "implication derivation," something they insisted needed to be done with the client, not for the client. Robert Blake and Jane Mouton's Managerial Grid fast became a research tool of choice because of its strong and clear visual presentation, making it immediately useful to both the consultant and the client.

If you look toward the middle of this line, you will note something called AAR, which means "after action review." It is a process the Army uses to review military engagements that have taken place. NTL had a process called EIAG, developed by early Episcopalian OD consultant/trainer Nancy Geyer. In this model, first you *Experience*, something "happens" or you do something. Next you *Identify* important points in that experience or action; you then *Analyze* that incident, using appropriate models or theories; and then you *Generalize*: What have I learned here that I need to apply to the next situation? Learning takes place in response to survey data, but learning can also be a process of discussing any activity or incident that occurs.

Survey feedback, although used by industrial psychologists, has been widely used in the OD field, not only with teams but also in assessing entire organizations. There are surveys that look at employee morale, perceptions of leadership, clarity about mission and strategy, and so on. Likert's scale, a Profile of Organization Characteristics, demonstrated that a method he termed a Systems Four method for making decisions (a participative process) was more likely to indicate a successful organization and satisfied employees. Blake and Mouton's

Managerial Grid looked at management's role in integrating concern for people with concern for productivity, using a system-wide approach. Data collected from managers through surveys were later used in workshops these managers attended to increase their ability to work with their subordinates, bosses, and peers.

One of the first applications of computers to assist in the action research process was *The People-Performance Profile* (PPP), developed by John Scherer and Bob Crosby in 1978. The PPP measured and fed back scaled information to the individual on personal factors (for example, exercise, nutrition, alcohol and drug use, stress management). Each work group received data on things like decision making, conflict management, or problem solving, and top management received data on strategic planning, physical environment, organizational stress, and other factors. In 1983, Ron Lippitt told the developers he considered the computerized PPP and the sophisticated employee-involvement process used to share the data with clients "one of the most significant contributions to applied behavioral science since Lewin." It will be interesting to see over time the impact of the Internet on action research and surveys. Organizations are now surveying their employees through the Internet. One such survey of organizational culture, developed by Dutch consultant Gert Hofstede, was a study of 130,000 IBM employees in forty different countries!

## Appreciative Inquiry (AI)

An interesting approach to action research is the integration of Appreciative Inquiry (AI). In brief, AI is a method that looks at the positive aspects of "what is working" in the organization through storytelling and extrapolates from these stories the "more" that is needed to sustain the positive into the future. It combines data collection with a large-group meeting (or meetings) where the stories gathered are used as building blocks to design new initiatives for the future.

Primarily through interviewing and storytelling, AI begins with exploring the best of the past, leading to enlivened images of what could be. AI searches for the best of "what is" (one's experience up to now) to provide the basis for imagining "what might be." The aim is to generate new knowledge that expands the "realm of the possible" and helps members of an organization to envision together a desired future. AI is treated in more detail in Chapter Seven.

## Group Dynamics

We have already described the birth of the T-group and its subsequent application to personal development. One element of a T-group was that participants were encouraged to share their perceptions of one another. As group members received feedback and discovered the impact they had on others, they also took the risk to reveal the impact that others had on them. It is important to note that, in Lewin's model, receiving and giving feedback on individual behavior was only one element of group dynamics training. Lewin was very interested that people learn about the dynamics of groups as models of larger social systems, what helped them function effectively, and what helped them make decisions that the group would willingly commit to. Lewin and his students saw small-group work as having a political aspect—a kind of training for democracy.

**How the T-Group Led to OD.** Saul Eisen, an OD "elder," gave us this account of how the T-group led to OD:

"Around 1955 a group of consultants, including Herb Shepard and Bob Tannenbaum, began a small-group project with a planned organizational change program. In the first phase, key managers were invited to participate in stranger labs at Western Training Laboratory (WTL) and National Training Laboratory (NTL). They viewed this as a seeding process to develop a culture of change. As a second phase, as these managers began asking for help with their own teams, one external consultant and one internal consultant with T-group experience were assigned to work with a manager and his/her team. The procedure they developed was to interview the manager and all team members about the team issues and needs requiring attention.

"They then took the team off-site for a week or so of intensive work together. The session began with a feedback presentation by the consulting team, which became the agenda for the off-site. These sessions had a strong T-group component, considering group and interpersonal interaction issues, but they were also grounded concretely in the task issues of the group. The sessions ended with specific action plans and decisions for how the team would work together toward their task mission when they returned 'home.' Sound familiar?

"These 'team labs' very quickly supplanted the 'stranger labs' of the first phase, and a large number of key project teams became involved, using what they had learned to tackle pressing organizational issues and tasks. Later a third phase began extending this approach to inter-group confrontation labs based on Dick Beckhard's model—and then into other whole system interventions involving larger organizational units. And that is how T-groups gave birth to OD."

## Interpersonal and Individual Skills

In the summer of 1947, The National Education Association sponsored Lewinian-type small-group training, which gave birth to The National Training Laboratory (NTL). Workshops have been held every summer since using the facilities of a boarding school in Bethel, Maine. During these early NTL sessions, in addition to social psychologists, many clinical psychologists came to the summer workshops and were often invited to be part of the staff. Some OD elders perceived that with the inclusion of clinical psychologists, the focus of the T-group changed. Before long the focus was more on interpersonal skills, receiving and giving feedback, and personal growth, rather than on the original focus on learning about groups and how they work. There is no question that many people found these therapeutically oriented groups helpful. Several of Lewin's old students were upset with this trend, holding a strong belief that something important was being lost. Lewin's original intent, coming out of Nazi Germany, was to give people the insights and the skills that would generate more democratic, participative processes in groups and teams.

The Western Behavioral Science Institute, formed shortly after NTL, took on more of the personal growth aspects. The western group had a strong focus on the individual, with The Esalen Institute being a well-known offshoot. There were tensions between those groups, those who wanted participants to learn about group processes and those who thought that personal development and personal growth should be paramount. In the 1970s, Hal Kelner organized a well-attended workshop at NTL called "A 1950s Group Dynamics Experience," a small-group experience to demonstrate what Lewin had intended.

Dick Beckhard used to tell his students, "In every team and organization there are issues around goals, roles, tasks—and interpersonal issues. Start with any of the first three, and the interpersonal will surface, but always in relationship to the first three" (personal communication). It was sanguine advice. It is not an either/or, but a polarity. Self-development and self-awareness are important, but so are the skills in working with groups, using participative processes, and helping groups make good decisions. These polarities are reflected in this book.

**Survey-Feedback-Based Skill Development.** As Lewin and his early "disciples" modeled, a number of different types of surveys were used to gather data feedback, both from the managers and from their subordinates and peers, often including something on their managerial style. This feedback was then used to provide training and development in the necessary skills. Data feedback surveys like Life Orientation (LIFO); Dominance, Influence, Steadiness and Conscientiousness (DISC); and Meyers-Briggs Type Indicator® (MBTI) were created and used for self-assessment. Other feedback surveys such as 360-degree feedback were developed to provide data from multiple sources on how their behavior was perceived. In addition to interpersonal and management skills, it was recognized that people need conflict resolution skills, systems thinking skills, and, more recently added, coaching skills.

Early on, people recognized the need to train people, internally and externally, in consulting skills. People in staff positions were encouraged to take training in how to consult with their internal client groups, and external people were given training in how to consult with client organizations. Interpersonal skills are often needed by people either in leadership roles or in positions where their influence is not based on their roles or titles.

## Systems Theory and Organization Change

Although the concept of systems theory was familiar to some of the founders of the field, much of the early work was done in small groups. There was a general belief that by working with groups of people in an organization, you could change the culture. Then, in 1958–1959, an interesting event took place at General Mills. Richard Beckhard, the external consultant, and Cy Levi, the internal, were set to work in "sensitizing" the first-line supervisors on the shop floor. The idea was to give them better interpersonal skills in managing the hourly workforce and to encourage more participative ways of managing. After the workshop was over, research was conducted to see whether the desired behavioral change had taken place. It had. There were very positive reports. There had been a definite shift in the culture.

Several months later, the researchers returned and, to their surprise, the situation was now worse than it had been before the workshops had occurred! What came to light was that nothing had been done with the managers who supervised the first level. A clear system theory message emerged: If you want to change an entire system, you must address the whole system. You cannot tamper with just a part of a system if you want it to change; you have to take into account the relationship of that small system to the whole. In order to promote an organization change, all the aspects of an organization have to be looked at, including such seemingly unrelated issues as the pay system, structure, physical arrangement, policies and procedures, and the way top management operates.

A seminal book appeared during this time, *The Social Psychology of Organizations*. In it, authors Katz and Kahn (1966) took the system theory of the biologist Ludwig von Bertalanffy and applied it to organizations. Von Bertalanffy, in writing about biological organisms, had written that organisms survive by their ability to work out a meaningful relationship with their environment. The OD application: Organizations survive to the degree that they can both externally and internally adapt to change.

Two Harvard professors, Paul Lawrence and Jay Lorsch (1969), developed a concept called Contingency Theory, which explored how an organization structures itself to meet the requirements of the external environment. The type of industry, and the stability or volatility of the market environment, may require different structures for different organizations. At the same time, they recognized that, as the organization structured itself to meet the demands of the external environment, there was a need to make changes internally and find mechanisms to integrate differentiated functions. This they called "differentiation and integration."

**Open System Planning.** Another process that developed as the impact of the larger environment became of greater concern was a process called Open System Planning, a methodology for recognizing and addressing external forces that impacted the organization, be they government agencies, customers, suppliers, or clients. The methodology recognized the need to adapt to emerging trends, but also the possibility of influencing some of the trends, to change or modify potential negative impact.

It is not coincidental that open system planning has increased in importance as the external environment has become more competitive and more demanding. After the end of World War II, there was such a dearth of consumer goods that companies focused on simply meeting the demand. It was a while before there was awareness of Japanese and German autos—as well as other imports—that were flooding the market. With the growth of the global economy, the need to be continually scanning the environment for important trends, at the same time working effectively with the demands of both external and internal stakeholders, placed enormous pressures on both profit and non-profit sectors. Large group intervention, the methodology of getting the whole system in the room around an issue that is important to the key stakeholders has been an effective way of working with the whole relevant system. (See Chapters Seventeen and Eighteen for more on large group interventions.)

OD started with small groups and action research as a means for creating organizational change. This was followed by an emphasis on changing the individual and leadership. Finally, there was recognition that change had to do with taking the whole system into account both internally and externally. This is how the field presents itself today.

## Early Adopters

Organizations had come out of World War II with a need to increase production and improve human relationships within work groups. It was important to train leaders to work with groups and to work with their employees and peers. It was natural that organizations and institutions would become interested in this kind of small-group training, asking, "How could we make a group of people working together on a task more effective?" In the early days of the National Training Laboratories, organizations began to send people to Bethel, Maine, to learn about groups. If you look at the bottom of the chart, you will see some of the early adopters. Esso, now Exxon, was one of the companies to send people, with Herb Shepard being one of the pioneers. There were General Mills, led by Douglas McGregor, and TRW Systems with Stan Herman. Industrial trainers and human resource/personnel people often represented these companies.

Another institution that embraced the newly emerging field, sending selected clergy and lay leaders to NTL Laboratories, was the Episcopal Church. Their enthusiasm spun off several organizations dedicated to spreading OD and the applied behavioral sciences into religious settings. Early NTL-trained Episcopal movers and shakers were Dick Byrd, David Jones, Bill Yon, and Mary Beth Peters, who came together with those of other faiths to launch The Association for Religion and Applied Behavioral Science (ARABS) in 1969: Lutherans

Otto Kroeger, Roy Oswald, and John Scherer; Catholics Father Gerard Egan and Roland Sullivan; Methodists Ken Mitchell, Bob Crosby, and Jay Olsen; and Presbyterians Newt Fink, Del Poling, and Arnie Nakajima. ARABS later morphed into the Association for Creative Change (ACC).

As you move across the chart, you will note that team- and group-oriented interventions were being used for a number of OD applications. As the civil rights movement took off, groups were used to sensitize people (more like sensitivity training) to deal with issues related to race and gender. As the United States found itself in a far more competitive market after World War II, groups were used to emulate some of the methods used in Scandinavia and Japan, such as Quality of Work Life and Total Quality Management. Procter and Gamble, in several of its plants, began experiments in self-managed teams. The increase in global teams has presented the field with some interesting challenges, such as meshing cultural differences and working with people spread across great geographical distances. The Internet has given birth to "virtual teams" as a way of managing globally dispersed people who have a common task or project. Team building continues today as one of the most-used OD interventions. (For more information on team building, see Chapter Fifteen.)

Most major organizations have used organization development, sometimes calling it, as does the military, "organization effectiveness." Some of the early adopters have been mentioned: Esso and TRW Systems, The U.S. Army, the U.S. Navy, the Chaplain's Corps, and the Episcopal Church being among the first.

Two of the people on the bottom line of the chart—Shel Davis from TRW Systems and Cy Levi from General Mills—took the risk to bring the newly emerging OD methodology into their organizations rather than simply sending people to workshops. There were several external consultants who are well known in the field, including Dick Beckhard (who taught at MIT) and Herb Shepard (affiliated with Case Western Reserve), mentioned previously. They were involved over many years in consulting with some of these same early adopting organizations, as well as in training the first and second generation of OD consultants.

One other important person to mention here is Ronald Lippitt, who spent his time focusing primarily on the non-profit sector. After the downturn of the auto industry in Michigan, Lippitt used large group interventions to work with citizen groups to change entire communities in Michigan. In one city, he involved three thousand people in re-creating their community. He also built into his work a process of focusing on a "desired future," rather then spending time solving tactical problems. Once you knew where you were and where you wanted to be, you could strategize how to close the gap. One important and less-well-known piece of his research showed what happened to a group's energy when they focused on problems (it tended to sag) and when they focused on what was working that could be improved (it grew). Appreciative Inquiry (Chapter Seven) and SOAR framework (Chapter Eighteen) are based in part on this premise. Lippitt also was one of the first to postulate the phases in the consulting process, something every OD consultant today knows like a favorite bedtime story.

## WHERE IS OD HEADED?

From its birth in the 1940s, OD has taken the shape of—or better, responded to—the environment in which it was happening. Looking ahead into the near-term future, which is all we can do these days, we see the following movements affecting the practice of OD:

- *Globalization* is going to continue to eat away at the "retiring" organizational models of hierarchical control and mono-cultures. The workforce in such a world will be more vulnerable as, in order to remain competitive—which means flexible and agile—radical change will become the natural state.

- *Speed* will continue to increase and will, as we are already seeing, ultimately affect every product or service, every department or function, and every business, large and small, private or public. "How can we go faster?"

- *Relevance* will become OD's rallying cry. In an era when relevance is measured in weeks or even days, Israeli OD consultant Allon Shevat reminds us, "Like a piece of solid, yet somewhat outdated piece of software, traditional OD will need to add applications and fix bugs, and eventually upgrade its platform, eventually reinventing itself and its original 'core code.'"

- *Eastern shift*. Born in North America, the emerging epicenter of OD is likely to be somewhere east of its birthplace, as it comes to thrive in cultures where norms around decision making, authority, and motivation are quite different.

- *Managerial Darwinism* may mean that tomorrow's executives are more ruthless as the pressure to compete and move more quickly in a rapidly changing marketplace weeds out the more humane candidates. This could open a place for the other pole of the polarity: "pockets" of high-performing/high-satisfaction in the organization, led by skilled managers who attend to the "people factor."

- *The human spirit* may increasingly become the focus of OD, as we learn how to connect the hearts and minds of employees with something of energizing and redeeming value in their work experience (Scherer, 1993). Quoting Allon Shevat again, "It is not inconceivable that a new post-modern union may appear. This new type of manager and union will provide OD with ample opportunities, provided we have morphed accordingly" (personal communication with the author).

# SUMMARY

A chapter revealing the roots of OD would not be complete without a definition of the field that has emerged. As you might imagine, every practitioner has a definition. Here is ours: "OD is the application of behavioral science, action research, and systems theory to organizations and larger human systems, using participative processes that involve all those affected, with the objective of increasing the internal and external effectiveness of the organization, especially in managing change."

We are standing on the shoulders of giants. It is now up to us, their descendants, to do what they did so many years ago: discover new principles and methods of assisting leaders and their organizations to be as effective as they can be.

# References

Beckhard, R. (1969). *Organization development: Strategies and models*. Reading, MA: Addison-Wesley.

Bennis, W. (1966). *Changing organizations: Essays on the development of human organizations*. New York: McGraw-Hill.

Bion, W. (1940). The war of nerves. In Miller & Crichton-Miller (Eds.), *The neuroses in war*. London: Macmillan.

Bradford, L., Gibb, J.R., & Benne, K.D. (Eds.) (1964). *T-group theory and laboratory method*. Hoboken, NJ: John Wiley & Sons.

Bunker, B., & Alban, B. (1997). *Large group interventions: Engaging the whole system for rapid change*. San Francisco: Jossey-Bass.

French, W.L., & Bell, C.H. (1999). *Organization development: Behavioral science interventions for organization improvement* (6th ed.). Upper Saddle River, NJ: Prentice Hall.

Herzberg, F., Mausner, B., & Snyderman, B. (1959). *The motivation to work* (2nd ed.). Hoboken, NJ: John Wiley & Sons.

Johnson, B. (1996). *Polarity management: Identifying and managing unsolvable problems*. Amherst, MA: HRD Press.

Katz, D., & Kahn, R.L. (1966). *The social psychology of organizations*. Hoboken, NJ: John Wiley & Sons.

Lawrence, P., & Lorsch, J. (1969). *Developing organizations: Diagnosis and action.* Reading, MA: Addison-Wesley.

Marrow, A. (1969). *The practical theorist: The life and work of Kurt Lewin.* Annapolis, MD: BDR Learning Press.

Maslow, A. (1965). *Eupsychian management: A journal.* Homewood, IL: Richard D. Irwin.

McGregor, D. (1960). *The human side of enterprise.* New York: McGraw-Hill.

Porter, L. (1974, Autumn). OD: Some questions, some answers: An interview with Beckhard and Shepard, *The OD Practitioner, 6*(3), 1–8.

Sashkin, M. (1980, June). Interview with Eric Trist, British interdisciplinarian. *Group & Organization Studies*, pp. 144–166.

Scherer, J. (1993). *Work and the human spirit.* Spokane, WA: Scherer Leadership Center.

Taylor, F. (1915). *The principles of scientific management.* New York: Norton.

Weisbord, M. (1987). *Productive workplaces.* San Francisco: Jossey-Bass.

Weisbord, M. (1992). *Discovering common ground.* San Francisco: Berrett-Koehler.

Weisbord, M., & Janoff, S. (2000). *Future search.* San Francisco: Berrett-Koehler.

CHAPTER FOUR

# Building Convergence Between Human Resource Management and OD

William J. Rothwell

According to thought leaders in the fields of human resource management (HRM) and organization development (OD) (Costello, Limbrick, Towle, & Warner, 2002), HRM and OD are converging (Sicard, Sicard Associates, Frank, & Insights, 2002). HR practitioners are increasingly expected to act like OD practitioners by effecting culture change and unleashing worker creativity (McBain, 2001). Conversely, OD practitioners must increasingly become knowledgeable about HR if they are to be most successful in helping clients. Some also believe that OD should take the lead in HR transformation (Rothwell, Prescott, & Taylor, 2008).

In making this point about the convergence of the fields, Sammut (2001, p. 9) writes:

> "Human resources (HR) and organization development (OD) share similar roots in the human aspect of organizations. In the past, distinct differences between HR and OD served to clearly differentiate the two disciplines. However, as each discipline has evolved, the differences between them have diminished. Currently, the fields of HR and OD are blurred, with no evident dividing line drawing distinction between these two disciplines."

This chapter addresses the following important questions:

- What are personnel management and human resource management?
- What do practitioners in the HR field traditionally do, and how are their roles changing?

- How does OD align with HR?
- Why are the two fields converging, and what are the implications of that convergence?

# WHAT ARE PERSONNEL MANAGEMENT AND HUMAN RESOURCE MANAGEMENT?

*Personnel management* means the traditional administrative functions of keeping personnel records and managing an employer's payroll. It is tactical in focus. It is also compliance-oriented, focused on ensuring employer compliance with governmental laws, rules, and regulations and employee compliance with an employer's policies and work rules.

*Human resource management* (HRM) is more strategic in its orientation than personnel management. It goes beyond personnel management to ensure that the organization's people are recruited, selected, managed, and developed in line with the organization's strategic objectives, not just applicable rules and regulations. Human resource management includes such people-oriented functions as:

- Human resource planning;
- Employee recruitment;
- Employee selection;
- Employee orientation;
- Work analysis;
- Competency assessment;
- Training;
- Career management;
- Performance management;
- Compensation management;
- Benefits management;
- Health and safety;
- Employee communications; and
- Labor relations.

The traditional foundation of all HR is usually work analysis and its products, the job description and job specification. However, many leading organizations are moving away from that foundation, basing HR instead on competencies so as to reap the possible differences in productivity between exemplary and average performers in every job level and category (Dubois & Rothwell, 2004).

In the HR field, it is common to distinguish between human resource management (HRM), which is broadest in its orientation and addresses all issues about people, and human resource development (HRD), which focuses on increasing individual and group productivity through learning (Brown, 2003). HRM emphasizes the utilization of existing people in their current jobs. HRD emphasizes the preparation of people for new roles and new jobs, their development in the current roles, and the unleashing of their creative potential.

# WHAT DO PRACTITIONERS IN THE HR FIELD TRADITIONALLY DO, AND HOW ARE THEIR ROLES CHANGING?

HR roles have been changing for some time. Historically, of course, HR practitioners have been expected to fill different roles in their organizations. Often, those roles have changed as management philosophies changed and have even, on occasion, conflicted (Rothwell, Prescott, & Taylor, 1998). However, numerous competency studies have demonstrated the requirements for success in the HR field (for instance, "More on what CEOs want from HR," 2003; Orr, 2001; Wright, 2001).

Today's HR professionals often have been depicted as dramatically different from the past. For example, they are expected to focus on, and guarantee, deliverables from deployment of HR practices that create value for their organization; develop organizational architectures and use them to translate strategy into action; perform organizational diagnosis by applying their organizational architectures to set organizational priorities; reengineer HR work through the use of technology, process reengineering teams, and quality improvements; be the employees' voice in management discussions, ensuring that employees feel that their issues have been heard; and be catalysts, facilitators, and designers of both cultural change and capacity for change, establishing a vision for the HR function that excites clients and engages HR professionals (Ulrich, 1997).

The six classic challenges for HR professionals outlined by Ulrich (1997) and his list of competencies indicate the closeness of HRM and OD. The six challenges are listed and described below.

*Challenge 1: HR Theory* HR professionals must master the theory behind HR work. Theories of learning, motivation, and organizational change should lay the foundation.

*Challenge 2: HR Tools* Improvements must continue in HR core technologies such as executive development, recruiting and staffing, training and education, rewards and recognition, performance management, employee relations, labor relations, and diversity. Five HR tools will become critical for the future: (1) global HR (focusing on the ramifications for HR of global business strategy); (2) leadership depth (defining and creating leaders for the future); (3) knowledge transfer (creating systems that will transfer knowledge throughout the organization to reduce cycle time and increase innovations and quality decisions); (4) cultural change; and (5) customer-focused HR.

***Challenge 3: HR Capabilities*** The new HR capabilities should include, in addition to the traditional ones, the following:

- *Speed*: Doing HR work quickly without sacrificing quality;
- *Implementation*: Turning ideas into actions;
- *Innovation*: Thinking creatively about problems; and
- *Integration*: Linking customer goals, strategic plans, and employee needs.

***Challenge 4: HR Value Proposition*** The HR investments in the future must focus on value creation and developing a value equation for HR services and products. HR practices affect employees in terms of their morale, commitment, competence, and retention; customers in terms of their retention, satisfaction, and commitment; and investors in terms of profitability, cost, growth, cash flow, and margin.

***Challenge 5: HR Governance*** HR professionals must improve how work is coordinated. They should also move away from transaction work, focused on routine processes, and move toward a more strategic focus in partnership with managers.

***Challenge 6: HR Careers*** HR professionals may work in one of four locations: site (plant); business unit (product line or country); corporate HR; or outside the HR function. They may be specialists or generalists, and they may function as individual contributors (working alone), integrators (coordinating the work of others), or strategists (directing policies and procedures).

Key HR competencies include the following:

- Knowledge of business (financial capability, strategic capability, technological capability);
- Knowledge of HR practices (staffing, development, appraisal, rewards, organizational planning, communication, and so forth);
- Management of change (creating meaning, problem solving, innovation and transformation, relationship influence, and role influence);
- Business mastery (knowing the unique nature of one business and the financial, strategic, technological, and organizational capabilities of the organization);

- Human resource mastery;

- Change and change process mastery; and

- Personal credibility (accuracy in all HR work; consistency or being predict-able; meeting commitments or doing what is promised on time and within budget; being personally comfortable with colleagues, subordinates, and supervisors; confronting appropriately; integrity; thinking outside the box; confidentiality; and listening to and focusing on the executive problems).

Personnel management, the predecessor of HR management, was born with the advent of government laws, rules, and regulations that affect organizations. In the United States, that began during World War I when employers were first required by government to track payrolls and keep personnel records. In Europe, it started even earlier (Bouchez, 1992). At the time, the dominant management philosophy was "scientific management," based on the work of Frederick Taylor. Taylor advocated establishing clear distinctions between managers and workers and rewarding people in line with their contributions. These early views of management led personnel managers of that time to focus attention on establishing job descriptions and devising rational pay systems.

For the most part, it is fair to say that, in the earliest role of personnel management, practitioners were expected to function as clerks who would track payroll, track benefits, and build record-keeping systems to track employers' actions with workers. That led to the role of paper-shuffling administrator, a part still played by HR practitioners in many organizations to this day. It also related to the HR practitioner's role as compliance officer, one who ensures that the organization's managers and employees function in ways that are legal. A compliance officer acts to make sure that the organization abides by the law.

Following the Hawthorne studies, personnel managers found themselves facing a new view: their role should be to maintain, or improve, good morale in their organizations. That was an important impact of the so-called human relations view of management, which followed scientific management. One key lesson of the Hawthorne studies was that people perform better when someone pays attention to them. While subsequent critics have questioned the value of the Hawthorne studies because the research designs may have been flawed, their impact seems clear. Personnel managers became the social directors of their organizations. They were expected to lead efforts to get people to work together more effectively by paying attention to them as people and the social side of the business.

The impact of that role today on HR is still apparent. HR is often tasked to lead company picnics and other social events, track employee morale through attitude surveys, address issues centering on employee wellness, manage cafeterias, supervise workplace security, oversee implementation of new government-required legal mandates, and generally oversee "employee welfare." It is no mistake that, in some British organizations, the HR director is called the "welfare officer." It is the legacy of this past.

In the 1950s and 1960s, modern human resource management was born. Following a difficult recession in the late 1950s, economists and management thinkers alike began discussing the importance of the human side of the enterprise. These thinkers emphasized that organizations should do more to unleash employee potential and should focus their humanistic efforts, made popular with the human relations school of management thought, toward improving productivity. It was an appealing philosophy that still impacts many organizations today.

The role of human resource management should be to create a work climate in organizations where individuals can realize their potential. The important focus of this role should be to strike a balance between organizational needs for productivity and profits and individual needs for increased autonomy. It was at this time that such terms as human resource management and human resource development were first coined to declare a new role for the old "personnel" function.

But more recent thinking about HR has reflected different schools of thought. One view is that HR should shift its focus to become more strategic in its thrust, relegating highly transactional efforts (such as processing forms or record-keeping) to outsourcing agents or delegating them to managers or employees to carry out. Another view is that HR should shift its focus to become more oriented to human performance improvement or performance consulting, which helps operating managers to troubleshoot and solve "people problems" that exceed their skills. A third view is that HR should shift its focus to help managers and workers to manage change, and that role links closely to OD.

One study of HR managers revealed their own opinions about how their roles are changing. According to the study results (Lipiec, 2001), HR managers perceive that their successors will increasingly focus on the following:

- Personnel management and managers' competencies (training, path of careers): 43.5 percent;
- Organization development (managing change, organizational culture): 41.8 percent;
- Employment policy: 33 percent;
- Employee cooperation: 21 percent;
- Personnel administration (pay, recruiting, work evaluation): 14 percent; and
- Social relations: 9 percent.

From these results it seems clear that HR managers in the study perceived that HR will have to focus more attention on building an organization's competitive advantage through focusing on human capital and on facilitating organizational change. HR has become (in some organizations) and is becoming (in other organizations) more strategically focused, seeking to align people with organizational direction and competitive advantage.

Ellis (2007, p. 32) found:

"The HR business partnering concept developed by Dave Ulrich, with its inherent shift to a strategic dimension, is now widely adopted in major organizations, so the boundaries between OD and HR are increasingly blurred. Sara Smart, manager, commercial and management development, at British Airways, cites the example of how a major restructuring benefits from OD input, but the consequences, such as appointing people to roles and managing individuals, fall to HR. Tina Takala, VP, organizational development and change at Nokia, comments: "HR is more and more doing OD-related work." In HP, OD consultant John Holland describes how HR strategic partner Kate Seeley's skills as an HR strategic partner make building relationships with the client team much easier. Developing a relationship across the HR and OD functions is important, whether or not the functions are internal or OD expertise is bought in."

# HOW DOES OD ALIGN WITH HR?

Organization development is fundamentally about change. Yet most of the policy levers for affecting change with people in organizational settings reside in the HR function. After all, HR tends to coordinate the policies and procedures for recruiting people, selecting people, orienting and training people, preparing people for promotion and for job transfers, compensating people, providing compensation adequate to maintain organizational competitiveness in external labor markets and internal equity across jobs inside the firm, planning for succession, reviewing current performance through performance management systems, and maintaining a work climate that encourages employee engagement and empowerment. Just about everything that an organization can do with its people is somehow coordinated by HR practitioners. HR must thus take the lead on change efforts like OD. HR should thus be closely aligned with OD efforts, and that is one of several choices in HR transformation (Rothwell, Prescott, & Taylor, 2008).

Some authorities believe that OD plays a specialized role in HR. According to one author, "Everything that OD is involved with is in support of and ties in directly with the vision and values of the organization and impacts management and supervisory practices and includes leadership, coaching and mentoring" ("Understanding HR management," 2008, p. 1).

Even in China, the importance of OD's influence on HR is being widely acknowledged. According to Prieur (2007, p. 20):

"Historically, HR's functions and responsibilities were in recruiting and orienting new employees. Today, HR in China can no longer take a back seat by providing just basic administrative services to the organization. It is also no longer just about retention; it focuses increasingly on productivity. To improve workforce productivity entails changing workforce demographics and a shift toward knowledge-based work. HR must now provide expertise on how to leverage human capital to create true differentiation within the marketplace for talent. Organization development (OD) is not just a singular concept. It is a process that HR must go through to figure out what really works within the work place. Concretely, HR must establish a workable OD that builds a disciplined but adaptive talent management process. This process will ensure that the company has the best talent in the industry that can take on the challenge of current and rapidly growing business opportunities."

# WHY ARE THE TWO FIELDS CONVERGING, AND WHAT ARE THE IMPLICATIONS OF THAT CONVERGENCE?

Few organizations operate in a stable, competitive environment. What is needed is a more systematic and strategic orientation to aligning people, and their creative abilities, to the organization's competitive objectives. That means OD must be integrated into HR practice. At the same time, many "levers" available to an organization's leaders to effect change in organizations reside in HR, including recruitment, selection, reward, feedback and appraisal systems, career pathing approaches, and much more. For that reason, those who set out to effect change must be masterful in their applications of HR.

The implications of convergence mean that OD practitioners must become more familiar with all aspects of HR, from strategic to tactical, and how they can be applied to improve productivity and organizational work climate. At the same time, HR practitioners should become more familiar with OD and its total system and humanistic approach to effecting change with people in organizational or group settings. While this whole book is about OD, it may be appropriate to present some of the HR approaches here to familiarize the OD practitioner with the thinking in the HR field. Some of the frameworks across the world are reviewed to provide appropriate background for the OD practitioner and to indicate how OD has already been tied to HR. Many frameworks and models to guide HR have come into existence in recent years. Some of these are briefly reviewed here.

## The Strategic HR Framework Approach

This framework, formulated by Ulrich and Lake (1990), aims to leverage and/or align HR practices to build critical organizational capabilities that enable an organization to achieve its goals. This framework offers specific tools and paths to identify how a firm can leverage its HR practices. Business strategy, organizational capabilities, and HR practices are the three important elements in this framework. Dave Ulrich (1997) presented a classic, and well-respected, framework for HR professionals in terms of four key roles: (1) managing strategic human resources; (2) managing firm infrastructure; (3) managing employee contributions; and (4) managing transformation and change. The activities for managing strategic human resources include aligning HR and business strategy, organizational diagnosis, reengineering organization processes, shared services, listening and responding to employees, providing resources to employees, managing transformation and change, and ensuring capacity for change.

To manage the firm's infrastructure, HR professionals must be heavily involved with examining HR processes for improvement, reducing unnecessary costs in HR efforts, and finding new ways to do old HR activities better. That requires HR professionals to design and deliver efficient HR processes for staffing, training, appraising, rewarding, promoting, and otherwise managing the flow of employees through the organization. To manage employee contributions requires HR professionals to listen and respond to workers and find ways to provide employees with resources that meet their changing demands. To manage transformation and change requires HR practitioners to identify and frame problems, build relationships of trust, resolve issues, set directions, and create and fulfill action plans.

## The Integrative Framework

The integrative framework offered by Yeung and Berman (1997) identifies three paths through which HR practices can contribute to business performance: (1) building organizational capabilities; (2) improving employee satisfaction; and (3) shaping customer and shareholder satisfaction. Yeung and Berman (1997) argue for dynamic changes in HR measures to refocus the priorities and resources of the HR function. They argue that HR measures should be business driven rather than HR driven; impact driven rather than activity driven; forward looking and innovative rather than backward looking; and instead of focusing on individual HR practices should focus on the entire HR system, taking into account synergies existing among all HR practices.

## Human Capital Appraisal Approach

This approach outlined by Friedman, James, and David (1998) of Accenture is based on the belief that there are five stages in managing human capital:

1. The clarification stage;
2. The assessment stage;

3. The design stage;

4. The implementation stage; and, finally,

5. The monitoring stage.

There are also five areas of human capital management:

1. Recruitment, retention, and retirement;

2. Rewards and performance management;

3. Career development, succession planning, and training;

4. Organizational structure; and

5. Human capital enablers.

A 5-by-5 matrix using these five stages and five areas could be used to evaluate and manage the human capital well. For example, during the clarification stage, the managers examine their human capital programs to fit them into their strategy and overall culture. They may also examine how each area fits into the strategy.

## P-CMM Approach

The People Capability Maturity Model (P-CMM) provides guidance in improving the ability of software organizations to attract, develop, motivate, organize, and retain the talent needed for continuous improvement of software development capability (Curtis, William, & Sally, 1995). The strategic objectives of P-CMM are as follows:

- Improving the capability of software organizations by increasing the capability of the workforce;

- Ensuring that the software development capability is an attribute of an organization rather than that of a few individuals;

- Aligning the motivation of individuals with that of the organization; and

- Retaining human assets (that is, people with critical knowledge and skills within the organization).

A fundamental premise of the maturity framework is that a practice cannot be improved if it cannot be repeated. Organizations act sporadically in their least mature state. The P-CMM describes an evolutionary improvement path from an *ad hoc* approach to a systematic and sustained approach. It helps an organization move from inconsistently performed practices to a mature, disciplined, and continuously improving approach that emphasizes the development of the knowledge, skills, and motivation of the workforce.

The P-CMM is intended to help organizations to:

1. Characterize the maturity of their workforce practices;
2. Guide a program of continuous workforce development;
3. Set priorities for immediate actions;
4. Integrate workforce development with process improvement; and
5. Establish a culture of software engineering excellence.

It is designed to guide software organizations in selecting immediate improvement actions based on the current maturity of their workforce practices. The P-CMM focuses on improving practices related to the work environment, communication, staffing, managing performance, training, compensation, competency development, career development, team building, and culture development. The P-CMM is based on the assumption that organizations establish and improve their people management practices through five stages of maturity: initial, repeatable, defined, managed, and optimizing. Each maturity level comprises several key process areas (KPAs) that identify clusters of related workforce practices. When performed collectively, the practices of a key process area achieve a set of goals considered important for enhancing workforce capability.

All these approaches share these questions in common:

1. Are systems-driven approaches that emphasize HR systems or subsystems or tools?
2. How much of an attempt is there to link HR practices with business goals?
3. How much recognition is there of the importance of HR professionals?
4. How much is the HR function itself recognized as important?

These frameworks indicate that HR is essentially a change-focused process. They also provide credence to the argument that the HR manager must be essentially a skilled change manager. OD skills therefore are needed to be a successful practitioner of HR. They indicate that OD and OD skills are essentially embedded into HR practice.

# SUMMARY

This chapter addressed important questions, such as:

- What are personnel management and human resource management?
- What do practitioners in the HR field traditionally do, and how are their roles changing?

- What is organization development as it relates to HR?
- What do practitioners in the OD field traditionally do, and how are their roles changing?
- Why are the two fields converging, and what are the implications of that convergence?

# References

Bouchez, J.P. (1992, September/October). 1880–1975: Emergence de la Fonction Personnel. *Revue Francaise de Gestion*, pp. 5–19.

Brown, D. (2003). Is T & D too important for HR? *Canadian HR Reporter, 16*(3), 22–23.

Costello, B.G., Limbrick, V., Towle, R., & Warner, S. (1996; revised 2002). *The role of the human resource manager as an OD practitioner*. Unpublished manuscript. Downloaded from the members-only Society for Human Resource Management website at www.shrm.org/hrresources/whitepapers_published/CMS_000431. asp-P-4_0 on 11 October 2003.

Curtis, B., William, E.H., & Sally, M. (1995). *Overview of the people capability maturity model*. Pittsburgh, PA: Software Engineering Institute at Carnegie Mellon University.

Dubois, D., & Rothwell, W. (2004). *Competency-based human resource management*. Palo Alto, CA: Davies-Black.

Ellis, F. (2007). The benefits of partnership for OD and HR. *Strategic HR Review, 6*(4), 32–35.

Friedman, B., James, H., & David, M.W. (1998). *Delivering on the promise: How to attract, manage and retain human capital*. New York: The Free Press.

Lipiec, J. (2001). Human resources management perspective at the turn of the century. *Public Personnel Management, 30*(2), 137–146.

McBain, R. (2001). Human resources management: Culture, commitment and the role of the HR function. *Manager Update, 13*(2), 22.

More on what CEOs want from HR. (2003). *HR Focus, 80*(4), 5–6.

Orr, B. (2001). HR competencies at a crossroads. *Canadian HR Reporter, 14*(15), 9.

Prieur, M. (2007). A new era awaits HR. *China Staff, 13*(8), 20–22.

Rothwell, W., Prescott, R., & Taylor, M. (1998). *Strategic HR leader*. Palo Alto, CA: Davies-Black.

Rothwell, W., Prescott, R., & Taylor, M. (2008). *Human resource transformation: Demonstrating strategic leadership in the face of future trends*. San Francisco: Davies-Black.

Sammut, A.C. (2001). HR and OD turf war: Highlighting the need to establish a clear definition of OD. *Organization Development Journal, 19*(2), 9–18.

Sicard, T., T.L. Sicard Associates, Frank, L.G., & Insights, F. (2002). Strategic partnerships. How the HR function can partner with other business functions to realize strategic potential and success: Linking HR and organizational development to succeed. *Strategic HR Review, 1*(5), 12–13.

Ulrich, D. (1997). *The human resource champions: The new agenda for adding value and delivering results.* Boston, MA: Harvard Business School Press.

Ulrich, D., & Lake, D. (1990). *Organizational capability: Competing from the inside/ out.* Hoboken, NJ: John Wiley & Sons.

Understanding HR management. (2008, May 26). *Businessline,* p. 1.

Wright, L. (2001). HR competencies: Getting them right. *Canadian HR Reporter, 14*(19), 20.

Yeung, A.K., & Berman, B. (1997). Adding value through human resources: Reorienting human resource measurement to drive business performance. *Human Resource Management, 36*(3), 321–335.

CHAPTER FIVE

# Competencies of OD Practitioners

Christopher G. Worley, William J. Rothwell, and Roland L. Sullivan

*Consulting competencies: Any list of the professional capabilities of an
OD consultant is extensive—something like a combination of the
Boy Scouts' law, requirements for admission to heaven, and
the essential elements for securing tenure at an Ivy League college.*
—Lippitt and Lippitt, 1978, p. 94.

Say "competency" in a management meeting and you are likely to have about the same effect as if you shouted "fire" in a crowded theater—however, instead of inciting a panic, confusion usually ensues. While competency modeling is supplanting work analysis as the foundation for human resource management and is therefore increasingly critical to those in human resource or related fields (Dubois & Rothwell, 2004; Lucia & Lepsinger, 1999), misunderstandings about the term are all too common (Brown, 2006; Mirabile, 1997). For organizational leaders, competencies are the underlying glue that holds talent management programs together (Kahane, 2008). For organization development (OD), the question of competency has been the subject of both ongoing efforts (Sullivan & others, 1992–2005; Worley & Varney, 1998) and empirical research (Bernthal, Colteryahn, Davis, Naughton, Rothwell, & Wellins, 2004; Shephard & Raia, 1981; Worley & Feyerherm, 2003).

This research has resulted in considerable confusion about whether competencies differentiate between effective and ineffective practitioners (Church, Burke, & Van Eynde, 1994), whether minimal levels of competence are required to practice OD (Worley & Varney, 1998), and whether competencies should be used as part of professionalizing the field (Church, 2001; Weidner & Kulick, 1999). In fact, these misunderstandings can be so severe that we often ask clients to stop the conversation and provide a definition whenever the term competency is used. Without clear understandings and shared definitions, productive conversation is usually not possible.

The purpose of this chapter is to explore OD competencies at the individual level of analysis. In addition to defining the term and its relevance to OD practice, we review prior OD competency studies and the history of a long-term effort to define them. The references in this chapter have been updated since the second edition of *Practicing Organization Development*. However, a search of literature in the OD field uncovered no new research-based studies on OD competencies between 2002 and the present. This chapter has been left largely unchanged, yet it is still thought-provoking as it stands.

Over a long period of time, we have been studying OD competencies. We have been focused on addressing two important questions. First, is there any underlying structure to the list of competencies? The list of competencies has grown quite large. Of both practical and research interest is whether a smaller number of reliable concepts adequately represent the longer list of specific competencies. Second, does the structure provide any increased utility to the field? That is, if there is structure to the list, are these smaller numbers of competencies more useful in defining the characteristics of an effective OD practitioner than the larger list of separate items or more useful than other competency studies? The chapter concludes with observations and suggestions for using OD competencies to guide practitioner development.

## COMPETENCIES AND THEIR IMPORTANCE

In the simplest business sense, a competency refers to—according to an often-cited definition—"an underlying characteristic of an employee (that is, motive, trait, skill, aspects of one's self-image, social role, or a body of knowledge) which results in effective and/or superior performance in a job" (Boyatzis, 1982, pp. 20–21). A competency is thus associated with an individual's characteristics in performing work and includes anything that leads to successful performance and results. It is not tied to work activities (as job descriptions are) or to the minimal entry requirements sufficient to qualify for a job (as job specifications are). In short, competencies are characteristics of people doing a certain kind of work (Krompf, 2007).

A competency model is thus a narrative description of the person who successfully performs a job (such as a supervisor), works in an organizational function (such as the marketing division), or works in an occupation or field (such as OD). Some competencies can be developed; others must be a target for recruiting and hiring people (Peterson, 2008). It is worth emphasizing that the competencies needed for success in OD may be different from those needed for success in HR or in learning and performance (Bernthal, Colteryahn, Davis, Naughton, Rothwell, & Wellins, 2004). Research by Grossman (2007) revealed that successful HR professionals must demonstrate abilities to function as credible activist, cultural steward, talent manager/organizational designer, strategy architect, business ally, and operational executor.

Applied to OD, the term competency must take into account the nature of the work being performed. Informed by early definitions of competence in the field (Lippitt & Lippitt, 1978), discussions among researchers and practitioners have produced the following definition: An OD competency is any personal quality that contributes to successful consulting performance. The term personal quality is intended to embrace areas of self, including values and driving principles; areas of knowledge, including fluency with relevant theories and models; and areas of skills and abilities, including the requisite behavioral capacity to perform certain tasks.

## The Motivation to Study OD Competencies

Several philosophies guide competency studies in general, including what should be described, who should be investigated, and the time span over which competencies should be studied. Approaches to competency modeling, if rigorous, can be quite technical (Cooper, 2000; Dubois & Rothwell, 2000). For the purposes of this chapter, the relevant philosophies guiding this research include: (1) What do we plan to do with the competency model? (2) What's the starting point? (3) How can competencies be measured? and (4) How should competencies be built?

The competency model created here was intended to provide newcomers to the field with an outline of the skills and knowledge required to effectively practice OD and to guide individual development or academic curriculum efforts. The starting point for this study is a competency list that has been under development for more than thirty years by Sullivan and his colleagues (McLean & Sullivan, 1992). Over time, this competency list has expanded and contracted. This study was undertaken to determine whether there was any structure underlying the current list. We hoped to provide some suggestions about how people might use the list for developmental purposes.

## The Importance of Competencies to OD

OD competencies are the characteristics that define successful performance; they provide a convenient means of distinguishing OD practitioners from managers or trainers. In short, OD competencies delineate who one needs to be, what one needs to know, and what one must be capable of doing. Thus, an OD competency model as a detailed description of an ideal performer has many practical applications.

For academicians, a competency model of the OD field could:

- Guide curriculum development;
- Provide students with a way to choose programs appropriate to their career goals;

- Provide a guide for accreditation of OD academic programs;
- Help faculty members identify their development needs in the field; and/or
- Provide a guide to the academic advising of students who are preparing to enter—or wanting to advance professionally—within the OD field.

For managers of in-house OD departments or functions, a competency model of OD could:

- Help to identify professional development needs of staff members by providing a foundation for comparisons in 360-degree assessments or performance management systems;
- Provide a starting point for devising recruitment and selection criteria; and/or
- Give clues about what interview questions to ask during selection interviews and what evidence to seek of competence during the selection process.

For clients, a competency model of the OD field could:

- Help in sourcing and selecting external OD consultants; and/or
- Provide a target or ideal set of skills and knowledge that might be transferred to the client system.

For individual OD practitioners, a competency model of the OD field could:

- Provide a starting point for self-reflection, a frame of reference against which to reflect on key personal strengths (that can be leveraged and used to mentor or coach others) and on areas needing development (that should be a focus of personal and professional development in the field);
- Provide a basis from which to seek coaching and mentoring by others; and/or
- Allow for distinctions to be made about different sets of competencies essential to practice.

For the field of OD, a competency model could:

- Help the field of OD establish a clearer identity; and/or
- Provide a method to determine qualifications to practice OD.

# PRIOR COMPETENCY RESEARCH IN OD

Much research has been focused on the competencies required for success in OD (see, for instance, Adams & Callahan, no date; Bushe & Gibbs, 1990; Church, Wadowski, & Burke, 1996; Eubanks, O'Driscoll, Hagward, & Daniels,

1990; Lippitt & Lippitt, 1978; McDermott, 1984; Neilson, 1984; Partin, 1973; Shepard & Raia, 1981; Varney, 1980; Warrick & Donovan, 1979; Worley & Feyerherm, 2003; Worley & Varney, 1998). We draw primarily from three studies. Shepard and Raia's (1981) OD competency study is one of the earliest reports. A Delphi study with seventy "OD experts" generated a list of eighty-three items in twelve categories. Varney and his colleagues (1998) developed a list of sixty-seven "entry level" competencies in four categories for academic programs, and Worley and Feyerherm (2003) explored twenty-eight OD competencies with the guidance of practitioners and researchers who were early founders of the field. More details on these three studies are provided below.

More germane at this point is a description of the competency study that serves as the basis for this chapter's empirical work. About 1974, a long-term effort to define OD competencies was initiated by Sullivan (1974). Over the past thirty years, he and his colleagues have worked with over 3,500 individuals internationally to generate, refine, and build a list of practitioner attributes. His intent was to define what knowledge and skills were essential to be regarded as a competent OD practitioner. The process began with a seven-item skill list for OD practitioners developed by Kenneth Benne at the National Training Laboratories (NTL) in the 1950s. Sullivan and Ron Lippitt expanded the list from seven to twenty-five items guided by the following change phases:

1. Development of a need for change ("unfreezing");
2. Establishment of a change relationship;
3. Working toward change ("moving");
4. Generalization and stabilization of change ("refreezing"); and
5. Achieving a terminal relationship.

In a subsequent iteration, and encouraged by OD founders Bob Tannenbaum and Richard Beckhard, Sullivan invited feedback from approximately fifty of the most recognized experts in OD. Their task was to review the list, add items they believed were missing, and delete items they believed were not central to good OD practice. The interest was great enough that it garnered a 90 percent response rate from that group.

Since that initial iteration, there have been more than twenty revisions of the list. In terms of participation, the revisions have included similar requests of the recognized experts with additional names added over time as well as the following efforts:

- Annual reviews were conducted at national OD Network conferences;
- Periodic reviews were held at the annual OD conference in Mexico;
- Reviews were conducted at local OD Network meetings and at ASTD chapter meetings;

- Sessions on OD competencies were delivered in Malaysia, Singapore, South Africa, Ireland, India, and Russia; and

- Feedback on the OD competency model was solicited from graduate OD classes at Pepperdine and Loyola Universities.

In addition, the list has been circulated and reviewed by over eighteen professional organizations, including the Academy of Management, Association for Quality and Participation, the National Training Laboratories, and the Gestalt Institute of Cleveland. Early on, the OD Institute (ODI) supported the competency modeling effort by establishing an advisory committee. ODI's belief that OD needed to become a profession led ODI to support efforts that clarified the field's ethics or established an essential body of knowledge and skills. Versions of the OD competency list have been published in the OD Institute's International Registry of Organization Development Professionals and Organization Development Handbook since 1992.

In terms of the list's content and length, it has expanded and contracted over the years. From the initial list of seven and then twenty-five items, the list grew to over 220 items in the early 1990s. In response to concerns over the length, the list has been reviewed and reduced by various processes and participants. Around the fourteenth or fifteenth revision in the mid-1990s, the list was organized around a version of the action research model, including such change phases as:

- Entry
- Start-up
- Assessment and feedback
- Action planning
- Intervention
- Evaluation
- Adoption
- Separation

Continued efforts to refine and revise the list were continued throughout the 1990s, with the last formal revision occurring around 1999. At that time, the list contained over 175 items.

This event history of the OD competency list leads to three assumptions about the current study. First, the list developed by Sullivan is exhaustive and inclusive. A large number of people, representing founders of the field, new practitioners, international practitioners, and academics, have reviewed, contributed to, and revised the list. The items on the list seem representative of the competencies OD practitioners should be expected to demonstrate. The list therefore has at least some face validity, and, as a result of the broad input from different OD constituencies, there's a fair chance that it has some content validity as well (Nunnally, 1978). Second, the list is still quite long and, in some cases, the items beg measurement. For example, what exactly does "prepare leadership for the truth" mean? Similarly, many generic items only appear in one section of the list. For example, the item "build trusting relationships" only appears in the marketing section but could easily appear in other stages of the change process. The current list may therefore be constrained in its description of OD competencies. Third, Sullivan's efforts have been qualitative and consensus building in purpose. He has been trying to get the field to develop and agree on the skills and knowledge necessary to practice OD. As a result, the list has not been subjected to any sort of quantitative testing—a requirement of any good competency modeling effort (Rothwell & Lindholm, 1999). We don't know, for example, whether contracting skills are any more or less important than implementation skills in successful OD practice.

The time seems right, therefore, to apply a more quantitative approach to determine whether any structure exists within the list and to explore the relative importance of various competencies.

## STUDY METHODOLOGY

To approach the purpose of this study—to explore the structure and utility of the competency list generated by Sullivan and his colleagues—the following methodology was applied.

First, the items were reviewed by the authors for use in a survey format. The items were screened for vocabulary (jargon), clarity, assumptions, and bias (Emory, 1980; Sudman & Bradburn, 1983). In particular, several items were "double barreled" and had to be split into two or more questions. For example, one of the original items in the list was "identify the formal and informal power in the client organization in order to gain further commitment and mobilize people in a common direction." This item was broken up into several items, including "identify formal power" and "confirm commitment of resources." On the other hand, many items were considered redundant and eliminated. The final number of items used in this study was 141.

Second, the questionnaire was designed. The survey was organized into sections similar to the most recent version of the OD competencies and roughly paralleled the action research process. The survey contained nine sections.

The first two sections, marketing and start-up, roughly correspond to the entry and contracting phase of the general planned change model. The marketing section contained eighteen items and the start-up section contained thirteen items. The third section was titled diagnosis and feedback and contained twenty-three items. The action/intervention planning section contained sixteen items. The fifth section, intervention, contained seven items. The next two sections, evaluation and adoption, contained thirteen and nine items, respectively, and corresponds to the evaluation and institutionalization processes of the Action Research model. The eighth section was titled separation and contained five items. The final section presented thirty-seven items under the heading of "other competencies" and represented a list of new items suggested by experts and other contributors to Sullivan's list of competencies.

Respondents were asked whether the competency was essential to success in OD today and, if so, the importance of the item to successful OD practices. The response format for the first question was "yes/no," while the importance scale ranged from 1 (not at all critical) to 5 (absolutely critical). The intent in the importance scale was to encourage the respondent to make discriminations between competency items that were "nice to have" versus "had to have" for success. The data analyzed here are the importance ratings of the 141 items.

Third, the survey was placed on the web and invitations to complete the survey were sent out to OD professionals. This occurred in a variety of formal and informal ways. For example, personal invitations were made during national and international presentations by the authors, the national OD Network invited people through its website home page, and an announcement and invitation were included in several issues of the OD Institute's monthly newsletter. In addition, electronic invitations were sent to Internet listservs operated by the OD Network, the OD Institute, the Appreciative Inquiry Consortia, ASTD, Pepperdine University's MSOD program, and the Association for Quality and Participation. Email invitations were sent to key OD leaders. Three hundred sixty-four people responded to the survey. The modal respondent was American, came from the private sector, and had a master's degree.

Fourth, descriptive statistics were calculated for each item. Then the analysis proceeded along two parallel tracks. The first track was an analysis of the items within a section of the survey, and the second track was an analysis of all the items together. In the first analysis, items within a section, such as marketing or adoption, were factor analyzed to determine whether items possessed any underlying structure. Clusters of items measuring a similar concept were created and labeled. As part of this process, items that did not correlate with other items in the section were identified. That is, a factor analysis includes information about items that either does not correlates well with other items or that is too generic and therefore correlates with too many items to be useful. For example, the item "build trusting relationships" in the marketing section, while no doubt important, was consistently a part of almost every cluster and therefore provided little discriminating information.

In the second analysis, all 141 items were submitted to a single factor analysis so that the items from one section could correlate with items in another section. As with the first analysis path, clusters of items measuring similar concepts were created and labeled, and any items that did not correlate with other items or correlated with too many items were identified.

In the final step, the two sets of clusters were compared. Where there was similarity between the two sets, a cluster was retained using as many common items as possible. Where unique clusters showed up in either set, the authors conferred and chose the clusters that seemed to best represent a broad scope of OD competencies. Based on this final set of clusters, the research questions concerning structure and utility of the list of competencies were addressed.

The process of labeling a set of items to represent an underlying competency is neither scientific nor quantitative. It is, in fact, quite subjective, and the authors toyed with different labels in an attempt to convey the essence of the items within a cluster. This was easy in some cases and much more difficult in others. In the first sectional analysis, we tried to use labels that acknowledged the phase of the process they represented. Thus, clusters from the diagnosis section were given labels with diagnosis in mind. In the pooled item analysis, we had free rein to provide labels reflecting nuances in the mix of items representing the competency. In the end, we chose labels that we thought were fair, but recognize that we should be cautious in believing that our labels are the "right" ones.

For the statistically minded reader, several assumptions were made about the data, including the ratio of sample size to the total number of items and whether generically worded items referred to a particular section of the survey. Any definitive OD competency study will have to substantially increase the sample size relative to the number of items. However, the exploratory nature of this study supports a more relaxed set of assumptions. We hope the data presented here can improve the efficiency of any future study. A complete output of this analysis is available from the authors.

# RESULTS

## Descriptive Statistics

The descriptive statistics from the survey displayed a very consistent pattern. Almost all of the items were rated very high (4) or absolutely critical (5). The range was from 3.5 to 4.9, with only 11 of 141 items having a mean below 4.0 and 51 items having means of 4.5 or higher. Despite the intent to steer respondents away from very high scores, nearly all of the distributions are skewed. This is not very helpful, and future studies need to take this into account. In other words, respondents were unable or unwilling to effectively discriminate between the items in terms of their importance. At some level, all of the OD practitioners in this sample are saying "all of these are really important." It is

Sullivan's belief that only high rates have survived because the list has been scrubbed and revised by so many practitioners over the years.

## Section-by-Section Analysis

In the first analysis, all items within a section were submitted together, but separate from other items and sections in the survey. The analysis produced thirty-two competency clusters using 116 of 141 items. The final results are shown in Table 5.1.

## Pool-Item Analysis

Table 5.2 describes the final competency clusters from the second analysis, where all items in the survey were submitted together. In this analysis, items from any section of the survey could correlate and form a cluster with items from any other section. The table identifies the name and the number of items in the cluster. In this analysis, thirty-three clusters were produced using 115 out of 141 items.

The first fifteen clusters all contained multiple items and ranged in size from two to thirteen items. Three of the clusters contained two items, while the remaining clusters contained between three and thirteen items. The last eighteen clusters contained between one and four items, with thirteen of these clusters only containing one or two items. In comparison, only eight clusters in the first analysis had one or two items. Thus, the distribution of cluster sizes is more skewed in the second analysis. Many competency clusters in Table 5.2 closely resemble those from the section-by-section analysis. As a result, and in the interest of space, we proceed to a comparison of the two analyses.

## Comparison of the Two Analyses

Table 5.3 presents a comparison of the clusters generated by each of the analyses. The table presents the two or more cluster name(s) and the number of items for each cluster where the cluster labels were similar. It then presents the number of items that were common to both clusters and the final list of items proposed to represent the competency concept. The final set of clusters includes labels that are both specific to a phase of the planned change process as well as generic skills that an OD practitioner should have. For example, the "keep information flowing" competency ensures that communications should remain open during all phases of the change process. Communication is, after all, key to success in organizational change (Ely, 2008).

The final set of competencies consists of twenty-four clusters and 104 items. Several competency clusters were nearly identical from the first analysis to the second and were retained in their original form. This lends some confidence to the integrity of the final proposed competencies. Clusters with good agreement between both analyses include (1) self-mastery, (2) ability to evaluate change,

Table 5.1. Section-by-Section Results

| | Competency Label | # of Items |
|---|---|---|
| Marketing | Ability to describe OD processes | 7 |
| | Quickly assess opportunities for change | 4 |
| | Clarify outcomes and resources | 3 |
| | Develop relationships | 2 |
| | Make good client choices | 1 |
| Start-Up | Set the conditions for change | 4 |
| | Address power | 3 |
| | Build cooperative relationships | 3 |
| | Clarify roles | 2 |
| Diagnosis/Feedback | Research methods | 6 |
| | Keep the information flowing | 5 |
| | Clarify data needs | 4 |
| | Keeping an open mind re: data | 3 |
| | Relevance | 1 |
| Action Planning | Creating an implementation plan – I | 4 |
| | Creating an implementation plan – II | 3 |
| | Facilitate the action planning process | 3 |
| | Obtain commitment from leadership | 2 |
| Intervention | Adjust implementation | 4 |
| | Transfer ownership of the change | 3 |
| Evaluation | Ability to evaluate change | 5 |
| | Use evaluation data to adjust change | 4 |
| Adoption | Manage adoption and institutionalization | 9 |
| Separation | Manage the separation | 5 |
| Other Competencies | Master self | 8 |
| | Be available to multiple stakeholders | 7 |
| | Ability to work with large scale clients | 4 |
| | Manage diversity | 3 |
| | Be current in theory and technology | 4 |
| | Maintain a flexible focus | 2 |
| | Possess broad facilitation skills | 2 |
| | Be comfortable with ambiguity | 2 |

Table 5.2. Pooled-Item Analysis Results

| Competency Label | # of Items |
|---|---|
| Self-mastery | 13 |
| Ability to evaluate change | 6 |
| Clarify data needs | 4 |
| Manage the transition and sustain momentum | 8 |
| Keep information flowing | 7 |
| Integrate theory and practice | 6 |
| Ability to work with large systems | 6 |
| Manage the separation | 3 |
| Participatively create a good action plan | 6 |
| Apply research methods appropriately | 4 |
| Manage diversity | 4 |
| Imagination skills | 2 |
| Focus on relevant issues | 5 |
| Clarify roles | 2 |
| Address power | 2 |
| Clarify outcomes | 1 |
| Keep an open mind regarding data | 2 |
| Stay current with technology | 2 |
| Apply effective interpersonal skills | 3 |
| Set appropriate expectations | 4 |
| Let data drive action | 3 |
| Manage ownership of change | 3 |
| Be mindful of process | 2 |
| Think systemically | 3 |
| Comfort with ambiguity | 3 |
| Action plan with results in mind | 1 |
| Involve leadership | 2 |
| Be credible | 2 |
| Be a quick study | 2 |
| Monitor the environment | 1 |
| Network your services | 1 |
| Make good client choices | 1 |
| Get leadership commitment | 1 |

(3) ability to clarify data needs, (4) managing transition and institutionalization, (5) integrating theory and practice, (6) staying current in technology, (7) the ability to work with large systems, (8) participatively creating a good implementation plan, (9) understanding research methods, (10) managing diversity, (11) clarifying roles, (12) addressing power, (13) keeping an open mind, (14) managing client ownership of the change, (15) being comfortable with ambiguity, (16) managing the separation, and (17) focusing on relevance and flexibility. In other words, more than half of the final competencies were reliably formed in both analyses. Another five competencies emerged as combinations of clusters from the two analyses.

# DISCUSSION

The results from Table 5.3 allow us to address the two research questions driving this chapter. First, is there any underlying structure within the list of OD competencies? Second, what utility does the refined list have for OD practitioners?

## Underlying Structure of the Competencies

The data generated and analyzed in this study strongly support an underlying structure in the list of competencies. In both analyses, the data were reduced to a smaller and more meaningful set of required skills and knowledge. The final analysis suggests that twenty to twenty-four competencies adequately describe the requirements of successful OD practitioners.

## Utility of the Competencies

Finding an underlying structure within a list of 141 competencies is not all that surprising. One of the primary purposes of factor analysis is to simplify and reduce complex data sets into their essential themes. As a statistical bludgeon, it has little trouble performing its task. The real issue is whether the proposed structure has any more utility than other competency models or provides better guidance to the field.

For this purpose, we compared our final competency list with the models generated by Worley and Varney (1998), Worley and Feyerherm (2003), and Shephard and Raia (1981). The Worley and Varney list was developed with support from the Academy of Management's OD&C Division and therefore represents a primarily academic view. The Worley and Feyerherm list was derived from interviews with veteran OD practitioners and researchers and therefore represents the view of founders of the field. The Shephard and Raia list was published in the early 1980s and therefore represents an historical baseline from which to compare the development of the field. The four lists are compared in Table 5.4.

**Table 5.3. Comparison of Competency Clusters**

| Sectional Analysis | Pooled Items Analysis | | Final | |
|---|---|---|---|---|
| Competence Name (# of items) | Competence Name (# of items) | # of Items in Common | Competency Label | Representative Items |
| Self-mastery (8) | Self-mastery (13) | 8 | Self-mastery | Be aware of how one's biases influence interaction |
| | | | | Clarify personal values |
| | | | | Clarify personal boundaries |
| | | | | Manage personal biases |
| | | | | Manage personal defensiveness |
| | | | | Recognize when personal feelings have been aroused |
| | | | | Remain physically healthy while under stress |
| | | | | Resolve ethical issues with integrity |
| | | | | Avoid getting personal needs met at the expense of the client |
| Ability to evaluate change (5) | Ability to evaluate change (6) | 4 | Ability to evaluate change | Choose appropriate evaluation methods |
| | | | | Determine level of evaluation |
| | | | | Ensure evaluation method is valid |
| | | | | Ensure evaluation method is reliable |
| | | | | Ensure evaluation method is practical |
| Clarify data needs (4) | Clarify data needs (4) | 2 | Clarify data needs | Determine an appropriate data collection process |
| | | | | Determine the types of data needed |
| | | | | Determine the amount of data needed |

| Sectional Analysis | Pooled Items Analysis | | Final | |
|---|---|---|---|---|
| Competence Name (# of items) | Competence Name (# of items) | # of Items in Common | Competency Label | Representative Items |
| Manage adoption and institutionalization (9) | Manage the transition and sustain momentum (8) | 4 | Manage transition and institutionalization | Help manage impact to related systems<br>Use information to correct negative change<br>Transfer change skills to internal consultant so learning is continuous<br>Maintain/increase change momentum<br>Mobilize additional internal resources to support continued change<br>Determine the parts of the organization that warrant a special focus of attention<br>Ensure that learning will continue |
| Stay current in theory and technology (4) | Integrate theory and practice (6)<br>Be current in technology (2) | 4 | Integrate theory and practice<br>Stay current in technology | Present the theoretical foundations of change<br>Articulate an initial change process to use<br>Integrate research with theory and practice<br>Communicate implications of systems theory<br>Utilize a solid conceptual framework based on research<br>Use the latest technology effectively<br>Use the Internet effectively |
| Ability to work with large-scale clients (4) | Ability to work with large systems (6) | 4 | Ability to work with large systems | Facilitate large group (70–2,000) interventions<br>Apply the skills of international OD effectively<br>Function effectively as an internal consultant<br>Demonstrate ability to conduct transorganizational development<br>Demonstrate ability to conduct community development<br>Consider creative alternatives |

**Table 5.3. Comparison of Competency Clusters**

| Sectional Analysis | Pooled Items Analysis | | Final | |
|---|---|---|---|---|
| Competence Name (# of items) | Competence Name (# of items) | # of Items in Common | Competency Label | Representative Items |
| Create an implementation plan – I (4)  Create an implementation plan – II (3) | Participatively create a good implementation plan (6) | 5 | Participatively create a good implementation plan | Co-create an implementation plan that is (1) concrete, (2) simple, (3) clear, (4) measurable, (5) rewarded, and (6) logically sequences activities |
| Understand research methods (6) | Apply research methods appropriately (4) | 4 | Understand research methods | Utilize appropriate mix of methods to ensure (1) efficiency, (2) objectivity, and (3) validity  Utilize appropriate mix of data collection technology  Use statistical methods when appropriate |
| Manage diversity (3) | Manage diversity (4) | 3 | Manage diversity | Facilitate a participative decision-making process  Be aware of the influences of cultural dynamics on interactions with others  Interpret cross-cultural influences in a helpful manner  Handle diversity and diverse situations skillfully |
| Clarify roles (2) | Clarify roles (2) | 2 | Clarify roles | Clarify the role of consultant  Clarify the role of client |
| Address power (3) | Address power (2) | 2 | Address power | Identify formal power  Identify informal power  Deal effectively with resistance |

| Sectional Analysis | Pooled Items Analysis | | | |
| --- | --- | --- | --- | --- |
| Competence Name (# of items) | Competence Name (# of items) | # of Items in Common | Final Competency Label | Representative Items |
| Keep an open mind (3) | Be patient (2) | 2 | Keep an open mind | Suspend judgment while gathering data<br>Suppress hurtful comments during data gathering |
| Transfer ownership of change (3) | Manage client ownership of change (3) | 3 | Manage client ownership of change | Reduce dependency on consultant<br>Instill responsibility for followthrough<br>Involve participants so they begin to own the process |
| Be comfortable with ambiguity (2) | Be comfortable with ambiguity (3) | 2 | Be comfortable with ambiguity | Perform effectively in an atmosphere of ambiguity<br>Perform effectively in the midst of chaos |
| Manage the separation (5) | Manage the separation (3) | 2 | Manage the separation | Be sure customers and stakeholders are satisfied with the intervention's results<br>Leave the client satisfied<br>Plan for post-consultation contact<br>Recognize when separation is desirable |
| Keep the information flowing (5) | Keep information flowing (7) | 8 | See the whole picture | Quickly grasp the nature of the system<br>Identify the boundary of systems to be changed<br>Identify critical success factors for the intervention<br>Further clarify real issues |
| Set the conditions for change (4) | Think systemically (3) | | | Link change effort into ongoing organizational processes<br>Begin to lay out an evaluation model<br>Know how data from different parts of the system impact each other |

Table 5.3. Comparison of Competency Clusters

| Sectional Analysis Competence Name (# of items) | Pooled Items Analysis Competence Name (# of items) | # of Items in Common | Final Competency Label | Representative Items |
|---|---|---|---|---|
| Monitor the environment for opportunities (4) | Be a quick study (2) | | | Be aware of systems wanting to change |
| | Monitor the environment (1) | | Set the conditions for positive change | Collaboratively design the change process |
| | | | | Clarify boundaries for confidentiality |
| | | | | Select a process that will facilitate openness |
| | | | | Create a non-threatening atmosphere |
| | | | | Develop mutually trusting relationships with others |
| | | | | Solicit feedback from others about your impact on them |
| | | | | Use information to reinforce positive change |
| Relevance (1) | Focus on relevant issues (5) | 3 | Focus on relevance and flexibility | Distill recommendations from the data |
| | | | | Pay attention to the timing of activities |
| Maintain a flexible focus (2) | | | | Recognize what is relevant |
| | | | | Stay focused on the purpose of the consultancy |
| | | | | Continuously assess the issues as they surface |
| Use evaluation to adjust change (4) | Data-driven action (3) | 1 | Use data to adjust for change | Use information to correct negative change |
| | | | | Use information to take next steps |
| | | | | Establish method to monitor change after the intervention |
| | | | | Use information to reinforce positive change |
| | | | | Gather data to identify initial first steps of transition |

| Sectional Analysis Competence Name (# of items) | Pooled Items Analysis Competence Name (# of items) | # of Items in Common | Final Competency Label | Representative Items |
|---|---|---|---|---|
| Develop relationships (2) | Set appropriate expectations (4) | 5 | Be available to multiple stakeholders | Collaborate with internal/external OD professionals |
| | | | | Balance the needs of multiple relationships |
| | | | | Listen to others |
| | Apply effective IP skills (3) | | | Interpersonally relate to others |
| | | | | Use humor effectively |
| | | | | Pay attention to the spontaneous and informal |
| Be available to multiple stakeholders (7) | Be mindful of process (2) | | Build realistic relationships | Build realistic expectations |
| | | | | Explicate ethical boundaries |
| | | | | Build trusting relationships |
| Good client choices (1) | Good client choices (1) | 1 | Good client choices | Match skills with potential client profile |
| Clarify outcomes and resources (3) | Clarify outcomes (1) | 1 | Clarify outcomes | Clarify outcomes |

**Table 5.4. Comparison of Final Competencies with Other Competency Studies**

| Final Competency List | Worley and Varney* | Worley and Feyerherm* | Shephard and Raia* |
|---|---|---|---|
| • Self-mastery<br>• Being comfortable with ambiguity | | • Clear knowledge of self<br>• Personal philosophies and values; Ability to operate within values | Intrapersonal Skills (including integrity, staying in touch with one's own purpose and values, active learning skills, rational-emotive balance, and personal stress management skills |
| • Managing transitions and institutionalization<br>• Participatively create a good implementation plan<br>• Managing separation<br>• Managing client ownership of change<br>• Setting the conditions for positive change<br>• Using data to adjust change | • Managing the consulting process<br>• Analysis and diagnosis<br>• Designing and choosing appropriate and relevant interventions<br>• Facilitation and process consultation<br>• Developing client capability | • Ability to design<br>• Ability to deeply understand an organization | General Consultation Skills (including entry and contracting, diagnosis, designing and executing an intervention, and designing and managing large change processes) |
| • Ability to work with large systems<br>• Staying current with technology | • Organization behavior (including culture, ethics, psychology, and leadership)<br>• Group dynamics<br>• Management, organization theory and design<br>• History of OD&C<br>• Theories and models for change | • Large systems fluency<br>• Core knowledge about the field | Organization Behavior/OD Knowledge and Intervention Skills (including group dynamics and (team building), OD theory, organization theory and design, open systems, reward systems, large system change theory, leadership, power, and sociotechnical analysis) |

| Final Competency List | Worley and Varney* | Worley and Feyerherm* | Shephard and Raia* |
|---|---|---|---|
| • Ability to evaluate change<br>• Ability to clarify data needs<br>• Understand research methods | • Research methods/statistics<br>• Evaluating organization change | • Evaluate and research<br>• Developing new models of change and organization | Research and Evaluation Knowledge and Skills/Research Design/Data Collection/ Data Analysis |
| • Being available to listen to multiple stakeholders<br>• Building realistic relationships<br>• Ability to work with and manage diversity<br>• Ability to clarify roles<br>• Ability to work with power<br>• Ability to keep an open mind | | • Interpersonal skills<br>• Ability to bring people together<br>• Consulting is saying the tough stuff<br>• Power and influence<br>• Considering multiple viewpoints | Interpersonal Skills (including listening, establishing trust and rapport, giving and receiving feedback, and counseling and coaching) |
| • Ability to see the whole picture | • Functional knowledge of business | • Broad education, training, experience<br>• Business orientation | Experience as a Line Manager/Major Management Knowledge Areas |
| | • System dynamics<br>• Comparative cultural perspectives | • Ability to see systems (systems thinking)<br>• Cultural experience | Collateral Knowledge Areas (including behavioral sciences, systems analysis, R&D) |
| • Ability to integrate theory and practice<br>• Able to focus on relevance and flexibility | | • Theory and practice<br>• Focusing on relevant issues | |
| • Clarifying outcomes | | • Specific competencies<br>• Luck and timing | Presentation Skills |

*Redundancies within the lists were eliminated and several minor competencies were omitted. The Worley and Varney list was divided into Foundational Knowledge Competencies, Core Knowledge Competencies, and Core Skill Competencies. The Worley and Feyerherm list consists of both current and future competencies.

Self-knowledge and self-awareness and understanding showed up in three of the four competency studies. Only the academically oriented study did not include self-awareness. The founders of the field and the early competency list strongly supported self-understanding. That importance was reiterated in the present study.

Consulting process competencies, especially competencies around the ability to diagnose and understand a system, design and execute interventions, and work with large systems, were included in all of the lists. The competency of managing the client's development also is in this section because we see the transferring of knowledge and skill from the OD practitioner to the client as a part of the consulting process. This specific competency was a central value in the early history of OD, but it isn't included in Shephard and Raia's list nor on the competencies described by the founders of the field. It is included in the academics' list and has always been a core item in the development of Sullivan's list. It could easily be listed independently or included with other competency categories, such as integrating theory and practice, and this classification warrants further discussion and research by the field. How important is the ability to transfer knowledge and skill to the client, and what is its relationship to other competencies?

All lists have competencies associated with academic knowledge and skills in organization behavior, management, and organization theory as well as specific knowledge and skill in OD. The current study possesses one competency within this category not found in any other list—the ability to stay current with technology. Worley and Feyerherm specifically noted the lack of awareness and mention of technology in their interviews with founders, and the academics do not mention technology either, although one might argue it is implied under the functional knowledge of business competence. In a related theme, three of the four lists identified experience and knowledge about business as a competence. Only Sullivan's list contained no items related to this dimension. The other three lists note that knowledge and experience represent sources of insight into client issues and opportunities.

All lists contain research methods competencies. Clearly, practitioners and academics, both new and old alike, see the ability to use appropriate data collection, analysis, and other design knowledge and skill as critical to the conduct of OD.

As an applied behavioral science, OD has always been concerned with interpersonal skills. As with the self-mastery competencies, the only group not specifically mentioning interpersonal skills is the academic list. The competencies in the current list are slightly richer in content and description than the other two. Shephard and Raia's list is very inclusive but somewhat generic, and the Worley and Feyerherm list has a mix of generic and interpersonally charged (for example, "consulting is saying the tough stuff") competencies.

All four studies indicate that OD practitioners should have knowledge and skills in collateral areas relevant to OD practice. Reflecting advancements in our theories and knowledge about change, competencies related to systems thinking show up in all four studies, although in much more specific and central ways in the three most recent competency studies. Similarly, the three most recent studies, reflective of a strong globalization trend in business and society, note the importance of working with diversity and having an appreciation of cross-cultural differences.

The current study and the competencies noted by the founders of the field suggest that OD practitioners be good at integrating, balancing, and applying both theory and practice together as well as staying focused on the relevant aspects of the change process. The academics and the early OD practitioners did not raise issues of relevance and the integration of theory and practice.

# CONCLUSIONS

Two initial conclusions are suggested by this comparison. First, the present competency list is only marginally different from other lists, suggesting a certain amount of convergent validity in our understanding of OD competencies and providing a solid basis for recommending OD practitioner development. Second, the relative stability in the competency list over the past twenty-five years presents a challenge to the field to move forward. Perhaps that can be done with new work around Appreciative Inquiry.

## Validity and Practitioner Development

The conclusion of convergence should be comforting to new entrants to the field or to current practitioners looking for development guidance. The fragmentation in the field and the lack of an agreed-on competency model have frustrated OD students and practitioners looking to improve their skills. An emerging consensus represents a positive and hopeful sign. So where does one begin?

The statistical process used in this study has at least one practical benefit: It orders the results in terms of their importance. Importance in this case means that, if an OD practitioner masters only the first competence, it will do more to move that person toward effective OD practice than any other competence.

As shown in Table 5.2, self-mastery is the most important competence for an OD practitioner to develop. Those familiar with the history and current state of the field will recognize this as a controversial recommendation. Some OD practitioners fear that giving personal growth and self-awareness such prominence will return the field to the days of T-groups and sensitivity training. They would be wrong, and their interpretation highlights one of the key reasons the field is fragmented: Too many groups both inside and outside of

OD confuse the technology of OD practice with the characteristics of effective practitioners.

Self-mastery is a competency, not an OD intervention. As an applied behavioral science, OD values helping organizations and their members change, increasing effectiveness, and improving the system's capacity for future change through people. It is grounded in theories of change and technologies of intervention and is often facilitated by a practitioner, change agent, or consultant. The practitioner's position in relationship to the client system determines, in part, the extent to which these valued outcomes are achieved. If practitioners unconsciously position themselves as experts, inappropriately substitute self-development for OD, or create interventions they believe the client "should" have, the likelihood of successful change, improved effectiveness, or learning is diminished. Under these circumstances, criticisms of the field are well founded and lead, understandably, to a belief that OD is a "touchy feely" process that is irrelevant to the strategic issues facing an organization. This difficult task is a function of the practitioner's self-knowledge, not the change intervention; it is a role-modeling task carried out by the practitioner, not the goal of the engagement.

Thus, self-mastery is the most important competency an OD practitioner can have and, rather than a source of irrelevance, provides the basis for delivering powerful results. Viewed not as an intervention in the system, but a characteristic of the person doing the work, self-mastery allows the practitioner to access and apply theories and models in a customized rather than a "canned" fashion; to create with the client system a future it desires rather than one imposed on it; to confront the client's resistance or contribution to the current situation rather than conspire with the client that it's "other people's" fault; to transfer knowledge and skill to the client system rather than breed the client's dependency; and to ensure implementation responsibility rests with the client rather than believing the system has to be told what to do and how to do it. Customizing a change management process to the client's situation, focusing on implementation and effectiveness, and thinking about helping the client to learn are the relevant and practical results that derive from this most personal competency.

This conclusion does not give OD practitioners license to gather clients into a circle to share feelings or to use coaching as a mask for therapy. It does say that every OD practitioner has the duty and responsibility to have an ongoing personal growth plan and to engage in an appropriate course of personal and professional development. This will be the focus of Chapter Six on "Mindful Leadership Development: Assessing Self for Leading Change." In addition to leadership development of OD, practitioners need to become clearer about their strengths and weaknesses, their psychological and behavioral idiosyncrasies, and their motivations for wanting to practice OD. For some that will mean deep therapy; for others, a T-group experience will be amazingly insightful; and for still others, journaling will represent a profound journey into self-awareness.

If the first recommendation about self-mastery was the most controversial, the second recommendation—to develop the ability to apply research methods—is surely the most surprising. Three of the top ten competencies in Table 5.3 are research related: the ability to evaluate change, to clarify data needs, and to apply research methods appropriately. Although this competency was mentioned in many prior competency lists, its importance in this list may reflect a recent trend in the field. More client organizations are asking for project justification and for evidence that OD processes will add value to the organization. The ability to collect data appropriately, analyze and draw conclusions from that data, and evaluate the effectiveness of change provides practitioners with a rationale and a vocabulary to do so. It also represents an interesting counterpoint to the self-mastery competence. The successful OD practitioner today must not only understand the self, an admittedly intrapersonal and "soft" skill, but must balance that skill with a cognitive, intellectual, and "hard" skill in research methods. The rational and positivistic approach of statistical thinking aligns well with today's short-term, logical, and analytic cultures in many organizations.

A third and final recommendation for practitioner development is the most obvious. OD practitioners must be competent in change management technologies. The competencies of managing the transition, keeping information flowing, integrating theory and practice, working with large systems, and creating a good action plan all speak to the ability to implement change. Curiously, diagnosis, long a staple in the OD repertoire, did not specifically make the top ten list, although "keep the information flowing" and "clarify data needs" were part of the diagnostic section of the survey. Diagnostic competencies, although not specifically identified as such, are thus not ignored in the list. Future revisers and studies of this list might consider making diagnosis a more explicit competence.

These three competencies represent a starting point for practitioner development. To assist readers in building their own personal and professional development plans, an assessment tool, based on this research, is available at this book's website. These competencies also can potentially serve as useful guidelines for curriculum development and governance of the field.

## Challenges to the Field

The second conclusion for this study is that the list of competencies challenges the field to move forward. The results of this study suggest that there are about twenty competencies of effective OD practitioners, and there is considerable agreement about those competencies across studies, samples, and time. Some competencies have evolved to reflect an increased understanding of human systems and the skills and knowledge necessary to change them according to a set of values espoused by the field. Other competencies have remained relatively stable over time, reflecting some of the more enduring aspects of OD practice and philosophy.

The positive aspects of that result were discussed above. But this result also challenges the field on two counts. First, if there is relatively good agreement on the competencies, is more competency research necessary? Second, if the competencies have not evolved dramatically, has the field matured or stagnated?

To the first challenge, we propose restricting future OD competency work to a more limited agenda. That is, there are a number of pressing issues facing the field that warrant increased attention, including a better understanding of the relationship between change and performance, better measures of change, and more development and sharing of intervention technologies. Among the suggestions for future research in the competency arena, we would support targeted work in three areas. First, how are external trends, including technology, globalization, and environmental sustainability, likely to affect OD competencies in the future? Second, do OD practitioners differ in their abilities in these areas and do those differences correlate with some measure of practitioner effectiveness? This will be a difficult piece of research because it requires that both successful and unsuccessful practitioners be identified. Third, do competencies differ by the practitioner's position? Are internal consultants different from externals; do line managers differ from full-time OD practitioners; and do international practitioners differ from domestic ones?

To the second challenge, the competencies reflect both a "forward to the past" and a more integrated view of OD practice. The list is most similar to Shepard and Raia's (1981) list and may therefore reflect a more traditional view of OD—some might say it's an old paradigm view. We see it as an evolution. The field began in the 1950s as part of the human relations influence in organization theory (Scott, 1981) and had a strong personal growth component. It expanded in the 1970s and 1980s to embrace more content-oriented concerns from work design, structure, and strategy. It moved away from its original roots and in many ways has become a fragmented field (Church, 2001). The current list therefore reasserts the roots of the field by noting the centrality of self-mastery as a competence of effective OD practitioners, not an OD intervention, and its key role in integrating content and process in the field. Our set of competencies also reflects the balanced view of the OD practitioner as an instrument of values, a holder of knowledge, and a person of action and ability (Lippitt & Lippitt, 1978). This balanced view of OD competencies reflects a mature view of what OD can be—a process of planned change intended to improve the effectiveness of the client system as well as the ability of that system to better carry out change in the future. It is a process, facilitated by people clear about their strengths and weaknesses, that involves other people in achieving positive visions of the future.

Organizations and the people in them are facing an enormous range of challenges, including new and more pervasive technologies, new competitors from existing and emerging economies, globalized financial and operating markets, and threats to the ecology, to name just a few. These change management challenges are at the top of most CEOs' "to do" lists; OD should be in a position to help. A more integrated field, one that understands what it can do, how it can help, the role OD practitioners can play, and (most germane to the purpose of this chapter) the characteristics of effective practitioners will be better positioned to bring out these desired and positive futures. Although tentative and not without weaknesses, we hope our work here has helped in a small way to pave the path toward this more integrated field of organization change.

# References

Adams, J.D., & Callahan, D.M. (No date). Self-assessment in OD consultation. Unpublished manuscript.

Bernthal, P., Colteryahn, K., Davis, P., Naughton, J., Rothwell, W., & Wellins, R. (2004). *Mapping the future: Shaping new workplace learning and performance competencies*. Alexandria, VA: The American Society for Training and Development.

Boyatzis, A.R. (1982). *The competent manager: A model for effective performance*. Hoboken, NJ: John Wiley & Sons.

Brown, T. (2006). Stop competency blunders. *Training & Development, 60*(1), 20, 22.

Bushe, G.R., and Gibbs, B.W. (1990). Predicting organization development consulting competence from the Myers-Briggs type indicator and stage of ego development. *The Journal of Applied Behavioral Science, 26*(3), 337–357.

Church, A. (2001). The professionalization of organization development: The next step in an evolving field. In R. Woodman & W. Pasmore (Eds.), *Research in organizational change and development* (Vol. 13). Amsterdam: Elsevier Science, pp. 1–42.

Church, A., Burke, W.W., & Van Eynde, D. (1994). Values, motives, and interventions of organization development practitioners. *Group and Organization Management, 19*(1), 5–50.

Church, A.H., Wadowski, J., & Burke, W.W. (1996). OD practitioner as facilitators of change. *Group and Organizational Management, 21*(1), 22–66.

Cooper, K. (2000). *Effective competency modeling and reporting: A step-by-step guide for improving individual and organizational performance*. New York: AMACOM.

Dubois, D.D., & Rothwell, W.J. (2000). *The competency toolkit* (2 vols.). Amherst, MA: Human Resource Development Press.

Dubois, D.D., & Rothwell, W.J. (2004). *Competency-based human resource management*. Palo Alto, CA: Davies-Black.

Ely, J. (2008). Big talk. *Training & Development, 62*(9), 34–37.

Emory, C. (1980). *Business research methods*. Homewood, IL: Richard D. Irwin.

Eubanks, J.L., O'Driscoll, M.C., Hagward, G.B., & Daniels, J.A. (1990). Behavioral competency required for organization development consultants. *Journal of Organizational Behavior Management, 11*(1), 77–97.

Grossman, R.J. (2007). New competencies for HR. *HRMagazine, 52*(6), 58–62.

Head, T.C., Sorensen, P.F., Armstrong, T., & Preston, J.C. (1994). The tale of graduate education in becoming a competent organization development professional. Organizational Development and Change Division. Academy of Management Conference Proceedings, pp. 3–4.

Kahane, E. (2008). Competency management: Cracking the code for organizational impact. *Training & Development, 62*(5), 70–-6.

Krompf, W. (2007, December). Identify core competencies for job success. *Info-Line,* 250712. Alexandria, VA: ASTD Press.

Lippitt, G., & Lippitt, R. (1978). *The consulting process in action.* San Francisco: Pfeiffer.

Lucia, A., & Lepsinger, R. (1999). *The art and science of competency models: Pinpointing critical success factors in organizations.* San Francisco: Jossey-Bass.

McDermott, L.C. (1984). The many faces of the OD professional. *Training & Development, 38*(2), 14–19.

McLean, G., & Sullivan, R. (1992). Essential competencies for internal and external OD consultants. In R. Golembiewski (Ed.), *Handbook of organizational consultation.* New York: Marcel Dekker, pp. 573–577.

Mirabile, R. (1997). Everything you wanted to know about competency modeling. *Training & Development, 51*(8), 73–77.

Neilson, E.H. (1984). *Organizational change.* Englewood Cliffs, NJ. Prentice-Hall.

Nunnally, J. (1978). *Psychometric theory* (2nd ed.). New York: McGraw-Hill.

O'Driscoll, M.P., & Eubanks, J.L. (1993). Behavioral competencies, goal setting, and OD practitioner effectiveness. *Group and Organization Management, 18*(3), 308–327.

Partin, J.J. (1973). *Current perspective in organization development.* Reading, MA: Addison-Wesley.

Peterson, D. (2008). Foundational traits vs. accelerators: What can and can't be taught. *Talent Management, 4*(4), 42–43, 64.

Rothwell, W., and Lindholm, J. (1999). Competency identification, modeling, and assessment in the USA. *International Journal of Training and Development, 3*(2), 90–105.

Scott, W.R. (1981). *Organizations: Rational, natural, and open systems.* Englewood Cliffs, NJ: Prentice-Hall.

Shepard, K., & Raia, A. (1981). The OD training challenge. *Training & Development Journal, 77,* 30–33.

Sudman, S., & Bradburn, N. (1983). *Asking questions.* San Francisco: Jossey-Bass.

Sullivan, R. (1974 ). Change-agent skills. *Minnesota Organization Development Newsletter*, pp. 4–7.

Sullivan, R., & others. (1992–2005, annually). *Competencies for practicing organization development. The international registry of organization development professionals and organization development handbook*. Chesterland, OH: Organization Development Institute.

Varney, G. (1980). Developing OD competencies. *Training & Development Journal, 77*, 30–33.

Warrick, D.D., & Donovan, M. (1979). Surveying organization development skills. *Training & Development, 33*(9), 22–25.

Weidner, C., & Kulick, O. (1999). The professionalization of organization development: A status report and look to the future. In W. Pasmore & R. Woodman (Eds.), *Research in organizational change and development* (Vol. 12). Amsterdam: Elsevier, pp. 319–371.

Worley, C., & Feyerherm, A. (2003). Reflections on the future of organization development. *Journal of Applied Behavioral Science, 39*(1), 97–115.

Worley, C., & Varney, G. (1998, Winter). A search for a common body of knowledge for master's level organization development and change programs: An invitation to join the discussion. *Academy of Management ODC Newsletter*, pp. 1–3.

# CHAPTER SIX

# Mindful Leadership Development

*Assessing Self for Leading Change*

Jacqueline M. Stavros and Jane Galloway Seiling

It is relevant that this chapter on leadership development for effectively leading change is written for those who have been termed *organization development practitioners*. Practitioners include those who offer professional services as internal or external consultants to clients *and* leaders and managers who are faced with being change agents and aspire to gain competence and confidence in effectively leading change.

Research in organization development (OD) has identified a mixture of personality traits, experiences, knowledge, consulting skills, relational skills, competencies, etc., important to leading change (Burke, 2008; Worley, Rothwell, & Sullivan, 2005). In addition, the psychological aspects of leading change (influencing skills, intrapersonal skills, and interpersonal skills) and building competency skills (abilities in managing the consulting process, general consultation skills, and knowledge of OD theory) are necessary. A sense of obligation to "do no harm" during leadership and OD consulting is also important. This obligation calls the OD person to, as noted by Eisen in Chapter Thirty, focus first on self as an instrument—to first look at oneself from the standpoint of change and development in order to effectively lead.

The assumption in this chapter is that the professional level of leadership performance is affected by practitioner learnings at the personal level. Personal level learnings affect interpretations made by the practitioner. Interpretations are ongoing during a change process as events are rarely static. This suggests that mindfulness to seemingly "normal" occurrences during change, an aspect receiving limited attention in OD and change literature because of the focus on crisis, is important to effective interpretive and sensemaking processes associated with personal and organizational change. Mindfulness, essential to resilience and staying the course during times of chaos and consternation, also calls for alertness for the unexpected (Weick, 1995).

This chapter starts with the importance of mindfulness and self-awareness, both essential to *knowing thyself*. Both are also of strong importance to effectively leading self and others. Then, Galpin's (1996, p. 70) "Key Attributes for Leading Change" are introduced and discussed. The third part of this chapter provides a leadership self-assessment process to discover how one can aspire to effectively lead change.

## MINDFULNESS AND SELF-AWARENESS

Weick and Sutcliffe's (2001) writings on mindfulness, as related to aircraft carriers, suggested including "a preoccupation with updating" (p. 44), can be adapted to convey the practitioner's need for updating personal understandings and skills in preparation for planning and leading change. According to Weick and Sutcliffe, one must reexamine discarded information by refining, differentiating, updating, and replacing misinformation with information that is relevant to a situation. They offer "a mouthful" definition of mindfulness as:

> "the combination of ongoing scrutiny of existing expectations, continuous refinement and differentiation of expectations based on newer experiences, willingness and capability to invent new expectations that make sense of unprecedented events, a more nuanced appreciation of context and ways to deal with it, and identification of new dimensions of context that improve foresight and current function." (p. 42)

This definition verifies Langer's (1997) suggestion that "When we are mindful, we implicitly or explicitly:

1. View a situation from several perspectives,

2. See information presented in the situation as novel,

3. Attend to the context in which we are perceiving the information, and eventually

4. Create new categories through which this information may be understood." (p. 111).

In this chapter, we pay attention to the mindfulness that the OD practitioner commits to when examining and reworking self prior to leading change. This includes attention to the practitioner's values, vision, and mission pertaining to work and how they impact performance as an OD practitioner. The self-assessment process will be discussed that supports the growth of OD practitioners' ability to lead and the expansion of their practices of "leading with" and influencing others during change. Unless noted, the terms "leader" and "practitioner" are interchangeable for this writing.

## Mindfulness in a Dynamic Environment

Weick and Sutcliffe (2001) studied people on aircraft carriers. This group was chosen because the dynamic nature of their work requires them to operate at a very high level of performance. In a constant state of high complexity and a high need for precision, carriers offer a unique environment for the study of change. The study concluded that this combination of complexity and precision required a high level of mindfulness.

First, they found that people working on aircraft carriers are *"preoccupied with failure"* and work to always accomplish their goal(s) (p. 47; italics in text). For practitioners leading change, preoccupation with identifying what needs to be done (and not done) to lead a successful change is essential. To avoid failure, preoccupation is an attribute the OD practitioner sorely needs.

Second, people on carriers are *"reluctant to simplify,"* while taking nothing for granted (p. 47; italics in text). OD practitioners know that to simplify can be a barrier to accomplishment of change. Simplification can lower the level of belief in need for change and lessen the intensity of purpose by the participants to move toward accomplishment of the targeted change.

Third, people on carriers *"maintain continuous sensitivity to operation."* They have an ongoing concern with the normal and the unexpected (p. 47; italics in text). Practitioners pay attention to process and know that development of a flexible process encourages a focus on the goal while knowing outcomes are unpredictable. Change is significant to growth and survival for the organization. Practitioner efforts for continual mindfulness are a top priority in order to maintain sensitivity to the interventions needed to accomplish change.

Fourth, the people on carriers have a *"commitment to resilience"* (p. 48; italics in text). Resilience is defined as the ability to demonstrate both strength and flexibility in the face of change (Barrett, 2004). Practitioners strive for resilience, recognizing that there will be times the process appears out of control and that good and bad surprises will occur. Comfort with chaos, disorder, and uncertainty is important.

And fifth, people on carriers *"maintain deference to expertise"* (p. 48; italics in text). Listening to and acknowledging those with a deep knowledge of technologies, people, and potential organizational capacities are important to a successful change process (and the avoidance of failure). The act of giving these potential hidden contributors a "voice of expertise" can influence them and others to support and contribute to efforts for change.

The above five characteristics identified in the study as being part of mindfulness offer valuable insights regarding leadership of change. For this reason, mindfulness will remain a topic of this chapter.

## Leadership of Change as a Process of Mindfulness

The practitioner's ability to create meaning (the creation of mindfulness around a particular change process) and get things done is filtered through choices made by people doing something the leader/practitioner may have requested or discussed. These choices include (1) which decisions are made, (2) the choice to make decisions happen—or not, and (3) the generation of personal responsibility and accountability to and with others regarding what has to be done together to make things work.

Quinn (1996) offers a set of questions about how to empower oneself for generating personal deep change and change in others. As practitioners, we (the authors) often use an adaptation of these questions to support leaders in becoming mindful of personal development needs, specifically about leading change:

1. How can I *become aware* of my own sense of meaning and task-alignment?

2. How can I *become aware* of my own sense of impact, influence, and power?

3. How can I *become aware* of my own sense of competence and confidence to rally efforts toward change in others?

4. How can I *become aware* of my own sense of self-determination and choice? (p. 228, adapted)

Quinn's original questions used the verb *increase*; we change it to "become aware of" to make the questions more reflective. Taking the time to write out the answers to these questions, specifically for yourself, can "shift the responsibility for our own empowerment from someone else to ourselves" (Quinn, 1996, p. 228).

Warner Burke (2008) believes there are as many diverse definitions of leadership as there are of "love." One's personal definition, he adds, will probably depend on past experiences with and/or observations of leaders and who one is talking to at the moment of definition. Burke offers the following explanation (not definition) of leadership: "Power is the capacity to influence others; leadership is the exercise of that capacity." He adds that "leadership [is] the act of making something happen that would not otherwise occur" (p. 228). Our challenge to this definition is: leaders cannot *make* things happen. What a leader *can* do is rally a group of stakeholders around a shared vision (direction), provide leadership and resources attuned to

**Figure 6.1.** Key Attributes for Leading Change

From T.J. Galpin, *The Human Side of Change*, 1996, p. 70.

a purpose (mission), and demonstrate a presence of personal values and motivation (inspiration) to get things done. Warren Bennis (1991) said it well: "A leader creates meaning. You start with vision. You build trust. And you create meaning" (p. 5). The ability and opportunity to rally a group require being mindful of one's *personal direction-setting capabilities*—your believed-in vision, which, according to Boyatzis and Akrivou (2006, p. 625), is based on the *ideal self* ("a core mechanism for self-regulation and intrinsic motivation") as an envisioned self in the future.

## LEADER-PRACTITIONER ATTRIBUTES FOR LEADING CHANGE

Galpin's (1996, p. 70) model of key attributes for leading change identifies areas for potential improvement for the leader/change-agent/consultant. Galpin's model (Figure 6.1) indirectly suggests that the leader is mindful of the *working with* approach (collaboration) in making change happen, instead of insisting that the members "work for" him or her, representing control, in bringing change. The italicized words that follow are Galpin's description of the key attributes in Figure 6.1 and are used for descriptive purposes (1996, pp. 71–73).

> *"Creativity, the first key attribute of change leaders,*
> *includes openness to the creativity of others."*

Encouraging the provision of new ideas and allowing people to "try things out" support creativity in ways that encourage and enroll members in the activities of change. Creativity requires removal of mental blocks, making it easier for people to see how other, previously ignored, ideas and opportunities can be utilized in ways not considered in the past (Dominowski & Dallob, 1995). Once discussion starts, other innovative thoughts begin flowing; problems get solved; issues disappear; and ideas emerge. Comments like "Tell us more," "Let's see how that might work," and "How do you think that might change things?" open the flood gates of creativity and higher levels of participation.

*"Team orientation demonstrates a manager's reliance
on the help of others to make change happen."*

Leaders cannot make change happen alone. They must enlist others, often in the form of teams, to consider issues, identify processes, and work on dealing with solutions. Otherwise, little energy will be exerted for change. Mindfulness to the "normal" and "unique" ideas of others often happens because of engaging others. The ability of the group or team to work well together is vital to success. The team leader helps to create belief that change through involvement can be beneficial.

Although some OD practitioners work alone instead of in teams, for optimal performance, they must know how teams work and are successfully managed. In Chapter Fifteen, Gibb Dyer and Jeff Dyer discuss various options available.

*"Listening is the attribute that communicates
to others that their opinions are valued."*

As noted throughout this book, communication is vital to nurturing and achieving change (Burke, 2008; Kotter, 1996; Palmer, Dunford, & Akin, 2009). Whether performing as an external OD practitioner or an internal leader, efforts to talk to and listen to others, and to have them willing to talk and listen, are important to creating practitioner legitimacy, stakeholder buy-in, and change acceptance.

*Generative listening* moves beyond empathic listening to mindful listening. Mindfulness that includes generative listening can create real connection between the speaker and listener. Listening on the part of the leader/practitioner helps him or her get a clearer understanding of the positives and negatives experienced by those involved, both during change and beyond.

*"Coaching is a powerful attribute for effecting change."*

Crucial conversations happen in the form of coaching conversations. Coaching is an art that uses ongoing developmental dialogue to help the person being coached to discover his or her strengths, solutions, opportunities, and ways to move forward. For OD practitioners, coaching for performance toward goals is hard work with less-than-perfect results. But it is also a primary role of the OD practitioner. Coaching abilities are important to achievement of change (Palmer, Dunford, & Akin, 2009).

Coaching is oriented toward achieving measurable results for the parties involved. According to the 2008 annual report by Workforce Management (p. 1), "Companies are investing in coaching in an effort to develop the next generation of leaders." The results from an American Management Society (AMA) survey of CEOs, HR managers, and other corporate executives at 1,030 international organizations in multiple industries stated: "Companies that use coaching report [they are] performing well on such measures as revenue growth, market share, profitability, and customer satisfaction. Individuals who received coaching were more likely to set work-related goals and subordinates trusted their leadership abilities" (p. 2).

The use of a personal coach by the OD practitioner can support personal growth and change efforts, but the coach must be chosen well. Chapter Fourteen, "Individual Development in OD," discusses how coaching can deepen empowerment for personal transformation.

*"Accountability in the context of change means
taking personal ownership for the success of the effort."*

In order for change to happen, all parties must be accountable for results. These parties include all those affected, not just the leader or person initiating the change. Change is often introduced by someone subordinate to the leader. This makes it important for the leader to be a partner, a catalyst, and a champion of the change effort, talking the language of change, taking part in the work, and demonstrating how the leader will also be accountable for outcomes.

A sense of being accountable in constructive ways on the part of those involved is important for accomplishment. *Constructive accountability* (CA) is defined as the exchange of sensemaking conversations and comments that create positive, shared accountability *during* the accomplishment of work (including during change) (Seiling, 2005). Constructive accountability occurs as a result of people willingly *acting with* others to make sense of what is occurring and what must occur to accomplish change. By communicating and creating mutual accountability for actions and outcomes, people mindfully work together to make things happen.

*"Appreciation allows change leaders to recognize and
reward employee efforts to make the change successful."*

Rath and Clifton (2004, p. 31) reported, "According to the U.S. Department of Labor, the number-one reason people leave their jobs is because they do not feel appreciated." They also noted a poll that found that "65 percent of Americans reported that they had no recognition for good work the year before" (p. 39). Obviously, there is an "appreciation gap" in America.

Cooperrider, Whitney, and Stavros (2008) define appreciation as "valuing—the act of recognizing the best in people or the world around us" (p. 4). The catalyst for members taking part in change is often appreciation (valuing) that has been demonstrated in the past for work well done. Waiting until the needed change is introduced to "become appreciative" is folly. Ongoing simple acts of appreciation and inquiry are generative, leading to getting a lot more accomplished than offering words or gestures of insignificance.

Organizational members want to be appreciated and feel valued for their ideas and contributions. Stavros and Torres (2005) suggest an *appreciative paradigm* for working together—"a perspective that invites us to attend to the positive dynamics in our relationships and communities" (p. 26). Any change led by leaders who have been obviously unappreciative in the past is likely to fail to gain the support of those previously dismissed as irrelevant. In some cases, it may be too late for the manager to change. There is no doubt that what he or she thinks, says, and does *over time* matters to whether his or her efforts to lead change (or daily efforts to lead) can be successful. There is information on the appreciative approach in Chapter Seven.

Within Galpin's (1996) model is the presence of *emotions* and the need for emotional intelligence (self-awareness, self-control, zeal, persistence, and the ability to motivate oneself; Goleman, 1995) when coping with the need to change personal leadership style. Unfortunately, when a leader alters past ways of leading and communicating, even with improvement, subordinates may become confused, asking themselves, "How do I act now?" Reassuring responses by the leader to this confusion are important to the willingness to "try out" new ways of working with this leader. Reassuring responses by others in response to new efforts to lead are also important to the leader's willingness to change.

Research in OD and leadership of change has identified a mixture of competencies, personality traits, experiences, knowledge, consulting skills, and relational skills. Galpin's (1996) change leadership attributes relate strongly to current interpretations of how to skillfully lead during times of change. They are offered as a way to be mindful of self-awareness.

# CREATING SELF-AWARENESS

If leaders are responding to a calling, as suggested by De Pree (1997), it follows that they must seek to prepare themselves for effective leadership. This is no less true of OD practitioners-as-leaders. They must be able to *be with* and understand the thoughts and intentions of change participants. This suggests that *all* activities (what we think, say, and do), whether by the change agent or change participants, *are interventions*, whether done intentionally or not. Thus, there are movements and transitional actions (small changes) occurring all the time. Regarding *transition*, De Pree (1997) states:

> "Transition is a matter and a process of becoming. Transition is a great deal more than change. It's a growing and a maturing and an understanding and wisdom-gaining process.... Transition is a marvelous polishing of our intellectual and spiritual and emotional faculties. It's a process of learning who we are." (p. 35)

Transition is an effort to "move toward" and to *continually be mindful* of the need to internalize learnings that make self-awareness possible. Transition includes the creation of *personal* and shared learning interventions. These efforts, if focused on learning about change, hopefully will result in accurate perceptions of one's level of knowledge and feelings—as they relate to how to lead change in others and organizations. The practitioner must first be able to transition toward self-awareness that makes it possible for transformational change to occur.

Of importance to change is the mindfulness essential to the ability to *see accurately* the complexities that exist both within self (attitudes and behaviors) and within relationships (whether existing within identified data, conceptual understandings, or the people involved). Not seeing accurately can be hampered by and result in biases that affect judgments and decisions that impact change-in-self and in leadership capabilities (Tannenbaum & Eisen, 2005). Additionally, being mindful of the existence of potential biases and addressing them is important to addressing existing self and relationship complexities.

Perceiving accurately contributes to the practitioner's knowledge of how personal evaluation biases, political behavior, past experiences, and educational background influence the practitioner's thinking and decisions. Burke (2008) states, "OD practitioners need to help change leaders to be as effective as they can be" (p. 26). Burke highlights the need for coaching leaders toward above-average self-awareness. Interventions that make awareness a reality are vital to self-development. Practitioner self-awareness is where the opportunity for use of self-as-instrument and coaching capacity begins.

In Chapter Five, self-awareness, self-knowledge, and self-understanding show up in three of the four competency studies that were reviewed. Pertinent to this information, the next part of this chapter presents a way to self-assess your leadership effectiveness based on your perception and the perceptions of your *trusted advisors*.

## KNOW THYSELF

The most basic competency of the change leader and/or practitioner is identifying his or her ability to "know thyself" before leading others. Knowledge of the processes for change is located in the *head*. Self-awareness of one's role and capabilities to address the emotions involved with loss, concern for the process, and authentic caring for the people involved in the change are located in the *heart*. As a reminder, we use the term "leader" in the following text as designation for either the practitioner/leader or the internal leader of change.

In order to legitimately and authentically lead, the leader must start first with looking at personal needs. At the end of the day, the leader should consider three questions:

1. Why would anyone want me to lead him or her?
2. How well did I lead today?
3. How can I lead better tomorrow?

As noted by Hesselbein (2002, p. 4), "Just as leaders are responsible for understanding their organization's strengths and preparing for its future, we must assess our personal strengths and take responsibility for planning our own development." This requires the leaders to do the hard assessment and retrospective thinking required to make necessary personal changes. They must "step back" and examine their basic understandings regarding their own values, vision (direction), and mission (purpose), and how they might impact their ability to lead others.

Leaders of change must understand their leadership style, including their personal strengths, weaknesses, and aspirations, and then be willing to make changes to further develop their personal model for leadership. Taking steps to continually improve their leadership style shows others that being mindful of personal development is ongoing—especially as it pertains to leading others. While emphasizing personal development and change, every leader can build trust, confidence, and rapport with those he or she serves in his organization.

Kotter's (1990; 1996) research and his book with Cohen (2002) emphasize that highly successful change efforts reflect a central challenge of transforming behaviors (leaders and others) in the direction needed to move the system. Achievement of transformational personal change, as ascribed in this chapter, involves deep thinking and reflection, interviews, and writing about the illogical and logical. It starts with hard work and awareness. The following briefly identifies the process that is discussed in the following chapter segments.

First, focusing on the self as the foundation, the journey begins with identifying your personal values. Second, you will write your vision and mission statements. Third, you will identify your leadership competencies and leadership style—being honest and forthright with yourself. Stew Friedman (2008) suggests that to improve performance, you should identify your vision and mission in all four domains of life—self, work, home, and community—to create alignment among them.

Once you have identified your values, vision, and mission, you will have conversations with two or three *trusted advisors*. The role of your "advisors" is to offer guiding information for learning and growth. You must be open to their feedback and insights. Reflect deeply on the feedback of your trusted advisors. This takes the form of a contemplative, honest, and forthright *written* leadership self-assessment.

Last, in the same assessment, identify a continuation of development that moves through specific areas of need for improvement, making commitments that are stretches to strengthen in years to come. If there are no stretches to strengthen, you will have fallen short of the opportunity for transformational leadership development.

# THE SELF-ASSESSMENT PROCESS

*Transformation* is change that can be seen, in this case, in a person's leadership behavior. *Change* is a departure from the status quo. Thus, significant *transformational change* by a leader can transform the nature of the organization and its members (Palmer, Dunford, & Akin, 2009).

As noted above, for personal and organization transformation to happen, leaders must first examine themselves. Self-assessment requires time, dedication, and a willingness to learn about *yourself* from others. And it is a futile effort unless there is a willingness to believe what has been heard and a desire exists to act on the assessment by taking steps toward change. The following expands on the above briefly described components of the self-assessment process.

## Values

While Meglino and Ravlin (1998, p. 354) characterized values as "oughtness" and how one ought to behave, Feather (2003, p. 34) conceived of values as "general beliefs about desirable ways of behaving or about desirable general goals." Identifying your values provides the foundation for writing your personal vision and mission statements. Values identification helps to answer the following questions:

- What do I want to live and work by each and every day?
- How do I want to treat others?
- What do I stand for?
- What do I care about?
- How do I show I care about others?

Values are only "good intentions" unless you take time to reflect on their impact on your actions each day—especially when making key decisions. Satisfaction with decisions comes with deciding while being mindful of your core values. In identifying your values, you should be able to locate your top ten to fifteen values without much thought or hesitation. The *Values Exercise* is posted on this book's website. (Friedman [2008, pp. 46–48] offers another listing in his book, *Total Leadership*.) Narrow the listing down to five or six core values. It is in reflection on why you have selected these values that supports identification of what will be important to you and where to focus in the future. Additional notes on values are included on the website.

Table 6.1 offers an example of a leader's value set. Later in this chapter, we will present how her values connect to her vision and mission, plus the values, vision, and mission of her boss and organization. She feels her values are based

### Table 6.1. Values Listing

| | |
| --- | --- |
| **History** | I grew up in a family of six in Detroit. We lived a simple life. There was plenty of love, a lot of sibling rivalry, and lessons learned while growing up. We lived in a flat above Grandma near a large automotive plant and next to a Union 76 gas station until my parents had enough money to move to the suburbs so we could attend public schools. Now my family and extended family provide unconditional love and support. |
| **Family** | In my family value, "family" includes close friends. For family to be real, it includes connection and belonging, feelings of acceptance, and feeling like my presence matters to those I care about. |
| **Integrity** | It provides the basis for living. Each of us has a purpose in life. And we need to model our purpose through being genuine and honest in our relations with self and others to gain trust and respect. Living with integrity makes it easy to sleep at night! |
| **Respectful-Kindness** | I strive to see a "sense of worth" in people and situations. In doing so, I strive to use consideration and kindness no matter how tough or frustrating the situation may get. This allows me to be honest with people and help them grow. |
| **Energy** | I value the energy that I awaken with each morning and the opportunity to renew it when I go to sleep at night. In order to live my values and take care of my family and career, I need a balance of physical, emotional, mental, and spiritual energy. If you find your passion and define your vision based on what you are passionate about, energy is fueled. You need energy to go after your dreams! I live my life trying to make sure that I have a full energy source. |
| **Humor, Health, and Humility** | Mental health (along with the field that I work in) requires that I live with the presence of ambiguity and uncertainty. My life never fails to give ample opportunities to encounter ambiguity. Laughter is healthy and I use it to diffuse situations. I try to bring humor and laughter into my life every day. |

on her history and experiences so they are also provided. Her values are bold. The additional information is her descriptions/meanings of her values.

In this case, her organization's values are: teamwork, integrity, excellence, respect, and sustainability. There is a connection between the core values of "integrity" and "respect." Although not an exact word connection, the values of "teamwork" and "family" connect. She sees an alignment of her values with her organization's values.

Ideally, there should be an opportunity for the leader to share her values with others in her organization and to have them do the same. The result can be a significant increase in respect, communication, patience, understanding—and accountability, over time.

## Vision

Leading scholars and practitioners have stated that *vision* is a key differentiating factor when comparing leaders to managers (Bennis & Nanus, 1985; Buckingham, 2005; Kotter, 1996). Vision is based on a person's values. We study values because it is that which enables vision to happen—how we create our futures and [impact the] futures of those we lead in our organizations (Boyatzis, 1997). The following questions should be considered in preparation for writing your vision:

- Think of a future you feel strongly about. What do you want your "ideal self" to be experiencing in this future? What is your vision as it relates to that future?
- What is your organization's vision? Is there alignment?
- Do you act as a symbol of your vision?
- How does your vision reflect your values?
- How could you communicate this vision to others?

Having a vision is about providing the power to take action toward reaching that future. Leaders use this mental image as power (energy) to fulfill their leadership roles and responsibilities and to inspire others. According to Kotter (1990):

> "The direction setting aspect of leadership does not produce plans; it creates a vision and strategies...it is...simply a description of something (an organization, a corporate culture, a business, a technology or an activity) in the future, often the distant future, in terms of the essence of what it should become." (p. 36)

Thus, the impact of a powerful vision is that it provides clear direction that *motivates movement forward*. This view is also supported by Tichy and Devanna (1986):

> "The vision is the ideal to strive for. It releases the energy needed to motivate the organization to action. It provides an overarching framework to guide day-to-day decisions and priorities and provides the parameters for playful opportunism." (p. 123)

At work, leadership is about aligning people, which includes getting the people behind an organization's vision (Kotter, 2002; Kotter & Cohen, 2002). The way the leader-change agent communicates the vision serves as a symbol of the authenticity of the vision. The leader is the central cheerleader for the vision. The leader must also work diligently to ensure that the stakeholders know where this vision is going and how it affects them. This includes asking for their insights and engaging them in dialogue about the vision so the vision is real to them.

People (and organizations) can have multiple visions that overlap. For example, a leader can have both a personal and a professional vision—and, as noted, they must be tied together to successfully achieve the two visions. Within an organization, different divisions that make different products may have different visions, but the *overriding* vision is the vision of the parent company—the dominant vision that must be shared and adhered to.

In an organization, visioning is a process of creating and communicating the direction of an organization as it impacts every stakeholder, especially the employees and customers. A process of education, training, questioning, and communicating must be used to bring the vision to life for each organizational member. The vision statement found in the strategic plan, on a website, or on the wall must find a way into the behavior, attitudes, purpose, and heart of the people.

Returning to our example, for the leader who presented her values above, her organization's vision is "to take a leadership role in preparing our students to be global leaders while achieving a just and sustainable society." The president's vision is "to create a more humane and sustainable world community by global thinkers and leaders." There is alignment of the president's vision with the organization's shared vision. The leader's vision is "to strive for authentic simplicity and engage in energizing relationships with a meaningful and sustainable purpose." Like her values, her vision aligns with the president's and with the organization's vision. There is a shared direction.

A person can have visions for different parts of his or her life, but a person's dominant vision can change/adjust other visions at any given time. Be aware of the connections between them. Ignoring them can create damaging disconnections between the multiple visions, creating a dilemma of contrast that can be difficult to work through. Having a meaningful personal vision provides "the ideal to strive for." It provides a basis for action and provides the motivation for creating and committing to one's direction. Being mindful of one's vision is crucial for it to have an impact on one's work and life.

Identification and communication of a set of core values and a vision (both personally and organizationally) are a strong start. Yet, a vision is only effective if actions taken reflect the meaning of the vision. The next step is to identify one's personal mission that stimulates action.

# Mission

Mission is purpose. It is what you do each and every day to *live* by your values. Also, a personal mission statement will support taking you where you want to go, to reaching your vision. A mission statement, like a vision statement, helps you to focus on what should be done. It can energize the highest and most creative energies to attain set goals. This suggests the benefits of writing a good *personal* and *professional* mission statement. Mission statements, like vision statements, take time to write and require deep reflection to achieve connection across one's values, vision, and mission. Consider the following example as a place to start in writing a personal mission statement.

*My mission (statement of purpose) is to* _____ _____ _____
*(use action verbs) for what:* _____ *(principal or cause)*
*to/with or for (whom)* _____

The question to be considered: What is the guiding purpose that pulls you closer to realizing your vision? Continuing with the above leader illustration, the organization's mission is "developing leaders through innovative and agile programs that focus on the sustainability and entrepreneurial issues for organizations." Sustainability is defined as including the whole system to collectively consider human and environmental capital as it relates to profit that can result in a better world for this generation and generations to come. The president's mission is "developing and delivering distinctive and innovative management programs that maximize student human potential." Our member wrote a mission that is simple yet significant to the organization's and president's mission. Because she is a faculty member who serves the students, her mission is "facilitating learning and serving with others to create a sustainable future for the students, myself, and my organization." There is alignment of her mission to both the president's and the organization's mission.

As noted above, one's mission statement is at the center of the process of knowing what you should be doing today (and tomorrow) as a leader of change. Thus, there are practical implications for writing a meaningful personal mission statement. Being fully engaged is essential to commitment to one's mission and to fulfill goals.

In order to go beyond just writing the words to design what Quinn (1996, p. 9) calls "rules of operation," one must be able to closely identify with and be continually mindful of the behaviors and actions that are reflected in the written statements. Because change, for our purposes, includes hearing challenges, resistance, and agreements, writing your mission statement can be a challenging activity—especially as it relates to personal change. Yet, according to Quinn (1996, p. 9), "Knowledge accumulates, assumptions are made, values formulate, competencies develop, and rules of operation are established." A person's rules of operation are best based on *written* vision and mission statements that gain full commitment by a determined writer.

As you have noted in the above exercises for identifying your values, vision, and mission statements, change takes strong awareness, effort, dedication, and concentration on the task. The next step is equally important. Next, you will think about leadership competencies. Many of your competencies have influenced and made possible the formation of your values, vision, mission, and the ability to lead effectively.

## Leadership Competencies

David McClelland has been noted as the founder of the modern *competency movement* based on his paper, "Testing for Competence Rather Than for Intelligence" (1973). In his paper, McClelland argues that (1) aptitude and intelligence tests are not all that valid and (2) it is best to identify "clusters of life outcomes," such as occupational, leadership, and interpersonal skills, in order to identify competencies. He suggests that identifying required competencies in a specific job is less useful than identifying a person who *fits* the organization. That job may disappear but the person may still be around. He also found evidence that you can develop individual and organization competencies by growing/training people already available in the organization. Therefore, identifying existing leadership competencies ("a cluster") is useful for new competency development as leaders of change.

It is no mystery that a leader's competencies will manifest themselves in demonstrated actions. The areas in which a leader is strong will receive more attention (action) and show through—whether or not they are beneficial competencies. A study by Stavros (1998) shows that outstanding capabilities come to the surface as the leader functions with organizational members. Skills, such as oral communications, networking, self-confidence, initiative, and attention to detail, may be the hallmark of a particular leader's activities. In her studies of leaders, the ability to take the initiative in creating a new vision, communicating the vision to others, giving attention to detail, presenting feedback, and having the confidence to move forward demonstrated the essence of effective leadership skills. These are noted as the competencies required in an organization for leadership of transformational change to happen. For identifying your leadership *core competencies*, Table 6.2, based on Boyatzis (1998), provides terms and definitions.

Taylor (2006) notes that the key to self-development is the *real self* being identified through accurate knowledge the person has of self and through gaining input from others that adds to self-knowledge. "This is because the individual and others have unique insights into the individual's real self, making their joint observations a more complete assessment than either assessment would

Table 6.2. Leadership Competencies to Effectively Lead Change

| | |
|---|---|
| Efficiency Orientation | The ability to perceive input/output relationships and the concern for increasing the efficiency of action. |
| Planning | The ability to define goals/objectives, strategy, tactics, and resources to be used to meet the purpose (mission). |
| Initiative | The ability to take action to accomplish something, and to do so before being asked, forced, or provoked into it. |
| Attention to Detail | The ability to seek order and predictability by reducing uncertainty. |
| Flexibility | The ability to adapt to changing circumstances, or alter one's behavior to better fit the situation. |
| Networking | The ability to build relationships, whether they are one-to-one relationships, a coalition, an alliance, or a complex set of relationships among a group of people. |
| Self-Confidence | The ability to consistently display decisiveness or presence. |
| Group Management | The ability to stimulate members of a group to work together effectively. |
| Developing Others | The ability to stimulate someone to develop his abilities or improve his performance toward an objective. |
| Oral Communications | The ability to explain, describe, or tell something to others through a personal presentation. |
| Pattern Recognition | The ability to identify a pattern in an assortment of unorganized or seemingly random data or information. |
| Social Objectivity | The ability to perceive another person's beliefs, emotions, and perspectives, particularly when they are different from the observer's own beliefs, emotions, and perspectives. |

Adapted from Boyatzis, 1998

be alone" (p. 644). Therefore, after identifying personal competencies, these competencies will be used in an interview process with three to four of your *trusted advisors*. These are people you respect and admire; people who have known you for a good while; people you have worked with in the past. Trusted advisors also may include a personal acquaintance such as a family member or close friend. These are people who want the best for you.

Prior to your conversations with your trusted advisors, you will ask them to identify your core values. Then you will share your values, vision, and mission and compare their perceptions with yours. This conversation will help you best understand your trusted advisors' perceptions of you and your leadership style and whether your actions reflect their understanding of your values, vision, and mission. The goal is together learn what *they* believe are your leadership competencies and then compare their list to yours. Seek trusted advisors who are willing to give straightforward answers regarding what leadership competencies they see you demonstrate in your personal and work environment and to be honest about where improvement is needed.

The openness of the trusted advisors will support future development efforts. It is helpful to rank these competencies listed as outstanding, above average, average, or needs improvement (see the matrix on the website for this book). The above definitions of core leadership competencies are not meant to be all encompassing. Nonetheless, they can be significant to one's ability to lead change in organizations. Competence in these areas can become more possible through *purposeful* development and attention to Galpin's (1996) attributes of leadership in change.

## Leadership Style

Identification of leadership style has become a focus in recent years. There are various tools available for this purpose. Style and competency are not the same. "Style," according to *Webster's Encyclopedia Dictionary* (in Rath & Conchie, 2008, p. 10), reflects "a characteristic mode of action or manner of acting." "Competency" is "possession of required skill, knowledge, qualification, or capacity" in a particular area. Without an awareness of core leadership competencies—and purposeful mindfulness to performance—"it's almost impossible for you to lead effectively."

A tool for identifying leadership style is the "Power Leadership Profile," designed by Bill Joiner and Stephen Josephs (2007) and available on their website, based on their book, *Leadership Agility*. The profile provides a report that describes the leadership style for the person taking the profile.

## Writing Your Leadership Self-Assessment

The (not so) final step in a journey to awareness is to write your findings regarding each step in this journey. Write it down. Don't miss anything, and make it a comprehensive account of your journey of leadership development.

The findings include putting your values, vision, and mission at the beginning and writing a narrative that is a personal message to yourself. The narration includes, among other things: (1) why the journey is occurring, (2) what you have done in the past in developing leadership capability, (3) how you expect to use the outcomes of the completed materials, (4) who and why you have selected your trusted advisors, (5) the outcomes of your assessment (the larger part of your written findings), and (6) a commitment to developing yourself in identified areas and how often you will revisit the materials to stay on track. Stay focused on your values, vision, and mission and their alignment with your work and your organization's. The written findings should minimally include:

1. Your values, vision, and mission statements. It should include why you chose the five values. Write comments from your trusted advisors' perceptions of your values, vision, and mission statements. What is the true reality? Is it yours, theirs, or something new?

2. Include why you are doing this assessment and what you hope to accomplish. Why does it matter?

3. Locate the values, vision, and mission of your organization. Is there alignment with your values, vision, and mission statements?

4. A report and commentary on your interviews regarding your leadership competencies and the evidence provided to support these competencies (the matrix). What competencies surprised you? Which ones disappointed you? How do you anticipate making improvements? What are your thoughts on what was said about your leadership competencies?

5. What will you do as a result of what was learned? What must you be mindful of regarding performance as a leader? Write a commitment describing how you will *specifically* use the information from the interviews and the collected materials from the process. What *specifically* will you do in the next weeks and months to achieve your vision and mission? How will you expand your leadership capabilities for your performance as a practitioner and change agent?

The goal in writing this self-assessment is to *make sense* of the possibilities that can arise from the learnings achieved from the assessment. Of importance is to remain alert to Galpin's leadership attributes and your quest for improvement regarding those attributes. The final question above is the essence of this learning process.

# SUMMARY

This chapter provides the materials to support an OD practitioner's self-development journey. Effective transformational leadership development requires an assessment. Because the field of OD and change is far from exact and far from mature—and the role of OD practitioner and leader of change is also less than exact—assessment for personal change is ever evolving. As noted by Pettigrew (2001, p. 697), the ability to understand "the dynamics and effects of time, process, discontinuity, and context" in the field of organization change is itself a complex process. The international nature of many organizations adds to the complexity of the field as well.

Yet, not to take this journey may in some way limit a practitioner's effectiveness in leading any kind of change. We acknowledge there are many ways to move through deep, personal transformational change. Living an effective life requires us to listen to the messages of "shoulds" offered by experiences, thinking, reflections, and personal learnings (Buckingham & Clifton, 2001). It also requires us to be mindful of how to successfully utilize those messages. According to Sethi (2009, p. 7), "Mindfulness at work is a key leadership competency, and leaders now more than ever need to live and lead mindfully, coach others to be mindful, and create a mindful organization." To become an effective, mindful change leader, these messages of shoulds, as provided by Weick and Sutcliffe's carrier study and Galpin's key attributes of change, when filtered through the leader's personal values, vision, and mission, are worth listening to. This is especially true as these messages are delivered during times when we, as OD practitioners and organizational leaders, are leading change.

# References

Barrett, F. (2004, Spring). Coaching for resilience. *Organization Development Journal*, *22*(1), 93–96.

Bennis, W. (1991, August). Creative leadership. *Executive Excellence*, pp. 5–6.

Bennis, W., & Nanus, B. (1985). *Leaders: The strategies for taking charge*. New York: Harper and Row.

Boyatzis, R.E. (2007, August 21). ORBH450: Executive leadership notes for class 1. Executive Doctorate in Management Program, Case Western Reserve University, Cleveland, Ohio.

Boyatzis, R.E. (1998). *Transforming qualitative information: Thematic analysis and code development*. Thousand Oaks, CA: Sage.

Boyatzis, R.E., & Akrivou, K. (2006). The ideal self as the driver of intentional change. *Journal of Management, 25*(4), 624–642.

Buckingham, M., & Clifton, D.O. (2001). *Now, discover your strength*. New York: Free Press.

Buckingham, M. (2005). *The one thing you need to know…about great managing, great leading, and sustained individual success*. New York: Free Press.

Burke, W.W. (2008). *Organization change: Theory and practice* (2nd ed.). Thousand Oaks, CA: Sage.

Cooperrider, D., Whitney, D., & Stavros, J. (2008). *The appreciative inquiry handbook: For leaders of change*. Cleveland, OH: Crown Custom Publishing.

De Pree, M. (1997). *Leading without power*. San Francisco: Jossey-Bass.

Dominowski, R.L., & Dallob, P. (1995). Insight and problem solving. In R.J. Sternberg & J.E. Davidson (Eds.), *The nature of insight* (pp. 33–62). Cambridge, MA: MIT Press.

Feather, N.T. (2003). Values and deservingness in the context of organizations. In S.W. Gilliland, D.D. Steiner, & D.P. Skarlicki (Eds.), *Emerging perspectives on values in organizations* (pp. 33–66). Greenwich, CT: Information Age Publishing.

Friedman, S.D. (2008). *Total leadership: Be a better leader, have a richer life.* Boston, MA: Harvard Business Press.

Galpin, T.J. (1996). *The human side of change: A practical guide to organization redesign.* San Francisco: Jossey-Bass.

Goleman, D. (1995). *Emotional intelligence.* New York: Bantum.

Hesselbein, F. (2002). Putting one's house in order. In F. Hesselbein & R. Johnston (Eds.), *On high-performance organizations.* San Francisco: Jossey-Bass.

Joiner, B., & Josephs, S. (2007). *Leadership agility: Five levels of mastery for anticipating and initiating change.* San Francisco: Jossey-Bass.

Kotter, J.P. (1990). *A force for change: How leadership differs from management.* New York: The Free Press.

Kotter, J.P. (1996). *Leading change.* Boston, MA: Harvard Business School Press.

Kotter, J.P. (2002). The marketing of leadership. In F. Hesselbein & R. Johnston, *On high-performance organizations* (pp. 19–29). San Francisco: Jossey-Bass.

Kotter, J.P., & Cohen, D. (2002). *The heart of change.* Boston, MA: Harvard Business School Press.

Langer, E.J. (1997). *The power of mindful learning.* Cambridge, MA: Perseus Books.

McClelland, D.B. (1973). Testing for competence rather than for intelligence. *American Psychologist, 28,* 1–14.

Meglino, B.M., & Ravlin, E.C. (1998). Individual values in organizations: Concepts, controversies, and research. *Journal of Management, 71,* 492–499.

Palmer, I., Dunford, R., & Akin, G. (2009). *Managing organizational change: A multiple perspectives approach.* New York: McGraw-Hill/Irwin.

Pettigrew, A.M. (2001). Studying organizational change and development: Challenges for future research. *Academy of Management Journal, 44,* 697–713.

Quinn, R.E. (1996). *Deep change: Discovering the leader within.* San Francisco: Jossey-Bass.

Rath, T., & Clifton, D. (2004). *How full is your bucket? Positive strategies for work and life.* New York: Gallup Press.

Rath, T., & Conchie, B. (2008). *Strengths-based leadership.* New York: Gallup Press.

Seiling, J.G. (2005). *Moving from individual to constructive accountability.* Published dissertation. Taos Institute/University of Tilburg, Netherlands.

Sethi, D. (2009, Winter). Mindful leadership. *Leader to Leader, 51,* 7–11.

Stavros, J.M. (1998). Capacity building: A relational process of building your organization's future. Dissertation, Weatherhead School of Management, Case Western Reserve University, Cleveland, Ohio.

Stavros, J.M., & Torres, C.B. (2005). *Dynamic relationships: Unleashing the power of appreciative inquiry in daily living.* Chagrin Falls, OH: Taos Institute Publishing.

Tannenbaum, T., & Eisen, S. (2005). The personhood of the consultant: The OD practitioner as human being. In W.J. Rothwell & R. Sullivan (Eds.), *Practicing organization development: A guide for consultants* (2nd ed.) (pp. 583–606). San Francisco: Pfeiffer.

Taylor, S.N. (2006). Why the real self is fundamental to intentional change. *Journal of Management Development, 25*(7), pp. 643–656.

Tichy, N.M., & Devanna, M.A. (1986). *The transformational leade*r. Hoboken, NJ: John Wiley & Sons.

Weick, K. (1995). *Sensemaking in organizations.* Thousand Oaks, CA: Sage.

Weick, K.E., & Sutcliffe, K.M. (2001). *Managing the unexpected.* San Francisco: Jossey-Bass.

Workforce Management 2008 Survey [www.workforce.com/archive/feature].

Worley, C., Rothwell, W., & Sullivan, R. (2005). Competencies of OD practitioners. In W.J. Rothwell & R. Sullivan (Eds.), *Practicing organization development: A guide for consultants* (2nd ed.) (pp. 583–606). San Francisco: Pfeiffer.

# CHAPTER SEVEN

# Appreciative Inquiry*

*OD in the Post-Modern Age*

Jane Magruder Watkins and Jacqueline M. Stavros

Appreciative Inquiry (AI) is a theory of change in human systems that shifts the perspective of every organization development (OD) method or model. AI practitioners are discovering that an appreciative perspective increases the power, effectiveness, and sustainability of any classical OD intervention, from strategic planning and organization redesign, to team building and diversity, to coaching and personal growth workshops such as NTL's T-group process. AI is being used world-wide in both small- and large-scale change initiatives (case studies, podcasts, and video clips are available at http://appreciativeinquiry.cwru.edu).

The *appreciative paradigm* is a perspective that attends to the *positive core* of relationships and organizations. The positive core lies at the heart of the AI 4-D cycle process (Discovery, Dream, Design, and Destiny) discussed later in this chapter. Each stage of inquiry and dialogue identifies and amplifies the organization's positive core, providing the whole organization an opportunity to value its history and embrace novelty to create positive possibilities for the future. The questions below, called the "four generic questions," are widely

---

*Appreciative Inquiry (AI) is a transformational gift to the field of OD from David Cooperrider. With the inspiration of Kenneth Gergen's work in social construction and the encouragement and collaboration of his advisor, Suresh Srivastva, and his colleagues at Case Western Reserve University's School of Organization Behavior, David's appreciative approach to Kurt Lewin's "Action Research Model" has become an organization change process for the post-modern world.

used and work well for the opening "interview protocol" in an AI process. The four questions seek the thoughts of the person being interviewed based on his or her experiences. These sample questions are focused on the topic of "Creating a High-Performing Team."

1. *Best Experience Question:* Tell me a story about a time when you were part of a high-performing team that really worked—an exciting time of high performance and success. Describe that experience in detail.

2. *Values Question:* What is it that you value most about high-performing teams and being a member of a high-performing team?

3. *Life-Giving Force Question:* From your experience and observations, what do you consider the core value, the *life-giving force* of a high-performing team?

4. *Wishes and Images of the Future:* Imagine that you are part of a high-performing team that fulfills all your expectations for excellence. Describe that team in detail.

Or you could ask: If you had three wishes for the best possible high performing team, what would those wishes be?

The shift is not in the methods and models of the change process itself, but rather in the perspective chosen to "see" the human system and to "inquire" into that system's strengths and successes. Examples of interventions with an appreciative perspective are discussed in Parts Three and Four of this book.

This chapter begins by defining AI, followed by a brief history of AI and how it fits with OD. The AI principles and the AI 4-D and 5-D models are introduced. There is a comparison of the classic and post-modern OD paradigms. The chapter wraps up with a discussion on the cyclical nature of AI.

# WHAT IS APPRECIATIVE INQUIRY?

Appreciative Inquiry (AI) has been described in many ways. It originated as a theory and qualitative research technique with five core principles: constructionist, simultaneity, poetic, anticipatory, and positive. The five principles move the foundation of AI from theory to practice.

David Cooperrider describes AI as a *causative theory* applicable to all OD and change methods:

"Appreciative Inquiry grows from the exciting challenge that is implicitly if not explicitly posed by the social constructionist and mentalist paradigms: that to a far greater extent than is normally acknowledged, we human beings create our own realities through symbolic and mental processes and that because of this, conscious evolution of the future is a human option. According to the mentalist paradigm, mind can no longer be considered the opposite of matter. Mental phenomena must be recognized as being at the top of the brain's 'causal control hierarchy' whereby, after millenniums of evolution, the mind has been given primacy over Darwinian bio-evolutionary controls that determine what human systems are and can become. Future reality, in this view, is permeable, emergent and open to the mind's causal influence; that is, reality is conditioned, reconstructed, and often profoundly created through our anticipatory images, values, plans, intentions, beliefs, and the like." (1999, p. 92)

AI has been called a philosophy, an approach, a method, a process, and a way of being for engaging people at any or all levels of an organization in an inquiry into its *positive core*. The positive core is that which makes up the best of an organization and its people. This positive approach leads to changes in the organization based on images of the best possible future as articulated and visualized by the people who make up the human system of the organization. The most commonly used practitioner definition says:

"Appreciative Inquiry is the cooperative co-evolutionary search for the best in people, their organizations, and the world around them. It involves the discovery of what gives *life* to a living system when it is most effective, alive, and constructively capable in economic, ecological, and human terms. AI involves the art and practice of asking unconditional positive questions that strengthen a system's capacity to apprehend, anticipate, and heighten its potential. AI interventions focus on the speed of imagination and innovation instead of the negative, critical, and spiraling diagnoses commonly used in organizations. The discovery, dream, design, and destiny model links the energy of the positive core to changes never thought possible." (Cooperrider, Whitney, & Stavros, 2008, p. 3)

Many articles, book chapters, and books have defined AI as an approach to organizational analysis, development, design, and learning. In this context, AI refers to:

- A belief that the future can be built on the lessons learned from the best of the past;
- A search for new knowledge to enrich the images of the future;
- A theory that acknowledges that collective action is a vital part of creating a way to enact the values and vision of a group, an organization, or a society; and
- A realization that human systems can create what they imagine.

No matter how AI is defined, it is deliberate in its *life-giving search*. It uses interview guides carefully constructed by the clients (with the guidance of the AI practitioner) to discover the positive core of what gives life to a system. The 4-D Process for applying AI in human systems is, like the classical OD process, based on Kurt Lewin's action research model. The major difference is in the perspective (appreciative) and in the role of the OD practitioner. Rather than the practitioner conducting interviews to identify problems and deficits in an organization, AI involves the whole system in interviews between members and stakeholders of the organization. The interviews focus on best experiences and are story-based. Instead of "analysis" of the information by the OD consultant, AI encourages story-sharing and dialogue to learn about the best of the past in order to understand what the people in the organization want more of; and to use that as a basis for imagining the most preferred future for their organization. When the whole organization aligns with a positive image of the future based on discoveries from the storytelling, dialogue, and images of the future, multiple projects are designed, agreed on, and implemented to create that future.

While classical OD processes generally are understood to be linear—from identifying the problem to planning how to rectify it—AI is cyclical in nature. AI moves from story to image of the future to planning how to create the future with the clear understanding that all "plans" are momentary solutions. Plans are made relevant and successful by keeping all options open and assuring that dialogue and "dreaming" are a continuous process.

Images and explanations of both the AI 4-D model and the AI 5-D model will follow the discussion of the principles. While the AI change process itself is described primarily with the AI 4-D model, this chapter written for OD practitioners includes a fifth D (define) added to the model for those facilitating an AI process to cover what OD practitioners call "contracting." "Defining" includes getting clarity on the focus for the inquiry process.

---

Ap-pre-ci-ate, a., 1. to recognize and like a favorable critical judgment or opinion; to perceive those things that give life (health, vitality, excellence) to living systems. 2. to feel or express gratitude. v., 3. to increase in value, e.g., the economy has appreciated in value. 4. to be fully aware of; realize fully. Synonyms: value, prize, esteem, and honor.

In-quire, v., 1. to explore and discover, n., 2. to question. 3. to be open to seeing new potentials and possibilities. Synonyms: discover, search, systematically explore, and study.

---

AI is based on several shared underlying assumptions (Hammond, 1998, pp. 20–21):

- In every society, organization, or group, something works well;
- What we focus on becomes our reality;
- Reality is created in the moment;
- The act of asking questions of an organization or group influences the group in some way;

- People have more confidence and comfort to journey to the future (unknown) when they carry forward parts of the past (known);
- The parts of the past we carry forward should be the best parts;
- It is important to value differences; and
- The language we use creates our realities.

How did we get to AI? It began with a story. Moreover, since stories are "foundational" to any AI OD-related intervention, the next section highlights the most "foundational" story about the creation and development of AI over the past twenty years.

# A BRIEF HISTORY OF AI

The birth and co-founding of AI happened in 1980, in the organizational behavior doctoral program at Case Western Reserve University. It was the result of collaboration between David Cooperrider and his advisor, Dr. Suresh Srivastva. As a doctoral student, David was involved with a group from Case working with the Cleveland Clinic in a conventional diagnosis or organizational analysis in search of "What's wrong with the human side of the organization?" In gathering his data, David was amazed by the level of positive cooperation, innovation, and egalitarian governance he was finding in the organization. Suresh noticed David's excitement and suggested going further with the excitement, making it the focus.

Having been influenced by earlier writings by Schweitzer on the idea of "reverence for life," David obtained permission from the Clinic's chairman, Dr. William Kiser, to focus totally on a life-centric analysis of the Clinic. This analysis focused on the factors contributing to the highly effective functioning of the Clinic when it was at its best and ignored everything else. The Cleveland Clinic became the first large site where a conscious decision to use an inquiry focusing on life-giving factors formed the basis for an organizational analysis. The term "Appreciative Inquiry" was first written in an analytic footnote in the feedback report of "emergent themes" by David Cooperrider and Suresh Srivastva for the Board of Governors of the Cleveland Clinic. The report created such a powerful and positive stir that the board called for ways to use this method with the whole group practice. The momentum set the stage for David Cooperrider's seminal dissertation, the first, and as yet, one of the best articulations of the theory and practice of Appreciative Inquiry (Cooperrider, 1986; Cooperrider & Srivastva, 1987).

From this beginning, AI has spread to become a global phenomenon. Today, many OD practitioners and scholars are advancing the theory and practice of AI as part of a historical shift in the social sciences toward more constructionist, strengths-based, and positive approaches to research, OD, and change. Thousands of organizations are embracing this positive OD revolution by applying AI in for-profit, non-profit, government, and social sectors. These range from global and government agencies, non-governmental agencies, Fortune 100 organizations, non-profits, and school systems to community planning organizations.

This is the promise of AI. Today, with nearly two decades of practice in every corner of the world and in every conceivable type of human system, we can assert with some confidence that we find AI to be aligned with and supportive of this new age of instant communication and global interdependence that so strongly impacts the way organizations need to organize and to function. AI is a process that respects and affirms both the differences and similarities in gender, culture, and nationality. It is a way to talk across all differences and to seek and find ways forward across these differences no matter how challenging the path. AI is an OD intervention that can have high cultural sensitivity and is adaptable across a wide variety of national cultures (Yaeger, Head, & Sorensen, 2006). (For a detailed timeline of the early development of AI, see this book's website.)

## HOW *AI* FITS WITH *OD*

Grounded in social constructionist theory, in new discoveries in the sciences about how the world works, in the nature and power of the human brain, and in the power of a positive mindset to create our most desired future, *AI challenges us to experience reality differently*. Such explorations lead us to realize that organizations are human systems more like the human body than like a mechanical machine.

This is not a casual or incremental notion of change in our understanding of human systems and how they work. This is a significant shift in the very "bedrock" beliefs imbedded in Western cultures about how human systems are structured and how they behave. This is a shift from the divisive notion that there is a right way and a wrong way, to the idea that form follows function. This suggests that organizations can, depending on the need, move organizational forms from pyramids to circles; hierarchy to radical democracy; destination to journey; certainty to curiosity; knowing to continuous learning—with full access to all parts of those seemingly dichotomous "choices." If pyramids fit the current situation and circles are required, in an AI environment, each choice is made and engaged as needed.

Once these ideas seep into our notions of reality, it becomes easy to shift the focus of OD practice from *fixing* what is broken to *creating* what is desired. As we broaden our understanding of human behavior and how human systems work when they are most successful and creative, we give up our belief that imposed order is always the best way. We move toward the amazing idea that human beings really can create systems wherein all voices are heard and valued and whereby the way forward and the responsibility for moving the organization along the path toward the future is truly the responsibility of each and every member of the organization. You can learn more ways AI is used in Chapter Fifteen: Team Building and the Four Cs of Team Performance; Chapter Eighteen: SOAR: Linking Strategy and OD to Sustainable Performance; and Chapter Twenty: Systemic Sustainability: Moving Sustainability from Ideas to Action.

# THE PRINCIPLES OF APPRECIATIVE INQUIRY

Appreciative Inquiry has, as an underlying guide to practice, a set of five original principles and an overall guiding principle of "wholeness." The practice of AI is a post-modern perspective, for OD is rooted and grounded in these principles. While the 4-D Model (Discover, Dream, Design, Deliver/Destiny) for applying AI is useful as a systematic approach, it is important to understand that variations on, or even alternatives to, this model (such as the AI 5-D Model) will inevitably emerge as each organization takes the AI approach and makes it its own. Once grounded in the AI principles, organizations inevitably become generative and creative, leading to even more innovation in the use and form of AI itself.

## The Overarching Principle of Wholeness

Appreciative Inquiry, rooted as it is in that which is strong and positive, leads to a *new way of thinking*. AI unleashes the imagination and provides a process for human beings to join and experience the idea that "Wholes precede parts!" as articulated in the book *Presence* (Senge, Scharmer, Jaworski, & Flowers, 2005).

It is said of Albert Einstein that he marveled at magnetic fields, gravity, inertia, and light beams. He felt that something deeply hidden had to be behind things. He retained the ability to hold two thoughts in his mind simultaneously, to be puzzled when they conflicted, and to delight when he saw an underlying unity. AI leads to this valuing of multiple realities.

AI makes apparent that what we define as "problems" can be resolved by looking forward toward a dreamed-of future rather than by looking backward to what was broken and needs fixing. Indeed, the very act of looking toward what is "wanted" and agreeing to move toward that goal includes the process of "fixing" those existing things that keep us from moving forward. AI helps us understand that human systems are different from mechanical systems and that the way forward is not by becoming the admired leader; rather, it is by empowering others to tap into their gifts and talents together "to create not just new worlds, but better worlds," as David Cooperrider articulates in the film, "A Fusion of Strengths."

Appreciative Inquiry is all about "wholes":

- Getting all parts of a system involved in imagining their preferred future;
- Getting all voices in the system into the conversation; and
- Recognizing that an organization is a "whole" and all parts are interrelated/entangled.

This is the challenge for an OD practitioner who wants to use AI—to help organizations begin to understand the interconnectedness of literally every part of the organization and to see it as an interconnected whole.

As with any approach to OD and change, one needs to know the essential principles (constructionist, simultaneity, anticipatory, poetic, and positive). Having an understanding of these core principles lets one apply and adapt the original AI 4-D cycle to any situation in which human beings play a key role (Watkins & Mohr, 2001).

## The Five Original Principles

The five core principles shown in Figure 7.1 are the beliefs and perspective that connect AI from theory to practice.

AI rests on these principles, originally discovered by David Cooperrider (1986). The practice of these principles in one's life and work will lead the OD practitioner to experience their relevance in creating strengths-based relationships and success in organizations and communities (Stavros & Torres, 2005).

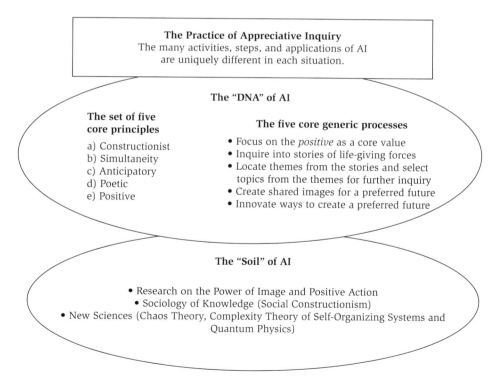

**Figure 7.1.** The Structure of AI

Adapted from Watkins and Mohr, 2001

***Constructionist Principle*** This is an understanding and acceptance of the social constructionist stance toward reality and social knowledge. For example, what we believe to be real in the world is created through our social discourse, through the conversations we have with each other that lead to agreement about how we will see the world, how we will behave, and what we will accept as reality.

The Constructionist Principle states that knowledge about an organization and the destiny of that organization are interwoven. To be effective leaders in any situation, we must be skilled in the art of understanding, reading, and analyzing organizations as living, human constructions. What we believe to be true about an organization, the way that we "know" it, will affect the way we act and the way we approach change in that system. The first task of any organization change process is Discovery—learning and making sense of what is believed and said about the system. Thus, the *way* we know *is* fateful (Gergen, 1995).

- The questions we ask are fateful;
- The questions determine what we find; and
- The questions and corresponding conversations create the world as we know it.

***Simultaneity Principle*** This principle works in harmony with the Constructionist Principle. There is a realization that *inquiry is change*. This means that the first question we ask is fateful in that the *organization will turn its energy in the direction of that first question*, whether positive or negative. As a result, the seeds of change are embedded in the questions we ask. The Simultaneity Principle recognizes that inquiry and change are not separate moments but are simultaneous. Inquiry is intervention. The seeds of change—that is, the things people think and talk about, the things people discover and learn, and the things that inform dialogue and inspire images of the future—are implicit in the very first questions we ask. One of *the* most impactful things a change agent does is to articulate questions. The questions we ask set the stage for what we "find," and what we "discover" creates the stories that lead to conversations about how the organization will construct its future.

***Poetic Principle*** This principle invites you to recognize that the meaning and energy generated in our conversations depend on the point of focus of the conversation. For example, you can focus an organizational conversation on moments of success, wisdom, and strength in your team. Or you can tell the story from a place of breakdown, dysfunctional dynamics, and weaknesses. The Poetic Principle provides an opportunity for your dialogue to enhance value and elevate your team's spirit and work. It brings to life the stories that empower positive relationships. The value of storytelling as a way of gathering holistic information is that it includes not only facts but also human feelings. This principle recognizes that stories (like good poetry) can be told and interpreted about any aspect of an organization's existence.

The Poetic Principle acknowledges that human organizations are open books. An organization's story is constantly co-authored by the people within the organization and those outside who interact with it. The organization's past, present, and future are endless sources of learning, inspiration, and interpretation, just as a good poem is open to endless interpretations. The important point is that we can study *any* topic related to human experience in *any* human system. We can inquire into the nature of alienation or the nature of joy. We can study moments of creativity and innovation or moments of debilitating stress. We have a choice.

***Anticipatory Principle*** This principle demonstrates that human beings act based on their "anticipation" of future events, and that this anticipation has an impact on themselves, the people, and systems in the organization. Anticipatory images help us understand that behavior and decisions are based not only on what we were born with or learned from our environment, but also on what we anticipate, what we think or imagine will happen in the future. Habits of the collective imagination, the mind, and the heart guide images of the future. Images are relational, public property, and dialogical.

The Anticipatory Principle says that the most important resources we have for generating constructive organization change or improvement are our collective imagination and our discourse about the future. It is the image of the future that guides the current behavior of any person or organization. Organizations exist, in the final analysis, because people who govern and maintain them share some sort of shared discourse or expectation about what the organization is, how it will function, and what it is likely to become. The power of this principle lies in action. When we act from an expectation, we move toward what we anticipate.

***Positive Principle*** This principle's core idea is that the more positive, bold, and affirmative the images we carry, the more likely we are to move toward those images. This final principle informs the other four principles. Positive images lead to positive actions. This principle shows us that, the more positive the image or questions asked, the more positive and long-lasting the results (Cooperrider, 1999).

There is power in positive questions, the affective side of transformation, and the dynamic of hope. Positive, grounded inquiry is *an antidote to cynicism*. The Positive Principle grows out of years of experience with AI. Momentum for change requires large amounts of *positive affect and social bonding—*emotions like hope, inspiration, and sheer joy in creating with one another. AI demonstrates that the more positive the questions used to guide a group process or organizational change effort, the more long lasting and effective the change effort (Bushe & Coetzer, 1995). Human beings and organizations move in the direction of what they inquire about. Widespread inquiry into "empowerment" or "being the best organization in the field" will have a completely different long-term sustainable impact for positive action than a study into "low morale" or "process breakdowns" done with the idea that those conditions can be cured.

These five original principles are central to AI's theoretical basis for OD work that is generative and strengths-based. The seminal article on these principles is "Appreciative Inquiry into Organizational Life" (Cooperrider & Srivastva, 1987).

### The Five Core Principles as Guidelines for Organizing—An Example

In the late 1990s, twenty-two AI practitioners began to meet regularly to explore the possibility of creating an organization based on a clear statement of purpose and a set of organizational principles. The organization, Appreciative Inquiry Consulting, created a global organization that operates as a loose confederation of people and groups who practice AI and are united in the purpose and principles to engage the "positive core" of all people and all living systems and to expand that rich potential, creating organizations that are themselves agents of world benefit. It took the group a few years of regular meetings to create this document and to formulate organization structure and form to fit this purpose and these principles. This organization is open to all who agree with the purpose and principles. Go to www.AIConsulting.org.

## THE CLASSIC AND POST-MODERN OD PARADIGMS

Since the 1940s, organizations have used the traditional deficit-based approach to solving problems. It starts with identifying problems, then diagnosing and analyzing the problems, and ends with a plan to fix the problems. AI provides an alternative to this traditional approach to a more affirmative, strengths-based way to look for what is working well in the organization. As Cooperrider, Whitney, and Stavros (2008) describe:

"In its most practical construction, Appreciative Inquiry is a form of organizational study that selectively seeks to locate, highlight, and illuminate the life-giving forces of the organization's existence. Appreciative Inquiry seeks out the best of 'what is' to help ignite the collective imagination of 'what might be.' The aim is to generate new knowledge that expands the 'realm of the possible' and helps members of an organization to envision a collectively desired future and to carry forth that vision in ways which successfully translate images of possibility into reality, and belief into practice." (p. xiii)

Organizations do not need to be fixed. They need constant reaffirmation. More precisely, organizations as heliotropic systems need to be appreciated. Every new affirmative projection of the future is a consequence of an appreciative understanding of the past or the present (Cooperrider, 1999).

It is in this context that the application of AI as an organization change process works. Table 7.1 describes traditional OD (Paradigm 1) and the AI post-modern OD version (Paradigm 2). Both paradigms are based on Kurt Lewin's "action research" process.

In the early days, the Paradigm 2 language was used for AI-type interventions. The AI process began with "appreciating the best of what is," moved to "envisioning what might be," engaged the group in "dialoging what should be," and ended by "innovating what will be." The process being used in the earliest applications was implemented, however, much like the traditional "deficit" based action research of traditional OD. The consultant did the interviewing, made sense of the data, and reported findings back to the "client" as a basis for a planning process. Several key innovations happened along the way.

In the mid-1980s, Dr. John Carter, a well-known and highly regarded NTL member and OD practitioner, was working with a large accounting firm in Canada. He knew about David's work and decided to use it for a "retreat" planning session that the firm wanted to have, including all five hundred of their major partners and staff. John was accustomed to the OD approach of the consultant, to interview those who would be attending the planning session. He knew that he wanted to experiment with AI, but the idea of interviewing five hundred people was daunting! So John pioneered the idea of having the participants interview each other, sharing stories, and, in small groups, sharing

#### Table 7.1. Paradigm 1: Traditional OD and Paradigm 2: Post-Modern OD

| Paradigm 1: Deficit-Based Research | Paradigm 2 (AI): Strengths-Based Research |
| --- | --- |
| Identifying Problems: What needs to be fixed | Appreciating the best of what is |
| Diagnosing: What are the causes | Envisioning what might be |
| Analyzing: What are possible solutions | Dialoging what should be |
| Planning/Proposing: What are the recommendations | Innovating what will be |
| Organizations (human systems) are problems to be solved | Organizations (human systems) are mysteries to be embraced |

and making meaning of what they had heard. This innovation became part of the AI process for gathering "data" and quickly spread.

In the late 1980s, David Cooperrider participated in an NTL conference in which he presented AI to the NTL-OD community for the first time. In a session about OD for international development agencies, David decided that it was time for AI to "go global." He persuaded the Case School of Organization Behavior to hold a conference focused on AI as a global social change process.

In preparation for the conference (held in 1989), five graduate students each volunteered to work with a global social change organization. Tojo Thatchenkery, then a student and now a professor at George Mason University, volunteered to be the consultant to the Institute for Cultural Affairs (ICA), a global organization dedicated to improving life for people around the globe. ICA is a community of dedicated and committed people who are innovative and eager to learn. Tojo, using the one-on-one (paired) interviewing process that John Carter had inadvertently made a part of the "application" of AI in large systems, was very pleased with the high level of participation. As John had done, Tojo asked those who had participated in the interview process to "give him the data." While the way of gathering the data was changing, it was still part of the AI practice for the consultant to take the data, to "make sense" of it, and to return it to the client system as a document identifying what needs attention. To his surprise, as Tojo reports, the ICA community said, "No." "It's our data," they explained, "and we will make sense of it!"

So the AI application as it is used today began to take shape. Often this is presented as the 4-D model (see Figure 7.2).

The underlying assumption of AI is that an organization is a *mystery to be embraced* rather than a *problem to be solved*. How to do this is shown in Figure 7.2 by starting with an affirmative topic selection like building a high-performance team. What follows are *Discovery* (appreciating what gives life), *Dream* (envisioning what might be), *Design* (co-constructing how it can be), and *Destiny* (sustaining what will be). These 4 Ds will be discussed later in the chapter, but first we want to introduce a change to the AI 4-D Model, the AI 5-D Model, as shown in Figure 7.3.

In the AI 5-D Model, a fifth D, *Define*, is added to the beginning of the cycle to cover what OD practitioners call the "contracting" phase of the process. Then, the application of AI to any organization change process follows the remaining 4 Ds: Discover, Dream, Design, and Destiny (originally Deliver). Whether you decide to use the AI 4-D or 5-D Model, both are actually a rearticulation of Kurt Lewin's action research model that is the very foundation of the OD field.

Table 7.2 explains the different processes for an OD intervention and describes the difference in assumptions and beliefs that underlie the classic OD action research approach and the action research AI 4-D process.

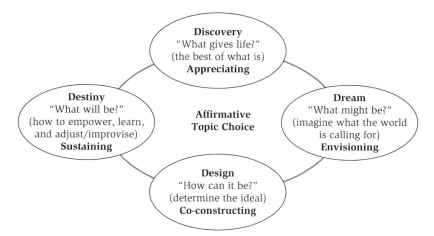

**Figure 7.2.** AI 4-D Model

While the steps for the application of AI in human systems are fairly concrete and understandable, the way those steps are carried out makes all the difference. It is essential that the AI process be "owned" by the client organization so that the consultant functions as coach and advisor. At every step, the people who are part of the organization do the essential "work" of the process. The data/information comes from the stories that they share with each other; the meaning they make of the information comes from group-level sharing and dialogue; the images of the future are ones they create; and, finally, the way forward is embodied in the plans they create for going forward.

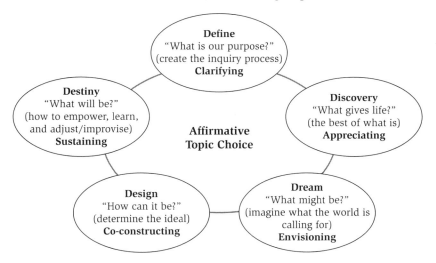

**Figure 7.3.** AI 5-D Model

**Table 7.2. Comparison of Action Research: OD and AI Assumptions and Processes**

| Action Research | Classical Organization Development (OD) | Appreciative Inquiry (AI) |
|---|---|---|
| **1. Study** | **Gather Data:** Discover what is not working in the organization (Deficits). | **Discover:** Discover what gives life to the organization (Strengths). |
| | **Assumption:** There are concrete problems that can be identified and "fixed" in order to return the organization to its ideal state. | **Assumption:** Every organization has a positive core—a set of beliefs and values that give it life and creates a core that gives guidance to the inevitable continuous change. |
| | **Process:** OD consultants work with the top people in the organization to create a "data-gathering tool" that the consultant can use to study the organization. The consultant interviews people in the organization and records what he or she hears. The search is for "facts." The questions are in search of what is not working well in the organization that is fixed. | **Process:** AI facilitators work with people in the organization to create a process for interviews done by the people themselves, generally working in pairs. The stories collected in these interviews enable the people in the organization to recognize and re-connect with the positive core of the organization—those values and ideals that give the organization life—so that an image is to guide the organization in its work. |
| **2. Make sense of what has been discovered** | **Analyze:** The consultant assembles the "data" gathered into categories that can be acted upon to "fix" the organization and return it to the ideal state.<br><br>The result of this "sense-making" is usually a report that can be shared with the leadership as a diagnosis of what needs attention that, once it is "fixed," will return the organization to health. | **Discover to Dream:** Dialogue groups make sense of the information in their stories and discover embedded in them the values that make up the "positive core" of the organization.<br><br>The result of this "sense-making" is usually the articulation of a guiding image (called a provocative proposition) of the organization's positive core that informs all organization planning and actions. |

| Action Research | Classical Organization Development (OD) | Appreciative Inquiry (AI) |
|---|---|---|
| **3. Use the information to decide on goals for next steps** | **Make a Plan:** Specific problems that were identified in Step 2 are addressed and goals are set. The goals often describe what the consultant and leaders believe is the desired state for the organization relevant to the identified problems. <br><br> The focus is generally on specific parts of the system that have been identified as not working well and the goals articulate the group's image of how it would be if they fixed it. This process, by its nature, works on discrete "parts" of the system. <br><br> The metaphor for this process is mechanical, the organization as machine. | **Dream:** Once the people in the organization agree on an articulation (provocative proposition) of the positive core, groups identify interest areas for focus and dialogue about multiple ways to move that interest area toward increased alignment with the Provocative Proposition. The focus is on the whole of the system and aligning every area with the life-giving positive core. The key is to understand the interconnectedness of all parts of the system and to inspire every person in the organization to constantly be aware of how aligned every action is or can be with their image of the most desired future. The metaphor for this process is organic, the organization as a stream. |
| **4. Plan how to achieve those goals** | **Make a Plan:** Generally, a document is created that describes each problem; identifies who will be working to solve that problem; lists the resources needed for that resolution; and sets a specific time line, often with written reports and other such tracking. | **Design:** Generally, people in the organization create dialogue groups around some interest area or environment and begin the process of discovering how that area would look when aligned with the positive core. Taking what they discover, the group creates an image of the ideal and begins multiple tasks or activities to move toward the image. If the situation requires written documents, those are prepared to inform others of their actions. |

**Table 7.2. Comparison of Action Research: OD and AI Assumptions and Processes**

| Action Research | Classical Organization Development (OD) | Appreciative Inquiry (AI) |
|---|---|---|
| **5. Begin to implement the plan** | **Implement:** In a traditional planning process, teams begin to implement their plans. Planning is understood to be a linear process that sequentially moves in a line from identifying what is wrong, articulating how it ought to be, deciding how to fix it in alignment with how it ought to be, and fixing it according to a pre-determined plan. | **Deliver/Destiny:** In AI, working groups repeat the process of Discovery, Dream, and Design with the focus being on the activity identified in the first iteration. Planning is understood to be a continuous process, circular in form, that moves from discovering the positive core of the enterprise and articulating what gives life in the system, deciding multiple ways to align all aspects of the system with that positive core, agreeing on processes that will continuously move the system toward the articulated ideal, and setting up a process for continuously re-examining and updating the activities and actions that are being carried out. |
| **What underlies the practices of these two approaches** | **Beliefs:** Human systems operate like mechanical systems that can be seen as parts, each of which can be removed, fixed, and returned to the whole. There is "one best way" for a person or an organizational function to behave. Structure is generally linear and clearly understood by all. Rules govern behavior and the right rules will assure order in the system. | **Beliefs:** Human systems are organic and operate as interconnected wholes, every part of which impacts every other part in hard-to-predict ways. "Best" behavior is determined by the combination of myriad variables, almost none of which is predictable. Structure is situational and is constantly emerging. Values govern behavior and the agreed upon values will guide the behavior of all who embrace the values. |

AI is the post-modern OD action research that is founded on the five original principles. To apply it to produce effective positive change, we have introduced both the AI 4-D and 5-D Models. While the AI 4-D model remains the most-often-used visual, it is important to remember that there should always be a conversation on *defining* the purpose of how and why AI will be used. The rest of this chapter highlights what happens at each phase.

# THE AI 4-D CYCLE

The application of AI can be visualized as a cycle through four phases of activity: *Discovery, Dream, Design,* and *Destiny*, as shown in Figure 7.2. Each of the Ds represents different activities and conversations with the common thread of ongoing dialogues that are generative. AI has been used in small groups and large groups for whole system change (Barrett & Fry, 2005). Chapters Sixteen and Seventeen present further information on large group interventions and whole system change.

## The *Discovery* Phase—The Best of What Is

The task in the *Discovery* phase is to inquire, learn about, and appreciate the best of "what is." The ability to collect strengths-based, life-giving, and future-oriented data is key to the Discovery phase.

To begin with, Discovery is conducted by having the interview pairs answer (as a guideline) the four "generic questions." The *first question* is to tell a story about a "peak experience" focused on the topic chosen for the inquiry. For example, if the inquiry is about creating a high-performing team, the question would be to tell a story about a peak experience working with a high-performing team. The *second question* is about values and often has two parts: (1) what one values about oneself and (2) what one values about working on a high-performing team. The *third question* asks about the life-giving factors of a high-performing team. Finally, the *fourth question*, referred to as the "wish" question, generally asks for three wishes that each person has for creating and sustaining a high-performing team.

The Discovery process has several important aspects. First is the importance of the story. It is through sharing stories that the participants get in touch with their ideas and beliefs about what makes a peak experience. According to recent research on the human brain, stories have the power of connecting the *left brain*, where reason and language reside, with our *right brain*, where our artistic nature, innovation, and creativity reside (Dew, 1996). By tapping into the whole brain, we access our full range of ideas and emotions, giving a powerful base to our images of an ideal state.

In this phase, interview pairs team up with, usually, two or three other pairs to share stories. As each person tells his or her partner's story, this person imparts to the group the key themes, feelings, and ideas heard in the story told. As the stories are shared, each person in the group makes a list of key themes and ideas in the story about what really matters to the storyteller. This activity is often called meaning-making for the group; it quickly identifies the important ideas in each story and provides a platform for finding key ideas from the whole group.

After each individual in the circle shares stories and identifies themes, the group makes a common list and has a dialogue to identify several key themes that have emerged from the stories. It is an amazing phenomenon each time it happens, but without fail, the group quickly sees a few key ideas and themes that are common in the stories and that indicate what the group really values.

Once the large group has identified, shared, and sorted these themes, the "story-sharing" groups focus on those themes that they see as the core values of their desired state for the subject of the inquiry (in this example, the team) and their images of this state at its best—images that come from the original stories. This step is accomplished in the Dream phase.

## The *Dream* Phase—What Might Be

The *Dream* phase is an invitation for the participants to amplify the positive core of the subject system by imagining possibilities for the future. The conversation centers on what a great team, organization, industry, or community might look like, based on the list of themes from the Discovery phase. This is often done with pictures, arts and crafts created images, or even skits. Following the visual images, the group is tasked with putting their image into words, which AI calls a *provocative proposition* (or sometimes, a *possibility statement*).

The Dream phase seeks to expand the organization's true potential. It is the time to "shift" the status quo. This phase creates momentum, synergy, and excitement among the participants of "what can be."

Dreaming is a significant activity that leads to higher levels of creativity, commitment, and enthusiasm for the organization's future. It is in these higher levels that participants access the ideas and energy for identifying and articulating specific tasks and actions in the Design phase.

## The *Design* Phase—How Can It Be

The *Design* phase, crucial in implementing the desired change, focuses on the best of the past as discovered in the stories (continuity) and moves toward future possibilities (novelty) in order to achieve (transition) the desired state as articulated in the Dream. The design steps vary depending on the complexity of the project, but generally include a two-step process.

**Step 1.** The whole group brainstorms a list of activities and ideas of things that the group wants to create in their ideal organization—activities and processes that can be planned and implemented in alignment with the dreams that were created in the previous Dream phase. Ideally, all organization systems can be "imagined" in alignment with the group's "dream." Once the brainstormed list is posted, the people in the room divide themselves into work groups according to their interests.

**Step 2.** Work groups focus on their chosen topic and, in line with their chosen task, begin by asking themselves the question: "How will we make this happen?" (If the work is for something as complex as strategic planning or other whole system change processes, certain models and processes within the purview of OD practice work well from an AI perspective.) The following steps are often useful for the planning process:

1. Review the "themes," "visual images," and "provocative propositions" created by the larger group.

2. Write a "possibility statement" for the goal or task that the group plans to work on to make clear the outcome that the group wants. Be sure to align each task possibility statement with the overall statement created by the larger group.

3. Using the possibility statement as a guide, brainstorm ways to "make it happen."

4. Make concrete plans for getting started, including plans for how to get the permissions and resources needed to go forward.

In client systems, the consultant or facilitator must consistently remind the planning group members that they are planning for things that they, themselves, will do. They will not be doing the traditional process of passing their ideas along to others to implement. Depending on the hierarchical nature of the organization, each planning group must include in its plan a way to get both the permissions and the resources needed to carry out its proposals. After groups complete their next-steps planning, each group presents the possibility statement for its project and its plan of action.

Of major importance is to make clear from the beginning that each group is planning for what its members, themselves, will do to bring about the lasting change they have identified as desirable. In traditional OD processes, large-group planning often has, as its outcome, a list of things that the group wants done with the expectation that some senior-level people will make it happen. In AI, each group identifies what ideal state its members want to work toward and decides how to get the permissions needed, how to get the required resources to carry out the plans, and what process to use for continuous examination of its goals and processes as work proceeds.

## The *Destiny* Phase—What Will Be

In this phase, participants have a conversation about how to *deliver* the dream and design based on the discovery and dialogue. Like the previous three phases, the *Destiny* phase continues with a dialogue. The possibility statements can be revisited and updated. Additional interviewing may take place. At regular intervals, it is wise for the group to reconvene and do a full inquiry using the 4-Ds to access how the project is proceeding and plan how to go forward. This review involves asking the group: "Tell a story about the best things that have happened in this project since we began." Often, if the planning team is small, the group simply shares stories around a circle and discusses what they value about the process they are in and what they wish for next steps and long term for the project. This review process also works well as a "valuation" process. Rich data emerge and can be presented to interested parties as information or as an evaluation (in AI, called a *valuation*) of the project.

Because of the continuous and rapid change in human systems, data gathered to assess how the project is going are often outdated before they can be reported. It is important in AI to think of valuation as a continuous process in the cyclical nature of AI. The *Destiny* phase transforms the organizational culture into an appreciative learning culture, and the cycle continues.

# THE RE-ITERATIVE NATURE OF THE 4-D CYCLE

The most important part of any AI process is for the "planners" to understand that every decision is a "rapid prototype"—in other words, in a world that is changing at the speed of imagination, what seems to be the "right" process one minute can be irrelevant a few minutes later. The "planning" skill in an AI world is to be ready for and, hopefully, to embrace the notion that every plan is flexible and susceptible to change, depending on the continuous and unrelenting stream of information that bombards all human systems today. It is useful continuously to ask one another, "How's it going?" and to be ready to shift gears at any moment.

For well over a decade, we in the OD world have been exposed to ideas like "continuous learning," "change at the speed of imagination," "rapid prototyping," and even more radical ideas from the new sciences, that is, the emerging ideas and perspective about how the world was formed and how it functions. The power of AI is in its flexibility and conviction that every human being is unique and every human system is not just unique, but is continuously and unpredictably changing. This means that no rigid and rigorous change models can be expected to work in all human systems. With AI, the process focuses on helping each human system identify and amplify the "best of what is" so it can continuously create the "best of what can be."

AI is all about continuous planning and action based on the social construc-tionist idea that we are continuously creating our images of and beliefs about the world through our conversations with each other. Thus, the AI planning process recycles the 4-D process at each step.

For example, using the high-performing team as the subject, a group might create a plan for being a high-performing team and begin to make it happen. As they go forward with ideas created in the planning process, team members may find that what they thought would work well does not. Then the next step is a new AI 4-D process. "Let's tell stories about times when what we have done so far is working well." Then, "Let's have a dialogue about what things we wish for that we might want to do differently. Perhaps we need to talk about how we are living our espoused values and see whether there are others to add or some that we clearly aren't interested in any longer." And, finally, "What is our plan for going forward from this 're-planning' activity?"

Such a cyclical process is the essence of AI. It *is* continuous learning. It is following the images of what we truly want rather than what we ought to want. It becomes a way of thinking, a way of being, and a way of practicing OD in this post-modern age.

# SUMMARY

Traditional OD, at its best, is about entering a system that is ready for change. And traditionally, OD practitioners have operated on the assumption that the "organization" (that is, most likely the leadership group in the organization) is ready for change—but the people in it are not. Further, OD practitioners often accept the assumption that it is part of their jobs to create an atmosphere in which people feel inspired and free to *change*. Helping organizations create such an atmosphere is an essential part of a "consultant's" work in traditional OD. Mayhew (2006) writes: "Resistance is reduced when a change plan is thoughtful and credible enough that people believe it will work and are willing to follow it" (p. 112).

Appreciative Inquiry holds a totally different assumption. The AI process shifts those assumptions about resistance and operates on the belief that the responsibility for change resides with the people. Traditional OD implies that the "people" and the "organization" are separate entities. In an AI process, it is the people themselves who *are* the organization and must be the creators of an atmosphere that embraces change. The shift begins with the "people" taking responsibility for the process through the story sharing and dialogue.

Even if some people are skeptical and believe, as they have been taught, that the consultants and organization's leaders are in charge of the process, it takes only that first story-sharing interview to shift energy and engage the whole organization in sharing responsibility for the future health and success of their enterprise.

Thomas Head (2000, p. 27) writes:

"Appreciative Inquiry, as a method for introducing and facilitating organization change, has proven itself a successful and robust methodology. In many ways, Appreciative Inquiry might be considered *organization development's aspirin*. It works for almost everyone and for almost any problem, but no one knows exactly why. One possible explanation, explored here, is that Appreciative Inquiry is successful because it almost entirely eliminates resistance to change."

All of which is to say that the first task in shifting into an AI approach to our practice is to grapple with the embedded beliefs and practices that have, in the past, made us successful in our field. As noted in this chapter, it is not that we have been "doing it wrong." For those of us who are OD practitioners trained in traditional OD methods, processes, and belief systems, it is to recognize that it is the very world around us—the global village, the interconnected communication systems, the speed of change, the massive expansion of knowledge—that is changing. And many of the methods and models that have served us well in the past may be no longer working so well for us in this new reality.

Our challenge is to notice our own assumptions and to open our minds to new possibilities. It is an "Isn't that interesting? I wouldn't have thought of it that way" approach to our practice and to practically everything in our lives these days. For the authors of this chapter, Appreciative Inquiry has provided that path.

# References

Barrett, F., & Fry, R.E. (2005). *Appreciative inquiry: A positive approach to building cooperative capacity*. Chagrin Fall, OH: Taos Institute Publishers.

Bushe, G., & Coetzer, G. (1995, March). Appreciative inquiry as a team-development intervention: A controlled experiment. *Journal of Applied Behavioral Science, 31*, 130–139.

Cooperrider, D. (1986). Appreciative inquiry: Toward a methodology for understanding and enhancing organizational innovation. Unpublished dissertation at Case Western Reserve University in Cleveland, Ohio.

Cooperrider, D. (1999). Positive images, positive action: The affirmative basis of organizing. In S. Srivastva & D.L. Cooperrider, *Appreciative management and leadership* (pp. 91–125). Euclid, OH: Lakeshore Communications.

Cooperrider, D., & Srivastva, S. (1987). Appreciative inquiry in organizational life. In W. Pasmore & R. Woodman (Eds.), *Research in organization change and development* (pp. 129–169). Greenwich, CT: JAI Press.

Cooperrider, D., & Srivastva, S. (1999). The emergence of the egalitarian organization. In S. Srivastva & D.L. Cooperrider, *Appreciative management and leadership:*

*The power of positive thoughts and action in organization* (rev. ed.). Euclid, OH: Lakeshore Communications.

Cooperrider, D., Whitney, D., & Stavros, J. (2008). *Appreciative inquiry handbook: For leaders of change.* San Francisco: Berrett-Koehler.

Dew, J. (1996, April). Are you a right brain or left brain thinker? *Quality Progress Magazine*, pp. 91–93.

Gergen, K. (1995). *Realities and relationships.* Cambridge, MA: Harvard University Press.

Hammond, S. (1998). *The thin book of appreciative inquiry.* Bend, OR: Thinbook Publishers.

Head, T.C. (2000). Appreciative inquiry: Debunking the mythology behind resistance to change. *Organization Development Practitioner: Journal of the OD Network, 32*(1), 27–35.

Mayhew, E. (2006). Organizational change processes. In B.B. Jones & M. Brazzel, *The NTL handbook of organization development and change* (pp. 104–121). San Francisco: Jossey-Bass.

Senge, P.J., Scharmer, C.O., Jaworski, J., & Flowers, B.S. (2005). *Presence.* New York: Doubleday.

Stavros, J.M., & Torres, C. (2005). *Dynamic relationships: Unleashing the power of appreciative inquiry in daily living.* Chagrin Falls, OH: Taos Institute Publishers.

Watkins, J.M., & Kelly, R. (2007). *Appreciative inquiry theory and practice: The resource book.* Williamsburg, VA: Appreciative Inquiry Unlimited.

Watkins, J.M., & Mohr, B.J. (2001). *Appreciative inquiry: Change at the speed of imagination.* San Francisco: Pfeiffer.

Yaeger, T., Head, T., & Sorensen, P. (2006). *Global organization development: Managing unprecedented change.* Greenwich, CT: Information Age Publishing.

PART TWO

# OD PROCESS TO GUIDE CHANGE

CHAPTER EIGHT

# Entry

*Marketing and Positioning OD*

**Alan Weiss**

Most OD practitioners fail to realize that they are in the marketing business. Superb consultants in this area cannot get work because they believe that marketing is not required. Average OD consultants are doing quite well because they recognize the importance of marketing and can do it. Consultants who are great marketers can name their fee. Which group would you rather be in?

Even on an internal basis, you can't sit back and wait for employee line areas to call you. You must be analyzing the organization from a business perspective and proactively recommending to key executives what can be done to improve productivity and performance.

You are not a firefighter. You are the fire marshal. This chapter will enable you to:

- Determine your value proposition;
- Identify your buyer;
- Establish routes to reach that buyer;
- Achieve conceptual agreement; and
- Create a proposal to close business.

# DETERMINING YOUR VALUE PROPOSITION

There are three critical factors to embrace when attempting to market professional services: (1) What's the market need? (2) What are your competencies? and (3) What is your passion?

## What Is the Market Need?

This is the essence of marketing. There must be a pre-existing need. For example, sales development or leadership improvement is always needed or a need you can create such as satisfying employees before satisfying the customer. Since OD is an often nebulous and inexact concept, it is vital to create a clear value proposition.

A value proposition is always a benefit for the potential client and never a description of your methodology. For example, here are good and poor value propositions:

| *Good* | *Poor* |
|---|---|
| • Improve retention of core talent | • Perform exit interviews |
| • Decrease time-to-market of new products | • Assess marketing/sales relations |
| • Merge acquisition and parent cultures | • Run focus groups for new people |
| • Improve customer response time | • Create customer survey |

You can embrace existing market need or else create new market need (which is what Akio Morita did at Sony when he created the Walkman® because no one knew they needed it until he educated them). Stephen Jobs and Apple are very adept at "jumping on the next big thing," in his words, and creating recombined new needs, the iPhone being a perfect example.

You must become proficient in articulating your value proposition in terms of a client outcome. Here is mine: "We improve individual and organizational productivity and performance." (The only legitimate response to this rather vague statement is, "What does that mean?" I reply: "Well, tell me something about your business, and I will be more specific." You cannot learn while you are talking, and the more you talk, the more the other person will tend to "deselect" you.)

One other point: You can anticipate need. In your organization or a client organization, is there a coming need to manage virtual teams that never see each other, or to change recruiting practices to hire completely different types of skills, or use an internal social networking medium? These are key OD marketing competencies.

# What Are Your Competencies?

Competencies are those combinations of skills, experiences, and behaviors that make you proficient in a given area. Your competencies cannot come from "store-bought" materials from training venders. Believe me, if they were sufficient, the company wouldn't need you.

If you do not have sufficient competencies, then the good news is that you can always acquire more. But what are you good at, and what would you like to become good at?

In terms of marketing (as opposed to content), Exhibit 8.1 lists the traits for a "rainmaker" (business developer/marketer) that I have discerned over the years. They may surprise you.

# What Is Your Passion?

Without passion, there is nothing but tedious work. Market need and competency must be fueled by passion. Isolate those competencies and needs you most favor and are most passionate about, and focus on them.

For example, I will not do any "downsizing" work whatsoever, because I am against it, since I consider downsizing to be a heinous act implemented to

## Exhibit 8.1. The Rainmaker Attributes

**Strategies for Marketing**

**The Rainmaker Attributes**

- Intellectual breadth
  - Able to discuss a wide variety of issues
- Sense of humor
  - Able to ease tension, maintain perspective
- Industry conversancy
  - Able to relate to and identify situational issues
- Superb communication skills
  - Able to command a room or a meeting
- Presence: *Sogomi*
  - Able to be accepted as a peer of the buyer
- Framing skills
  - Able to quickly describe problems and opportunities
- Innovation
  - Able and willing to raise the bar, seek new paths
- Resilience
  - Able to accept rejection and reject acceptance
- Life balance
  - Able to view life holistically

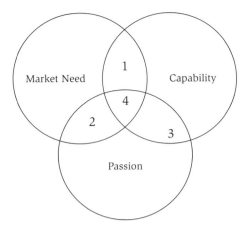

**Figure 8.1.** Three Areas and Four Conditions for Value

compensate for executive error. I am passionate about developing leadership, so I actively seek out work in that area.

If you refer to Figure 8.1, you will see four possibilities:

1. Need and capability without passion create drudgery. You are a hired hand with little motivation and no "ownership" of outcomes.

2. Market need and passion without competency make you a snake oil seller, hawking your potions but without the real medicine needed to cure the ills.

3. Capability and passion without market need make you a dilettante, offering aesthetic solutions to problems no one cares about unless you can convince them otherwise.

4. The combination of these elements makes you an effective marketer.

If you have these elements in place, then you need only respond to the following questions—and the good news is that marketing is difficult but not complex—to arrive at your marketing strategy:

1. *What is my value proposition?* What outcomes do you provide for the client? Consider another way to ask this question: After you walk away, how is the client better off? How has the client's condition been improved?

2. *Who is likely to write a check for that value?* This is what I call the "economic buyer" or the "true buyer." He or she has the budget to authorize, approve, and launch your project. In large organizations, there are scores (or even hundreds) of economic buyers. In small organizations, there may be just one or two. If your contact must go

elsewhere for approval or to "seek budget," you are not talking to an economic buyer.

3. *How do I reach that buyer?* A key problem in marketing is that too many consultants go directly to point 3 without understanding the first two points. But the only way to arrive at point 3 is after establishing the first two realities.

## IDENTIFYING AND REACHING THE ECONOMIC BUYER

There are two types of "buyers" in organizational settings:

1. *Economic buyer*: Possesses the power and authority to approve a check for your services and to fund the project.

2. *Feasibility buyer*: Provides opinion and analysis of the project's appropriateness in terms of culture, scope, credentials, content, and other relative clients.

Now hear this: Most consultants fail at marketing because they spend too much time with feasibility buyers—who cannot say "yes" but can say "no"—and not enough time (or no time at all) with economic buyers who can say "yes." That is why the attributes mentioned above are so important. You must be able to relate to economic buyers on a peer basis. Your content and OD skills are not sufficient for that. You must have business acumen and conversancy. This means that within organizational walls, you cannot confine yourself to a staff cave. Ergo, the proactive seeking of improvement noted above.

When you encounter feasibility buyers—"gatekeepers" and "filters"—you must endeavor to go around or through them to the economic buyer. You can do this in three ways, in descending order of effectiveness.

1. *Appeals to rational self-interest.* Try to convince the feasibility buyer that it would be dangerous to proceed even with a tentative plan or preliminary proposal without hearing from the true buyer's lips exactly what his or her expectations are. Explain that your experience about this is unequivocal: The economic buyer must be brought into the discussion, however briefly, as early as possible, and certainly preliminary to creating a proposal. Attempt to form a partnership with the feasibility buyer to accomplish this.

2. *Guile.* Use some device to get past the feasibility buyer. Here is my favorite, and quite honest, alternative: "Ethically, I must see the person who has the fiduciary responsibility for the project, since I need to understand exactly what his or her expectations are before deciding whether to bid on this work." Another: "It is unfair of me to expect

you to market on my behalf, especially if there may be adverse reactions. Let me take that responsibility."

3. *Power.* Ignore, circumvent, or blast through the gatekeeper. Although this will create bad relations, you are not going to get the business in any other way. Send a letter, email, fax, or phone message informing the economic buyer that you have enjoyed working with the gatekeeper but must have twenty minutes of his or her time before submitting a proposal. Provide your contact information and hope for the best.

If you content yourself with people who are willing to see you but cannot help you (for example, cannot say "yes"), you will fail as a marketer (and as an effective OD practitioner). A strong value proposition will capture the attention of an economic buyer if you can reach that person.

When people are empowered only to say "no," that is what they will inevitably say. Find the person who can say "yes" or "no," which at least gives you a fighting chance.

## ESTABLISHING THE ROUTES TO THE ECONOMIC BUYER

The best way to market is to create a "gravity" that draws people to you. This changes the entire buying dynamic. Instead of having to prove how good you are, you instead engage people who are interested in what you can do for them. This is why branding, reputation, and word-of-mouth are so important. After all, no one enters a McDonald's to browse. The buying decision has already been made before entering the store. Figure 8.2 lists a variety of ways to create gravity, and these are discussed in the following sections in more detail. Internally, you can build powerful brands. It's not unusual to hear an executive request, "Get Jane Hudson on this. We need her to help us find the right solution."

### Pro Bono Work

Pro bono work for marketing purposes should have the following characteristics:

- A cause or objective in which you believe and wish to support;
- Relatively high-profile non-profit or charity;
- Public events and media coverage;
- Significant potential buyers or influencers are volunteers and/or key exhibitors (for example, the editor of the local newspaper, the general manager of the electric company, the senior vice president of a major bank); and
- Involvement will be interactive, and not individual.

Seek out a leadership position or fill a difficult position in the organization. Typically, fund raising, managing volunteers, and publicity are vitally needed

**Figure 8.2.** The "Gravity" Concept of Marketing OD Services

and tough to do well. You want a high-visibility position and one in which you can rub elbows with your potential buyers and influencers. Take on the difficult jobs, but do them extremely well. Make the reports at the meetings, give interviews to the media, and shower credit on your colleagues.

When the time is right, suggest to the executive you have worked with or the publisher you have supported that it might make sense to have lunch some time and compare notes about your two organizations. Pro bono work like this automatically builds relationships and allows others to see your abilities on neutral turf. That is why you should do the tough jobs and do them well. Excellent organization ability, strategies, management of others, fiscal prudence, and similar traits translate well into the needs of your pro bono colleagues.

Pro bono work is especially powerful for those living in fairly major markets and who wish to reduce their travel and work closer to home. I have done work for everyone from the League of Women Voters to a shelter for battered women to local theater groups.

***Basic Rule:*** You should be engaged in at least one pro bono activity each quarter.

## Commercial Publishing

A commercially published book can provide a strong credibility statement. For successful consultants endeavoring to reach the next level, this may be the shortest route.

Early in my career, I published books that addressed the issues I wanted to be hired to consult about: innovation, behavior and motivation, and strategy. Later in my career, I published books that capitalized on my established expertise: marketing, consulting, and speaking professionally. An entirely new career was launched for me when I published *Million Dollar Consulting*, for example, which established me as a "consultant to consultants."

What part of your existing practice would you like to propel forward, or what new aspect would you like to create?

Writing a business book is not like writing a novel. You need a topic, ten or twelve chapters, and a half dozen key points supported by facts, stories, and anecdotes in each chapter. If you do not believe me, pull any ten random business books off the shelf and take a look. Create a treatment for the book, which should take about a week or two, and get it off to an agent or a publisher.

Another aspect of commercial publishing involves articles and interviews in the popular and trade press. You should be circulating article query letters and manuscripts regularly. Get used to the rejection. It happens to everyone. Successful consultants, in particular, with a raft of client experiences and case studies, should be able to create powerful, vivid pieces that, in turn, will draw interested readers to want to know more.

Try to include an offer to contact you in your articles of research studies, visits to your website, email responses to questions, and so on, enabling readers to continue to connect with you in more personal ways.

*Basic Rule:* You should set a goal to publish one article per quarter, meaning that you should be proposing four articles per quarter in different publications. (Another goal might be to create a book proposal in the next ninety days and send it to a publisher or agent.)

## Position Papers

I often refer to these as "white papers." These are powerful tools that can be used for:

- Content in your press kit;
- The basis for an article to be published;
- The basis for booklets;
- Web-page content;
- Handouts at speeches; and/or
- Giveaways for inquiries.

Position papers are two- to six-page discussions of your philosophy, beliefs, findings, experiences, and/or approaches. They are not and should never be self-promotional. Instead, they should provide credibility through the impact of their ideas and the applicability of their techniques.

Try to provide as many pragmatic and immediately useful ideas as possible. The best position papers are applicable, not esoteric. The reader should come away from them saying, "I would like to apply this, and I would like to hear more from the author."

Position papers are one of the absolutely most economical, high-impact, and versatile aspects of the gravitational field. Right now, you probably have sufficient experience and ideas to create several dozen. Create some short ones that are "plain vanilla" and straightforward and some longer ones with graphs and charts.

*Basic Rule:* Create one white paper every month.

## Radio and Television Interviews

You should be doing radio and even television appearances at any point in your career. They are relatively easy to do, since there is a constant need for fresh voices and faces to provide expert commentary on issues ranging from management fads to business etiquette to how to retain key talent.

As with the entire gravitational field, do not evaluate media interviews in terms of number of "hits" or new business. Regard them strategically as an ongoing part of your major thrust to create recognition and higher levels of credibility. Some radio appearances are worthless in terms of short-term business, but you never know who will hear you and pass your name on or what other media professional might then invite you to a more appropriate setting.

Radio interviews should be done, with rare exception (for example, National Public Radio and some major syndicated shows), from your home and over the phone. Television shots are done in the nearest local affiliate. For a memorable interview (most TV shots are only five to eight minutes, while some radio interviews can last for an hour), follow these rules:

- Provide the interviewer and/or segment producer with detailed background about you, including pronunciation of your name, and key "talking points" or questions to ask.

- Research the topic so that you can quote a few dramatic statistics and anecdotes. The media love pithy sound bites. In fact, practice short responses to all questions so that more questions can be accommodated.

- Always have two or three points in mind that promote you that you can work into responses no matter what the question. Do not rely on the host to promote you, no matter what the promises. Example: If the question is, "Alan, what is your opinion of large scale downsizing and its impact on our society?" then answer this way: "One of the reasons I am asked to work with executives from top-performing organizations is that they want me to help them retain key talent, not throw it away. So let me answer from their perspective...." If you have written a book, then say, "As I point out in Chapter Four of my newest book, *Good Enough Isn't Enough....*"

- Obtain a tape or MP3 download. Usually, asking the station in advance will do it, but always back it up with another taken from the actual airing by a friend. Splice these tapes/downloads together for a "highlights" reel of your media work, which will sell more sophisticated media outlets and just might get you on national TV. The tape is also quite impressive with prospects.

Radio and television work requires a promotional investment for ads and listing, but it is well worth it when you have reached the stage where your experience and accomplishments make you an "authority."

*Basic Rule:* Appear in a minimum of one major listing source with at least a half-page ad annually.

## Electronic and "Social Media"

Aside from your website, you have the potential to use blogs, Facebook, Linkedin, and any number of these so-called "social media" to reach out to people, network, and strut your stuff. You're best off if you already have a brand, because people will follow you. But if you don't, consider a well-done (not generic or formulaic) blog to convey your intellectual property, ideas, reactions, and guest commentary. Use social media to keep people informed of what you're doing and why. You never know where your next lead may come from.

*Basic Rule:* Don't spend more than a few hours a week on these areas. You can become consumed in electronic communications, and they are *not* your main source of leads. Executives do not troll the web to find consultants; they rely on peer referrals and more public visibility.

## Speaking

Early in people's consulting careers, I advocate that they speak wherever and whenever they can to improve credibility and visibility. However, for the experienced consultant, professional speaking is not only a key gravitational pull but is also extremely lucrative.

Most consultants are lousy speakers because they become wrapped up in their methodology and the content of their message. But the fact is that audiences need to be captivated and even entertained a bit if they are to accept any message more easily and readily.

Moreover, the keynote spot at major conferences or in-house company meetings provides a terrific platform for hundreds (and sometimes thousands) of potential buyers and recommenders to establish the beginnings of a relationship with you at one time. This is not the place to go into the details of developing a professional speaking career, but we can examine a few of the key steps you should take since the synergy with consulting is so powerful.

- As a keynote speaker or concurrent session speaker, you should continually cite your experience and other organizations with which you have worked so that the audience can think about how you might be helpful to them. Always *make it clear that you are a consultant who happens to speak at such meetings and not a speaker who also consults.*
- Provide handouts with your company's name and full contact information.
- Obtain a participant list of everyone in your session.
- Come early and stay late so that you can network with the organizers, senior management, participants, exhibitors, and others.
- Charge a high fee for your speaking, just as you would for your consulting. I suggest a three-part fee of increasing amounts for keynotes, half-days, and full days.

I used to speak for free as a method to publicize what I do. Then I realized that not only were others being paid, but that the speakers doing the most important spots were always the highest paid. Today, it is not unusual for a client to say, "I would like you to address our annual meeting, and then let us explore how you can work with us to implement the theme."

Here is an excellent resource if you want to find out which associations are holding meetings, who the executive director is, what the themes will be, who will be in the audience, and what the budget is: National Trade and Professional Associations of the United States (Columbia Books, Inc., www.columbiabooks.com)

*Basic Rule:* You ought to be speaking at least once a month in front of groups that include potential buyers.

## Website and Electronic Newsletters

At this stage, your website should be state-of-the-art from a marketing standpoint, not necessarily a technical one. It is not the bells and whistles that matter but the "draw" and appeal for potential customers. I often tell prospects to "be sure to visit my website" only to hear "That is where I just came from." A high-powered website should follow these tenets:

- Sufficient search engine presence using appropriate generic and specific key words to drive people to the site;
- A user-friendly initial page—with immediate appeal and options for the visitor;

- Easy navigation and no "traps" that force visitors to hear more about your methodology than they would ever need to hear;
- Immediate value in the form of articles to download; links to related, high-quality sites; tools and techniques; and so forth;
- An opportunity to contact you easily at any time;
- Products to purchase that you preferably own on a secure page; and
- A compelling reason to return and to tell others about the site.

By posting an article each month (still more utility provided by the position papers discussed earlier), new lists of techniques, and other value-added additions, you create a site useful to the visitor. No one is interested in visiting sites to hear people talk about themselves. Develop and upgrade your site with the potential buyer in mind. (And visit the sites of your colleagues and competitors to understand what they do well and how you can do even better.)

Electronic newsletters are wonderful means by which to reach more buyers, since readers routinely pass excellent newsletters along to colleagues as a favor. Start with your current database, create a sign-up spot on your website, and offer the newsletter in your signature file on your email. An excellent electronic newsletter should:

- Be brief—on average, no longer than a single screen;
- Be non-promotional—and simply carry your contact information at the bottom;
- Enable people to subscribe and unsubscribe easily (which is also required by law);
- Contain high-value content that is immediately applicable for most readers;
- Go out at least monthly and regularly on the same day. Consistency and constancy are everything; and
- Be copyrighted.

Use an ISSN number to protect your newsletter (the equivalent of an ISBN number on books): www.issn.org/.

One of the people in my mentoring program began with a modest list and soon had thousands of subscribers to his sales skills newsletter, which addressed "sales acceleration." He closed a piece of business with a bank in Toronto that he never would have even spoken to without someone in the bank finding the newsletter and realizing that the bank's loan officers needed this kind of sales help.

Commercial list servers can automatically deliver the newsletter and add and delete subscribers for less than $50 per month.

***Basic Rule:*** You should have a newsletter of some kind—either a monthly electronic one or at least a quarterly print version.

## Word of Mouth, Referrals, and Third-Party Endorsements

All of us need to keep fueling the "buzz" that surrounds our names and our approaches. I have found that consultants become blasé about endorsements and testimonials after a while, but they are our stock-in-trade.

In every engagement, ask the client for a referral, a blurb for a product you are creating, to serve as a reference, and to provide a testimonial letter. If you do not ask, they generally do not happen.

Write letters to magazines, newspapers, and electronic sources that rely on your credibility for the point you make, pro or con, relative to a recent article. Stand up at business, social, civic, and professional meetings to make your point. Take controversial and "contrarian" stands if you must.

Once you have an established reputation, it is far easier to maintain the momentum of word of mouth, which is a powerful lead source. But we often do not bother any longer, which is ironic, since it is now easier than ever. And this leads into other parts of the gravitation field. It is likely, for example, that some of your high-level buyers can place you in front of the trade associations to which they belong as a featured speaker at the next convention or meeting. Are you pursuing these connections?

*Basic Rule:* Your current, active clients should be providing a minimum of one testimonial and three highly qualified referrals every month. Not nearly enough practitioners and consultants ask for these very reasonable resources.

## Trade Association Leadership

At this point in your career, when you may feel that you are not getting anything out of professional associations and trade associations (and justifiably so, since most members will be at a lower level), it is time to use them differently. It is time to take a leadership position.

In the first case, the association and its membership can use your expertise and experience. In the second, it is a good way to "pay back" the profession that has been so kind to us. But third, the visibility will be a tremendous source of gravity.

You do not have to take on time-consuming national duties. You can simply serve as an officer at the local or chapter level, head a committee, organize an event, or sponsor an initiative. Whatever it is, your status within the industry will be enriched. I find that many of my referrals come from other consultants who feel they cannot handle the assignment and hope that I will either reciprocate some time or involve them in the project, both of which I am quite happy to do.

Since very few capable people ever seek these offices, it is almost guaranteed that you can be as responsible and as visible as you choose.

***Basic Rule:*** You should at minimum belong to the Institute of Management Consultants (IMC: www.imcusa.org/) or the Society for Advancement of Consulting (SAC: www.consultingsociety.com) and be known to your local membership, presenting a session at least once a year at a scheduled meeting.

## Teaching

You will establish an entirely new circle of references and contacts through teaching part-time at a university, college, or extension program. And you are now in a position to do so with a minimum of difficulty.

You can earn the title of "adjunct professor" in most cases and arrange to teach one evening a week. The ideal is to teach at the graduate level, where you will be challenged by students and receive a diversity of opinion that you might not experience in business life. These positions add immeasurably to your ability to become published, gain higher levels of credibility, and receive references from the university (and, in some cases, from the students).

You can almost always find a junior college or trade school to start out if you are uncertain and want to test the waters easily—or do not possess the requisite doctorate for work at a senior institution. I was on the extension faculty at Case Western Reserve University in Cleveland and received several pieces of business as a result.

***Basic Rule:*** Teach as a guest lecturer at least three or four times a year at local institutions or by contract at national sites.

## Alliances and Networking

I have placed these two together for discussion purposes since alliances are often the result of effective networking. Interestingly, and short-sighted, experienced consultants sometimes feel that their networking days are behind them. But that is only if you see networking as a tactic instead of a marketing strategy—and strong aspect of gravitation. Among those who constitute networking potential for you are

- Buyers
- Media people
- Key vendors
- Mentors
- Endorsers
- Meeting planners
- Recommenders to buyers
- Bankers
- Key advisors
- High-profile individuals in your business
- Trade association executives
- Community leaders

Networking is far easier than ever, utilizing email, voice mail, instant messaging, social networking, and other communication alternatives, but nothing is as effective as the face-to-face interaction that allows for personal chemistry to develop. If possible, networking should be done in person. It should then be followed up or reinforced through other communications avenues.

Here is a sequence for networking, whether at a trade association meeting, civic event, business conference, recreational outing, or nearly any other activity that you know in advance you will be attending.

1. Learn who will likely attend the event. Obtain a participant list, a brochure, the names of the committee members, or make an educated guess. Prepare yourself for whom you are likely to encounter and create a "target list" of the best prospects. For example, if you know the local business page editor is attending a charity fundraiser, you may want to make his or her acquaintance so that you can eventually suggest an article. If the general manager (and a potential buyer) for the local utility is at the dance recital, you may want to try to identify him or her and begin a casual conversation during intermission.

2. Begin casual conversations during the gathering, both to identify those targets you have chosen and to learn who else might be there who could be of help. For example, you might want to introduce yourself to another consultant whose web pages you think are excellent to explore whether she might make her web designer's number available to you or approach a local designer because you would like to understand how he might work with you even as a novice.

3. Introduce yourself without describing anything about your work and simply listen. If in a group, which is likely, do not attempt your personal networking. Wait until you can find the person alone later and approach him or her one-on-one, preferably where you will have a few minutes in private. That is all you need. Do not talk to someone while your eyes work the rest of the room. Talk only as much as required to get the other person talking. You want to hear about him or her, and his or her views and preferences.

4. When you are able to spend a few minutes one-on-one, offer something of value based on what you have heard. For example, if the person is a potential buyer who has mentioned the problem she is having with attracting and retaining good people, suggest a book that you would be happy to pass along or a website that you will send by email that has articles on the subject. If the person is a graphic artist, ask permission to give his or her name to some people you know who need literature designed. The key here is to provide value to the other person.

5. In the event you are asked what you do, practice providing very succinct responses. Here is a dreadful response:

"I am a consultant who focuses on interactions of teams, especially cross-functionally, raises sensitivity to synergies possible in greater

collaboration, and implements processes to enhance team connectedness. I use many instruments."

Here is a terrific response:
"I assist clients in improving individual and organizational performance."
If the other person says, "That is a bit vague. How do you do that?"
then you reply, "Well, if you tell me something about your organization
and the issues you are facing, I will show you how the approaches may
apply specifically to you."

6. Exchange a card or somehow gather the other person's contact information so that you can send the promised material or information. At
   a minimum, get a phone number and email address. DO NOT provide
   brochures, materials, or any other gimmicks or "stuff." No one wants
   to lug around material at any kind of event, and this stuff usually
   winds up in the nearest garbage can.

7. Immediately, the next morning at the latest, deliver what you promised. If you are providing the other party as a resource to someone
   else, then copy that person on the email or correspondence, or mention to her that you have given her name to the individuals you had
   mentioned.

8. In a week or so, follow up to see whether the material was helpful, the
   reference worked out, the prospects called, and so forth. Ask if there
   is anything further along those lines that might be helpful. Then summarize or reaffirm your offer of further help with a letter accompanied
   by your promotional material and literature. Suggest to the other person
   that you thought he or she might want to learn a little more about you
   and what you do.

9. In a few weeks, send still more value in the form of a contact, potential
   customer, or article of interest.

10. If the other party replies with a "thank you" for your latest offer of
    value, then get back to him and suggest a brief meeting, breakfast,
    lunch, or other opportunity to get together at his convenience. Sim-
    ply say that you would like to learn more about what he or she does
    and also get his or her advice about what you do. If he or she has not
    responded with a "thank you" of any kind, then wait one more week,
    call to see if he or she received the additional value you sent, and then
    suggest the meeting as described above. (An active response simply
    enables you to shorten the waiting time.)

***Basic Rule:*** You should be networking at some event at least twice a month,
and you should establish at least one useful contact from each one.

# ESTABLISHING CONCEPTUAL AGREEMENT

Whether you reach out to people or they approach you due to "gravitational pull," you must achieve conceptual agreement on three basic issues prior to submitting a proposal. Most practitioners submit too many proposals too soon in the marketing process. Conceptual agreement means that you and the economic buyer agree on:

1. *Objectives*. What are the outcome-based business objectives to be achieved through this project? There are usually no more than a handful in a cogent project. Keeping them tightly described avoids "scope creep" (the gradual enlargement of projects as clients keep asking for more and more tasks to be accomplished) through the focus on very specific, mutually agreed-on goals.

2. *Measures of success*. What are the metrics that will indicate that you have made progress and/or reached the goals? Agreeing on these means that your proper contribution will be noted and the proper time to disengage has arrived.

3. *Value to the client*. What is the worth and impact of what you are accomplishing, *and is it annualized*? By stipulating to the value of the project, the client is focused on value and not fee and can make an appropriate ROI determination. If you are discussing fees and not value, you have lost control of the discussion.

Figure 8.3 shows the role of conceptual agreement in the overall marketing process. You can see two factors in Figure 8.3. First, conceptual agreement is the heart of the process. Second, the proposal should not be submitted until after conceptual agreement is gained, since it is merely a summation and not an exploration. Let us conclude, then, by considering powerful proposals.

# CREATING PROPOSALS THAT CLOSE BUSINESS

Let us begin with the parameters of what proposals can legitimately and pragmatically do and not do. Proposals can and should do the following:

- Stipulate the outcomes of the project;
- Describe how progress will be measured;
- Establish accountabilities;
- Set the intended start and stop dates;
- Provide methodologies to be employed;
- Explain options available to the client;

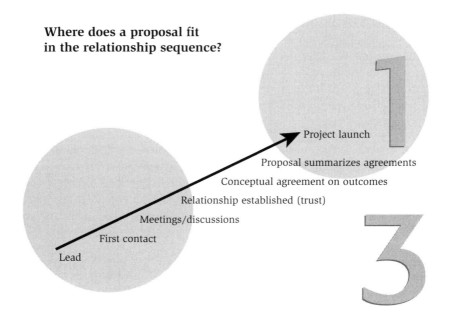

**Where does a proposal fit
in the relationship sequence?**

Project launch

Proposal summarizes agreements

Conceptual agreement on outcomes

Relationship established (trust)

Meetings/discussions

First contact

Lead

**Figure 8.3.** Conceptual Agreement as the Key to Closing New Business

- Convey the value of the project;
- Detail the terms and conditions of payment of fees and reimbursements;
- Serve as an ongoing template for the project;
- Establish boundaries to avoid "scope creep";
- Protect both consultant and client; and
- Offer reasonable guarantees and assurances.

Proposals cannot and/or should not do the following:

- Sell the interventions being recommended;
- Create the relationship;
- Serve as a commodity against which other proposals are compared;
- Provide the legitimacy and/or credentials of your firm and approaches;
- Validate the proposed intervention;
- Make a sale to a buyer you have not met;
- Serve as a negotiating position;
- Allow for unilateral changes during the project;

- Protect one party at the expense of the other; or
- Position approaches so vaguely as to be immeasurable and unenforceable.

There are nine steps to a great proposal, which you can find in my work, *How to Write a Proposal That Can Be Accepted Every Time*, or you can find the steps on this book's website.

# SUMMARY

We have discussed how to: (1) determine your value proposition; (2) identify your buyer; (3) establish routes to reach that buyer; (4) achieve conceptual agreement; and (5) create a proposal that will close business.

Marketing is the first of the OD phases to plan and facilitate change. The following chapters will take you through the pre-launch and launch phases of an OD intervention and beyond. However, unless you market effectively, there will be no projects.

CHAPTER NINE

# Front-End Work

*Effectively Engaging with the Client System*

David W. Jamieson*

When a consultant initially enters into and engages a client system for the purpose of facilitating change, there are a number of early outcomes that must go well. The activities in the front-end phase serve as the platform for all subsequent organization development (OD) work. The quality and clarity of the foundation (agreements, expectations, relationships, and feelings) that are established at the outset can strengthen subsequent work phases. Often, challenges encountered later in change work can be traced to missed or flawed outcomes during this front-end phase. Much is at stake in the beginning of any change effort. It is common to encounter:

- Minimal visible support in the organization;

- Managers and employees who feel vulnerable;

- Differing and biased perspectives about what is working, what is not working, and what needs to be done;

- More "unknowns" than "knowns";

- Mixed motives for seeking a consultant's help (desire to change, financial trouble, need for a scapegoat, and so forth); and

- A past history of bad change experiences.

---

*I would like to thank David Shechtman for his helpful comments on an earlier draft.

In the beginning, it is usually not clear what the consultant will need to do, who he or she will need to work with, how he or she will conduct the process, how fast it will need to occur, or what the results should look like. However, within this context, consultants must work with their clients to establish rapport, develop credibility, validate the issues and needs, contract for the work, and begin developing working relationships within the organization.

All consulting engagements, whether internal or external, problem-focused or potential-focused, require a sound beginning regardless of philosophical orientation, style, or approach. Any consultant has to contract for the work, build relationships with clients, and understand both formal and informal aspects of the organization.

While internal consultants may have more knowledge of the client and the organization, they can also be enmeshed in the culture and see the world as the clients do. They should not make early assumptions about what needs to be done or what has to be clarified. External consultants generally have to do more to become familiar with the organization and contract financial arrangements. However, both must establish a sound platform during front-end work.

## THE DILEMMA OF FRONT-END WORK

The front-end phase rarely falls neatly or sequentially between the marketing and closing activities and the assessment and diagnosis work. In fact, some elements discussed in this chapter can occur while obtaining the work and continue throughout the engagement. Likewise, preliminary assessment is necessary when entering an organization in order to understand it, validate issues, confirm visions, and hypothesize initial plans. For the purpose of this chapter, *front-end work begins when a consultant clearly has a client with a desire to do work, and when the activities associated with marketing, selling, and closing have been completed. It concludes when the consultant and client have clarified the nature of the change effort, their working relationships, their expectations, and their contract, and when they are ready to proceed with more extensive diagnosis or other initial activities.*

The phrase "front-end work" is intended to capture a series of outcomes that comprise an ongoing effort, like any relationship development, in which there is a concentrated focus in the beginning. Some of the outcomes actually begin during marketing, and some will need further attention as the engagement unfolds. While marketing, consultants are learning something about the organization and its present issues and opportunities, must establish their competence and credibility and create the first stages of relationship(s) with one or more people. Additionally, as they move into designing, launching, and ongoing implementation, the consultant will learn still more about the organization and continue to refine the assessment and design needed action.

As new clients develop within the organization, a consultant will once again need to establish competence/credibility, build relationships, enter new groups, and contract for work and working relations. When new issues arise during interventions or the scope of the work changes, continuing discussions will be required to clarify new expectations or to re-contract the work. So even though elements of front-end work have to be done well up-front to establish the right foundation, the cyclical nature of OD requires entry and contracting throughout the engagement.

In the early years of OD, the concept of planned change was useful in that one was intervening in a systematic, planned approach to effect some desired change, and the environment was relatively placid. Today, most change is too complex to be planned, and the environment is anything but placid! The inherent complexities, uncontrollable variables, unanticipated events, and speed of environmental change will undoubtedly affect modifications in outcomes and any change plans (Jamieson, 2003).

"Planned change" may never have been completely relevant in complex systems, yet it was the essence of OD for many years. This led to the use of phased models, implying separate and distinct stages. It also led to the importance of Lewin's change model of "unfreezing, changing, and refreezing." Some front-end activities ordinarily create some "unfreezing," but most organizations today are already in rapid, continuous change, chaos, and uncertainty—and quite "unfrozen." However, the usefulness of Lewin's concept remains viable when applied to operating beliefs, attitudes, and mindset.

As Burke (2005) has emphasized, much of the work of implementing change is about managing reactions of people and organizations; balancing multiple interventions simultaneously; managing interaction of complex variables, unintended consequences, and adaptation—or creating the positive future needed to survive in the ambiguous, turbulent environment envisioned (Watkins & Mohr, 2001). So a consultant can't actually plan change or work in sequential phases, yet still must accomplish certain outcomes involving entry and contracting, both at the beginning and throughout the engagement.

# THE ESSENCE OF THE FRONT END

The essence of the front-end phase is to enter the organization, build a platform for engaging in change work with the client, and to contract for work, methods, relationships, and exchanges. The consultation really begins here. Everything the consultant does to obtain these early outcomes is an intervention, affecting some change in the client system (Bruce & Wyman, 1998). Schein (2005) has emphasized that first contacts, early questions, discussions, and meetings are the beginning of intervention and provide diagnostic information and system change even while front-end outcomes are being pursued.

At the front end, we need some understanding of the organization, its visions, values, and needs; identification of initial clients and sponsors; a preliminary assessment of helpful or hindering forces; agreement on work tasks and methods; and the start of relationships characterized by mutual openness, trust, and influence. Achieving these outcomes is critical to the success of the change effort. To conduct an effective project and use everyone's resources effectively, the consultant must ensure that he or she has created a client-focused project and is working on the "right" path within the appropriate boundaries with the right relationship, using the correct methods, working within the specified time, and eliciting the proper support. Since resources such as time and money are valuable, it is the responsibility of both the consultant and the client to avoid misusing them by conducting sound front-end work.

# THE ELEMENTS OF FRONT-END WORK

In building the foundation for working together on change, certain issues have to be addressed and certain agreements have to be made. Much of this material comes from classic works that have stood the test of time. Few have written new material on the essence of front-end work. The issues and agreements can be organized into the following seven outcomes that have to be realized at the outset as well as at other key junctures during the engagement:

1. Identifying the client(s) and sponsor(s);
2. Becoming oriented to the client's world;
3. Establishing the consultant's competence and credibility;
4. Developing an open, trusting, and aligned relationship;
5. Completing a preliminary diagnostic scan;
6. Contracting for the work, working relations, and exchange; and
7. Introducing the engagement and consultant(s) to the larger organization.

## Identifying the Client(s) and Sponsor(s)

The consultant should clarify as early as possible who the client(s) will be. It is not always possible to know immediately who the relevant players in the client organization will be or who will have to be involved, but those who are known and those who are possible key players should be the consultant's early focus of attention (French & Bell, 1999). Of course, the consultant may find that there is an individual client, a group client, or even multiple clients. The consultant may also find that whoever is the client at the outset of the OD intervention is replaced by subsequent clients as the intervention progresses (Cummings & Worley, 2001).

Burke (1994) offers another perspective on identifying clients. He suggests that the relationship and/or interface between individuals or units comprise the client. Thus, identifying the interactions and interrelationships that are contained in the issues or are the central focus of a desired future would identify the relevant players. This concept is supported from the classic work on consulting as intervention by Argyris (1970): "To intervene is to enter into the ongoing system of relationships, to come between or among persons, groups, or objects for the purpose of helping them" (p. 15).

The importance of client identification is further illustrated by Schein (1997), who defined the following six basic types of clients in complex systems:

1. *Contact clients*: The individual(s) who first contact the consultant with a request, question, or issue.

2. *Intermediate clients*: The individuals or groups that get involved in various interviews, meetings, and other activities as the project evolves.

3. *Primary clients*: The individual(s) who ultimately "own(s)" the issue being worked on or the desired future being developed; they are typically also the ones who pay the consulting bills or whose budget covers the consultation.

4. *Unwitting clients*: Members of the organization or client system above, below, and laterally related to the primary clients who will be affected by interventions but who are not aware that they will be impacted.

5. *Indirect clients*: Members of the organization who are aware that they will be affected by the interventions but who are unknown to the consultant and who may feel either positive or negative about these effects.

6. *Ultimate clients*: The community, the total organization, an occupational group, or any other group that the consultant cares about and whose welfare must be considered in any intervention that the consultant makes. (pp. 202–203)

For many in OD, the health and vitality of the whole organization, its various subsystems, and its members are the primary concern, thus defining the "client" in the broadest sense.

It is also possible to distinguish sponsors (those who initiate and often pay for the work, but have minor participation) from clients (those with direct or indirect participation and impact). However, it is best when anyone who is initiating or paying is also participating, and consultants often need to ensure those involvements.

Although no two interventions start or progress in the same way, the first step is usually a meeting or phone conversation with one person from the organization. The second step often is a meeting with a small group of key sponsors, a management team, or an employee committee. These group members may or may not continue as clients, but they could remain as engagement sponsors. Depending on how the set of interventions is designed, a new group, such as a design team, may become the client. The consultant may also be asked to work jointly as a co-consultant with others from inside or outside the organization or department.

Some consultants contracted with a company that was one of three owned by a parent company. The consultants believed that their clients were the president and the senior staff. Not long after the intervention began, the president of the parent company began to make telephone calls to the consultants for information about the client organization and to ask how well the president and senior staff members were working with the consultants. It was no longer clear to the consultants who the client was, so they called a meeting with the two presidents. The consultants were able to clarify in the meeting that the primary client was the company in which direct intervention was occurring but that the parent company was, indeed, a secondary client or sponsor. An arrangement was made for the consultants to meet monthly with both presidents to update them on the intervention.

Clients and sponsors can have different perspectives, work styles, and levels of influence. Sometimes the consultant may need to work with people who cannot make necessary intervention-related decisions, requiring the involvement of other decision-makers. The consultant's direct clients may not be in agreement with a key sponsor. If all the players are known, all viewpoints should be included. If (unknowingly) the consultant is not in contact with all the key players, the consultant may embark on inappropriate courses of action or be derailed by powerful groups or persons who were excluded. Thus, one important goal at the front end is to identify and create alignment in the contracting among all the clients and sponsors.

## Becoming Oriented to the Client's World

People in organizations operate from their own perceptions of reality. Many things influence their perceptions, such as past experiences; history and culture; work technology, methods, and processes; and beliefs and assumptions about their organization, the industry, and competitors. The consultant must understand and appreciate how the clients perceive their world.

Becoming oriented to the client's world involves asking questions about it, observing it, and reading about it. Some key questions that the consultant might explore include:

- What is happening in the client's environment (for example, issues involving regulation, competition, increased or decreased customer demand, changing customer profiles, globalization, and the economy)?
- What statements are made in the client organization's annual report, state-of-the-organization messages, recent studies, or website?
- How is the industry structured?
- Who are the competitors?
- What are the organization's strategy, core competencies, and competitive advantage?
- What does the organization do particularly well?
- What crises and/or achievements has the client experienced?

In addition to the client's external context and history, consultants should also familiarize themselves with the characteristics of the client system, including the organization's work, structure, technology, culture, and people. This is a significant part of what Margulies and Raia (1978) called "mapping." Because organizations are systems, their parts and interconnections must be understood, and change must be viewed in its largest context. The following questions can help ascertain that context:

- Who is asking for this work and who else supports it?
- What other departments, functions, or people will the change influence?
- What can help or hinder the change?
- What alignments are needed to make change work?
- What does the organization produce or do?
- How does the organization make its products or provide its services?
- How is technology used?
- How is the organization structured?
- What challenges/issues does the organization typically have to deal with?
- What are the organization's greatest strengths?
- What values and behavioral norms operate in the workplace?
- Who are the key players in the formal or informal social network?
- What was the client's previous experience with other consultants and change efforts?

The change effort has to be integrated and coordinated with the efforts of different units. It must be positioned and linked to what is already or will be occurring.

> *The owner of a successful, growing service business contracted with a consultant to look at her company's future prospects, facilitate strategic planning, and develop the senior management team. After the consultant had collected data, designed a process that worked well in terms of planning and team building, and conducted the intervention, the participants, including the owner, expressed satisfaction with the work, plans, and future commitments. A few months later, the owner sold the company to a competitor. The consultant and the other participants felt blindsided and betrayed since this option was never even discussed.*

Becoming oriented to the client's world provides the consultant with an understanding of the client's language, fears, desires, frustrations, and present state. This gives the consultant a basis for relating to the client(s), and introducing alternative thinking, different frameworks, and new ideas. It demonstrates that the consultant cares, and it helps him or her to connect with people through their reality. This connection with the client's reality can be very powerful since, as Shepard (1985) has said, consultants should "start where the system is."

> *While working with a utility company, an OD consultant found it helpful to have someone explain the current drive to develop alternative energy sources and the trend toward deregulation. She was able to use this information to support needed change in the culture toward innovation, risk-taking, and entrepreneurial behavior.*

In the front end, the consultant will not have detailed information about the client organization. Subsequent assessment activities, discussed in Chapter Ten, will fill in gaps and deepen information about the organization and its dynamics, needs, and issues.

## Establishing the Consultant's Competence and Credibility

The competence and credibility of the consultant rest in the eye of the beholder: the client(s). The client has to perceive the consultant as competent and credible, *for the organization and change situation,* for the consultant to be influential. Consultants depend on influence since they have no formal power or authority. Influence derives from the social power (French & Raven, 1959) they receive from clients that is based, in part, on their developing competence and credibility in the clients' eyes. Clients may have different criteria in mind when they assess a consultant's competence. For example, experience in organizations like theirs, knowledge of a specific methodology, or previous experience.

The client is also vulnerable during a change effort and is rightfully concerned about receiving the appropriate help. Lundberg (1997) even suggests that "help" in the context of consultation can be defined as client anxiety reduction, which often starts with a positive perception of the consultant's competence and credibility. On the other hand, the client's anxiety is increased when the consultant's credibility is questionable—either in performing the necessary work or in working effectively with the client. While it is important for the consultant to know the client's world, the client will find it equally important to learn about the consultant's background, experience, and values. The client should also know how consultants acquired their expertise, what they have done that is related to the change effort, what they know that is relevant to the intervention, and how they feel about the possibilities for success.

> *In an entry situation, a client was particularly impressed and put at ease when she learned of the consultant's previous work in the same industry. They proceeded to discuss some common industry issues and quickly were into discussing the client's specific issues.*
>
> *In another situation, the consultant was asked to identify some of the clients he had worked with before. He consciously chose to describe a variety of types of organizations in different industries. The client then commented about wanting someone with varied industry experience who could bring a different perspective and new ideas because management was "too insular."*

The consultant's knowledge, skills, experience, values, and work style must fit the OD intervention and the client's needs. The consultant must be appropriate for the work and client situation (Lippitt & Lippitt, 1986). The consultant is just as responsible as the client in determining an appropriate match (Greiner & Metzger, 1983). Few clients are sophisticated enough to understand differences in expertise and specialties. It is an ineffective and unethical use of resources for a consultant to work on an OD intervention for which he or she lacks the necessary competence.

Consulting competence may come from various areas. It may result from expertise in a particular content area required for the intervention, such as total quality management or work-process redesign. Competence also may result from the consultant's expertise in process design and facilitation, such as the ability to involve people, run large groups, generate new ideas, or reach consensus.

It also may be based on the outcomes of the consultants' previous work, their understanding of the client's situation, or their writings or teachings.

Authenticity, honesty, and confidence contribute to a consultant's credibility. Consultants may not have worked with many clients before, but they may have compelling ideas about how to approach the client's situation. They may even have conducted a similar intervention before that did not work well, but from which they learned valuable lessons that could affect the success of the current change effort. The consultants' credibility can also be enhanced when they describe their strengths and limitations with the clients, voice their concerns, and express confidence about the engagement.

> In one situation, the consultant was honest about not having performed a particular type of work before. The consultant shared the approach she planned to use and asked for the client's approval and commitment to the change effort. The consultant's honesty engendered client trust and permitted important collaboration between them.

Credibility is associated with more than just having the right knowledge and competencies. It also stems from the client's trust in the consultant, and the consultant's ability to relate to the client and to complete activities leading to a successful change effort. Credibility grows from the consultant's ability to organize action, such as what steps to take and how to sequence them. It reflects how clients feel about the potential for success and takes into account their ability to work well with the consultant. Ultimately, the success of an OD intervention will depend both on what is done and on the effectiveness of the client-consultant relationship.

> In one client situation, a consultant found it necessary to assume a leadership role in the first meeting. She pulled out a piece of paper and drew a simple model so she could discuss with her clients the relationship among the concerns that the client organization was experiencing. These clients were confused and wanted to feel that they were receiving expert help, and the consultant was able to provide this by guiding the clients to a better understanding of the problem(s).

Clients' continuous and obsessive questioning of background, past experience, credentials, or approaches is often a sign of resistance, dressed as concern for competence. It could stem from feelings of vulnerability or lack of commitment to the intended project. Usually, it needs to be challenged early or inquired about in order to surface and name what it really is so that it can be dealt with appropriately.

## Developing an Open, Trusting, and Aligned Relationship

Developing an effective working relationship is essential for a consultant to gain client trust, build support from power brokers, and ensure appropriate consultant influence. It is also important because it is through the relationships that much of the consultation actually occurs (Jamieson, 1998). There needs to be *engagement* in the client-consultant relationship in order for the consultant to add value and to create change (Jamieson & Armstrong, 2008). The client-consultant relationship is also key to the work in that it provides an understanding of the culture and provides continual data on the progress of the work (Schein, 2005). Old (1995) describes the nature of the needed relationship as "partnering." The client-consultant relationship must be built on a foundation of mutual confidence, openness, and trust (French & Bell, 1999). Confidence comes from each party's perception of competence and credibility, as discussed earlier. Openness is important to the relationship because the client and the consultant have to share all information affecting the change effort. This includes important information about the organization and the personal concerns, fears, and opinions of key clients, sponsors, and the consultant. Trust is essential for both parties to feel their resources are being used effectively and the client's best interests are paramount. Consultants often need to take the lead in being role models for the relationship.

In creating openness and trust, the consultant will find it helpful to discuss the following with the client:

- Expected timelines;
- Real barriers or challenges;
- Personal hopes;
- Helpful and hindering behaviors;
- Possible roadblocks;
- Alternative ways for the client to think about what is possible;
- Possible risks in the change effort; and
- Personal commitments and values as they relate to the change.

One consultant found it useful to alert a top manager about issues that could surface about his role and its contribution to the situation. This lead-in enabled the leader to share his concerns about his contribution and to express a willingness to change.

In another initial meeting, the consultant challenged the client's description of the presenting problem and implied solutions. She helped the client to think differently about the possible interrelationships among causes of the present state and opened up his possible paths to change. She was hired on the spot. He appreciated her openness, courage, and thinking.

Openness and trust also emanate from a foundation of alignment (seeing things the same way), honesty (saying what is real), and authenticity (reflecting who you really are). To establish such a foundation, the client and the consultant must maintain a continuing dialogue about what is meaningful, significant, compelling, or frightening. Openness and trust grow from sharing experiences authentically. The client and the consultant should talk about specific issues as they arise. They must also talk about what forces support the success of the OD intervention, what forces will hinder the intervention, what motivations underlie the change effort, and what they find exciting about the desired future.

Values are also an important part of achieving alignment. The consultant has to know which of the client's values are relevant to the change effort—about people, work, success, diversity, and so on, and about what the client is changing for or changing to—and how compatible these values are with those of the consultant (Jamieson & Gellermann, 2005).

Those entering a change effort rarely do so from a value-free perspective; rather, everyone operates with desired methods and results in mind. OD consultants often bring to a change effort their perspectives, which are loaded with such value-based principles as a high regard for employee involvement, employee empowerment, and respect for human dignity. Although the consultant's values should not singularly drive the OD intervention, the client and the consultant may not work together effectively if their values are incompatible. Without some alignment, unhealthy conflict is likely to result over the intervention's goals and means.

---

*One client was interested in improving the effectiveness of his department. However, when the consultant suggested group meetings with employees at different levels to get their input, the client was adamant that the consultant only needed to talk to the managers. There were clearly incompatible values related to participation, manager roles, and systems thinking.*

---

Clients often experience mixed feelings (including desire, fear, inadequacy, and vulnerability) about a change effort. Consciously or unconsciously, these feelings can lead the client to resist closure on contracting. Consultants can either be helpful in dealing with these feelings or aggravate them. In addition, if clients find it difficult to understand or work with consultants, additional barriers are created. Feelings of satisfaction and comfort during OD interventions are affected by how clients want to be included and informed, how they want to receive inputs from consultants, and what consultants want from their clients. Many of the feelings experienced by clients and consultants are associated with their feelings of vulnerability, interpersonal needs, availability to one another, their priorities, and their levels of commitment to the change effort.

It is possible to experience a mix of support and resistance from clients as different aspects of their feelings about the work are triggered. For example, they can be elated by a discussion of intended end-states and uncomfortable after a discussion of a methodology based on values that differ from their preferences or normal approaches. If the consultant doesn't attend to appropriate contracting, readiness checking, and commitment testing throughout the early interactions, many forms of passivity, slowness, discomfort, or sparring that show up can actually be resistance to the work or relationship.

Margulies and Raia (1978) earlier stressed the importance of the consultant-client "fit" and described the quality of the relationship as dependent on their value systems, the consultant's competence and ability to "help" the client with the perceived challenge, the client's experience with other consultants, expectations about the consulting role and process, their personalities and interpersonal styles, and the compatibility of their needs and objectives. Massarik and Pei-Carpenter (2002) describe the client-consultant relationship as interconnecting "selves" with the amount of overlay defining the congruence of styles, needs, objectives, and values.

> *In one consulting relationship, the client was very controlling and directive and acted as if the consultant was one of his employees (whom he also treated inappropriately). Normally, a consultant would straighten this situation out, re-contract, or quit. However, this consultant was putting up with it. On deeper discussion with a consulting colleague, it was determined that this consultant still had some authority issues hindering his challenging the client and that financially he needed the work. In this case, their needs and styles played into each other, blocking the potential for growth or improvement.*

In developing open, trusting, and aligned consultant-client relationships, the consultant's ultimate value is in maintaining a boundary position (Cummings & Worley, 2001) with marginality and objectivity (Margulies & Raia, 1978). Becoming intimately involved with the culture of an organization or group, yet remaining apart from it, provides the kind of detachment and objectivity required for effective consulting. It involves balancing the ability to understand and empathize with the client system while avoiding becoming so acculturated that the consultant mirrors the same biases and subjectivity as the client. The consultant's ability not to be absorbed by the culture (French & Bell, 1999) and to remain free from the organizational forces that might distort his or her view of the organization and its issues should not be compromised in the process of developing a quality client-consultant relationship.

*Friendship is often an issue in developing quality client-consultant relationships. Some consultants have grown so close, personally and socially, with a particular client that they have lost neutrality, objectivity, and marginality in the eyes of other clients in the system. On the other hand, some consultants have managed to remain effective with the client system while maintaining a friendship with the primary client, by openly discussing the situation, keeping boundaries very visible, and behaving in accord with all contracts.*

The client and the consultant do not have to agree on everything at the outset of the change effort, but they do have to be candid, confront their differences, and clarify how they will proceed.

## Completing a Preliminary Diagnostic Scan

In a preliminary diagnostic scan, the consultant and the client are "scouting" (Kolb & Frohman, 1970), which involves developing a general understanding of:

- The current state (presenting issues and needs, the culture, the basis they have for developing their vision);
- The potential sources of resistance and support;
- The apparent power and political system; and
- A perception of the organization's readiness, commitment, and capability.

**The Current State.** Initially, the consultant attempts to learn enough about the clients and their change desires to contract effectively for the initial work. It is important to approach this aspect of consulting with a spirit of inquiry and neutrality, accessing one's ignorance (Schein, 1997) and avoiding any inappropriate assumptions or premature conclusions about the situation. It is best to treat hunches as hypotheses at this point. Consultants should seek information from more than their initial contact. They may find it helpful to hear from or about people who have various stakes in past problems or new desired futures.

When a project is deficit-focused, the consultant might, for instance, seek information to answer such questions as:

- What is the issue or the different interpretations of the issue?
- What is the apparent cause(s) of the challenge?
- Why does the present state exist?
- What are the likely consequences if the issue(s) is not resolved?
- What would success look like?
- How do people feel about the current situation?

However, when projects take a positive, developmental stance to help the organization move toward an exciting new future vision, then it's important to consider other questions, such as:

- What has made us great so far?
- What do we have that will help us reach our vision?
- What is going well in the organization?
- How can these strengths be leveraged?
- What are the likely possibilities if our strengths can be further developed?

Whenever possible, the consultant should obtain this information directly from those closest to the situation. At a minimum, consultants should be able to question credible sources for their perceptions about how the people involved in the problems or future vision would answer these questions.

> *After an initial meeting with the head of a division, a consultant asked to talk informally, at no charge, with a handful of key players, after which he would meet again with the head person to discuss the project and his "fit" with the proposed work and client, and then explore contracting. Another approach is to do phased work—to do the same, but charge for the initial work.*

In a preliminary scan, consultants should not strive to obtain great detail; rather, they should seek to understand the issues and possibilities and the relationships among them, generally. In part, consultants are trying to achieve clarity and elevate their confidence about what to work on and how, while serving as an organization mirror (Bruce & Wyman, 1998), sharpening clients' understanding. Consultants are also trying to establish the validity of the current state (Cummings & Worley, 2001) and determine the commonality of perceptions or distinctions among different viewpoints.

Sometimes consultants are trying to scope the situation in order to design a diagnostic approach or scope the possibilities and strength of resources to plan an appreciative process. They want enough knowledge of the organization's issue(s), resources, and desires to enable the two parties to make informed choices about proceeding with the engagement (Cummings & Worley, 2001). In this process they should talk to a few key people or meet with key stakeholder groups. Consultants may have to facilitate discussions so as to surface real strengths and issues and challenge beliefs. Consultants may also review studies, memos, or other documents that relate to the issues, needs, and viewpoints. Consultants may find it helpful to observe some regular meetings or to tour work areas to see the operations, interactions, and culture at work. Investing a little energy in the preliminary scan will help consultants to contract for, and place the OD intervention on, the right path.

> *Touring the work facility of a small design and manufacturing company where creative artists, engineers, and construction people needed to collaborate helped to explain their status issues (very different offices and work space) and some of their conflict (physical distances affecting psychological distances).*

**Support, Resistance, Power, and Politics.** Consultants should also note who appears to support or resist the change effort and why they feel the way they do. Identifying supporters and resisters helps to crystallize motives and personal agendas. Supporters and resisters may also dramatize the real hurdles to be encountered or identify key considerations in designing the content and process of the change effort.

> *While scouting in a large department with numerous specialists, a consultant discovered some very different perspectives on the presenting problem and some very logical feelings of resistance. In a subsequent meeting with the initial client, the consultant was able to provide a more accurate description of the "starting point," which expanded the client's view of the situation and led to contracting for a different initial phase of work to deal with the differences and build consensus for any change.*

Resistance can be an indicator of missing information, lack of understanding, poor prior involvement, disagreement with some aspect of what's planned, a power assertion, or a violation of existing political norms. In any case, it is valuable data and should be addressed in order to redirect the work, create new alignments, provide for better inclusion, improve communication, and/or build further support.

It is also important to identify potential leverage points for change (Burke, 1994) by understanding the organization's power system (the people who have influence or authority over key systems and processes, rewards and incentives, and people) and its political dynamics (Greiner & Schein, 1988). They must find out who has significant influence, how decisions are made in the organization, and who has expertise pertinent to the change effort. Consultants must also learn about the motives, perspectives, and values of those in power in the organization to understand the political dynamics inherent in its culture (for example, coalitions, dependencies, tradeoffs, deals, and incentives).

Powerful people attain their status through formal and informal means (for example, position, information, expertise, intimidation, access, or amicability).

Consultants must learn about the power/political dimensions of the organization and gain access to key people in appropriate ways during early stages of work. Greiner and Metzger (1983) refer to this aspect of consulting as "meeting the power structure." A consultant's knowledge of the power structure can be used to help leverage change (Cobb, 1986; Cobb & Margulies, 1981; Greiner & Schein, 1988).

> *In one consulting situation, an OD intervention was terminated when a pending invoice was rejected because a new chief financial officer (CFO) had not been involved in the early stages of the intervention. The client and the consultant had proceeded without paying attention to a key change in the power system and, in this case, the emergence of a new perspective on the value of the work being performed.*
>
> *In another intervention, the human resource client got into trouble with the head of data processing by launching an OD intervention on people issues for implementing technological change without first obtaining the support and approval of the high-powered head of data processing. Even the organization's president, who initially supported the OD intervention, overlooked the importance of involving this power player. The head of data processing discredited early work in the intervention, and it was terminated after the initial phase. In this case, the consultant should have tested the political system rather than relying on the client's belief that everyone necessary supported the OD intervention.*

**Readiness, Commitment, and Capability.** Consultants should assess the organization's readiness (motivation to change), level of commitment (attitude and energy toward change), and the capability of its members (their knowledge and skills needed for the change effort). It is also important to know the extent of resources (money, people, technology) available to support the change effort (Burke, 1994). Knowing the commitment of key stakeholders is important because it helps consultants determine whether the organization is ready for change or if other steps will be required to create the necessary impetus. Commitment can be viewed as levels of energy applied toward or against change. People can be against the change direction, somewhat neutral about letting it happen, passively for it, or wanting to make it happen (Beckhard & Harris, 1987). Assessing the commitment to change by those involved in the issues helps the consultant ascertain how much readiness building is needed and the strength of the change champions.

> *After beginning down a path toward a change program, a consultant and client were informally collecting data about readiness and commitment. To their surprise, they discovered a lot of neutrality and passive support. Clearly, such*

*attitudes would not support a large and significant change process. Everything was put on hold until the chief executive client could have some individual and team meetings to gain alignment or change in thinking about what was needed for the future.*

The capability of organizational members is measured by their knowledge and experience with change and change processes and their level of required skills, such as their ability to participate, work productively in groups, function in an open way, think creatively, and demonstrate flexibility. Change could be utterly new to some organizations, participation could be counter-cultural, and the people may be highly rigid. However, other organizations may be accustomed to change, their members may have undergone extensive training in interpersonal communication and small-group management, and these organizations may have employees who seek variety and innovation. A consultant who is familiar with an organization's change competence can more easily determine how much education or skill building should be included in the intervention strategy and how to use the organization's human resources during the change.

A preliminary diagnostic scan will often move the client from a simple presenting issue to a more complex understanding and different change targets or methods. Present-state descriptions may be full of attributions and can be seen more accurately only by surfacing the real causes of why a system is not working, why products are of poor quality, why services are fraught with delays, or why the organization is stymied from reaching its potential. The consultant may also find that some form of education or readiness building is essential prior to launching because of the level of capability or the real potential for sabotage.

When determining whether a good match exists to work with a specific client, consultants may also wish to consider these questions:

- Can I work with this client?
- Do I have the right competencies?
- Will this client keep agreements?
- Can this client be honest with him- or herself, others, and me?
- Is this client open to bad news, new ideas, and change?
- Are the client's motives, commitments, resources, and values appropriate?
- Are the client's expectations realistic?
- Do I believe we can be successful?

The results of skipping or short-cutting the preliminary diagnostic scan can be disastrous. Without a good understanding of the "reality," the subsequent work can be off-target, designed too narrowly, or end up as "a hammer looking for nails." If a consultant hurries to begin the intervention, resistance may be elevated, necessitating unnecessary remedial work. The consultant must, therefore, help the client pinpoint real needs and intentions. Only then is it possible to contract appropriately and design diagnostic and action strategies effectively.

## Contracting for the Work, Working Relations, and Exchange

The information learned so far provides a foundation for the contracting process and data for identifying the content of the work and psychological contracts (Boss, 1985). The word "contract" is often thought of only in formal and legal terms, but in OD it can be formal, informal, oral, or in a letter of agreement. Contracting means establishing and clarifying expectations about the change effort, the working relationship(s), consulting support needs, and financial or other arrangements. The process of contracting must be a primary focus during the front end, but will be continuous in some respects and reopened as conditions change.

Block (2000) refers to contracting as an explicit agreement about what the consultant and the client should expect and how they should work together. That agreement results from discussions in which the wants, offers, and concerns of the client and the consultant are clarified. Differences are negotiated and agreement is reached. Weisbord (1973) defines contracting as an explicit exchange of expectations, clarifying for the consultant and client what each expects to obtain from the relationship, how much time each will invest, when, and at what cost, and the ground rules under which the parties will operate.

Contracting is intended to allow good decisions to be made about how to carry out the change process (Beer, 1980) and sets the tone for the entire OD intervention (Block, 2000). It establishes the clarity needed to have an effective working relationship and avoid subsequent surprises or problems that derail projects. With whom consultants should contract will depend on who is identified as the different types of client(s), sponsor(s), and other key player(s) in the power system. Consultants may sometimes need to perform primary contracting for all aspects of a change effort and working relationships with some client(s), but auxiliary contracting for parts of the change effort or limited relationship needs with other client(s).

**Contracting for the Work.** The consultant should start the OD intervention by agreeing with the client about the initial understanding of the situation, desired results or intended outcomes, measures of success, the value proposition for the work, and the options, methods, timing, and accountabilities anticipated. As part of these discussions, the consultant and the client should be sure to establish critical success factors (what it will take to be successful) or organizational effectiveness criteria that can later be used in evaluating success (Smither, Houston, & McIntire, 1996).

Critical success factors and effectiveness criteria can include objective, measurable outcomes, such as reduced turnover, higher margins, or quality improvements, and more subjective attitude or behavior outcomes, such as more participation among a group's members, improved morale, or shared perceptions of what is valued and rewarded. Caution may be needed, however. There is no guarantee of improvement in human systems work; often, there is no way to show that the changes emerged from the intervention, and there is no control over external factors that can negatively impact the change, such as an unfriendly takeover or downturn in the economy. Additionally, no matter how well the consultant does, there can be no change or improvement without the full support and committed participation of the client organization. Boss (1985), Lippitt and Lippitt (1986), and Schein (1988) have all stressed the importance of emphasizing the joint responsibility of clients and consultants during contracting.

Developing consensus on the strategy and methods of the change effort will produce more detailed information on the project boundaries, work tasks, and data requirements; with whom to work directly; whom to include in various ways; where the OD work will take place; in what sequence activities should happen; when the work should be performed and at what pace; how technology will be used in data collection or ongoing communication; deliverables to be produced; and approximately how long the change effort will take.

The consultant should be sure that flexibility is incorporated in the contractual language because, at the time of contracting, there are still many unknowns and it is impossible to know how many and what type of interventions will be used. Even though there may not be a separate assessment/diagnosis phase, it is still important to contract for how data will be generated and used. For interventions to be effective, they still require valid and useful data, free and informed choice, and internal commitment (Argyris, 1970).

The result of this part of contracting is often a plan that may be more specific and detailed for the immediate next steps, such as diagnosis or preliminary education, and more general for the subsequent cycles of design, intervention, and implementation. It is often helpful to include key decision points in the change plan for client-consultant review or modification. Sometimes contracting for the work is actually broken into phases, such as education, diagnosis, design, and implementation work, or preparation, design, and execution for a large-scale event.

*In one organization, the initial work contract was structured to include a design group drawn from a wide cross-section of the organization that would identify all the relevant stakeholders, select people for invitation, and prepare all the communications and pre-work materials to be sent to the invitees for a fairly comprehensive, multi-day, diagnostic and planning meeting. The executive team would be included along the way and at the meetings. The design group would also compile the work from the large stakeholder meeting and determine communication and feedback mechanisms to share with and involve the rest of the organization.*

**Contracting for Working Relations.** The most in-depth relationship contracting occurs with the consultant's direct client(s). In contracting with the direct client(s), consultants must address the full range of relationship issues and develop a working relationship. In addition, consultants will find it essential to clarify what roles they and clients will have, what they should expect from each other, how they should plan and work together, and how they should reach critical decisions.

In developing working relations, the consultant and client are contracting primarily for the psychosocial aspects of the relationship and creating an interpersonal relationship for changing the client's organization (Bruce & Wyman, 1998). This includes—but is not limited to—roles and expectations, commitments, needs for involvement, information needs, access, control, work styles, and the ground rules or principles that will be used as the consultant and the client work together. Unless there is mutual understanding and agreement about the process, there is significant risk that one or both of the parties' expectations will not be met (Bellman, 1990).

It is reasonable to expect that roles and needs will change during the life of the project through client growth, transfer of skills, and growing mutual confidence and trust. This type of contracting requires recycling, the consultant and the client asking for what they want or need (Block, 2000; Boss, 1985), and each having self-awareness and clarity of his or her motives and values (Burke, 2002; Smither, Houston, & McIntire, 1996). "Self as an instrument of change" (Jamieson, 1991, 2003) is of critical importance in contracting and was introduced in Chapter Six and will be discussed later in Chapter Thirty.

> In one situation, a client and consultant developed a contract that included a weekly meeting for updating and decision making; a monthly meeting with the top team to present progress; no written reports; client-consultant access at any time for emergencies, otherwise during work hours; both would be visible in project events, but the client would handle other internal communications (related divisions, the board, and so forth); neither required a lot of detail in their discussions; a quarterly review of what had changed in the project, how they were working together, and any changes to their contract; the client asked for "brutal honesty" and challenges; the consultant wanted administrative support for the project and monthly billing with thirty-day payments.

Consultants have numerous orientation, role, and style choices based on who they are and what the client system requires (Jamieson, 1998). These are also part of establishing expectations and fitting with the client. For example, they might position themselves in the foreground, more central in the change work and visible in the client system, or more in the background, working through the client(s); more oriented to educating the client(s) and building their capability or more protective of their skills and expertise; or more task or process oriented (Margulies & Raia, 1972). Consultants can be more or less directive, supportive, confrontive, or facilitative (Jamieson, 1998; Lippitt & Lippitt, 1986). They can serve as experts, pairs of hands, or collaborators (Block, 2000). As Harrison (1970) put it, the change agent is continuously confronted by the dilemma of whether to "lead and push, or to collaborate and follow." These choices create very different dynamics in the client-consultant relationship and can meet very different client system change needs and client and consultant personal needs.

When consultants contract their roles and relations with the client, it is instructive to keep in mind what one study identified as the client's view of the ideal consultant: the person listens, but does not sell; fits into the organization and embraces its mission and culture; teaches the internal staff and helps them achieve independence; provides good customer service; protects confidentiality; challenges assumptions; is a recognized expert; provides perspective and objectivity; and celebrates with the internal staff (Bader & Stich, 1983).

It is equally important to clarify the client's role. For example, is the client a project manager, a co-consultant, or a decision-maker? The implications of these role choices are critical. The more consultants act as experts on substantive content issues, the less effective they will be on managing process (French & Bell, 1999) and the more they intrude on a needed client role. If the client acts in a co-consultant role, he or she loses some of the power and context of being the decision-maker.

Sponsors and key power players may want roles with different levels of involvement. Some may join in the change effort; others may be interested observers. Generally, contracting for these relationships involves determining how much sponsors and key power players wish to participate; what and how much information they want to receive; how much faith they have in the consultant's ability to pursue the objectives they seek; and how much information, support, and involvement the consultant wants from them. The consultant or primary client will have to keep the power players informed and obtain their input.

If consultants know that other people will be impacted or involved in the change effort later, they may find it helpful to brief them on what will be happening, determine how to keep them informed, estimate when and in what ways the change effort may impact them, and discuss, if appropriate, what they can do to prepare for participating in the change effort.

---

*In one OD intervention, the direct clients consisted of a group of senior managers. The sponsor was an executive vice president, and there were about six other key power players. The consultant defined the direct clients' roles as compiling and analyzing data, and he defined his role as educating the organization, providing input options, being on call for assistance, and facilitating review and integration meetings. They agreed on what type of information to share. Agreements were also reached about the value of timeliness and the ground rules for meetings. The sponsor agreed to attend the periodic review and integration meetings, wanted frank discussions with the consultant about the OD intervention's progress, and requested a written report at the end of the intervention. In a meeting, the other power players were informed of the project's purpose and their roles. Their initial inputs and advice were sought. They were also reassured about confidentiality and told that the sponsor would keep them informed and share project results with them.*

Once the OD consultant's and the client's roles have been discussed, their working process and expectations can be clarified. Will the intervention be jointly planned or planned chiefly by the consultant or the client? Will meetings be client-led or consultant-led? The consultant and the client also will need to clarify how often they will meet, what information will be communicated, how they will communicate (for example, phone call, email, presentation, or memo), and when the consultant and the client will be accessible.

*In one project, a client was expecting a written report from the consultant. The consultant, however, had prepared an oral presentation with a PowerPoint and a handout. Shortly thereafter, the client began to quarrel with the consultant over billed time because the client did not believe that the consultant was using his time appropriately. There was obviously lack of clarity and agreement about how the report should be presented and how time was to be used.*

People's work styles also must be considered, especially in joint and collaborative relationships. Some people require very detailed designs and discussions; others work well with general outlines. Some people require everything to be data-based; others work well from intuition, a concept, value, or vision.

Other style issues that have to be considered include how quickly each key person learns and works; whether each person works better alone or with others; and how tolerant each is about ambiguity, flexibility, and risk taking. Sometimes, work styles are compatible and relationship contracting is easy. When the consultant's and the client's work styles are not compatible, clarity and compromise may be necessary to minimize tension and frustration.

Principles or ground rules for working together often originate from work styles, involvement, and information-sharing discussions. Agreements such as

"It is okay to call me at home if we need to talk" or "We will tell each other everything and avoid surprises" provide both parties with an understanding of what is acceptable and effective. Other principles might relate to anticipating problems, listening, equality, timeliness, or how each party can grow and develop in the OD intervention. No matter what each includes in contracting, the consultant and the client will have to clarify and agree on how they will work together in a trusting, productive, and rewarding relationship.

> *In some contracts, the client and the consultant agree to have follow-up meetings after key steps in the OD intervention, to discuss and enhance learning about the conceptual base of the OD intervention, and to discuss specific situations or emerging problems. In other situations, clients and consultants have held monthly breakfasts, weekly meetings, and periodic three-way meetings with sponsors. Consultants and clients also have used written status reports or presentations at executive staff meetings.*

The consultant should also discuss the termination options (both unexpected and planned) with the client during contracting and include considerations such as:

- Who can end the OD intervention or consulting relationship? How?
- What circumstances will breach their contract or cause a termination?
- How will transfer of expertise and planned termination occur?
- What does each party owe the other party if a termination occurs?

**Consultant Support Needs.**   In some OD engagements, consultants need support services. These can be described as any help needed to see the OD intervention or change effort through to a successful conclusion. These services often include clerical help, presentation support, data analysis, office space, travel arrangements, or other administrative assistance and should also be contracted.

If questions about support are left unanswered at the outset of the OD intervention, they may result in misunderstandings or lead to a situation in which support tasks are not carried out and aspects of the engagement are handled poorly.

**Consultant-Client Exchange.** The last aspect of contracting involves what is being exchanged. Most engagements involve financial payments, but it is possible to barter for exchanges, such as the use of developed materials, an exchange of services, or consultation for equity. When financial arrangements are used, the client and the consultant must reach agreement on the following issues:

- What is the consultant's rate(s)?
- What consulting expenses are covered?
- What time is billable (for example, will travel time be billable and at what rate)?
- How is time calculated (for example, nearest quarter hour, hour, half-day)?
- How much time and money are estimated for the OD intervention?
- When should the consultant's invoices be sent?
- How should the invoices be prepared?
- What information should the invoices contain?
- Who should the invoices be sent to?
- What is the estimated timing for payments?
- Will late fees be charged?

There are often sensitivities and misunderstandings related to the money, so it is extremely important that the client and the consultant be clear about the billing and payment procedures, and often these should be documented in writing.

> *In one situation, a consultant arranged an exchange that included a lower fee and ownership of all materials developed. In another, the consultant and the client bartered for an exchange of services—the consulting help in exchange for the development of a computer system tailored for the consultant's firm. One project required invoicing that separated consulting from training work since they would be paid out of different budgets.*

Both parties should discuss any changes that will affect the financial arrangement, such as using up budgeted amounts faster than anticipated or unanticipated budget cuts by the organization. The consultant and the client should also discuss, periodically, the relationship between what is being accomplished in the change effort and the expenditures. When the cost-benefit relationship does not seem correlated, the client's concerns may grow: People do not want to spend substantial sums of money without witnessing visible progress toward their goals!

> *In one consulting situation, the consultant found it helpful to explain to the client why more billable consulting days would occur earlier in the intervention rather than later, and that the early bills would be larger than subsequent ones. Because the client was informed, the consultant's first invoices did not surprise her.*

Throughout contracting, there is a constant need to pay attention to ethical issues in order to establish the right boundaries, relationship, and work methods. Earlier, White and Wooten (1983) summarized the types of ethical dilemmas in OD: misrepresentation and collusion, misuse of data, manipulation and coercion, value and goal conflicts, and technical ineptness. Later, Page (1998) added client dependency and Egan and Gellermann (2005) include competing rights, obligations, and interests. It is common in OD to ensure that participation is voluntary, that participants are protected from harm, that information collected from individuals is kept confidential, that individual data are owned by individuals, and that the organization owns non-confidential and non-anonymous data (Smither, Houston, & McIntire, 1996). Consultants should not say they can do things that they cannot, require clients to depend on them too much, or collude with one part of an organization against another part.

With contracting, consultants need to remember that there are so many different systems and clients that contracting is always a process of customizing. Both parties must meet their individual and mutual needs in order to be satisfied. The contracting process should enhance the working relationship and requires sensitivity, skill, and flexibility.

## Introducing the Engagement and Consultant(s) to the Larger System

Introducing the OD engagement and the consultant(s) can be difficult. The consultant must know the organization's culture and systems in order to know how to present the intervention properly. If people are not informed about the intervention before the consultant arrives, they might resist it. Who introduces the intervention and how it is done affect its credibility. If the wrong person introduces the OD intervention or uses the wrong method of communication, the intervention will begin poorly.

> *In one communication that was not designed or monitored by the consultant, a client sent out a memo announcing the start of an OD project that referred to the consultant as an "efficiency expert" and the project as "improving the efficiency of their operations." There were obviously some different understandings in the contracting!*

An introduction can benefit from the use of more than one medium. It may include a notification to everyone, followed by small-group sessions. The rationale for the intervention should be clear: what is being started and why. The involvement of key members of the organization in the introduction helps others to see the work as important, cross-organizational, and not "owned" by one person, group, faction, or department. The consultant, client, and sponsors can all have roles in the beginning of the OD intervention. Part of the introduction should be in writing in order to have a clear statement without multiple interpretations (Greiner & Metzger, 1983). Technology can be used effectively. For example, the project introduction and rationale might be posted on the company intranet, and comments could be posted to a specially designated forum.

Consultants can also meet key people informally before the introduction to build comfort and rapport while minimizing feelings of concern. Providing personal as well as professional information about themselves at the outset of an intervention can also help portray them as human beings. These actions build the consultant's credibility and the larger client's confidence.

How various parts of the organization will be involved or affected by the intervention should determine how much time and effort should be devoted to its introduction. Some people should just be informed; others should be involved in two-way forums to be sure they understand the intervention and know what to expect. The consultant should know how the organization usually introduces information, but if its method is ineffective, the consultant may want to differentiate the change effort by creating a new introduction process.

> *At the onset of a fairly large engagement, the people who would be affected were invited to a large presentation in an auditorium. This was led by the president and the top team. It included an introduction to the consultant, who also described the process and what people could expect. This large-group introduction was followed by small-group meetings in each department to answer questions and clarify their participation, the intended outcomes, and the rationale for the change approach being used. These department meetings were facilitated by the consultant and the head of each department.*

# SUMMARY

Numerous difficulties arising in OD interventions can be traced to flaws in the front-end phase. Difficulties can stem from misunderstanding the organization, ignoring issues associated with the power structure, disagreeing about work methods, not reaching agreements on consulting rates or time commitments, or clashing work styles. These setbacks and issues can be avoided if addressed early on.

Consultants must work carefully in surfacing organizational issues or in starting down a new path with a client. At the same time, they should work to instill trust and match their personal styles to the expectations of multiple players. Starting OD projects takes on great significance because change is inherently risky and both parties face a considerable amount of risk, uncertainty, and ambiguity. Consultants can be lured by feelings of competence, unworthiness, or dependency to engage in agreements that are not appropriate or in their best interest. Change can engender feelings of vulnerability, guilt, or inadequacy in clients, intensifying emotions in ways that complicate helping relationships.

OD consultants are change agents who have to rely on their thoughts, feelings, strengths, and weaknesses throughout their work. Quade and Brown (2002) expound on this concept in discussing the importance of being "conscious consultants" who enlarge the awareness of who they are; their own styles and ways of thinking, working, and interacting; and who actively track and change implicit models and assumptions in their work. In each engagement, one is using "self" and growing "self."

The consultants' authenticity and skills are central to establishing effective working relationships that contribute to successful change. Consultants cannot be too needy or too greedy, too passive or too controlling. They have to remain marginal to the system yet remain close enough to the change effort and the people to obtain valid data and to instill trust and confidence.

The work that consultants do is affected by how quick they are to judge, criticize, or conclude. Communicating, listening, and probing effectively will increase their understanding and ease client fears. Confronting others appropriately and giving timely and effective feedback will increase their clients' clarity about issues and their authenticity in approaching problems and solutions. How well consultants adapt to their clients' cultures may determine the success of their interventions. Moreover, OD consultants' front-end work—entering and contracting—will be greatly improved by their ability to elicit hope, facilitate discussions, work collaboratively, empathize, and assert their points of view.

In the final analysis, consultants can see only what they have prepared themselves to see and do only what they have developed themselves to do.

# References

Argyris, C. (1970). *Intervention theory and method: A behavioral science view.* Reading, MA: Addison-Wesley.

Bader, G., & Stich, T. (1983). Building the consulting relationship. *Training & Development Journal, 43,* 55–60.

Beckhard, R., & Harris, R. (1987). *Organizational transitions* (2nd ed.). Reading, MA: Addison-Wesley.

Beer, M. (1980). *Organization change and development: A systems view.* Santa Monica, CA: Goodyear.

Bellman, G. (1990). *The consultant's calling.* San Francisco: Jossey-Bass.

Block, P. (2000). *Flawless consulting: A guide to getting your expertise used* (2nd ed.). San Francisco: Pfeiffer.

Boss, W. (1985). The psychological contract: A key to effective organization development consultation. *Consultation, 4*(4), 284–304.

Bruce, R., & Wyman, S. (1998). *Changing organizations: Practicing action training and research.* Thousand Oaks, CA: Sage.

Burke, W. (1994). *Organization development: A process of learning and changing* (2nd ed.). Reading, MA: Addison-Wesley.

Burke, W. (2002). *Organization change: Theory and practice.* Thousand Oaks, CA: Sage.

Burke, W. (2005). Implementation. In W. Rothwell & R. Sullivan (Eds.), *Practicing organization development* (2nd ed.). San Francisco: Pfeiffer.

Cobb, A. (1986). Political diagnosis: Applications in organization development. *Academy of Management Review, 11*, 482–496.

Cobb, A., & Margulies, N. (1981). Organization development: A political perspective. *Academy of Management Review, 6*, 49–59.

Cummings, T., & Worley, C. (2001). *Organization development and change* (7th ed.) Cincinnati, OH: South-Western College Publishing.

Egan, T., & Gellermann, W. (2005). The ethical practitioner. In W. Rothwell & R. Sullivan (Eds.), *Practicing organization development* (2nd ed.). San Francisco: Pfeiffer.

French, J., & Raven, B. (1959). The bases of social power. In D. Cartwright (Ed.), *Studies in social power* (pp. 150–167). Ann Arbor, MI: University of Michigan, Institute for Social Research.

French, W., & Bell, C. (1999). *Organization development: Behavioral science interventions for organization improvement* (6th ed.). Englewood Cliffs, NJ: Prentice-Hall.

Greiner, L., & Metzger, R. (1983). *Consulting to management.* Englewood Cliffs, NJ: Prentice-Hall.

Greiner, L., & Schein, V. (1988). *Power and organization development.* Reading, MA: Addison-Wesley.

Harrison, R. (1970). Choosing the depth of organizational intervention. *Journal of Applied Behavioral Science, 6*(2), 182–202.

Jamieson, D. (1991, March). You are the instrument. *OD Practitioner, 23*, 20.

Jamieson, D. (1998). Your consulting style. *Consulting Today, 2*(1), 1–2.

Jamieson, D. (2003). The heart and mind of the practitioner: Remembering Bob Tannenbaum. *OD Practitioner, 35*(4), 3–8.

Jamieson, D., & Armstrong, T. (2008). Client-consultant engagement: What it takes to create value. Paper presented at AOM Management Consulting Conference, Client-Consultant Cooperation: Coping with Complexity and Change. Copenhagen Business School.

Jamieson, D., & Gellermann, W. (2005). Values, ethics and OD practice. In M. Brazzel & B. Jones (Eds.), *The NTL OD resource book: Understanding the essence of organization development.* San Francisco: Pfeiffer.

Kolb, D., & Frohman, A. (1970). An organization development approach to consulting. *Sloan Management Review, 12,* 51–65.

Lippitt, G., & Lippitt, R. (1986). *The consulting process in action* (2nd ed.). San Francisco: Pfeiffer.

Lundberg, C. (1997). Towards a general model of consultancy: Foundations. *Journal of Organizational Change Management, 10*(3), 193–201.

Margulies, N., & Raia, A. (1972). *Organization development: Values, process and technology.* New York: McGraw-Hill.

Margulies, N., & Raia, A. (1978). *Conceptual foundations of organization development.* New York: McGraw-Hill.

Massarik, F., & Pei-Carpenter, M. (2002). *Organization development and consulting: Perspectives and foundations.* San Francisco: Pfeiffer.

Old, D. (1995). Consulting for real transformation, sustainability, and organic form. *Journal of Organizational Change Management, 8*(3), 6–17.

Page, M. (1998, August). Ethical dilemmas in organization development consulting practice. Unpublished master's thesis. Malibu, CA: Pepperdine University.

Quade, K., & Brown, R. (2002). *The conscious consultant: Mastering change from the inside out.* San Francisco: Pfeiffer.

Schein, E. (1988). *Process consultation (Vol. I): Role in organization development* (2nd ed.) Reading, MA: Addison-Wesley.

Schein, E. (1997). The concept of "client" from a process consultation perspective: A guide for change agents. *Journal of Organizational Change Management, 10*(3), 202–216.

Schein, E. (2005). Taking organization culture seriously. In W. Rothwell & R. Sullivan (Eds.), *Practicing organization development* (2nd ed.). San Francisco: Pfeiffer.

Shepard, H. (1985, December). Rules of thumb for change agents. *OD Practitioner, 17,* 2.

Smither, R., Houston, J., & McIntire, S. (1996). *Organization development: Strategies for changing environments.* New York: HarperCollins.

Watkins, J., & Mohr, B. (2001). *Appreciative inquiry: Change at the speed of imagination.* San Francisco: Pfeiffer.

Weisbord, M. (1973). The organization development contract. *OD Practitioner, 5*(2), 1–4.

White, L., & Wooten, K. (1983, October). Ethical dilemmas in various stages of organization development. *Academy of Management Review, 8,* 690–697.

CHAPTER TEN

# Launch

*Assessment, Action Planning, and Implementation*

D.D. Warrick

The "launch" phase of organization development (OD) is an interesting, valuable, and potentially high-impact phase of OD and is the heart of the OD process. If done well, the probability of successful change will be very high. If done poorly, the aftermath can be far-reaching.

The term "launch" is a term coined by Warner Burke (2008, p. 257). It is a phase of OD where valuable information is gathered and analyzed. A collaborative approach is used to evaluate the information and plan actions around a sound change process, and actions are implemented that may be directed at specific changes but have the ultimate goal of improving the health, effectiveness, and self-renewing capabilities of an organization.

## THE PURPOSE OF LAUNCH

While assessment and action planning may be used informally in the Pre-Launch phase of OD and more formally in the Launch phase, they are, in fact, used in various ways throughout OD efforts. In the same way, implementation is a dynamic process that often requires frequent adjustments and may involve going back to the assessment and action planning phases. In other words, these three phases of OD are interactive as are all phases of the OD process. The purpose of the launch phase is

1. To discover present realities and future possibilities and the gaps in between.

2. To understand the strengths (major assets and what is working) and opportunities for improvement (what is not working or could be improved) of organizations, groups, and individuals and what it will take for each to succeed.

3. To collect relevant information for use in designing (action planning), managing, and monitoring the change process and improvement efforts. Monitoring progress is especially an important and often overlooked function as corrections can be made if it is known that the desired progress is not being made.

4. To develop action plans based on a sound change process.

5. To know how to successfully implement change so there is a high probability for success.

6. To involve and engage people in the change process.

7. To evaluate the success of OD efforts and plan future actions.

# A MODEL FOR ASSESSING ORGANIZATIONS, PLANNING ACTIONS, AND IMPLEMENTING CHANGE

The model presented in Exhibit 10.1 and discussed in more detail in the remainder of this chapter can be used for working with whole organizations, groups, or individuals and is intended to provide guidelines rather than rigid steps. In applying the model, several considerations should be kept in mind:

1. The potential uses of the assessment, action planning, and implementation processes go far beyond traditional OD literature. For example, while much of the OD literature deals primarily with existing organizations and groups, the processes may be used in forming new organizations, groups, and alliances; in preparing for and integrating merged organizations; and in working on social, political, or international issues or with geographically dispersed or culturally diverse groups.

2. Technology has opened up many new alternatives for assessing organizations, groups, and individuals; for guiding the action planning process; and for implementing change. Examples include electronic questionnaires, real-time messaging, conferencing, and action planning

Exhibit 10.1. Assessment, Action Planning, and Implementation Guidelines

| Assessment | Action Planning | Implementation |
|---|---|---|
| **Planning** | **Involve Key Stakeholders** | **Keep the Big Picture in Mind** |
| 1. Involve the right people in the project. | 1. Involve those who are in the best position to understand and utilize the assessment and lead needed changes. | 1. Keep focused on the specific change and the big picture, which includes improving the health, effectiveness, and self-renewing capabilities of the organization. |
| 2. Clarify the desired goals and outcomes of the assessment. | 2. Ensure that someone will lead the change effort and, if needed, develop a change team to plan and manage the change process. | **Choose the Right Interventions** |
| 3. Agree on what and who will be assessed. | | 2. Learn to think in terms of individual, group, and whole systems interventions. |
| 4. Choose methods. | **Evaluate and Prioritize Relevant Data** | 3. Use strategic involvement to economize the time of the participants. |
| 5. Determine how to best collect data. | 3. Develop a process for evaluating, prioritizing, and making the assessment information manageable and useable. | 4. Consider multiple interventions to accelerate the change process. |
| 6. Determine how to analyze and report the data. | 4. Clarify the focus of change efforts (whole organization, group or inter-group, individual, structural, technological, etc.). | **Use a Sound Change Model to Plan and Manage the Change Process** |
| 7. Determine how to feed back and utilize the data. | 5. Consider the level of desired change (fine-tuning, incremental, or transformational). | 5. Use the action planning plan and model to guide and manage the change process. |
| 8. Agree with leaders on the process and how the results will be utilized and coach the leaders on their role in making the assessment successful. | 6. Focus on present realities and future ideals and possibilities and explore alternatives for achieving greater success. | 6. Build in feedback mechanisms so you will know what is working and not working and adjustments can be made. |
| 9. Develop milestones for getting things done. | | |
| **Data Collection** | | |
| 10. Assure that anyone involved in performing the assessment is properly trained. | | |
| 11. Prepare the organization for the assessment. | | |
| 12. Perform the assessment. | | |

## Assessment

### Data Analysis

13. Develop a strategy for analyzing and presenting the assessment results in a user-friendly way.
14. Prepare a simple-to-understand and use presentation of the findings.

### Data Feedback

15. Design a feedback strategy for determining who gets what information, how, and when.
16. Prepare the appropriate people on how to use the results for helpful and not harmful purposes.
17. Decide on when and how to connect the feedback to action planning.
18. Prepare people for how to understand and utilize the data in helpful and positive ways to diffuse anxiety and ensure that the process will be a beneficial and useful one.

## Action Planning

### Agree on the Changes to Be Made

7. Agree on the actions to be taken, recognizing that it is better to do a few things well than many things poorly.
8. Evaluate the change from a systems perspective, considering the implications of the changes and the alignment needed.

### Develop a Change Strategy

9. Identify any forces working for or against the desired change.
10. Explore strategy alternatives.
11. Develop a change process based on a sound change model.

### Clarify Roles and Follow-Through Responsibilities

12. Clarify the roles and follow-through responsibilities of all involved in the change process.
13. Commit to keeping the change process as clear and simple as possible and to improving both the health and effectiveness of the organization.

## Implementation

### Keep People Engaged and Make the Incentive to Change Greater Than the Incentive to Stay the Same

7. Target early and continued wins.
8. Communicate progress.
9. Keep those involved focused and energized.
10. Continuously look for ways to make the incentive for change and involvement greater than the incentive to stay the same or to avoid involvement.

### Identify and Manage Resistance to Change

11. Be aware of significant resistance to change and take positive steps in overcoming resistance.
12. Deal with continued resistance as quickly and constructively as possible.

### Follow Through and Learn from the Process

13. Follow-through until the desired goals of the change is achieved.
14. Build in ways for the change to be sustained.
15. Learn from the process and share what has been learned.

without geographical constraints, and many other technologically driven alternatives.

3. In assessing organizations, doing action planning, and implementing change, there is always the ideal and the reality with which to deal. Approaches and methods need to be tailored to fit the realities, such as what leaders are willing to do, available resources, time constraints, and political, geographical, and technological considerations. For example, it may be desirable both to survey and interview people, but the leaders are only willing to allow interviewing. A skilled OD practitioner can usually work within the boundaries given, but there may be times when the boundaries will not provide valid results, and the client must be told so.

Every possible effort should be made to make the Launch phase and all phases of OD as clear, simple, time efficient, and value added as possible. OD efforts sometimes die of their own weight because they have become too complex and time-consuming or lose sight of the ultimate goal of OD to improve organizational effectiveness and health (Beckhard, 1969).

# DEVELOPING AN ASSESSMENT, ACTION PLANNING, AND IMPLEMENTATION PHILOSOPHY

Significant and sometimes radical changes in the environment in which organizations must compete and changes in the field of OD itself make it important to develop a sound philosophy for assessing organizations and planning actions. Philosophies may run, for example, from a more deficit or problem-centered philosophy (focusing on weaknesses and what is wrong and broken and how to fix the problems) that characterized some of the early OD efforts to a more positive Appreciative Inquiry (AI) type of philosophy that focuses on stories of best practices and experiences and discovering the life-giving properties present when organizations are performing optimally.

While it would be difficult to find supporters for the deficit or problem-centered approach to the exclusion of other approaches, a healthy and continuing debate exists about whether a balanced approach that looks at both the positives and negatives is most appropriate or if an AI type of approach should become the exclusive approach of OD practitioners. Some OD practitioners are concerned about a one-size-fits-all strategy and others have become very strong advocates for the exclusive use of a positive OD approach. In either case, every OD practitioner needs to become a student of these various philosophies and to develop a sound and defensible assessment, action planning, and implementation philosophy as it will significantly influence the approach used.

# THE IMPORTANCE OF UNDERSTANDING ORGANIZATIONS AND WHAT IT TAKES TO BUILD THEM

Important to any effort to assess organizations, plan actions, and implement change is an understanding of organizations and what makes them successful. Fundamental to the Launch process is knowing what to look for to understand an organization and what it takes to build a successful organization capable of succeeding in today's changing environment.

## Understanding Organizations Before Trying to Change Them

Organizations are much like people. They have beliefs, values, attitudes, habits, strengths, and weaknesses. Like people, they can be very different. Some are exceptionally focused, healthy, productive, vital, innovative, quick to adapt to change, willing to learn and grow, and great places to be. Others are confused, unhealthy, dysfunctional, rigid, slow to learn and grow, resistant to change, and great places to avoid. Some organizations live by simple and straightforward principles and are easy to understand, and some are complex and difficult to understand and are somewhat schizophrenic with multiple and conflicting personalities.

Also, like many people in today's fast-moving and unpredictable environment, organizations can go from champ to chump and success to failure in a short time if they don't keep improving and adapting. All of this is said to emphasize the importance of understanding organizations before trying to change and improve them so that the strategies fit the unique characteristics, needs, and circumstances of each organization. Otherwise, strategies are likely to fail or underachieve what is possible.

In trying to understand organizations, it is helpful to have a model or framework that can be used in knowing what to look for. Models can also be used in designing an assessment strategy, developing interview questions and questionnaires, and organizing and presenting information in a useful and understandable way. Several such models are described below:

1. *The Diagnosing Organization Systems Model* (Cummings & Worley, 2005). This is perhaps the most comprehensive of the models for understanding organizations. It is a systems model that looks at Inputs, Design Components (often called Processes in other models), and Outputs at the Organization, Group, and Individual levels. This is discussed in Chapter Seventeen.

2. *The Six Box Model* (Weisbord, 1978). Weisbord identified six organizational components that can be used to understand organizations. The components are organizational (1) purposes, (2) structures, (3)

relationships, (4) rewards, (5) leadership, and (6) helpful mechanisms. These six components influence and are influenced by the environment in which the organization functions.

3. *The Organization Dynamics Model* (Kotter, 1976). Kotter's model focuses on seven major organizational components to understand organizations. These are (1) key organizational processes, (2) external environment, (3) employees and other tangible assets, (4) formal organizational arrangements, (5) social systems, (6) technology, and (7) dominant coalition (top management).

## Criteria for Building Successful Organizations

It would seem logical that OD practitioners should have a clear understanding of the fundamentals of building successful organizations as a framework for everything they do. Many efforts have been made to study best-run organizations and to identify what separates these organizations from the rest. For example, it would be good to review the research of Cameron, 2008; Collins, 2001; Collins and Porras, 1994; Hamel and Prahalad, 1995; Kotter, 2009; Slater, 2001; and *Fortune* magazine's annual list of America's Most Admired Companies, The Global Most Admired, and The 100 Best Companies to Work For in looking for patterns.

While every organization is different, there are many consistent themes in research and in experts' views on successful organizations. For example, the best typically perform far above the industry average and tend to focus both on building a great organization (organization health) *"and"* on getting great results (organization effectiveness). The rest have a plan for neither or become preoccupied with only one or the other, which typically means being preoccupied with performance while doing little to build a healthy organization.

Developing a well-researched list or model of the fundamentals of building successful organizations can be very useful to the OD practitioner. However, it should be pointed out that the application of the criteria may differ from organization to organization and culture to culture. Some organizations find unorthodox ways of succeeding, and the unique characteristics and circumstances of each organization must be taken into account in planning and implementing changes. An example of the Fundamentals is shown in Exhibit 10.2.

# ASSESSMENT

Prepared with a model that provides guidelines on assessment, action planning, and implementation, an understanding of the purpose of these important aspects of the OD process, a sound change philosophy to guide and provide consistency to your thinking and choices, ideas about how to understand organizations, and

## Exhibit 10.2. Fundamentals of Building Successful Organizations

1. Lead the Way
   - Good leadership is the major key to success.
   - Top-level leaders have a passion for excellence and are humble, competent, visible, approachable, trustworthy, straightforward, and skilled at providing vision, direction, and inspiration. They walk the talk.
   - Top-level leaders are close to the organization and function like a united, focused, results-oriented top leadership team.
2. Develop a Strategy for Succeeding and Get Everyone Using the Same Play Book
   - The vision, mission, core values, and strategic goals are clear, energizing, and known throughout the organization.
   - The strategy includes a strong emphasis on both people and performance.
   - Everyone knows how he or she can contribute and is empowered to do so.
3. Structure the Organization for Results
   - The right people are in the right places doing the right things.
   - Everything is aligned to support the goals and values.
   - Simple, flat, non-bureaucratic, adaptable, responsive design that is effective, efficient, and results oriented.
   - Processes, systems, technology, and practices make it easy to get things done.
4. Build a High-Performance Culture
   - Values-driven culture that encourages excellence and frees people to be their best.
   - Culture encourages teamwork and being self-directing.
   - Culture values disciplined action and entrepreneurship.
   - Culture encourages being open and straightforward, treating people with respect, and doing what is right.
   - High level of trust.
   - Culture values innovative thinking.
5. Develop Value-Added Managers
   - Managers at all levels are expected to add value, get results, and make things happen.
   - Managers are empowered to get the job done and are expected to do the same with their people.
   - A strong emphasis is placed on the continuous development of the leadership and management skills of present and potential managers.
6. Take Care of Your People
   - Having a committed, motivated, and well-trained workforce is a top priority of the leaders.
   - People at all levels are treated with value.
   - Efforts are made to attract, retain, develop, and fully utilize committed and talented people who are a good fit with the organization.
   - Efforts are made to make working conditions and the work environment a plus rather than a minus.

**Exhibit 10.2.** *Continued*

7. Take Care of Your Customers
   - Being customer driven to both internal and external customers is a high priority.
   - Employees from top to bottom are encouraged to know their internal and external customers and their needs.
   - Building good relationships with present and potential customers is valued.
   - The organization has a reputation for treating customers well.
8. Build Teamwork
   - Teamwork is encouraged and developed at the top, within teams, between teams, and outside the organization with groups key to the success of the organization.
   - There is a one-team mentality with minimal barriers between groups.
   - Involvement and collaboration are a way of life.
9. Never Stop Learning, Improving, and Building a Great Organization
   - A strong emphasis is placed on continuous learning, improvement, and development at the individual, group, and organization levels.
   - Many opportunities are provided for people to share ideas and make improvements.
   - Complacency and maintaining the status quo are not options.
10. Keep Score and Get Results
   - Measures of excellence are simple and clear and allow the organization to know where it stands regarding performance, human resource indicators, culture, customers, and other important measures.
   - Decisive decisions are made to make needed adjustments to get the best results without damaging the culture or compromising the core values.

a one-page description of the fundamentals of what it takes to build a successful organization, the OD practitioner is now ready to begin the assessment process. As shown in the model in Exhibit 10.1, there are four major steps:

1. Planning
2. Data Collection
3. Data Analysis
4. Data Feedback

While this chapter is designed to provide an overview of the assessment process, there are many good sources that provide the details. Three excellent sources are David Nadler's (1977) classic *Feedback and Organization Development: Using Data-Based Methods*; Church and Waclawski's (1998) *Designing and Using Organizational Surveys*, which provides a comprehensive analysis of the positives and negatives of methods using technology such as emails or websites; and *Appreciative Inquiry Handbook* by Cooperrider, Whitney, and Stavros (2008), which addresses assessment from an AI perspective.

## Planning the Assessment

A well-planned assessment can provide valuable information that can be used in making organizations, groups, and individuals successful. It can confirm what is being done right and may also uncover blind spots or potential opportunities that, when addressed, result in significant improvements or even a turnaround situation. A poorly planned assessment, however, can demoralize people and cause division. Therefore, it is very important that someone with experience and expertise lead the planning process.

The size and scope of the assessment, the level of expertise of the person or persons leading the assessment process, and the commitment needed to make the assessment successful will determine who and how many should be involved in the planning process. A known, trusted, and experienced internal or external OD practitioner may be able to plan an assessment with minimal involvement. However, many efforts require considerable involvement in establishing goals, agreeing on what and who will be assessed, choosing methods, deciding on how to collect the data, and fulfilling the other steps in the planning process.

## Data Collection

Technology has made it possible to collect and analyze data very quickly. However, every situation must be analyzed to determine the most effective and realistic way to collect data. For example, while a wealth of information can be collected and quickly analyzed through questionnaires, people may be more open in face-to-face interviews and communicate things that cannot be picked up in questionnaires.

The most frequently used methods of data collection are available information (an organization's vision, mission, values, strategic goals, organization charts, turnover rates, and so forth), using questionnaires and interviews (individual and group), and observations. Ideally, both quantitative and qualitative data are preferable. *Quantifiable* (most quantifiable data are still subjective) data, which typically are collected through questionnaires, make it possible to know the magnitude of an issue. An average of 2.5 on a 7-point scale, with 7 being the highest favorable score, has a far different meaning than a 6.5. However, quantitative data will not always tell you what is behind the numbers. *Qualitative* data are generally collected through one-on-one or focus-group interviews that make it possible to pick up information and impressions that explore a wide range of issues, including what is behind the issues.

# Data Analysis

The OD practitioner or practitioners leading an OD process usually compile, analyze, and prepare a report of the assessment results. Technology has made it possible to automate the compilation and analysis part of an assessment, and with large numbers of people being assessed, this is almost a necessity for efficient assessment. The data go in and a report comes out, complete with attractive charts and graphs. However, no matter how dazzling the technology and resulting report may be, of much greater importance—regardless of how the data are analyzed and presented—is that the analysis should provide valid and useful information. This information should be presented in a way that is brief and easy to follow and utilize. Some question whether this can be done solely by machine or without an experienced expert or experts doing the analysis. Nevertheless, the point is that this part of the assessment and action planning process is extremely important, and a poor analysis or presentation of the results will lead to a low use and/or misuse of the assessment.

# Data Feedback

If and how data are fed back has a significant impact on OD efforts. Feedback properly handled can energize people, create momentum for change, and ensure that organization members trust and own the data. However, if feedback isn't properly handled, it can undermine present and future OD efforts. For example, leaders may not like what they see and choose to forego the feedback process, or too much time may be allowed to elapse before providing feedback, which will likely result in the data losing its relevance and motivating potential. The important point is that properly planned feedback is very important to the OD process, and poorly planned feedback can have many consequences such as a loss of credibility and trust in the OD process.

The feedback process, must be designed for each unique situation, but typically includes some version of the following steps:

1. A strategy is developed by the OD practitioner in collaboration with the appropriate people about who receives what information, how, and when.

2. If appropriate, training is provided for those leading feedback sessions so that there will be consistency in philosophy, methods, and outcomes in each session.

3. The top-level leader involved will usually be briefed on the findings and coached on behaviors that tend to help or hinder the feedback process and what the feedback process consists of.

4. The feedback then is usually presented to the primary group it is intended for or cascaded down the organization, starting with top

management. Each group receives the information that is appropriate for it to see and respond to. There are exceptions where a "bottom-up" approach is used, with recommendations eventually formulated to present to top management.

While some feedback sessions at this point are designed simply to brief people on the results, most follow a presentation of the results with some phase of the action planning process. For example, a group may be used to evaluate, validate, and prioritize data and brainstorm alternatives and then pass this on to an action planning group, or they may serve as the action planning group and develop specific actions. Whatever method is used, it is important to make the feedback process a positive, helpful, and energizing experience that accurately presents present realities but keeps the focus on what is possible and what it will take to move forward.

# ASSESSMENT METHODS

One of the many interesting aspects of assessing organizations is that a variety of methods can be used to find out what is going on and what is possible. Each method has advantages and disadvantages. For example, interviews and questionnaires are the most frequently used methods, but have advantages and disadvantages. Interviews make it possible to collect a wide variety of data, find out what is behind issues, and see and dialogue with respondents, but may suffer from interviewer bias. They also can be time-consuming and expensive if a consultant is used and large numbers of people are interviewed. Questionnaires make data quantifiable but may suffer from respondent bias and are not likely to reveal what is behind the numbers. A summary of the major advantages and disadvantages of various assessment methods is shown in Exhibit 10.3, and a brief discussion of the methods follows.

***Examining Existing Data*** This part of the assessment begins when an OD practitioner gets involved and starts learning about an organization. It serves as a first step in the assessment process, even though it often precedes a formal assessment. It could include, for example, studying past and present information available on the organization, including information published by or about an organization, such as an organization's history, reputation, past and present success, and brochures or publications that may describe the organization's vision, mission, core values, strategic goals, organization chart, and products and services. It could also include information on turnover rates, absenteeism, or even prior assessments.

***Interviews*** Interviewing is a most interesting and important part of OD. A skilled interviewer could go into most organizations, spend a day talking to

## Exhibit 10.3. Advantages and Disadvantages of Organization Assessment Methods

| Method | Advantages | Disadvantages |
|---|---|---|
| ***Examining Existing Data*** | | |
| • Past and present published information<br>• Brochures<br>• Vision, mission, values, goals statements<br>• Organization charts<br>• Available data on profits, sales, turnover, etc. | • Information already exists<br>• Generally easy to access<br>• Quickly familiarizes the person doing the assessment with the organization<br>• Efficient and inexpensive<br>• Relatively objective | • Reality between what is stated and what is may differ<br>• Some existing information may be difficult to access<br>• Gives only a surface view of the organization |
| ***Interviews*** | | |
| • Structured (specific questions designed to elicit specific responses)<br>• Non-structured (open-ended questions)<br>• Individual<br>• Group<br>• Face-to-face<br>• Phone or electronic | • Makes it possible to collect rich, valuable, in-depth information<br>• Can be used for a wide range of assessment purposes<br>• Makes it possible to probe and elaborate on information and pursue new lines of questioning<br>• Can build empathy, trust, support for OD efforts | • Can be time-consuming and expensive if large number of respondents involved<br>• Subject to interviewer bias and influence<br>• Interpreting and summarizing information from interviews can be difficult<br>• May not give a sense of magnitude or importance of information collected<br>• Risks inconsistencies in interviewing style and interpretation of the results if more than one interviewer involved |
| ***Questionnaires*** | | |
| • Used to gather data on whole organizations, groups, or individuals, or a specific focus<br>• Quantifiable<br>• Open-ended questions | • Make it possible to quantify and objectively analyze results<br>• Can survey and involve large numbers of people<br>• Numbers and a sense of magnitude can be strong motivators for change<br>• Relatively inexpensive<br>• Can seed the organization for change<br>• Can compare before and after results | • Misses qualitative data, especially if open-ended questions not included<br>• May not reveal what is behind the numbers<br>• Lacks the flexibility of interviews<br>• Subject to respondent bias, especially if respondents lack knowledge pertaining to some questions<br>• Interpreting and summarizing data may require a high level of expertise |

| Method | Advantages | Disadvantages |
|---|---|---|
| *Observations* | | |
| • Formal (specific things to observe and information to collect)<br>• Informal (observing, talking, attending meetings, etc.) | • Organization behavior, processes, and systems can be observed first-hand<br>• Can obtain a better feel for the culture of the organization or group<br>• Real-time data<br>• Flexibility in terms of what is observed | • Not always easy to arrange and can be distracting to those being observed<br>• Possible observer bias in interpreting what is observed<br>• Can be expensive and time-consuming for the value received<br>• May be difficult to analyze what is observed |
| *Live Assessments* | | |
| • Data collected and analyzed live at meetings and workshops<br>• Data collected and analyzed in real time electronically | • Interesting, engaging, real time, and provides fast turnaround and use of information<br>• With skilled facilitator can be used with large groups of people<br>• Quickly involves people and builds commitment to change | • May miss valuable information that comes from a variety of sources over time<br>• Dependent on having key people present or commitment may be lost<br>• Somewhat risky in the event that unforeseen things can happen that undermine the process |

key people, and probably have a reasonably good idea of the strengths and weaknesses of the organization and have some preliminary ideas about what it would take to move the organization to a higher level. According to Cummings and Worley (2005, p. 119), interviews are the most widely used method for collecting data in OD. Interviewing offers many advantages for collecting information because of the ability to see people face-to-face, probe for clarification and possible alternatives, and build personal credibility and trust. However, it can also be time-consuming and expensive.

Interviews can be classified as structured or non-structured, individual or group, and face-to-face or non-face-to-face. Structured interviews contain prepared questions asked in a particular order that are designed to elicit responses in specific areas. Unstructured interviews consist of open-ended questions followed by probing based on what the respondent says. Most OD practitioners use a blend of the two, with prepared questions designed to cover a number of specific areas and the flexibility to go with the flow as the interview unfolds. Interviews can also be done with individuals or groups or a combination of both. Respondents are likely to be more open in individual interviews, but group interviews, of course, make it possible to reach and involve far more people. While most interviews are done face-to-face, when this is not possible, there are still other options, such as telephone, teleconference, videoconference, or synchronous (or even asynchronous) chats on the Internet. Exhibit 10.4 offers some guidelines on conducting interviews, and Exhibit 10.5 provides a list of possible interview questions.

***Questionnaires*** Questionnaires can be used to understand whole organizations and groups and provide valuable information in forming organizations and groups. They can also be used to address specific areas such as organization structure, culture, and communications; the leadership or interpersonal skills of leaders; how people are dealing with intercultural issues; or for evaluating important issues such as a lack of teamwork and cooperation between groups. There are, of course, many other possible uses. Ideally, questionnaires should be easy to understand, brief enough to motivate people to complete them yet comprehensive enough to solicit valuable information, and based on a theory or model that makes it possible to easily understand, interpret, and utilize the results.

***Observations*** Data can also be collected by observing organizational dynamics. This can be done in a formal way with specific things to observe or information to collect such as observing a top management meeting and evaluating roles, relationships, and group dynamics, or informally by walking around or spending time with individuals and groups.

***Live Assessments*** A high-interest and fast way to collect data is to do so live in workshops or meetings or even electronically by linking tele- or audioconferencing with the technology to collect and tabulate data, and to make decisions instantly, even though the participants may be dispersed worldwide. This method is particularly used in large group meetings where data are collected, fed back, organized, and used for decision making and action planning. Many of these types of meetings, such as the Search Conference, Future Search, and Real Time Strategic Change, are described in Bunker and Alban (1997) and Holman, Devane, and Cady (2007).

Live data gathering can be especially effective when brief questionnaires are used and the results immediately tabulated by technology or by hand so that it can be immediately discussed. For example, you can have each team member complete a questionnaire on how the team is functioning, shuffle the questionnaires so that each team member receives a questionnaire at random (or produce the results electronically, if the technology is available), and have team members read off the results for each item and then discuss the findings.

## Exhibit 10.4. Interviewing Guidelines

1. Provide a comfortable and private place where there will be no interruptions. There should be few barriers such as a desk between you and the interviewee.
2. Introduce yourself and ask for the name, department, and job of the interviewee. You may also want to know the name of the interviewee's immediate supervisor. Briefly describe the purpose of the interview. Point out that you are looking for trends and will not report any information that would identify the source without permission from the interviewee. Ask for permission to take notes. Interviewing provides a good opportunity for you to personally build credibility and to promote the program you are involved in.
3. Try to be as natural, warm, and friendly as possible and do not over-react to what is said. Over-reactions will stimulate or hamper continued discussion on a subject. An alert body posture and good eye contact are important.
4. You should be aware that the questions you ask and comments you make are likely to be reported to others after each interview.
5. If a survey is also being used, it is best to administer the survey first so the results can be used in developing questions for the interview. It is also helpful to use questions that will serve as a cross-check with the survey and reveal the subjective data behind the numbers.
6. Take notes so you can remember what was said. Skip quickly over unimportant items. Your objective is to (1) identify major strengths and opportunities for improvement; (2) solicit supporting information; and (3) ask for possible solutions to opportunities for improvement. Learn to take notes without losing eye contact with the interviewee.
7. Make sure that you encourage the interviewee to talk about strengths and creative ideas. Dwelling primarily on weaknesses is likely to produce guilt and discouragement.
8. Objectivity is extremely important! You must record what is being said—not what you were primed by others to believe ahead of time or what you want to hear. Check out your perceptions thoroughly if you have any doubts about what is being said.
9. You can end an interview at any time by asking, "Is there anything else that you think I should know?" Don't prolong an interview when a person has little to say. When you finish, thank the interviewee for his or her time.
10. Summarize the interview at the conclusion of the day according to the following format: (1) major strengths; (2) major issues along with their supporting facts and possible solutions; and (3) miscellaneous information.

# ACTION PLANNING

Action planning is the collaborative process of systematically planning a change effort using sound strategies, change models, and change principles. When done effectively, it can energize and mobilize people and significantly improve the impact of a change or improvement and accelerate the time needed to

## Exhibit 10.5. Sample Interview Questions

1. What words or phrases would you use to best describe your organization at this time?
2. If you were to rate how successful your organization is at this time on a 10-point scale with 10 high and 1 low, what number would you choose?
3. If you were to rate morale on a 10-point scale, what number would you choose?
4. On a 10-point scale, rate your organization as a place to work. How well does your organization treat employees? How would you describe the working conditions such as pay, fringe benefits, facilities, and the things you need to do your job well? What words or phrases would you use to describe the culture or work environment here?
5. Describe your leader and how well-regarded he/she is in your organization. How would you describe his/her management style? What are his/her major strengths and weaknesses? What could he/she do to be more effective? If important, do the same for other senior leaders.
6. How clear are the vision, mission, values, and goals of your organization?
7. In your opinion, what are the major strengths of your organization? What are the major weaknesses or opportunities for improvement? What are the major concerns you have or hear other employees talking about?
8. What is going well in your organization? What is not going well or could be improved?
9. If you could only choose three things your organization could or should do to become more effective or successful, what would they be?
10. Now do some creative, bold, breakthrough thinking and list a few additional things your organization could do to go from good to great or become a one-of-a-kind organization.
11. Is your organization structured for results with the right organization design and the right people in the right places?
12. What does your organization do to provide training and professional development for leaders and employees?
13. How client-centered and service-oriented is your organization? What would your clients likely say about your organization?
14. What words or phrases would you use to describe the culture or work environment here?
15. How effective is your organization at communicating with employees, keeping them informed, and encouraging open communications?
16. How good is the organization at teamwork at the top, within teams, and between teams?
17. What are some of the major frustrations or obstacles you face in getting things done?
18. How are changes typically made in your organization?
19. What kinds of behaviors are rewarded and are discouraged in your organization?
20. Does your organization do a good job of providing training and professional development opportunities?
21. If you were to rate how free you feel to be open on a 10-point scale with 10 representing very open and 1 very guarded, what number would you choose?
22. What does your organization do to encourage innovative thinking, new ideas, and improvements?

23. How does a person get ahead in your organization?
24. What does the organization do to value, recognize, and reward people for their contributions?
25. What are some of the major motivators and de-motivators in your organization? What would motivate you more?
26. What do you consider to be the major issues facing the future of your organization?
27. Is there anything else you would like to comment on?

accomplish the desired actions. When done ineffectively, action plans will generate little commitment and have a low probability of being implemented and may, in fact, create unintended negative side-effects.

## Understanding Action Planning

Even though action planning is an integral part of any OD effort, surprisingly little has been written about the details of action planning. Action planning first appeared in the pre-OD days of Kurt Lewin in his action research concept, which is basically a process of gathering data, organizing and feeding data back, and using the data to explore ways to improve.

Beckhard and Harris (1977, p. 28) offer one of the most detailed descriptions of action planning. They describe it as a process of developing strategies and action plans to manage the transition between present and future states. They list four steps in the action planning process:

1. Determine the client's degree of choice about change (How much control do clients have in deciding whether to change and how to change?).

2. Determine what needs to be changed.

3. Determine where to intervene.

4. Choose intervention technologies.

Beckhard and Harris also provided guidelines for developing an activity or process plan (pp. 51–52). Their seven guidelines for developing a process plan are as follows:

1. The activities should be clearly linked to the goals and priorities of the identified change.

2. The activities should be clearly identified rather than broadly generalized.

3. Discrete activities should be linked.

4. The activities should be time-sequenced.

5. Contingent plans should exist in case unexpected forces develop during the change process.

6. The change plan should be supported by top management.

7. The plan should be cost-effective.

David Nadler (1977, pp. 156–158) listed six characteristics that are important for successful action planning meetings:

1. *Motivation to work with the data*. People must feel that working with the data will lead to positive results.

2. *Assistance in using the data*. Someone, usually an OD practitioner, needs to be familiar with the data and how to interpret and utilize them.

3. *A structure for the meeting*. An agenda, usually planned by an OD practitioner or collaboratively developed with the involvement of an OD practitioner, should provide a useful process for dealing with the data and for planning actions.

4. *Appropriate membership*. The right people should attend the meeting. This could include, for example, those who most need to buy into the action planning process and who can best contribute to planning relevant actions.

5. *Appropriate power*. Membership should also include one or more persons with the power to make needed changes.

6. *Process help*. A skilled facilitator, usually an OD practitioner, is needed to guide the process and observe how the group is working.

## The Action Planning Process

The action planning process shown in Exhibit 10.1 includes five steps:

1. Involve key stakeholders.

2. Evaluate and prioritize relevant data.

3. Agree on the changes to be made (actions to be taken).

4. Develop a change strategy.

5. Clarify roles and follow-through responsibilities.

Much of the action planning process is just good common sense. This is true of the entire OD process, just as it is of good leadership and of building a successful organization. However, common sense is not so common and often requires a high level of expertise to discover and implement. In just about every endeavor in life, whether we are talking about OD practitioners, leaders, athletes, musicians, teachers, or parents, those who are highly skilled make what they do seem almost effortless. This is definitely the case with action planning. When done well, it makes sense and has a natural flow to it. However, to do it well requires a clear understanding of at least the five steps presented above.

**Involve Key Stakeholders** Stakeholders include people at all levels of an organization and occasionally people outside an organization who are influenced by and/or can influence or contribute to the success of change efforts. When key stakeholders are involved in the action planning process, the plans tend to be sound and realistic, and those involved tend to have a strong commitment to assuring the success of the planned actions. When key stakeholders are not involved, commitment may be lacking from those who can make or break changes, time and planning required to convince key players to support the actions can be excessive, and the plans are often well-intended but faulty because those developing the plans may lack the wisdom and insight of those close to the action. Therefore, the first step in the action planning process is to evaluate who should be involved in various action planning efforts. It is assumed that the OD practitioner guiding the OD effort will facilitate or be involved in the selection process and most action planning efforts. In deciding who should be involved, consider the following:

- *Givens*: Start with the givens, that is, people who would be expected to be involved.

- *Expertise*: Who possesses the knowledge and skills necessary to contribute to successful action planning?

- *Position, power, and influence*: Who has the ability to mobilize necessary resources and make change happen?

- *Track record*: Who has been involved in past successful change efforts?

- *Structure*: Who has responsibility for approving changes, and who will be impacted most by the changes?

- *Ideal involvement*: Explore the ideal and plan for the real while compensating as much as possible for gaps.

Either before or after decisions are made on involvement, a *change agent* or *change champion* should be appointed to assure that someone will have responsibility for leading any change effort. And, if necessary, appoint a *change team* to assist the change agent or change champion in planning and managing the change process. Change agent is another name for an OD practitioner. A change champion is a person at any level of the organization who is skilled at championing needed change and who in the action planning process is assigned the responsibility for assuring that planned actions are accomplished. A change team is often assembled to assist the leader of a change or improvement effort in planning and managing the change or improvement process. A change team is a team of representative people assigned to work with a change agent or change champion in helping plan and manage the change process and assure that planned actions are accomplished.

In some cases the change agent (OD practitioner) involved will lead the action planning and follow-through efforts, including leading a change team when one is involved. However, in most cases the change agent will facilitate and help guide the action planning and follow-through efforts and coach a change champion who is formally appointed to lead follow-through efforts. The actual names assigned to roles, such as change agent, change champion, and change team, will vary with different organizations depending on the names that best fit the culture of the organization.

**Evaluate and Prioritize Relevant Data** It takes a skilled OD practitioner to facilitate action planning meetings where data can be evaluated, prioritized, and turned into action plans. This is true of working with a small group like the top management team or in facilitating large-group meetings. Even highly experienced OD practitioners will have to do some or perhaps a great deal of planning to make an action planning meeting run smoothly. Some of the issues that must be considered in preparing for action planning follow:

- Who will facilitate the meeting or meetings (more than one facilitator may be required)?

- How much time is available in total and how much time will it take for each part of the process?

- Will the meeting include training, data feedback, and action planning or be totally devoted to action planning?

- What kind of a meeting room is necessary and what type of equipment is required?

- What will be done to prepare the participants to understand the big picture of the OD effort and to work effectively together?

- How will the data be presented and what processes or decision-making techniques will be used to evaluate and prioritize the data?

- Is the desired outcome of the action planning meeting to leave with completed plans or to allow a follow-up group to put the finishing touches on the plans?

The data used in action planning may be simplistic or sophisticated, and the process used to evaluate and prioritize data may range from easy-to-use and understand processes to far more complex processes. However, whatever the methodology used, the approach should be tailored to the particular audience and purpose selected. *It is also important to clarify the focus of change or improvement efforts (whole organization, group or inter-group, individual, structural, and technological) and to consider the level of desired change (fine-tuning, incremental, and transformational).* Once this is done, the evaluation and prioritization processes are likely to follow some variation of (1) discovering present realities, (2) considering future ideals or possibilities, and (3) evaluating and prioritizing alternatives for change.

**Agree on the Changes to Be Made** The key to choosing actions that will make a difference and have a high probability of being successful is to choose a *"few"* actions where the need, energy, or incentive to accomplish the action is high and to assure that changes are considered from a systems perspective. This approach usually takes skillful coaching and guidance from the OD practitioner to keep people focused, stress the importance of doing a few things well rather than many things poorly, and to understand the importance of systems thinking.

In regard to choosing a few actions, the action planning process tends to generate an abundance of ideas so the temptation is to over-commit on what can be accomplished. This raises the probability of failure no matter what follow-up process is used. It is important to consider that people are often already over-committed and have difficulty doing what is presently on their plates without adding more. Therefore, be selective in committing people to additional actions.

Systems thinking considers the big picture implications of actions chosen and the need to assure that current systems (anything in place that would support or undermine the success of a desired change or improvement) that would affect the desired outcome are aligned for support. For example, a change in structure may have significant cultural, interpersonal relations, and group relations implications. In the same way, present systems, such as reward systems, may not be aligned to support the desired change and may need to be adjusted.

**Develop a Change Strategy** Developing a change strategy for implementing the desired change is as important as the actual changes. Even the right changes implemented the wrong way will fail and may have far-reaching consequences for present and future change efforts. This important part of the action planning process can significantly increase the probability of success, not only of the action planning process but also of the entire OD process. It cannot be emphasized enough how essential this step is in action planning. It is the part of action planning where OD makes the most unique and strongest contribution, and yet it is also the part that is often left out altogether!

One way to begin developing a change strategy is to do a force-field analysis. This is a technique developed from the work of Kurt Lewin that analyzes the forces working for change and the forces working for maintaining the status quo or resisting change (Lewin, 1951). In its simplest form, this involves listing the forces working for and against the desired change and then planning ways to increase the forces for change and reducing the forces against change.

The next step is to plan the change. Ideally, you need four things to plan a change:

1. *A change model.* Figure 10.1 shows an example of a three-stage model for change (Warrick, 2005). Keep in mind if you use a three-stage model that these models recognize the dynamic nature of change and were never intended to be viewed as static or linear models of change (Schein, 1987).

2. *A change checklist* based on the selected change model. A checklist is useful in knowing what to consider in planning and implementing changes and is especially useful for those who may not be well trained in OD. Exhibit 10.6 provides an example based on the Warrick change model shown in Figure 10.1.

3. *A list of change principles* to assure that the change plans follow sound change principles. Change principles are valuable truths, lessons, or guidelines that are useful in planning and implementing changes. Examples would be
   - You must create compelling reasons to change to motivate change.
   - The incentive to change must be greater than the incentive to stay the
   - same.
   - How change is accomplished is as important as what changes are made. (An example of change principles has been placed on this book's website.)

4. *A change planning form* that provides a systematic way to plan the change. A change planning form should be brief and consistent with the change model and checklist. In most cases, one page will do for developing a general change plan. Some of the things that could be included on the change planning form are
   - Reasons for changing;
   - Who will champion the change;
   - The desired goals or outcomes; and
   - What will be done in each stage of change. (An example of a change planning form has been placed on this book's website.)

The four-step process for planning changes can be quickly learned and used by change agents, leaders, and others involved in planning changes. In fact, the

# Exhibit 10.6. Change Management Checklist

## Stage I—Preparation

### Exploration

1. Identify a need or opportunity for improvement or change.
2. Involve one or more change champions, change agents, a change team, or some combination of each in a preliminary needs assessment and consideration of alternatives for change.
3. Clearly identify the key stakeholders and explore ways to involve them in planning and managing the change process.
4. Build support and seed the organization for change (develop advocates, share information and ideas, etc.).
5. Contract for change by involving the appropriate people in designing and negotiating a change strategy that provides a clear vision of what has to be done.

### Diagnosis and Planning

6. Develop a plan for gathering the necessary data and information needed to clarify present realities and future ideals, and how to achieve the ideals.
7. Implement the diagnosis.
8. Utilize the results of the diagnosis for problem solving, action planning, and modifying the change strategy.

### Commitment Building

9. Clarify the roles of the key players in the change process (change leaders, change agents, change champions, and change teams) and involve each as much as would be appropriate in the design and implementation of the change program.
10. Communicate the change vision to the appropriate people who can impact or will be impacted by the changes, educate them on the change process, involve them when appropriate in the change process, and address their concerns and suggestions.

## Stage II—Implementation

### Managed Change

11. Educate and train the key players in the paradigms (thinking patterns and models) and skills needed to implement the changes.
12. Select and implement the appropriate strategies and changes.
13. Manage resistance to change.
14. Build in reliable feedback mechanisms to monitor and manage the change process and make necessary adjustments.
15. Keep people focused on the vision.

## Stage III—Transition

### Planned Follow-Through

16. Ensure that enabling structures are aligned to facilitate and reinforce the desired changes. A team could be appointed to carry out this important task.
17. Ensure that the change is accomplished, supported, and sustained.
18. Reinforce, reward, and communicate successes; learn from mistakes or failures; make adjustments; keep people informed about program progress; and integrate changes into the culture.

### Change Evaluation

19. Conduct a follow-up diagnosis and use the results to evaluate the program, improvements, and opportunities for further improvement, and what can be learned from the change process.

### Renewal

20. Develop a renewal plan for maintaining the gains, planning future actions and improvements, sharing what has been learned with other parts of the organization, monitoring progress, and being prepared to respond quickly to the need for new directions.

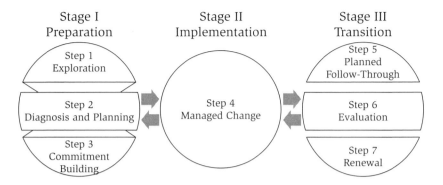

**Figure 10.1.** The Planned Change Process

ideal situation is for an organization to develop its own change model, checklist, principles, and planning form that can be used throughout the organization and by doing so make the change planning process a way of life in the organization.

**Clarify Roles and Follow-Through Responsibilities** The final step in the action planning process is to ensure that follow-through roles and responsibilities are clear. Exhibit 10.7 shows the typical roles that must be covered in change efforts. It is important to keep in mind that—depending on the scale of the change and the training and skills of available resources—one or more persons may play multiple roles and not all roles are needed for all changes. In fact, the roles required and the persons fulfilling the roles may change throughout a change effort.

In evaluating the roles that need to be filled, consider that a *change agent* (OD practitioner) should be engaged in action planning when a specialist is needed to guide the change effort or to serve in an advisory capacity. Change agents can be internal or external to the organization or a combination of both. A *change leader* is a person in a leadership position whose involvement and support are important in achieving the desired change. A *change champion*, as mentioned previously, is an internal person who is responsible for championing the change effort and who works with a change agent or has enough training or natural skills to lead a change effort. When a leader also assumes the role of change champion, the change effort is greatly accelerated. A *change team*, as you may recall, consists of the appropriate combination of change agents, change champions, change leaders, and key stakeholders who are responsible for planning, managing, and championing the change effort. Some members may be regular attendees at change team meetings, and others, such as leaders or change agents, may be involved when needed. A *change supporter* is a person who supports a change effort by being as involved as needed and by encouraging the front-line players in change efforts.

## Exhibit 10.7. Roles in Successfully Managing Change

*Change Agent:* A person who is a specialist in organization development and change.

*Change Leader:* A person in a leadership position who can significantly influence the success or failure of a change effort and provide the support and the leadership necessary for change to succeed.

*Change Champion:* A person who champions needed changes. An organization needs to develop change champions at all levels of the organization. However, it is particularly important to have change champions at the top.

*Change Team:* A team that is responsible for planning, managing, monitoring, and championing a change effort.

*Change Supporter:* A person who supports needed changes in attitude and actions, offers valuable assistance in accomplishing change, and encourages the change agents, leaders, and change champions.

Note: The same person may play multiple roles in some situations, several people may occupy a role, and while at least one Change Champion is always needed, Change Agents and Change Teams may or may not be needed depending on the nature of the change.

What roles are needed and what they are called depend on the needs and culture of the organization. However, whoever is involved in leading the change effort must ensure that the roles that are needed are adequately covered and that a good balance is achieved between too much and too little involvement and too much and too little delegation when considering those who have roles. It is also important to keep the change process and involvement as stream-lined and results-oriented as possible, while avoiding any tendencies to create a change bureaucracy that impedes rather than facilitates change.

# IMPLEMENTATION

In the change process, assessment plays an essential role in assessing present realities and future possibilities. Action planning plays a very valuable role in planning changes so that they have a high probability of success. However, implementation would be considered by many OD practitioners as the most important role. If changes are not successfully implemented, the rest of the change process will count for little.

Six steps are recommended for the implementation process (see Exhibit 10.1):

1. Keep the big picture in mind.

2. Choose the right interventions.

3. Use a sound change model to plan and manage the change process.

4. Keep people engaged and make the incentive for change greater than the incentive to stay the same.

5. Identify and manage resistance to change.

6. Follow through and learn from the process.

When implementation is done well, it energizes people, results in needed changes, and produces confidence in the change process. However, it is also filled with many challenges, as conditions may frequently change and guiding changes to successful completion requires considerable skill and persistence.

## Keep the Big Picture in Mind

Keeping the big picture in mind in implementing changes has several meanings in OD. First, always have the end goal in mind in everything you do in OD. The end goal has been defined differently, but usually describes some variation of increasing the health, effectiveness, and self-renewing capabilities of the organization. Keeping the end in mind gives purpose to everything you do and can create opportunities that might be overlooked. For example, leadership development can be turned into interventions in the organization by having each participant commit to one personal, team, and organizational improvement. Or a seminar on stress management can be turned into an opportunity for improving the organization by evaluating what the organization is doing that stresses employees most.

Another aspect of keeping the big picture in mind is having a *systems perspective*. Seeing the big picture from a systems perspective has always been one of the major contributions of OD. *Stated in simple terms, systems thinking as applied to OD means viewing organizations as whole systems with many interacting parts and recognizing that a change in one area of a system is likely to result in changes in other areas, and changes in one area are not likely to be sustained without support in other areas.* Understanding systems thinking is very helpful in implementing changes. For example, it is important to understand that a change in one part of the organization may affect other parts of the organization; that a change in technology may also affect individual, group, and whole organization behavior; or that a structural change may also result in a cultural change.

## Choose the Right Interventions

Some changes require basic interventions that can be performed by HR specialists, change champions, or consultants trained in a few fundamental interventions. Most, however, and especially large-scale changes, require multiple interventions guided by skilled and knowledgeable OD practitioners. One way to think about interventions is to think of them as fitting into *individual, group*, or *organization interventions*. In this classification group, interventions would include inter-group activities and organization interventions would include inter-organization activities. A list of possible interventions organized by this classification is shown in Exhibit 10.8. A number of other classifications are available for your consideration (for example, see Massarik & Pei-Carpenter, 2002, p. 120; French & Bell, 1999, p. 165; and Cummings & Worley, 2005, p. 147).

In choosing interventions, two things are especially important to consider. In today's fast-moving environment where pressures to perform are high and time is scarce, it is important to *strategically plan involvement and activities to economize the time of participants*. For example, brief brainstorming meetings can be held to generate ideas, while a smaller group or even a change agent can be used to analyze and summarize the results. Also, *using or inventing interventions that will accelerate the change process* is also important. One way to do this is to combine activities. For instance, OD strategies can be thought of as *inside-out strategies* (focusing on individuals, then groups, and then the whole organization), *outside-in strategies* (focusing on the organization, then groups, and then individuals), or *integrative strategies* (focusing on individuals, groups, and organizations simultaneously).

In the early days of OD, it was not uncommon to move from developing leaders (individual change), to developing groups (group change), to developing organizations (organization change) and to take several years or more to do so. This process can be greatly accelerated by an integrative approach whereby all of these areas are addressed simultaneously, with many activities addressing all three areas.

## Use a Sound Change Model and Action Plan to Manage the Change Process

This part of the implementation process includes using the previously developed action plan that was developed around a sound change model to guide and manage the change process and adapting the plan to changing conditions. For smaller projects this may be as simple as having a change agent or change champion use and modify the action plan to manage the change process and keep the appropriate people informed and involved. For larger or more complex changes, the responsibility for managing the change process would likely be the responsibility of a change team.

One of the often overlooked keys to successfully implementing changes and managing the change process is to build into the process feedback mechanisms so you will know what is working and what is not. *It is not uncommon for changes to not be working and for those who initiated or are managing the change to be unaware of how the changes that made such good sense to them are being experienced*. Issues that could have been identified with good feedback mechanisms and quickly addressed and resolved go undetected for months, years, or more and often leave a path of unresolved issues, demoralization, and distrust of any future changes. Feedback mechanisms could include, for example:

**Exhibit 10.8. Types of OD Interventions**

| Individual Interventions to Improve Individual Health and Effectiveness | Organization, Inter-Organization, and Trans-Organization Interventions to Improve Organizational Health and Effectiveness |
|---|---|
| • Leader development and training in OD and change management | • Organization assessment, feedback, action planning, and improvements |
| • Change agent and change champion training and coaching | • Organization change programs within organizations |
| • Leader assessments, feedback, counseling, coaching, succession planning, and life and career planning | • Organization change programs between organizations |
| • Conflict resolution between individuals | • Trans-organization development programs |
| • Individual role clarification | • Organization transformation programs |
| • Using self-awareness tools | • Organization visioning, goal setting, and strategic planning |
| • T-groups and other self-awareness training | • Force-field analysis applied to organizations |
| • Gestalt OD applied to individuals | • Culture change programs |
| • Grid OD phase 1 | • Large scale systems change |
| | • Grid OD phases 4, 5, and 6 |
| | • Process and systems improvement efforts |
| | • Efforts to create learning organizations |
| | • Efforts to create more innovative organizations |
| | • Organization design, alignment, and restructuring |
| | • Appreciative–inquiry applied to organizations |
| | • SOAR approach to strategic planning |
| | • Gestalt OD applied to organizations |
| | • Sociotechnical systems applied to organizations |
| | • Future search conferences |
| | • Parallel learning structures |

## Group and Inter-Group Interventions to Improve Group Health and Effectiveness

- Facilitating various team meetings and activities
- Team training and development
- Team assessments, feedback, action planning, and improvements
- Team building within teams
- Team building between teams
- Team visioning, goal setting, and strategic planning
- Process consultation
- Force-field analysis applied to groups
- Team and team member role analysis
- Team conflict resolution
- Large group methods
- Appreciative—inquiry applied to groups
- Gestalt OD applied to groups
- Sociotechnical systems for groups
- Grid OD phases 2 and 3

- Periodic surveys, interviewing people impacted by changes, or occasional focus group interviews;
- Having key people appointed and given the responsibility for monitoring changes;
- Involving people affected by change on change teams responsible for managing changes; or
- Involving leaders more closely in the change process so they know first-hand.

## Keep People Engaged

Anyone who has been involved in making changes knows how challenging it is to keep people engaged in the change process. Leaders get busy and preoccupied with other tasks, key players often have too much on their plates to stay focused and carry out their responsibilities, and changes in leadership can present major obstacles to keeping changes alive.

Some things can be done to keep people engaged. Early wins, especially ones that are visible and have tangible benefits, are very important to target so the change process will have credibility. Keeping key people informed about progress is also important. Often only those directly involved in the change process are aware of any progress being made. Communications is also important when things are not going well and there is a need for leaders to energize the change process or to involve the appropriate people in addressing issues. It is also important to frequently remind people of the change purpose and goals and what needs to be done, and to be a cheerleader in encouraging, recognizing, and motivating people for their efforts.

An area that is seldom addressed in the change process but that is extremely important in keeping people engaged and involved is to explore ways to make the incentive for change greater than the incentive to stay the same. *The reality is that many if not most changes are only designed to benefit the organization and often simply translate to more work and no benefits for those involved in or affected by the change.* Add to this the fact that, because most changes are poorly managed and are likely to not be successful, there is little incentive to become or stay involved. Simply stated, those involved in initiating, planning, and managing change need to strongly consider ways they can make the incentive for change greater than the incentive to stay the same. The incentive for change could involve challenging and worthy goals, knowing that changes include improving working conditions, providing tangible incentives, or having those affected by change explore possible incentives. It is particularly important to provide opportunities during the change process for people to evaluate ways to reduce workload, unnecessary bureaucracy, busywork, and other unproductive activities, and to provide opportunities to think, plan, and share ideas.

# Identify and Manage Resistance to Change

There are, of course, many reasons why people resist change. Some prefer the status quo to having to adapt to something new. Some resist for the sake of resisting. Some may resist for political, ideological, or self-serving reasons. Most resisters, however, resist for perfectly logical reasons: most changes are not successful, the reasons for change are not made clear, the leaders are not vested in making the change succeed, and so on. Exhibit 10.9 shows a number of reasons why people are likely to resist change. It should be clear from this list that, while leaders tend to label some resisters as if they are the problem, most of the resistance comes from poorly managed change.

It is not enough to know why people resist change. It is also important to take a proactive approach to overcoming resistance to change. Exhibit 10.9 also shows a number of ways to overcome resistance to change. Most if not all of these ways are simply ways to manage change right in the first place, which will quickly

### Exhibit 10.9. Why People Resist Change and Overcoming Resistance to Change

**Why People Resist Change**

- Lack of vision and purpose regarding the change
- Organizational memory about past change efforts
- Leaders not effectively leading or supporting the change
- Lack of involvement in the change process
- Lack of incentive to change
- Fear of unknown
- Personal threat or possible loss
- Work overload
- Change overload
- Ideological differences or concerns
- Political or self-serving reasons
- Lack of resources or institutional support
- Lack of skills to make the needed change
- Lack of information
- Poor timing

**Overcoming Resistance to Change**

- Communicate compelling reasons for change
- Demonstrate visible and convincing leadership involvement and support
- Appoint a capable and respected champion
- Involve key stakeholders and contributors
- Make the incentive for change greater than the incentive to stay the same
- Educate, train, and prepare people for change
- Communicate, regarding the vision and progress
- Listen to and address concerns and obstacles
- Use assessments and data to motivate change
- Target early wins and use pilot projects to gain confidence
- Be sensitive to time and action requirements
- Take a positive approach to dealing with issues and resistance, but know when to bite the bullet

break down resistance and give people greater incentives to become involved in changes and make changes succeed.

One other thing should be noted about resistance to change. While some resistance is natural and logical and some resisters should be listened to, continued resistance that undermines the change process should be dealt with, and earlier better than later when it has already taken its toll and gathered reinforcements. Naturally, taking a positive approach, such as trying to win the resisters over or inviting possible solutions to their objections, is preferred. However, at some point leaders must be leaders and confront and deal with the resistance and consider consequences for continued non-compliance.

## Follow Through and Learn from the Process

This last phase of the implementation process is perhaps the most obvious and yet least practiced. It takes considerable discipline and perseverance to assure that changes succeed and will last, and considerable persuading of the leaders to stay with the process until the desired goals are achieved, and especially to take the time to learn from the process.

In addition to following through and achieving the desired changes, this phase requires building in ways to sustain changes. Sustaining changes for whatever period they need to be sustained requires having those who were guiding the change take responsibility for sustaining changes or appointing a person specifically for the purpose of sustaining changes. Unfortunately, if no one is paying attention to the need to sustain changes, the organization often regresses back to the former state before the changes, and it confirms for many that efforts to change won't be successful.

Another important phase of the implementation process is to evaluate the change process and what has been accomplished and what remains to be accomplished, and to use this valuable information to learn from and improve on the process, share what was learned with others, and plan for future actions that are needed. It is the practice of the military to debrief and learn from activities, but private and public-sector organizations rarely engage in this important practice.

It should be apparent by now that effectively implementing changes is hard work! However, it should also be apparent that when managed well, the probability of successful change can be quite high and the benefits to an organization and the people in them quite substantial. How effectively organizations implement change can affect their competitive advantage and even their survival. Knowing how to effectively implement change is a skill set that is so important that, like many OD skills, it should be taught to leaders as well as OD practitioners.

# SUMMARY

The Launch phase of OD is the heart of OD. Discovering present realities and future possibilities can be fascinating, making it possible to focus on the right things to improve the health, effectiveness, and self-renewing capabilities of an organization. Action planning can be very energizing, as you now have an opportunity to develop plans that can make a difference and know that, if the plan is designed around a sound change process, the probability for success is quite high. Implementing change is without a doubt the most challenging phase of the Launch process. While it can be a difficult and constantly changing endeavor, with knowledgeable implementers who are capable of selecting and facilitating appropriate interventions and who are guiding the implementation process using a sound action plan, the probability of success is again quite high. In short, Launch is a critical part of the change process, and how it is managed will make or break changes.

# References

Beckhard, R. (1969). *Organization development: Strategies and models*. Reading, MA: Addison-Wesley.

Beckhard, R., & Harris, R. (1977). *Organization transitions: Managing complex change*. Reading, MA: Addison-Wesley.

Bunker, B.B., & Alban, B.T. (1997). *Large group interventions*. San Francisco: Jossey-Bass.

Burke, W. (2008). *Organization change*. Thousand Oaks, CA: Sage.

Cameron, K. (2008). *Positive leadership: Strategies for extraordinary performance*. San Francisco: Berrett-Koehler.

Church, A.H., & Waclawski, J. (1998). *Designing and using organizational surveys*. San Francisco: Jossey-Bass.

Collins, J. (2001). *Good to great*. New York: Harper Business.

Collins, J., & Porras, J. (1994). *Built to last: Successful habits of visionary companies*. New York: Harper Business.

Cooperrider, D.L., Whitney, D., & Stavros, J. (2008). *Appreciative inquiry handbook*. Brunswick, OH: Crown Custom Publishing, and San Francisco: Berrett-Koehler.

Cummings, T.G., & Worley, C.G. (2005). *Organization development and change*. Cincinnati, OH: South-Western College.

*Fortune*. America's most admired companies, The global companies most admired, and The 100 best companies to work for. [printed annually]

French, W., & Bell, C. (1999). *Organization development*. Upper Saddle River, NJ: Prentice Hall.

Hamel, G., & Prahalad, C.K. (1995). *Competing for the future*. Boston, MA: Harvard Business School Press.

Holman, P., Devane, T., & Cady, S. (2007). *The change handbook*. San Francisco: Berrett-Koehler.

Kotter, J. (2009). *A sense of urgency*. Boston, MA: Harvard Business Press.

Kotter, J. (1976). *Organization dynamics and intervention*. Reading, MA: Addison-Wesley.

Lewin, K. (1951). *Field theory in social science*. New York: Harper & Row.

Massarik, F., & Pei-Carpenter, M. (2002). *Organization development and consulting*. San Francisco: Pfeiffer.

Nadler, D.A. (1977). *Feedback and organization development: Using data-based methods*. Reading, MA: Addison-Wesley.

Slater, R. (2001). *Get better or get beaten! 29 secrets from GE's Jack Welch*. New York: McGraw-Hill.

Schein, E. (1987). *Process consultation: Vol. 2. Its role in organization development*. Reading, MA: Addison-Wesley.

Warrick, D.D. (2005). Organization development from the view of the experts. In W.J. Rothwell & R. Sullivan (Eds.), *Practicing organization development* (2nd ed.). San Francisco: Pfeiffer.

Weisbord, M.R. (1978). *Organization diagnosis: A workbook of theory and practice*. Reading, MA: Addison-Wesley.

# CHAPTER ELEVEN

# Situational Evaluation

Steven H. Cady, Julie Auger, and Marguerite Foxon

*Did it work … was it worth our time and
money … are we better off … what next?*
Leader

The question "Did it work?" addresses the age-old issue of cause and effect. A person or group develops an intervention. One or more people agree to pay money while allocating time and energy for implementation. Efforts are made to evaluate its impact. As organizations evolve, dramatic events and trends sweep the world, new technologies emerge, profit margins shrink, market demographics change, competition ebbs and flows … leaders are exerting more and more pressure to see the value-added of interventions.

Evaluation in an organizational setting examines the impact of an intervention—an intentional action taken to create change in a system. Interventions can be proactive or reactive, and they come in a variety of forms: training sessions, social programs, policy creation, education initiatives, strategic planning, organization redesign or restructuring, cost-cutting initiatives, new product development, life and career coaching, succession planning, implementing or upgrading technology, and more. We ask ourselves, "Was it worth our time? Are we better off? What's next?" In seeking to answer these evaluation questions, we uncover layers of complicating issues.

In this chapter, we provide a foundation for you to initiate an evaluation or take your evaluation process to the next level. We begin with a review, examine a paradox we uncovered, provide a model for selecting an evaluation strategy, and then propose a simple step-by-step evaluation process.

# THREE ROOTS OF EVALUATION

Evaluation has a unique history. The need to evaluate the impact of interventions is not the domain of one field or industry. Some industries deliver a product or service, and some support the delivery. When looking at supporting disciplines, it is often said, "When times get tough, HR, OD, training [etc.] is the first budget to get cut." Others argue that it is in tough times that these functions are the most important. This is where evaluation comes into play. Over the past fifty-plus years, evaluation has emerged in three distinct fields or disciplines.

## Education and Social Programs

Before the 1940s, evaluation was primarily used to assess education and was performed mostly by university affiliated social science researchers (Russ-Eft & Preskill, 2001).

In the 1840s Horace Mann, a member of the Boston Board of Education, led the way by not only evaluating student achievement but also teacher and institutional effectiveness (University of Chicago Press, 1886). Evaluations in education became uniform, and by the 1930s many states had a variety of state-wide-standardized tests. In 1942, Ralph Tyler, referred to as the father of educational objectives, introduced a multi-purpose model of educational program evaluation based on the notion of identified behavioral objectives (Scriven, 1991). Under Tyler, the focus moved from student outcomes and test norms to using evaluation as a tool for process improvement (Russ-Eft & Preskill, 2001).

With the emergence of social programs following the Depression and World War II, the government's push for assessment of these programs sparked research in evaluation. Yet the use of evaluation as standard protocol for programs did not come about until Senator Robert Kennedy led the passing of a bill requiring the measurement of success of government-funded programs. Consequently, after 1965 the field of evaluation began to grow in all disciplines. Gradually, major universities began to establish programs teaching evaluation. The American Evaluation Association was founded in 1985 and remains the major evaluation professional association today.

## Organization Development

Decades earlier, Frederick Taylor had begun to direct his attention to the business community. As early as 1893, Taylor focused on management's responsibility to develop an efficient workforce in the manufacturing world. Marvin Weisbord refers to Taylor's rational systems technique as "Taylorism" and describes Taylor's book *The Principles of Scientific Measurement* (1911) as possibly "the first ever human resources textbook" (Weisbord, 2005, p. 3).

Kurt Lewin, a refugee from Nazi Germany, played a significant role in the early stages of OD evaluation (Beckhard, 1997). Lewin shifted attention from an individual to a group dynamics approach in developing "action research" (Cady & Caster, 2000). After World War II, he began studying individual behaviors in relation to social dynamics and the environment. Along with Ronald Lippitt, Lewin researched the effects of leadership style on group dynamics. Their conclusion that group behavior rather than individual variation produced change led to the creation of T-groups (Lewin, 1946). The National Training Lab was then formed in order to evaluate and teach change and motivation methods in groups or T-groups. From this came action research, a data-based reflective approach for progressive problem solving. What it omitted, however, was an evaluation of the improvement process (Beckhard, 1997; Kleiner, 1996).

In the 1960s and 1970s, Robert Stake's responsive evaluation approach looked through the lens of the audience and their intended use for information. He used the term "stakeholders" and focused on program success and on improving the process (Stake, 1975). At the same time, Michael Scriven proposed goal-free evaluation with its emphasis on actual outcomes and not the intended outcomes. Scriven coined the terms "summative and formative evaluation" to describe two approaches to data collection and recognized the need to integrate both identity standards and performance data (Russ-Eft & Preskill, 2001; Scriven, 1991).

At the organizational level, a collaborative approach has been integrated into the evaluative process over the past fifteen years. For example, Michael Patton's (1997) utilization-focused evaluation guides organizations in making decisions about evaluation purpose, design, and focus, as well as what data should be collected and who should be involved. Patton strongly advocates collaboration between the evaluator and the intended user of the findings in the organization.

## Training and Development

In 1959, Donald Kirkpatrick published a series of articles outlining his four levels of evaluation to assess the effectiveness of training (Kirkpatrick, 1969). His *Evaluating Training Programs: The Four Levels* (1998) is an updated version of his approach and can be adapted to the systems thinking of OD. Each level brings a deeper and more rigorous measurement standard and analysis of training programs. Both summative and formative forms of data collection are used. Jack Phillips added a fifth level, measuring return on investment (ROI), expressed as a cost-benefit ratio analysis. Phillips' Level 5 addresses an organization's accountability for the outcomes of training (Phillips, 1996). Both Kirkpatrick's four levels and Phillips' Level 5 are discussed later in the chapter.

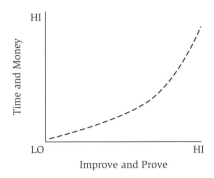

**Figure 11.1.** The Paradox of Competing Demands in Evaluation

# THE PARADOX OF COMPETING DEMANDS

Curious about what the evaluation community is focused on today, we conducted a review of blogs, discussion boards, and literature in practice and research. There seems to be an underlying assumption that, in an ideal world, it is best to perform rigorous high-quality evaluations of all interventions. Yet, a theme in the dialogue presents competing demands suggesting that this is not practical (see Figure 11.1): *prove and improve* versus *time and money*.

## Prove and Improve

When considering the "why" or purpose of an evaluation, it boils down to two aims. First, *prove* that the intervention worked. Proving is important to those who are responsible for the intervention's impact. In some cases, it is about accountability for results, and in others it's about making the business case. Here are some key factors that influence the need to prove the intervention's impact:

- The number of stakeholders connected to the intervention;
- Funding opportunities for the future of the intervention;
- Legal and governmental oversight for the intervention; and
- Political implications, posturing, and debate surrounding the intervention.

The second "why" is to evaluate an intervention in order to *improve* it for the future. A future focus is based on a need to understand how interventions work, identify the relative importance of a technique or method, advance theories, and create more robust approaches to change. Here are some key factors that influence the need to improve an intervention for the future:

- The potential impact of the intervention on key decisions and next steps;

- The number of iterations or times the intervention will be used in the future;
- Intended use of the intervention in other settings; and
- The comprehensive impact of the intervention on the health of people or the system.

## Time and Money

Conducting evaluations can be costly for all stakeholders involved. And this means time and money. If either or both are too high, it may lead the client and the consultant to decide against conducting an evaluation altogether. In terms of *time*, leaders will need to pull people away in order to fill out evaluations, be interviewed, and provide data. Here are key time and money factors to consider:

- The detail going into the design, data collection, and reporting;
- Requirements of leadership and management in the evaluation process;
- Who else needs to be involved in the evaluation and how; and
- The number of projects and initiatives that are under way.

Some interventions produce outcomes that are not easily measured; to do so takes *money*. Move up to higher levels of evaluation and you will find the required sophistication often surpasses the expertise of those responsible for the intervention. Here are some factors to consider:

- Opportunity costs in the form of lost revenues from doing the evaluation;
- The consulting fees and staffing costs;
- Technology and software required; and
- Materials and other supplies.

## The Competing Demands

The paradox is that, as an organization wishes to increase the *proving and improving* of an intervention, it will cost more in terms of *time and money*. Which do you choose: the intervention or the evaluation? Are they not one and the same?

On one hand, there is a costly intervention that has important implications for the organization or community. If there are long-term plans for the intervention, then the intended impact is vital to the future. Further, continued funding will depend on demonstrating results in some objective fashion. On the other hand, evaluation will take time away from implementing the intervention. There is no money in the budget allocated to the evaluation. Some believe that funds would be better spent on additional interventions. Some might even argue that evaluation is not necessary and it does not add value to the intervention. It is just a bureaucratic mechanism for show. The perception is that the outcomes of the process are so obvious it is not necessary to conduct an evaluation.

These competing demands have implications for the level of evaluation conducted. Think of levels in terms of invasiveness or how far or deep the evaluation goes. Two particularly user-friendly models are Kirkpatrick's Four Levels of Evaluation (1998) and Phillips' ROI (1996). While originally intended for the field of training, they have been applied to a variety of change initiatives (Russ-Eft, Bober, de la Taja, Foxon, & Koszalka, 2008). Consider the following in terms of before and after an intervention:

- Level 1: reaction—how satisfied are people?
- Level 2: learning—what do people know?
- Level 3: behavior—what are people doing?
- Level 4: results—what outcomes have been achieved?
- Level 5: return—what monies have been generated compared with what was spent?

While the higher levels provide more improving and proving data, they also cost more in terms of time and money. Some may argue that it is unrealistic to expect practitioners to conduct comprehensive evaluations in every situation. They would argue that one should settle for evidence rather than seek proof (Kirkpatrick, 1977). In this case, the evaluation will need to be less rigorous and less formal, while in other cases, it will be more formal and more rigorous. Table 11.1 provides examples of what quantitative and qualitative evaluations would look like for each level of evaluation.

The scope of Levels 1 and 2 includes participants in the moment (view top of Figure 11.2). An example would be satisfaction surveys and quick multiple-choice testing done in the classroom during a training program. The scope focuses on the *specific* training program in isolation from the application context. Level 3 brings the evaluation into the organizational setting, by evaluating whether the initiative when implemented leads to actual change beyond reaction and learning. However, it doesn't indicate if there are benefits to organizational processes and productivity. Levels 4 and 5 provide that scope of data because they move from evaluating the specifics of an intervention to examining the intervention's impact on the *whole* organization.

The challenge to be resolved is for evaluation to be fully utilized as a practical tool in the organizational toolkit. Consider utilization trends. Practitioners agree that Level 4 and 5 evaluations are the most desirable, yet they appear to be the least done. Twenty years ago, Foxon (1989) found that 30 percent of training practitioners considered evaluation to be one "of the most vexing problems" of the job (p. 89). She found that more than 75 percent of organizations conducted

Table 11.1. Quantitative and Qualitative Evaluation Examples

| Evaluation | Informal—Less Rigorous | Formal—More Rigorous |
|---|---|---|
| **Level 1 - Reaction** | *Quantitative* – Prepare a quick flip chart survey with 2 to 3 scaled questions and 1 to 2 open-ended questions seeking feedback on aspects of the intervention. Ask participants and leaders to give you a verbal satisfaction score between 0 and 10. <br><br> *Qualitative* – Hold a group debrief at the intervention's close to gain general feedback on items of interest such as usefulness, what work worked well or not well. Ask the leaders and those who approved the intervention if they are happy with how things are going and what they think. Take some notes down, debrief with key stakeholders team, and make a list of themes that seem relevant. | *Quantitative* – Conduct a survey with Likert-scaled and open-ended questions, along with demographics, administered at the end of the session. Choose validated survey questions. Consider doing a pre- and post-assessment to get at the change in attitudes and beliefs about the intervention. <br><br> *Qualitative* – Conduct structured interviews or focus groups to gain feedback and assess reactions to the intervention. The data is taped, transcribed, analyzed using qualitative analysis procedures and software. Panels are used to categorize responses to ensure reliability. |
| **Level 2 - Learning** | *Quantitative* – Administer a simple quiz on a flip chart or verbally given to check the understanding or awareness (e.g., critical data, key skills, etc.). Conduct spot checks throughout the organization to see what people know and have learned. Quantify the assessment by percentages of those who answered the questions correctly. <br><br> *Qualitative* – Observe performance in practice activities such as informal groups, role-plays, town hall meetings, etc. Ask people what they have learned. Ask questions with groups or individuals to assess comprehension. Take some notes on what people are getting out of or know about the change initiative (i.e., intervention). | *Quantitative* – Develop a formal test that is piloted for reliability and validity. Randomly administer the test across the organization to ensure it is a representative sample. Again, do pre- and post-assessment of a change in knowledge, competencies, awareness, etc. <br><br> *Qualitative* – Provide a team with a stretch assignment as a form of action learning to assess learning of skill and knowledge in an applied setting. Two trained observers rate performance in role-plays or activities according to performance criteria. Inter-rater reliability is established. Observe post-training performance using a checklist to assess mastery of skill or process. Experts agree on pass/fail score. |

**Table 11.1. Quantitative and Qualitative Evaluation Examples**

| Evaluation | Informal—Less Rigorous | Formal—More Rigorous |
|---|---|---|
| **Level 3 – Behavior** | *Quantitative* – Distribute a short survey listing the intervention objectives or topic areas and ask them to check any they are using. Provide examples of key behaviors and get participants to check off what they are doing now compared to before. Do a straw poll in meetings or in other informal situations.<br><br>*Qualitative* – Evaluate 'by walking around,' observing, engaging in conversation, talking with participants' managers, to subjectively assess how much performance change has occurred since the training. Reconvene the trainees for a group discussion about how much they are applying. | *Quantitative* – Observe each individual using a detailed checklist prepared by experts (e.g., to assess transfer of learning about operating equipment). Administer 360 tools to assess behavior change by comparing pre- and post-intervention profiles. Measure key behaviors at Time 1 and Time 2.<br><br>*Qualitative* – Undertake structured interviews of participants and managers in relation to application of specific skill and knowledge. Specific instances of application required. Determine the frequencies of comments in order to quantify or ascertain changes in behaviors that are the focus of the intervention. |
| **Level 4 – Results** | *Quantitative* – Email participants asking them to report outcomes or organizational results from the intervention. Obtain some quick measures from spot checks related to goals or intended outcomes of the intervention.<br><br>*Qualitative* – Ask managers if they have noticed any outcomes that can be traced to the intervention. Gather some quick stories, testimonials, and other examples that appear to support the positive, negative, or neutral impact. | *Quantitative* - Use a short survey to identify those whose application of the training has had an impact. Collect results-oriented data pre- and post-intervention to show impact. Use longitudinal analysis to show a change over time.<br><br>*Qualitative* – Build on the quantitative analysis above. Interview these respondents to validate and quantify the extent of the impact. Provide action-learning projects with built-in metrics for tracking progress and results. Monitor progress by meeting with team members, checking metrics, reviewing project outcomes. Use the Success Case Method (Brinkerhoff, 2003) to analyze impact cases' and illustrate value to organization. |

only Level 1 evaluations. More recent data suggest little has changed. Rossett (2007) reports that Level 1 to 4 evaluations are being conducted 94 percent, 34 percent, 13 percent, and 3 percent of the time, respectively.

# CHOOSING AN EVALUATION STRATEGY

Figure 11.2 addresses the challenge of competing demands. It is based on the notion of satisficing—pick the best of the least best alternatives, while doing no harm. The model proposes that there are combinations of rigor and scope.

The higher the rigor, the more formal and planned the evaluation. It can be argued that, in these cases, the results are valid and reliable. As for scope, the more whole the focus, the more the evaluation moves beyond examining the participants' experience to the intervention's impact on the entire system. These options provide the practitioner with four basic evaluation strategies:

- **Crude:** In this evaluation strategy, an informal and imprecise evaluation is conducted, most likely at Level 1 and 2. It is unlikely that a Level 3 would be conducted. Use this strategy when there is an interest in the performance of the specific intervention with individuals participating in the process, but less concern with proving or demonstrating the impact. For example, you want to assess reactions to a coaching seminar (Level 1) and check if the coaching model is understood (Level 2). You might

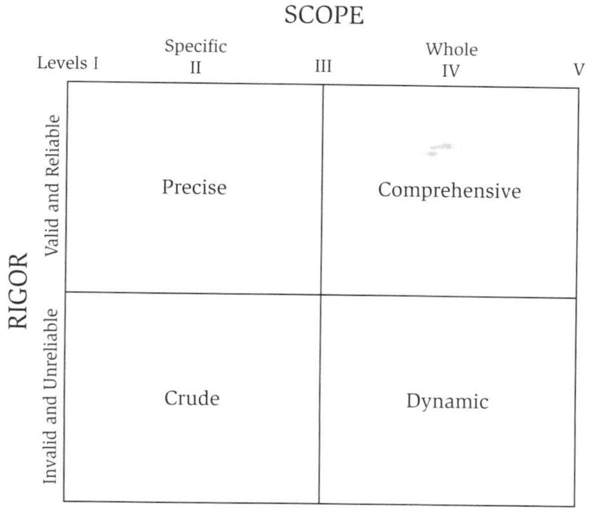

**Figure 11.2.** Four Evaluation Strategies

use three questions on a flip chart to assess satisfaction, and ask them to write down the coaching model components to check learning.

- **Precise:** This is a more formal and narrowly focused strategy. The evaluation is more robust and the results can be tested for reliability and validity. This may include a Level 3 evaluation. The focus is on examining the specific application of the intervention with no regard for how the whole system is impacted. In the case of our coaching seminar, this might involve carefully constructed formal surveys to assess reactions (Level 1) and application after six weeks (Level 3), and a standardized test at the course close (Level 2). Participants' reactions, learning, and post-course performance are assessed; the data and results are validated with a report provided.

- **Dynamic:** With this strategy, it becomes a more complex or organic mix of rigor and scope. The intention is to formally prove the intervention has specifically impacted individuals, while informally understanding how to improve the intervention's broader connection to the whole organization. It is not intended to validate the fact that the intervention has impacted the entire system, yet information is needed by the designers to make important improvements for the future. The first two to three levels of evaluation are therefore undertaken in a formal and precise fashion, with less formality and precision used for Levels 4 and 5. For example, in collecting Level 4 and 5 data about the coaching seminar, the evaluator may walk around the organization noticing things, asking questions, seeking personal input about the perceived impact of the coaching approach. The evaluator may make some assumptions about impact, estimate the cost savings and revenue generation, and estimate an ROI.

- **Comprehensive:** This strategy, just as the name implies, is the most invasive and extreme. The evaluation in this quadrant seeks robust data needed to make high-leverage improvements in the intervention while also proving its impact on the whole system, including its ROI. In other words, how effective is the coaching seminar, how can it be made more effective, what measurable difference has it made to the whole organization, and what costs have been saved or revenues generated because of the seminar? All five levels of evaluation are done in the most formal and valid fashion. It will be well documented and most likely conducted by research-trained professionals.

Which of the four strategies do you pick? By incorporating the competing demands, we propose the Situational Evaluation Model to assist in the decision making. It is based on the premise that each situation has a unique combination of demands that require a customized solution. The model identifies four

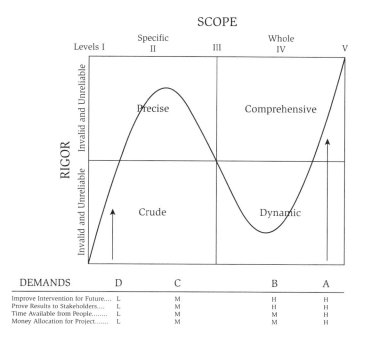

**Figure 11.3.** A Situational Evaluation Model for Assessing Interventions

degrees of demand with "A" being the most demanding. We added a curved line to the model to simplify the strategy selection process (see Figure 11.3). Draw a line straight up from "A" and you hit the curved line in the upper-right-hand quadrant (Comprehensive). In the lowest degree of demand, you find "D" and a vertical line intersects with the line in the lower-left-hand quadrant (Crude). The model provides a way of thinking about these competing demands and the trade-offs that have to be made. Choosing the appropriate evaluation strategy is subtler than this. While we propose four distinct strategies, there are areas of grey in between that may be more realistic for you to choose. For example, the model shows that there is no realistic way to conduct Level 4 or Level 5 evaluations if time and money are limited. Hence, you may have to go back to the drawing board and rethink what is most important. And this may require renegotiating expectations with key leaders and other stakeholders.

## A FOUR-STEP EVALUATION PROCESS

An evaluation typically follows a four-step process we propose as an evaluation cycle (see Figure 11.4). Begin with planning the evaluation and then move to execution (data collection, analysis, etc). The key in these two steps is the

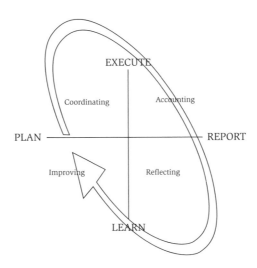

**Figure 11.4.** The Evaluation Cycle

coordination of work to be completed by the key stakeholders. Moving from execution to reporting the evaluation results, there is a level of accountability. The reporting, if used properly, will lead to learning and continuous improvement. Here, sense-making becomes relevant in reflecting on what the results mean. If learning from the evaluation has occurred, you will be equipped to make changes to improve future instances of the intervention. In addition, you will be able to review the evaluation process and determine how best to evaluate for the next application. This brings you full circle back to the beginning in crafting a new plan for iteration.

## Step 1—Create a P.L.A.N.

*Purpose and outcomes* are about assessment priority. Create a clear statement of purpose with a list of outcomes for the evaluation. Purpose is a one-sentence answer to the question: What is to be different from conducting the evaluation? Outcomes are more specific end-results that together, when achieved, lead to the evaluation purpose being realized. Be careful to focus purpose and outcomes on the evaluation and not the intervention. That is, there are purpose and outcomes for the intervention and there are separate, yet connected, purpose and outcomes for the evaluation. Given the space limitations of this chapter, we will give more attention to this first step, as it is the most important and attracts the most questions.

For example, consider an intervention on distance or online teaming. The purpose of the program is for people to improve their online collaboration skills in order to increase efficiency on projects, whereas the purpose of the evaluation may be to verify that people are using the teaming tools and the broader impact in order to obtain the necessary support to deliver the program globally.

Crafting purpose and outcomes can be a challenge. People want to move to action without getting at the "why" and as a result risk commencing an evaluation without purpose. Try creating the list of outcomes first, and then move to purpose. Ask the question: If we achieve these outcomes, what will be different? The answer is the purpose. Make sure the outcomes are results-oriented and not action-oriented. So if someone states an outcome as "to have people fill out the satisfaction survey online," recognize that this is an action step. Instead, ask: Fill out the survey online in order to what? The answer to this question will get you closer to the outcome you seek (Holman, Devane, & Cady, 2007).

A fundamental principle in OD is to involve people in the design of their future. The primary reason is *not* to reduce resistance or create buy-in. Buy-in is a by-product of engagement. The real reason is to ensure the best evaluation strategy is chosen. Determining purpose with others can lead to some consternation, political posturing, and compromise. It can also lead to intervention clarity, process improvement, and long-term success. Ultimately, this creates a more inspired commitment to a better design.

**Leading—Who Else Needs to Be Involved?** Answering the question of "who" defines the boundaries for the evaluation. As boundaries are explored, purpose is further clarified. Who should perform the evaluation: the client organization, the consultant, or a third party? Typically, the responsibility falls equally with the consultant and the client. Regular, ongoing evaluation will provide continuous feedback, if so designed, and will allow the consultant and the client to partner to maximize the potential in the intervention. An evaluation can begin anywhere. Often you will find an evaluation beginning with a person or persons located in a lower level or peripheral location in the organization.

**Action Steps—Develop a Road Map** The goal in this step is to develop a clear action plan for collecting, analyzing, and reporting on the evaluation. The evaluation needs to complement and integrate within the implementation of the intervention. While separate, intervention and evaluation are interconnected. Most action steps in evaluation will include the following:

- Model creation—review published research along with expected cause and effect relationships (hypotheses).
- Selection of Measures—levels of evaluation and evaluation strategy.
- Data Collection—who, what, when, and where.
- Data Analysis—entering data, analyzing data, and testing hypotheses.
- Reporting of Results—written reports, charts, graphs, and presentations.

The process by which data are gathered and stored can be overwhelming. The focus of this step is to get the most reliable and relevant data in the most efficient way. Creating a comprehensive model requires that all information be centralized. There are exceptions to this, but they should be explicitly addressed and agreed on. Data warehousing is a centralized function in which the collection process can be decentralized. Because there are various ways to measure the same thing, the previous steps should be used to choose the best measurement protocol. As for the timing of data collection, decisions have to be made about frequency, dates, and times.

### Needs

As mentioned in the competing demands paradox, there are needs that must be filled in order to complete the action steps successfully and realize the purpose and outcomes. There are four basic areas of needs:

- Money
- Time
- Tools and Materials
- Advocacy

The first three were discussed earlier, so we will discuss only advocacy here. This term refers to the support required from leaders and other stakeholders as well as to the support needed to report the results to the key stakeholders and participants. It also refers to the support required to ensure the results lead to tangible improvements. This may include political support to maneuver through defenses and political posturing.

> Bottom line—Is leadership willing to work with the larger stakeholder group to objectively review the results and commit to concrete action? This is the link-pin of the whole evaluation process.

## Step 2—Execute the Evaluation

Evaluation is dependent on the robustness of the planning. The more solid the plan, the more robust the design. The more robust the design, the more valid the results. As is often the case, evaluation plans unfold in unexpected ways. It is important, therefore, to include scenario planning for a variety of "what if" events.

Scenario planning was originally used for strategic planning and policy making. For evaluation, it involved taking a systems thinking approach by anticipating the many factors that could arise. The aim is to look at the various situations that may surprise you. Determine the plausibility, create story lines as a sequence of events that could occur, and then develop thoughtful responses. The benefit is that when the unexpected happens, you will spend less time figuring out what to do and more time on adapting your plan to meet the immediate needs of the situation (Schwartz, 1991).

Finally, document, document, and document again. If necessary, note potential validity issues and report the results describing limitations to the findings. This will add credibility to the people and the process.

## Step 3—Report the Results

Having data is not enough. Data and the corresponding results can be compelling to the person conducting the evaluation but to no one else. When the results from an evaluation are well presented, key stakeholders understand the data in a way that empowers them to take action. A variety of tools is available to report results:

- *Charts and Graphs*—pictorially presented data that give the viewer a comparative appreciation for the numbers. Charts and graphs show how the measures compare to each other and aggregated measures such as the mean and standard deviation, which can be reported from the existing data or other relevant data from such stakeholder groups as another department, competitors, industry, and society.

- *Scorecards*—a summarized or key set of measures that is important for everyone to see and track over time. These measures are often able to be seen on one page and address such things as satisfaction, productivity, learning, and profit (for more detail, see Kaplan & Norton, 1996).

- *Metaphors*—a story or picture that captures the meaning of the data and relationships among key variables. An example of this approach as applied to major corporations can be found at Root Learning (www.root-learning.com). Their motto is a picture is worth a thousand words, and a metaphor is worth a thousand pictures.

- *Predictive Models*—a diagram that shows the relationships among a variety of key measures that flow to important end-result outcomes. This concept was popularized by Sears, which developed the concept of the employee-customer-profit chain (Rucci, Kirn, & Quinn, 1998).

Each item above can support existing interventions and can lead to both proving and improving. It is important to weave together these tools in order to provide a more whole system performance model of the intervention's impact (Cady & Lewis, 2002).

## Step 4—Learn from the Evaluation

Feeding back the results from an evaluation can be both productive and challenging (Cady & Caster, 2000). First, agree on the relevant facts. Facts are the objective data collected, along with analysis in the form of measurable and observable information. Second, draw judgments or conclusions from agreed-on facts. Judgments are value-laden opinions related to the relative importance of the information. The modeling process provides facts related to causal relationships among the soft and hard measures. These facts can be helpful in evaluating longstanding judgments that have existed in the organization. With empirically based facts, the judgments are more objective and the emotional ramifications can help to build consensus. Therefore, it is important to clearly connect facts to judgments and to share the emotions that are surfacing as the facts are shared and judgments are formed (happy, sad, mad, fear, and guilt). Using the results to facilitate the sharing of emotions can be helpful in eliminating the static (defensiveness, blame, and other things) that can interfere with interpersonal communication. Finally, focus on next steps that can be taken in the short term to address the learning. What do we choose to do from here? Often, the next steps involve specific decisions with regard to the competing demands of *proving and improving* versus *time and money*.

## THE FUTURE OF EVALUATION IN OD

It is evident from our review of the literature, both scholarly and anecdotal, that evaluation is still a vexing area for most practitioners. The intention to do more robust and broader scope evaluations is there, but the practice is not. Invariably, this is because of the inability to align the competing demands. It is also a reflection of the lack of training in evaluation—practitioners feel overwhelmed at the prospect of determining the impact of an intervention on an organization. Our four-quadrant Situational Evaluation Model and the Evaluation Cycle are intended to help break down the process into manageable steps in relation to the constraints faced.

The process of evaluating interventions is about determining whether the path you are on has been the most effective strategy efficiently executed for the system you are in. In turn, this will influence how you move forward into the future. The fundamental premise of good evaluation is self-awareness on a large scale. Any sized system—from a small group to an entire organization—will be amenable to change when all relevant data are understood. If people and the system are self-aware, then they will be wise enough to know what to do next.

The more a client system is able to understand itself, the more likely it is that the system will take ownership in determining how to best move forward. Within this context, key change agents are more able to influence the system with data that demonstrate success and failure. Success and failure are concepts critical to creating a learning organization, and this is where the consultant as intervener has an important role. In providing the system with a better understanding of itself through rigorous evaluation, the system will begin to change its thinking paradigm. When the system begins to change its thinking paradigm, the learning has begun and "action learning" occurs. This shift in thinking or learning is what will lead to sustainable new organizational habits that result in long-term health and prosperity.

# References

Beckhard, R. (1997). *Agent of change: My life, my practice.* San Francisco: Jossey-Bass.

Brinkerhoff, R.O. (2003). *The success case method: Find out quickly what's working and what's not.* San Francisco: Berrett-Koehler.

Cady, S.H., & Caster, M. (2000). A DIET for action research: A problem and appreciative focused approach. *Organization Development Journal, 18*(4), 79–93.

Cady, S.H., & Lewis, M.J. (2002). Organization development and the bottom line: Linking soft measures and hard measures. In J. Waclawski & A.H. Church (Eds.), *Organization development: A data-driven approach to organizational change* (pp. 127–148). San Francisco: Jossey-Bass.

Foxon, M. (1989). A process approach to the transfer of training. *Australian Journal of Educational Technology, 5*(2), 89–104.

Holman, P., Devane, T., & Cady, S. (2007). *The change handbook.* San Francisco: Berrett-Koehler.

Kaplan, R.S., & Norton, D.P. (1996). *The balanced scorecard.* Boston, MA: Harvard Business School Press.

Kirkpatrick, D. (1969). Techniques for evaluating training programs. *Training and Development Journal, 13,* 3–9.

Kirkpatrick, D. (1977). Evaluating training programs: Evidence vs. proof. *Training and Development Journal, 31*(11), 9–12.

Kirkpatrick, D. (1998). *Evaluating training programs: The four levels.* San Francisco: Berrett-Koehler.

Kleiner, A. (1996). *The age of heretics: Heroes, outlaws, and the forerunners of corporate change.* Garden City, NY: Doubleday.

Lewin, K. (1946). Action research and minority problems. *Journal of Social Issues, 2,* 34–46.

Patton, M. (1997). *Utilization-focused evaluation* (3rd ed.). Thousand Oaks, CA: Sage.

Phillips, J. (1996). *Measuring ROI: The fifth level of evaluation.* Alexandria, VA: American Society for Training and Development.

Rossett, A. (2007, February). Leveling the levels. *Training and Development,* 49–53.

Rucci, A.J., Kirn, S.P., & Quinn, R.T. (1998). The employee-customer-profit chain at Sears. *Harvard Business Review, 76*(1), 82–97.

Russ-Eft, D.F., & Preskill, H.S. (2001). *Evaluation in organizations: A systems approach to enhancing learning, performance, and change.* New York: Basic Books.

Russ-Eft, D., Bober, M., de la Taja, I., Foxon, M., & Koszalka, T. (2008). *Evaluator competencies: Standards for the practice of evaluation in organizations.* San Francisco: Jossey-Bass.

Schwartz, P. (1991). *The art of the long view.* Garden City, NY: Doubleday.

Scriven, M. (1991). *Evaluation thesaurus* (4th ed.). Thousand Oaks, CA: Sage.

Stake, R. (1975). *Evaluating the arts in education: A responsive approach.* Columbus, OH: Charles E. Merrill.

Taylor, F.W. (1911). *The principles of scientific management.* New York: W.W. Norton.

University of Chicago Press. (1886). *Journal of proceedings and addresses of the 35th annual meeting.* National Education Association. Buffalo, New York.

Weisbord, M.R. (2005). *Techniques to match our values.* Remarks prepared for Organization Design Forum, San Francisco.

CHAPTER TWELVE

# Closure

*Freeing Up Energy to Move Forward*

Ann M. Van Eron and W. Warner Burke

The last step or phase in the organization development (OD) process is closure. This final phase is important but is rarely conducted in a careful, planned manner. Few consultants or researchers write or speak about this phase of the OD process (Golembiewski, 2000; McLean, 2006). However, given the fast pace of change today when most leaders and organizations are faced with multiple challenges and the need to be innovative and responsive to external pressures, the benefit of attending to closure is magnified. More than simply separating from the OD process, there are benefits in consciously closing the process, reflecting on learning, and mobilizing energy for moving forward. By stopping and reflecting, meaning can be made that will support future initiatives.

We begin this chapter with a case example when closure was not successful and some related reasons for endings of OD projects. Next, we explore an effective closure process. We then highlight the importance of managing and freeing up energy to move forward after closing an OD engagement. We caution about need to foster independence with clients and explore related psychological issues in closure. We also provide guidelines for handling the closing process, including questions to explore with clients and how to determine the next actions. As a summary, we provide an example of a successful closure process.

# CASE EXAMPLE

While not atypical, the following synopsis of an actual OD effort provides an illustration of a consultant's managing the final phase rather poorly. The OD consultant had worked with his client for about nine months conducting the usual steps. Data had been collected via interviews from a majority of management and key staff personnel. The data were reported back to the CEO and his direct reports, followed by a similar summary of the interview results to the larger system.

The OD consultant's diagnosis was that most of the data collected were symptoms and that the major underlying cause was the existence of two "camps" within top management who vehemently disagreed with one another as to how the company should be managed and what business strategy was best regarding the future. The consultant held an open discussion concerning the two-camp issue with the CEO alone and then with the entire top group of executives. The group verified that the consultant's diagnosis was correct and that action should be taken to do something about this serious conflict. The CEO was very supportive of participation, that is, he wanted consensus within his top team. As a result, he was immobilized by the seemingly intractable differences of opinion, particularly regarding strategy. The OD consultant provided coaching with suggestions for action steps. Changes within the top group needed to be made. But no action was taken. Time went by, with the CEO continuing to be in a "frozen" state. The OD consultant became exasperated.

The CEO did eventually modify the organizational structure somewhat and fired a key executive, but the OD consultant believed that these changes were largely cosmetic and would not lead to the fundamental changes that were needed for significant improvement in organizational performance.

The OD consultant had other clients at the time who were more demanding, and, therefore, he allowed this client to drift away rather than pursuing potential options for change and working on his relationship with the CEO. Closure in this case occurred, not due to a planned process, but rather as a function of time passing and inadequate motivation on either the consultant's or the client's part to try harder or to agree in a deliberate way to discontinue the relationship.

While real and not necessarily unusual (see Burke, 1991, for more detail), we are not recommending this case example as an exemplary one for the closure phase. The fact that a careful closure phase is not common is no reason to overlook the importance of this final phase in OD practice.

Closure is not easy, and, in any case, we should be clear that separations occur more often as a consequence of, say:

- A change in leadership due to retirement, a new and perhaps sudden assignment, or leaving the organization for "greener pastures." For example, one of us had been a consultant to a large, global corporation for well over three years and had worked closely with the CEO and the head of HR. Both of these gentlemen retired at about the same time. The succeeding CEO, who had been with the corporation for a number of years, made it clear to the consultant that he would no longer be needed. In the eyes of the new CEO, the consultant had been "too close" to the retired CEO and the HR executive, and he needed to establish his own direction and bring in a new consultant who would not be seen as "linked to the old regime." Although not planned by the consultant, separation occurred.

- Acquisition or merger where new leadership takes over and perhaps changes many of the old ways of doing things, including changing consultants.

- Sudden change in organizational priorities due to an unforeseen crisis, for example, the Bhopal disaster, Enron's financial "errors," an economic downturn, or perhaps some sudden change in technology that drastically affects the business.

These examples represent frequent unplanned separations and, therefore, are rarely under the control of the OD consultant. We will now address the closure phase in a more consciously planned manner.

## THE CLOSURE PROCESS

Done properly, the closure phase will be linked back to the contracting phase. What did the initial contract (probably revised a number of times along the way) call for? For external consultants, the contract covers the work to be done, of course, and is usually accompanied by specifications regarding time and money. This process may be less defined for internal consultants, since they are often considered to be "on call" much of the time. Yet internal OD consultants can conduct their practice in much the same way as externals, that is, moving through the phases from entry and contracting to closure. It's just that separation for internals is more like a clearly demarcated ending of a project but not ending a relationship with the client. Given that internal consultants are likely to be working on other OD projects, it is useful to take the time for closure in order to free up energy of the consultant and the client to work on new projects. It is valuable to complete or close any unfinished business and reflect on learning that can be applied in the next initiatives.

In any case, closure is planned as a function of the content in the contracting phase. Good contracting on the part of the OD consultant consists of agreements of who does what when and the specification of "deliverables"—the work to be performed—and how long everything is expected to take. So here is where the separation phase begins, that is, when the work has been completed to the client's satisfaction.

The *Cycle of Experience* developed by the Gestalt Institute of Cleveland (2003) identifies the closure and withdrawal phase to be a critical part of the change or consulting process. Closing—identifying what has been achieved and what remains undone—supports learning and integration (Mackewn, 2003). Moving toward closure and separation doesn't imply that the work has been unsatisfactory, but that it is time to move on. By closing the engagement, there is space for new awareness and mobilizing energy for new beginnings. Closing must happen with the client and the consultant. Each should pause and reflect on what went well, what is unfinished, and what was learned.

The closure process begins with the contract phase of OD consulting by identifying what the "deliverables" will be. Once these deliverables are achieved, then ending the consulting project and client relationship is in order. But, as noted already, separation is difficult.

## MOBILIZING ENERGY

Effective closure mobilizes energy for new initiatives and next steps. Given the fast pace of change, it is easy to quickly shift focus and fail to effectively close an OD effort. For example, in one organization, where one of us supported a cultural change effort with a focus on creating a respectful environment for employees and customers, much progress was made. The organization dramatically improved its rating by an external publication, internal employee surveys had marked improvement, and customers gave positive ratings about their experience of respect and service. As part of this initiative, managers participated in workshops emphasizing how to communicate and create a respectful environment. In this large organization, managers continued to request the workshop for their teams after the initiative was completed. Nevertheless, there was confusion about how the focus on the workshops fit into the next initiative. Without a clear sense of closure and completion, energy was tied up in seeing how the initiative was effective. Organization members can easily become tired of initiatives when they don't have the space for clear closure and meaning making.

When we were able to clearly announce that the formal part of the cultural change effort was being completed, managers were able to appreciate the progress they made and understand that supporting respect would be an ongoing part of their focus with their teams. With a clear sense of closure, managers were able to value the organizational initiative rather than complaining about too many initiatives. Without the conscious effort of closure, making meaning and withdrawal, energy is tied up as if stuck in a dammed river. After a clear closure conversation, there can be a sigh of relief and the freeing up of energy for what is next.

For example, when something is unfinished, such as the need to write a paper, pay taxes, or complete something, our energy is tied up with what we need to do. When we complete the task, we often have a sense of relief and a release of tension. We can redirect our attention and energy to the next project. Formally closing an OD effort frees up this energy for what is next.

We believe that a clean closure supports mobilizing energy. Just as it is useful to literally clean out our closets and offices to create space for new things, clear closure leaves the consultant and the client with a greater sense of meaning and space for the next initiative.

When we don't take the time for closure, energy is tied up in the process and we don't feel completely finished and ready to move on. One of us had a premature closing to an initiative to bring together various parts of an organization where leaders were creating similar programs, thus duplicating efforts. It was a successful initiative to come to agreement on working together, presenting a cohesive message, and reducing costs dramatically. A new leader was assigned to the business, and the OD initiative using the consultant was abruptly ended. Meetings with the consultant were stopped without an effective closure process. The incomplete process took psychological energy of the client team and the consultant. It was not until later that the consultant and client were able to formally close. After the dialogue, both felt satisfied and ready to move on. The client had the same dialogue with the leaders of the organization, and all were more prepared to move forward.

Just as there is value of getting organized and clearing out old materials, we are able to become unstuck from things that are taking up space and energy. The cleaning-up process creates more energy for new opportunities. Closure supports coming to terms with an experience that was felt or lived over time. By sharing emotions about what was finished and what was not completed, we are more able to move on.

We have closing ceremonies when we graduate from school, when we get married, or when we experience significant changes in our lives, such as birth or death of a loved one. The opportunity to stop and reflect supports us in closing one experience and having the energy for moving to the next experience. When we fail to have such a ritual, it can take longer to mobilize our energy to go to the next phase or new beginning.

## FOSTERING INDEPENDENCE

A part of the value system and folklore of OD is that effective consultants work themselves out of jobs. It is important for OD consultants to transfer their skills to clients and to identify resources in client organizations to carry on change efforts. When independence is fostered, closure comes more easily for all involved. At the same time, consultants must avoid becoming dependent on their clients as a means to meet their needs for work, money, or affiliation, because these needs can lead to unnecessary change efforts and wasted resources. Consultants should respond to actual needs in client organizations rather than to their own needs. Given the growing need for internal OD consultants with numerous change initiatives, it is useful to have clear closure of projects. In this way, clear lines of responsibility are established and confusion avoided.

As consultants embark on the closure process, they should be aware of their "need to be needed" and refrain from encountering or encouraging dependence (Bell & Nadler, 1979). To avoid dependence, consultants have to train those in client organizations to continue their own change efforts.

In practice, one project with a client often leads to other projects. An effective consultant develops a good working relationship with his or her client and identifies new opportunities within the client organization. At the same time, the OD consultant should continue to transfer his or her skills to organizational members so that they are capable of facilitating their own change efforts.

The notion of dependence in the OD relationship has its origin in the assumption that the consulting relationship is equivalent to the relationship between a therapist and patient. Although both are helping relationships, the situations are quite different. The client for an OD consultant is often an organizational system, and the OD consultant tends to work with many people from the client organization and with the interfaces between people and units. This mitigates personal dependence issues with the consultant. On the other hand, a prolonged project can create some dependence on the consultant. That is why appropriate training of organizational members is so important to effective closure.

# PSYCHOLOGICAL ISSUES

Ideally, the consultant and client mutually agree that it is time to close the engagement. Otherwise, there are challenges when only one party sees the need to close. The client and the consultant can experience a sense of loss that may result in depression and dependence as a positive working relationship comes to a close (Block, 2000; Kelley, 1981). In some societies, endings often initiate anxiety, discomfort, sadness, or depression. Therefore, some people may avoid terminating relationships. They may postpone completing projects by beginning new projects or by procrastinating in completing assignments.

The client and the consultant may have shared important experiences and are likely to have developed a mutual interdependence. It is important that the consultant initiate a discussion to address and deal with the emotions associated with disengagement. Otherwise, these feelings may not go away (Kelley, 1981), and they could lead to anger or an unproductive extension of the consulting process (Dougherty, 1990).

In a healthy but terminating OD relationship, the client may miss the confidential, candid, and stimulating discussions he or she had with the consultant. Both the client and the consultant can experience the loss of friendship. The consultant may also sense a loss of challenge. The process of jointly determining the appropriate time to terminate the relationship allows the client and the consultant an opportunity to share their feelings and perspectives. An open discussion about the discomfort in separation is important and healthy. The consultant and the client will find it valuable to understand the stages and the behavioral outcomes of the mourning process for long-term relationships. Bridges' (1980) book on transitions presents one view of this process.

The consultant may express concern about the well-being of the client. In addition, discussing future possibilities for working together can ease the stress of termination (Dougherty, 1990) and can validate the friendship.

## GUIDELINES FOR THE CLOSING PROCESS

A simple but useful process for closure is having the client and the consultant reflect on a few simple questions. We have found it useful to share these questions in advance and then meet with our clients in a conducive environment where we can take the time to reflect and talk about the questions. The more we make the closing clear, the more impact we experience. Sometimes we talk about the questions over a meal. Sometimes we may share symbols or tokens to remember our work together with a photo of the team or some other small reminder of our work together.

Possible questions include:

- What stands out for you about the initiative?
- What meaning are you making of the project?
- What feels complete and finished for you?
- What do you feel good about?
- What have you learned?
- What feels unfinished and incomplete?
- How have we worked together? What can we appreciate?
- What could we do better or differently next time?
- Are there actions to take?
- What else needs to be said for closure?

- What should be the next steps for the organization?
- What are next steps for our relationship?

We have found these and similar questions to be useful when we make the time for reflection with our clients. Taking the time for reflection supports learning, and the ritual of reflection frees up energy for the transition.

One of us recalls being surprised by the meaning the client was making and taking from the initiative. The client came to the meeting with a well-thought-out list of learnings that made the entire effort more meaningful for us and for the client. In another situation, discussing what was unfinished, such as not sharing findings with a key constituency, could be planned for. This satisfied both the consultant and the client. Often, simply stating what is unfinished frees up energy to move on.

We strongly recommend having a closing conversation or ritual with each project. You don't need to wait until the final end of a project; you can also take time for closing after different phases of a project. For example, you can evaluate and close after meetings with key constituents.

More than being an evaluation of a project, the closure process frees up energy and releases the tension from what is unfinished. The closure process offers an opportunity to celebrate our work together. Often not much time is taken to savor the successes and the potential meaning and learning. Certainly, given the fast pace of change in organizations, there are often things that were not fully completed. It is useful for those involved to speak from their experience and how they are making meaning rather than from an accusatory or judgmental stance.

# DETERMINING NEXT STEPS

After the client and the consultant have reviewed the initial agreement or contract and determined the results of the change effort, they can then identify any remaining tasks and determine whether to continue the services of the OD consultant. The client and the consultant should develop an outline of next steps and decide who will be involved in these. If the goals of the change effort were not realized, the consultant and the client will have to redefine the challenge or desired state and/or generate new intervention options. Even if the goals of the effort were realized, there still may be additional or related work for the consultant. In this case, the process moves to one of exploring needs and contracting anew. Alternately, the consultant and client may decide that additional work is not required at this time, but they may still wish to retain some type of relationship.

One way to stay in touch with clients is to contract for a different relationship as the OD consultant departs. We have coached clients after the completion of change initiatives on a regular basis or for quarterly check-ins to assess progress. Even when a formal arrangement is not made, it is useful to touch base with clients to renew friendships and engage in dialogue regarding initiatives and developments. When a successful closure is made, it is not uncommon for clients to call even years later for another engagement. After we assisted a client with a large cultural change effort, she called for assistance with an even more complex cultural change process when she moved to a different organization five years later. Because time had been spent to evaluate and successfully separate, the client had positive feelings about the work and we were able to start a new process in an efficient manner. We were able to recall our learnings from the first project and build the structures and support needed to be successful. In addition, we had a basis of trust.

A consulting project with a different organization was successful, but the client became very busy and time was not taken to effectively separate. A few years later the client was grateful when the consultant stopped to visit and they then were able to adequately close when he had more time and energy. It is likely he did not call for additional projects because he felt awkward about the ending. It's often not too late to close. One of us had the chance to more formally close with one client a few years after an effort. Even at this late stage, we found it meaningful to have the closing conversation. We both left feeling more satisfied and with enhanced learning from this reflection. The client shared some developments in the company and helped to clarify some previous issues. Both of us were able to appreciate our work together.

Some ways to stay in touch and maintain a relationship include sending periodic notes and emails, visiting the client when nearby, encouraging the client to call at any time, helping a client find resources, suggesting articles and books, providing recommendations for opportunities that may be of interest, such as conferences, and calling to ask to use the client's name as a reference for other projects (Biech, 1999).

It is useful for all involved to pause and appreciate the successes and challenges associated with the project. We continually remind people to pause and reflect, even briefly. With the fast pace of organizational change, it is easy for people to become burned out. Building in the structure of pausing, learning, and celebrating along the various milestones of a change initiative make final closure a more natural part of the change process.

The consultant should plan to fill the emotional gap that he or she experiences when a major project is completed. It is not uncommon for consultants to experience a sense of loss after successfully completing major projects. Many OD consultants immediately begin new and challenging projects; others plan relaxation time. It is helpful to acknowledge that low feelings are natural and to learn how to manage them (Kelley, 1981).

# SUMMARY

We'll conclude with a more successful case of closure to change the organization's culture. The project involved working with the organization's leadership team to develop a vision, strategy, and implementation plan. Part of the process was supporting the executive leadership team's development and providing executive coaching to the CEO and his direct reports. The consultant assisted the leadership team in developing and communicating the vision, values, desired behaviors, and plans to the large organization. After implementation teams were in place and the organization was experiencing the benefits of the OD process, the consultant began to reduce her role and support those in the organization taking on more of the responsibility to ensure implementation.

The consultant had several meetings with the CEO to review the original contract and dialogue about their achievements, the meaning each were creating, what went well, and what was unfinished. Both agreed that the initiative had been successful in building the case for the need for change, building a strong leadership team (where the opposite had been the case), enhancing morale, and generating excitement and commitment for the changes being made. They regretted that perhaps too much energy was focused on a leader who did not support the change and that it had taken some time to find strong internal OD support. Both the client and the consultant shared what they learned from working together. The reflection allowed the client and the consultant to appreciate their efforts and accomplishments.

The consultant and client then focused on identifying next steps. A plan was made to transition facilitation of the team meetings to the CEO and the internal OD leader. The internal OD leader agreed to follow the structure and format for the meetings that the consultant had introduced. The consultant coached the internal OD person for a period of time. The OD leader agreed to follow up on the development plans of the leaders the consultant coached. The consultant and the OD leader met with those she coached to review goals and actions. Some of those being coached continued with the consultant for an additional period. A clear transition was made to having the internal OD person facilitate executive leadership team meetings. Together, the consultant and the leadership team reflected on their successes and learning. The leadership team also identified next steps for the team going forward. It was agreed that the consultant would meet with the leadership team once a quarter for the rest of the year to check in on progress on the actions and how the group was functioning.

The clients and consultant recognized the emotional component of closure. Some members of the team were sad about the transition. The consultant provided empathy and support. The consultant experienced both satisfaction with the project as well as sadness in reducing her involvement and connection with members of the organization. It was useful to identify the mixed feelings and find support; the consultant talked with colleagues about her experience of loss. At the same time, the consultant appreciated the friendships with the leaders, noted the successes of the organization change effort, and identified what she learned from the process.

The consultant followed up with the team and leader to check in on progress. In addition, the consultant periodically called members of the organization to check in. She later resumed coaching with some members who moved on to other roles and organizations. Over time, the consultant was invited to work on a number of projects by those she worked with, both for the same organization and for other systems.

Taking the time for reflection about fulfillment of the contract and the process, recognizing the emotional component of closure, agreeing on next steps, saying good-bye, and following up enable the client and the consultant to benefit from this last phase of the OD process.

# References

Bell, C.R., & Nadler, L. (1979). Disengagement and closure. In C.R. Bell & L. Nadler (Eds.), *The client-consultant handbook* (pp. 210–214). Houston, TX: Gulf.

Biech, E. (1999). *The business of consulting: The basics and beyond.* San Francisco: Pfeiffer.

Block, P. (2000). *Flawless consulting: A guide to getting your expertise used* (2nd ed.). San Francisco: Pfeiffer.

Bridges, W. (1980). *Transitions: Making sense of life's changes.* Reading, MA: Addison-Wesley.

Burke, W.W. (1991). Engineered materials. In A.M. Glassman & T.G. Cummings (Eds.), *Cases in organization development* (pp. 68–77). Homewood, IL: Richard D. Irwin.

Dougherty, A.M. (1990). *Consultation: Practice and perspectives.* Pacific Grove, CA: Brooks/Cole.

Gestalt Institute of Cleveland. (2003). *International gestalt coaching program: An organization and systems development center training program.* Cleveland, OH: Gestalt Institute of Cleveland.

Golembiewski, R. (2000). *Handbook of organizational consultation* (2nd ed.) New York: Marcel Decker.

Kelley, R.E. (1981). *Consulting: The complete guide to a profitable career.* New York: Charles Scribner's.

Mackewn, J. (2003). *Developing gestalt counselling.* London: Sage.

McLean, G.N. (2006). *Organization development: Principles, processes, performance.* San Francisco: Berrett-Koehler.

PART THREE

# LEVELS AND TYPES OF CHANGE

# CHAPTER THIRTEEN

# Taking Organization Culture Seriously

Edgar Schein

Culture as a concept impacts organization development (OD) in two fundamental ways. First, it is increasingly evident that practitioners of OD must learn to deal with the cultures and subcultures of client systems. This requires conceptual models and intervention skills that realistically deal with what culture is and how culture works.

Second, OD as an occupational community has developed a culture and subcultures within itself and must learn what its strengths and weaknesses are. Of particular importance is the recognition that the subcultures within OD may be in conflict with each other but may not be aware of it. In this chapter, a working model of culture is presented and these two OD issues are analyzed.

## WHAT IS CULTURE AND HOW DOES IT WORK?

The simplest way of thinking about culture is to liken it to personality and character in the individual. As we grow up, we learn certain ways of behaving, certain beliefs, and certain values that enable us to adapt to the external realities that face us and that give us some sense of identity and integration. As a group or organization grows and succeeds, it undergoes the same kind of growth and learning process. The initial beliefs and values of the group's founders and leaders gradually become shared and taken for granted if the group is successful in fulfilling its mission or primary task, and if it learns how to manage itself internally. The group's culture consists of its accumulated learning, and if the group builds up a history, the beliefs, values, and norms by which it has operated become taken for granted and can be thought of as shared assumptions that become tacit and non-negotiable.

When we take this model to the level of organizations, the same logic applies, but with additional elements. The young organization develops shared beliefs, values, and norms based on what its founders brought with them, what the people they hired have brought, and what worked in solving problems of survival, growth, and internal integration. However, as organizations grow and age, they also develop subunits, in which the learning process described above occurs as well, since they have different tasks and different issues of internal integration. An organization will, therefore, eventually develop both an over-arching culture and subcultures that will vary in strength and degree of congruence with the total organization culture.

The strength of a given culture or subculture will depend on several factors:

- The strength of the convictions of the original founders and subsequent leaders;
- The degree of stability of the membership and leadership over a period of time; and
- The number and intensity of learning crises that the group has survived.

The stability of the leadership and membership is the most critical in that high turnover, especially of leaders, would keep the organization from developing a shared set of assumptions in the first place. Beliefs and values would continue to be contested between various subgroups which would prevent the kind of consensus that would, over time, lead to shared tacit assumptions.

The *content* of a given culture is generally the result of the *occupational* culture of the founders and leaders of the group or organization. Since the mission or primary task of an organization is to create products or services that its societal context wants and needs, successful organizations usually reflect some congruence between the core technology involved in the creation of the products and services and the occupational skills of the founders and leaders. Thus, a computer company tends to have been founded by electrical engineers, a chemical company tends to have been founded by chemists and chemical engineers, and a bank or financial institution tends to have been founded by people trained in the management of money. There will be many exceptions, of course, such as IBM, which was founded by a salesman, but ultimately there will be congruence between the core technology and the core occupations of the founders and leaders.

An occupational culture can be thought of as the shared beliefs, values, and norms of an occupational community, based on their formal training and practical experience in pursuing the occupation, leading to shared tacit assumptions that govern the occupation. In the traditional professions, such as medicine or law, these beliefs, values, and norms are codified and formalized, including codes of ethics designed to protect the vulnerable client from professional exploitation. Underneath these codes are the tacit assumptions such as "a doctor must do no harm" or "a scientist must not misrepresent data." As new occupations such as OD have evolved, they have sought to professionalize themselves by developing formal educational and training programs for future practitioners and by developing codes of practice and ethics designed to reassure clients and set standards.

The process by which this happens is the same as in the growth of other group cultures. OD founders and leaders, such as Kurt Lewin, Lee Bradford, Rensis Likert, Ron and Gordon Lippitt, Eric Trist, A.K. Rice, Tommy Wilson, Harold Bridger, Elliot Jacques, Doug McGregor, Chris Argyris, Richard Beckhard, Herb Shepard, Warren Bennis, Bob Blake, and Bob Tannenbaum—to name a few of the first generation of forerunners—have shared certain beliefs, values, assumptions, and practices that they have taught to successive generations.

However, as this long list of OD leaders indicates, the process of forming consensus around occupational norms takes longer and is more complex because the client systems respond differently to different practices that come from the same occupational community. And in this way an occupation spawns subgroups and subcultures in the same way that a given organization does. For example, the Tavistock group, built around A.K. Rice, developed very different theories and assumptions about how to work with groups and organizations than the Lewinian group that developed in Bethel, Maine, or the Human Potential group that evolved in California around Bob Tannenbaum and John and Joyce Weir.

Even the OD group working in Bethel eventually divided over the issue of whether to stay focused on leadership training and community building or to become more individually oriented. Within ten years this group had divided into at least two factions—those wanting to continue to work with organizations and managers and those who saw in sensitivity training the potential for therapy for "normal" individuals and who allied themselves with the human potential movement.

The field of OD today is, therefore, considered to be more of a confederation of subcultures trying to become a single occupational community rather than a profession in the more traditional sense. It is missing a core content that would be embodied in a formal training program and licensing process, and there is little consensus on what is an appropriate or inappropriate form for working with client systems. The same statement applies to the larger field of consultation, especially management consultation, where it is obvious that consulting companies and individual consultants are quite diverse in what they advocate is the "correct" way to deal with clients and what they think the goals of consultation should be.

In making an analysis and critique of OD practices, I am not indicting the whole field, but I am trying to set a standard that is undoubtedly already held by many OD practitioners. The critique is warranted, nevertheless, because published accounts of what OD practitioners advocate are still, in my view, both scientifically and practically out of line with what we have come to learn about the cultures of our client systems.

Certain practices that I observe, hear about, and read about show a complete lack of understanding of how culture works in the organizations in which these practices are pursued. Furthermore, this implies a complete lack of self-consciousness about the degree to which those practices reflect a given subculture of a given set of OD practitioners, rather than an accepted consensus in the larger OD community.

## IS OD STILL HOOKED ON DIAGNOSIS AND DATA GATHERING?

This analysis and critique are directed at the models of consultation that take it for granted that, before one makes an intervention, one should make some kind of diagnosis of what is going on. That diagnosis is typically based on several things: (1) the consultant's insights based on prior education and experience, operating in the form of mental models that structure expectations, predispositions, stereotypes, and communication filters; (2) the consultant's personal style and preferences in the sense that those preferences will predispose the consultant initially to perceive the new situation in a way that is comfortable for that person; (3) the here-and-now "online" interpretation of spontaneous reactions by the client to whatever the consultant does, and the consultant's reactions to what the client says and does; and (4) formal or informal activities by the consultant in the form of questions, surveys, or observation periods designed to elicit data (most models talk about a stage of data gathering) that are then interpreted by the consultant as a basis for deciding how to intervene.

It is my belief that the first and second factors, the consultant's theoretical biases and personal style, are inevitable and ever-present sources of whatever diagnostic insights the consultant possesses. It is also based on my experience, that the third factor, the immediate "online" interpretation of here-and-now events as the consultant and client interact, is the only valid basis for diagnostic insights. And by implication, it is my belief that the fourth factor, the active diagnostic activities that consultants engage in for gathering data, is, in fact, interventions in disguise that, if not treated as interventions, change the system in unknown ways and, thereby, invalidate whatever is found by the interviews, surveys, or observations in the first place. In other words, formal diagnostic processes launched by the consultant through surveys, assessment processes, tests, or interviews are neither scientifically valid nor good practice.

When we engage in any kind of interaction with another person or group, whether in the role of a consultant, friend, casual acquaintance, or stranger, we are in a process of dynamic, mutual influence that simultaneously reveals data to be interpreted and learned from and changes the situation as a result of the interaction. Even if we take a completely passive listener's role, like the psychoanalyst sitting in a chair behind the patient on the couch, our silence is still an intervention that influences the patient's thoughts, feelings, and behaviors. When therapists talk of transference and counter-transference, they are talking of the reactions both in the patient and in the therapist, through their ongoing interaction.

For some reason, in the OD field, many practitioners have deluded themselves that they can engage in data gathering prior to intervention and have, thereby, created a monumental fantasy completely out of line with reality, that data gathering precedes intervention.

Let me illustrate. A CEO calls me to help him figure out what some of the cultural realities are in his organization and how to institute more of a culture of teamwork. I express some interest since this is my field, so I have already intervened by altering his expectations about my potential involvement. He invites me to visit the organization and talk to some of his colleagues. Some proponents of OD theories and models would argue that I should accept this invitation and gather data to decide how to proceed and whether or not to take on the project. It is my assertion that this would be totally inappropriate. Why?

First, I do not know what the CEO's motives are in bringing me in as a consultant. Second, I do not know what the CEO means by "culture." Third, I do not know what problem is motivating the CEO to explore this area. And fourth, I have no idea what the CEO has told the organization and, therefore, have no idea what the impact would be from my showing up there to gather data. What then should I do?

I should intervene with the intention of having my intervention produce some data that might help me to figure out where to go next and how to build a relationship with this CEO that would be trusting enough for me to find out what is really going on. My intervention goal is simultaneously to build a relationship and to learn more (gather data), but note that I start with intervention, not with diagnosis. So I inquire, get interested, and try to communicate to the CEO that I will work with him but will not take the monkey off his back. I will not visit him unless we can talk out what he has in mind, why a visit would be helpful, and how it would be arranged. All of the initial interventions are geared to building a trusting relationship with him, not for its own sake but in order to facilitate accurate communication between us. If it turns out that the project really involves a vice president and her group, the CEO and I have to decide jointly how to involve her, how to present me to her, and how to build a sense of joint ownership of what we do next. These steps need not take a great deal of time, but the relationship building should be the focus of the initial interventions.

What I am arguing against in the strongest possible terms is consulting theories that start with some notion of up-front "contracting" followed by a period of data gathering or scouting in preparation for some kind of intervention.

Eventually, the field of OD will have to disassociate itself from the field of assessment, especially quantitative assessment, where such techniques are advocated as preceding the building of a relationship with clients that permits valid concerns to be worked on. Assessment will eventually be a different field but will never work if culture is not taken into account.

## IS TOO MUCH OD BASED ON INDIVIDUAL COUNSELING MODELS?

This critique is directed at two groups of OD practitioners—those who are helping with individual assessment, 360-feedback, and coaching, and those who try to fix organization-level problems by interventions designed for individual counseling. For example, some of the most sophisticated coaching projects involve interviewing the client's role network to gather extensive information about that individual, without giving any thought to the potential impact of all this interviewing on the network.

Only experimental psychologists trained in pre-Milgram days would treat others as simply sources of data without analyzing what it means to them to be asked to give opinions about a colleague or what might happen if they choose to compare notes and create consensus opinions where none existed before. Only organizationally naïve consultants would assume that you can create the conditions for colleagues to give honest and useful feedback without understanding more about the politics and culture of the organization in which this is taking place.

A more disturbing issue is the question of who is paying for the coaching, the organization or the individual, and what the implications are if the organization is paying. Is the coach supposed to influence the client toward organizationally valued behavior? Will the organization accept a coaching process that leads a valued executive to decide to leave the organization? Does the coach have to report to higher management if he discovers in the client certain traits that clearly go against company values? Who owns the data from the 360-feedback process, and are the colleagues who provide feedback warned about who will or will not see the data?

My fear is that the answers to all of these questions are based on maximizing the supposedly scientific accuracy of the data and what is good for the individual client, with virtually no consideration of organizational implications.

The same issues apply, of course, to the ever-popular survey process. It has always amazed me that survey projects intended to improve morale and connectedness between management and employees tell the respondents that their answers will be kept completely confidential. Isn't this a confession that management assumes that employees would not give honest opinions unless they were guaranteed anonymity and confidentiality? Does this not convey mistrust and cynicism in a situation in which the goal is to build up trust?

The use of surveys and assessment tools, especially in the area of culture and climate, has a second problem—the assumption that a lot of individual responses can be amalgamated into a picture of something that is organizational. Many OD practitioners, especially those coming from quantitative sociology or psychology, assume that one can build valid conclusions from adding up the responses of samples of employees. I think it is naïve to assume that if we guarantee anonymity, we will then find the truth. The scared employee will still try to be positive, the angry employee will still exaggerate on the negative side, the alienated employee will be a non-respondent, and the survey analyst will use sophisticated statistical tests to prove that 40 percent of a group, that is itself a sample of 25 percent of the total population, reacting a certain way, is or is not something that management should pay attention to.

After management and the survey analysts have reached certain conclusions, they pay lip service to OD values by sending the data back down through the organization by requiring every supervisor and his or her group to meet and go over the data that have been provided from the master database. It is even possible that, under certain conditions and in certain cultures, this process now starts some useful discussions at the employee level, but the message is very clear that it is management that is deciding what and how to discuss it.

Would it not be better if supervisors got together with their employees in the first place, either in open discussion or with survey data gathered from that group right after it has been gathered?

My view is that this kind of session can happen in residential team-building labs. If morale improvement, teamwork, and problem solving are the goals, the method should reflect those goals, and employees should be involved from the outset in groups, not as individuals. The individual respondent method gives management a lot of numbers that they do not know what to do with and consultants a lot of money for providing potentially useless information.

But that is not the worst of it. The survey stimulates thought, gets discussion going among employees, sets up expectations that management will listen and fix things. In the traditional survey method that I am criticizing, management does not have to make any up-front commitments so there is a great danger that morale will get worse while management tries to figure out what to do.

# DOES OD MISAPPLY NATURAL SCIENCE MODELS TO HUMAN SYSTEMS?

One set of criteria for deciding how to intervene in the organization at the outset derives from the assumption that consultants are "scientists" who have to gather valid information in order to make valid diagnoses so as to give valid advice. What is hidden in this generalization is that the word "scientist" has different meanings in different subcultures. If we adopt the natural science model, we start with the assumption that it is essential to ask questions that minimize the respondent's bias that give minimal cues as to the consultant's opinion and that can be asked in a standard format so that responses can be compared and combined. But is this possible? Can one gather objective data in a human relationship? Or are cultural predispositions, prior expectations, and preconceptions always operating and, therefore, always biasing not only what the respondent will tell you but also what you are capable of hearing? The most dangerous source of bias is lack of mutual involvement. If the consultant plays a minimal role as an intervener, being just an objective data gatherer, there is a good chance that the client will feel like a guinea pig or a subject of study and will give only the most minimal and self-protective responses possible.

A further assumption of the natural science model is that the respondent and the data gatherer are independent entities so that "objective" data can be gathered. An alternative assumption that I believe fits the work with human systems much better is that the consultant and the client must form a relationship out of which come new ideas and new data. But those data reflect the relationship, not the client as a unique and independent agent. In fact, most theories of therapy, such as modern psychoanalysis and Gestalt therapy, assume that growth comes out of transference and counter-transference, not out of insight on the part of the patient.

From this point of view, the entry of the consultant into the system is the first intervention and the system will never be the same. This is consistent with most traditional theories of OD. We have somehow overlooked in some of our OD subcultures the fact that the Heisenberg principle applies to all systems, so why would we assume that we can study systems without changing them? I agree completely with Kurt Lewin's dictum that you do not really understand a system until you try to change it.

# WHAT SHOULD OD'S STANCE BE VIS-A-VIS SUBCULTURES? WHAT IS ORGANIZATIONAL HEALTH?

Having been critical of some OD practice, let me now shift to a more positive view. How should OD evolve as an occupation? What basic mental models should it operate from? If OD consultants care about the developmental part of that label, they must have a concept of organizational health.

Organizations are dynamic systems in a dynamic environment. My preferred model of health is, therefore, a systems model of the coping process. What does a system have to do to cope with a perpetually changing environment? There are five critical processes to be considered, and each of them provides some mental models of what the consultant should pay attention to strategically.

First, the system must be able to sense and detect changes in the environment. The organizational therapist can intervene by observing or inquiring whether or not the organization is in touch with its relevant environments.

Second, the system must be able to get the information to those subsystems that can act on it, the executive and operating subsystems. The sales force or the purchasing department may detect all kinds of environmental trends, but if senior executives devalue the opinions of those employees, they will not be able to assess and cope realistically. The organizational therapist can intervene by inquiring whether appropriate channels of communication exist and whether relevant information circulates.

Third, if the information requires changes in one or more subsystems, if new products have to be developed, if manufacturing processes need to change, or if refinancing is required, can the system change in the appropriate direction? Is there systemic flexibility? Can the system innovate? Many an organization knows exactly what it must do to survive, has sufficient insight, but is unable to make the necessary tradeoffs to create real change, just as many individuals prefer to live with their neuroses because of secondary gain and the difficulties involved in relearning. The organizational therapist can intervene by inquiring about present transformational processes and help the client to design and facilitate major transformations.

Fourth, the system must have the capacity to export its new productions. This issue should focus the therapist on the whole sales and marketing function to inquire about whether changes made actually are effectively externalized.

Finally, the system must close the cycle by observing accurately whether its new products, processes, and services are achieving the desired effect, which is again an environmental sensing process.

Of course, this is a perfectly good model of an individual human, seen in systemic terms. What makes it more complex in organizations is that the subsystems develop their own cultures that often are in conflict or at least out of alignment with each other. All organizations are subject to schizophrenia or multiple personalities as they age and grow. The subcultures form around units that have enough independence to do their own learning and that exist in different environments, such as geographical units or functional units. All organizations also have what you might think of as three fundamental generic subcultures that must be aligned:

1. *An operator culture, the line organization that delivers the basic products and services.* This would be production and sales in businesses, nursing and primary care in hospitals, the infantry in the army, and so on. These units are always built around people and teamwork and are embedded in the organization.

2. *An engineering or design culture, the research and development function and/or the design engineering function.* This culture is not embedded within the organization but in the larger occupational community that constitutes their profession. It is their job to design better products and processes, which often means engineering the people out of the system through automation, because it is people who, in their view, make mistakes and foul things up. These are the design engineers in business, the experimental surgeons in the hospital, and the weapons designers in the military. Their solutions are often expensive, which reveals the third critical culture.

3. *The executive culture, the CEO, whose primary job is to keep the organization afloat financially.* The CEO culture is also a cosmopolitan culture that exists outside the organization in that the CEO is most responsive to the capital markets, to the investors, to Wall Street and the analysts, to the board of directors, and, paradoxically, to the CEO's peers. CEOs believe their jobs to be unique and feel they can only learn from other CEOs.

## A NEW ROLE FOR OD CONSULTANTS

I have mentioned these three subcultures because they redefine the job of the organizational therapist and OD consultants in a fundamental way. Instead of helping the operators and trying to get the engineers and the executives to pay more attention to the human factors, which is typically what we do, why not help the engineers to be better designers and help the CEOs be better money managers? Instead of pitting the operator culture against the other two, which our value premises often lead us to do, why not define our job as getting these three cultures to communicate with each other so that everyone recognizes that all three are needed and must be aligned with each other?

We sometimes tend to forget that society advances through design improvements and that, without good fiscal management, organizations and the jobs they provide disappear.

# SUMMARY

To take culture seriously, we must start with understanding the occupational culture in which we are embedded and that we take for granted. Having understood that, we can then examine the cultures and subcultures of our client systems and decide whether or not there is enough value congruence to proceed with the project. If we pass that test in our own minds, we can proceed to help the client by intervening in a helpful, constructive way to build a relationship with each part of the client system that will reveal cultural strengths and weaknesses on the path to helping the clients with whatever problems they want us to help with.

Our growing awareness of organizational cultures and subcultures will ensure that all our interventions are jointly owned with the client so that whatever further actions are taken are feasible within the existing culture and take advantage of its strength. If we encounter elements of the culture that are hindrances, then we will work realistically with our client to launch the much more difficult and time-consuming process of changing that element, always being mindful of using other elements of the culture as sources of strength for the change program.

## Resources

Schein, E.H. (1987). *The clinical perspective in fieldwork*. Thousand Oaks, CA: Sage.

Schein, E.H. (1987). *Process consultation, Vol. 2: Lessons for managers and consultants*. Reading, MA: Addison-Wesley.

Schein, E.H. (1996). Three cultures of management: The key to organizational learning. *Sloan Management Review, 38*(1), 9–20.

Schein, E.H. (1999). *The corporate culture survival guide*. San Francisco: Jossey-Bass.

Schein, E.H. (1999). *Process consultation revisited*. Englewood Cliffs, NJ: Prentice-Hall.

Schein, E.H. (2003). *DEC is dead; Long live DEC*. San Francisco: Berrett-Koehler.

Schein, E.H. (2004). *Organizational culture and leadership* (3rd ed.). San Francisco: Jossey-Bass.

# CHAPTER FOURTEEN

# Individual Development in OD

*Human-Centric Interventions*

*Udai Pareek, Lynnea Brinkerhoff, John J. Scherer, and Rick Flath*

Every day, thousands of people in organizations are being coached, mentored, and trained under the banner of OD. But is this actually OD? Under what circumstances does individual development (ID) become OD? What does it take for an intervention intended to develop an *individual* to become something that benefits the *organization* and vice versa? The authors explore this and other questions in this chapter, developing further distinctions and highlighting dilemmas in conducting ID as OD.

First, we offer a working definition, value and goals of ID, and emphasize the business advantage of employing ID strategies. The Polarity Model™ is used to illustrate the necessity of holding the tension of opposites between the individual and the larger system, especially during the transformation effort. Client examples and a chart offering an array of ID interventions, their benefits and considerations, assist in reframing current understanding of the field. Notably, we seek to underscore the hypothesis of our co-author, Dr. Udai Pareek, that today's emphasis in ID is to move away from what is wrong with people to what is right, to move from vulnerability to resilience.

## INDIVIDUAL DEVELOPMENT (ID) DEFINED

ID is any activity aimed at enhancing awareness levels of the individual (intrapersonal); raising shared meaning and interactions among colleagues (interpersonal);

performance-based action in the world (performance-based/behavioral); and seeing oneself within and acting upon a larger system (system-wide). These levels are displayed in Figure 14.1, The Four Quadrants—Arenas of Development. Higher levels of ID include: witnessing the phenomenon of being an individual in an organization, demonstrating concern for and taking action on behalf of the whole, and galvanizing forces from all four quadrants (integral leader).

Founder of the "integral" movement, Ken Wilber (2001) seeks to understand humans and society by combining scientific insights with other fields of study. Below, he offers a comprehensive view to use as a backdrop for this chapter, further defining the levels of system potentially activated in ID interventions.

When engaging in ID activities, practitioners must engage the whole person. This means *enriching the inner life* of employees (individual interior (II)), offering opportunities for *meaningful and transparent dialogue* with colleagues (collective interior (CI)), measuring and *reinforcing observable behaviors* (individual exterior (IE)), which ideally considers "*self, other and the larger mission*" of the organization and its business results (collective exterior (CE)). McKinseyquarterly.com in February 2007 offered that "[Integral] leaders can have an impact in four ways: making the transformation program meaningful, often by making it personal; inspiring others as a role model; building a strong

**Figure 14.1.** The Four Quadrants—Arenas of Development

Adapted from Wilber, 2001

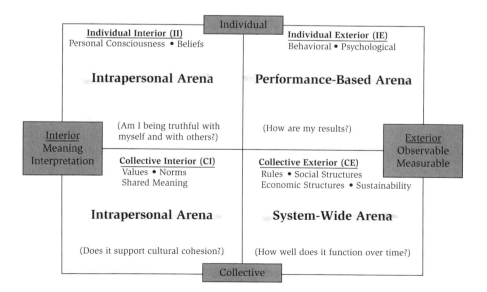

and committed top team; and getting involved when significant financial and symbolic value is at stake. A CEO who pays only lip service to a transformation will find everyone else doing the same.

Some of the interventions utilized in service of this goal that will be reviewed in this chapter include:

- Coaching;
- Mentoring;
- T-groups;
- Orientation;
- Performance development;
- Assessments;
- Rewards; and
- Feedback

# BENEFITS FOR EMPLOYING ID

On average, 75 percent of all change efforts in organizations fall significantly below desired expectations on the part of leaders. Research also indicates that two-thirds of employees in organizations undergoing change activities would choose not to become involved at all (Long, 2008, p. 32).

CEOs across the board state routinely that their companies are most challenged by:

- Attracting and retaining talented employees;
- Changing organizational culture and employee attitudes;
- Changing leadership and management behaviors; and
- Improving workforce performance.

We live in a highly matrixed world. There is no denying the interdependent ecosystem of earth and its people linking us inextricably to one another's fates. In this digital global age, leaders are required to be "weavers," that is, facilitating networks of virtual teams. They are not serving as authority figures, but are coordinating disparate groupings of trusted others to share innovations and complementary skills (Miller, 2004, p. 12).

Developing integral leaders of this sort at every level in business, government, and household would enable higher-level solutions to emerge with greater ease and frequency. They would show themselves as people with the ability to soberly confront realities with grace, without bias, and to weave strongly held viewpoints and values of their group or constituency toward life-giving resolutions for many.

> "The movement of our 'self-sense' from ego-centric to ethno to world-centric is part of the evolutionary growth of organizations. At each step along the road from ego to ethno to world-centric, the perspective gets larger and as our perspective grows, our ability to take in more information, to see more clearly into the future and to evaluate the utility of different points of view enlarges as well. Many of our leaders find themselves in over their heads because they do not have the capacity to hold a large enough perspective, or the skills to seamlessly shift perspectives under pressure. These deep seated abilities are the keys to learning, innovation and sustainable success." (Conversation with Rev. Michael Pergola, MBA, JD)

Figure 14.2 depicts the movement from a less productive mindset to one that is welcome in today's complex environment. Given that an equal capacity to destroy civilization as well as to evolve it lies in the hands of many diverse parties, to be world-centric can literally save lives. The power of accelerating technology has outrun our collective ability to exercise qualities of the human heart. We are reaching what systems philosopher Ervin Laszlo calls a "chaos point" or a decision-window (Laszlo, 2006).

Our global corporate complex is an infrastructure already in place with billions of people inhabiting them daily, taking cues from the higher-ups regarding the ethics of how to live their lives, and making decisions about what is important to value. Feedback is everywhere, and the results are still largely dismal. The corporation, stemming from the Latin word "corpus," meaning "a body of people," is the perfect control group to test hypotheses that all humans have in them the capacity to rise above their comfort levels for a greater good.

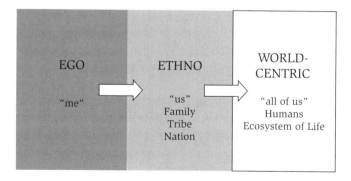

**Figure 14.2.** From Me to We

Adapted from Wilber, 2001

---

**Case in Point**

A major financial Institution offers their employees a performance management process that focuses on "being-based competencies." They have everyone fill out their own 360-degree feedback sheet and structure a respectful dialogue between supervisor and direct report. They then issue everyone a coach of his or her own to help them prepare for those conversations and get clear on their strengths, areas for improvement, key resources, write a development plan, and learn how to assert their needs in an emotionally intelligent manner. In that environment, the best and the brightest "thoroughbreds" from around the globe are found, and they are not used to losing at any game. When it comes to EI, they often prefer IT. Their careers often plateau if they fail to identify, use, understand, and manage their emotions.

By choosing the mindset of limited resources, by choosing to focus on outcomes rather than process, and by making faulty comparisons with others, we become little more than robots. The true individual is characterized by openness to the new, is always reclassifying the meaning of knowledge and experience, and has the ability to see his or her daily actions in a bigger, consciously chosen perspective.

---

Co-author John Scherer (1980) maintains that the workplace is the perfect "laboratory" for personal development.

> "The workplace could be a 'classroom' for profound development that, if taken in the right vein, can strengthen the human spirit daily. All the 'stuff' that happens each day is the perfect 'curriculum' for us, and our perfect 'faculty' (the people we work with) gathers every day, ready to 'teach' us what we need to learn. It is all available as 'grist for the mill' of our development into the human beings we are capable of being." (2009, p. 3)

The questions that may need to be asked:

- Is the workplace an appropriate venue for this kind of thinking?
- How would an organization be able to build this kind of context?
- Would employees be willing to engage in this broader context?
- Even if people thought it was a good idea, would they be capable of operating in this manner?
- Can we afford not to ask these questions?

According to *Training* magazine's 2007 Industry Report, $58.5 billion a year is spent on executive training development with a focus on improving performance through intra/interpersonal skills, which indicates a vital need for new ways of relating and defining success.

# ID OR OD: WHICH ONE IS BEST?

If OD is about how to use system-wide interventions and ID is about how to develop the individual to enhance overall performance, then which one is the best to focus on? Barry Johnson's (1992) repeated theme is that organizational effectiveness is not something we should choose sides over. It is not an *either/or*, a problem to solve, but rather is a polarity to be managed, a *both/and*. Johnson describes a polarity as an issue to be managed, creating a situation in which a position taken strongly on one side requires an opposite position to be managed.

"In a polarity, the more we focus on one pole or position, the more important the opposite pole or position becomes" (Johnson, 1992, p. 4). This is evidenced by asking ourselves, for instance, which kind of love is best to raise a child with, tough love or unconditional love? Is there one answer or does the presence of one necessitate the existence of the other? They each have a place in meeting the overall goal of raising a healthy child. So the question for an OD practitioner of whether to focus on the individual or the system has only one answer: Yes.

Figure 14.3 describes, pictorially, the natural movement of one point of view holding fast to its positive "upsides" and inevitably, over time, slipping into its negative "downsides" of maintaining its point of view over the other pole. And so the dance of life continues. More deeply satisfying resolutions to age-old dilemmas are possible, as long as this dialectic is acknowledged and is used to inform productive dialogue.

## SOCIAL PHENOMENA AFFECTING BREAKTHROUGHS ABOUT INDIVIDUALS IN SYSTEMS

Cutting-edge OD practitioners are creating powerful new personal development approaches standing on the shoulders of Kurt Lewin. But they have gone beyond his breakthrough theories of the 1940s. Lewin's principles were a timely counterbalance to the attraction of personal therapeutic models of Freud and Jung and to behavioral psychologists like Skinner. Of crucial importance was Lewin's classic formula of a person's relationship to his or her environment;

$B = f(P, E)$, where behavior (B) equates to the function (f) of the person (P) plus his or her environment (E).

'His formula implies that individuals are not isolated entities *behaving* in a vacuum (individual internal); rather, they interact with and are shaped by what is going on around them (collective internal).

As many OD practitioners know—sometimes from painful experience—attempting to change a person's attitudes or behavior in isolation from the environment may limit long-term success. Like many addicts who go away to

## Polarity Management® Map

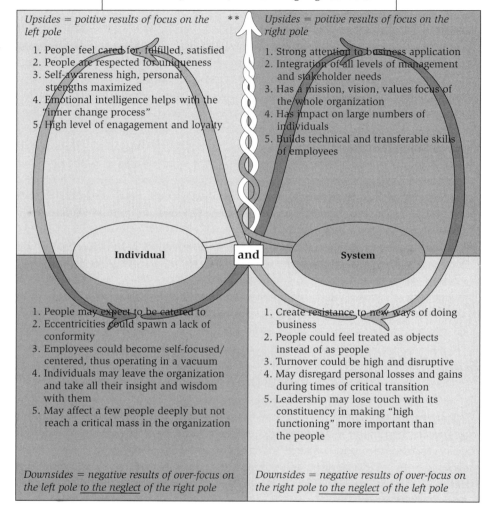

The Goal That Makes Managing This Polarity Worthwhile
**Productive, Effective, and Fulfilling Organizations**

Upsides = poitive results of focus on the left pole
** 
Upsides = poitive results of focus on the right pole

1. People feel cared for, fulfilled, satisfied
2. People are respected for uniqueness
3. Self-awareness high, personal strengths maximized
4. Emotional intelligence helps with the "inner change process"
5. High level of enagagement and loyalty

1. Strong attention to business application
2. Integration of all levels of management and stakeholder needs
3. Has a mission, vision, values focus of the whole organization
4. Has impact on large numbers of individuals
5. Builds technical and transferable skills of employees

**Individual**        and        **System**

1. People may expect to be catered to
2. Eccentricities could spawn a lack of conformity
3. Employees could become self-focused/ centered, thus operating in a vacuum
4. Individuals may leave the organization and take all their insight and wisdom with them
5. May affect a few people deeply but not reach a critical mass in the organization

1. Create resistance to new ways of doing business
2. People could feel treated as objects instead of as people
3. Turnover could be high and disruptive
4. May disregard personal losses and gains during times of critical transition
5. Leadership may lose touch with its constituency in making "high functioning" more important than the people

Downsides = negative results of over-focus on the left pole to the neglect of the right pole
Downsides = negative results of over-focus on the right pole to the neglect of the left pole

**Figure 14.3.** Polarity Management Map

Polarity Map © 1992, 2008 Management Associates LLC.

get "clean," then often relapse upon returning to their family systems, individuals in organizations who are "'sent away to be changed" usually revert to their former patterns of behavior on re-entry to the work situation. Lewin's advice still applies: instead of trying to change the individual, it's better to focus on changing elements in the larger system that would more likely modify their behavior permanently (external collective).

# ARRAY OF ID INTERVENTIONS

To choose the anciently contested path of "via positiva" versus "via negativa" is an act of faith in life and in people. This focus on enhancing the strengths of others in ID interventions is intended to build positive psychological capital. As the leverage for change, it consists of future-oriented strategies, searching positive aspects, rather than diagnosing problems, working toward collaboration rather than competition. Such interventions have successfully brought about widespread attitudinal change in organizations and individuals. We briefly outline such interventions in Table 14.1.

# KEY LEVERAGE POINTS FOR INTERPERSONAL DEVELOPMENT

Using a conceptual model adapted from Richard Bolles by co-author John Scherer, many individual development efforts in the workplace focus on the Work Content Area and somewhat on the Functional/Transferable Area in the pyramid shown in Figure 14.4. These skills are more directly connected to a person's effectiveness

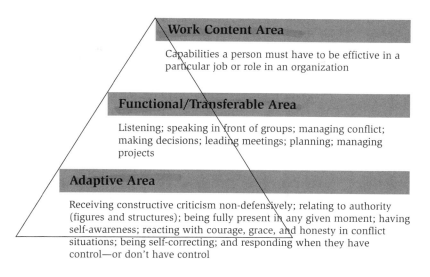

**Figure 14.4.** Skill Level Pyramid

**Table 14.1. Array of ID Interventions**

| | Description | Benefits | Considerations |
|---|---|---|---|
| Coaching | Every successful athlete has a coach. So should managers. A coach works with a client or coachee to enhance the person's effectiveness, assisting in bringing out the best the person has in him or her and applying it in life and/or work. Coaching concentrates on where the clients are now and what they are willing to do to get where they want to be in the future. | Coaching accelerates the client's progress in life and work by helping him or her create greater focus, awareness, and increased options. Since the coach, unlike the mentor, does not work with the client, there is greater safety in revealing potentially career-damaging issues. The client does not have to worry about looking good and can therefore work at deeper levels in enhancing effectiveness and fulfillment. | Because coaching is a professional relationship existing outside the organization's structure, there will be *cost* involved. Because coaching is an ongoing process, *time* is required, taking the coachees away from their work for an hour or two on a regular basis. It is important to focus on transferable and adaptive skills (see below) so that results are visible to the investors. |
| Mentoring | A more senior manager takes a more junior manager under his wing and, through regular one-on-one meetings and conversations, assists the person in navigating the way through the politics of the organization, guides the person's decision making about career issues, and does what he can to foster the person's capabilities and perceived value to the organization. | Career-Enhancement. Having one or more politically savvy senior executives in various specialty areas guiding one's career path and helping make tough career-oriented decisions enhances the likelihood that someone will make wise choices and move more smoothly through the organization. | By hitching herself to the star of a specific senior mentor, the mentee runs the risk of being tarred with the same brush if the mentor should fall from favor. The mentee is also not likely to reveal sensitive issues, thus the need for coaching. Today's complexities invite the concept of a team of champions instead of just one person. |

|  | Description | Benefits | Considerations |
|---|---|---|---|
| T-Group | Usually a seven-to-ten-day residential experience with a small group of ten to sixteen people who come together to learn about themselves in the context of a group, where the designated leader(s) or facilitator(s) do not lead or facilitate in a traditional way. Instead of managing the conversation, they make occasional observations about the group's process and give brief input on group dynamics, leaving it up to the group to manage its own affairs and learn from what is happening. | Self-Awareness: The group becomes a laboratory wherein people can try new behaviors and learn the effect of their old behavior through giving and receiving feedback. In confronting the blank slate of a leaderless group, people fill in the vacated space with their own agendas—revealing their inner needs and insights. In skilled hands, people also learn about group dynamics, the original agenda of the T-group. Unfreeze—Change—Refreeze. | As history clearly shows, if people attend T-groups with colleagues, there is the potential for what happens to be used in negative political ways back at work. In the hands of less-skilled facilitators, it is possible for participants to get in over their heads and experience emotional disintegration with no help in putting things together again. This results in Unfreeze—Change—with no Re-Freezing. Key organizational sponsors can be appointed to receive and integrate the person back into the system, helping translate insights into action. |
| Orientation | Activities carried out with new employees (and managers) to assist them in coming to understand the culture of the organization and their places in the system. Often includes face-to-face visits with key leaders and managers, as well as question-and-answer sessions. The objective: accelerate the getting on board process and have people ready to dig in and go to work ASAP. | What is often a perfunctory and obligatory experience can, in the hands of an ID expert, create positive psychological capital and a positive cultural readiness. Rules to ensure this sticks: be simple, communicating the core idea; do the unexpected, grabbing attention; be concrete, using vivid, hard-to-hear truths and helping them understand; be credible, by bringing in experts; be emotional, helping them care; use stories, detailing possibilities of how things could be better. | Orientations are easy to mess up. HR staff can forget to include the more challenging human needs of their new employees and end up de-motivating them and/or burying them in organizational messes. You have about ten minutes to set the tone you want people to take away from the orientation, so make the beginning as interesting and as human as possible. Ask yourself: What would *I* need at this point in my employment? This serves as a way to initiate new employees into the cultural DNA of the organization. |

**Table 14.1. Array of ID Interventions**

| | Description | Benefits | Considerations |
|---|---|---|---|
| Assessments | Mentoring, coaching, and training can be enhanced with the use of some kind of data-gathering instrument or assessment, which can be as simple as a single page of questions or a full-blown diagnostic tool with research-based numeric or qualitative data base. The focus can be on things like communication, leadership, personal/ management style (MBTI), or sometimes the data is gathered from colleagues and fed back to the user in a 360-degree process. | Using an instrument with a "hard" research base gives the respondents a more objective sense of where they are. The same instrument can be used at some time in the future, giving the respondents a clear picture of their progress. Involving colleagues in the data-gathering and feedback process creates a better application or transfer of learning environment—feeling trusted, colleagues are more likely to support the user's development. | The map is not the territory. It is possible to become so enamored with hard data that subtle aspects of a client's reality can be overlooked or downplayed. In a low-trust environment, gathering data from colleagues bent on sabotaging someone's career to enhance their own, the data gathered can be skewed to show a more negative picture than is real. In the hands of a less-skilled consultant, the process (especially the 360) can leave a trail of bodies if the data is not worked through deeply enough to become truly useful. What does this data *mean*? |
| Rewards | These are ways people are recognized and/or given something of value as an incentive to greater performance and effort. It can be as simple as a "Nice job" or as complex as a profit-sharing system or monetary spiff given for a job well done. Research shows that money is a *satisfier*—not a *motivator*—how the reward is offered is more of a factor in the long run. | Linking rewards to specific behaviors that create the outcomes the organization is aiming for motivates people to do what is necessary for success. When a person knows that a reward (that is meaningful to him or her) comes when he or she does X, it increases awareness and interest in doing X as well and as often as possible. Performance management builds on this principle. | Rewards must be given as close in time to the behavior being reinforced as possible. Otherwise, it becomes a mystery and the psychological connection is lost between the behavior and the reward. When a reward comes in a "currency" that is not valued by an employee, it is lost on the person. When giving away monetary rewards in the absence of conversations of encouragement, over time the money is wasted. |

on the job. Technical training, a huge commitment in many organizations, is aimed at this area. We all know people, however, who have mastered the *work content skills* for their jobs, yet fail dismally as members of the organization. There is more to individual effectiveness than this level of skill.

*Transferable skills*, on the other hand, apply to more than one specific job role. There is a high correlation between these skills and delivering on concrete results. Most ID efforts focus here with adequate results. There is another level, however, that is fundamental to the other two: the most hidden and most powerful area of personal development. The *Adaptive area* refers to the habitual ways of thinking, feeling, and behaving that a person developed early in life in order to survive and be successful in his or her family of origin (Kerr & Minno, 1999). How did they learn to adapt to what was happening around them and how will they modify these thoughts and behaviors for greater personal impact? These characteristics are more about *who a person is* than about what he or she thinks or does. Here is a sampling of skills in these areas used to assess and train leaders and managers in client systems.

It is a rule of work life that people get hired for their work content and functional skills and fired (or promoted) for their adaptive tendencies.

## Great Versus Average Performance

"Via positiva" begs for the change leader to plan for health and scan for disease in a client system. Goleman (2003) found that the difference between average and great performance is also essential to successful ID interventions. It is referred to as the Intentional Change Process. First, we must have a *vision* of the ideal self. Second, we need to experience the self in reality, having a clear view of our strengths and gaps in competence. Third, we must be willing to practice new ways of being in the workplace. Fourth, perhaps most critically, it is the receiving of iterative feedback from trusted, credible sources and having solid relationships over time with people who can assist us to have the "real view" of the self. It is this that allows us to grow our adaptive areas most effectively enhancing our capacity to become a "world-centric integral leader.".

---

### Case in Point

An experiment took place in which scientists took swabs of the cells inside of a person's mouth and flew them in a Petrie dish to Australia from the United States. Two weeks later, they evoked emotions in the person still in the United States and found that the cells five thousand miles away were reactive in the same way as the subject was. This process is termed "correlating."

A global consulting firm employs this principle in teaching meeting management to executive teams. They insist that the purpose of meetings is not to exchange energy but rather to correlate or "attune" with each other, thereby setting the "contagious tone" of how they will operate when they are virtual. The entire meeting becomes the laboratory for how they function when they are separate and on task in several locations.

They use this as their source of observing and setting feedback loops into their performance improvement process and do it in real time around real subjects that concern them all. They understand that *what does not happen in the meeting will not happen in real life*. It is their diagnostic tool of choice and their clients do not leave the room until they are adequately attuned with each other.

# FEEDBACK IN INDIVIDUAL DEVELOPMENT

Feedback is a fundamental element in every training program or mentoring and coaching relationship. A person does not have to be in a program to receive feedback. In every healthy organization, informal feedback occurs continuously in all kinds of ways, and usually addresses above-the-waterline work content issues—things like how well a report went or the accuracy of an email or measurements of a person's productivity. There is a tacit opening and expectation that someone will give you feedback on your performance. It comes with the job. To paraphrase Charles Seashore (Seashore & Weinberg, 1997), feedback is information about past behavior, delivered in the present, in a way that allows it to influence future behavior.

## Cognitive Dissonance

As Lynton and Pareek (1990) have shown, one reason the T-group, for instance, works to change participants' attitudes and behaviors is the result of cognitive dissonance. Cognitive dissonance exists whenever there is a perceived difference between *what is* and a key belief about *what should be* happening. Cognitive dissonance is what happens inside you when someone makes a comment about you and you spontaneously disagree. Internal discord can rise, which, by nature, we are driven to reduce, sometimes at great cost to the relationship. This is where adaptive skills are most helpful. Dissonance usually occurs when someone's self-concept, his or her expectations of a situation, actual behaviors, and the reactions of others are at odds.

The key point to remember here is that, whether a practitioner is designing a training program or setting up a coaching or mentoring relationship and wants deep learning to occur, one proven approach is to *make sure that there is cognitive dissonance in the experience*. The practitioner or facilitator must find a way to confront participants with whatever gaps are present between their concept of things and reality (for example, how trustworthy others perceive someone

### Table 14.2. Checklist for Offering Feedback Effectively

| Is Effective | Not Effective | Example |
|---|---|---|
| Descriptive | Evaluative | "X happens, which confuses me" vs. "That's ridiculous" |
| Focused on the behavior | Focused on the personality | "When you did X" vs. "When you are a very controlling person" |
| Concerns behavior that is modifiable | Focus on the unchangeable | "Making a funny sound in your throat" vs. "That limp of yours…" |
| Specific and based on data | General and based on impressions | "Yesterday, the way you handled X" vs. "You're never nice to my friends" |
| Based on data from the provider's experience | Hearsay | "I noticed X" vs. "Stacey said that you are…" |
| Reinforces positive new behavior and what the recipient has done well | Begin with negative | "Opening your presentation with that overview seemed to create a receptive listening" vs. "That…" |
| Suggest | Prescribe improvement avenues | "I wonder what would happen if you did X" vs. "Just handle it" |
| Continual | Sporadic | Informally, constructive, and positive, every day vs. once every six months at performance review time |
| Based on need and requested by the recipient | When you alone are ready | "Are you willing to receive feedback now?" vs. "Get ready, here it comes" |
| Intended to help | Intended to wound | "I feel you could be even more effective if…" vs. "You're just not enough" |
| Satisfies the needs of both provider and recipient | Damaging to relationship | "I bet we would both benefit from some honesty" vs. "Just get out" |

to be). This requires that both participants and the OD practitioner be highly skilled at offering and receiving feedback.

## Offering Feedback Effectively

Interpersonal feedback involves at least two people: one who gives feedback and one who receives it. The main purpose of feedback is to help the recipient increase personal and interpersonal effectiveness (individual internal/collective internal). The effectiveness of feedback depends on the *behaviors* and *responses* of both the feedback provider and the feedback recipient and should follow the suggested guidelines set out in Table 14.2. While the skill of offering and receiving feedback is vital, more importantly, the intent behind it must be one of *serving the other person* with helpful insights.

## Receiving Feedback Effectively

The effectiveness of feedback depends as much on how it is received and used as on how it is given. If the feedback disconfirms an expectation of the recipient (for example, concerning his or her self-image), dissonance is created. According to dissonance theory, disconfirming an expectation stimulates psychological tension, which sets up a "moment of truth" when learning can happen. The feedback recipient may reduce dissonance by reacting in either a defensive or an open/confronting manner. If the fight or flight stress response is intense, it is an indication that there may be a threat to the person's core identity. This is where the adaptive skills and taking a larger perspective become most useful. Groundbreaking researcher Clare Graves' concept of tribalism indicates that most people fear that negative feedback leads to their being unduly on display as an outcast and thus ostracized. Therefore, creating a supportive, emotionally safe environment makes the difference (Beck & Cowan, 1996).

# SUMMARY

Organizations around the globe are finding that what they thought was unconventional five years ago has become mainstream today. The longer the traditions of the companies, the more innovative they must be to meet the demands of a changing society. Call it "the strengths revolution," "natural capitalism," or "triple bottom-line," recent economic and social upheaval is also spawning opportunities to redefine the workplace. The authors have taken the view that deep engagement at the level of the individual, using a wide array of already existing ID activities, can have system-wide impact and yet must be leveraged through the four arenas of development (seen in Figure 14.1) in order to be referred to as OD. Rick Flath, co-author, has observed in twenty-five years of interacting with client systems that most successful organization change efforts begin with individual development before engaging the full organizational system.

As the globe shrinks, the speed of proximity to the unfamiliar is surrounding each of us with other generations, cultures, and belief systems that force us to become more compassionate and inclusive or burn up in the cauldron of the laboratory called the workplace. The business of exchanging goods and services is ultimately a human process, supported by solid technology. We are here to serve one another and, in doing so, have an opportunity to develop our own talents and character along the way. The better human being is the result of good business practices. Business philosopher Peter Koestenbaum (2002) emphasizes that personal maturity makes good business sense. And it is through the consistent positive intent and skilled feedback of trusted colleagues that each of us is shaped.

We believe it possible to live as a healthy community of individuals while turning a decent financial profit and doing social good. The assertion is that to enact OD processes with strengths-based ID principles can produce a more world-centric view, thus encouraging a healthy and peaceful global environment. While most OD practitioners are by nature empathetic to the role of ID in their work, we hope that this chapter has brought to light complementary perspectives that allow the reader to become even more human-centric. As co-author Lynnea Brinkerhoff reminds us, "No matter what the mission of our organization, we are all in the business of IS-ness!"

# References

Beck, D., & Cowan, C. (1996). *Spiral dynamics: Mastering values, leadership and change*. Malden, MA: Blackwell.

Goleman, D. (2003). *Emotional intelligence at work*. New York: Bantam.

Johnson, B. (1992). *Polarity management: Identifying and managing unsolvable problems*. Amherst, MA: HRD Press.

Kerr, B., & Minno, D. (1999). Unraveling the knot. In P.M. Senge, A. Kleiner, C. Roberts, G. Roth, R. Ross, & B. Smith (Eds.), *The dance of change: The challenge of sustaining momentum in learning organizations*. New York: Currency/Doubleday.

Koestenbaum, P. (2002). *Inner side of greatness, A philosophy for leaders*. San Francisco: Jossey-Bass.

Laszlo, E. (2006). *The chaos point: The world at a crossroads*. Charlottesville, VA: Hampton Roads Publishing.

Long, S. (2008). #1 reason 75% of organizational change efforts fail & how you can be part of the 25% that succeed. Ezine Articles [http://ezinearticles.com/?1-Reason-75%-of-Organizational-Change-Efforts-Fail-and-How-YOU-Can-Be-Part-of-the-25%-That-Succeed&id = 1416793]

Lynton, R., & Pareek, U. (1990). *Training for development* (2nd ed.). West Hartford, CT: Kumarian Press.

Miller, R. (2004). *The millennium matrix*. San Francisco: Jossey-Bass.

Scherer, J.J. (1980). Job-related adaptive skills. Toward personal growth. In J.W. Pfeiffer & J.E. Jones (Eds.), *The 1980 annual handbook for group facilitators*. San Francisco: Pfeiffer.

Scherer, J.J. (2009). Five questions that change everything: Life lessons at work. Fort Collins, CO: Bibliocast Press.

Seashore, C.C., & Weinberg, G. (1997). *What did you say? The art of giving and receiving feedback*. Columbia, MD: Bingham House.

Wilber, K. (2001). *A theory of everything: An integral vision for business, politics, science, and spirituality*. Boston, MA: Shambhala Publications.

2007 Industry Report. (2007, October 25). *Training*, p. 2.

# CHAPTER FIFTEEN

# Team Building and the Four Cs of Team Performance*

*W. Gibb Dyer and Jeffrey H. Dyer*

One of the key interventions used by organization development (OD) practitioners almost since the field's inception has been "team building" whose primary purpose is to improve team performance. Over the past several decades, as we have consulted with teams and conducted research on team performance, we have come to the conclusion that there are four factors—"Four Cs"—that must be understood by OD practitioners in order for them to do effective team building.

These factors, depicted in Figure 15.1, are

1. The *context* for the team;
2. The *composition* of the team;
3. The *competencies* of the team; and
4. The *change* management skills of the team.

In this chapter, we will discuss the importance of these four factors in determining team effectiveness and then discuss various options available to OD practitioners who want to engage in team building to improve team performance.

---

*This chapter is adapted from W.G. Dyer, W.G. Dyer, Jr., and J.H. Dyer. *Team Building: Proven Strategies for Improving Team Performance.* San Francisco: Jossey-Bass, 2007.

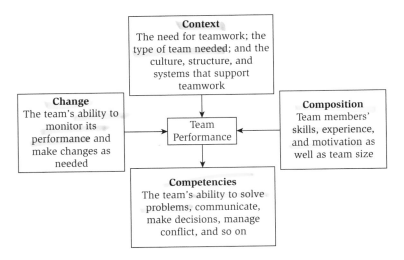

**Figure 15.1.** The Four Cs of Team Performance

# CONTEXT FOR THE TEAM

Team context refers to the organizational environment in which the team must work. Understanding context, and how it influences team performance, requires an understanding of the answers to the following questions:

1. Is effective teamwork critical to accomplishing the goals desired by the organization? If so, what are the measurable team performance goals around which the team can organize?

2. Does the organization's reward systems, structure, and culture support teamwork?

Experience has shown that the teamwork required to achieve high performance is much more important when the team must complete a complex task characterized by a high degree of interdependence. In addition, we have found that some organizations deploy formal organization structures or reward systems that become barriers to effective teamwork. For example, reward systems that provide strong individual incentives often create strong disincentives to engage in cooperative behavior within a work team.

High-performing teams manage context effectively by: (1) establishing measurable team performance goals that are clear and compelling, (2) ensuring that team members understand that effective teamwork is critical to meeting those goals, (3) establishing reward systems that reward team performance (more than individual performance), (4) eliminating roadblocks to teamwork that formal organization structures might create, and (5) establishing an organizational culture that supports teamwork-oriented processes and behaviors.

# COMPOSITION OF THE TEAM

The composition of the team concerns the skills and attitudes of team members. You have to have the "right people on the bus" to make things happen as a team and achieve top performance (Collins, 2001). To effectively manage the composition of the team, team leaders must understand that team leadership and processes differ depending on the answers to the following questions:

1. To what extent do individual team members have the technical and interpersonal skills required to complete the task?

2. To what extent are individual team members committed to the team and motivated to complete the task?

3. Is the team the right size to successfully complete the task?

Teams saddled with members who are not motivated to accomplish the task, or who do not have the skills to achieve team goals, are doomed to failure from the outset. Of course, "team composition" also refers to assembling a group of individuals with complementary skills. High-performing teams utilize the complementary skills and abilities of each team member in a synergistic way to achieve high performance. Team members of high-performing teams clearly understand their roles and assignments and carry them out with commitment. Team size also plays a significant role in team effectiveness. A team that is too large may be unwieldy and cause team members to lose interest due to a lack of individual involvement. Too few team members may place unnecessary burdens on individual team members, and the team may not have the resources needed to accomplish its goals.

High-performing teams effectively manage team composition by: (1) establishing processes to select individuals for the team who are both skilled and motivated, (2) establishing processes that develop the technical and interpersonal skills of team members as well as their commitment to achieve team goals, (3) cutting loose individuals who lack skills and/or motivation, (4) managing the team differently depending on the skills and motivation of team members, and (5) ensuring the team is "right sized," which usually means making sure the team is not too large or small to accomplish the task.

# COMPETENCIES OF THE TEAM

We have found that successful teams have certain competencies that exist independent of any single member of the team but that are embedded in the team's formal and informal processes—its way of functioning. High-performing teams have developed processes that allow the team to:

1. Clearly articulate their goals and the metrics for achieving those goals;

2. Clearly articulate the means required to achieve the goals, ensuring that individuals understand their assignments and how their work contributes to team goals;

3. Make effective decisions;

4. Establish accountability for team and individual assignments;

5. Effectively manage meetings;

6. Effectively communicate, including giving and receiving feedback;

7. Build trust and commitment to the team and its goals;

8. Resolve disputes or disagreements;

9. Create mutual respect among team members;

10. Encourage risk taking and innovation;

Thus, while the context and composition of the team set the stage, these competencies propel it to high performance. If the team hopes to be extraordinary, it must develop competencies at goal setting, decision making, communicating, trust building, and dispute resolution.

# CHANGE MANAGEMENT SKILLS OF THE TEAM

High-performing teams must change and adapt to new conditions to be effective over time. Factors related to team context, composition, and competencies may need to be changed for the team to succeed in reaching a new goal. A team that is able to monitor its performance and understand its strengths and weaknesses can generate insights needed to develop a plan of action to continually improve. Toyota, a company that we've researched extensively, uses the "kaizen" or continuous improvement philosophy to help its teams identify the "bottlenecks" they are facing and then develop strategies to eliminate the bottlenecks (Dyer & Hatch, 2004). They are never fully satisfied with the team's performance because, once they've fixed one problem, they know that continuous improvement requires that they find, and fix, the next one. However, unlike Toyota, we have found that teams in most companies are oblivious to their weaknesses or, even when they do recognize them, they do not have the ability to manage change effectively to overcome those weaknesses. It is possible to view "change management skills" as just another team competency, but this "meta-competency"—what we call "team-building skills"— is so important that it deserves special attention.

High-performing teams have developed the ability to change by: (1) establishing team-building processes that result in the regular evaluation of team context, team composition, and team competencies with the explicit objective of initiating needed changes in order to better achieve the desired team goals; and (2) establishing a philosophy among team members that regular change is necessary in order to meet the demands of a constantly changing world.

# STAGES OF A TEAM-BUILDING PROGRAM

Now that we have briefly discussed the Four Cs of team performance, we will discuss what to do at each stage of a team-building program to ensure its success. These stages are labeled: Preparation, Start-Up and Data Gathering, Data Analysis and Problem Solving, Giving Feedback, Action Planning, and Follow-Up. In each stage there are a variety of alternatives available depending on the nature of the problem and the circumstances of the team.

## 1. Preparation

*Goals.* The goals are to explain the purpose of team building, gain commitment for participation, and do preliminary work for the team-building workshop. Commitment will increase if people understand clearly *why* the team-building program is being proposed and whether they have an opportunity to influence the decision to go ahead with the program.

Questions of deep concern probably will not be eliminated but may be reduced as a supportive climate is established and as people "test the water" and find that plunging in is not very difficult. Experience will be the best teacher, and people will allay or confirm their fears as the session proceeds. Those conducting the session should anticipate such concerns and raise them prior to the first meeting to reduce any extreme anxiety by openly describing what will happen and what the anticipated outcome will be.

## 2. Start-Up and Data Gathering

*Goals.* The goals of this stage are to create a climate for work; to help people relax; to establish norms for being open with problems, concerns, and ideas, for planning, and for dealing with issues; and to present a framework for the whole experience. The climate established during the start-up phase will, of course, influence the rest of the program. Here are some ideas about how you might begin:

1. The manager or team leader can give a short opening talk, reviewing the goals as he or she sees them and the need for the program, emphasizing his or her support, and reaffirming the norm that no negative sanctions are intended for any open, honest behavior.

2. The role of the consultant can be explained by either the manager or the consultant.

3. Participants are asked to share their immediate here-and-now feelings about the meetings. Their responses should be listed on a white board and discussed by the team.

The purpose of this type of beginning is to set the norm that the whole program is centered on data gathering, data analysis, open sharing, and trying to plan with data. This also allows group members to test the water about simple, immediate data rather than more sensitive work-group issues, to see how people will respond and react to the questions.

Another approach to starting a team-building program would be to ask team members the following: "In order for us to see a picture of how you see our team functioning, would each of you take a few minutes to describe our team as a kind of animal or combination of animals, a kind of machine, a kind of person, or whatever image comes to mind." Some teams in the past have been described as

- *A hunting dog—a pointer.* We run around and locate problems, then stop and point and hope that somebody else will take the action.
- *An octopus.* Each tentacle is out grasping anything it can but doesn't know what the other tentacles are doing.

As people share such images and explain what elicits the image, some questions may be asked: What are the common elements in these images? Do we like these images of ourselves? What do we need to do to change our image? Discussions aimed at answering these questions become the major agenda item for subsequent group meetings.

A third alternative is to ask the team to work on a major decision-making problem—such as the arctic or desert survival activities or TinkerToy tower building (Miller, 2004). The consultant acts as a process observer. After the exercise, the consultant has the group members review their own processes and determine both their strengths and their deficiencies in solving problems. The consultant shares his or her observations with the group. In some instances we have found it useful to videotape the team doing the exercise and then replay the videotape for the team so that team members can actually see how they performed. As the exercise is reviewed, lists of positive and negative features are compiled.

The agenda for the following session is set based on the question, "How do we maximize our strengths and overcome deficiencies?" Of course, it is also appropriate to use more traditional methods of data gathering such as interviews or surveys to gather data about the team. In cases in which there is some reluctance on the part of team members to share data openly, the OD consultant will likely gather data from the team via personal interviews or a survey (see Dyer, Dyer, & Dyer, 2007, for various team surveys).

## 3. Data Analysis and Problem Solving

*Goals.* One goal is to take action on the problems identified in the previous phase. Assignments are made and dates are set for the completion of work. Another goal is for the team to practice better problem-solving, decision-making, planning, objective-selecting, and delegation skills.

Whatever the start-up method or combination of methods used, this third phase usually involves two parts: (1) the team begins to engage in the problem-solving process and (2) the OD consultant helps the group look at its competencies in working on problems as an effective team, as a prelude to improving its problem-solving capabilities. Some of the common problems we find in teams are

- Domination by the leader;
- Warring cliques or subgroups;
- Unequal participation and uneven use of group resources;
- Rigid or dysfunctional group norms and procedures;
- A climate of defensiveness or fear;
- A lack of creative alternatives to problems;
- Restricted communications—not all have opportunities to speak; and
- Avoidance of differences or potential conflicts.

Such conditions reduce the team's ability to work together in collective problem-solving situations. The role of the consultant is to help the group become aware of its processes and begin to develop better group skills. Specifically, after becoming aware of a process problem, the group needs to establish a procedure, guideline, or plan of action to respond to the negative condition.

One approach that we've found helpful in the data-analysis and problem-solving stage is, instead of presenting data from prior data-collection methods to the team, data about the conditions or problems of the team can be raised at the team meeting. Each person is asked to come prepared to share his or her perception of the following: (1) What keeps this team from functioning at its maximum potential? (2) What keeps you, personally, from doing the kind of job you would like to do? (3) What things do you like in this team that you want to have maintained? (4) What changes would you like to see made that would help you and the whole team? Team members or the leader may have other items they would like to put on the agenda.

Each team member takes a turn sharing information. The responses are listed and common themes are identified. The most important issues are listed in priority, and they become the items for discussion.

Regardless of the approach taken, the team should, by this point, have identified a series of problems, concerns, or issues. The team next must move into a traditional problem-solving process by engaging in the following kinds of activities:

1. Put problems in order of priority and select the five or six most pressing problems to be addressed during the workshop.

2. Begin the classic problem-solving process: clearly define the problem, describe the causes of the problem, list alternative solutions, select the alternative to be implemented, develop an action plan, perform the action, and evaluate the results.

3. Conduct a force-field analysis (Lewin, 1958). Identify the existing level of team performance on a set of performance metrics, formulate a specific goal to improve performance, identify the restraining forces (the factors that are barriers to better performance), and develop a plan to remove the restraining forces.

4. Begin role negotiation (Harrison, 1971). Negotiate between people or subunits that are interdependent and who need to coordinate well with each other to improve effectiveness.

5. Set up task-force teams or subunits. Give each team a problem to work on. Set up a plan of action, carry out the plan, and assess the results.

6. After all problems have been listed, the team can sort them into categories based on the nature of the problem: (a) we can work on the problem here within our team; (b) someone else must handle the problem (and identify who that is); or (c) we must live with this problem, since it appears to be beyond our ability to change.

7. Set targets, objectives, or goals. The group should spend time identifying short- or long-range goals it wishes to achieve, make assignments, and set target dates for completion.

## 4. Giving Feedback

A major issue that often arises following the identification of problems is the sharing of feedback with individuals, subgroups within the team, or the team as a whole. Certain actions, functions, personal styles, or strategies on the part of one or more people may be hindering teamwork and preventing other team members from achieving their goals or feeling satisfied with the team. If such is the case, it may be legitimate to engage in an open feedback session.

*Goals.* This phase is designed to share feedback among individual team members in such a way as to help them improve their effectiveness and to give feedback to the whole team with the same objective in mind. The goal of a feedback session is to share data about performance so that difficulties can be resolved. It is critical that a feedback session *not* slip into name calling, personal griping, or verbal punishing of others. All feedback should reflect a genuine willingness to work cooperatively: "My performance suffers because of some things that happen in which you are involved. Let me share my feelings and reactions so you can see what is happening to me. I would like to work out a way that we all can work more productively together." The following are some ways group members might go about sharing feedback with one another:

1. *Each person has a sheet of newsprint on the wall.* Each team member writes on the sheets of other members' items in three areas: (a) things that person should *begin* doing that will increase his or her effectiveness; (b) things the individual should *stop* doing; and (c) things he or she should *continue* to do.

2. *Envelope exchange.* Each person writes a note to the others, covering the same issues as in Item 1, and gives the notes to the other team members.

3. *Confirmation-disconfirmation process.* Group members summarize how they view themselves and their own work performance—their strengths and areas that need improvement. Others are asked to confirm or disconfirm the person's diagnosis.

4. *Management profile.* Each person presents the profile of his or her effectiveness from previously gathered data (there are a variety of profile instruments). The group confirms or disconfirms the profile.

5. *Analysis of subunits.* If the team has subunits, each subunit is discussed in terms of what it does well, what it needs to change, and what it needs to improve.

6. *Total unit or organizational analysis.* The group looks at how it has been functioning and critiques its own performance over the past year, identifying things it has done well and areas that need to be improved.

7. *Open feedback session.* Each person who would like feedback may ask for it in order to identify areas of personal effectiveness and areas that need to be improved.

8. *Prescription writing.* Each person writes a prescription for others: "Here is what I would prescribe that you do (or stop doing) in order to be more effective in your position." Prescriptions are then exchanged.

## 5. Action Planning

The end result of all the activities mentioned so far is to help the team identify those conditions that are blocking both individual and team effectiveness so that the team can begin to develop plans for action and change. Action plans should include a commitment to carry the action to completion.

*Goals.* The goals of this phase are to pinpoint needed changes, set goals, develop plans, give assignments, outline procedures, and set dates for completion and review. Often the plan is a set of agreements on who is willing to take a specific action. All such agreements should be written down, circulated, and followed up later to ensure that they have been carried out.

*Options for action planning.* Following is a set of actions that are possible during this phase:

1. *Personal improvement plan.* Each person evaluates his or her feedback and develops a plan of action for personal improvement. This plan is presented to the others.

2. *Contract negotiations* (Boss, 1989). If there are particular problems between individuals or subunits, specific agreements for dealing with conflict issues are drawn up and signed.

3. *Assignment summary.* Each person summarizes what his or her assignments are and the actions he or she intends to take as a follow-up of the team-development meeting.

4. *Subunit or team plans.* If development plans have been completed, they are presented and reviewed.

*Schedule review.* The team looks at its time schedule and its action plans. Dates for completion and dates for giving progress reports on work being done are confirmed. The next team meeting is then scheduled. If another team-development workshop or meeting is needed, it may be scheduled at this time.

## Another Approach to Team Building: Appreciative Inquiry

Up to this point we've focused on using a "problem-centered" approach to team building: the team identifies the problems it faces and then engages in problem solving to improve its performance. An alternative team-building approach is to focus on the more positive aspects of the team using Appreciative Inquiry (AI) (Cherney, 2005).

The AI approach to team building starts with the assumption that every team has some positive characteristics that can drive it to high performance. The issue for the team is how to discover and tap into these positive characteristics. Thus, rather than focus on the negative—the problems experienced by the team—this team-building approach focuses on the positive characteristics of the team. To begin the team-building activity, the manager, team leader, or consultant asks team members to answer the following questions (Cherney, 2005):

1. Think of a time when you were on a hugely successful team, a time you felt energized, fulfilled, and the most effective—when you were able to accomplish even more than you imagined. What made it such a

great team? Tell the story about the situation, the people involved, and how the team achieved its breakthrough.

2. Without being humble, what was it about you that contributed to the success of the team? Describe in detail these qualities and what you value about yourself that enables team success.

3. It is one year from today and your team is functioning more successfully than any of you imagined. What are we doing, how are we working together differently, what does this success look like, and how do we make it happen?

Members of the team pair up and share their answers to these questions. They then can move into larger subgroups and share their stories, or the entire team can be brought back together to report their stories and their feelings about the future of the team. Professor Gervase Bushe, who uses the AI approach, explains how one team improved its performance through AI:

> "In one business team I worked with, one member talked about a group of young men he played pick-up basketball with and described why they were, in his opinion, such an outstanding 'team.' He described their shared sense of what they were there to do, lack of rigid roles, [and] easy adaptability to the constraints of any particular situation in the service of their mission. But what most captured the team's imagination was his description of how this group was both competitive and collaborative at the same time. Each person competed with all the rest to play the best ball, to come up with the neatest move and play. Once having executed it and shown his prowess, he quickly 'gave it away' to the other players in the pick-up game, showing them how to do it as well. This was a very meaningful image for this group as a key, unspoken, tension was the amount of competitiveness members felt with each other at the same time as they needed to cooperate for the organization's good. 'Back alley ball' became an important synthesizing image for this group that resolved the paradox of competitiveness and cooperation." (Cherney, 2005)

By sharing such powerful images, a team may be able to envision a different way of functioning from its current pattern and create new values and beliefs that will enable the team to plot a new course. The role of the team leader or consultant is to help the team identify those images and metaphors that can be incorporated by the team as it seeks to improve its performance. The team should ask and answer the following questions: (1) How can we as a team become like the high-performing teams that we've experienced in the past? and (2) How can I, as a member of this team, contribute to helping our team achieve its full potential? As the team and its members answer these questions, commitments are made to change the team in a positive direction. The team can use the images of team excellence to motivate the team to a higher level of performance.

The AI approach is often useful when a team tends to focus on the negative, continually bringing up negative images of the team and complaining about other team members. Such a positive approach can give energy to an otherwise impotent and demoralized team. However, when using AI, the team should still be willing to confront important problems and not see the world completely through rose-colored glasses.

## 6. Follow-Up: What Happens After Team Building?

Assuming that a team-building program began with a block of time that resulted in some agreements to change or improve the way team members have been functioning, how does a good follow-up program proceed? There must be some method of following up with team members on assignments or agreements and then some form of continuing goal setting for improved performance. These follow-up activities can be done by the whole team together, one-to-one between team members, or a combination of the two. Fortunately, some excellent research has been done that describes the kinds of follow-up processes that have proved to be successful.

Professor Wayne Boss (1989) of the University of Colorado became interested in the "regression effect" following a team-building session. He observed, as have others, that during a two- or three-day intensive team-building activity, people become very enthusiastic about making improvements, but that within a few weeks, the spark dwindles and people regress to old behaviors and performance levels. Boss wondered, "Is there a way to keep performance high following the team-building session and to prevent the regression phenomenon from occurring?" He began to experiment with a one-on-one follow-up meeting he called the Personal Management Interview (PMI). The PMI has two stages: first, a role negotiation meeting between boss and subordinate (usually one hour) during which both clarify their expectations of each other, what they need from each other, and what they will contract to do for each other. Second, following the initial role negotiation session, the two parties meet regularly. Boss found that these meetings have to be held on a regular basis (weekly, biweekly, or monthly), but if they are held and follow the agreed-on agenda, performance stays high without regression for several years. States Boss, "Without exception, the off-site level of group effectiveness was maintained only in those teams that employed the PMI, while the teams that did not use the PMI evidenced substantial regression in the months after their team-building sessions" (Boss, 1983, p. 75).

What goes on in these interviews that makes such a difference? Despite some variation, each interview tended to deal with the following issues:

- Discussion of any organizational or work problems facing the subordinate;
- Training or coaching given by the supervisor to the subordinate;
- Resolution of any concerns or problems between supervisor and subordinate;

- Information sharing to bring the subordinate up-to-date on what is happening in the team and organization; and

- Discussion of any personal problems or concerns.

These were common agenda items, but the first part of every meeting was spent reviewing assignments and accomplishments since the last session. Time was also spent making new assignments and agreeing on goals and plans to be reviewed at the next PMI. These assignments and agreements were written down, and each party had a copy that was the basis of the review at the following meeting.

Boss has the following suggestions for conducting an effective PMI:

- The PMI is most effective when conducted in a climate of high support and trust. Establishing this climate is primarily the responsibility of the superior.

- The interviews must be held on a regular basis and be free from 'interruptions.

- Both parties must prepare for the meeting by having an agreed-on agenda; otherwise, the PMI becomes nothing more than a "rap" session.

- When possible, a third party whom both the supervisor and the subordinate trust should be present to take notes and record action items.

- Meetings should be documented by use of a standard form to make sure the key issues are addressed in a systematic way. Both parties agree on the form.

- The leader must be willing to hold subordinates accountable and to ask the difficult "why" questions when assignments are not completed.

Boss has found that performance drops off if these meetings are not held but will increase if meetings are started, even if they have never been held before or had been stopped for a time. Boss has tracked the use of PMIs in 202 teams ranging from three months to twenty-nine years (personal communication, 2006). His research indicates that regular PMIs can significantly decrease, and even prevent, regression to previous levels of team performance for as long as twenty-nine years with no additional interventions after the original team-building sessions. Certainly the evidence is compelling enough to indicate that this is an effective way to follow up on the decisions made during a team-building session.

## Follow-Up Team Sessions

We have known for many years, since the early research of Rensis Likert (1967), that follow-up team sessions can also help to sustain high performance. In his research on sales teams, Likert described the elements of follow-up team meetings that make a significant difference in the performance of members on a sales team. The research was done with sales offices from a national sales organization. The top twenty sales units were compared with the bottom twenty to see what made the difference in their performance. Likert found the following to be the most important factors:

- The team leader (the sales manager) had high personal performance goals and a plan for achieving those goals. Team members saw an example of high performance as they watched the team leader.
- The team leader displayed highly supportive behavior toward team members and encouraged them to support one another.
- The team leader used participative methods in supervision. That is, all team members were involved in helping the team and the members achieve their goals.

The major process for achieving high performance was holding regular, well-planned meetings of the sales team for review of each person's performance. In contrast to Boss's PMI, which is a one-on-one follow-up, the units in the Likert research used team meetings as the follow-up process. Those team meetings had the following major features:

- The team met regularly—every two weeks or every month.
- The sales manager presided over the meeting but allowed wide participation in the group. The main function of the manager was to keep the team focused on the task, push the team to set high performance goals, and discourage negative, nonsupportive, ego-deflating actions of team members.
- Each salesperson presented a report of his or her activities during the previous period, including a description of the approach used, closings attempted, sales achieved, and volume and quality of total sales.
- All the other team members then analyzed the person's efforts and offered suggestions for improvement. Coaching was given by team members to one another.
- Each salesperson then announced his or her goals and procedures to be used for review at the next team meeting.

The researchers concluded that this form of team meeting results in four benefits:

1. Team members set higher goals.
2. They are more motivated to achieve their goals.
3. They receive more assistance, coaching, and help from their boss and peers.
4. The team gets more new ideas on how to improve performance as people share, not hide, their successful new methods.

It seems possible, then, to have either one-on-one follow-up meetings or a series of follow-up team meetings as a way of maintaining the high performance of team members. The key issue is that team building requires a continuous effort to monitor the team's ability to improve team performance. The key person is the team leader, who must build into the process some type of follow-up procedure.

# SUMMARY

In this chapter, we have described the Four Cs of team performance and the basic elements of a team-building program. These elements include describing the purposes of the team-building program and addressing any concerns or fears of team members. Common steps in team building are as follows:

- Data regarding the performance of the team is generated by examining archival data, observing the team perform a particular task, interviewing team members, or surveying members of the team. A variety of alternatives are available to generate such data.

- The team then engages in a problem-solving process to come up with solutions to the problems that have been identified. An AI approach is an alternative to the traditional problem-solving model.

- Action plans are developed and implemented by the team. Commitments are generally written down and assignments clearly communicated to team members.

- To ensure that changes in the team persist over time, team leaders should engage in regular personal management interviews with members of their team or conduct regular team meetings to review commitments made in the team-building sessions and to make changes as needed.

# References

Boss, R.W. (1983). Team building and the problem of regression. The personal management interview as an intervention. *Journal of Applied Behavior Science, 19*, 67–83.

Boss, R.W. (1989). *Organization development in health care*. Reading, MA: Addison-Wesley.

Boss, R.W. (2006, May). Personal communication.

Cherney, J.K. (2005). Appreciative teambuilding: Creating a climate for great collaboration. [www.teambuildinginc.com/article_ai.html].

Collins, J. (2001). *Good to great*. New York: HarperCollins.

Dyer, W.G., Dyer, W.G., Jr., & Dyer, J.H. (2007). *Team building: Proven strategies for improving team performance*. San Francisco: Jossey-Bass.

Dyer, J.H., & Hatch, N. (2004, Spring). Using supplier networks to learn faster. *Sloan Management Review*, pp. 57–63.

Harrison, R. (1971). Role negotiations: A tough-minded approach to team development. In W.W. Burke & H. Hornstein (Eds.), *The social technology of organization development*. Washington, DC: NTL Learning Resources.

Lewin, K. (1958). Group discussion and social change. In E.E. Maccoby, T.M. Newcomb, & E.L. Hartley (Eds.), *Readings in social psychology*. New York: Holt.

Likert, R. (1967). *The human organization*. New York: McGraw-Hill.

Miller, B.C. (2004). *Quick team building activities for busy managers: 50 exercises that get results in just 15 minutes*. New York: AMACOM.

# CHAPTER SIXTEEN

# Interventions in Large Systems

*Thomas G. Cummings and Ann E. Feyerherm*

Interventions in large systems help organizations implement changes that satisfy the demands of rapidly changing and highly competitive environments. For example, change programs may involve redesigning an organization's structure to make it leaner and more flexible, linking key suppliers and customers closer to the organization, or establishing a reward system that closely links pay with gains in business-unit performance.

This chapter details a coherent set of actions, which generally proceed from assessment and action planning to implementation of changes in large systems, such as the total organization or its major divisions. It defines interventions in large systems, describes their characteristics, and presents examples of these change methods.

## DEFINITION OF LARGE-SYSTEM INTERVENTIONS

The purpose of an OD intervention in a large system is to make significant change in the character and performance of an organization, a stand-alone business unit, or a large department. The *character* of an organization includes the pattern of exchanges between the organization and its environment and the design of the organization's internal structures, processes, and procedures that produce desired products or services. The *performance* of an organization is measured by its productivity, return on investment, environmental impact, and employee satisfaction and retention.

An organization's character directly affects its performance. Specifically, when exchanges between the organization and its environment are effective and its internal-design features fit together and reinforce strategic behavior, performance is likely to be high (Mohrman et al., 1990; Worley, Hitchin, & Ross, 1996).

Figure 16.1 illustrates these two major components of organizational character: organization-environment relations and internal-design components. The figure relies heavily on open-systems theory which views organizations as embedded in a larger environment (Cummings & Worley, 2008). The environment provides an organization with inputs (such as raw materials) that are converted by transformation processes (such as manufacturing) into outcomes (such as products and services). The environment also provides feedback to the organization about how well it is performing. The organization's transformation processes include several interrelated design components. A key concept in open-systems theory is congruency or fit among the components. They must fit with one another to attain the most effective results (Hanna, 1988; Mohr, 1989). Interventions that include more of these components increase their chance of effectiveness (Macy, Bliese, & Norton, 1994).

The open-systems model applies to different levels within an organization, as well as the whole organization. It is an appropriate model for large-system change because its components must be viewed with the total organization in

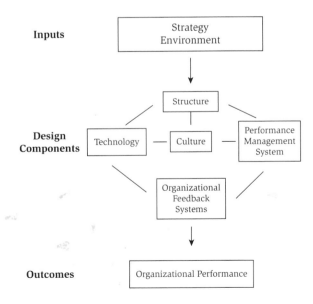

**Figure 16.1.** Model of a Large System Organization

mind. The environment must provide the organization with needed inputs; the design components must promote effective and efficient performance; and the feedback system must provide knowledge of results.

A large-system intervention aims to improve the two key aspects of an organization's character: the organization-environment relationship (how well the inputs are appropriate for the organization) and the internal-design component (how well the design components match each other). An intervention directly influences the organization's character which, in turn, affects organizational performance. Examples of large-system interventions are described later in the chapter. First, the two areas are defined further.

## Organization-Environment Relationship

The organization-environment relationship is defined as the fit or symbiosis between an organization's inputs and design components. The key inputs include strategy and environment.

*Strategy* defines how an organization will use its resources to gain a competitive advantage in the environment (Chaffee, 1985; Hill & Jones, 2004). It includes choices about which functions the organization will perform, which products or services it will produce, and which markets and populations it will serve. By its nature, strategy defines the relevant environment within which the organization chooses to compete (Porter, 1985).

Consequently, the *environment* consists of external elements and forces that affect an organization's ability to attain its strategic objectives. The environment includes suppliers, customers, competitors, and regulators. It also includes cultural, political, technical, and economic forces.

Environments range along a continuum from static to dynamic (Emery & Trist, 1965). A dynamic environment changes rapidly and unpredictably. It requires organizational strategies and designs that are different from those appropriate in a static environment. Research suggests that when an organization's strategy results in a highly dynamic environment, the organization's design should be organic with flexible design components (Burns & Stalker, 1961; Lawrence & Lorsch, 1967). A static environment calls for a more formalized structure that supports standardized behavior and predictability. Organizational members need to assess their organization's environment in order to plan a large-system intervention.

## Internal-Design Components

In addition to the organization-environment relationship, an organization's performance depends on the alignment among its design components. The following five design components are shown in Figure 16.1: technology, structure, organizational feedback systems, performance-management systems, and culture.

*Technology* includes the methods an organization uses to convert raw materials into products or services. It involves production methods, equipment, and work flow. Total-quality processes, such as statistical process control, are also part of technology.

*Structure* is the way in which an organization divides tasks into departments or groups and coordinates them for overall task achievement. Alternative structures are departments differentiated by function (such as engineering, manufacturing, and sales), by product and service (such as detergents, food, and paper), or by a combination of these (a matrix). Structures can also be based on business processes (such as product development, order fulfillment, and customer support).

*Organizational feedback systems* are the methods an organization uses to gather, assess, and disseminate information relevant to organization performance. Management information systems help an organization ensure that each subunit's activities are consistent with its objectives. Performance-review systems serve the same function with employees and teams.

*Performance management systems* focus on selecting, developing, and rewarding people. These systems help shape employees' behavior and activities within an organization. For example, reward systems induce people to join, remain, and work toward specific objectives. They provide employees with incentives for achieving the organization's goals.

*Culture* includes the basic assumptions, values, and norms shared by organizational members (Schein, 1985). It guides and coordinates members' decisions and behaviors by providing a shared understanding of what actions are needed for successful performance. Because culture is so pervasive and central to an organization's design and can significantly impact success or failure of strategic change, it is central among the design components shown in Figure 16.1 (Abrahamson & Fombrun, 1994; Cameron & Quinn, 1999).

Research suggests that organizations achieve high performance when all five design components fit with one another and mutually reinforce behaviors needed to achieve the organization's strategic objectives (Galbraith, 1973). For example, when an organization's strategy and environment demand innovation and change, its design elements should promote flexibility and experimentation, such as those found in high-involvement organizations (Ashton, 2000).

While we have structured this chapter using open systems theory, complexity theory may also be a useful framing for OD practitioners. Complex systems display characteristics of learning and adaptability, spontaneous self-organizing, and emergent phenomenon from interactions among agents in the system (Axelrod, 1999). The paradox or tension between freedom and control in complex systems can be an avenue for creativity and innovation. OD interventions based on complexity theory seek to create greater connectivity among organizational members and significant stakeholders external to the system. This results in organization designs that encourage self-organizing, learning, and self-motivation (Brodbeck, 2002; Styhre 2002).

# CHARACTERISTICS OF LARGE-SYSTEM INTERVENTIONS

Large-system interventions have a number of common features that distinguish them from other OD interventions. These characteristics are as follows:

- They are triggered by environmental jolts and internal disruptions;
- They provoke revolutionary or transformational change;
- They incorporate new organizing paradigms;
- They are driven and led by senior executives;
- They require an organizational learning system; and
- They involve multiple organization levels and large numbers of members.

Environmental jolts and internal disruptions can be compelling reasons for large-system change. Such interventions generally occur in direct response to at least three kinds of disturbance (Tushman, Newman, & Romanelli, 1986):

1. Industry discontinuities such as dramatic changes in legal, political, economic, and technological conditions that shift an organization's ground rules;

2. Changes in a product's life cycle that require different business strategies; and

3. Internal organizational dynamics such as changes in size, strategy, or leadership.

These disruptions jolt an organization at a fundamental level and, if they are identified correctly during diagnosis, they can provide the strong "felt need" necessary to embark on large-system change.

Large-system interventions involve revolutionary changes that dramatically reshape an organization. Such changes generally transform all of the organization's design components. Although evolutionary changes that fine-tune an organization can also occur during large-system interventions, the primary focus is revolutionary change (Greiner, 1972; Tushman & Romanelli, 1985).

Most large-system interventions attempt to restructure or redefine organizations. The goal is to create commitment-based organizations that are better suited than the old compliance-based organizations to adapt to rapidly changing conditions. Commitment-based organizations have many mutually reinforcing elements, including the following:

- Lean and flexible structures;
- Information and decision making diffused throughout the organization;
- Decentralized teams and business units accountable for specific products, services, processes, or customers;

- Participative management and teamwork;
- Strong customer orientation; and
- Total-quality concepts and practices.

An organization's senior executives must lead and take an active role in large-system interventions (Kotter, 1996). Change leadership generally involves the following three critical roles (Tichy & Devanna, 1986; Tushman, Newman, & Nadler, 1988):

1. *Envisioner.* Someone who articulates a clear and credible vision of the new organization and its strategy and generates pride and enthusiasm.

2. *Energizer.* Someone who demonstrates excitement for changes and models the behaviors linked to them.

3. *Enabler.* Someone who allocates resources for implementing change, uses rewards to reinforce new behaviors, and builds effective top-management teams and management practices.

The innovation and problem solving necessary for large-system change require considerable organization and personal learning (Mohrman & Cummings, 1989; Quinn, 1996; Senge, Kleiner, Roberts, Ross, Roth, & Smith, 1999; Shani & Docherty, 2008). Learning helps to manage the uncertainty involved in major change by bringing new information to the organization and by providing a constructive element of control. Unlearning old ways is equally important as people's traditional values, worldviews, and behaviors are challenged and replaced with new ones. Because members spend considerable time and effort in learning how to change themselves, organizations need to create processes, procedures, and norms that support a learning orientation for the whole organization.

Large-system interventions require heavy involvement and commitment from members throughout the organization. Consequently, OD practitioners attempt to involve everyone or at least a cross-section of the organization when planning and implementing large-scale change. Ideally, this involves getting all or a majority of organization members at the same time, in the same room. As members of the system directly communicate and interact with each other, they begin to understand the issues confronting the system and to devise better responses to them.

Increasingly popular methods for bringing members together for large-system change are *large-group interventions* (Bunker & Alban, 1996; Owen, 1997; Purser & Griffin, 2008). These include such techniques as "conference boards," "future searches," "open space technology," and "Appreciative Inquiry," each having its own proponents and rhythm. Manning and Binzagr (1996) discuss common values and assumptions that underlie these large-scale interventions, which include the belief that people in the system have the capacity to self-organize, perception becomes the reality, and the organization is seen as the "whole system."

While pragmatically having the whole system in the room at the same time may sometimes be impossible to accomplish, at least representatives of all relevant stakeholders should be included. This technology has been used in organizations to bring people together to discuss plans for plant closures, strategies for creating innovative products and methods, restructuring organizations, and a host of other issues that potentially involve all organizational members (Barros, Cooperrider, & Chesterland, 2000; Coghlan, 1998; Purser, Cabana, Emery, & Emery, 2000; Watkins & Mohr, 2001).

# EXAMPLES OF SELECTED INTERVENTIONS

Organization development interventions that apply to large systems generally fall into two categories: those that create changes in the organization-environment relationship and those that reshape the internal-design components of an organization. Examples of both interventions are presented in the following sections.

## Organization-Environment-Relationship Interventions

Two interventions that are used to restructure organization-environment relationships are dynamic strategy-making and network organizations.

**Dynamic Strategy-Making.** Today's fast-paced environments require rapid strategic responses. Yet, conventional approaches for planning and executing strategy are highly formal, detailed, and time-consuming. They create, often unintentionally, obstacles to swift thinking and action. Dynamic strategy-making is a new type of OD intervention aimed at overcoming the problems with traditional strategic planning. It provides organizations with the capability to strategize continuously and to execute quickly (Greiner & Cummings, 2009). It enables them to engage effectively with rapidly changing environments.

Dynamic strategy-making addresses both the content (the what) and the process (the how) of strategy-making. It treats them as inseparable and integrates strategic content and process to create strategies that are relevant and implementable. Dynamic strategy-making forges a strong link between strategy and execution, addressing them together rather than separately. It builds strategy-making and implementation into the design of the organization—its structure, systems, and culture—so strategic behaviors are constantly directed and reinforced.

Dynamic strategy-making involves organization members directly in creating strategic content—what the organization intends to do to achieve specific outcomes in a particular marketplace. Determining strategic content involves two broad activities. The first is *strategic assessment*, which involves collecting and analyzing data about the organization and its environment to inform strategic choice. The organization is examined to identify core capabilities and resources; the environment is scanned to discover opportunities whereby the organization can gain competitive advantage. Based on this assessment, the second activity involves drafting a *statement of strategic direction*. It includes the business model for how the organization will gain competitive advantage and the strategic goals that will direct and motivate members' behavior. The statement also contains guidelines for structuring the organization's activities, and an action plan for implementing strategic initiatives.

Dynamic strategy-making also addresses strategic process—those activities used to create, execute, and update strategic content. Choices about process can powerfully affect whether strategic content is relevant, timely, and accepted throughout the organization. Strategic process identifies the key stakeholders who should be involved in strategy-making and organizes their interaction and decision making. It includes two key issues. The first has to do with *strategic leadership and change*, which are essential for guiding strategy-making and making sure the strategy is enacted effectively throughout the organization. Strategic leaders show behaviorally how to create the strategy and make it happen. They hold themselves and others accountable for changing the organization to enact the strategy and to keep it up-to-date.

The second issue involves *guided involvement*, which helps members rapidly assess the organization and its environment, share their knowledge and experience, and choose the right strategic direction. Guided involvement is generally carried out by OD practitioners with skills and experience in both the content and process of strategy-making. They help organizations involve key stakeholders in strategy-making, facilitate their interactions and choices, and encourage wider understanding and commitment to the strategic content throughout the organization. In Chapter Eighteen, you will be introduced to the SOAR framework and approach, which is one way to build and execute dynamic strategy.

**Network Organizations.** A consultant can use concepts of networking to help an organization join in partnerships with other organizations to solve problems and perform tasks that are too complex and multisided for single organizations to handle alone (Boje & Hillon, 2008; Chisholm, 2008; Cummings, 1984; Gray, 1989; Snow, 1997). Such multi-organization partnerships are used increasingly to respond to the complexities of today's dynamic environments (Rycroft, 1999). Examples include joint ventures, research and development consortia, public-private partnerships, and customer-supplier networks. Four basic types of networks have been categorized: an internal market network, a vertical market network, an inter-market network, and an opportunity network (Achrol, 1997; Chisholm, 1998; Halal, 1994). The opportunity network tends to be the most loosely coupled, nonhierarchical, and under organized. Consequently, it requires OD interventions that help members recognize the need for such partnerships and develop mechanisms for organizing their joint efforts.

OD interventions to create and develop network organizations generally follow four stages that are typical of planned change in under-organized settings: identification, convention, organization, and evaluation.

In the *identification* stage, a consultant identifies potential network members. The organization or person that begins a networked organization generally takes the lead, which is key in the early stages. The main activities during this stage are determining criteria for membership and identifying organizations that meet them. Often a network of leaders emerges that mimics the characteristics of the network (Feyerherm, 1994).

In the *convention* stage, the consultant brings potential members together to assess the feasibility of forming a network organization. At this point, the potential members evaluate the costs and benefits of forming, and determine an appropriate task definition. Key activities in this stage include reconciling members' self-interests with those of the network collective and working through differences.

In the *organization* stage, the network takes shape. Members organize themselves for task performance by creating key roles and structures. Legal obligations and member rights are determined at this point.

In the *evaluation* stage, the consultant gives the members feedback about their performance so they can start identifying and resolving problems. The members assess how the network is working and how it can be improved.

## Internal-Design-Component Interventions

This section describes four interventions that reshape the internal-design components of an organization so they fit better with one another. These interventions are sociotechnical systems (STS), structural design, reward systems, and built-to-change organizations.

Each intervention emphasizes different design components. Sociotechnical systems involve technology and performance-management elements; structural design addresses structure and technology; reward-system interventions include performance management and feedback systems; built-to-change organizations affect most design components.

**Sociotechnical Systems (STS) Interventions.** STS is based on the premise that a work system is comprised of social and technical parts and is open to its environment (Cummings & Srivastva, 1977; Dyck & Halpern, 1999; Trist, Higgin, Murray, & Pollack, 1963; van Eijnatten, Shani, & Leary, 2008). Because the social and technical elements must work together to accomplish tasks, work systems produce both physical products and social/psychological outcomes. The key is to design work so that the two parts yield positive outcomes; this is called *joint optimization* (van Eijnatten, Eggermont, de Goffau, & Mankoe, 1994).

In addition to joint optimization, STS is also concerned with the work system and its environment. This involves *boundary management*, which is a process of protecting the work system from external disruptions while facilitating the exchange of necessary resources and information (Pasmore, 1988). OD consultants use the following guidelines to design sociotechnical systems (Attaran & Ngyen, 2000; Barko & Pasmore, 1986; Cherns, 1987; Taylor & Felton, 1993):

- Work is organized in a way that is compatible with the organization's objectives. This often leads to a participative process that promotes employee involvement in work design.

- Only those minimal features needed to implement the work design are specified. The remaining features are left to vary according to the unique technical and social needs that arise in the work setting. This provides employees with the freedom necessary to control technical variances quickly and close to their sources.

- Employees who perform related tasks are grouped together to facilitate the sharing of information, knowledge, and learning. This typically results in self-managed work teams.

- Information, power, and authority are vested in those performing the work to reduce time delays in responding to problems and to enhance employee responsibility.

- Workers are trained in various skills so they have the necessary expertise to control variances and the flexibility needed to respond to changing conditions.

**Structural-Design Interventions.** Structural-design interventions focus on the structure of an organization (Galbraith, 1973; 2008). They involve dividing the organization's tasks into specific groups, units, or processes and then coordinating them to achieve overall effectiveness. This results in four basic organizational structures: functional, self-contained units, matrix, and networked. When selecting a structure for an organization, OD consultants consider the following four factors: environment, size, technology, and goals (Daft, 2004).

The functional structure is hierarchical. Different specialized units, such as research, engineering, and marketing, report upward through separate chains of command and join only at the organization's top levels. This structure offers several advantages: it reinforces specialized skills and resources; it reduces duplication of scarce resources; it facilitates communication within departments. The major disadvantages of a functional structure include a short-term focus on routine tasks, narrow perspectives, and reduced communication and coordination among departments. The functional structure works best when the organization's environment is relatively stable, the organization is small to medium size, and it is engaged in routine tasks that emphasize efficiency and technical quality (McCann & Galbraith, 1981).

The self-contained-unit structure is organized around a product line, geographical area, customer base, or common technology. Employees with all the needed functional expertise are internal to the unit. The major advantage of this organizational structure is that the key interdependencies and resources within each unit are coordinated toward an overall outcome. The major disadvantage is that there is heavy duplication of resources and expertise. The self-contained-unit structure works well in large organizations facing dynamic environments and having multiple products and customers (Mohrman, Cohen, & Mohrman, 1995).

Matrix organizations are designed to take advantage of both the functional and self-contained-unit structures by imposing a lateral structure of product or program management onto the vertical, functional structure (Joyce, 1986). Consequently, some managers report to two bosses. A matrix structure works best in a large organization that faces an uncertain environment, has high technological interdependencies across functions, has product specialization and innovation goals, and employees who are good at lateral working relationships (Bartlett & Ghoshal, 1990). This structure offers the advantage of managing interdepartmental interdependencies and allowing for skill diversification and training. Its primary disadvantages are that it is difficult to manage and control, and employees face ambiguous roles and inconsistent demands (Larson & Gobeli, 1987).

A networked structure consists of separate units that are either internal or external to an organization. Each unit specializes in a business task or function and is held together by ad hoc (internal) or contractual (external) arrangements. Internal networks consist of temporary project teams that use specialists from throughout the organization. This results in a flat, information-based structure that has few levels of management or a more "boundaryless organization" that enhances coordination and information flow across the firm as well as with key segments of the environment (Ashkenas, Ulrich, Jick, & Kerr, 1995; Drucker, 1989).

Externally networked structures are similar to network organizations described previously, such as joint ventures, research and development consortiums, and licensing agreements across national boundaries. Networked structures are highly flexible and enhance the distinctive competence of each member organization (Charan, 1991; Miles & Snow, 1986). The major disadvantages of a networked structure are that it is difficult to manage lateral relationships across many organizations and to sustain member commitment to the network over time (Galbraith & Kazanjian, 1986).

**Reward-System Interventions.** These interventions focus on rewarding desired behaviors and work outcomes and are increasingly seen as an integral part of OD (Lawler, 2000). Because people generally do those things for which they are rewarded, rewards can powerfully shape work behavior. Rewards can be both tangible and intangible, and can be given at a variety of levels, from individual to team to business unit. Rewards are especially effective when they satisfy basic needs, are viewed as equitable, and fit individual motivations. Reward-system interventions attempt to satisfy these conditions and to ensure that rewards reinforce appropriate work behaviors and outcomes (Kerr, 1975).

Reward-system interventions generally involve three kinds of rewards: pay, opportunity, and benefits. Money can have a profound effect on employees' behavior. Traditionally, pay is based on job classification and seniority. Although this reinforces allegiance to a particular job, it may not promote the high levels of flexibility and performance needed in today's business environment. An organization may find that alternative pay systems such as skill-based pay and pay for performance may be more appropriate for its situation. In skill-based systems, employees are paid based on the number of skills they have mastered or jobs they can perform; this results in a flexible labor force with high skills. Performance-based pay ties rewards directly to measurable performance outcomes that employees can impact. Many organizations reward team or business-unit performance, which, in turn, reinforces teamwork and cooperation (Welbourne & Gomez-Mejia, 1995).

Rewards based on opportunity traditionally include promotions. Given the current trend toward downsizing, however, promotions are less plentiful in today's organizations. Instead, organizations are using opportunities for increased learning, task-based empowerment, special work projects, and wider job experiences as motivators and rewards for exemplary performance.

Rewards that focus on benefits can help an organization attract and retain talented employees. Benefits include early and flexible retirement, pre-retirement counseling, on-site services, childcare, educational funding, investment plans, and flexible work hours. These benefits are sometimes administered through cafeteria-style plans that give employees some choice over benefit options (Lawler, 1981). This method helps to tailor fringe benefits to individual needs, thus increasing the motivational impact of such rewards.

Reward-system interventions may influence an organization's other design components. For example, an organization may need to modify its training and appraisal systems if it uses skill-based pay to reward employees.

**Built-to-Change Organizations.** One of the newest interventions aimed at internal-design components involves designing organizations for change, not just for normal operations (Lawler & Worley, 2006; Worley & Lawler, 2006). Built-to-change organizations are designed to compete in rapidly changing environments in which constant change is essential for success. Their design elements and managerial practices all promote and reinforce change. These contrast with traditional organization designs that support stability and reliability, which can be a recipe for failure in a fast-paced world.

Built-to-change organizations include the following design components: talent management practices that select quick learners and provide them with constant training and development; reward systems tied to change goals and continuous learning; flat, lean structures that promote flexibility and innovation; transparent information systems that move information rapidly to where it is needed; and shared leadership that disperses power and control throughout the organization.

Developing these features can be a daunting task, especially for organizations that have been designed for stability. The following interventions can help the transition to a built-to-change organization (Lawler & Worley, 2006):

- *Create a change-friendly identity*. This addresses the core values, norms, and beliefs shared by organization members that can either hinder or support change. Existing values and norms are surfaced, they are assessed for their relevance to change, and appropriate adjustments are made. Attention is directed at creating values and norms that help members see change as necessary and natural.

- *Pursue proximity*. This helps the organization get closer to current and possible future environments by focusing outward to gain a clearer picture of environmental demands and opportunities. Scenarios of possible and desired future environments are developed, and a strategy for moving the organization and its environment in the desired direction is developed.

- *Build an orchestration capability*. This facilitates the organization to build its own change capability. It develops members' change management skills, builds an organization design and change function into the firm, and helps members learn how to apply their change capability by engaging in organizational changes and reflecting on that experience.

- *Establish strategic adjustment as a normal condition*. This helps organizations constantly work at changing and coordinating all of the organization design elements to fit changing conditions. It includes empowering members to make relevant decisions, sharing information widely, giving them the necessary skills and knowledge, and measuring and rewarding the right things.

- *Seek virtuous spirals*. This helps organizations continually build on their change capabilities to create even better organization designs and competitive strategies. This results in a series of competitive advantages as organizations improve their capabilities and designs to take advantage of emerging prospects.

# SUMMARY

The large-scale OD interventions described in this chapter touch all aspects of the organization, although each of them arises from different needs and demands and targets a specific element of the organization. An important consideration for OD practitioners is to deftly assess what intervention is most appropriate. For example, interventions at the boundary of the organization (such as networks and dynamic strategy-making) will differ from those directed at internal design components (such as sociotechnical or rewards systems). However, OD practitioners must be aware that changing a significant aspect of an organization will have implications for the whole organization, and thus it is essential to plan how a large-scale intervention may cascade throughout the organization.

## References

Abrahamson, E., & Fombrun, C.J. (1994). Macrocultures: Determinants and consequences. *Academy of Management Journal, 19,* 728–755.

Achrol, R. (1997). Changes in the theory of interorganizational relations in marketing: Toward a network paradigm. *Journal of the Academy of Marketing Science, 25,* 56–71.

Ashkenas, R., Ulrich, D., Jick, T., & Kerr, S. (1995). *The boundaryless organization.* San Francisco: Jossey-Bass.

Ashton, C. (2000, November/December). KI Pembroke succeeds through teamwork, empowerment and rewards. *Human Resource Management International Digest,* pp. 21–23.

Attaran, M., & Nguyen, T.T. (2000). Creating the right structural fit for self-directed teams. *Team Performance Management,* pp. 25–33.

Axelrod, N.N. (1999, October/December). Embracing technology: The application of complexity theory to business. *Strategy and Leadership.* pp. 56–58.

Barko, W., & Pasmore, W. (1986). Sociotechnical systems: Innovations in designing high-performing systems. *Journal of Applied Behavioral Science, 22* (Special issue 1), 195–360.

Bartlett, C., & Ghoshal, S. (1990, July/August). Matrix management: Not a structure, a frame of mind. *Harvard Business Review,* pp. 138–145.

Barros, I.O., & Cooperrider, D. (2000). A story of Nutrimental in Brazil: How wholeness, appreciation, and inquiry can bring out the best in human organization. *Organization Development Journal, 18*(2), 22–29.

Boje, D., & Hillon, M. (2008). Transorganizational development. In T.G. Cummings (Ed.), *Handbook of organization development* (pp. 651–664). Thousand Oaks, CA: Sage.

Brodbeck, P.W. (2002). Complexity theory and organization procedure design. *Business Process Management Journal*, pp. 377–402.

Bunker, B., & Alban, B. (1996). *Large group interventions: Engaging the whole system for rapid change.* San Francisco: Jossey-Bass.

Burns, T., & Stalker, G.M. (1961). *The management of innovation.* London: Tavistock.

Cameron, K., & Quinn, R. (1999). *Diagnosing and changing organizational culture.* Reading, MA: Addison-Wesley.

Chaffee, E. (1985). Three models of strategy. *Academy of Management Review, 10*(1), 89–98.

Charan, R. (1991, September/October). How networks reshape organizations—for results. *Harvard Business Review*, pp. 104–115.

Cherns, A. (1987). Principles of sociotechnical design revisited. *Human Relations, 40*(3), 153–162.

Chisholm, R. (1998). *Developing network organizations: Learning form theory and practice.* Reading, MA: Addison-Wesley.

Chisholm, R. (2008). Developing interorganizational networks. In T.G. Cummings (Ed.), *Handbook of organization development* (pp. 629–650). Thousand Oaks, CA: Sage.

Coghlan, D. (1998). The process of change through interlevel dynamics in a large-group intervention for a religious organization. *Journal of Applied Behavioral Science, 34*, 105–120.

Cummings, T. (1984). Transorganizational development. In B. Staw & L. Cummings (Eds.), *Research in organizational behavior: Vol. 6* (pp. 367–422). Greenwich, CT: JAI.

Cummings, T., & Srivastva, S. (1977). *Management of work: A sociotechnical systems approach.* San Francisco: Pfeiffer.

Cummings, T., & Worley, C. (2008). *Organization development and change* (9th ed.). Cincinnati, OH: South-Western.

Daft, R. (2004). *Organization theory and design* (8th ed). Cincinnati, OH: South-Western.

Drucker, P. (1989). *The new realities.* New York: Harper & Row.

Dyck, R., & Halpern, N. (1999). Celestica, Inc. *Journal for Quality and Participation. 22*(5), 36–41.

Emery, F., & Trist, E. (1965). The causal texture of organizational environments. *Human Relations, 18*(1), 21–32.

Feyerherm, A. (1994). Leadership in collaboration: A longitudinal study of two interorganizational rule-making groups. *Leadership Quarterly, 5*(3/4), 253–270.

Galbraith, J. (1973). *Organization design.* Reading, MA: Addison-Wesley.

Galbraith, J. (2008). Organization design. In T.G. Cummings (Ed.), *Handbook of organization development* (pp. 325–352). Thousand Oaks, CA: Sage.

Galbraith, J., & Kazanjian, R. (1986). *Strategy implementation: Structure, systems and process* (2nd ed.). St. Paul, MN: West.

Gray, B. (1989). *Collaborating: Finding common ground for multiparty problems.* San Francisco: Jossey-Bass.

Greiner, L. (1972, May/June). Patterns of organizational change. *Harvard Business Review, 45*, 119–130.

Greiner, L., & Cummings, T. (2009). *Dynamic strategy-making.* San Francisco: Jossey-Bass.

Halal, W. (1994). From hierarchy to enterprise: Internal markets are the new foundation of management. *Academy of Management Executive, 8*(4), 69–83.

Hanna, D. (1988). *Designing organizations for high performance.* Reading, MA: Addison-Wesley.

Hill, C., & Jones, G. (2004). *Strategic management: An integrated approach* (6th ed.). Boston, MA: Houghton Mifflin.

Joyce, W. (1986). Matrix organization: A social experiment. *Academy of Management Journal, 29*(3), 536–561.

Kerr, S. (1975). On the folly of rewarding A, while hoping for B. *Academy of Management Journal, 18*(4), 769–782.

Kotter, J. (1996). *Leading change.* Boston, MA: Harvard Business School Press.

Larson, E., & Gobeli, D. (1987). Matrix management: Contradictions and insights. *California Management Review, 29*(4), 126–139.

Lawler, E. (1981). *Pay and organization development.* Reading, MA: Addison-Wesley.

Lawler, E. (2000). *Rewarding excellence: Pay strategies for the new economy.* San Francisco: Jossey-Bass.

Lawler, E.E., & Worley, C. (2006) *Built to change: How to achieve sustained organizational effectiveness.* Hoboken, NJ: John Wiley & Sons.

Lawrence, P., & Lorsch, J. (1967). *Organizations and environment.* Cambridge, MA: Harvard University Press.

Macy, B., Bliese, P., & Norton, J. (1994). Organizational change and work innovation: A meta-analysis of 131 North American field experiments—1951–1990. In R. Woodman & W. Pasmore (Eds.), *Research in organizational change and development: Vol. 7.* Greenwich, CT: JAI Press.

McCann, J., & Galbraith, J. (1981). Interdepartmental relations. In P.C. Nystrom & W.H. Starbuck (Eds.), *Handbook of organizational design: Remodeling organizations and their environments: Vol. 2*, 60–84. New York: Oxford University Press.

Manning, M.R., & Binzagr, G.F. (1996). Methods, values, and assumptions underlying large group interventions intended to change whole systems. *International Journal of Organizational Analysis, 4*(3), 268–284.

Miles, R., & Snow, C. (1986). Network organizations: New concepts for new forms. *California Management Review, 28*(3), 62–73.

Mohr, B. (1989). Theory, method, and process: Key dynamics in designing high-performing organizations from an open sociotechnical systems perspective. In W. Sikes, A. Drexler, & J. Gant (Eds.), *The emerging practice of organization development* (pp. 199–211). Alexandria, VA: NTL Institute for Applied Behavioral Science/San Francisco: Pfeiffer.

Mohrman, S., Cohen, S., & Mohrman, A. (1995). *Designing team-based organizations.* San Francisco: Jossey-Bass.

Mohrman, S., & Cummings, T. (1989). *Self-designing organizations: Learning how to create high performance.* Reading, MA: Addison-Wesley.

Mohrman, A., Mohrman, S., Ledford, G., Cummings, T., Lawler, E., & Associates. (1990). *Large scale organizational change.* San Francisco: Jossey-Bass.

Owen, H. (1997). *Open space technology: A user's guide.* San Francisco: Berrett-Koehler.

Pasmore, W.A. (1988). *Designing effective organizations: The sociotechnical systems perspective.* Hoboken, NJ: John Wiley & Sons.

Porter, M. (1985). *Competitive advantage.* New York: Free Press.

Purser, R., Cabana, S., Emery, M., & Emery, F. (2000). Search conferencing: Accelerating large-scale strategic planning. In M. Anderson (Ed.), *Fast cycle organization development.* Cincinnati OH: South-Western College Publishing.

Purser, R., & Griffin, T. (2008). Large group interventions: Whole system approaches to organization change. In T.G. Cummings (Ed.), *Handbook of organization development* (pp. 261–276). Thousand Oaks, CA: Sage.

Quinn, R. (1996). *Deep change.* San Francisco: Jossey-Bass.

Rycroft, R. (1999, May/June). Managing complex networks: Key to 21st century innovation success. *Research-Technology-Management*, pp. 13–18.

Schein, E. (1985). *Organizational culture and leadership.* San Francisco: Jossey-Bass.

Senge, P., Kleiner, A., Roberts, C., Ross, R., Roth, G., & Smith, B. (1999). *The dance of change: The challenges of sustaining momentum in learning organizations.* New York: Doubleday.

Shani, A.B., & Docherty, P. (2008). Learning by design: Key mechanisms in organization development. In T.G. Cummings (Ed.), *Handbook of organization development* (pp. 499–518). Thousand Oaks, CA: Sage.

Snow, C. (1997). Twenty-first century organizations: Implications for a new marketing paradigm. *Journal of the Academy of Marketing Science, 25,* 72–74.

Styhre, A. (2002). Non-linear change in organizations: Organization change management informed by complexity theory. *Leadership and Organization Development Journal*, pp. 343–351.

Taylor, J.C., & Felton, D.F. (1993). *Performance by design: Sociotechnical systems in North America.* Englewood Cliffs, NJ: Prentice Hall.

Tichy, N., & Devanna, M. (1986). *The transformational leader*. Hoboken, NJ: John Wiley & Sons.

Trist, E., Higgin, B., Murray, H., & Pollack, A. (1963). *Organizational choice*. London: Tavistock.

Tushman, M., Newman, M., & Nadler, D. (1988). Executive leadership and organizational evolution: Managing incremental and discontinuous change. In R. Kilmann and J. Covin (Eds.), *Corporate transformation* (pp. 102–130). San Francisco: Jossey-Bass.

Tushman, M., Newman, W., & Romanelli, E. (1986, Fall). Managing the unsteady pace of organizational revolution. *California Management Review*, pp. 29–44.

Tushman, M., & Romanelli, E. (1985). Organization evolution: A metamorphosis model of convergence and re-orientation. In L.L. Cummings and B. Staw (Eds.), *Research in organizational behavior: Vol. 7* (pp. 171–222). Greenwich, CT: JAI.

Van Eijnatten, F., Eggermont, S., de Goffau, G., & Mankoe, I. (1994). *The sociotechnical systems design paradigm*. Eindhoven, The Netherlands: Eindhoven University of Technology.

Van Eijnatten, F., Shani, A.B., & Leary, M. (2008). Sociotechnical systems: Designing and managing sustainable organizations. In T.G. Cummings (Ed.), *Handbook of organization development* (pp. 277–310). Thousand Oaks, CA: Sage.

Watkins, J., & Mohr, B. (2001). *Appreciative inquiry: Change at the speed of imagination*. San Francisco: Pfeiffer.

Welbourne, T.M., & Gomez-Mejia, L.R. (1995). Gain-sharing: A critical review and a future research agenda. *Journal of Management, 21*(3), 559–609.

Worley, C., Hitchin, D., & Ross, W. (1996). *Integrated strategic change: How organization development builds competitive advantage*. Reading, MA: Addison-Wesley.

Worley, C., and Lawler, E.E. (2006). Designing organizations that are built to change. *Sloan Management Review, 48*(1), 19–23.

CHAPTER SEVENTEEN

# Whole System Change

*What It Is and Why It Matters*

**Emily Axelrod, Steven H Cady, and Peggy Holman** *

*Change is not merely necessary to life—IT IS LIFE*
—Alvin Toffler

There is a new story of change being born even as the old story is dying. At its heart, that new story stays true—and enlarges upon—the old story's core intention to increase organization effectiveness and health using behavioral-science knowledge (Beckhard, 1969). The new story not only expands its focus from organizations to include communities and other social systems, but also goes about its work in a new way: equipping people to engage in and create their *own* outcomes. This chapter offers some history of how Whole System Change has evolved; presents a framework to distinguish it from other change strategies; sets some expectations for leading change; and provides insights into how to get started.

## A LITTLE HISTORY

Perhaps the earliest roots of the field began when, fleeing from the Nazis, German-born social psychologist Kurt Lewin brought Gestalt psychology to the United States in the late 1930s. He was concerned that psychology might lose relevance to social problems (Bunker & Alban, 1997). His introduction of field theory, in which a dynamic field of forces influences human behavior, helped to create experimental social psychology as a new discipline.

---

* The authors are listed in alphabetical order as they contributed equally to the creation of this chapter.

Another significant contributor to the organizational change movement was Ron Lippitt, whose work was described by Art Kleiner (1996) in *The Age of Heretics*, a history of the 20th Century social movements. Lippitt was described as one of the heretics from the dominant institutions who, in the late 1950s, saw the value of human relationships and community. Lippitt believed that there was a void of human spirit, making it difficult for corporations to perform at their full potential. This view went against the attitudes of institutions at that time. Lippitt saw the world as a whole system and began using his concepts to help cities and organizations become what they yearned to be.

Lippitt, like other organizational consultants of the 1950s and 1960s, had studied with Kurt Lewin and used his processes with organizations. While studying with Lewin at MIT, Lippitt joined several of Lewin's doctorate students to form the Institute for Social Research at the University of Michigan, as well as the National Training Labs (NTL) of Bethel, Maine. Ron Lippitt believed that there was an important dynamic that could be released from people in organizations by combining their yearnings for the future of the organization. Lippitt brought a creative genius to the design of processes by focusing on uncovering a preferred future that leads to energy creation (Bunker & Alban, 1997; Kleiner, 1996).

During the social transformation of the 1960s, organization development (OD) was established at NTL, drawing from the developments in social psychology and the behavioral sciences (Beckhard, 1997). NTL began teaching people how to engage in this new process, named "organization development" by Dick Beckhard, Douglas McGregor, Peter Vail, and others. Whole systems thinking emerged in both Europe and the United States during this time in philosophy, science, and organizational change (Bunker & Alban, 1997).

In the 1960s, OD strategies were primarily based on small-group behavioral science theory and actions. The state-of-the-art method of changing a system was top to bottom, with senior management using a hierarchical process to send down "the word" on changes through the organization. Such sequential, incremental change was slow, largely because a small number of people made the decisions and expected the rest of the system to follow orders to implement the changes.

In the 1980s, a new approach began to emerge in which the people of a system—across functions and hierarchy—participated in both making the decisions and implementing the changes. Such an approach creates a sense of wholeness that accelerates change because people act from their collective image of their desired future as they begin to experience themselves as a whole system. This whole system methodology began to take hold on the fringes of OD, its processes influenced by open systems theory. As data were shared with the system, change began to occur rapidly, sometimes simultaneously. Some practitioners began innovating, bringing new methods that expanded on the small group theory and interventions that currently existed. They also assembled larger, more diverse groups from communities and organizations

(Weisbord, 1987). These were the beginnings of Whole System Change as a new body of knowledge.

The leaders who have significantly contributed to the evolution of whole system change include: Ronald Lippitt and Ed Lindaman (Preferred Futuring, 1969), Fred Emery and Eric Trist (Search Conference, 1960), Marvin Weisbord and Sandra Janoff (Future Search, 1982), Kathleen Dannemiller (Whole Scale Change, 1982), Harrison Owen (Open Space Technology, 1985), David Cooperrider (Appreciative Inquiry, 1987), and Richard and Emily Axelrod (The Conference Model, 1991). It is important to note that these leaders were all influenced by Emery and Trist of the Tavistock Institute in London, Kurt Lewin's groundbreaking research on leadership, and Ron Lippitt's whole community thinking and other behavioral science theories developed and tested at NTL in the 1950s and 1960s.

## PUTTING WHOLE SYSTEM CHANGE IN PERSPECTIVE

The founders mentioned above broke new ground, discovering the means to create dramatic shifts in a system when needed. They provided insight into handling increasing complexity and diversity so that change could be undertaken by the people in a system more rapidly and with a much greater likelihood of success. Given the increasing dislocation of many of our social systems—education, health care, the economy, to name a few—these pioneers have helped prepare us for the times we face today. The framework that follows puts this type of complex change in perspective, illustrating when Whole System Change is most useful and why.

Change, any change, begins with a disturbance. It can be caused by something as small as a broken promise or as large as a hurricane sweeping across a populated city. It could be something perceived very positively such as a new job, a new contract, a new baby; or experienced with dread like the loss of a job, a contract, a life. No matter what the disturbance, because it moves us, it evokes a response—a change.

We draw on three common patterns when responding to a disturbance. The more conscious we are of our options, the greater the likelihood of successfully navigating the waves of changes that seem to be moving through our lives at an increasing pace.

### Just Do It

Take a moment to notice a disturbance in your world. For most of us, our first response is to act from habit (Figure 17.1), to ignore or suppress everything but the symptoms that confront us, to fix it and get back to business as usual. Beyond the obvious fix, how do you know whether there is more to do? For most of us, we discover something else is called for when the disturbance gets louder.

**Figure 17.1.** Acting from Habit

Image drawn by Paul Dupree, www.unisonconsulting.com

## Take Charge

Perhaps a broken promise leads to diminished trust and a breakdown in communication. And then the distrust ripples further. When the volume is sufficiently loud that the situation can no longer be ignored, the strategy most commonly associated with change efforts is called upon—to act from certainty and manage it! (See Figure 17.2.)

This is where traditional OD tools shine, providing both quantitative and qualitative ways of working to study the disturbance, state recommendations, set targets for outcomes, plan the work, work the plan, and harvest the results. Recognizing the importance of involving people, some facilitate focus groups with customers, suppliers, employees, community members, or others to influence the recommendations.

## Time for Something Completely Different

Our social systems are currently rife with disturbances such as failing financial institutions, rising gas prices, rising food prices, and skyrocketing incarceration rates (particularly among African-American men), to name a few. Our most cherished assumptions about change—and our ability to manage it—are break-

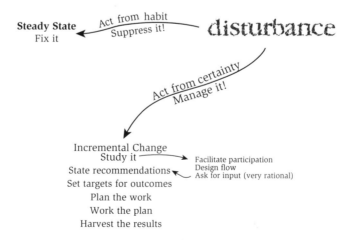

**Figure 17.2.** Acting from Certainty

Image drawn by Paul Dupree, www.unisonconsulting.com

ing down, eliciting a very common and human response. Many are throwing up their hands and saying, "I'm stumped. I don't know what to do." Business as usual is over. More and more leaders and change agents are asking for help.

This degree of dislocation calls for a dramatic change in how we address change. Successful responses require accessing not just our rational minds, but much more of ourselves. Not only that, but once we begin, we may awaken to the best in ourselves and connect to the best in others. In so doing we discover that the power of what we can be and do together is impossible alone. These times are calling forth a shift in how humans organize themselves to accomplish meaningful purpose. The methods of Whole System Change are providing one of the most promising routes to addressing the complex challenges many organizations, communities, even whole industries such as health care, education, and journalism are facing. (See Figure 17.3.)

Addressing discontinuous change is radically different from the predictable flow of managed change. It requires a willingness to face the unknown with equanimity and to be curious, receptive, and humble. It is the work of asking questions that focus our attention toward deeply felt, collective aspirations. It involves creating hospitable conditions that invite the diversity of the system to step in and take initiative, knowing that clear intentions create an organic

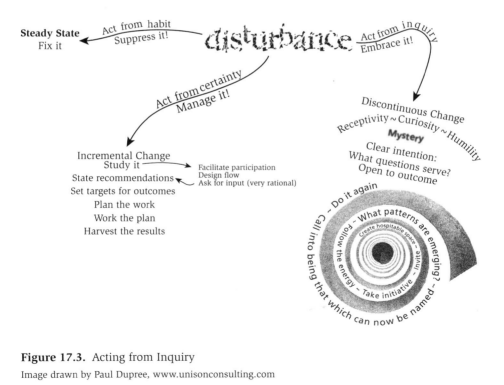

**Figure 17.3.** Acting from Inquiry

Image drawn by Paul Dupree, www.unisonconsulting.com

boundary for the work to be done. By following the energy that emerges, sensing the patterns taking shape, and calling those patterns into collective awareness, novel and often unpredictable solutions appear. Who could have imagined the remarkable public response to the people of New Orleans after Hurricane Katrina when the U.S. government fell short of what was needed?

Achieving a successful result does not always mean that new ways of working together are sustained. For many, such experiences set a new high-water mark of what is possible for a diverse group to accomplish. Making the process visible with a focus on what went right can set the stage for new habits. Practicing what it takes to successfully enter into the unknown yet again is essential. With repetition, new behaviors become familiar and integrated.

## SIX CAPACITIES FOR LEADING WHOLE SYSTEM CHANGE

Such shifts in behavior begin with those leading the change. No longer is it enough for people with position power to "lead the charge" telling the rest to "take that hill." Here are six aspects of the changing work of change agents and those leading a change effort.

*First, leaders must walk their talk or they will not be trusted.* The primary relationship is that of supervisor-employee. If the employees do not trust the supervisors, they will not voice their ideas and opinions or willingly follow the lead of their supervisors. Integrity is the key to good leadership, and this means aligning words with actions (Simons, 2008). Simons has examined the bottom-line value of integrity; he found in his research that it drives the profitability and overall success of organizations.

A good example of this was a values rollout in a manufacturing company. The CEO visited the plants and talked about what the values meant to him, how they would be implemented, and answered questions. He did this with groups of about twenty-five people each. Now ten years later, people in that organization continue to hold their leaders accountable for living the values. A vice president in this organization was productive but not holding to the ethical values. While the management team was deliberating what to do about this, some of the employees met and communicated their ideas to the leader. The VP was let go. The leadership had been wrestling with the issue, and the employees reminded them of the values they all had to live by.

*Second, change is messy and difficult.* Leaders must be able *to use the messiness of the change creatively.* They must be role models for others whose eyes will be focused on them. They need to be honest about their frustrations, as they are human, too. But they need to be clear about the belief in supporting the outcomes of the process. In the redesign of a mortgage bank during the last hours of a whole system meeting, a suggestion was made to lend money geographically. The leader of the bank stood up and said he had never in his experience seen this work, but he was willing to consider it and would reconvene the meeting in two weeks to continue the conversation. In this he was honest and open while providing resources to get to the best outcome in the messy process of change.

*Third, leaders must be able to convene others to confront issues in the achievement of their goals.* This is an anchor for change processes and daily leadership. There are two issues here. One is to convene the right stakeholders; the other is to support them in achieving their goals. Effective Whole System Change leaders recognize that their job is to create a hospitable environment, ask appreciative questions that provide clear focus, invite the diversity of people in the system to step in and then let go, and make room for innovative answers to emerge.

*Fourth, leaders must be willing to listen and learn.* Most systems today are too complex for any one person to see the whole picture. The need to think systemically and understand the implications of change on different parts of the organization and its members, customers, or suppliers has never been greater. It requires a degree of humility to know that you cannot go there on your own. While many leaders have this ability, others come to a more open attitude and systemic thinking after unsuccessfully trying top-down, sequential change methods.

*Fifth, leaders must support people with time, resources, guidance, and actions.* If the change effort is compelling enough for the organization to take it on and involve the number of people such efforts usually require, then the leader must be involved and supportive from the outset. Leaders do not want to fail. Determining support and resource needs is an important point of discussion when contracting for the work. If that conversation does not occur, then leaders can be caught off guard and appear unsupportive because the requirements have not been clear. It is essential that leaders have resources in the right place at the right time and that they support and listen to others as the situation evolves.

Jim Shelton (2008), program director at the Gates Foundation, shared an African proverb that is used throughout their organization.

If you want to go fast...go alone.
If you want to go far...go with others.

One underappreciated key to the sustainability or long-term viability of a change initiative is the staffing. For example, consider establishing a dedicated team providing communications, logistical support and road shows between events, and including as much of the organization as possible.

Ten years after a Whole System Change process in a Canadian printing plant, the consultants contacted the organization again. They discovered that the current leaders were the ones who had stepped up to lead during the reorganization of the company ten years earlier! By supporting and nurturing those who step forward to take on the work of change, hidden talents are discovered. People become more engaged when they have a say in their work world. Typically, roles change and opportunities open up for employees to take on different roles. Leaders need to support and nurture those who adapt to the shifting roles.

*Finally, one of the most talked about issues with these processes is letting go of control and being willing to be changed by what occurs.* This does not mean abdication of responsibility; rather it reframes leadership as a form of engagement. Some organization and community leaders have been hurt by turning over decision-making control. When decision making is delegated well, it is done with appropriate boundaries in which alignment, internal controls, and monitoring mechanisms are present. When certain decisions are distributed to groups, they may actually provide more control because people are watching for positive overall outcomes. The groups also have ownership and want to do a good job. Such experiences can be life-changing for formal leaders, as they discover how responsible and capable most people are when invited to be and do their best.

In a telephone utility company, the customer service department was redesigning itself. The leader decided to use one of the whole system approaches in order to increase the speed of change and because he understood the importance of engaging everyone in the process. He declared at the outset that he liked to retain control and that this was a new experience for him in letting go of control. He worked with the design team to set boundaries so that others could engage in meaningful work, and he provided support in terms of time and resources so that people could get the work done. As a result, the people gave extra time and energy to the project.

When leadership is recognized as a broadly held capacity that can emerge from anywhere, organizations begin to operate in a more fluid and life-affirming way. They make room for a different kind of organization, one that enables collective leadership to emerge. By recognizing and embracing the potential inherent in disturbances, both formal and informal leaders develop the skill to ask powerful questions. When issues arise, someone takes responsibility to convene a gathering, inviting whoever cares to address it on behalf of the whole. There is growing confidence that, when diverse people follow that which has heart and meaning, when they embrace the dynamic tensions that emerge among them, and when they reflect collectively on what unfolds, then unexpected and innovative insights cohere into clear intentions and meaningful action. As a result, many are changed by the experience, growing in self-confidence and willingness to trust others.

# GETTING STARTED

Over the last fifty years, the pioneers of Whole System Change have led the way in creating methods for engaging the people of the system in creating their future. There are many practices now in use and more are emerging all the time. Some widely used methods are Appreciative Inquiry, Conference Model, Future Search, Open Space Technology, Whole-Scale Change, and World Café (Holman, Devane, & Cady, 2007). No matter which method is chosen, there are some common aspects to consider when getting started with this work. The questions that follow highlight some of these themes.

## What Are These Methods and Why Would I Use Them?

These methods *engage* others in doing what each of us cannot do alone. We are able to productively use people's time to pursue opportunities and turn problems into solvable possibilities. They help us provide:

- A structure whereby people reach a common understanding of an issue, can take ownership, and commit to actions to make a difference in the life of the organization and their lives;

- A structure for communicating large amounts of information which creates energy for change;

- A systematic way to capitalize on internal desires to participate and develop quality results;

- A space for people who think differently, or come from different cultures and traditions, to work together and explore common ground that benefits them individually and benefits the organization or community; and

- An opportunity for people to give voice to what matters to them, to make sense of information together that creates meaning, and to take action around their common ground.

## How Do I Learn These Methods?

Think of it as a journey traveling through three phrases, where one masters methods, blending, and invention. A person begins as an apprentice of a methodology, develops mastery, and then, using an understanding of the principles that inform the methods he or she has mastered and internalized, begins blending aspects of those methods (Figure 17.4). When the combinations lead to predictable results, then a new method or tool emerges. Then the next phase begins as an apprentice, and so forth. The exciting aspect is the iterative nature of learning.

We are all novices at something most of the time. We have different learning styles. Know your styles so you can use your strength to educate yourself. Choose a method that attracts you. Read, watch videos, talk with practitioners,

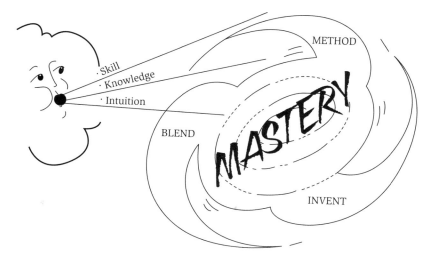

**Figure 17.4.** The Cycle of Mastery

Image drawn by Christine Valenza, www.christinevalenza.com

and learn the history and theory of that method. Create a personal library. Be sure to embody the values. People are sensitive to those who do not truly believe in giving voice, from including more stakeholders to connecting to each other to co-creating. Practice the method and get into your comfort zone. Practice until the method is a part of you.

Then choose another method. With each practice, it gets a little easier. It is a bit like language acquisition. Acquiring a fourth or fifth language becomes simpler because there is an intuitive grasp of some deeper pattern. As practitioners internalize and integrate more essential practices, they tap an underlying stream of why things work—the social psychology of Whole System Change. From this foundation, it is possible to wisely blend different processes.

## What Is the Nature of This Type of Change?

Unlike traditional change processes where specific targets are set, plans are established and executed, Whole System Change unfolds as people follow the energy of the desired intention. In other words, these methods are emergent, with specific outcomes unknown when the work begins. While the details may not be known, creating a clear intention, often expressed as a question, provides direction. Additionally, a road map of some sort is created to orient the work. Unfortunately, road maps do not always indicate where the construction is that will slow you down or where the detours might be. Whole System Change road maps are dynamic in nature. The first part of the map can be filled in with more detail and the latter grows sketchier, as we lack all the information we need.

This is known as the "headlights effect." What we can see in our headlights is what we pay attention to. So we give our best guesses and march on with the information and research we have.

In a printing plant that was redesigning the whole organization, the plan for iterative conferences was established, the implementation roll out was planned, and the leadership was totally supportive of the effort. However, the charismatic leader received a job offer and left before the first conference. He hired a replacement with the understanding that he was to lead this effort. The lead consultant had emergency surgery. The plant's main customer threatened to go to another competitor if service did not improve immediately. Such things are not usually on the road map. The plant focused on straightening out the issues with the customer, someone stepped in for the lead consultant, the leadership on the design team took on many of the leadership roles, which the new leader supported, and the change process was successful.

## How Do I Use These Methods to Address an Issue?

The way to put these methods to use is to become clear on purpose, boundaries, and whom to involve. In many organizations, becoming clear on the purpose is called the "business case for change" and is the logical level of purpose. The one that is usually most impactful is when people can speak to why the purpose is important to them personally and what meaning it has for them at the heart level.

In one situation, a school district planning team's discussion turned to why changes needed to occur. When members of the team shared their personal reasons, they talked about improving test scores, providing a better educational experience for students, and balancing the social emotional needs. As they probed deeper and asked why it was important to achieve these goals, one of the teachers had tears in her eyes. Someone asked, "Why?" She told the story of a student shot and killed on his way home from school. This was a good student, a well-liked and well-rounded young man. Through her tears, the teacher said, "This is more important than improving test scores. This is about saving kids. That is what we are about. That is the difference we have to make."

## How Do You Create a Compelling Purpose?

Bring together a microcosm of the organization representing diverse voices. Talk about the need for change and enlist everyone's help. Working together, co-create a logical case for change and a case for meaning at the heart level. Ask questions such as: "What do you want to be different in the organization because of this change?" "What do we want to be different for ourselves because we are working on this task?" "What are we willing to sacrifice to make this happen?" "What is it about the purpose that has meaning and would be worth doing for me personally?"

Revisit your purpose. Rarely do we figure it out on the first try. A week later, ask yourself: "Does this engage me? Does it have meaning? Does it have depth? Does it engage others?" Test it on those you want to engage. Revise and make changes based on their reactions.

Purpose also defines the boundaries of the work. People need boundaries so they know what is up for discussion and what is not. Boundaries are real. People do not have unlimited resources and time. The legal considerations need to be clear. The planning team needs to spell these out for people.

## Whom Do We Involve and How?

We focus on these three questions:

- How do I involve more than the usual people?
- How many people should I include?
- Should the same people be involved throughout all the work?

In the book *You Don't Have to Do It Alone* (Axelrod, Axelrod, Beedon, & Jacobs, 2004), the authors share a helpful framework for addressing how to involve more than the usual people. They suggest you consider six important categories: people who care, people with authority and responsibility, people with information and expertise, people who will be impacted, people with diverse points of view, and people who are considered troublemakers. Some brainstorm a list of these people by stakeholder group and by individuals' names. Some create a visual map or make lists. Typically, we think of more people than we can possibly invite.

## How Many Should I Include?

A large group is very useful when you want to create a critical mass for change in an organization or community. Smaller groups are most effective for doing detail work and working on smaller jobs.

A large health authority found after several mergers that the referral process was not working and decided to use a Whole System Change process to transform the process. They used various groups at different points in the process:

- A leadership team and a microcosm totaling twenty people determined the purpose, boundaries, whom to include, and the design of the process.
- A large group of three hundred met twice to understand the process and the issues, and then created a new process.
- Task forces of four to twelve people worked on the details of the process.
- Functional groups spread the word.
- Conversations of two or three contributed to spreading the word as the work progressed.
- The planning team functioned as a coordinating team for the task forces.

### Want to Join the Journey?

This is a young and rapidly developing field. One aid to its evolution is the "Nexus for Change," a conference held periodically among people interested in the practices of Whole System Change (www.nexusforchange.org). Nexus, by definition, is a connector or center of something. The Nexus conference is just that—a gathering of practitioners, researchers, activists, leaders, students, and educators who come together to further conversations concerning the creation and structure of Whole System Change and its ability to make a difference in the world. The Nexus Conference has met twice, in 2007 and 2008, at Bowling Green State University. Future conferences will use a mix of virtual and face-to-face gatherings to meet locally and converge globally online.

# SUMMARY

This chapter began with history, talked about what distinguishes Whole System Change, described some expectations for leading change, and offered some suggestions for starting. It concludes with some reflections on what might unfold as this field continues to evolve.

With Whole System Change, we enter the terrain of emergence: acting from inquiry, when, once we really "get it," we embrace disturbance because we know the promise of creative and innovative answers on the other side of the unknown. To enter is to acknowledge that mystery is a given. It is to be receptive. After all, when we do not know what to do, what else can we be? This turns out to be a very active, albeit unfamiliar state. It is not easy to be receptive to the unknown when we have been trained to "just do something." It is to be humble; discovering that finding our way through is not a solo act and demands more than input. It takes whole-hearted (and whole-minded) involvement from people from the many aspects of the system touched by disturbance. The greater our capacity to be curious as we become clear about our intentions and stay unattached to the form the outcomes take, the greater our ability to ask the questions that attract the diversity of a system to join in the quest.

What happens when a system becomes whole? What are the benefits? We believe the system knows the right thing to do and moves fast in doing it. Everybody matters in this universe, everyone has a place, and everyone has a meaning. And in that connectedness, healing occurs. What possibilities are achievable if we work as a whole system? What do we gain by integrating divided parts of an organization? And why is it particularly important in these times to be able to achieve system-wide success?

As organizations evolve, they tend to shift into a more mechanistic mode of thinking in response to their operating environment. We often see this happening at a time when a founding leader is replaced (think of Steve Jobs). The board will often pick a successor who will be more orderly and less entrepreneurial and uncontrolled. Frequently, these pressures result in the loss of the originating identity of the organization. Our challenge is not to attempt to alter the environment, but rather to uncover and release the shared organizational identity that has existed from the beginning.

We cannot think globally without thinking whole system. The notion of "find and fix" belonged to the last century; in this century the focus is on seeing the need for change and making it happen. The truths presented in this chapter provide an array of hues to incorporate into the underpinnings of a new generation of leaders, consultants, and educators in OD. You can use these colors as the foundation for beginning a successful transformation and include your own experience and attributions in order to move ahead.

As you look to the future in terms of research and collaborative thinking on Whole System Change, go outside the box and broaden your domain of interest. New thinkers are emerging, new methods from diverse fields are being developed, and new applications are being explored. A broader framework is in order, one that truly capitalizes on what each of us knows and reaches out to these new and emerging areas of interest. Yours will be the shoulders from which the 22nd Century practitioner, scholar, and student will leap.

# References

Axelrod, E., Axelrod, R., Beedon, J., & Jacobs, R.W. (2004). *You don't have to do it alone*. San Francisco: Berrett-Koehler.

Beckhard, R. (1969). *Organization development: Strategies and models*. Reading, MA: Addison-Wesley.

Beckhard, R. (1997). *Agent of change: My life, my practice*. San Francisco: Jossey-Bass.

Bunker, B., & Alban, B. (1997). *Large group interventions*. San Francisco: Jossey-Bass.

Holman, P., Devane, T., & Cady, S. (2007). *The change handbook*. San Francisco: Berrett-Koehler.

Kleiner, A. (1996). *The age of heretics: Heroes, outlaws, and the forerunners of corporate change*. Garden City, NY: Doubleday.

Simons, T. (2008). *The integrity dividend: Leading by the power of your word*. San Francisco: Jossey-Bass.

Shelton, Jim. [Jim.Shelton@gatesfoundation.org]. (2008, September 5). Education initiative. Private email message to Steve Cady [steve@stevecady.com].

Weisbord, M.R. (1987). *Productive workplaces: Organizing and managing for dignity, meaning and community*. San Francisco: Jossey-Bass.

# CHAPTER EIGHTEEN

# SOAR

*Linking Strategy and OD to Sustainable Performance*

Jacqueline M. Stavros and Daniel K. Saint

T his chapter discusses the intersection between organization development (OD) and strategy. Specifically, we describe SOAR and its application within a global professional services firm. This firm subsequently achieved significant positive change across all measures of operational excellence, client satisfaction, employee engagement and retention, and financial results. SOAR is an OD strengths-based, whole system approach to strategic planning and execution. The acronym SOAR stands for **S**trengths, **O**pportunities, **A**spirations, and **R**esults. It begins with a *strategic inquiry with an appreciative intent* into what is working well and what are the possible opportunities for growth. It engages a whole system perspective and involvement in the strategic planning process. This chapter tells the story of a service organization with quantified results. First, we discuss the convergence of research and management practice in strategy and OD. Then, we present the SOAR framework and approach. Finally, we let the story speak for itself.

## CONVERGENCE OF STRATEGY AND OD

As the OD field evolves, practitioners serve organizations using emergent theories, methods, and tools of planned change. Recent advances in the OD and strategy fields include Appreciative Inquiry (AI), positive organizational scholarship (POS), whole system change, organizational learning, sustainability considerations, and strengths-based perspectives. Similarly, strategic leadership is transitioning to encompass practices designed both to capture the knowledge of all employees and to engage employees in the creation, execution, and ownership of strategy. Intersecting OD and strategy significantly improves the effectiveness of strategic planning and change (Worley, Hitchin, & Ross, 1996).

The SOAR approach integrates AI, POS, whole system, and strengths-based change to create a *strategic* transformation process. In the SOAR framework, the foundations of AI are applied with a focus on strategic thinking, creating, and implementing. As highlighted in this book, AI is one of today's leading OD and change philosophies. It engages the whole system in shaping the organization's future. Appreciative Inquiry has been successfully used by thousands of organizations to identify possibilities and then to design and deliver a future path based on the whole system's contributions.

The term *strengths-based* is newer to the strategy field. Nonetheless, researchers have collected data related to strengths development in hundreds of studies over the last thirty years from the Gallup Organization. The results of this research have appeared in the popular business press with books like *Good to Great, Now Discover Your Strengths, Positive Leadership, Blue Ocean Strategy*, and *Strengths-Based Leadership*. Peter Drucker's description of leadership captures the idea (personal communication): *"The task of leadership is to create an alignment of strengths, making our weaknesses irrelevant."* Strengths-based thinking shifts the focus to building upon strengths rather than improving weaknesses. The idea is to build teams with complementary strengths and allow individuals to do what they do best. The intended result is excellence, high performance, and successful managers, employees, and teams across a wide range of industries—all strengths-based issues (Cameron, Dutton, & Quinn, 2003).

Whole system involvement captures holistic information upon which to improve strategic decision making. SOAR invites the whole system, or at least its representatives, into the strategy process. In order to gain perspective and act effectively, the knowledge and perspectives of the whole system must be understood. Stakeholder involvement, buy-in, and commitment add perspective and deepen engagement. Involvement begins with identifying the key stakeholders in the value chain and the impact of the organization's strategies and activities on these stakeholders. Stakeholder value "is becoming a way to achieve competitive advantage based on the economic, ecological, and social impacts a company has on its diverse constituents" (Lazlo, 2008, p. 21). Research overwhelmingly indicates that consideration of broader stakeholder needs creates shareholder value (Margolis & Walsh, 2003).

Leading practitioner publications and scholarly journals reflect this parallel shift in thinking. A recent *Harvard Business Review* article observes that knowledge-based organizations in the information age create value differently from prior models of control-oriented management systems. In a learning environment where employees' participation and ideas are invited and welcomed, employees engage with customers and within the organization more meaningfully. "They will offer innovative ways to lower cost and improve quality—thus laying a more solid foundation for their organization's success" (Edmondson, 2008, p. 67).

An article in *The McKinsey Quarterly* states that over 70 percent of senior executives identify innovation as one of the three strategic imperatives for their companies. McKinsey research shows that engaging employees is a more effective path to generating and sustaining innovation. Relying on predictable strategy practices and conventional processes and structures is ineffective in inspiring innovation (Barsh, Capozzi, & Davidson, 2008). If there is a growing demand for strategy to be more innovative and to be implemented more rapidly, then an organization must create and communicate strategy and plans that invigorate stakeholders with a shared set of values (ways to operate together), vision (future direction), mission (present purpose and organization offering), and a set of strategic initiatives (foundations for goal and objective setting).

Core to SOAR is engaging employees in a series of conversations to further discover strengths, opportunities, and collective aspirations leading to commitment to a series of strategic initiatives and results. For organizations that can bring in external stakeholders, SOAR can engage stakeholders from the start. The key is for relevant stakeholders to be identified and effectively connected within the conversations. The SOAR framework optimizes value by balancing the needs of the current customers, new customers, employees, suppliers, partners, the community, and shareholders. By engaging stakeholders (*or ensuring their voices are represented*), an organization accelerates its strategic planning efforts by understanding what it does best (strengths) and then identifying the potential market, product, or service opportunities.

Contemporary organization theory indicates that our ways of working and organizing are trending increasingly toward collaboration. Current thinking about strategy development and operational control is evolving toward relational processes and structures. Several factors are leading to collaboration in business, including the emergence of an information-based economy where knowledge is the key value-creating asset (Thatchenkery, 2005); a growing body of theory signifying that we co-create our futures in relationships (Anderson, Cooperrider, Gergen, Gergen, McNamee, & Whitney, 2008; Shotter, 2008); and the disintegration of loyalty as a force holding organizations together (Barker, 2007).

Recent theorizing into strategy finds that integrative strategizing helps senior managers to be more effective in influencing and contributing to strategic organizational change (Jarzabkowski, 2008). The SOAR framework and its processes encompass the concept of integrative strategizing. SOAR concurrently engages employees in developing strategy and establishing the organizational structure and controls to implement the strategy.

From this brief review of emerging strategy research and practice, several questions begin to develop:

- How can we invite and welcome employees' participation and ideas?
- What new and innovative methods do we have to engage employees?
- How can we build on the trend toward collaboration to generate and leverage new relational processes and structures?
- In what ways can we simultaneously develop strategy while engaging employees and establishing the organizational structure and controls to implement the strategy?

Next we will provide a brief overview of what SOAR is and how to apply it. Then, the story of a business unit of a global professional services firm will provide an example of bringing theory to practice.

# THE SOAR FRAMEWORK

## What Is SOAR?

SOAR is a strengths-based framework with a participatory approach to strategic analysis, strategy development, and organizational change (see Figure 18.1). The SOAR framework enhances and guides strategic planning and implementation processes with its positive guiding approach to *inquire* into the organization's strengths, opportunities, aspirations, and measurable results; *imagine* the organization's desired future; *innovate* strategies, plans, systems, designs, and structures; and *implement* the strategy innovations developed in the three previous phases to build a sustainable culture.

The appreciative paradigm led to shifting to a new acronym to support strategic analysis, evolving SWOT into SOAR. The traditional SWOT approach begins with a scan of internal strengths and weaknesses and an external scan of opportunities and threats. SOAR places the focus on finding a strategic fit between positive aspects of internal environment (strengths) and external environments (opportunities).

From the recent advances in OD theory, we realized that any consideration of strengths implicitly considers weaknesses and, similarly, opportunities are developed in consideration of threats. There is also an intentional shift in language from problems to possibilities that is subtle yet powerful when engaging in strategic conversations. Rather than focusing attention on weaknesses and threats directly, organizations can reframe their perspective to optimize their path toward their highest possible achievements.

From the disciplines of POS and AI, SOAR applies a similar line of thinking. While applying and reflecting about the SOAR framework and approach, it struck us that, instead of stating a weakness such as "We have significant problems with

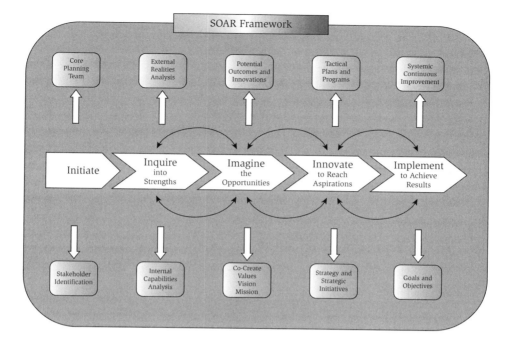

**Figure 18.1.** SOAR Framework and 5-I Approach

distribution," an organization could reframe this as an opportunity: "We have an opportunity to create a more effective distribution channel." SOAR doesn't ignore an organization's challenges; it reframes them into possibilities, thus creating a strengths-based *opportunity approach* to the strategic plan.

The following questions are offered as an illustration for the SOAR components of Strengths, Opportunities, Aspirations, and Results:

- What are our collective organizational strengths? What are our greatest assets?

- What are the possible market and product (service) opportunities? What potential do you see or recognize?

- What are our collective aspirations? What dreams do we have for our organization? What could you imagine for our best possible future?

- What measurable results can we achieve together? What results are the most meaningful?

- How will we know we are on track to accomplish our goals?

- What are the rewards and resources required to achieve the results?

These questions and their responses can start the journey to understand and apply SOAR as a flexible framework to make sense of our past and present situation and to co-create a most preferred future for our organizations. The questions are designed to drive intentionally positive conversations in small groups, followed by reports to the larger group to create collective understanding. The workshops and summits we have conducted have had a wide range in number of participants and duration of participation required to answer these or similar questions. The situation dictates what is appropriate. The specific questions used by the professional services firm will be provided in the story that follows.

The principle is to ensure that stakeholders' voices are represented and that there is sufficient information and time to inquire, imagine, innovate, and make decisions for implementation. It has been our experience that you can design a SOAR session with twenty to hundreds of participants, with the sessions ranging from a half-day to three days. The difference in the ranges depends primarily on what the organization wants to achieve.

SOAR offers a wide range of options for its application (see Table 18.1) so that the framework (Figure 18.1) can be built upon and applied appropriately to the strategic need.

## How to Apply SOAR

A 5-I approach guides the SOAR process: Initiate, Inquire, Imagine, Innovate, and Inspire (Implement) that can be used to guide the delivery of the questions highlighted above. The phases are briefly defined below:

**1. Initiate.** The organization's leadership team or a core strategic planning team meets to determine how to use SOAR. They identify the relevant stakeholders to invite and discuss ways to engage stakeholders in and throughout the process. This is where the core strategic planning team is typically created and/or identified.

**2. Inquire.** This is a strategic inquiry into values, mission, vision, internal strengths, external environment to create opportunities, and conversations of aspirations and results. The "as is" state of the organization and "might be" of future possibilities are explored in this phase.

**3. Imagine.** A dialogue takes place that considers the combination of strengths and opportunities to match the aspirations to create a shared vision. Participants use the power of positive images of the future as a basis for envisioning actions and results. These images and supporting dialogue create the inspiration and excitement to fuel strategic initiatives and aligned action.

**4. Innovate.** Strategic initiatives are identified and prioritized that may result in new or changed processes, systems, structures, and culture as required to support the new goal. These changes are designed by taking advantage of the identified strengths and opportunities to achieve the aspiration and results.

**5. Implement.** Energy, commitment, and tactical plans emerge to implement the new strategic plan. Implementation involves many people with different skills and competencies aligned and working on linked projects. Because the original inquiry and strategic dialogue connected each person to what to do, why to do it, and how to do it, he or she is more likely to be motivated to contribute to the resulting service to stakeholders. The rewards are not only tangible in terms of a successful result in the marketplace or in financial returns, but also in knowing the work served others in a positive way.

Table 18.1. Selected Examples of SOAR Applications

| SOAR Framework and 5-I Approach | Brief Description of Work |
|---|---|
| Biological Conservation Charity | To create a strategic plan with priorities that serve as a living document |
| BAE Systems | To create a strategic plan for an acquired division |
| Cathedral Foundation | To bring stakeholders together to design a plan to serve all of its community members |
| DBC—National Healthcare Board | To use appreciative strategy processes in co-creating an engaging leadership team that develops a shared vision for its national planning board |
| FCI Automotive | To discover a strategy to improve supply chain management and inventory quality |
| Hayes-Lemmerz–Cadillac | To discover how the plant can be environmentally profitable while decreasing operational costs and improving plant efficiencies |
| Jefferson Wells | To engage the whole practice in strategy development and execution to create a positive impact on financial results |
| John Deere | To align strategy at corporate, business, and functional areas |
| Metropolitan Library System | To bring about a strategic integration of a Chicago metropolitan library system |
| Orbseal Plymouth Tech Center | To align a newly created technology center with corporate strategy |

Since SOAR is a framework, it provides the flexibility of application in many different situations and levels, as illustrated earlier in Table 18.1. A goal of this section has been to provide you with a new way of thinking to craft and implement strategy. We have found that creating strategy from a strengths-based, whole system perspective builds confidence and momentum to move people forward in an uncertain environment. The following story brings this concept to life.

# POSITIVE TRANSFORMATION

## Overview

This story is set within a global professional services firm specializing in finance and accounting, internal audit, tax, and technology risk management. The firm has approximately fifty offices across North America, Europe, and Asia. It is a subsidiary of a Fortune 100 company.

In the Great Lakes Region (GLR), positive organization approaches, including SOAR and AI, were used over three years to build and develop a team of professionals committed to serving clients and each other. By 2008, the GLR had grown to be the global firm's largest cash-flow generator. GLR also ranked first of all practices in both client satisfaction and employee engagement.

## The GLR Story

At the beginning of 2005, GLR was viewed as a solid operation. It ranked eighth in total revenues and twelfth in operating profit out of twenty-five profit-and-loss centers globally. Given the relative size of the market and lagging Midwest economy, performance was seen as admirable. Employee engagement as measured by annual survey was high, as was employee retention. With an annualized employee turnover rate of 32 percent, GLR ranked sixth in the firm for retaining employees. The previous office managing director (MD) had recently been promoted to vice president of operations.

A new human resources director and a new MD joined GLR in early 2005. They were joining a local leadership team of fourteen. Although annual employee turnover at 32 percent placed the practice in the top quartile of the firm, they saw improvement in retention as a key lever for overall improvement.

The new MD and HR director worked intentionally with the rest of the leadership team to have meaningful dialogue with all primary stakeholders as soon as possible. The MD's goal was to meet every one of the approximately 150 professionals within the first two months of joining the practice; they met many at the client organizations where they were working. Meeting clients, corporate managers, and other stakeholders was also on the agenda.

# Discovering the Positive Core

During those initial meetings, the two new members of the leadership team asked each person to tell his or her story and they shared theirs. They asked questions to uncover the positive core of the organization: *When our firm is operating at its best, what does that look like?* They asked people to tell of their peak experiences: *How long have you been working here? What is your best experience in that time?* They asked questions to get a better sense of the values in use of the firm: *What do you value most about the firm? What do you value most about yourself as a member of the firm?* Some of the questions were asked to uncover what could be improved and to consciously begin moving toward a preferred future: *Imagine it is three years from now, and everything has gone exceptionally well. What does our practice look like? What clients are we now serving? How many people now work for the practice? If you could change one thing about the practice, what would it be?* The MD and HR director also asked questions to get a better sense of their role and how they could best serve the team: *If we are exceptionally successful, what would it look like to you? How can we best serve you?* Clients and other community organizations, including local universities and charities, were asked to tell of their best experiences working with GLR and to imagine how they could be better served.

Some of the initial meetings were held in the offices of GLR and at client work sites, while others occurred in restaurants over breakfast, lunch, dinner, and evening social gatherings. The data uncovered from those meetings told of people feeling closely connected to the practice. Employees believed that the management team cared about them. Clients expressed thankfulness that GLR did not gouge them for fees, as other firms had when Sarbanes-Oxley (SOX) requirements initially caused a shortage of accountants and auditors. Clients also expressed that the combination of the firm's "outstanding people" and fair prices provides an excellent value. They also conveyed the idea of relationship and partnership.

The leadership team wanted to uncover a positive core upon which to build. The questions were designed to identify and amplify what was already working well in the system. They were consciously co-constructing a positive future as part of their team.

As the year 2005 closed, the practice was growing quickly and the team felt that they were headed in the right direction. Annualized employee turnover declined from 32 percent to 26 percent. Operational and cost measures also began to improve considerably. Revenues for the year increased 49 percent, and profits were up 53 percent, which resulted in the practice moving from eighth to fifth place in revenue and from twelfth to seventh place in profitability.

## From Top-Down to Whole System Strategic Planning—Learning to SOAR

In the next year, 2006, the leadership team decided to use SOAR to build on the practice's financial and operational successes. SOAR seemed appropriate for a professional services organization because of its whole system nature and its relationship to research into both strategy and positive organizational scholarship (POS).

The corporate office provided a standardized strategic planning template for each office to complete. The regional offices had autonomy in using any processes to develop their plans. GLR began the strategic planning process for 2007 in early third quarter 2006. The SOAR journey into strategic planning unfolded through five phases: Initiate, Inquire, Imagine, Innovate, and Implement.

**1. Initiate.** The leadership team of sixteen people set aside time in several of their weekly meetings to begin the process. The team faced new challenges in developing their plan. In previous years, the MD developed the plan with input from select members of the leadership team. As more people were brought into the process, a degree of control was lost. The team outlined some measures to ensure the plan stayed aligned with the corporate strategy and timeline. During those meetings, they identified a core strategic planning team and nominated other managers, professionals, and administrative support team members to participate on the core team. The core team had ten people, including an external consultant. The consultant facilitated the process so that everyone could participate. The team proposed a plan for the process and addressed questions such as how to keep the process on time and manage the logistics of inviting the whole system to participate.

In a professional services firm, the cost of every meeting is apparent. Every meeting increases cost and decreases revenue by taking employees away from serving clients. GLR's value proposition is based on delivering experienced, skilled professionals at a relatively low price. This balance was carefully considered before scheduling any meeting.

The deliverables from the Initiate phase included the identification and development of a core strategic planning team, creation of a planning process outline, and identification of stakeholders.

**2. Inquire.** Considering the potential disruption in client service, the planning team initially decided to limit the summit meeting to the practice's extended leadership team of about fifty people. In the summit meeting, the group explored the SOAR phases of inquiry, imagine, and innovate, and an initial direction for implementation.

The directors, business development managers, engagement managers, and administrative team attended the first summit meeting. The ideas generated from bringing that team together were clearly value creating, but the energy and engagement were exciting. They felt that something special was occurring. The planning team decided to extend the process to all two hundred employees in the region. The summit for all employees was similar to the summit held for the extended leadership team, except now members of the leadership team served as table facilitators.

The Appreciative Inquiry that began in August 2005 provided a good foundation of data from a broad base of stakeholders. Building on the learning from that period, the planning team developed the protocol to guide the strategic inquiry. In the summit meetings, participants paired with someone with whom they did not normally work. Each participant asked the other the questions and took notes, and then the roles were reversed. Figure 18.2 shows the question protocol from the interview guide.

After an hour, the groups came together in tables of eight. Each person shared the stories he or she heard. One of the table participants, acting as a recorder, captured the emerging themes and ideas.

Interesting dialogue occurred at each table. Participants discussed a mix of stories of exceptional client service, of times when they really felt engaged

---

1. *What Attracted You?* Think back to when you first decided to join the firm. What attracted you? What were your initial excitements and impressions?

2. *High Point.* During your time in the firm, I'm sure you've had some ups and downs, some peaks and valleys, some highs and lows. I'd like you to reflect for a moment on a high-point experience, a time when you felt most alive, most engaged, and most proud of yourself and our firm. Tell the story. What happened? What was going on?

3. *What Enabled Your Success?* What was it about you, others in the firm, and/or our clients that made your peak experience possible?

   • What were your best qualities, skills, approaches, values, and so on that made it a great experience?
   • Who else played a significant role and how did he or she contribute?
   • What were the most important factors in the organization that helped (for example, strategic focus, leadership qualities, best practices, traditions, structures, processes, skills, relationships)?

4. *Positive Core.* When the firm is at its best, what are the core factors (our strengths) that give life to our organization—without which the firm would cease to exist?

5. *Future Vision.* Close your eyes; imagine it is 2012. Where is the GLR five years from now? What new market segments, services, or process innovations have been successfully created and launched. What opportunities have we seized? And how did you and your team help to get us there?

6. *Three Wishes.* If you could change or develop anything you wanted about our firm, what three things would you do to heighten its capacity to grow our competitive advantage?

---

**Figure 18.2.** GLR SOAR Interview Guide

and part of the firm, and of new business development and growth success. When the energy finally shifted from the tables back to the whole, each team recounted some of the stories and themes that emerged. The following strategic themes were identified for the next phase:

1. Growth by expanding service offerings into existing clients and developing new clients;

2. Client service excellence;

3. Employee engagement, retention, and team development;

4. Individual professional development and personal growth; and

5. Managing the economics of the practice.

**3. Imagine.** In the third (imagine) and fourth (innovate) phases of the summit meeting, strengths, opportunities, aspirations, and measuring results were discussed. The framework in Figure 18.3 was used to guide the conversations.

The key strengths identified previously were discussed. The depth of relationships among the people on the team and clients was clearly foundational. People on the team felt as though they were part of something and valued the close relationships and professional camaraderie. The clients appreciated the value created for them and supported the organization's further growth. When asked, clients provided introductions and references internally within their organizations and externally with other companies.

As noted above, implicit in the discussion of strengths and opportunities were considerations of weaknesses, mission, and long-term goals. A primary long-term goal was profitable growth, so what in the strengths presented

| | **Strengths** | **Opportunities** |
|---|---|---|
| STRATEGIC INQUIRY | • What are we doing well?<br>• What are our greatest assets? | • What are our best possible market opportunities?<br>• How are we to best partner with others? |
| APPRECIATIVE INTENT | **Aspirations**<br>• To what do we aspire?<br>• What is our preferred future? | **Results** (measurements)<br>• What are our measurable results?<br>• What do we want to be known for? |

**Figure 18.3.** SOAR Matrix

opportunity? From strengths, the team found areas in which change likely would bring opportunity. One consideration was to reevaluate the sales strategy and incentive system that encouraged client relationship professionals to focus on bringing in new client companies rather than fully developing existing clients. The deep relationships and a solid reputation in several large current clients were acknowledged, such as GM, GMAC, DTE, Comerica, and Chrysler. One opportunity came from changing the focus for several client relationship professionals to focus strategically when there was already success and significant opportunity.

From the broader summit, it also became evident that GLR had a broad network of relationships from client service professionals that had not been fully tapped. The new client development strategy became very focused on potential clients for which GLR has top management access and high probability of creating value.

The themes developed related to value-creating aspects of the business. They also connected the identified strengths with market relevancy. From that, the opportunities related to strengths are shown in Figure 18.4.

Although this paper lays out the phases in linear form for explanatory purposes, the summit discussions were ongoing and iterative. Aspirations, and even

|  | Strengths | Opportunities |
|---|---|---|
| **STRATEGIC INQUIRY** | • Deep client perception of value creation and reference support<br>• Broad untapped professional relationships<br>• Experienced, committed, competent leadership team<br>• Professional workforce desiring growth, learning, and personal relationships | • Penetrate and significantly grow accounts that have large account potential<br>• Improve profitability margins<br>• Adapt organizational structure to support continued growth<br>• Workforce and team development |
| **APPRECIATIVE INTENT** | **Aspirations**<br>• To be the recognized trusted advisor to our clients<br>• Serve 60% of companies with over $1 billion in revenue<br>• Place four clients in the firm's top ten clients<br>• Be in the top decile of the firm in measures of client satisfaction, employee engagement, employee retention, profitability, and revenue<br>• Serve our clients and our team so well that we are selected as Office of the Year | **Results** (measurements)<br>• Achieve client satisfaction of less than 1.5 on a scale of 4.0<br>• Add two large clients (capability of over $5 million in revenue) and increase total revenues by 20%<br>• Improve net profit margin by 8 percentage points<br>• Achieve employee engagement score above 90% and employee turnover below 12% |

**Figure 18.4.** Strengths, Opportunities, Aspirations, and Results

desired results, were created as the opportunities list was developed. In some cases, inquiry started with desired results in mind and worked backward or started with aspirations or even opportunities. Or opportunities related to one set of strengths were discussed and then the conversation moved straight to aspirations and results. For example, increasing revenues was a desired result from the beginning. From that desired result, the inquiry was designed *in reverse order* from SOAR. Another important point to reinforce is that in all discussions of strengths, weaknesses and threats were considered when discussing opportunities.

**4. Innovate.** The aspirations and results flowed from the strengths and opportunities. For example, uncovering the strength of deep client perception of value led to identifying an opportunity to significantly grow revenues in large client organizations that were being served well but in a limited way. From that opportunity, an aspiration was developed to grow two additional clients to a revenue target that would put them in the top-ten list of the firm's global clients. They already had two on the list of the firm's top ten. How the team would set and measure that goal is expressed in the result "Add two large clients (capability of $5 million in revenue)." Figure 18.4 presents the SOAR working outline of the strategic plan.

Necessary changes emerged for organization structure, processes, systems, and compensation plans. The "how and what" of realizing the strategic plan was done next. The opportunities were narrowed to the four shown in Figure 18.4. Those four opportunities became the overarching goals that drove the future strategic action. There were now both strategic direction and ideas on how to get there.

**5. Implement.** Moving to execution of the plan, GLR staff showed high energy and broad commitment to the plan. Many team members came together to work on projects linked to the goals. Execution groups were generally self-organized. People migrated to where their interests and abilities were. The team was confident that they were on the right track and saw how their contributions were really valued and implemented.

To realize each of the goals, a supporting team was needed. For example, in some way, everyone became active in moving to achieve the first overarching goal: penetrate and significantly grow accounts that have large account potential. Client perceptions of services provided successfully to large clients were analyzed. The subsequent action, to penetrate other large companies using the strength of client perceptions of value creation, was defined. Next, a targeting plan was developed for all companies that fit the profile. All members of the team were asked to identify any relationships they had in the targeted companies. Relationships were mapped, causing some sales territories to shift and assignment of directors to each client or prospect. The team then aggressively pursued developing and advancing relationships to advance or establish work in the targeted companies.

The entire team created a second goal of improving profitability margins, even though initially that seemed to be completely in the hands of the business development managers (BDMs), directors, and MD. Improving pricing was as much a change management initiative as a market-focused adaptation. Improving profit margins was communicated internally as a need to improve pricing and to build confidence *based on the value clients had perceived and realized*. The professionals entered into what was previously closed pricing dialogue. They became more aware of what clients were being charged. They began to push negotiating teams to ask for higher rates based on the value they produced. Now the BDMs and directors who worked directly in pricing services in negotiations not only were feeling downward pressure from clients to reduce prices, but were feeling upward pressure to increase prices from the client service teams.

The team also moved to be involved in the workforce development goal. Attracting, hiring, and retaining high-quality staff members were critical elements to the workforce development strategy. A high priority was placed on candidates with advanced degrees in business, accounting, law, and taxation, and certifications in auditing, accounting, and technology security. By involving everyone in the discussion, the practice experienced significant growth in qualified employee referrals. In the following year, GLR had the highest participation rate in the firm for employee referrals. Building and retaining a highly professional team supported the first and second overarching goals of increasing penetration in large clients and increasing profit margins.

After the summits and subsequent planning meetings, the GLR team was well on the way to executing the plan, even before it was completed and presented to the corporate senior leadership team.

## Results

Through the series of leadership team meetings, planning team meetings, client interviews, employee summit meetings, and follow-up cross-functional meetings, the strategic plan was completed. Although the first draft of the plan did not result in any groundbreaking new ideas, there was a new positive flow of energy and engagement. Everyone in the organization had some degree of ownership, belief, and pride in the future direction of the firm locally. The dissemination and implementation of the strategy had begun simultaneously with the Initiate Phase of SOAR.

From year-end 2004 through 2007, GLR doubled in size to become the firm's largest and most profitable operation. The practice moved from twelfth place in profits and eighth place in total revenues in 2004 to first place in both financial measures by year-end 2007. Along with the increase in profits, GLR moved into first place in client satisfaction scores, employee engagement, and employee retention.

Table 18.2. Change in Relative Position

| | *Relative Rank of GLR Within Global Firm* | | | |
|---|---|---|---|---|
| | 2004 | 2005 | 2006 | 2007 |
| Employee Engagement | 6th | 1st | 1st | 1st |
| Employee Retention | 6th | 3rd | 1st | 1st |
| Client Satisfaction | 8th | 8th | 6th | 1st |
| Revenue | 8th | 5th | 4th | 1st |
| Income | 12th | 6th | 2nd | 1st |

As mentioned at the beginning of the story, annualized employee turnover at the end of 2004 was 32 percent, and that placed GLR in the top quartile of the firm. By 2007, employee turnover dropped to a low of 7 percent and the practice ranked first of all offices in achieving the lowest turnover and highest employee engagement as measured among all large offices globally by Corporate. Table 18.2 shows the progression of GLR relative to the other offices in the firm.

In 2005, the team was awarded the Manpower Global Power Award for Operational Excellence, an award given to the practice that best serves its clients and team. For 2006 and 2007, the practice received the firm's highest award, Office of the Year. The GLR was also named in 2008 by the *Detroit Free Press* as one of the top three places to work in the Great Lakes Region for companies with 150 to 500 employees.

Staff within the GLR practice displayed a sense of relationship and sincere care for each other, the clients, and the community. These results show the positive impact of creating sustainable value by leveraging social and economic considerations within strategy development to achieve financial success.

Culture is also a strategic lever for financial improvement. While any conclusions drawn from this data are anecdotal, the GLR team hypothesized that improving employee retention and employee engagement improved client satisfaction, and improving employee and client satisfaction led to increased revenue growth and profitability. They also believed that the AI philosophy and SOAR framework had a positive impact on improving employee engagement and retention.

Over the three-year period, the leadership team applied these appreciative, strengths-based OD-related concepts and methods to enable and inspire the organization to grow, change, and achieve greater effectiveness by channeling the passion, skills, and engagement of the team. Of course, AI and SOAR did not account for all of the changes in results over time. Having a talented, committed team and great clients to serve were probably the larger variables in the equation.

# SUMMARY

## Leveraging Culture to Build Sustainable Value

Conventional strategic planning methods emanate from modern, scientific management. They assume the environment is knowable and the future predictable. Based on a metaphor of management as control, strategy originates from the center-top of the hierarchy. Experts analyze market forces and then predict the behavior of customers, suppliers, and competitors. From the analysis and prediction, transformational change initiatives are planned and a top-down budget showing increasing revenues is derived. The strategic plan is complete. In this conventional strategy setting/change model, the thinking is separated from the acting. The thinking is done by somebody and the work is done by someone else.

SOAR brings a post-modern perspective to strategic thinking, planning, and implementing. SOAR assumes that organizations are socially constructed by people in relationship to one another. It also begins with an assumption that those who work in the organization care about the organization and understand the nature of their work and their customers better than do outside experts. The employees have a "stake" in the organization and will put their energy and commitment behind its success.

SOAR provides leaders with an expanded capability for helping organizational members make sense together of the environment and the organization. Within SOAR is an awareness of purpose to engage the whole system—employees, customers, suppliers, and other relevant stakeholders—together in dialogue. Participants make meaning of their stories of relationship and share their sense of commitment and aspirations for the organization. They are invited to surface innovations in products and services, structure, process, and methods through relationship. They not only craft positive visions of success and preferred potential futures for the organization, they simultaneously begin moving toward those visions. As the strategic planning process unfolds, implementation *with inspiration* begins.

## References

Anderson, H., Cooperrider, D., Gergen, K.J., Gergen, M., McNamee, S., & Whitney, D. (2008). *The appreciative organization* (Vol. 2). Chagrin Falls, OH: Taos Institute Publishing.

Barker, J.R. (2007, June). Review of the firm as a collaborative community. *Administrative Science Quarterly*, pp. 326–330.

Barsh, J., Capozzi, M.M., & Davidson, J. (2008, January). Leadership and innovation. *The McKinsey Quarterly*, (1).

Cameron, K., Dutton, J., & Quinn, R.E. (2003). *Positive organizational scholarship: Foundations of a new discipline*. San Francisco: Berrett-Koehler.

Edmondson, A.C. (2008, July/August). The competitive imperative of learning. *Harvard Business Review*.

Jarzabkowski, P. (2008). Shaping strategy as a structuration process. *Academy of Management Journal, 51*(4), 621–650.

Lazlo, C. (2008). *Sustainable value*. Sheffield, UK: Greenleaf Publishing.

Margolis, J.D., & Walsh, J.P. (2003). Misery loves companies: Rethinking social initiatives by business. *Administrative Science Quarterly, 48*(2), 268–306.

Shotter, J. (2008). *Conversation realities revisited*. Chagrin Falls, OH: Taos Institute Publishing.

Thatchenkery, T. (2005). *Appreciative knowledge management for strategic change*. Chagrin Falls, OH: Taos Institute Publishing.

Worley, C.G., Hitchins, D.E., & Ross, W.L. (1996). *Integrated strategic change*. Reading, MA: Addison-Wesley.

PART FOUR

# SPECIAL ISSUES IN OD

# Positive Organizational Change

*What the Field of POS Offers to OD Practitioners*

### David S. Bright and Kim Cameron

This chapter describes the emerging field of "positive organizational schol-arship" (POS) and its connection to organization development (OD). The story of the Rocky Flats Nuclear Arsenal shutdown provides an illustration of what is meant by positively deviant performance, a key focus of POS research. A framework for POS is described as a model for differentiating between "abun-dance" versus "deficit" approaches to OD. The chapter concludes with examples and implications of research findings on the heliotropic effect, positive climate, and positive energy.

## THE ROCKY FLATS STORY

The Rocky Flats Nuclear Arsenal was a top-secret nuclear weapons produc-tion facility, opened in 1951 just sixteen miles northwest of downtown Denver, Colorado. During its heyday, Rocky Flats played a key role in the U.S. cold war strategy. Beginning in the late 1960s, however, the work at Rocky Flats generated increasing worry among officials in other government agencies and in the general public. Questions were fueled by the secretive nature of the work, several industrial accidents, and the antagonistic relationships between the managing contractors and the workforce on site. These and other concerns culminated in a 1989 FBI raid that froze production activities across the site. No production work was allowed, and eventually the entire six-thousand-acre facility was downgraded and slated for closure. In 1995, CH2M Hill, an environmental engineering firm, won the contract to clean up and decommission the facility (see Cameron & Lavine, 2006, for the complete story).

## From Extraordinary Problems...

At the onset of cleanup, the prognosis for success was bleak by nearly every expert's prediction. For starters, this was the first cleanup of a nuclear weapons production facility in world history—no one in this industry knew how to accomplish this task. In addition, the site had a long track record of bitter union/management conflict. Grievances from workers were common, expectations for life-long employment were the norm, and a high degree of pride existed among workers regarding their skilled labor. Whereas employees previously felt a sense of purpose and patriotism, imminent closure meant that they were now working without a clear mission. Cleanup also meant that they would literally work themselves out of a job. The FBI raid turned employees from being labeled patriots to being labeled criminals.

To make matters worse, Rocky Flats was one of the most polluted nuclear sites in North America: hundreds of tons of nuclear-grade material, tens of thousands of liters of liquid radioactive solutions, and a half-million cubic yards of low-level radioactive waste were present. A special ABC "Nightline" television program rated two Rocky Flats buildings as "the most dangerous site in America" (Marash, 1994). More than a dozen rooms were labeled "infinity rooms" because radiation levels exceeded the calibration of measuring devices.

To resolve a problem of this magnitude, studies projected that it would require no less than seventy years to clean up at a cost of more than $36 billion. These factors were compounded by a history of conflict between Rocky Flats contractors, government regulatory agencies, environmental groups, community leaders, and citizen groups. The culture was one of secrecy, protectionism, and concealment, and political wrangling had already caused numerous bureaucratic delays. The situation could only be described as bleak and highly dysfunctional—a classic case of severe organizational decline.

In light of these ominous challenges, the prospects of a successful closure and cleanup at Rocky Flats in the seventy-year time frame were labeled as optimistic by the U.S. Department of Energy Secretary.

## ...to Extraordinary Results

Fast-forward ten years. By October 2005, the project was completed, and after thorough testing to ensure that the site was completely clean and safe, the land was turned over to the Bureau of Land Management and is now a wildlife refuge. All on-site buildings had been demolished, all surface level waste removed, and soil and water remediated to a level that exponentially surpassed initial federal standards. The total cost for the project was less than $7 billion, nearly $30 billion under budget and more than sixty years ahead of schedule.

More telling, many former critics—including citizen action groups, the environmental community, local and state governments, city mayors, and regulating agencies—transitioned from being protestors and adversaries to becoming advocates, lobbyists, and partners. The state of labor relations among the unions and management was at its highest level in the history of the facility. A culture of life-long employment and employee entitlement transitioned to one in which the workforce enthusiastically worked itself out of a job as quickly as possible. More than two hundred technological innovations were produced in the service of faster and safer performance. The theme of the facility, "making the impossible possible," represented performance that exceeded all standards by a wide margin. In sum, the Rocky Flats cleanup was an extraordinary achievement by nearly any standard (Cameron & Lavine, 2006).

## POSITIVE ORGANIZATIONAL SCHOLARSHIP

Stories such as the Rocky Flats cleanup illustrate the research interests of scholars in the field of POS. Starting in 2001 at the University of Michigan, the concept of POS was originated as an alternative to the dominant scholarly paradigm at the time. POS is distinct from traditional organizational studies in that it seeks to understand what represents and approaches the best of the human condition. *Positive* refers to (1) positive deviance (such as explaining extraordinary positive outcomes and the processes that produce them); (2) an affirmative orientation (such as focusing on strengths rather than weaknesses or on flourishing relationships rather than problematic relationships); and (3) virtuousness and elevating processes (such as doing good in addition to doing well). *Organization* is the context in which these positive phenomena occur; the dynamics of the workplace are centrally important. Finally, *scholarship* describes the intention of grounding all findings and prescriptions in rigorous, theoretically based research in order to understand what makes these kinds of positive dynamics and organizational breakthroughs possible (Cameron, Dutton, & Quinn, 2003).

Although not without critics (Fineman, 2006; George, 2004), POS scholars are helping to develop an understanding of organizations that nurtures flourishing (Fredrickson & Losada, 2005), thriving (Spreitzer, Sutcliffe, Dutton, Sonenshein, & Grant, 2005), optimal functioning (Keyes, 2002), capacity-building (Dutton & Glynn, 2007), and general excellence in the human condition (Cameron, 2003). POS scholars focus on understanding enablers and motivators, as well as "the outcomes or effects associated with positive phenomenon" (Cameron, Dutton, & Quinn, 2003, pp. 3–4).

Because OD is grounded in a humanistic values orientation (McLean, 2006), POS research is of particular interest to OD practitioners. Indeed, POS and other related research efforts such as "positive psychology" (Seligman & Csikszentmihalyi, 2000), Positive Organizational Behavior (Luthans & Youssef, 2007), and Appreciative Inquiry (Cooperrider & Srivastva, 1987) have been described as the scholarly foundation for a number of common OD practices and innovations (Bushe, 2007; DiVirgilio & Ludema, 2008). This chapter describes the POS orientation in more detail, some of the major findings from this research perspective, and a few implications for the field of OD.

# A POS FRAMEWORK

Why is there a need for scholarship that specifically focuses on positive organizing? First, as suggested by Figure 19.1, there is reason to expect that unique dynamics are associated with positive organizing that differs from normal organizing processes.

Loosely speaking, we can think of people and organizations in terms of three states: negative deviance, ordinary, and positive deviance. At the extreme left end of the continuum is negative deviance, or the dysfunctional state. In this state, people experience illness, and organizations are unprofitable, ineffective, and inefficient. Quality is problematic and errors in production are customary. Unethical behaviors may be evident. Interpersonal relationships between people are often toxic. Metaphorically, this condition might be characterized by individuals or organizations in need of a hospital.

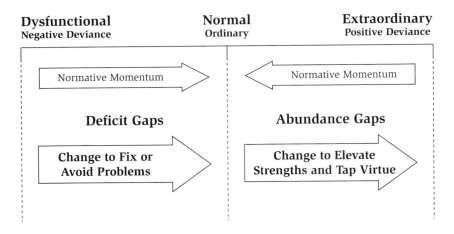

**Figure 19.1.** Differences in States of Organization and the Dynamics of Change
*Source:* Bright, 2005

At the right end of the continuum is positive deviance, or an extraordinarily functional state. People in this condition are filled with vitality and experience *flow* in their work (Csikszentmihalyi, 1990). Extraordinary organizations thrive and contribute extraordinary value; they are not merely effective but excellent. Virtuousness characterizes organizational practices. Quality is error-free, people honor one another, and flourishing occurs at every level, "achieving the best of the human condition" (Cameron, 2008c). Metaphorically, this condition might be characterized by individuals or organizations functioning like an Olympic athlete.

The Rocky Flats story exemplifies both extremes. At the beginning of cleanup, the site was clearly in a negatively deviant, highly dysfunctional condition. By the time of site closure, Rocky Flats had become a positively deviant, extraordinarily performing organization.

It is highly unusual for organizations to function at either extreme of deviance, as illustrated by the "normative momentum" arrows in Figure 19.1, which point toward the center. The act of organizing is usually an act of reducing variance or deviance, usually stimulated by the emergence of difficulties, uncertainties, or constraints. Generally speaking, organizations are designed to generate stability, steadiness, and predictability (March & Simon, 1958; Parsons, 1947; Weber, 1992). In order to function in such as way, organizational leaders continually work to set expectations, strategies and goals, rules, processes, procedures, strategies, and structures—all of which reduce uncertainty as they increase predictability and dependability. The effect is that most leaders and organizations, by nature and by default, focus on maintaining performance at the norm or center of the continuum. Success becomes a measure of how effectively the organization creates predictable trends, reliable functioning, and profitable operations. As a result, most performance is neither positively nor negatively deviant (Quinn, 2004; Spreitzer & Sonenshein, 2003).

## A POS LENS IN THE PRACTICE OF OD

Because OD practitioners focus on the creation and implementation of change, the POS model provides a framework for identifying the two fundamental motivations for change. Specifically: Is the change intended to fix a dysfunctional aspect of the organization (closing deficit gaps), or is the change intended to extend or elevate the strengths in the organization (closing abundance gaps)?

With respect to the first motive, the resolution of deficit gaps, many professional OD practitioners note that they are typically brought into an organization when dysfunction exists (Burke, 2002). The OD professional functions much like a physician in diagnosing the issues, prescribing solutions, and working to heal the organization from its ills. Basically, in this type of change, the organization's starting point for change is assumed to be in a state of negative deviance, and thus the intention of change is to fix things. In this endeavor, the OD practitioner encourages processes that work *with* the normative momentum to overcome deficit gaps and fix problems, essentially helping to overcome negatively deviant organizational habits while reinforcing expected norms and routines. Many change experts, for instance, advocate the need to create urgency for change (Kotter, 2008) or the importance for "diagnosis" (Cummings & Worley, 2009), tacitly acknowledging the normative power of identifying a common concern and the motivating potential that may come in the process of overcoming such challenges (Cameron, 2008a).

The second motive for change is a transformation past an ordinary, expected state to an extraordinary, positively deviant state. This means changing from normal performance to extraordinary performance—unleashing the latent positive energy in a system so that thriving and flourishing can occur (Spreitzer, Sutcliffe, Dutton, Sonenshein, & Grant, 2005). As illustrated in Figure 19.1, however, extraordinary performance works *against* the normative momentum to remain at the center of the continuum. Just as an Olympic athlete immediately experiences decline toward the ordinary state if he or she ceases training at the highest level, extraordinary organizations also quickly slip into a pattern of ordinariness that is consistent with expected, average performance. Extraordinary performance is always dynamic and difficult to sustain.

In light of these different motivations for change, it is important to be clear about two things. First, the starting point for change on the continuum in Figure 19.1 may differ for every person and every organization. What is normal, ordinary, or expected for one may not be the same for another, and the expectations of internal constituencies may not be the same as those of external constituencies. Traditional OD change strategies, when focused primarily on closing deficit gaps, will rarely alter the standard of effective or expected performance. Positively deviant change, conversely, can be understood as both change internal to an organization that transforms the normal point for insiders and as change that exceeds the norms as defined by those external to the organization. Positively deviant change alters both internal and external norms and expectations.

Second, POS research firmly acknowledges that positively deviant organizations are not ignorant of negative conditions or situations when mistakes, crises, deterioration, or problems are present. Rather, extraordinary organizing is pursued not just when conditions are favorable, but even—and perhaps especially—when conditions are grave or difficult. Extraordinary performance is often motivated by the presence of problematic and difficult circumstances. Indeed, as described in an extensive analysis by Cameron and Lavine (2006), the Rocky Flats case is exemplary precisely because there was such a strong potential for continued stagnation and dysfunction. Sometimes, the attributes of extraordinary organization are apparent only in response to obstacles, challenges, or detrimental occurrences.

# THE HELIOTROPIC EFFECT AND OTHER INSIGHTS FOR ORGANIZATION DEVELOPMENT

In biology, the *heliotropic effect* refers to the phenomenon whereby plants track the sun as it moves across the sky. In a human sense, it is the tendency to both seek and draw on sources of positive energy (Cooperrider, 1990). Empirical evidence confirms that human beings have a natural inclination toward, and thrive most when exposed to, the positive (Cameron, 2008b).

When considering questions of organizational change, the idea of heliotropism fits with the Lewinian concept of force fields (Lewin, 1951). In essence, Lewin postulates that change occurs when the forces *against* change are overcome by the forces *for* change. Where heliotropism exists, it serves as an energy force that draws people toward extraordinary activity in organizational life. Ironically, however, both common human experience and abundant scientific evidence (Baumeister, Bratslavsky, Finkenauer, & Vohs, 2001) support the idea that *bad is stronger than good*. Human beings *react* more strongly to negative phenomena than to positive phenomena. Early in life individuals learn to be vigilant in responding to the negative and to ignore positive occurrences. People react to the negative more readily and more forcefully than to the positive because of survival instincts. Human organizations, similarly, are designed to do the same. They are organized so as to protect against the negative. Hence, positive change requires significantly more positive energy than neutral or negative energy, and emphasis on the positive must be pervasive and sufficiently strong enough to draw people toward it with compelling force. OD interventions intent on enabling positive change, therefore, must pay particular attention to the elements in organization that generate heliotropic-inducing energy.

In this regard, recent scholarship builds on and clarifies the foundations of heliotropism, and how it shapes and influences organizations (for examples, see Bright, 2005; Bright, Cameron, & Caza, 2006; Bright, Cooperrider, & Galloway, 2006; and Cameron, 2003). The following sections, drawn substantially from Cameron (2008c), provide a sampling of insights from research that highlights the factors that influence heliotropism and its effects on organizations.

## Example 1: Positive Climate and Virtue-Based Organizing

*Positive climate* describes a social condition in which positive emotions predominate over negative emotions (Denison, 1996; Smidts, Pruyn, & Van Riel, 2001). Numerous studies show that the positive emotions, which comprise positive climate, are associated with optimal individual and organizational functioning (Bagozzi, 2003; Fredrickson, 1998, 2001, 2003; Fredrickson & Joiner, 2002).

For example, Fredrickson (1998) was among the first to document the "broaden and build" phenomenon, in which positive emotions "broaden people's momentary thought-action repertoire and build their enduring personal resources" (Fredrickson, 2003, p. 166). Positive emotions (such as joyfulness, love, or appreciation) enlarge cognitive perspectives. In other words, people are literally able to take in more information when they experience positive emotions. Individuals can attend to more information, make richer interpretations, and experience higher levels of creativity and productivity (Isen, 1987). People become more creative, experimental, and playful. In contrast, negative emotions narrow people's thought-action repertoires and diminish their cognitive abilities.

A positive climate enables people to cope with negativity in productive ways (Bright, Fry, & Cooperrider, 2006). Performance is positively affected by a positive climate (Mathieu & Zajac, 1990; Schneider, 1991), yet stress, anxiety, and other forms of negativity are always present in organizations. In extraordinary organizations, positive emotions counter the potentially negative effects of fear, anger, sadness, or anxiety (Fredrickson & Levenson, 1998). Positive interpretations can predominate over negative interpretations to generate a sense of hope. Thus, positivity nullifies the harmful consequences of negativity, allowing for regenerative, rather than dysfunctional, outcomes when negativity occurs.

The release of positive energy occurs when an OD intervention emphasizes positive change (closing abundance gaps), rather than emphasizing problem solving or returning to a normal state. Organizations may invoke such excellence when they appeal to fundamental, human virtues such as courage, gratitude, compassion, and justice (Bright, Cameron, & Caza, 2006; Cameron, Bright, & Caza, 2004). Organizational virtue generates human impact because it encourages thriving people and communities. Practices such as organization courage, integrity, compassion, and forgiveness promote a positive climate because they are contagious and inspire morale elevation. When people witness exemplary behavior in others, they feel emotionally elevated and are inspired to engage in exemplary behaviors themselves. A reinforcing, upward spiral takes root and becomes self-sustaining. Such virtuous cycles have been documented as illustrating the heliotropic effect, especially when positive change is pursued.

## Example 2: Positive Energy Networks

Research by Baker, Cross, and Wooten (2003) has shown that individuals can be identified as "positive energizers" or "negative energizers" and that the difference has important implications. Positive energizers create and support vitality in others. They uplift and boost people. Interacting with positive energizers leaves others feeling lively and motivated. Positive energizers have been found to be optimistic, heedful, trustworthy, and unselfish. Interacting with them builds energy in people and is an inspiring experience. Positive energizers benefit their organizations by enabling others to perform better. In fact, a comparison among people's locations in information networks (who obtains information from whom), influence networks (who influences whom), and positive energy networks (who energizes whom) revealed that position in the energy network is far more predictive of success than position in information or influence networks (Baker, 2004). A positive energizer is four times more likely to be a success than the person who is at the center of an information or influence network (Baker, Cross, & Wooten, 2003).

Positive energizers also help others become better energizers. In fact, high-performing organizations have three times more positive energizers than average organizations, enabling leveraged interpersonal relationships that build better coordination and collaboration, and efficiency of work (Cross, Baker, & Parker, 2003). Moreover, positive energizing is a learned behavior, not a personality attribute.

In contrast, negative energizers deplete the good feelings and enthusiasm of others. They sap strength from and weaken people. They leave others feeling exhausted and diminished. Negative energizers have been found to be critical, inflexible, selfish, and untrustworthy (Cross, Baker, & Parker, 2003).

Not everyone is a positive energizer for everyone else, of course, and an individual may positively energize certain people but not others. Hence, conducting an analysis of the positive-energy network in an organization helps to identify positive-energy hubs, black holes, and peripheral members who may need development (Baker, 2000).

A very simplistic, but still useful diagnosis is to ask employees to write down the names of the two or three most energizing people in the organizational unit. The results are then tabulated so that the most frequently named individuals are identified—the positive energizers—as well as the names of individuals not mentioned who can be mentored and developed.

## Example 3: High-Quality Relationships

Building on the idea of positive energy networks, the strength of interpersonal ties between people in organizations is also an important enabler of positive change (Dutton & Heaphy, 2003). Positive relationships refer to those that are a "generative source of enrichment, vitality, and learning" for both individuals and organizations (Dutton & Ragins, 2007, p. 5). Positive relationships mean more than people "getting along" or avoiding toxicity in their interactions. Positive relationships, rather, serve as enablers of positively deviant outcomes physiologically, psychologically, emotionally, and organizationally.

High-quality relationships enable flourishing and resilience in organizations. They are characterized by positive regard between the participants, mutuality, the feeling that each party is engaged and fully participating, and a feeling of vitality or aliveness. While these connections may be temporary, they can leave a lasting impression and effect, and sustained high-quality connections become high-quality relationships. This connectivity is the means by which resources flow and coordinated action takes place (Losada & Heaphy, 2004). Coordinated exchange, in turn, enables higher productivity and higher-quality performance because it facilitates the formation of needed social capital and synchronicity (Dutton & Heaphy, 2003; Fredrickson & Levenson, 1998; Fredrickson & Losada, 2005; Losada, 1999; Fredrickson, Mancuso, Branigan, & Tugade, 2000). High-quality interpersonal connections have also been linked to the outstanding performance of leadership teams (Losada & Heaphy, 2004). In sum, healthy organizations strive to establish a context in which high-quality connections may flourish, regenerate, and proliferate (Golembiewski, 2003; Kleiner, 2007).

Also of interest, a common assumption is that, when people receive love, support, and encouragement (that is, when their psychological and emotional needs are met), they tend to feel secure and their performance is therefore elevated. What has actually been found, however, is that *what people give* to a relationship, rather than *what they receive* from the relationship, accounts for the positive effects (see Brown & Brown, 2006; Brown, Nesse, Vinoker, & Smith, 2003; Grant, Dutton, & Rosso, 2008).

# SUMMARY

This chapter introduces the concept of positive organizational change, which has emerged from the field of positive organizational scholarship (POS). The research suggests that what is currently known about dysfunctional organization (deficit gaps) is vastly greater than what is known about extraordinary organization functionality (abundance gaps). POS attempts to address this imbalance, not to the exclusion of problem-based scholarship and practice, but as a complementary extension. Implications for expanding the practice of OD through POS are numerous, and we have focused in this chapter on briefly reviewing research that can lead to positive change interventions.

Both positive and negative factors may perpetuate positive change, but when both are present, the negative tends to dominate, so positive energy must be emphasized in order for positive change to be stimulated. This helps explain why a historical bias exists in OD toward deficit- over positive-oriented change (Cameron, 2008b). Positive climate, positive energy, and high-quality relationships, however, unleash the heliotropic effect in individuals and organizations, and this, in turn, produces extraordinary performance. We hope that this chapter will serve as a stimulus to encourage more positive change practices by OD practitioners.

# References

Bagozzi, R.P. (2003). Positive and negative emotions in organizations. In K.S. Cameron, J.E. Dutton, & R.E. Quinn (Eds.), *Positive organizational scholarship: Foundations of a new discipline* (pp. 176–193). San Francisco: Berrett-Koehler.

Baker, W. (2000). *Achieving success through social capital*. San Francisco: Jossey-Bass.

Baker, W. (2004). Half-baked brown bag presentation on positive energy networks. Unpublished manuscript. Ann Arbor, MI: University of Michigan Business School.

Baker, W., Cross, R., & Wooten, M. (2003). Positive organizational network analysis and energizing relationships. In K.S. Cameron, J.E. Dutton, & R.E. Quinn (Eds.), *Positive organizational scholarship: Foundations of a new discipline* (pp. 328–342). San Francisco: Berrett-Koehler.

Baumeister, R., Bratslavsky, E., Finkenauer, C., & Vohs, K.D. (2001). Bad is stronger than good. *Review of General Psychology, 5*(4), 323–370.

Bright, D.S. (2005). Forgiveness and change: Begrudging, pragmatic, and transcendent responses to discomfiture in a unionized trucking company. Unpublished dissertation, Cleveland, OH: Case Western Reserve University.

Bright, D.S., Cameron, K., & Caza, A. (2006). The amplifying and buffering effects of virtuousness in downsized organizations. *Journal of Business Ethics, 64*(3), 249–269.

Bright, D.S., Cooperrider, D.L., & Galloway, W.B. (2006). Appreciative inquiry in the Office of Research and Development: Improving the collaborative capacity of organization. *Public Performance and Management Review, 39*(3), 285–306.

Bright, D.S., Fry, R.E., & Cooperrider, D.L. (2006). Forgiveness from the perspectives of three response modes: Begrudgement, pragmatism, and transcendence. In C.C. Manz, K.S. Cameron, K.P. Manz, & R.D. Marx (Eds.), *Journal of Management Spirituality and Religion*, 3(Special Issue), 78–103.

Brown, S.L., & Brown, R.M. (2006). Selective investment theory: Recasting the functional significance of close relationships. *Psychological Inquiry, 17*(1), 1–29.

Brown, S.L., Nesse, R.M., Vinokur, A.D., & Smith, D.M. (2003). Providing social support may be more beneficial than receiving it: Results from a prospective study of mortality. *Psychological Science, 14*(4), 320–327.

Burke, W.W. (2002). *Organization change: Theory and practice*. Thousand Oaks, CA: Sage.

Bushe, G. (2007). Appreciative inquiry is not (just) about the positive. *OD Practitioner, 39*(4), 33–38.

Cameron, K.S. (2003). Organizational virtuousness and performance. In K.S. Cameron, J.E. Dutton, & R.E. Quinn (Eds.), *Positive organizational scholarship: Foundations of a new discipline* (pp. 48–65). San Francisco: Berrett-Koehler.

Cameron, K.S. (2008a). A process for changing organizational culture. In T.G. Cummings (Ed.), *Handbook of organizational development* (pp. 429–445). Thousand Oaks, CA: Sage.

Cameron, K.S. (2008b). Paradox in positive organizational change. *Journal of Applied Behavioral Science, 44*(1), 7–24.

Cameron, K.S. (2008c). *Positive leadership: Strategies for extraordinary performance.* San Francisco: Berrett-Koehler.

Cameron, K.S., Bright, D.S., & Caza, A. (2004). Exploring the relationships between organizational virtuousness and performance. *American Behavioral Scientist, 47*(6), 766–790.

Cameron, K.S., Dutton, J.E., & Quinn, R.E. (2003). Foundations of positive organizational scholarship. In K.S. Cameron, J.E. Dutton, & R.E. Quinn (Eds.), *Positive organizational scholarship: Foundations of a new discipline* (pp. 3–13). San Francisco: Berrett-Koehler.

Cameron, K.S., & Lavine, M. (2006). *Making the impossible possible: Leading extraordinary performance: The Rocky Flats Story.* San Francisco: Berrett-Koehler.

Cooperrider, D.L. (1990). Positive image, positive action: The affirmative basis of organizing. In S. Srivastva & D.L. Cooperrider (Eds.), *Appreciative management and leadership: The power of positive thought and action in organizations* (pp. 91–125). San Francisco: Jossey-Bass.

Cooperrider, D.L., & Srivastva, S. (1987). Appreciative inquiry in organizational life. *Research in Organizational Change and Development, 1*, 129–169.

Cross, R., Baker, W., & Parker, A. (2003). What creates energy in organizations? *MIT Sloan Management Review, 44*(4), 51–56.

Csikszentmihalyi, M. (1990). *Flow: The psychology of optimal experience* (1st ed.). New York: Harper and Row.

Cummings, T.G., & Worley, C.G. (2009). *Organization development and change.* Mason, OH: South-Western Cengage Learning.

Denison, D.R. (1996). What is the difference between organizational culture and organizational climate? A native's point of view on a decade of paradigm wars. *Academy of Management Review, 21*(3), 619–654.

DiVirgilio, M., & Ludema, J. (2008). How can I help you succeed? Leading change by asking questions that generate energy for action. Paper presented at the 2008 Academy of Management Annual Meeting in Anaheim, California.

Dutton, J.E., & Glynn, M.A. (2007). Positive organizational scholarship. In C. Cooper & J. Barling (Eds.), *Handbook of organizational behavior.* Thousand Oaks, CA: Sage.

Dutton, J.E., & Heaphy, E.D. (2003). The power of high-quality connections. In K.S. Cameron, J.E. Dutton, & R.E. Quinn (Eds.), *Positive organizational scholarship: Foundations of a new discipline* (pp. 263–278). San Francisco: Berrett-Koehler.

Dutton, J.E., & Ragins, B.R. (2007). *Exploring positive relationships at work: Building a theoretical and research foundation.* LEA's organization and management series. Mahwah, NJ: Lawrence Erlbaum Associates.

Fineman, S. (2006). On being positive: Concerns and counterpoints. *Academy of Management Review, 31*(2), 270–291.

Fredrickson, B.L. (1998). What good are positive emotions? *Review of General Psychology, 2*, 300–319.

Fredrickson, B.L. (2001). The role of positive emotions in positive psychology: The broaden-and-build theory of positive emotions. *American Psychologist, 56*(3), 218.

Fredrickson, B.L. (2003). The value of positive emotions. *American Scientist, 91*(4), 330–335.

Fredrickson, B.L., & Joiner, T. (2002). Positive emotions trigger upward spirals toward emotional well-being. *Psychological Science, 13*(2), 172–175.

Fredrickson, B.L., & Levenson, R.W. (1998). Positive emotions speed recovery from the cardiovascular sequelae of negative emotions. *Cognition and Emotion, 12*(2), 191–220.

Fredrickson, B.L., & Losada, M. (2005). Positive affect and the complex dynamics of human flourishing. *American Psychologist, 60*(7), 678–686.

Fredrickson, B.L., Mancuso, R.A., Branigan, C., & Tugade, M.M. (2000). The undoing effect of positive emotions. *Motivation and Emotion, 24*(4), 237–258.

George, J.M. (2004). Positive organizational scholarship: Foundations of a new discipline. *Administrative Science Quarterly, 49*(2), 325–330.

Golembiewski, R.T. (2003). *Ironies in organizational development/Robert T. Golembiewski* (2nd ed., rev. and expanded). Public administration and public policy; No. 100. New York: Marcel Dekker.

Grant, A., Dutton, J.E., & Rosso, B.D. (2008). Giving commitment: Employee support programs and the prosocial sensemaking process. *Academy of Management Journal, 51*(5), 898–918.

Isen, A.M. (1987). Positive affect, cognitive processes, and social behavior. *Advances in Experimental Social Psychology, 20*, 203–253.

Keyes, C.L.M. (2002). The mental health continuum: From languishing to flourishing in life. *Journal of Health and Social Behavior, 43*(2), 207–222.

Kleiner, A. (2007). Organizational circulatory systems: An inquiry. *OD Journal, 39*(3), 4–8.

Kotter, J.P. (2008). *Sense of urgency*. Cambridge, MA: Harvard Business School Press.

Lewin, K. (1951). *Field theory in social science*. New York: Harper and Row.

Losada, M. (1999). The complex dynamics of high performance teams. *Mathematical and Computer Modeling, 30*, 179–192.

Losada, M., & Heaphy, E. (2004). The role of positivity and connectivity in the performance of business teams. *American Behavioral Scientist, 47*(6), 740–765.

Luthans, F., & Youssef, C.M. (2007). Emerging positive organizational behavior. *Journal of Management, 33*(3), 321–349.

Marash, D. (Reporter). (1994, December 20). *ABC News Nightline: The most dangerous building in America*. [Television broadcast]. New York: ABC News.

March, J.G., & Simon, H. (1958). *Organizations*. Hoboken, NJ: John Wiley & Sons.

Mathieu, J.E., & Zajac, D.M. (1990). A review and meta-analysis of the antecedents, correlates, and consequences of organizational commitment. *Psychological Bulletin, 108*(2), 171.

McLean, G.N. (2006). *Organization development*. San Francisco: Berrett-Koehler.

Parsons, T. (1947). *Max Weber: The theory of social and economic organization* (1st paperback ed.). New York: The Free Press.

Quinn, R.E. (2004). *Change the world*. San Francisco: Jossey-Bass.

Schneider, B. (1991). *Organizational climate and culture*. San Francisco: Jossey-Bass.

Seligman, M.P., & Csikszentmihalyi, M. (2000). Positive psychology. *American Psychologist, 55*(1), 5–14.

Smidts, A., Pruyn, A.H., & Van Riel, C.B.M. (2001). The impact of employee communication and perceived external prestige on organizational identification. *Academy of Management Journal, 44*(5), 1051–1062.

Spreitzer, G., Sutcliffe, K., Dutton, J., Sonenshein, S., & Grant, A.M. (2005). A socially embedded model of thriving at work. *Organization Science, 16*(5), 537–549.

Spreitzer, G.M., & Sonenshein, S. (2003). Positive deviance and extraordinary organizing. In K.S. Cameron, J.E. Dutton, & R.E. Quinn (Eds.), *Positive organizational scholarship: Foundations of a new discipline* (pp. 207–224). San Francisco: Berrett-Koehler.

Weber, M. (1992). *The protestant ethic and the spirit of capitalism* New York: Routledge.

CHAPTER TWENTY

# Systemic Sustainability[SM]

*Moving Sustainability from Ideas to Action**

### Mona A. Amodeo and C. Keith Cox

Today's savvy business leaders understand that the next wave of business transformation, the "sustainability revolution" (Edwards, 2005), is rapidly becoming a source of unprecedented business opportunity. A company's serious commitment to sustainability can result in a tremendous upside, including: (1) an enhanced corporate reputation, more powerful brand, and increased customer goodwill; (2) a reduction in costs coupled with an increase in production; (3) a competitive edge in the "war for talent"; (4) a more energized and vision-guided workforce; and (5) a "green" values-driven organizational culture that opens the door for rapid business innovation. Taken together, one has a very compelling business case for sustainability that is hard to ignore.

Yet, sustainability is a lot like the idea of democracy; everyone is in favor of it but somehow it gets defined differently depending on who you talk to (Kielstra, 2008). Based on our research (Amodeo, 2005; Cox, 2005; Ludema & Cox, 2007; Schrader, 1995) and experience, we have concluded that sustainability derives its greatest power and potential in organizations when it is embraced as

---

*We are grateful for the many thought-provoking conversations with leaders of companies at the forefront of the sustainability movement such as: Interface, Inc., The Body Shop, 3M, ShoreBank, Seventh Generation, Green Mountain Coffee Roasters, Honest Tea, Trillium Asset Management, Organic Valley Farms, Calvert Group, Wild Oats, White Dog Café, Church & Dwight Company, Inc., as well as a host of others. We also thank our colleague and generative thinking partner Dave Schrader, Ph.D. (www.leading-work.com/), for his wisdom and involvement in our work.

a set of core values that uplift and integrate economic prosperity, environmental stewardship, and social responsibility, sometimes referred to as people, profit, and planet. When an organization embraces these sustainability values and weaves them into every facet of the business, it becomes definitional—revealing itself in every aspect of behavior.

However, incorporating the values of sustainability into the cultural assumptions of the organization is an intentional and incremental process that occurs over time. Each organization must arrive at its own shared understanding of what sustainability means and create its unique path to bring those values to life through words and actions (Amodeo, 2008; Cox, 2008).

The objective of this chapter is to introduce the Systemic Sustainability[SM] Framework as a way of embracing sustainability and integrating the associated beliefs into the conversations and actions of the organization. In doing so we will highlight the organization development (OD) concepts, techniques, and methods that serve as a catalyst throughout the sustainability journey and provide a recent case study as an example of how the framework can be applied. Finally, we will provide some concluding thoughts on the future of OD research and practice and how those emerging frontiers may expand our understanding of how organizations repurpose and reinvent themselves in order to become more sustainable.

## SYSTEMIC SUSTAINABILITY FRAMEWORK OVERVIEW

We have discovered that to successfully make sustainability an organizational reality, leadership must put forth bold visions while engaging their organization in different, deeper conversations about the purpose and responsibility of business. Moreover, there must be proactive engagement of the whole system in such a way that: mental models become explicit; multiple stakeholder perspectives are incorporated into the process; and collective interaction yields new knowledge, structures, processes, practices, and stories that can drive the organization forward. The bottom line is that there simply must be a willingness to go far beyond surface-level change to challenge assumptions and some long-held beliefs, or what we call *transformative dialogue* around the sustainability agenda. The Systemic Sustainability Framework (SSF) was specifically designed for this purpose.

The SSF (see Figure 20.1) is divided into four overlapping, perpetual phases: (1) Exploration and Foundation Building, (2) Expanding Engagement, (3) Innovating and Integrating, and (4) Refine, Refocus, and Reenergize. Each revolves around a series of collaborative conversations, transformational interactions, and cross-pollinating relationships that are fostered within individual learning experiences and cutting-edge, small- and large-group facilitated sessions, workshops,

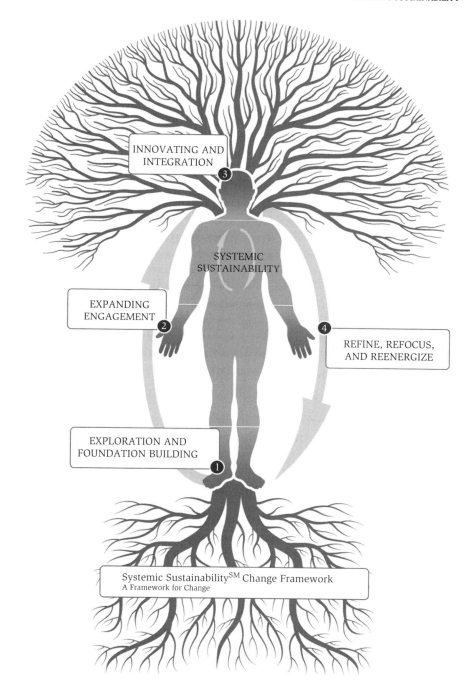

**Figure 20.1.** Systemic Sustainability Change Framework

and seminars. As an organization translates the meaning of sustainability into behavior, ongoing connections, relationships, and networks begin to flourish through an infusion of knowledge, wisdom, and grassroots experience. Skepticism gives way to understanding as the organization confirms the validity of the values through the successes experienced. Over time, this new way of thinking, believing, and doing is incrementally embedded into the organization's cultural assumptions. These new paradigms lead to innovations that emerge in the form of: technical advances, sustainable business practices, and new leadership capacity.

The culmination of this hard work is a solid foundation of a culture steeped in sustainable understanding, thinking, believing, and acting. The following sections provide a synopsis of each phase of the SSF.

## Phase 1: Exploration and Foundation Building

The first phase of the SSF begins with engaging leadership in answering questions required to undertake the sustainability journey. This is a time of energy, activity, intense questioning, and soul searching. The work occurs at both the individual and organizational level and revolves around addressing the following questions:

- What do "we" collectively know about sustainability?
- Where are we today?
- Am I willing and able to make a difference?
- Is this a journey we are ready to embark upon?
- What are the next steps?

This initial activity, deep reflection, and inquiry is really the beginning of a transformation process, which, if ignored, ensures the "creative tension" required for change is lacking and the intense commitment, courage, and dedication needed for success fleeting, leaving sustainability to become the latest "flavor of the month." Moreover, this step focuses on intimately building bridges between the individual leader and the broader global issues and the organizational sustainability agenda, which is paramount for success. Some of the activities used to facilitate this critical learning at the individual level may include individual values assessment, vision/mission development, 360-degree feedback, service learning, outdoor experiential learning, coaching, and peer-to-peer mentoring, among various other deep learning exercises.

The "completion" of this first series of conversations/activities creates a strong foundation moving forward, and the success of the entire sustainability agenda is directly correlated to the quality of work put into this preparatory phase. Next, with groundwork laid for achievement, the emphasis shifts to expanding stakeholder engagement both inside and outside the organization.

# Phase 2: Expanding Engagement

Involving others effectively is about creating the space and context for meaningful conversations to occur, bringing disparate voices together, embracing spontaneity, working within paradox, and facilitating the change process when required. It is about building broader, deeper stakeholder connections, inside and outside the organization, much more so than the typical product/service alliances and partnerships or the employee suggestion boxes found in the mainstream business world. It is in this phase the organization begins to move sustainability from ideas to the actions that will define each organization's individual sustainability journey.

The focus for expanding engagement is centered on the following questions:

- What do we need to learn?
- Who else needs to be in on this?
- What behaviors will define our journey and how will we measure success?
- How will we communicate our journey to our internal stakeholders?
- How far are we prepared to go?

The work of answering these questions revolves around a common mantra in the OD world: people will only defend and support that which they help build and create (Weisbord & Janoff, 1995). Furthermore, as Senge (1990) reminds us, organizations are like complex puzzles in which the whole cannot be understood until all the pieces are viewed systemically, nor can the whole be changed until the collective is assembled to work together to shape a new potential future.

When sustainability becomes the core driver of the firm's strategic intent, this emphasis on joint exploration and co-creation becomes paramount (Senge, Lichenstein, Kaeufer, Bradbury, & Carroll, 2007). Phase 2 taps into the creative intelligence of the organization and its stakeholders through realized diversity, purposeful dialogue, collaborative inquiry, community building, and cutting-edge change methods that support new ways of thinking and transforming relationships.

In order for sustainability to become more than just an intellectual exercise, extended conversation, and good intentions, it must be synthesized into the organizational DNA, the cultural core. This becomes the focus in the next phase of the framework: Innovating and Integrating.

# Phase 3: Innovating and Integrating

Sustainability will not thrive if it is positioned as a stand-alone strategy or program confined to the domain of a single staff group (Googins, Mirvis, & Rochlin, 2007; Kielstra, 2008). Instead it must be aligned, integrated, and institutionalized into corporate systems, structures, and processes. Therefore, this SSF phase addresses the following questions:

- Where will we start?
- How will we accelerate progress through organizational learning?
- How will we expand our communications to our external stakeholders?
- How will we continuously recognize, reward, and celebrate success?

However, the reality is that an organization's sustainability journey leads down many paths, some successful and some not. Therefore, the work at this juncture centers on leveraging OD knowledge and practice to design and facilitate conversations, large-group dialogues, "local experiments," and learning experiences that address the individual, organizational, and technical demands of bringing sustainability to fruition in practice (see Table 20.1).

As a result, new structures, systems, processes, and business practices emerge as individuals continually question the status quo and simultaneously infuse the declared sustainability-driven purpose, principles, vision, and values of the organization into the culture and ongoing conversation of becoming "green."

### Table 20.1. Sample Activities in the Innovating and Integrating Phase

| | | |
|---|---|---|
| • Expand sustainability leadership network | • Redesign operating strategies/practices; organization structure/reporting relationships; HR policies, procedures, programs; and board/corporate governance to support sustainability journey | • Develop and execute strategic communications |
| • Increase networking, coaching, role modeling, mentoring, and peer-to-peer community development | | • Introduce technical changes to support sustainability journey (air, water, waste, energy, health and safety, information technology, physical space and facilities, products/services, etc.) |
| • Deepen individual mind, body, and spirit work | | |
| • Align internal "talk" and "walk" (values integration) | • Create new sustainability metrics, standards, and environmental performance management system | |
| • Amplify stakeholder engagement (for example, increase memberships, partnerships, and collaborations) | • Generate a sustainability report | • Obtain third-party program feedback, reviews, verifications, and certifications (where applicable) |
| • Accelerate introduction of new ideas or experts in the field | | • Employ continuous improvement processes |
| | | • Celebrate successes |

Furthermore, the simultaneous processes of trial and error, experimentation, and developing creative alternatives create impacts, outcomes, and "ripple effects" throughout the organizational system. The results of these sustainability efforts are highly contextual and influenced by a number of individual and organizational variables. No two organizations will have identical sustainability outcomes such as business practices, programs, or metrics, among others.

So the road to innovative solutions and integrating sustainability into the heart and soul of the organization can be a long one, rife with twists and turns along the way that arise in the form of dilemmas, mistakes, paradox, uncertainty, combined with the constant challenge of "bureaucracy creep" and the always tempting desire to lapse back to a dependence on more traditional ways of thinking and managing the firm (such as command and control). Therefore, it is imperative that all stakeholders remain vigilant about monitoring the implementation processes in the present; co-creating and sharing learning; and maintaining the spirit of discovery, even when the way forward seems clear. It is this emphasis on reinforcing, refining, refocusing, and reenergizing that signals the transition into the fourth stage of the SSF.

## Phase 4: Refine, Refocus, and Reenergize

As an organization's sustainability initiatives take root, undoubtedly the playing field changes as the broader sustainability movement grows. This constant state of flux, expanding and shifting, produces new ideas and innovations. Leaders quickly begin to realize that crossing the finish line in the race to sustainability never really happens. Instead they come to accept the fact that, to a degree, their organization is a grand business/social experiment in progress, one that will require regular attention, perseverance, and nurturing over the long term. Therefore, this SSF phase addresses the following questions:

- How do we refine, refocus, expand, and continually embrace the values of sustainability?

- How will we know we've succeeded?

The prevailing wisdom for an organization at this point in its journey is to lift up celebration and improvisation while simultaneously focusing on reorientation. In other words, while there is overt recognition of the progress achieved and a continued push for entrepreneurial thinking and innovative solutions, there is also the need to once again gauge the pulse of the organization, its stakeholders and society, and determine if a course adjustment is required.

Some frame this work as charting the next leg of the sustainability journey, others implementing as Sustainability 2.0. But whatever you call it, it is propelled by methods grounded in whole system change (Holman, Devane, & Cady, 2007; Piderit, Fry, & Cooperrider, 2007), complexity theory (Olson & Eoyang, 2001; Wheatley, 2005), organizational learning (Senge, 1990; Senge, Lichenstein,

Kaeufer, Bradbury, & Carroll, 2007; Senge et al., 2004), and personal commitment (Quinn, 2000, 2003). In practice, the emphasis is on large group visioning and strategic planning; innovation summits, team building, and leading conversations around topics such as how to introduce new green products and services; improving sustainability measurement and reporting, environmental supply chain management, and the like.

Like life's connection with the four seasons of the year, Phase 4 is a time of renewal and rebirth, the beginning of another cycle in the ongoing, iterative, overlapping sustainability process and the SSF. In the next section we present a recent case study, Interface, Inc. (NASDAQ:IFSIA), that builds on the original research and illustrates an approach to Phase 4 of the framework.

# SSF CASE STUDY: INTERFACE, INC.

Even when values of sustainability are alive and well in organizations, as they are today at Interface, continued dialogue focused on celebration, reflection, and planning are needed to ensure the value remains robust and consistently translated into action through strategy. Long-heralded as a sustainability exemplar, Interface recently found itself needing to take a step back and reflect on its accomplishments and to map the next leg in its sustainability journey. The authors helped them through the first of a series of Phase 4 activities. (The original write-up of the Interface Next Ascent appeared in the *AI Practitioner* in August 2008 at www.aipractitioner.com.)

## Historical Context

In 1994 Interface took the first steps on its sustainability journey, incrementally transforming itself from a self-proclaimed "plunderer of the earth" to a recognized, pioneering leader of industrial sustainability. The GlobeScan (2007) Survey of Sustainability Experts think the Interface sustainability journey has also proven to be a smart thing to do from a bottom-line perspective. The first quarter of 2008 marked the best financial performance in the company's history, demonstrating that a sustainability-based culture can offer a new and more profitable business model. While not the only factor in its success, incorporating sustainability as a core-defining value substantially improved competitiveness with respect to brand/reputation, cost/productivity, access to talent, associate engagement, and innovation.

Our research has led us to conclude that sustainability's greatest potential is realized when businesses shift from "greening" their products and processes to greening the organizational mindset. Over the ten-year period examined in the original Interface research study, we found dozens or hundreds of congruent activities, behaviors, incentives, training sessions, personal reflections, and leadership messages coalesced into a fundamental shift in mindset. With these new eyes, the company began to see new risks, new challenges, and most importantly new opportunities. Understanding of sustainability replaced skepticism, and belief produced commitment as doing shifted to being.

Phase 4 of the SSF acknowledges the importance of ongoing vigilance in order to sustain the forward momentum of the change process by intensifying focus on the vision relative to accomplishments. In many ways, Phase 4 represents the next iteration of the activities in Phase 2. Once again the goal during this phase is to get the voices in the room, ask powerful questions, and allow the organization to co-create the next step in the process.

In the following section we share the framework of a recent summit held with Interface (Amodeo & Hartzfeld, 2008). Our goal was to celebrate the accomplishments of the sustainability journey while bringing energy, focus, and passion to charting the next leg of the journey.

## Interface: Refine, Refocus, Reenergize

For much of the Interface family, 2007 was a banner year with respect to financial success and in demonstrating solutions to some of its biggest technical sustainability challenges. Yet to many there was a growing angst about the need to reinvent itself again, both due to increasing competition and to establish the trajectory to meet its Mission Zero goals. Dan Hendrix, CEO of Interface, Inc., and successor to founder Ray Anderson, determined the time was urgent to imagine and plan Interface's "next ascent" up Mt. Sustainability. He saw that this "next ascent" will demand that Interface climb higher than ever on some familiar fronts, but also require its leaders to think deeply and together in some important new areas.

InterfaceRAISE, the consulting arm of Interface, Inc., engaged us to support the development and facilitation of a strategic planning summit. The gathering brought together sixty of the Interface top executives from around the globe to reflect upon accomplishments and plan the next leg of the journey to "Mission Zero"—a promise to eliminate any negative impact the company may have on the environment by the year 2020. This mission will be accomplished by scaling the Seven Faces of Mt. Sustainability, a metaphor for a complex combination of measurable results that defines success (for more details, visit www.interfaceglobal.com).

## Design and Implementation

The phrase "Mission: The Next Ascent" was coined to define the next leg of the organization's journey. This mission was conceptualized as a process of imagining, planning, and implementing success. The summit design incorporated a 5-D Appreciative Inquiry framework (Watkins & Mohr, 2001) and World Café (Brown & Isaacs, 2005), two widely respected, strength-based organization development and change processes. In addition, the summit design integrated principles from the U Process (Senge, Scharmer, Jaworski, & Flowers, 2005). The combination of these methods created a context for positive engagement, interactivity, creativity, connection, and motivation of summit participants, while providing the leadership a composite view of stakeholder perspectives about strategic factors that will ensure the organization reaches the summit of Mt. Sustainability by the appointed date. To provide the optimum context for this dialogue, the session was held over three days in the Blue Ridge Mountains. Green-meeting standards were also followed.

## Mapping the Positive Core: Discovering the Best of What Is

***Summit: Day 1.*** Since 1994, Interface has made amazing strides toward its sustainability objectives. By engaging participants in exploring the best of what is, we began to focus on strengths and possibilities and to move the organization in the direction of bold ideas and innovations. Thus, our objective was to discover forces and factors that have propelled the successes of Interface to date. After one-on-one interviews and small-group conversations, we asked participants to share in plenary session key themes underlying strengths that had been discovered. Interface founder and sustainability pioneer Ray Anderson participated in this part of the summit, as well as the evening interactive presentation/discussion by social activist Majora Carter.

## Discover the Best of What Is and the Possibilities of What Can Be

***Summit: Day 2.*** The World Café format provided an excellent framework for building on the positive core identified during the first day and for sharing knowledge and for stimulating innovative thinking around topics identified in the pre-summit interviews: culture, technology, leadership, and image. AI-structured questions were developed to explore areas of inquiry within each of the areas identified in pre-summit interviews as foundational to a successful next leg of the climb. Summit attendees contributed their best thinking in four rounds of self-selected World Café conversations. Café hosts provided continuity between each of the group conversations.

The ideas from each Café were summarized during creative, experiential exercises to encourage participants to move beyond the analytical, objective, logical left-brain activities by activating the intuitive, creative, and subjective spheres. This assignment was incorporated at the end of the second day to keep the energy high during the ongoing and intensive dialogue process.

The creative presentations communicating the emergent thinking were performed in plenary sessions, and participants were asked to provide additional feedback through notes given to each group. Ideas framed during creative presentations provided a springboard for the dialogue on day three. The evening of the second day was intentionally unstructured to allow time for individual discussion, reflection, and relaxation.

## Dream: Imagine What Might Be

**Summit: Day 3.** Building on what was discovered during Days 1 and 2, summit participants prepared a final five-minute high-level summary of the ideas generated during the four rounds of World Café. They were asked to imagine they were presenting recommendations to the senior management team. The report included: (1) provocative propositions; (2) recommended initiatives; (3) recommended next steps; and (4) recommendations for continued dialogue.

**Next Steps.** These recommendations were reviewed during a senior leadership meeting, summarized, and communicated to the entire organization using an internal website. It is important to note that all of the senior leadership participated in the summit. The senior officers' meeting provided time for additional reflection and discussion about priorities and alignment of resources. Each member of the senior leadership team took responsibility for engaging the business units in action in one of the areas of strategic focus. The CEO, Dan Hendrix, continues to provide leadership for the overall process.

## In Sum

This summit design emerged as a powerful and effective means to create focused, yet emergent dialogue between high-level organizational members. The process reinforced our belief in the potential for positive change and dialogue-based processes to drive the radical transformation of business necessary to meet the growing social and environmental challenges of society. While it is fundamentally necessary for every business to have a sharp understanding of the negative consequences (mostly unintentional and external) of its operations (the worst we have been), strength-based conversations provide a powerful tool to directly tap into the creativity and energy of companies when they have been at their best. When we think about those moments when we were the most proud of our companies or institutions, we find amazing and seemingly impossible accomplishments. When we look deeply into the characteristics of those peak performances, we find inspiring stories of vision, alignment, planning, courage, tenacity, and purpose. When we recognize that we can tap these very same characteristics to address today's seemingly intractable environmental or social challenges, they seem much more achievable—not necessarily easy, but doable.

# SUMMARY

Our friend and colleague, Ken Murrell, once reminded us: "Now are the times that test our soul and they are telling us the world needs even more from us [the OD field].... Our work is to create other more life-affirming options for humanity and models for how we can learn to move beyond the conflicts and differences and find our greater destiny" (Murrell, 2002, p. 15). With those sentiments as guiding inspiration, we believe that the Systemic Sustainability Framework is an innovative values-based approach to creating sustainable organizations. It represents the best of what we have learned from our research and ongoing conversations with progressive organizations and their leaders. This framework provides theoretically grounded, empirical support to those interested in building sustainability-based cultures and consultants wishing to facilitate this type of deep cultural change.

Moreover, we also believe we are in our infancy in understanding how systems, especially organizational ones, become more life affirming, sustainable, and restorative. Yet, what we are sure of is that the complex web of interrelationships and human dynamics we encounter in the pursuit of sustainability must be approached with not only the best of what the OD field has offered over the past sixty years, but with latest thinking and cutting-edge practice that we find in the pages of this book.

There is no single, detailed path to sustainability; each organization's journey will be unique. For organizations not born with the values of sustainability as part of their cultural core, the introduction of this value set, which is very different from foundational values found in most organizations, is required. Therefore, we must change the conversations we have with ourselves and throughout the organization and explore new worldviews contrary to the business wisdom born in the industrial revolution.

Fortunately, a variety of OD approaches offer powerful discovery processes to engage the best thinking of stakeholders. We can find a full range of strengths-based, whole-system change methods ideally suited to guide organizations to explore answers, rather than leaders or consultants entering the system with predetermined "how to" answers. We are learning the dance of chaos and complexity theory and looking to other disciplines and fields to find ways to accelerate change and to produce more lasting transformations. We are even rediscovering ancient traditions of indigenous cultures for clues on how to live in community, harmony, and balance with the biosphere.

So like the sustainability movement and the companies we work with and study, our journey is continually unfolding. Our contribution may be small, but as we combine it with those who have come before us, our colleagues and friends we rely on today, and those great ideas just beginning to see the light of the sun, we hope to be a little closer to the human prosperity the OD field has always sought to engender.

# References

Amodeo, R.A. (2005). Becoming sustainable at Interface: A study of identity dynamics within transformational culture change. Unpublished doctoral dissertation. Lisle, IL: Benedictine University.

Amodeo, R.A. (2008). Interface Inc.'s journey to sustainability. In P. Docherty, J. Forslin, & A.B. Shani (Eds.), *Creating sustainable work systems* (2nd ed.). London: Routledge.

Amodeo, R.A., & Hartzfeld, J. (2008, August). The next ascent using appreciative inquiry to support Interface's continuing sustainability journey. *AI Practitioner*, pp. 6–13.

Brown, J.D., Isaacs, D., & the World Café Community. (2003). *The World Café: Shaping our futures through conversations that matter*. San Francisco: Berrett-Koehler.

Cox, C.K. (2005). Organic leadership: The co-creation of good business, global prosperity and a greener future. Unpublished doctoral dissertation. Lisle, IL: Benedictine University.

Cox, C.K. (2008). Organizational visions of sustainability. In P. Docherty, J. Forslin, & A.B. Shani (Eds.), *Creating sustainable work systems* (2nd ed.). London: Routledge.

Edwards, A.R. (2005). *The sustainability revolution: Portrait of a paradigm shift*. Gabriola Island, BC: New Society Publishers.

GlobeScan, Inc. (2007). *The GlobeScan survey of sustainability experts 2007*. www.GlobeScan.com.

Googins, B.K., Mirvis, P.H., & Rochlin, S.A. (2007). *Beyond good company: Next generation corporate citizenship*. New York: Palgrave Macmillan.

Holman, P., Devane, T., & Cady, S.H. (2007). *The change handbook: The definitive resource on today's best methods for engaging whole systems* (2nd ed.). San Francisco: Berrett-Koehler.

Kielstra, P. (2008). *Doing good: Business and the sustainability challenge*. London: Economist Intelligence Unit.

Ludema, J.D., & Cox, C.K. (2007). Leadership for world benefit: New horizons for research and practice. In S.K. Piderit, R.E. Fry, & D.L. Cooperrider (Eds.), *Handbook of transformative cooperation* (pp. 333–374). Stanford, CA: Stanford Business Books.

Murrell, K.L. (2002). The new century for global organization development: Responding to the challenges of the day. *OD Practitioner, 34*(1), 9–15.

Olson, E.E., & Eoyang, G.H. (2001). *Facilitating organization change: Lessons from complexity science*. San Francisco: Pfeiffer.

Piderit, S.K., Fry, R.E., & Cooperrider, D.L. (Eds.). (2007). *Handbook of transformative cooperation*. Stanford, CA: Stanford Business Books.

Quinn, R.E. (2000). *Change the world: How ordinary people can accomplish extraordinary results*. San Francisco: Jossey-Bass.

Quinn, R.E. (2003). Building the bridge as you walk on it: Taking yourself and others through the process of deep change [Conference Presentation]. Cleveland, Ohio: University of Michigan.

Schrader, D.A. (1995). Toward the environmentally sustainable corporation: The challenges of implementing change. Unpublished doctoral dissertation. Cleveland, OH: Case Western Reserve University.

Senge, P.M. (1990). *The fifth discipline: The art and practice of the learning organization*. New York: Doubleday Currency.

Senge, P.M., Lichtenstein, B.B., Kaeufer, K., Bradbury, H., & Carroll, J.S. (2007). Collaborating for systemic change. *MIT Sloan Management Review, 48*(2), 44.

Senge, P.M., Scharmer, C.O., Jaworski, J., & Flowers, B.S. (2004). *Presence: Human purpose and the field of the future*. Cambridge, MA: The Society for Organizational Learning.

Watkins, J.M., & Mohr, B.J. (2001). *Appreciative inquiry: Change at the speed of imagination*. San Francisco: Pfeiffer.

Weisbord, M.R., & Janoff, S. (1995). *Future search*. San Francisco: Berrett-Koehler.

Wheatley, M.J. (2005). *Finding our way: Leadership for an uncertain time*. San Francisco: Berrett-Koehler.

# CHAPTER TWENTY-ONE

# The Global OD Consultant

Therese F. Yaeger, Peter F. Sorensen, Perla Rizalina M. Tayko,
and Eric Gaynor-Butterfield

A special issue confronting the field of organization development (OD) today is the phenomenon of globalization, as reflected in world markets in which corporations strategize, produce, and market across national boundaries. Countries that once seemed absent on the global stage now have an exciting and growing global presence in the world of business. China, Pakistan, India, and Southeast Asia represent the new ways in which the world does business. But it is not just globalization in terms of business that is changing rapidly—the world is also changing in terms of the importance of different beliefs and ideologies, the global impact of religious beliefs, and the implications of both of these for world peace or conflict. The increased impact on and the protection of our environment are global considerations, along with the increased globalization activities and consequences of these activities, is the changing and expanding role of OD.

Global OD is a process for changing an organization to improve its effectiveness. *Global* refers to being cognizant that there are political, economical, technological, and cultural factors that may influence a change initiative or may alter the OD approach. The OD field is changing in terms of the need for new professional competencies, for new concepts and understandings required to work effectively in a world that is vastly more complex, and in the need for the skills and concepts that OD has to offer. What a wonderful time to be an OD professional, to be a member of a field dedicated to the implementation and effective change within a set of uncompromising human values at a time when we see massive changes at an ever-accelerating rate.

In this chapter we present what we feel are some of the most important issues, current activities, concepts, and approaches for the consultants who work globally. We begin with an overview of the issues in terms of the questions the global OD* professional or consultant needs to ask and then provide a brief overview of critical issues and how these issues can influence the work of the OD professional. Then, we address the competencies, skills, and abilities required of the OD professional in the increasingly complex and rapidly changing world.

It is important to remember that our field originated and developed based on the recognition of differences in culture and ideology as experienced by Kurt Lewin—differences he experienced between Nazi Germany and the United States, differences that led to the fundamental core values of our field.

National cultural values and OD continue to represent fundamental questions for the OD professional:

- What are the core values that define the field of OD?

- To what extent am I as an OD professional committed to these values?

- To what extent are national cultural values compatible with the core values of OD?

- What is my role as an OD professional in working within cultures with national cultural values opposed to the values of OD?

The questions above represent a significant source of debate within the profession. The following list of questions serves as a guide to the practice of global OD:

- How is OD perceived in the host nation? How will I be perceived, and what is expected of me? Are the clients expecting a facilitator, or an expert? Am I entering a potentially hostile environment? Does the nation have a positive history of OD?

- How am I to be perceived by the client as an OD consultant? What are the perceptions of my age, gender, status, and credentials?

- What are the client organization's values as reflected in a particular country's culture? Are they compatible with my values as an OD practitioner?

- Is the culture stable, or is it in transition? Cultures experiencing significant change are frequently very difficult situations. It is particularly important that the OD practitioner be sensitive to the dynamic nature of the environment.

*In this chapter, we use global OD and international OD interchangeably.

- What is the level of sophistication for business and management in general, and specifically for OD consulting?

- What is the level of economic development? This is an area of knowledge that is essential for determining the appropriate OD intervention.

- What is the nature of the political system? Lack of understanding of a political system is often the cause of inappropriate OD interventions.

- What is the appropriate OD process? What needs to be modified? This is at the heart of what OD professionals do.

- What interventions are appropriate? What needs to be modified?

# CRITICAL ISSUES AND THEIR INFLUENCE ON GLOBAL OD

Many would be surprised at the success rate of OD both in the United States and internationally. The best-documented work on OD success is the work of Robert Golembiewski (Golembiewski & Luo, 1994). He presents more material on this topic in Chapter Thirty-Six. Golembiewski reports success rates for OD at approximately 90 percent, with relatively comparable success rates for OD in developing countries and in Southeast Asia. Golembiewski's work is supported by other studies reporting high rates of success for OD (see, for example, a summary of other studies in Yaeger, Sorensen, & Bengtsson, 2005, or for other information see Yaeger, Head, & Sorensen, 2006). But what are the issues and questions that we need to ask in terms of successful international OD?

## Culture

The role of national cultural values and OD has received a fair amount of attention. Probably the most influential work, and the work which is most helpful to OD professionals in understanding how cultural values impact their work, is that of Geert Hofstede (1997, 2001) and his concepts regarding societal orientation in terms of power, uncertainty, masculinity, and individualism.

- *Power distance* is the extent to which a society accepts the fact that power in institutions and organizations is distributed unequally.

- *Uncertainty avoidance* is the extent to which a society feels threatened by uncertain and ambiguous situations.

- *Individualism* is a loosely knit social framework in which people are supposed to take care of themselves and their immediate families only, while *collectivism* is characterized by a tight social framework in which people distinguish between in-groups (relatives, clan, organizations) to look after them, and in exchange for that they feel they owe absolute loyalty.

- *Masculinity* is the extent to which the society is assertive and aggressive rather than contemplative (indicative of a feminine culture).

Culture has important implications for the global OD consultant in that national cultural values play a major role in terms of differences in resistance to change, the nature of leadership roles, organizational structure, and the application of OD techniques such as team building, survey feedback, job redesign, and large group methods.

## Economic Development

Although Golembiewski reports high levels of success in developing countries, there are, nevertheless, a number of questions that are important for the OD professional. A country's level of economic development places constraints on the application of OD in terms of the existence of technology and information systems, employee and management skill levels, project planning and organizing, and motivational and reward systems, among others (Cummings & Worley, 2009).

These include:

- What is the economy's base: agricultural, manufacturing, or diversified?
- What is the skill level of the labor force?
- What are the labor costs (wages, benefits, social programs)?
- What is the general quality of life? Quality of work life?
- What is the native managerial skill level?
- Is technology cost-effective?
- What problems create significant costs for the employer?

## Legal Issues

Probably one of the areas that has not received sufficient attention but which is critical for the practice of global OD is issues of legality. Some of the questions we feel the OD professional needs to ask include:

- What are the national laws that the client must follow?
- Which laws are enforced by the government and which are not?
- Should I suggest the client comply with the laws, even when such compliance is not needed?
- What are the national laws the consultant must obey?
- What unique elements are in the nation's legal system, particularly with regard to commercial codes?
- Is the consultant prepared to deal with ethical dilemmas that might occur?

On a more personal level, questions that the OD professional may want to ask include:

- What are the visa requirements for the business traveler?
- Is it possible to enter the country on a regular visitor's visa, or is a special business visa required?
- Are there any restrictions on traveling between locations within the client's country?
- Will my copyrights be valid and actively protected?
- Will I encounter any problems in being compensated for my services?
- Will I have access to the information I require to make good decisions?

Answers to these questions can help the OD professional when undertaking work in other countries.

# THE ROLE OF CULTURE IN GLOBAL OD

Let us return to the role of culture in global OD. The topic of culture is huge and exists at multiple levels, for example, national cultures, corporate cultures, etc. This chapter focuses on the role of national culture values. Culture serves to shape the other elements of legal and economic development. Does culture make a difference in terms of how we practice OD globally? There are three answers: yes, no, and maybe. There has been a considerable amount of work on matching national cultural values to the core values of OD. The basic question is not "Can OD be successful in different countries with different values?" That has been answered by the work of Golembiewski cited earlier. The yes it works, no it does not, and the maybe answers are more complex. The maybe answer deals with changing national cultural values and the question: "Do we have OD approaches that transcend national cultural values?"

## Matching OD Practices with Cultural Values

The matching approach to global OD is based on work by Jaeger (1986), who compared the national cultural values established by Hofstede, defined as low power, collectivism, feminine, and low on uncertainty avoidance, with the core humanistic values of OD, such as trust, respect, and collaboration (Tannenbaum & Davis, 1969). How compatible national cultural values are with the values of OD has important implications.

Those countries with values most compatible with OD were identified as Denmark, Sweden, and Norway. Countries with values moderately different from those of OD included Australia, France, Germany, Great Britain, India, Singapore, South Africa, Turkey, and the United States. Countries that differ the most were identified as Argentina, Belgium, Greece, Hong Kong, Italy, Japan, Mexico, Pakistan, Taiwan, and Thailand.

Matching values has important implications for the global OD professional. For example, the Scandinavian countries are characterized by values that are not only compatible with, but reinforce, the values of OD. These countries have a long history of OD-related activities, including early work on industrial democracy in Norway, the Saab-Scania/Volvo work on work redesign, self-managed work teams in Sweden, and projects at the Department of Education and Welfare. In these countries, resistance to change would be expected to be low, so a full range of OD interventions would be appropriate, ranging from job redesign to sociotechnical change and large-group interventions.

Countries with values moderately consistent with OD also provide a favorable environment for the global OD professional. Many have a rich history of contributions to the field. Here a wide range of OD interventions is appropriate. These nations' cultural values suggest, however, that interventions would frequently be more conservative than in the Scandinavian countries. Team building needs to be more explicitly task-focused, and autonomous work groups would require more attention to development and implementation. Management by objectives would not have the same degree of employee involvement. Transition and change to a more organic organization would require greater time, effort, and preparation.

In countries with values least consistent with the values of OD, greater attention needs to be given to the choice of interventions, the method of implementation, and the role of the global OD professional. In these countries the acceptance of the OD professional is based on a demonstration of "expert" knowledge. In these countries the OD professional will be challenged and may need to find innovative and creative ways of resolving value dilemmas. The implementation of any change may very well be more directive and less inclusive and participatory. Appropriate interventions may have to be more task-oriented and structured. Appropriate interventions include job enrichment and job redesign, management by objectives, survey feedback, and use of The Managerial Grid. The emphasis in each of these would have to concentrate on structure, task, and quantitative data (for example, survey feedback).

Is OD universal or situation-specific? There are good arguments on both sides. The matching approach suggests that OD is universal but needs to be tailored to national cultural values. But it is not quite that simple. First, are we seeing the emergence of a truly universal approach to the practice of OD, and second, what about changes in national cultural values? As demonstrated in the above discussion, national cultural values represent an important consideration for OD consultants working in the global environment.

# THE POWER OF AN INCLUSIVE CULTURE

One of the fundamental elements for sustainable change and transformation that must be addressed is organizational culture: how people interact with each other, the dominant styles that are reinforced in a million informal ways each day, and the mindsets and behaviors that drive people. Culture gives leadership to an organization and defines how it functions. No matter how much a new program or procedure is reinforced, it won't succeed if it is at odds with the organization's culture. Culture trumps policy and strategy every time.

Culture is transferred from generation to generation. It is comprised of the oral histories that are shared about what and who is valued. People learn much more about an organization's culture by walking through the halls than through formal policies or on-boarding programs. It is the general "vibe" one gets after spending time in an organization.

An inclusive culture is a critical ingredient for organizational breakthroughs that foster higher levels of performance. Our definition of inclusion is

> A sense of belonging: feeling respected, valued, and seen for who we are as individuals; and a level of supportive energy and commitment from leaders, colleagues, and others so that we—individually and collectively—can do our best work.

An inclusive culture is one that enables ideas, perspectives, and experiences to be fully leveraged, creating a wide bandwidth for problem solving and innovation (Miller & Katz, 2002). In the past, people were rewarded for getting business results by any means; in contrast, an inclusive organization recognizes that results are obtained through people. There is an acknowledgment that the more people are engaged, the more they will contribute not only their primary energy, but their discretionary energy and ideas. In the past, it was acceptable to utilize and "go to" the top 20 to 25 percent of people, while in an inclusive organization there is a recognition that talent and ideas reside at all levels and within all people. The challenge is how to tap into the wisdom that resides throughout the organization. By overutilizing some and underutilizing others, organizations fail to tap into all existing talent, wasting some people's talent and overburdening others. The result is that some people never receive opportunities to grow and develop, while others burn out or leave.

What most prevents people from being able to do their best work, both individually and collectively, is a sense of not being included in the flow of the organization. They feel their ideas and perspectives do not matter and are not particularly wanted. They experience pressure to not express differing points of view, to simply do what one is told, to leave the thinking and decision making to those at the top. At a time when organizations need everyone's ideas to address complex problems, when there are many unknowns, that mindset and culture are at odds with what is needed for success.

Several important hallmarks distinguish an inclusive culture as a place where people can bring their thinking and contribute their best work:

- *People are respected.* Regardless of job title, seniority, identity, or other characteristics, everyone in the organization is treated with dignity and honor. There is respect for people's time, talents, needs, and life outside the organization.

- *People are valued.* All people are important members of the organization whose contributions are essential for overall success.

- *People are seen.* There is no need to hide certain elements of one's identity in order to fit in or climb the ladder. An inclusive culture acknowledges and values who people are and sees their background and experiences as providing organizational capability.

- *People speak up.* People feel safe to share their ideas. Contributing ideas and perspectives is expected—it is seen as essential for leveraging the talents of all members of the organization.

- *People offer peer-to-peer leadership.* While a managerial hierarchy may still be in place, it is understood that leaders and expertise exist at every level in the organization—titled or not—and that each member has influence and knowledge to bring to her or his work teams and day-to-day interactions.

- *People are willing to be BIG, step out, and be bold.* Individuals are no longer hiding out and waiting for others to initiate. They take leadership where and how they can (Katz & Miller, 2008).

# BREAKING THROUGH: INCLUSION AS THE *HOW* FOR HIGHER PERFORMANCE

A result of an inclusive culture is that breakthroughs in operations and individual and team performance occur daily. Inclusion is not an end-point in itself; it is a means to an end. It is *how* organizations can continually raise the bar on performance and perpetuate an environment that is as limitless and resourceful as the members themselves. It establishes new mindsets and expectations for how people treat each other, operate within the enterprise, and obtain results. A key outcome of inclusive mindsets, behaviors, and practices is the creation of a more connected workforce—specifically, the creation of a Connected Organization.

## The Connected Organization

The Connected Organization is one in which people focus on the work to be done and the partnerships necessary to achieve collective goals. Rather than focusing primarily on reporting relationships as the cornerstone of who and

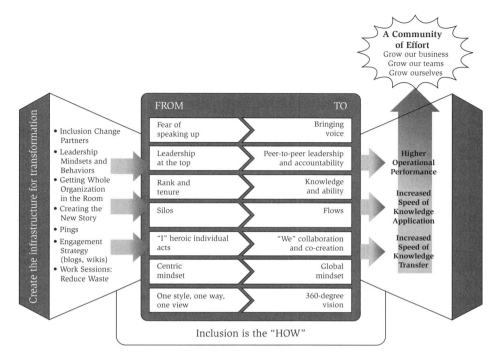

**Figure 22.1.** KJCG Methodology for Transformation

# GETTING THERE: A METHODOLOGY
# FOR CULTURE TRANSFORMATION

So how can leaders and OD practitioners go about facilitating inclusion as a means for organizational breakthroughs and creating the Connected Organization? In our work, we have leveraged the following methods and strategies to create organizational transformation (as illustrated in the Methodology for Transformation diagram in Figure 22.1):

- Shift mindsets about how to achieve culture transformation.
  - *from* training programs          *to* interventions
  - *from* senior leaders acting alone    *to* engaging everyone
  - *from* edicts and speeches        *to* collective input of all people
  - *from* incremental change        *to* bold leaps
- *Connect to the business imperative.* Culture change cannot be disconnected from the operations of the organization. It cannot be positioned as something

"nice to do," but instead must be seen as essential for organizational success. Its impact on the bottom line must be explicit. The desired culture must be seen as the *HOW* for achieving operational results.

- *Create the organizational infrastructure for transformation.* Few significant change efforts ever occurred through the current organizational chart. Similarly, with an inclusion transformation, the organization needs to create a temporary, enabling infrastructure necessary to lead and implement the change effort. This includes the appropriate level of leadership and resources to shepherd and infuse the effort.

- *Identify the current state through a process of discovery.* Critical to the success of the effort is to have a solid diagnosis of the current state of the culture and to establish appropriate metrics. The implementation of a discovery process that includes interviews (face-to-face as well as via telephone where needed) and the use of a quantitative survey provide the foundation for the effort and for the establishment of a *FROM ⟶ TO* culture vision. The discovery process itself is an intervention that begins to engage people in the effort and can identify early adopters. The discovery data must be shared with the senior leadership team as a way to create buy-in and identify the aspirational culture that the organization needs to move "TO." This is critical for mapping out strategy and establishing a baseline against which to measure.

- *Create the new story.* Culture is passed down as legacy—in the stories, mythologies, and histories that carry from generation to generation. The change effort has to generate new stories, with new messages that become a part of the new culture. The organization also needs to be creative in how it proliferates new stories. Critical to success is highlighting how inclusion is impacting results and making visible what is often invisible. It is essential to highlight both small and big successes in moving to the "TO" state. Communication channels include wikis and blogs that enable co-creation of various elements of the message by everyone.

- *Utilize the FROM ⟶ TO culture vision to provide a gap analysis.* All interventions need to be targeted to close the gap between the *FROM ⟶ TO* (for example, *from* a relationship culture *to* a performance culture). A list of six to ten *FROM ⟶ TO* items needs to be developed with the input of senior leaders and then enhanced by the larger organization as the intervention rolls out. This creates the first clear understanding of the work at hand—how far the organization needs to travel along the change path to achieve its goals. Some examples of a *FROM ⟶ TO* culture vision follow:

| From | To |
|---|---|
| Too little acceptance of differences | Global mindset and skill set to effectively engage differences |
| Command-and-control culture that causes people to wait for direction | Empower people to make decisions, take action, and be accountable |
| Working and thinking in silos | Cross-divisional, cross-functional, cross-regional high-performing teams |
| Individuals competing "against" colleagues | Individuals and teams competing together |
| Information is protected and only shared with certain people and groups | Information is openly shared and team members are more informed |

- *Align senior leaders.* Although the effort will need to engage people at all levels, getting senior leaders on board and on the same page is an essential early step. Leaders themselves cannot make change happen, but their buy-in, early adoption of the needed mindsets and behaviors, and support for the effort as it moves forward are critical. Leaders must also understand that a more inclusive culture and Connected Organization are critical to achieving business results and how they must grow themselves as leaders.

- *Identify the mindsets and behaviors necessary for the new culture.* Mindsets are one of the key underpinnings to the transformation process. Often, interventions have focused only on behaviors, thereby limiting success. Explicitly identifying the new mindsets is critical for creating a breakthrough, since moving to the "TO" state will not happen without the conscious shift of mindsets. In many organizations, mindsets have coalesced over the years without anyone paying attention to them. By identifying the cognitive cornerstones of the organization and the behaviors that flow from them, the organization can begin to move forward.

- *Find the self-interest for change.* Everyone has something to gain in the new culture, even those who thrived in the old one and may feel threatened by change, because everyone is valued and respected in the new culture. Everyone benefits from increased performance and organizational success. Identifying and helping people to buy into the "what's in it for me" component of a more inclusive culture is a crucial step.

- *Educate and disseminate the change through peer-to-peer leadership and accountability.* To create critical mass for change, 10 to 15 percent of the organization needs to be engaged, creating advocates for change who can exert peer-to-peer leadership and enroll their colleagues in the effort. Of that 10 to 15 percent, a small group must be educated in an intense, multi-part, multi-day education series to enable them to develop the new mindsets and learn and practice in real time the behaviors needed for transformation. The role of these people is to reach out to colleagues with whom they work to begin bringing inclusion into the day-to-day operations and interactions of the organization. These members then similarly engage their colleagues, using peer-to-peer leadership as a way to create waves of change and to hold each other accountable for living the new mindsets and behaviors. They are not expected to become trainers. Rather, they bring new mindsets and behaviors into day-to-day operations so that inclusion becomes the *HOW* for doing business. At the same time, education sessions need to be held to bring the entire organization together to provide information about why the change is needed (business imperative) and where the organization needs to go (culture vision and *FROM ⟶ TO*), to hear their thinking about what needs to change in their areas of responsibility, and to create buy-in to the effort and shared accountability.

- *Conduct ping surveys.* These are brief (typically five to eight questions) electronic surveys that allow quick feedback from as many people as possible to not only monitor progress, but to help shape strategies going forward. They also demonstrate inclusion by soliciting the voices and opinions of people throughout the organization on substantial issues. Pings are conducted weekly or monthly and provide valuable real-time data to adjust and shift the change strategy more rapidly.*

- *Model and promote conscious inclusion by living the Twelve Inclusive Behaviors listed below.* These should be promoted as the "ground rules for interactions" that everyone in the organization is expected to model:
    1. Greet people authentically—say hello.
    2. Create a sense of safety for yourself and your team members.
    3. Work for the common good and shared success.
    4. Listen as an ally—listen, listen, listen, and engage.
    5. Lean into discomfort—be willing to challenge yourself and others.
    6. Put your stake in the ground and be willing, eager, and able to move it.
    7. Link to others' ideas, thoughts, and feelings.
    8. Create 360-degree vision: Ask others to share their thoughts and experiences and accept their frame of reference as true for them.

---

*Thank you to John Shoolery of Datacycles (www.datacycles.com) for his groundbreaking work on using pings as a change facilitation tool.

9. Address misunderstandings and resolve disagreements.
10. Speak up when people are being excluded.
11. Ask who else needs to be in the room to understand the whole situation.
12. Build trust: Do what you say you will do and honor confidentiality.

# SUMMARY

The kind of organizational transformation we have identified takes committed leaders who understand the goals of the effort and, most importantly, the business payoff for change. It requires people at all levels of the organization who are willing to change and grow themselves into new kinds of leaders. It also takes committed followership.

One of the central tenets of inclusion is the competitive advantage of all people in the organization being able to contribute their best to create a whole much greater than the sum of the parts. It will take peer-to-peer leadership and accountability to create a truly collaborative, co-owned culture in which all people are respected, seen, and heard. The crucial sense of belonging has to come from within the organization, not from above.

Creating a sense of belonging and a culture of inclusion starts with trust, which is the necessary ingredient for achieving breakthroughs like knowledge transfer, adopting new mindsets, and building a *connected organization*. With these elements in place and inclusion as a way of life, organizations can start to achieve the breakthroughs necessary for success in an ever-changing workplace and marketplace.

## References

Katz, J.H., & Miller, F.A. (2008). *Be BIG: Step up, step out, be bold*. San Francisco: Berrett-Koehler.

Miller, F.A., & Katz, J.H. (2002). *The inclusion breakthrough: Unleashing the real power of diversity*. San Francisco: Berrett-Koehler.

# CHAPTER TWENTY-THREE

# Organization Design

Amy Kates

Organization design is a field that is of increasing interest to many organization development (OD) professionals. Businesses are developing ever-more-complex strategies that often require multi-dimensional global organizations to execute. In addition, constant technological improvements have created higher expectations for organizations to process information and make decisions faster.

As a result, business managers are looking for assistance in making smart decisions about the shape of their organizations. They expect that their HR generalists and specialists will be knowledgeable about organization design frameworks, methods, and tools. Business clients also expect that their HR partners will have the time and capability to help them sort through these complicated and high-value decisions.

This chapter will define organization design and its relationship to OD work. It will present key organization design concepts and principles to introduce the OD practitioner to the language of organization design and provide an essential tool—design criteria—for linking strategy to organizational capabilities. Finally, the chapter will highlight some of the competencies of organization design so that the reader can begin to assess his or her own interest in and aptitude for the field.

# THE RELATIONSHIP OF ORGANIZATION DESIGN TO ORGANIZATION DEVELOPMENT

The first question to address is, "What is organization design?" Organization design is what John Boudreau calls a "decision science" (Boudreau & Ramstad, 2007, p. 15). In many fields there is a decision science that focuses on setting frameworks and making sound choices among competing alternatives. Those fields often have a complementary "practice area" that is focused on implementing the appropriate tools and interventions to successfully execute on the selected framework. For example, *marketing* is a decision science: where and how we compete, how we differentiate our products and services. *Sales* is the complementary practice area, which identifies how we use our skills and tools to execute on our marketing plans. Another example can be found in the distinction between *finance*, which is the decision science for evaluating and making investment decisions, and *accounting*, the practice of ensuring that those decisions are based on accurate data.

*Organization design* is a decision science for selecting among competing alternatives in order to match the optimal organizational model to the strategy. Making good design choices is not enough, of course, to successfully carry out a strategy. *Organization development* can be thought of as the discipline (or "practice area") of implementing these design choices. Organization design constitutes the link between business strategy and OD, as illustrated in Figure 23.1.

Without organization design, there is no framework within which to determine what OD activities will have the most impact and when they should be carried out. Therefore, even if the OD practitioner is not involved directly in organization design decisions, adding this knowledge to his or her toolkit is useful. Understanding organization design concepts and options and being able to analyze existing designs and anticipate the predictable consequences of various choices will aid practitioners in making better decisions regarding what OD interventions will be most effective and how best to carry them out.

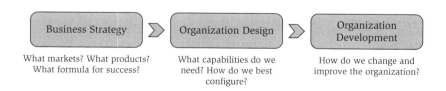

**Figure 23.1.**  From Strategy to Organization

Many experienced OD practitioners are seeking to learn about organization design because it moves them up the value chain in their discussions with their business clients. Taking part in the discussion places them closer to strategic decisions and in a position to more fully influence OD work.

One can also define organization design by its relationship to talent. An analogy is that of city planning to architecture. Architecture is about individual buildings and their relationship to one another. City planning is about urban systems; it not only deals with the built environment, but with political, social, economic, and transportation networks as well. In the same way, organization design is about complex, interconnected systems that create the conditions in which individuals and teams—that is, "talent"—can succeed.

Finally, we should focus on the word "design." Organization design is a creative, integrative activity based on an understanding of patterns of organizational behavior. Good organization design embodies the same values of good design found in more common objects: balance, proportion, and unity. The key difference between organization and industrial design is that the organization being designed is invisible, yet everyone has to understand its intentions and their place in this unseen web of work relationships.

In most companies, organization design is considered an adjunct of OD work and is housed in the HR department. However, many people come to the field from a strategy, process, or business background. Given the close relationship of organization design to strategy and the discipline's focus on systems, some companies are examining the option of housing their organization designers in a strategy execution group along with specialists in project management, business process reengineering, systems requirements management, and change management. While there is debate about where organization design should reside within a firm (and whether it is even an HR activity), today it remains most often an HR offering and a part of the OD specialist's role.

## KEY CONCEPTS IN ORGANIZATION DESIGN

The key elements to consider in organization design are illustrated in the Star Model, which was developed by Jay Galbraith in the 1970s and is shown in Figure 23.2. There are many versions of the Star Model in use, as well as similar models, such as McKinsey's "Seven S." We use the Star Model here because it has proven over the years to be both comprehensive enough for experienced practitioners to apply and clear enough for line managers to understand and use.

The Star Model provides the basic elements that must be considered in any organization design effort: strategy, structure, process, metrics, and people. Notice that, although culture is an essential part of an organization, it is not

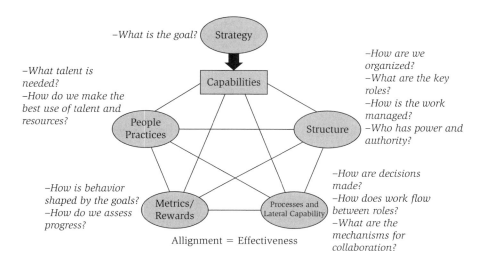

*–What is the goal?* Strategy

*–How are we organized?*
*–What are the key roles?*
*–How is the work managed?*
*–Who has power and authority?*

*–What talent is needed?*
*–How do we make the best use of talent and resources?*

Capabilities

People Practices

Structure

*–How is behavior shaped by the goals?*
*–How do we assess progress?*

Metrics/ Rewards

Processes and Lateral Capability

*–How are decisions made?*
*–How does work flow between roles?*
*–What are the mechanisms for collaboration?*

Allignment = Effectiveness

**Figure 23.2.** The Star Model

Adapted from Galbraith, 2002, p. 15

an explicit part of the model, as the leader cannot design the culture directly. An organization's culture consists of the common values, mindsets, and norms of behavior that have emerged over time and that are shared by most employees. It is a product of the cumulative design decisions that have been made in the past and of the leadership and management behaviors that result from those decisions. Only those a leader has direct influence over are included in the model.

In addition to the "what" of organization design summarized by the Star Model, there is also a "how to" that is emerging as a core design methodology in the field. A decision that is made early in a process will constrain the choices that can be made later, foreclose avenues of exploration, and eliminate alternatives. Making good decisions at early, critical junctures requires both a sound theoretical framework and a process that makes use of all the data and experience available to the decision-makers. Figure 23.3 summarizes the core organization design process.

The process of organization design starts with *design criteria* to determine differentiating capabilities upon which the strategy is built. The next step is an *assessment* to identify gaps between the current state and the future envisioned by the strategy. The assessment is followed by *option generation and evaluation* to test scenarios and make tradeoffs. The final stage of the process is the selection among various identified design alternatives and implementation.

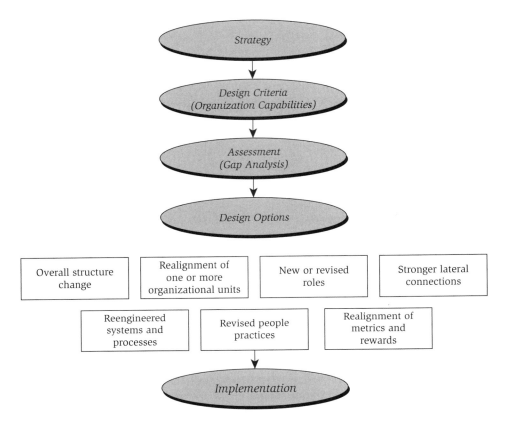

**Figure 23.3.** The Organization Design Process

# ORGANIZATION DESIGN PRINCIPLES

All good organization design follows a set of core principles. Those that provide the broadest guidance are summarized below:

- *Alignment.* The idea of alignment is fundamental. Each component of the organization should work to support the strategy. The more that the structure, processes, rewards, and people practices reinforce the desired actions and behaviors, the better positioned the organization is to achieve its goals.

- *Reconfigurability.* Just as important as initial alignment is the ability to realign as circumstances change. An organization's internal rate of change has to match the rate of change in its external environment. But the larger the organization, the harder it is to change. Leaders' first instinct is often to change structure, as that is the most visible and tangible action. However, structural changes are frequently disruptive, distracting, and excessive. Rather, an organization's ability to quickly assemble the right people around risks or opportunities is its most powerful means for changing direction. Through robust project teams, cross-organization processes, and lateral collaboration, management decisions and actions can be rerouted to shift priorities and redirect organizational energy. The underlying structures can stay the same.

- *Requisite complexity.* An organization should be as complex as its business requires (Ashby, 1952). Business leaders are pulled between responding to the increased demands of the market and the speed of competition while keeping their organizations manageable. The organization designer has to challenge the desire of managers to oversimplify. Designers must ask business leaders some hard questions:
    - Have we simplified too much in a desire to make the leadership task easier?
    - Have we failed to build an organization that can achieve all aspects of our strategy?
  Conversely, some questions may arise about whether an organization is too complex:
    - Have we exceeded human limitations?
    - Have we created too many interactions and interfaces for our people to manage?
    - Can we achieve the same outcomes more simply, and only introduce complexity when absolutely necessary?
- Organizations can be designed so that managers have simple roles in a complex structure, or, alternatively, so that managers work in a simple structure but end up with highly complex jobs. Complexity cannot be avoided—it is a fact of the modern business environment—but it can be intelligently designed and managed.
- *Complementary sets of choices.* There exist numerous choices among structures, processes, rewards, and people practices. However, once a strategic path is set, the number of suitable choices for each design element will be reduced. The organization designer learns what sets of complementary choices work best together and assists the organization's leaders in building, aligning, and optimizing these alternatives.
- *Coherence, not uniformity.* A large, complex organization—particularly one that spans geographic boundaries—rarely has a simple or single structure. Leaders can make their organizations responsive to local conditions and at the same time remain coherent by differentiating where appropriate and then using integrative mechanisms to link the organization into one cohesive system. Beware of a desire by managers to create uniform structures when they are not called for simply because they make the management task easier.

- *Clear interfaces.* To manage complexity, spend time designing and clarifying interfaces. When interfaces between units are numerous and unclear, the amount of communication that takes place can become overwhelming, and coordination suffers. Help the people who will be working at the interfaces understand the intentions and implications of the design. Role clarity happens not at the core of the work but at the interface between one role and another.

- *Organize, rather than reorganize.* Successful companies are continually evaluating and adjusting their organizations. Leaders of these firms form and communicate a picture of the envisioned future state and move toward it continuously. Rather than periodic reorganization events that lurch the organization forward, leaving employees with whiplash, aim for 80 percent initial alignment, with a plan for how to continue organizing toward the ideal.

# HOW TO USE ORGANIZATION DESIGN TO BUILD STRATEGIC CAPABILITIES

As was noted above, the organization design process is made up of a series of choices and decisions. In any decision-making process, clear criteria serve the purpose of allowing alternatives to be evaluated against agreed-upon standards. The criteria that should be used to make organization design decisions are the organizational capabilities that will differentiate the organization and help it execute its strategy. Therefore, the terms *organizational capabilities* and *design criteria* can be used interchangeably.

Organizations compete on the basis of different strategies and different capabilities. For example, a pharmaceutical company developing novel prescription drugs requires a strong research and development capability and an ability to build relationships with physicians. On the other hand, a pharmaceutical company that specializes in selling over-the-counter medicines needs efficient manufacturing processes and a strong consumer marketing capability.

In general, strategic organizational capabilities are

- Unique, integrated combinations of skills, processes, and human abilities; these are not simple programs or technologies that can be copied from other companies.

- Created by and housed within an organization; they are not bought or conferred by regulation or location or monopoly position. Rather they are developed, refined, and protected internally.

- Factors that differentiate the organization and provide competitive advantage. This is important, as there are many areas in which a company needs to match its competitors, but just a few for which it truly needs to be significantly better.

Different strategies require different capabilities, and therefore different organization designs. The process of identifying the most important organizational capabilities is the first step in drawing connections between the firm's strategy and the decisions about the form of its organization. Once the capabilities have been identified, then a set of organizational implications can be generated to form the basis for a discussion of alternatives. Each design decision can be tested against the design criteria to determine whether it will be helpful in creating the desired strategic capabilities. Metrics can then be set as a way to gauge progress.

Design criteria serve another purpose, however: they focus the organization on developing strengths, not just on correcting flaws or gaps. Organizational capabilities are fundamentally positive attributes of the organization. They embody what the organization can and must do better than its competitors. When the design criteria have been clearly articulated, employees at every level can understand why the organization will be configured in a certain way, why various investments will be made, and why resources are allocated as they are. To continue with the pharmaceutical example, one would expect to see a large and well-resourced consumer marketing group in the over-the-counter company and a large and well-resourced direct sales group in the prescription-based company that sells primarily through physician influence. These are the organizational manifestations of the capabilities that are required by the two companies' very different strategies.

The identification of organizational capabilities is carried out by the leader or leadership team that has ultimate responsibility for the design decisions. This is not an activity that can be delegated, as it requires the broad strategic perspective that is available only at the leadership level. These organizational capabilities will become the criteria against which all subsequent design decisions are judged, so they must be agreed on at the highest level of the organization being designed.

Once the design criteria are in place, there is a question that can be asked at each step in the design process: Which option will better help us preserve or build the organizational capabilities we have said are critical to our success? We suggest that the leaders identify no more than five organizational capabilities to serve as design criteria. It is the act of generating possible capabilities and then narrowing them down into those that can truly differentiate the company that creates healthy discussion and debate about what direction is truly most important to the organization. The *Developing Design Criteria* tool located on this book's website provides detailed guidance on identifying, selecting, and using organization capabilities in the design process.

# What Makes a Good Organization Designer?

As OD practitioners seek to add organization design to their service portfolios, it is worth reflecting on what defines a skilled organization designer. The good news is that the field has matured and coalesced in the past ten years. Designers can draw upon a robust set of models, tools, guides, and methodologies that are readily available (see the list of suggested resources at the end of this chapter). But, as in any field, knowledge is not enough. Organization design requires a particular set of competencies and skills.

**Diagnostic and Analytic Skills.** The organization designer must have the ability to ask the right questions and make sense of the answers. Like a physician who sorts through symptoms that may have many causes and determines the correct underlying disease, the organization designer has to be able to determine the root causes of performance issues in the system. The designer then analyzes what changes will have the most impact with the greatest likelihood of success in this particular context.

**Deep Curiosity About Organizations as Systems.** Effective organization designers are fascinated by the complexity of business and organizational life. They like to solve multi-faceted problems and do not stop at easy answers or one-dimensional solutions. It is important to be able see an organization as more than a collection of individuals and to be able to discern the interconnected political, social, and information networks that have formed. Organization designers tend to be wide-ranging in their personal interests, read on a broad range of topics, and be inquisitive about how things work below the surface.

**Design Mindset.** Designers—whether of organizations, buildings, information technology systems, or functional objects—share a common ability to conceive of and articulate how their designs will work. They take problems and frame them so that the right questions are asked, a wide range of options is generated, and the best solutions are chosen. They know that the process is rarely linear, but rather iterative and enhanced by contributions from different perspectives. Designers are often ambidextrous thinkers, comfortable with solving for both the possible and the practical.

**Pattern Recognition.** Organization design is not for the neophyte. One must have enough hands-on, personal experience working with a variety of organizations to build the expertise to recognize and sort patterns. While one can become familiar with frameworks from training programs and reading, pattern recognition cannot come from a book. It grows from experience and structured reflection that turns data into wisdom. Organization design is typically a field

Mergers and acquisitions are shrouded in secrecy. Executives putting a deal together have to keep a very tight lid on their intentions, for both competitive and legal reasons. This is in stark contrast to the research evidence, which shows how full and early communication enhances employee understanding of and support for organizational changes (Smith, 1998). Kotter (1995) cites the value of coalition building in successful organizational change management. However, managers in the midst of a merger or acquisition adopt very political behaviors in hopes of exercising control over an uncertain situation and protecting their positions, perks, projects, and people (Marks & Mirvis, 1985). And culture clash produces "us versus them" dynamics that pull partners apart rather than bring them together and, as a result, interferes with effective teamwork, planning, and decision making (Mirvis & Marks, 1986).

# THE MERGER SYNDROME

Many factors account for the dismal M&A track record: buying the wrong company, paying the wrong price, making the deal at the wrong time, and so on. However, research findings repeatedly reveal that the factor that matters most in eventual merger or acquisition success is the *process through which the partner companies are integrated* (Schweiger & Goulet, 2000).

Through an action research program that has spanned thirty years, we have identified the "merger syndrome" as a primary cause of the disappointing outcomes of otherwise well-conceived mergers and acquisitions (Marks & Mirvis, 1998). The syndrome is triggered by the often unavoidably unsettled conditions in the earliest days and months following the announcement of a deal and encompasses stress reactions and development of crisis management in the companies involved.

## Personal Signs of the Merger Syndrome

The first symptom of the merger syndrome is heightened self-interest—people become preoccupied with what the combination means for themselves, their incomes, and their careers. They develop a story line about the implications, but often it is a mix of fact and fantasy. No one has real answers and, if there are any, the answers are apt to change. Not only do people become fixated on the combination, but they tend to focus on the costs and ignore the gains. Soon after a combination announcement, the rumor mill starts and people trade on dire scenarios.

Combination stress takes its toll in people's psychological and physiological well-being. Reports of tension and conflict increase at the workplace and at home—spouses and children worry about their fates and grow anxious, too. Rates of illness and absenteeism rise in workforces going through combinations. Interviews with executives in the early stages of a combination are colored with reports of headaches, cold and flu symptoms, sleeplessness, and increased alcohol and drug usage.

## Organizational Signs of the Merger Syndrome

To cope with the many tasks of combining, teams of executives in both the lead and target companies typically lurch into a crisis management mode. The experience is stressful yet exhilarating, and many liken themselves to generals in a war room. Decision making in these top groups can be crisp and decisive. However, top management is generally insulated during this period and often prepares self-defeating gambits. They cut themselves off from relevant information and isolate themselves from dissent. All of this is symptomatic of what psychologist Irving Janis termed "groupthink"—the result of accepting untested assumptions and striving for consensus without reality-testing the possible consequences.

While the executive teams are in their respective war rooms, people in one or both organizations are adrift. Decision-making powers become centralized and reporting relationships clogged with tension and doubt. Priorities are unsettled and no one wants to make a false move. Meanwhile, downward communications tend to be formal and unsatisfactory. Official assurances that any changes will be handled smoothly and fairly ring hollow to a worried workforce.

## Cultural Signs of the Merger Syndrome

All of this is exacerbated by the clash of cultures. By their very nature, combinations produce an "us versus them" relationship, and there is a natural tendency for people to exaggerate the differences as opposed to similarities between the two companies. What is noted first are differences in the ways the companies do business—perhaps their relative emphasis on manufacturing versus marketing or their predominantly financial versus technical orientation. Then differences in how the companies are organized, say their centralization versus decentralization or their differing styles of management and control, are discerned. Finally, people ascribe these differences to competing values and philosophies—with their company seen as superior and the other as backward, bureaucratic, or just plain bad.

Ironically, a fair amount of diversity in approaching work aids combinations by sparking productive debate and discussion of desired norms in the combined organization. When left unmanaged, however, the clash of cultures pulls sides apart rather than joins them together.

# THE OD ROLE IN MAKING MERGERS AND ACQUISITIONS WORK

Organization development (OD) professionals have worked with executives to put combinations on the path toward strategic and financial success. "Generic" OD practices—such as collecting valid data, feeding it back, and engaging clients in using the findings to develop insights and plan interventions—apply here. In addition, OD interventions have been developed at the individual, group, and organizational levels specifically for M&A situations. While an exhaustive listing of OD interventions for making mergers and acquisitions work cannot be presented in this chapter, we can provide a sample of the ways in which OD activities have enhanced M&A outcomes.

## Individual Level: Managing the Merger Syndrome

Helping individuals adapt to a merger or acquisition involves moving them from being preoccupied with the event to integrating it into their lives (Schlossberg, 1981). This occurs through a two-step process of, first, minimizing the undesirable impact or debilitating aspects of the transition and, second, maximizing the growth or developmental opportunities inherent in the transition (Marks, 2007).

The work of Tannenbaum and Hanna (1985) in facilitating the process of "holding on" and "letting go" guides OD interventions aimed at facilitating employee adaptation to M&A. They cite the value of "consciousness raising" in helping employees acknowledge what they are personally holding on to and become aware of their reasons for doing so. *Workshops* that include content on the emotional aspects of living through a transition promote consciousness raising in ways such as educating employees on the difficulties of transitions and making the internal process of adaptation explicit to them.

The reasons for and implications of holding on become more fully understood when they are expressed experientially. Talking through where they have been and what they are currently experiencing as a result of the merger or acquisition helps employees bring their feelings to a conscious level. A carefully facilitated *venting meeting* can get people to open up in a supportive and safe environment. Even for employees who do not speak up, vicariously listening to others express similar views is beneficial in weakening the negative emotions left over from living through a difficult transition (Marks, 2003). Letting go is completed through an active mourning of what is being left behind—old ways of seeing and doing things, abandoned hopes and expectations, and the loss of what was once satisfying, meaningful, or simply familiar. People need ways to honor and then let go of the pain and loss that result from merging or being acquired, and they often benefit from doing this in a shared public ritual (Frost, 2003). Thus, adaptation to M&A is further facilitated through *symbolic events*, such as mock funerals or graduation ceremonies that mark the transition from the old to the new.

## Group Level: Managing Culture Clash

The primary method for minimizing the unintended consequences of culture clash is establishing a basis of respect for the partner cultures. This is true even if the ultimate intention is to absorb a company and assimilate its culture. Managers who display a consideration for their partner's way of doing things, rather than denigrate it, are likely to gain a reciprocal sense of respect for their own culture. In mergers in which a new culture is being built—either through transformation or by selecting the best from both organizations—a tone of cross-cultural consideration helps employees open up to different ways of doing things rather than tightly hold onto their ways.

One OD tactic we have used at the work group level to build cultural under-standing and minimize culture clash is a hands-on *cultural mirroring* activity. The activity is built around each partner group making three lists: (1) how we view our organization's culture, (2) how we view the other side's culture, and (3) how we think the other side views our culture. The rosters include business practices, interpersonal behaviors, and values. The ensuing discussion brings the language being used behind closed doors when one side discusses the other out in the open. For example, what one side values as "push back," the other may distastefully regard as "rude." We have used this activity to enhance cultural respect among merging senior leadership teams, human resources teams, sales teams, operational teams, and so on.

## Organizational Level: Managing the Transition

The upside of a merger or acquisition is the opportunity to generate breakthrough ways of thinking that can leverage the strengths of both partners to accelerate the achievement of business strategy. This requires an effective *transition man-agement structure* that creates a forum in which the parties can study and test whether or how hoped-for synergies can be realized, contributes to relationship and trust building across partners, and involves people close to the technical aspects and key business issues implicated in the combination. OD practitioners contribute by facilitating transition decision-making meetings, providing credible and rigorous issue identification and decision-making processes, and accelerating the development of teamwork across typically sparring partners.

# SUMMARY

The global economic crisis is expected to bring an increase in the number of mergers and acquisitions as organizations combine to cut costs and expand into new markets. Organization development interventions can help organizational leaders minimize the unintended human, cultural, and organizational consequences of integrating previously independent entities, while maximizing opportunities to use the combination to build a truly new and better organization.

# References

Carwright, S., & McCarthy, S. (2005). Developing a framework for cultural due diligence in mergers and acquisitions. In G.K. Stahl & M.E. Mendenhall (Eds.), *Mergers and acquisitions: Managing culture and human resources*. Stanford, CA: Stanford Business Books.

Frost, P.J. (2003). *Toxic emotions at work*. Boston: Harvard Business School Press.

Harding, D., & Rouse, T. (2007). Human due diligence. *Harvard Business Review, 85*, 124–131.

Haspeslagh, P., & Jamison, D.B. (1991). *Managing acquisitions: Creating value through corporate renewal*. New York: Free Press.

Kanter, R.M., Stein, B.A., & Jick, T.D. (1992). *The challenge of organizational change: How companies experience it and leaders guide it*. New York: Free Press.

Kotter, J.P. (1995). Leading change: Why transformation efforts fail. *Harvard Business Review, 72*, 59–67.

Lipton, M. (1996). Demystifying the development of an organizational vision. *Sloan Management Review, 37*(4), 83–92.

Lovallo, D., Viguerie, P., Uhlaner, R., & Horn, J. (2007). Deals without delusion. *Harvard Business Review, 85*, 92–99.

Marks, M.L. (2003). *Charging back up the hill: Workplace recovery after mergers, acquisitions and downsizings*. San Francisco: Jossey-Bass.

Marks, M.L. (2007). A framework for facilitating adaptation to organizational transition. *Journal of Organizational Change Management, 20*(5), 721–739.

Marks, M.L., & Mirvis, P.H. (1985). Merger syndrome: Stress and uncertainty. *Mergers and Acquisitions, 20*(2), 50–55.

Marks, M.L., & Mirvis, P.H. (1998). *Joining forces: Making one plus one equal three in mergers, acquisitions, and alliances*. San Francisco: Jossey-Bass.

Mirvis, P.H., & Marks, M.L. (1986). Merger syndrome: Managing organizational crises. *Mergers and Acquisitions, 20*(3), 71–77.

Schlossberg, N.K. (1981). A model for analyzing human adaptation to transition. *The Counseling Psychologist, 9*(2), 2–18.

Schweiger, D.M., & Goulet, P.K. (2000). Integrating mergers and acquisitions: An international research review. In C. Cooper & A. Gregory (Eds.), *Advances in mergers and acquisitions* (Vol. 1). New York: Elsevier Science.

Smith, D. (1998). Invigorating change initiatives. *Management Review, 87*(5), 43–48.

Stahl, G.K., & Mendenhall, M.E. (2005). *Mergers and acquisitions: Managing culture and human resources*. Stanford, CA: Stanford Business Books.

Tannenbaum, R., & Hanna, R. (1985). Holding on, letting go, and moving on: Understanding a neglected perspective on change. *Human Systems Development*.

Thomson Financial. (2007). *Global M&A financial advisory review*. New York: The Thomson Corporation.

Wiley, J.E., & Moechnig, S.A. (2005). The effects of mergers and acquisitions on organizational climate. Paper presented at the annual meeting of the Society of Industrial/Organizational Psychologists, Los Angeles.

CHAPTER TWENTY-FIVE

# Human Systems Dynamics

*Competencies for a New Organizational Practice*

Glenda H. Eoyang

Today's organizational challenges are different from those of the past. Agents of organizational change must find radically new ways to respond to different demands. As organization development (OD) professionals, we and our clients are striving to cope with global diversity, virtual relationships, unpredictable outcomes, and unflinching demands for performance, profitability, and sustainability. We are called on to help others manage change that is instantaneous, unpredictable, and cross-functional. While familiar, hierarchical roles and relationships are being transformed into more collaborative styles of leadership, the drive toward measurable outcomes and lean performance continues to escalate. While global virtual teams work together toward common goals, cultural conflicts erupt in communities and organizations. While cycle time and client expectations for response time shrink, processes and procedures to ensure consistent quality expand. These and many other tensions drive our clients' organizations and our own.

Such an environment requires that we rethink the theory and practice of OD and our roles as practitioners. Many emerging theories and practices help us adapt to this new and less stable environment. Barry Johnson talks about the many polarities that shape individual, social, organizational, and community realities (Johnson, 1992). Lisa Kimball (2008) writes about positive deviance, which seeks to identify and optimize existing resource and solutions within the community to solve community problems. Harrison Owen (2008) expands Open Space. Large-scale intervention techniques are transformed to meet local needs and resources

465

(Bunker & Alban, 2006; Holman, Devane, & Cady, 2007). Many other innovative tools and methods are emerging to help our practice evolve to meet the demands of this transformed marketplace, but something is still missing.

OD needs more than just new tools and methods to meet the challenges of tomorrow. Any innovative tool or method can be brought into a traditional OD practice. It can be integrated into the process that we trust and that we repeatedly ask our clients to trust. We can co-opt even the most radical approach and adapt it—tame it—to fit with our tried-and-true approaches. While this path allows us to stretch our toolkits, it will not prepare us to meet the challenges of a radically different organizational ecology and a transformed professional services market. Around the world, OD practitioners and their clients and client systems are dissatisfied with the standard OD theories and practices. Many people find that, even with an assortment of radically new methods, they are unprepared to meet the challenges of this emerging world. Sometimes native abilities and deep intuitions lead practitioners and their clients in the right direction, but even that sometimes-reliable strategy can break down at the most inopportune times.

These practitioners are as frustrated as they are experienced. They realize that effective OD practice of the future will require a new foundation of assumption, method, and theory. This new foundation must adapt to local and changing requirements, support rapid response, and integrate the use of a wide variety of tools and practices. To make such a significant and meaningful difference, practitioners have to re-examine our common notions and question our expectations. We have to take a risk and challenge our fundamental practices and assumptions with new ways to think about change. We have to consider our options and our roles as responsible, active agents of change.

This chapter outlines a theory base that is both radical and familiar. While it fits the intuitions of the most experienced OD practitioners, it breaks through some locked-in assumptions of traditional OD practice. This new approach to organizational practice has emerged from the new sciences of nonlinear dynamics, chaos, and complexity. It incorporates a wide range of philosophies and social science disciplines. It has been tempered with grounded theory and successful practice. It is an open and adaptive approach to dealing with the unpredictability of OD in the 21st Century. It is human systems dynamics.

# HUMAN SYSTEMS DYNAMICS DEFINED

Human systems dynamics (HSD) is a field of research and practice that emerges at the intersection of complexity and social sciences. It is grounded in the assumption that human systems—at all levels of organization from intrapersonal to national—are complex adaptive systems. A complex adaptive system

## Exhibit 25.1. Human Systems Dynamics Competencies for a New Organizational Practice Self-Assessment

Who are you?                                    What is today's date?

Describe a recent project and/or client interaction:

In this interaction, I…(Check one column for each question.)

|  | Strongly Disagree | Disagree | Neither Agree Nor Disagree | Agree | Strongly Agree |
|---|---|---|---|---|---|
| Taught clients/ colleagues to see new things in new ways |  |  |  |  |  |
| Taught clients/ colleagues to act in new ways |  |  |  |  |  |
| Learned something surprising about myself |  |  |  |  |  |
| Learned something new about my client |  |  |  |  |  |
| Learned something new about my professional field |  |  |  |  |  |
| Identified strengths of individual clients |  |  |  |  |  |
| Reinforced strengths of individual clients |  |  |  |  |  |
| Identified strengths of groups of clients |  |  |  |  |  |
| Reinforced strengths of groups of clients |  |  |  |  |  |
| Identified my own strengths |  |  |  |  |  |
| Reinforced my own strengths |  |  |  |  |  |
| Applied existing, received theory |  |  |  |  |  |
| Developed or extended existing, received theory |  |  |  |  |  |

| | Strongly Disagree | Disagree | Neither Agree Nor Disagree | Agree | Strongly Agree |
|---|---|---|---|---|---|
| Applied practices I've found useful in the past | | | | | |
| Developed new practices I will find useful in the future | | | | | |
| Gave value for value | | | | | |
| Received value for value | | | | | |
| Defined and attended to the part | | | | | |
| Defined and attended to the whole | | | | | |
| Defined and attended to the greater whole | | | | | |
| Engaged in joyful practice | | | | | |
| TOTAL number of checks in each column: | | | | | |

Which HSD competencies should I focus on in the future?

What actions will I take to reinforce my strengths?

What actions will I take to strengthen my weaknesses?

# References

Bunker, B., & Alban, B. (2006). *The handbook of large group methods: Creating systemic change in organizations and communities*. San Francisco: Jossey-Bass.

Eoyang, G. (2001). Conditions for self-organizing in human systems. An unpublished doctoral dissertation. Cincinnati, OH: The Union Institute and University.

Holman, P., Devane, T., & Cady, S. (2007). *The change handbook: The definitive resource on today's best methods for engaging whole systems*. San Francisco: Berrett-Koehler.

Johnson, B. (1992). *Polarity management: Identifying and managing unsolvable problems*. Amherst, MA: HRD Press.

Kimball, L. (2008). Positive deviance webcast [groupjazz.com/html/gj-news.html].

Owen, H. (2008). *Wave rider: Leadership for high performance in a self-organizing world*. San Francisco: Berrett-Koehler.

# CHAPTER TWENTY-SIX

# Seeing and Influencing Self-Organization

Kristine Quade and Royce Holladay

This chapter is based on Human Systems Dynamics (HSD), an emerging field of study and practice. HSD emerges at the intersection of complexity theory and social sciences, using metaphors and perspectives from complexity to understand and influence human interactions. We provide a basic definition of two foundational principles of HSD: complex adaptive systems (CAS) and patterns, along with tools from HSD to help understand how constraints influence pattern development across a system. We believe tapping into new theories such as HSD will become paramount for OD practitioner skills to remain cutting edge and influential in complex systems.

## GENERATING AND RESPONDING TO PATTERNS

In complex adaptive human systems, individuals and situations interact in interdependent, responsive, and adaptive ways. The degree of interdependence, both internal and external to the system, determines how responsive and adaptive the total system remains. Through this process of responding and adapting, the system finds its most productive and appropriate "fit" in a volatile and challenging landscape.

# Defining Complex Adaptive Systems (CAS)

A CAS is a collection of semi-autonomous agents interacting in interdependent ways, such that their interactions create system-wide patterns. Those system-wide patterns, in turn, influence behaviors of agents in the system (Eoyang, 2001). Breaking this definition into its components is important for understanding how patterns are generated and reinforced. Figures 26.1 through 26.4 illustrate this concept.

Semi-autonomous is simply an ability to choose. In a human system, agents are individuals with options for how they interact with each other within their environments. They choose to follow rules of the whole or to be independent. They choose excellence or expedience. They choose purposeful, intentional actions in service to the greater whole, or they choose to optimize their own situations and standing.

Striving for control and predictability in a system is an illusion of leadership, especially when it comes to individual decisions and actions at a given point in time. Overall mission, vision, values, and ethics standards can guide interactions, not control them. Performance goals, measurements, and accountabilities can heighten expectations, not predict organizational outcomes.

When semi-autonomous agents come together, they respond to each other in interdependent ways. They form groups, develop inside jokes and language, learn from each other, come into conflict, and reach new understandings. Each agent makes choices about how to interact, sometimes following established norms and rules, and sometimes not. Interactions are unpredictable and interdependent, with new meaning emerging constantly.

Pattern formation refers to emergence of patterns of thought, behavior, and response. Over time, actions and interactions in a complex adaptive system are

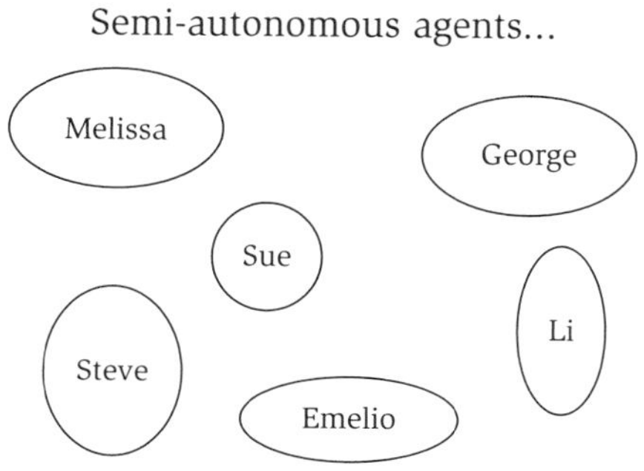

**Figure 26.1.** Semi-Autonomous Agents

Interact in interdependent
ways...

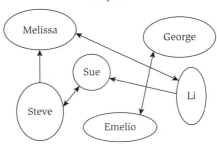

**Figure 26.2.** Interact in Interdependent Ways

repeated enough to form patterns, defined as "similarities, differences, and relationships that have meaning across space and time" (Eoyang, 2008). If prevalent behaviors are respectful and tolerant, patterns across the organization will reflect encouragement of differences, inclusion of new ideas and people, and acceptance of change. If individuals are secretive, isolated, or risk-averse, patterns across the organization will reflect strong competition, subversion, and possible unethical actions. The presence and "feel" of these patterns are often referred to as the culture of the group or organization.

Such that their
interactions form
system-wide patterns....

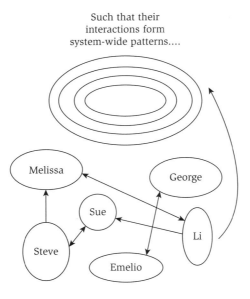

**Figure 26.3.** Forming System-Wide Patterns

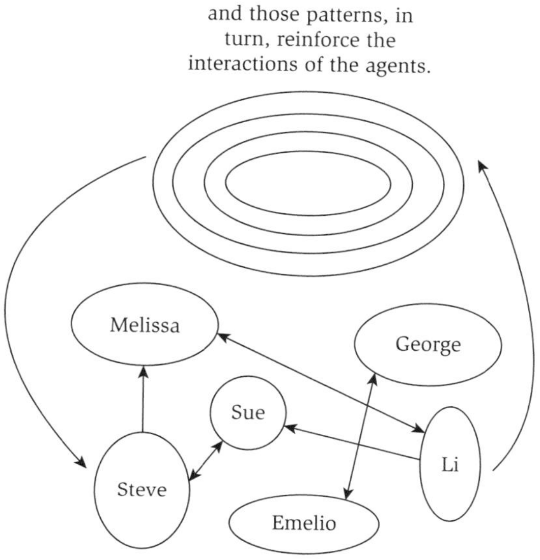

and those patterns, in
turn, reinforce the
interactions of the agents.

**Figure 26.4.** Patterns Reinforce Interactions of Agents

As system-wide patterns form, they, in turn, influence behavior across the system. A leader who consistently demonstrates thoughtful and probative questions will reinforce the same in others and begin to develop a pattern of questioning for the purpose of inquiry. Over time, this can change the interactions with others outside the organization. Another leader, appearing to make inconsistent decisions, will create distrust in the organization, risk aversion among others, and "wait-and-see" behavior by decision-makers positioned lower in the organization.

## Why Study Complex Adaptive Systems

Working from a deep understanding of CAS provides a greater value to organizations than traditional understandings of systems. It heightens awareness of various patterns that influence action inside the system. This deeper understanding of systems is necessary because of the increased complexity and diversity in systems as compared to organizations in earlier times. While systems thinking was deeply embedded in theory developed by the founders of OD, in more recent years, emphasis in the field has moved toward toolkit development, without a clear understanding of the massively entangled complex systems and underlying patterns and dynamics that trigger, support, and maintain the culture of a system.

# THE LANDSCAPE DIAGRAM

Activities inside CAS can be characterized in one of three ways: organized, self-organizing, and unorganized. At any given time, each of those descriptors is appropriate to different activities throughout the organization. All three are important and necessary in every organization. Most traditional management theories emerged from a mechanistic perspective in which control is an important goal. Developmental theories assume a constant, identical, and predictable process of change for every organization. Even the process of developing mission, vision, and values statements is designed to create manageable control in the organization. In a system that is constantly adapting to changes in its environment, this level of control in all parts of the system is simply not possible.

The Landscape Diagram (Holladay, 2002) is a tool for understanding complex activity and provides a picture of the "lay of the land" in organizational work. It is designed to illustrate necessary similarities, differences, and relationships in activity (patterns) across an adaptive organization. A landscape diagram (Figure 26.5) is a way to "see" patterns that form and re-form, based on Agreement and Certainty.

## Landscape Dimensions

When considering any question or action, two considerations exist—Agreement and Certainty. *Agreement* refers to the degree to which people are aligned with each other about action. They can be anywhere on a continuum from "close to" or "far from" Agreement, as indicated on the Y-axis of the diagram. *Certainty* refers to the degree of possibility that something will actually happen, ranging

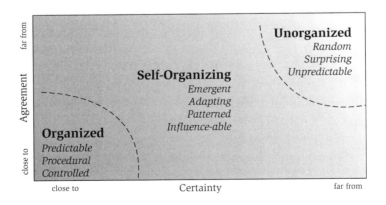

**Figure 26.5.** The Landscape Diagram

from "close to" or "far from" Certainty, as indicated on the X-axis of the diagram. Organizational activities can be plotted on the diagram according to these two dimensions.

When a system is close to Agreement and close to Certainty, system activities are organized, predictable, and controlled and operate in the "Organized Zone." Some functions in the organization require strict conditions to function successfully. In high-tech manufacturing processes, people have to be close to Agreement about steps in the manufacturing process and how to respond to defects. They must be close to Certainty about what will be produced in each cycle of the process. Clear processes and procedures, expectations, and performance outcomes reduce variation and ensure consistency.

Activities far from Certainty and Agreement operate in the "Unorganized Zone." Each customer service call represents new opportunity. No one can predict, with any degree of Certainty, what the call will be about (Holladay & Quade, 2008). Nor will there be unanimous agreement about the system's response. This zone represents possible trends outside the organization, new opportunities for responding and adapting, and different types of information-seeking communication channels and networks. This is the zone in which organizational leaders pay attention to blips and trends to inform strategic planning.

In the middle, between Organized and Unorganized, is a zone of emergent patterns called the "Self-Organizing Zone." This is the arena of interaction, learning, and pattern formation as experienced in cross-functional teams. It is where change happens in the system. While organized work is critical to an organization's functioning, it is in the Self-Organizing Zone that leaders and practitioners find their greatest challenges.

## Using the Landscape Diagram

The Landscape Diagram helps explain value and contributions of patterns that occur in each of the three Zones: Organized, Self-Organizing, and Unorganized. It represents strong interaction between zones as patterns emerge and shift. Options for action can be developed from a deep understanding of how activities flow across the diagram.

The Landscape Diagram is useful for understanding patterns at personal, process, and system levels. On a personal level, practitioners use the diagram to identify individual mindsets and response mechanisms. Some people work best in situations of predictability and control; some like the freedom of emergence and response; still others prefer randomness of ideas and information before patterns form. Using the Landscape Diagram, practitioners can help others understand personal preference, mindset, and impact so viable expectations and agreements can be established about work.

At a systems level, processes and procedures move from zone to zone, depending on the constraints. For example, a research and development process begins in the Unorganized Zone as an unconstrained activity of disconnected ideas and exploration of random possibilities. As random ideas become more fully formed, they appear as a pattern to be messaged, tested, and investigated in the Self-Organizing Zone and become more constrained as they become prototypes or plans. Finally, in the Organized Zone, prototypes and plans take on specifications for standardized implementation and manufacturing, a highly constrained system.

All levels of activity along the spectrum from uncontrolled to controlled are necessary, yet different activities across the spectrum often become the subject of misunderstanding or conflict. Those who work in the Organized Zone to produce a final product may not understand the need for free and wide-ranging exploration of possibilities. Those who work in development must, at some point, discontinue new exploration and work from ideas they have at hand. Helping participants in the process see similarities and differences across the zones more clearly provides opportunity to build appropriate structures and expectations throughout the organization.

At the systems level, a vibrant organization allows for differences across the Landscape, to ensure engagement with possibilities, responsiveness to the new and novel, and a heightened awareness of the necessity for knowledge transfer at all levels.

## Application of the Landscape Diagram

Practitioners can help others understand the Landscape Diagram by engaging them in a physical activity. Using masking tape, a practitioner can form the Landscape Diagram on the floor of a large space. After explaining the dimensions and zones, practitioners invite participants to stand in the zone that represents personal preference in their daily lives and then debrief by asking why individuals placed themselves as they did.

This exercise can be repeated, asking individuals to stand in the zones in which they experience the majority of their work assignments. Participants could be asked to notice shifts from personal preference to work assignment requirements. The activity can be debriefed through discussion about what is supported or given up between personal preferences and work assignments.

The Landscape Diagram can be used to discover preferences within a team or for choosing new team members to ensure diverse perspectives. To determine team members' confidence about a decision quickly, practitioners can ask individuals to indicate their personal Agreement with the decision and their Certainty that the decision will result in desired outcomes. Individuals can indicate where they think the rest of the team is in relationship to the decision, discussing ways the two sets of data are aligned or misaligned. Using the Landscape Diagram, change practitioners can

- Help leaders adjust their styles and behaviors to provide effective supports and oversight;

- Support employees in developing a repertoire of responses and actions appropriate to the various zones; and

- Work with the entire system to establish appropriate policies, procedures, and expectations.

# CONSTRAINING THE SYSTEM

Movement and location of activities on the Landscape Diagram are determined by the ways the system is constrained. "Constraints" are the degrees of freedom or limitations that emerge from interactions and activities of the system itself. Some examples of system constraints are patterns of behavior; rules, policies, and procedures; clarity of vision and mission, or the nature of relationships in a system.

Constraints are not inherently "naughty or nice" (Holladay & Quade, 2008). Different levels of constraint are appropriate at different times and in different situations. Appropriate degrees of constraint depend on sustainability of the system. The question to ask is, "What level of constraint is necessary to help this system adapt to its environment in productive and sustainable ways?"

When a system requires precise and uniform outputs, high constraints are necessary. Specifications must be clearly articulated. People communicate frequently with a common vocabulary. Rules must be followed, and personal freedoms are relinquished in context of work to be accomplished. This high level of constraint moves that part of the system into the Organized Zone.

When a system is exploring new trends to identify new products, constraints must be low. People must be free to examine multiple sources, seek wide ranges of experiences, challenge assumptions, and be creative. The system is constrained not by rules, regulations, or specifications, but by alignment with organizational mission and goals. Lack of constraints moves that part of the system into the Unorganized Zone.

When constraints are not appropriate to a system's work, imbalance occurs. In the earlier example of high constraint, if procedures are vague, communication is unclear, or important rules are ignored, the system is under-constrained and cannot accomplish its work appropriately. There may be times as well when the system becomes over-constrained. When engaged in strategic

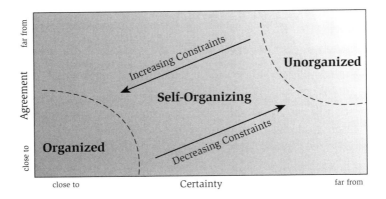

**Figure 26.6.** Landscape Constraints

thinking, too much constraint—limited scope of exploration, lack of support for risk, or quick formation of groupthink—results in a lack of creativity.

### Using Constraints and the Landscape Diagram

If a process in the Organized Zone is not working as desired, the process is assigned to those who can "find the fix that fits" by reducing or changing set rules and looking for how to make the process work—reducing constraints. This shifts the work to the Self-Organized Zone. As an activity requires greater constraints, it will move toward the Organized Zone on the Landscape Diagram. Figure 26.6 reflects how shifting levels of constraint move activities or issues across the Landscape Diagram.

## HOW TO INFLUENCE PATTERNS USING CONSTRAINTS

When faced with a need to bring about a desired change, focus should be on constraints that form the pattern of behavior, process, or relationship that is dysfunctional. Traditional approaches by change practitioners included tools that sometimes worked, but perhaps with limited success. Practitioners were left with few resources to understand why their interventions worked or how to search for a new tool that might work better.

As a result of her dissertation research, Glenda Eoyang developed a model to help practitioners understand the dynamics of change. The Eoyang CDE Model (Olson & Eoyang, 2001) offers options for influencing patterns of constraint in organizations. Eoyang identified three conditions—containers, difference, and exchanges—that influence the speed, path, and direction of self-organization.

## Containers

Containers hold the system together until a pattern can emerge. They form a boundary that can take one of several forms. Physical containers (locations, space, building structures) define what is in or out of a system. Organizational containers can be functions, departments, teams, or levels of management. Conceptual or psychological containers include affinities, charismatic leaders, organizational missions, or beliefs. To understand which container to influence, practitioners consider questions:

- What is the container? Is it too large or too small?
- How would I see the problem if I looked at a different container? What would that accomplish?
- What will I watch for as I shift the container?

## Difference

Differences provide texture or substance that manifests into patterns and enable movement or change across the organization. In a painting, differences of texture, shading, and color bring forth an image and make it compelling. The same is true in a system. Differences among agents establish patterns. Such differences may be personal, such as experience or educational differences, or they may be organizational, such as the difference between research and development staff and production staff. Differences may be more global, such as purchasing cycles aligned with specific holidays.

Having differences within a system enables it to adapt and fit with its environment. Without rich contrasts of difference, a system can slip into "sameness" or "groupthink" and miss opportunities to adapt and be flexible.

When working with difference as a change dimension, practitioners choose significant variables to watch or they look at differences a variable creates over time. For example, in a group of new employees, practitioners can watch for leadership skills to emerge, affinities to form, or how people differentiate themselves. Or they can choose one variable such as leadership skills and observe how those skills grow over time.

To understand which differences to influence, practitioners might think about these questions:

- What significant differences do I see in this system?
- How might the differences shift if amplified (made stronger) or dampened (lessened)?
- What do differences tell me about the larger system or its agents?
- How are differences over-constrained? Under-constrained?
- How are differences contributing to this system's fitness with its environment?

# Exchanges

Exchanges are ways the system shares information, energy, time, and other resources. Exchanges can be language-based—talking and listening, email, or newsletters. They can be a source of organizational culture—performance feedback, input, or participative decision making. Exchanges can flow one direction and have only directional impact, but change practitioners must pay attention to those exchanges that are transformative–changing both the sender and the receiver because of what is learned by both.

To understand exchanges, practitioners might think about these questions:

- Is the challenge I am facing a result of an exchange?

- How are people sharing information or resources? What is being shared?

- What impact do I notice as a result of exchanges?

- What exchanges are needed to bring about a different outcome?

# Influencing the System Using the CDE Model

Being able to see, understand, and name patterns is one part of the change practitioner's role. Using the Eoyang CDE Model to become aware of the dynamics of a system is a first step toward understanding and influencing it. Practitioners can then identify specific patterns to work on as well as the conditions to shift to influence the pattern. Table 26.1 can be used to name relevant containers (C), differences (D), and exchanges (E).

Looking at relevant containers, differences, and exchanges, practitioners can determine appropriate constraints of the system. Differences and exchanges should be specific to a given container to ensure a connection between intervention and resulting shifts. Without the direct link between a container and its differences and exchanges, entanglements in the system are more difficult to identify, and the situation will appear more complicated than it may be. Table 26.2 represents the impact of constraints on container, differences, and exchanges. Because issues are massively entangled across levels in an organization, what appears as a difference at one level will be a container at another level. For example, if practitioners consider all people in an organization as a container, a difference that makes a difference could be "experience." If they look at all experienced people in the organization, experience becomes a container, and "level of expertise" could be a difference that matters.

# Shifting the Conditions to Influence Patterns

To shift constraints in the system, practitioners can choose to develop interventions addressing one or more conditions of the Eoyang CDE Model.

## Table 26.1. CDE Identification Examples

| | *Ideally Constrained* | *Over-Constrained* | *Under-Constrained* |
|---|---|---|---|
| Definition | System is aligned with its environment and adapts smoothly and responsively to external and internal changes | System has limits in its ability to self-organize and adapt in alignment with environmental fitness | System has too much freedom in its options for adaptability and cannot settle into patterns of self-organization |
| C (Container) | Container holds the system together while patterns form to move the system toward fitness | Container is too limiting, forcing the system into patterns that exhaust its energies too quickly, preventing effective self-organization. *Sample:* Sometimes projects have limited success because they are over-constrained by budget, time, and/or lack of expertise in the team | Container is too expansive, preventing the system from settling into productive patterns. *Sample:* Some projects that have too many expectations and a broad scope with too few workers and not enough resources |
| D ((Difference) | The important differences are balanced, enabling the system to adapt appropriately to its environment and move toward fitness | Differences are limited in the system and patterns become limiting forces. *Sample:* Committees or teams that have been together a long time often fall into "groupthink" | There are too many differences in the system, or the differences are so large that system-wide patterns of adaptation cannot form to move the system toward fitness. Sample: New committees or teams spend some time coming to group agreements across their various differences |

*Continued*

### Table 26.1. CDE Identification Examples

| | Ideally Constrained | Over-Constrained | Under-Constrained |
|---|---|---|---|
| E (Exchange) | Exchanges in the system move information and other resources, allowing effective adaptation in the environment, moving it toward fitness | Exchanges in the system control the availability of resources and information to the point that the system is unable to respond flexibly and adapt to changes in the environment<br><br>*Sample:* During a merger, employees proliferate rumor and fear by sharing information quickly and limiting time to check facts | Exchanges in the system are "loose" and limited such that they do not move information and other resources at a rate that allows the system to use them to support adaptation toward fitness so that information and other resources move too slowly<br><br>*Sample*: During a merger, the leadership of the organizations don't share information quickly enough or deeply enough to fight the rumors that are flying around |

Table 26.3 offers a summary of common interventions and how they are most likely to affect group dynamics. This tool is not intended to be definitive, but a suggestive beginning for practitioners to add their own skills in working with the CDE.

The Eoyang CDE Model helps practitioners analyze situations to understand dynamics driving emergent patterns. It provides a framework for practitioners to complete their question sets by asking about containers, differences, and exchanges. When one condition shifts, it will impact all the others. Practitioners can use an intervention to change one condition, observe how the system adjusts, and use that information to determine their next intervention. Many practitioners have a tendency to use exchange interventions first because they are well known and popularly held, but other conditions may be more effectively shifted. By looking at the conditions in the system, practitioners can determine patterns of interaction.

Table 26.2. Shifting Conditions

| | Increase Constraint | Decrease Constraint |
|---|---|---|
| Container | Clarify goals and mission<br>Reduce number of people<br>Move to smaller space<br>Shorten meetings<br>Tighten agenda<br>Define projects/project management<br>Clarify roles and responsibilities<br>Rewrite job descriptions | Brainstorm new options<br>Include more stakeholders<br>Lengthen meetings<br>Use large-scale interventions<br>Engage in scenario building<br>Encourage cross-functional teams<br>Encourage different work venues, such as telecommuting |
| Difference | Focus on similarities<br>Set a dress code standard<br>Standardize operating procedures<br>Hire to complement existing skills and competencies<br>Institute balanced scorecard<br>Enforce standards<br>Reduce turnover | Focus on significant differences<br>Relax standards<br>Encourage creativity<br>Train on global and cultural sensitivity<br>Tell personal stories<br>Use Appreciative Inquiry approaches<br>Implement training on a new topic |
| Exchange | Build communication templates<br>Use standard communications<br>Have periodic communication<br>Increase two-way communication<br>Clarify norms<br>Institute specifically targeted rewards and recognitions (for example, sales goals)<br>Simplify/enforce performance appraisals<br>Change sequence of talk (round-robin, talking stick)<br>Give and receive constructive feedback<br>Measure outcomes and process<br>Evaluate meeting effectiveness | Increase options for interaction (breakout groups)<br>Focus on informal exchanges<br>Encourage social interaction<br>Enliven commons areas<br>Open online conversations<br>Ask authentic, challenging questions<br>Perform environmental scans<br>Introduce dialogue practices<br>Observe in silence<br>Encourage personal reflection<br>Open access to information<br>Encourage pro and con discussion in meetings<br>Conduct town hall meetings |

### Table 26.3. Summary of Common CDE Interventions

|  | *Increase Constraint* | *Decrease Constraint* |
|---|---|---|
| Container | Clarify goals and mission | Brainstorm new options |
|  | Reduce number of people | Include more stakeholders |
|  | Move to smaller space | Move to larger space |
|  | Shorten meetings | Lengthen meetings |
|  | Define projects/project management | Large-scale interventions |
|  | Institute balanced scorecard | Scenario planning |
|  | Clarify roles and responsibilities | Encourage cross-functional teams |
|  | Rewrite job descriptions | Encourage telecommuting |
| Difference | Focus on similarities | Focus on significant differences |
|  | Introduce dress code | Relax standards |
|  | Introduce standard operating procedures | Encourage creativity |
|  | Hire to match existing staff | Train on cultural sensitivity |
|  | Enforce standards | Tell personal stories |
|  | Reduce turnover | Use Appreciative Inquiry techniques |
|  | Deliver system-wide training | Implement creativity training |
|  | Implement automation of core business |  |
|  | Orient new employees |  |
| Exchange | Build communication templates | Increase options for interaction |
|  | Use standard communications | Focus on informal exchanges |
|  | Have periodic communication | Encourage social interaction |
|  | Increase two-way communication | Hang out in commons areas |
|  | Clarify norms | Open collaborative online conversations |
|  | Institute rewards and recognitions | Ask authentic and challenging questions |
|  | Simplify/enforce performance appraisals | Perform environmental scans |
|  | Enforce sequence of talk (round-robin) | Introduce dialogue practices |
|  | Increase communications skills | Observe in silence |
|  | Give and receive feedback | Encourage personal reflections |
|  | Measure outcomes and process | Open access to information |
|  | Improve meeting management | Encourage discussion in meetings |
|  | Encourage shared jargon |  |

# SUMMARY

Seeing systems as unique, complex, and adaptive, with their own histories, characteristics, driving forces, and adaptability, will open the capacity for change practitioners to go beyond traditional tool kits into a realm of deep systems change. Using the Landscape Diagram, practitioners are able to identify and observe patterns as they emerge and shift through constraining forces. Using the Eoyang CDE Model will aid in decision making about how best to bring about lasting change—moving a system toward fitness with its environment.

New approaches to bringing about change are emerging from a deeper understanding of underlying dynamics of CAS. By seeing and understanding patterns as the root of opportunity for systems change, practitioners can choose their interventions to match the dynamics at work in teams, organizations, and communities. Shifting the dynamics of a system toward fitness ensures a coherence of action at all levels. This skill provides practitioners greater options for action to establish and build sustainable systems in today's uncertain and volatile environments.

# References

Eoyang, G. (2008). Verbal definition provided in Human Systems Dynamics' professional certification course. Wayzata, MN: Human Systems Dynamics.

Eoyang, G.H. (2001). Conditions for self-organizing in human systems. [Unpublished dissertation]. [www.winternet.com/ ~ eoyang/dissertation.pdf]

Holladay R., & Quade, K. (2008). *Influencing patterns for change: A human systems dynamics primer for leaders*. Scotts Valley, CA: CreateSpace.

Holladay, R. (2002). HSD@Work: *Frequently asked questions about HSD*. Circle Pines, MN: Human Systems Dynamics Press.

Olson, E., & Eoyang, G. (2001). *Facilitating organization change: Lessons from complexity science*. San Francisco: Pfeiffer.

# CHAPTER TWENTY-SEVEN

# Values, Ethics, and Expanding the Practice of OD

William Gellermann and Terri Egan

T he past three decades have seen a number of formal and informal dialogues, discussions, and debates about the nature of organization development (OD) and the values, ethics, and practices on which it is based. A classic article on the future of the field of OD suggested that, in contrast to a certain clarity around values that characterized the early days of OD, we have experienced a period of confusion and ambiguity—leaving practitioners in the position of having to rely on their individual ethical frameworks rather than an agreed-on set of ethical standards (Worley & Feyerherm, 2003). At the same time, the boundaries of what we include in the OD field remain unclear.

In this chapter we explore the meanings of OD and human systems development (HSD); OD/HSD viewed as a "profession" or a "field of practice"; values and ethics in OD/HSD; and the potential expansion of this field.

## THE MEANING OF ORGANIZATION DEVELOPMENT (OD)

Before examining questions related to establishing values and standards of ethical practice, it will help to briefly reflect on the history of OD to give a perspective for thinking about what we mean by OD as it relates to HSD. To do that, we begin by retelling a slightly modified version of a story told by the late Bob Tannenbaum in introducing a plenary address to an annual

OD Network conference (as remembered by Bill Gellermann and confirmed by Frank Freidlander at the 2008 OD Network Conference).

"A woman went into an ice cream store and said to the clerk, 'May I have a quart of chocolate ice cream?' The clerk replied, 'I'm sorry, lady. We don't have any chocolate ice cream.' She paused and then said, 'Well. How about a pint of chocolate ice cream? Can I have that?' And he replied, 'I'm sorry, lady. We just don't have any chocolate ice cream!' Again, after another pause, she asked, 'Well. How about a chocolate ice cream cone? Can I have that?'

"The clerk thought a moment and then, with a bit of impatience in his voice, said: 'Lady. How do you spell the van in vanilla?' And she said, 'V A N.' Then he asked, 'And how about the straw in strawberry?' And she said, in a hesitant tone of voice, 'S T R A W.' Then he asked, 'And how about the f--- in chocolate?' And she replied adamantly, 'There's no f--- in chocolate!' And he responded, 'Lady! That's what I've been trying to tell you!!!'"

After the laughter subsided, Bob then said, "There is something I have been trying to tell our profession—and I'm going to try one more time. OD is not about our kit of tools. *OD is about the way we lead our lives!*"

In our view, "the way we lead our lives" is an extraordinarily important way of thinking about the nature of OD, since, on reflection, it contrasts with many of the prevailing views of what "organization development" means.

For us those words focus on *the way people within organizations live their lives*—and it also extends to *the way "we" (human beings throughout the world) live our lives*. The first way of thinking is consistent with the focus on developing organizations and the second way is consistent with the emerging, expanded view of our "field of practice," namely the field of HSD.

One of the places where "human systems development" emerged as a way of thinking about our field was in meetings called by Herb Shepard, one of OD's founders. Participants were representatives of the major OD-oriented practitioner organizations (such as the OD Network, OD Institute, International OD Association, and Academy of Management OD Division). Their purpose was to find ways of improving collaboration among those organizations. At their first meeting, Bill Gellermann (co-author of this chapter) asked for their support of a process for developing a statement of values and ethics for OD professionals that the group did endorse. (The statement that emerged is described at this book's website and discussed later in this chapter.) At their second meeting several months later, the group, which had initially called itself "The Inter-Organization Group," changed its name to "The Human Systems Development Consortium" because several representatives reported that they had a significant number of members for whom the term "Organization Development" was not appropriate, such as people working with countries, communities, and regions.

# ALIGNMENT: A META VALUE FOR LEADING OUR LIVES

One concept for thinking about the meaning of the way we lead our lives is "alignment," namely "energy moving in the same direction." Energy moving in the same direction has enormous potential and can be thought of as coherent and impactful. Energy moving in different directions—or anti-coherent energy—is wasteful and actions that emerge from anti-coherence may have unintended consequences. (*Note*: a laser is an example of coherent light beams, which, because of their coherence, are able to cut through steel.)

For *individuals*, living in alignment has an internal and external component. Internal alignment means that our awareness includes the intellectual, emotional, intuitive, physical, and spiritual aspects of self. We commit to the development and integration of each of these dimensions, and we understand how each dimension impacts our capacity for ethical practice. External alignment is the extent to which we express our internal state of coherent energy into our personal and professional actions.

For an *organization*, alignment means that all of the organization's members are motivated to serve a shared purpose and vision or, at least, purposes and visions that are complementary. In other words, their motivations are moving them in the same direction. For example, the Johnson & Johnson Credo illustrates one way an organization can contribute to creating the conditions under which people are all motivated to move in the same direction. That credo begins: "We believe our first responsibility is to the doctors, nurses, and patients, mothers, and fathers, and all others who use our products and services." In contrast, Coca-Cola's mission (purpose) begins: "We exist to create value for our share owners on a long-term basis." In our view, the J & J mission is more likely to evoke motivation throughout the organization that is aligned in a common direction than the Coca-Cola mission. We do not mean that Coca-Cola's mission of "long-term shareholder value" is not important, but only that it is less likely to energize motivation in a shared direction than J & J's mission, which makes serving customers primary.

# ALIGNMENT AND HUMAN SYSTEMS DEVELOPMENT (HSD)

Although the mental leap from OD to HSD can seem large, the conceptual leap is relatively clear. Namely, when OD is conceived of as the process of facilitating alignment among all organization members, then HSD involves the process of facilitating alignment among all system members.

In HSD, alignment takes on even greater importance. As the size of the system increases, the opportunity for misalignment, and the impact of misalignment, increases. Consider that the majority of collaborative efforts fail as a result of misalignment in mindsets, goals, resources, cultural values, and so forth at the individual, group, and organizational level. As the world increasingly calls for the power of collaboration, the issue of alignment becomes even more vital.

For example, although it is an extraordinary conceptual leap, alignment of all members of the global community is conceivable. The means of achieving global alignment may be beyond our present ability, but activities of the United Nations can conceivably be steps in that direction. For example, creating a Global People's Assembly (composed of representatives of "the people") as a subsystem of The United Nations to complement the General Assembly (composed of representatives of governments) would be an example of HSD. Other examples of HSD are:

- *Avaaz* (www.avaaz.org) "has grown to almost 3.4 million people from every country of the world, an average growth of over 40,000 people per week. Working in thirteen languages, Avaaz members have taken nearly eight million actions" [per e-mail message dated August 28, 2008].

- *Wiser Earth* (www.wiserearth.org) "is a community directory and networking forum that maps and connects non-governmental organizations (NGOs), businesses, governments, and individuals addressing the central issues of our day: climate change, poverty, the environment, peace, water, hunger, social justice, conservation, human rights and more." According to its website, it includes more than 109,200 organizations, 16,400 people, and 780 groups (with shared focus).

- *We, The World* (www.wetheworld.com) describes itself as "a place where many movements for social change come together in an ongoing mass public education and mobilization campaign for 'Peace on Earth' and 'Peace with Earth,'" and its website specifies that it forms international networks of collaboration and action.

In view of the fundamental similarity of OD and HSD, we find it clarifying to conceive of them separately and simultaneously (as OD/HSD). In view of our earlier discussion, we view the practice of OD/HSD more as facilitating the process of alignment in OD/HSD than as the development process itself. In other words, according to this view, *OD/HSD practitioners do not "do" OD/HSD*; rather, they *facilitate* it.

## OD/HSD: PROFESSION OR FIELD OF PRACTICE?

Over the years of OD/HSD practice, conflict has emerged over the issue of whether or not "we" are a profession. Some have resisted our becoming a profession on such grounds as concern about standardization, barriers to entry, and a shift to valuing the interests of the profession above those of our clients (which has emerged in the history of many other professions, such as law and medicine). On the other hand, some have urged our becoming a profession on such grounds as improving the quality of our practice by establishing procedures for certifying qualification, standards of competence and a code of ethics, and procedures for enforcing both competence and ethical practice.

We prefer a third alternative based on a view suggested by Dick Beckhard, one of the founders of OD. In Dick's opinion, we are a "field of practice" and not a profession (personal communication). With that view, it is possible for us to collaborate in developing standards of competence as well as values and ethics and to support one another in establishing practice consistent with those standards. But we are more oriented to supporting one another in practicing in accord with such standards than to enforcing compliance with such standards.

Also, although we may choose not to view ourselves as a "profession," we can view ourselves as "professionals," by which we mean simply that our practice in the field of OD/HSD is a way of earning our living and not something we do "just for the fun of it." As a community of professionals, we also acknowledge our responsibility to other professionals and our field of practice, but without subordinating ourselves to a profession.

The question remains: What is the boundary of our field? In our view, alignment is a critical component of "the way we live our lives" and a fundamental mark of OD/HSD practice. The boundary of our field is a question of how far "our lives" extend—and in this definition lies the web or network of relationships and considerations that we include when considering what is ethical in the field of OD/HSD.

# VALUES, ETHICS, AND OUR FIELD OF PRACTICE

"Values" and "ethics" are widely used words, but their meanings are not widely shared, although people tend to assume shared meanings. For our purposes here, "values" are "standards of importance" and "ethics" are "standards of good/bad or right/wrong behavior based on values." For example, respect, integrity, authenticity, honesty, truth, profit, shareholder value, and stakeholder value are values. These values can be expressed through such ethics as "Respect yourself and others," "Act with integrity and authenticity," "Be honest," "Be true to yourself," "Seek to maximize profit and shareholder value," and "Seek to maximize stakeholder values." [For "A statement of Values and Ethics by Professionals in Organization and Human Systems Development," see the website for this book, and for discussions of several cases involving values and ethics, see the book, *Values and Ethics in Organization and Human Systems Development: Responding to Dilemmas in Professional Life* (1990) by William Gellermann, Mark Frankel, and Robert Ladenson.]

## Values and Ethics in Organization Development

As noted earlier, OD practitioners are currently experiencing a period of confusion and ambiguity about their shared values. Concurrent with escalating uncertainty about OD values, we have entered a period marked by a growing crisis in public confidence directed at one of our largest domains of practice— publicly held corporations. As a series of ethical scandals has unfolded, a parallel concern has emerged about the role of practitioners in supporting, or at a minimum overlooking, ethical misdeeds. The role of professional organizations as mediators between the interests of the public at large and the interests of practitioners is increasingly important.

Tension over seemingly incompatible values in the field of OD is highlighted in a study by Worley and Feyerherm (2003), who interviewed twenty-one pioneering OD thought leaders regarding the past, present, and future of the field of OD. In their discussion of the field's boundaries, the authors identify two camps: the traditionalists and the pragmatists. Traditionalists support the field's traditional humanistic values, while pragmatists are concerned with integrating the strong process competencies that defined the early stages of OD with more systematic approaches to strategy and organizational design. While traditionalists worry that the pragmatic approach may sell out to power and influence in large corporations, pragmatists are concerned about the relevance of the human process approach.

While the debate in various professional organizations continues about the extent to which the field is or should be based on an established code of ethics, the day-to-day challenges of developing an ethical practice as an OD/HSD practitioner offer a rich opportunity for self-discovery and development. The current tension and ambiguity that characterize our field demand a more rigorous examination of our individual values and ethics and how they relate to our practice. In the absence of such personal clarity, we run the risk of drifting toward a form of rationalized choice based on unexamined self-interest.

Our purpose in this chapter, and its associated website, is to help you review current thinking about values and ethics in the practice of OD/HSD. We will do this by providing frameworks to help you reflect on (1) your place as a practitioner in the context of values and ethics relevant to our field and (2) the potential for expanding our field of practice.

## Ethical Challenges for Global Practitioners

Globalization as a trend impacts the process by which the values and ethics of OD/HSD professionals develop. Practitioners must understand areas in which their personal and professional values may conflict with the values of the organizations and cultures in which they are working.

For example, business ethics scholars (Robertson & Fadil, 1999) have proposed a relationship between national culture and ethical behavior. Focusing primarily on Hofstede's (1980) cultural dimension of individualism versus collectivism as a measure of cultural variation, the authors suggest that managers from individualistic cultures will reason at levels different from managers from collectivist cultures. By extension, ethical decision making may also be impacted by national culture. For example, the authors suggest that individualistic cultures may be less ethically oriented than collectivist cultures. While the evidence for the specifics of this assertion is quite limited, it poses at least two questions for practitioners. First, to what extent is your ability to reason shaped by the basic assumptions of your national culture? Equally important, to what extent do you understand how your theories of practice may need to be adjusted to be appropriate outside of the culture in which they were developed?

So we are left with the question: "To what extent are the largely humanistic traditional values that characterized the early stages of the field's development still important for today's OD practitioners?" In practice, the evolution of a profession or field of practice and ethical practice within that field are largely social constructs (Cottone, 2001). This is reflected in several ongoing initiatives designed to codify, clarify, and provide practitioners with standards for ethical practice in the field of OD. Several such initiatives are described on the book's website for this chapter.

- Discussion About Values and Ethics in OD
- OD Network Conversations About Values and Ethics
- Code of Ethics for Our Field
- Overview: An Annotated Statement of Values and Ethics by Professionals in Organization
- Human Systems Development
- Developing Our Ability to Think and Act Ethically
- Individual Factors That Influence Ethical Judgment and Practice
- Common Ethical Dilemmas

## EXPANDING OUR VIEW OF HUMAN SYSTEMS DEVELOPMENT

As noted earlier, we consider OD and HSD inseparable and, in previous sections, we focused on OD as a subsystem within the more inclusive concept of HSD. Then we gave examples of how our view of our field could expand beyond OD (and *individual* organizations) to include systems that are more inclusive than single organizations (such as Avaaz, Wiser Earth, and We, the World).

Clearly, many of the ways of thinking and practicing associated with OD can be applied to facilitating the development of more comprehensive systems, such as communities, industries, nations, networks, meta-networks (networks of networks), and mega-networks (networks of meta-networks). For example: Al Gore's meta-network (see www.wecansolveit.org), which lists about seventeen organizations/networks, encompassing more than 1,500,000 people, who share a focus on coping with the climate crisis.

Even more comprehensively, if, as suggested by Bob Tannenbaum, our field of practice encompasses *"the way we live our lives,"* then OD/HSD practice can be conceived as encompassing *all human beings on Earth* and can even be expanded to include *all life on Earth* (of which "we human beings" are a subsystem).

## Expanding Our World View

Expanding our view of what constitutes OD/HSD practice is consistent with thinking that has been emerging from a number of different sources, although they have not focused specifically on OD/HSD. In *Towards A New World View: Conversations at the Leading Edge*, Russell DeCarlo (1996) interviewed twenty-seven "seminal thinkers" about "realignment of our most basic assumptions about the way things are...about the subtler nuances of both the old world view and the one that is emerging" (p. i).

> *Marilyn Ferguson*, author of the classic *Aquarian Conspiracy*—"Right now we would be wise to focus our attention on how basic human beings behave in basic selfish ways.... Nothing short of being imaginative, creative, and compassionate is going to save us.... As I see it, either we are going to have a very rapid decline into a 'worst case' scenario, or else the dream of a new Renaissance will be made a reality. The choice is ours." (p. 13)
>
> *Richard Tarnas*, author of *The Passion of the Western Mind* (described by Joseph Campbell as "the most lucid and concise presentation of the grand lines of what every student should know about history") (p. 20)—"A change in a world view is never something that can be simply imposed from without or that takes place simply due to instruction by an external person or book. It is something that is ready to emerge, ready to be born within the individual's consciousness. (p. 23)...We...have a freedom to evolve in a certain way, to choose what kind of a world and world view we will grow within....(p. 29). We are just starting to see that within each individual human being, his or her psyche is rooted in a much larger psyche, that our consciousness participates in a collective consciousness that is shared by all human beings and is rooted in nature, the world, and the cosmos." (p. 32)

*Willis Harman*, president of the Institute for Noetic Sciences (founded in 1973 by Apollo astronaut Edgar Mitchell to expand knowledge regarding the mind and spirit and to apply that knowledge to advance health and well-being for humankind and the planet) (p. 38)—"What is really at issue is a total world view and the beliefs we hold at unconscious levels. Every one of us resists the change of our own internalized assumptions. We're being called to answer the deeper questions, like 'What is the nature of reality?' (p. 40)… I think we really have two fundamental problems. One is ecological sustainability. And the other involves the coherence of our society (p. 44)…. The combination of those two is going to require a total redefinition of society and the social contract…. Our main task [is] discovering… our own oneness with the Oneness." (p. 44)

Two years later (1998), in his book *Global Mind Change*, Harman gave a comprehensive overview of the challenges we face and what we need to do to respond to them. In his introduction, Harman says, "A change is taking place at the most fundamental level of the belief structure of Western industrial society…. However we view it, the present-day world situation is hazardous for civilization. The passengers on planet Earth have a rough passage ahead. Our ability to travel that passage together without a wreck depends on keeping levels of understanding high and anxiety low. Whatever conclusions one reaches participating in this dialogue will increase the needed understanding."

In addition, we would add, OD and HSD professionals are uniquely prepared to help us (passengers on planet Earth) move beyond understanding to collaborative action so that our concept of "we" shifts to encompass all life on Earth, a shift that will enable us to co-create "a world that works for all." Even more fundamentally, our view of who "we" (the community of OD/HSD professionals) are has the potential for helping us transform ourselves into being truly a global community whose members are aligned in ways that will give our energy coherence of the kind that gives light beams the ability to cut through steel.

# SUMMARY

In conclusion, we would like to repeat, for emphasis, that we place higher value on a *process for developing* shared values, ethics, and standards of competence with which practitioners can freely align themselves than on a *process for enforcing compliance* with standards. It is clear to us that our preferred process is much more likely to inform practitioners' actual practice. Our hope is that this chapter will be a contribution to that process.

# References

Cottone, R. (2001). A social constructivism model of ethical decision making in counseling. *Journal of Counseling and Development, 79,* 39–45.

DeCarlo, R.E. (1996). *Towards a new world view: Conversations at the leading edge.* Epic, PA: Epic Publishing.

Gellermann, W., Frankel, M.S., & Ladenson, R.F. (1990). *Values and ethics in organization and human systems development: Responding to dilemmas in professional life.* San Francisco: Jossey-Bass.

Harman, W.W. (1998). *Global mind change: The promise of the 21st century.* San Francisco: Berrett-Koehler.

Hofstede, G. (1980). *Cultures consequences: International differences in work-related values.* Thousand Oaks, CA: Sage.

Robertson, C., & Fadil, P. (1999). Ethical decision making in multinational organizations: A culture-based model. *Journal of Business Ethics, 19*(4), 385–392.

Worley, C., & Feyerherm, A. (2003). Reflections on the future of organization development. *Journal of Applied Behavioral Science, 39,* 97–115.

CHAPTER TWENTY-EIGHT

# Technologies to Support Interactive and Connective OD in a Virtual World

Richard G. Bush and S. Alan McCord

Inclusion of information technology (IT) in the literature and teaching of organization development (OD) is a recent development, and often fails to articulate how OD can benefit from the use of IT in practice (Yaeger & Sorensen, 2006). IT, however, is important to the study and practice of OD as it contributes to the overall performance of organizations and also can support a range of OD initiatives including management development, on-demand learning, and data analysis (Church, Gilbert, Oliver, Paquet, & Surface, 2002).

Recent developments in consumer electronics, wireless communications, and Web 2.0 technologies—the creative application of web technologies to support group collaboration—have changed the organization by making it more virtualized and personalized. These collaborative technologies call into question some traditional assumptions about how OD is carried out within organizations.

OD depends on the creativity, problem-solving ability, and social competencies of members of the organization. Technologies that facilitate collaboration, manage change, accelerate learning, improve project management, and capture organizational knowledge are requisites for success in our global economy. Whereas businesses in the past could dictate how technology would be used to transact business, today's customers and partners exercise their power over communication and collaboration methods.

This chapter discusses some of the roles played by IT in the context of OD practice. We discuss how organizations use communication and collaboration technologies and how OD practitioners can use these technologies to improve the quality of their interventions. We close with speculation about the future impact of technology on organizations and on the practice of OD.

# THE SOCIO-TECHNOLOGICAL PERSPECTIVE

Technology cannot exist in isolation within an organization. Technology alone cannot create value, and people do not benefit from technology without thoughtful implementation and planning for organizational change. Technology must therefore be viewed from a socio-technological perspective. This perspective was articulated by Leavitt (1965) and has developed into a dominant view of how people interact with technologies in organizations. Technologies—hardware, software, and networks—require substantial social, intellectual, and organizational energy to realize their full value.

In the socio-technological perspective, the technical subsystem focuses on the technological, physical, and formal capabilities of technology (Chen & Nath, 2008). From this viewpoint, technologists are concerned with issues such as efficient computation, data storage, access, network infrastructure, data flow, security, and reliability.

In contrast, the social subsystem focuses on how organizations develop and implement technology to impact individual behavior and organizational performance (Chen & Nath, 2008). From this viewpoint, change agents are concerned with how individuals and organizations perceive and use information and how organizations derive true benefits from their technology investments.

Considering both the technical and social perspectives broadens our view of technology from a focus on systems development to include behavioral issues that surround the development and use of technology (Alban & Scherer, 2005). Adopting a socio-technological view ensures a more holistic approach to managing technology, resulting in a better fit between technology and organizational goals.

## Impact of Technological Trends on Organizations

The Internet, only available to the general public since 1995, has dramatically changed how organizations communicate and collaborate by providing new communication channels, driving down costs, and bringing global communication to each employee's desktop.

Until the late 1990s, economists struggled to demonstrate that technology investments improved economic performance: the so-called "IT productivity paradox" (Brynjolfsson, 1993). More recent analyses show that IT has contributed significantly to increased productivity and economic growth, and in some sectors is the primary driver of growth (Hagemann, 2008).

New organizational and personal capabilities to use technologies wisely provide significant opportunities to create competitive advantage. The old adage that "people are our most valuable resource" requires modification to accommodate today's realities of mass outsourcing, partnering, global operations, and mergers and acquisitions. Technology provides the framework needed to thrive in today's global economy. While people are valuable, communication and collaboration technologies provide the "reach" necessary to succeed globally. Talented and skilled people are certainly "sufficient" requirements for success, but appropriately applied technology has become "necessary" for success.

Some of the major organizational capabilities enabled by today's communication and collaboration technologies include:

1. Connecting with talent across the globe through virtual workplaces, communication, knowledge management, and collaboration;

2. Improving automation and efficiency through business process reengineering and knowledge management; and

3. Creating innovation and intellectual property through new global partnerships.

Enterprise technology initiatives are complex undertakings as they often integrate disparate processes, connect people who have historically worked in isolation, and require changes to management mindsets (McDonagh & Coghlan, 2006; Scherpereel & Lefebvre, 2006). While the benefits of enterprise technologies are compelling, many enterprise technology initiatives still focus largely on technical and financial aspects at the expense of organizational performance, thereby ignoring the socio-technical perspective (Kontoghiorghes, 2005). Such technology initiatives are primarily concerned with technologies, timelines, deliverables, and budgets and less so with organizational change. This is an important dilemma to keep in mind when working as an OD practitioner in technology-enabled organizations or when using technology tools to support OD initiatives.

The neglected socio-technological perspective represents a significant opportunity for OD practitioners: applying OD principles to improve the success rate of strategic technology initiatives, which may in turn improve organizational capabilities. OD issues to be considered when implementing enterprise technology initiatives include gap analysis, organizational change planning, coaching, and benefit tracking (Thach & Woodman, 1994).

## The Virtual Workplace

Workplaces are increasingly virtual, driven by the need to collaborate to create innovation and competitive advantage. Prior to 1995, most enterprise technology applications, including basic services such as email, used client-server technology that required specialized software to be loaded on users' computers.

The general availability of the Internet, followed by the explosion of personal communication technologies, has resulted in employees who are Web-based and inherently virtual, even when working inside office buildings, in hotel environments with other workers (Church, Gilbert, Oliver, Paquet, & Surface, 2002), or at remote customer or partner locations.

Today's virtual employees are accustomed to accessing data as they move from place to place, and organizations attempt to provide a technology infrastructure that supports pervasive and mobile computing while ensuring the integrity and security of enterprise data. Because of their skills in using web-based services, knowledge workers also expect to be able to personalize their technology environment, which runs counter to the traditional "one size fits all" model of providing enterprise technologies.

McCord and Boone (2008) classify today's virtual work technologies into three broad categories:

1. Communication tools—telephony, email, personal productivity tools, enterprise file systems, informational websites, and corporate intranets;

2. Conferencing tools—tools to promote real-time meetings, including audio, video, and web conferencing; and

3. Collaboration tools—tools to support true virtual work environments, including document management, project management, and knowledge management tools to help collect, assemble, and publish enterprise knowledge.

Most enterprise technology solutions are no longer implemented as unique systems developed by in-house technologists. Most organizations acquire and implement commercial software such as enterprise resource planning systems, which provide common basic business services. Many enterprises use open source software in their data centers for operating systems, databases, and web services (Schindler, 2008). These enterprises may collaborate with their partners or their competitors to share in the development of open source tools. Furthermore, business units sometimes implement open source software in addition to standard enterprise technologies. Some enterprises supplement or even replace their traditional systems with web services, which operate outside the traditional enterprise data center. The nature of enterprise technology services, from both technological and social perspectives, is an important consideration for OD practitioners when assessing organizational competencies, practices, and needs.

## The Human Side of Technology and OD

Communication and collaboration technologies can enhance an organization's competitiveness if they align with the organization's strategic objectives to improve efficiency and effectiveness (Lucas, 2005). The return on technology investments is directly related to how seamlessly technology is incorporated into the lives of employees and customers (DiVanna, 2003).

As technologies are introduced to drive change, Sarmento (2003) suggests that we ask two important diagnostic questions:

- What are the current levels of technology literacy and systems knowledge?
- How much training do employees need to acquire to use the new technologies and implement the proposed changes?

As we can see, the linkage between strategy and performance depends on organizational and personal change, and OD practitioners can help make these changes happen. Later in this chapter we address how OD practitioners can use communication and collaboration tools to support their change efforts.

The implications of the virtual workplace for OD practitioners conflict with some assumptions of traditional OD practice, such as working face-to-face with clients or even having the opportunity to meet clients. How can OD be practiced in environments that focus more on business than on human processes? How can OD be practiced effectively in environments in which clients are anonymous? One technology that holds promise for future OD practitioners is social networking, which can reduce anonymity and enrich interpersonal relationships, even across distance, language, and cultural boundaries.

# COMMUNICATIONS AND COLLABORATION IN THE NETWORKED ORGANIZATION

Technology facilitates communications and collaboration between organizations, clients, and suppliers to reduce the amount of time needed to develop and produce products and services (DiVanna, 2003). Today's networked organizations extend traditional organizational boundaries by leveraging communication and collaborative technologies to broaden and speed the transfer of information and knowledge (Pearlson & Saunders, 2006; Willis, 2002). Several ways in which organizations leverage technology are discussed in this section.

## Managing Global Teams

In virtual and networked organizations, individuals are geographically separated and often isolated from direct supervision (Pearlson & Saunders, 2006). Technologies to proactively communicate with members include email, video or web conferencing, employee monitoring software, document management systems, and social networking software.

Managers of virtual teams must demonstrate proactive leadership, good project management skills, open and frequent communication, and personal attention to team members (McCord & Boone, 2008). Managers of virtual teams need to focus on building clarity, setting clear objectives and responsibilities, facilitating professional virtual discourse, and interpreting virtual work in context of enterprise objectives. OD practitioners can collaborate with managers to improve their virtual management skills.

## Communities of Practice

While managing on-site and virtual teams is a key skill for succeeding in our global business climate, people are increasingly organizing into self-governing "communities of practice" to share knowledge within and outside organizational boundaries.

Traditional communities of practice and other approaches such as change agent networks (Vales, 2007) can be virtualized through use of communication and collaboration technologies. These communities leverage technologies provided through enterprise or professional association web portals, chat rooms, and personal networking sites to share knowledge and solve problems (Pearlson & Saunders, 2006). OD practitioners can use these tools to extend their own networks and implement change initiatives.

## Knowledge Management

There is greater need for knowledge management in organizations competing in complex global markets. Knowledge management helps organizations understand their capabilities, products, and services to maximize development of collateral knowledge, products, and services. Knowledge management tools provide the ability to locate, analyze, ingest, annotate, store, and retrieve knowledge. Without the appropriate technologies, knowledge management in large virtual organizations is simply not possible.

Knowledge is only useful to a community when it circulates through a community and attracts the attention of community members (McDermott, 1999). Knowledge management, therefore, is directly related to the success of communities of practice. In addition to knowledge management tools, communication technologies such as instant messaging can be important components of knowledge management programs (Zhang & Fjermestad, 2008).

Team activity and learning orientation, two outcomes of successful OD initiatives, contribute to the development of knowledge management capabilities (Yu, Kim, & Kim, 2007). Organizations choosing to develop knowledge management capabilities must provide higher levels of "IT diffusion" represented by pervasive communication and collaboration services focused on gathering and disseminating knowledge (Lin, 2007; Lucas & Ogilvie, 2005). OD practitioners can contribute to the development of these capabilities by focusing on the social aspects of the technologies.

What implications do these new communication and collaboration tools hold for OD practitioners? First, they represent a different way of working that enterprises need to survive in the 21st Century. Second, employees already use these systems, learning from them and changing their work habits. It is not unusual for employees to work on significant projects without meeting the manager or members of the project team. Third, the flattening of today's organizations means that work is becoming "disintermediated," with fewer layers of management between employees and their work. (Communication and collaboration technologies are replacing middle managers and project managers in many enterprises.) OD practitioners can learn to evolve their intervention practices to bring them more in line with today's technologically enhanced and disintermediated workplace.

# TECHNOLOGIES SUPPORTING OD

In addition to supporting workplace communication and collaboration, technology can also be used to support inquiry. Wyssusek and Schwartz (2003) suggest that our use of technologies has little or no effect on our perceived reality, but can enable us to communicate, collaborate, analyze data, and gain a better view of the larger picture.

Which technologies can help OD practitioners be more successful in implementing change in today's virtual workplace? This section provides an overview of several technologies available in the workplace or to practitioners in the field.

As we explore these technologies, it is important to keep the socio-technological perspective in mind. Simply because we have the capability to deploy a technology to address a problem does not mean that we should do so. Does the technology solve a real problem or is it simply in search of a problem? Can we identify real benefits from using a technology, and can we develop metrics to understand its real benefits? Do we have the organizational and personal skills to effectively use the technology? Is the technology mature, or should we assume the risks and potential benefits associated with using emerging technologies?

## Enterprise Applications

There are a number of enterprise-level technologies that can support OD initiatives. These systems fall into two general classes: communication and collaboration technologies and human resources technologies. We have already discussed communication and collaboration technologies. Examples of enterprise human resources technologies include enterprise human resource management systems, competency management and certification systems, succession planning systems, recruitment and placement systems, employee intranets, and systems to manage employee assistance programs.

We recommend that OD practitioners work with their clients to develop an inventory of existing enterprise applications to determine which of these systems can be queried or leveraged to support OD initiatives. Understanding an organization's enterprise technologies also helps the OD practitioner understand the overall technology capabilities of the enterprise and its employees.

## Project Management and Team Management Software

Project management software is used to identify tasks, schedule resources, establish timelines, and manage work in progress (Gordon & Tarafdar, 2007). Most organizations make significant use of project management software to manage both on-site and virtual projects, and many employees expect that project management software will be used to help manage complex initiatives. We recommend that OD practitioners become skilled in using project management software to help manage their change interventions.

Most enterprises have selected a commercial project management suite such as Teamcenter, Primavera, or Microsoft Project to manage their projects. Several Web 2.0 project management applications are available that increase communication and collaboration by utilizing the Internet to identify tasks, allocate resources and times, manage tasks, and communicate progress.

OD practitioners can often make use of enterprise project management tools during engagements, and may also wish to use personal copies of commercial or web-based tools to help manage change interventions.

## Productivity and Collaboration Software

The promise of Web 2.0 is not that it is a new technology, but that it improves how existing web technologies are used to leverage the network effects of people and of data. This is in contrast to the Web 1.0 technologies whereby people interacted directly with static websites to display content and conduct transactions.

A number of technologies are used by enterprises to support group collaboration and communication. These include enterprise solutions such as SharePoint, Teamcenter, and WebEx, as well as group and individual tools such as Groove, Google Docs, Microsoft Office Live, and Yahoo! Groups. Other Web 2.0 tools include social networking tools such as MySpace and Ning, social bookmarking tools such as Delicious and Digg, community media tools such as YouTube and Flickr, and professional networking sites such as LinkedIn. OD practitioners, once they are familiar with the capabilities of these tools, will be able to maintain their contact information, manage projects from virtually anywhere, share ideas, and seek answers to questions from a larger community.

What does this mean for OD practitioners? First, practitioners should strive to understand the technology environment provided in the organization within which they will practice, as the technologies in use affect how employees work. Second, OD practitioners should consider using the same enterprise systems, project management systems, and collaboration software deployed for employee use. Using the tools with which employees are familiar reduces the time needed for employees to participate in the intervention. Of course, this means that OD practitioners need to change the tools they use depending on the client's technology environment. Adapting to the technology climate of the clients helps embed the practitioner within the environment and may help legitimize their efforts.

# FURTHERING THE PRACTICE OF OD

Communication and collaboration are critical to the success of change, and to the ability of OD practitioners to help "tell the story." To accomplish this, the OD practitioner should select an appropriate tool kit of technologies and learn to use these tools as part of his or her practice. Moreover, the technologies in the tool kit must be easy and comfortable to use. Several tools may be needed to adequately communicate with clients and colleagues. Personal productivity software such as Outlook, Goldmine, ACT, and others can help practitioners maintain appointments, tasks, email, and project documents. Another way to communicate a complex idea is through concept maps, graphics, and charts. These visual communication methods help clarify concepts and simplify the complexity of change initiatives. In addition, online tools that enhance practitioners' communications and productivity help them stay connected via the Internet. This section will briefly discuss tools for personal productivity, visual and concept mapping, and survey tools.

## Personal Productivity Tools

OD practitioners need never miss another important communication when away from the office. Personal productivity software can consolidate and organize emails and faxes, call contacts via your cell phone or over the Internet, synchronize important contact data with smart phones and personal digital assistants, and link to community portals and websites that reflect shared interests and needs. Tools such as Outlook, FrontRange GoldMine, ACT, eFax, Google Calendar, Google Mail, Plaxo, LinkedIn, and TimeBridge can improve OD practitioners' productivity.

Communication is a key factor in the overall success of change initiatives, and staying connected is an essential capability for OD practitioners. The benefits of using these tools include:

- Integration—using one application for email, faxes, contacts, and calendaring;
- Synchronization—information can be shared and synchronized between a computer, a website, a cell phone, or other devices;

- User interface—a common user interface is emerging across many productivity products available, making them easier to learn and use;

- Online meetings—services and web tools help practitioners connect with colleagues and clients without traveling; and

- Preparation—searching and reviewing previous communications aids in preparing for the next encounter with clients.

These are only a few of the benefits of integrating personal productivity tools into the OD practitioner's tool kit. These tools will help keep the OD practitioner connected and communicating throughout the change process.

## Visual and Concept Mapping Tools

Visual and concept mapping tools enable OD practitioners to quickly communicate change plans to clients. Tools such as Mindjet's MindManager, Microsoft Visio, Draw Anywhere, Flowchart, and Google SketchUp can be used to communicate graphically the concepts and activities of an intervention.

Visual and concept mapping tools can support OD interventions that use Six Sigma, business process improvement, and other process-related methodologies (Ahmad, Francis, & Zairi, 2007; Jeffery, 2005). These tools allow the practitioner to communicate across cultural and languages boundaries with less reliance on written or verbal communications. Graphic tools allow clients to quickly grasp large issues, identify patterns, and understand dependencies. These tools are by nature more inclusive than written communication and may increase communication and collaboration between clients.

## Survey Tools

OD practitioners often need to collect data quickly from large groups. Online or web-based survey applications are convenient and powerful tools to help OD practitioners design and collect data, making it easy for most anyone to do a survey. Survey tools such as Survey Monkey, Zoomerang, SurveyGizmo, and ZAPSurvey allow practitioners to send invitations via an email list, send follow-up invitations, track participation, analyze results, and prepare graphics. Many of these tools allow personalization or branding.

The benefits of using online or web-based survey tools include:

- Simplicity—Most survey administration is automated, making invitation, follow-up, and tracking easy to manage. These tools provide a consistent "look and feel" for participants (Dillman, Smyth, & Christian, 2009; Lippert, 2003; Mann & Stewart, 2000).

- Scalability—Survey tools support gathering responses from large or small populations (Dillman, Smyth, & Christian, 2009).

- Response rates—While useful, online surveys tend to have lower response rates than traditional paper-based surveys deployed in traditional environments. Online surveys may yield a 20 percent or better response rate (Dillman, Smyth, & Christian, 2009). Past research comparing paper and pencil and electronic surveys range from 6 to 70 percent better response with online surveys (Lippert, 2003).
- Rapid data capture—Most survey responses will occur within the first forty-eight hours following invitation (Lippert, 2003).
- Flexible design—Survey tools address survey complexity, ease of use, attractiveness, and overall cost (Lippert, 2003).

Of course, web-based survey tools will not guarantee that you will devise a good survey. Dillman, Smyth, and Christian (2009) suggest a tailored survey design that links closely with the elements of social exchange required to produce higher quality surveys and achieve higher response rates. OD practitioners should develop a sound understanding of good survey design practices, rather than simply begin using online survey tools as a "gimmick."

As you can see, there is a wide range of technology tools available to the OD practitioner. These tools can increase efficiency and effectiveness, improve communication, and extend the reach of the practitioner within the enterprise. Many of these tools are free or available at low cost due to the vast economies of scale available to global technology vendors. We encourage you to experiment with these tools, evaluate them individually and collaboratively with your peers, and use whatever set of tools you believe will help your practice.

Legacy productivity tools such as word processing, spreadsheet, and presentation software have been in use for many years and still maintain some of the look and feel of their ancestors. Today's Web 2.0 tools behave in very different ways, change their feature sets frequently, and evolve quickly into new product offerings. OD practitioners should be prepared to experiment with and use many different emerging technology tools, learning from each to expand their skills and constantly add more tools to their tool kits.

# SUMMARY

We have reviewed several overarching trends driving the nature of the future workplace. These trends have significant impact on the traditional practice of OD within organizations. OD practitioners must be prepared to design interventions appropriate to virtual workplaces. We have also laid out a range of technologies used by today's enterprises, and we recommend that OD practitioners familiarize themselves with the technologies used by their clients before designing change interventions. Finally, we have introduced a range of software that OD practitioners can use to enhance their productivity and skills.

any one learning journey. These concern *what kind of* community you want to build, *when*, and for *what* purpose.

For instance, a journey can have specific aims: to signal a new direction; educate leaders on some aspect of business, leadership, the environment, geopolitics, and such; raise concerns or celebrate progress; and so on. At that time of its first journey, Unilever Foods Asia was just being formed and a new management board and leadership cadre were coming together for the first time. Key aims of its initial journeys were to build ownership for strategy development and create cohesion in the group by experiencing a new culture taking shape in China. The trip to India, in turn, helped to establish a fresh, new direction and sense of purpose. "Why did we come to India?" Tex noted, "To figure out how to move to be a mission-driven company."

## Locales and Theme

In programs I helped to design for a Dutch branch of Unilever, there was a clear analogy between the locale and theme of the journey and the actual business "journey" of the firm (Mirvis, Ayas, & Roth, 2003). This work included travel to the Ardennes, to relive the Dutch spirit during World War II, to Scotland, to see how "clans" might come together rather than compete with one another, and to Petra, Jordan, to reflect on how an ancient trading center went to ruin by failing to adapt to its marketplace (when the Silk Road was replaced by sea travel in the 1400s).

In other cases, a trip to Brazil emphasized access to health and included hands-on community service in myriad health centers in a major city, meetings with health officials in Brasilia, and time with indigenous tribes to look at natural medicine and issues of sustainability. In turn, a trip to Dubai for private equity specialists took us from traditional markets to the modern stock exchange, across twenty business ventures ranging from the national airline to the Palm real estate island, and into deep conversation with civic activists about the state of the natural environment and status of women in this fast-growing commercial center wrapped in a traditional, royal culture.

## Places and People

Ideally, a journey takes place in nature and/or at a locale that has historical, cultural, or spiritual significance. In addition, it should ideally be at a place where the bulk of participants have never been. Key reasons are to ensure elements of surprise and awe—and also make it a gift to participants. It is important, too, that participants move physically from place to place—by hiking, via car, train, and/or boat, or, for an added experience, by riding a horse, camel, donkey, or mule.

It also helps to expose business leaders to children, older people, everyday workers or caregivers, or to indigenous peoples. This all helps to reconnect people to what is universal about humanity. It is helpful, too, to experience communities first-hand. The intent is to open minds and eyes to social conditions around the globe and to encourage them to reflect individually and collectively on what they found and what implications this might have for themselves and the business.

Before the experience, it is important that you brief people on what they are about to experience and what you want them to focus on during the experience. Afterward, you ask people to reflect individually and collectively on what they found and what implications this might have for themselves and for the business.

# THE LEARNING EXPERIENCE

Journeys run the risk of seeming to be like corporate tourism. Thus, it is important to emphasize learning within and from the experience. My preferences are for "action" learning—whereby people first participate in an experience and then reflect on its meaning and implications. This means there is not much in the way of explanation or theorizing before we embark on an activity, and lots of individual and collecting reflecting afterward.

Managers typically have little time to reflect on experience individually, let alone collectively. One of the key elements of a journey is to build in time for people to reflect individually and collectively on who they are, where they want to go, and how they may get there. There are various tools to stimulate reflection, including journaling, preparing a lifeline, writing a letter to parents, talking about heroes, and so forth. It is important to give people the right space (time and place) to reflect deeply.

Finally, it is important to recall Weick's (1995) commentary that experiences are not what happens to us, but what we do with what happens to us. This reminds us that the experiences themselves do not engage participants, stretch them, or instruct them. The onus of transforming activities into mind-expanding, heart-rending, and soul-stirring encounters is on the participants. They do the work and learning of asking provocative questions, challenging assumptions, surfacing contradictions, and confronting themselves and one another.

On this count, I've helped groups to use the principles of dialogue whereby they speak to the "group as a whole" and build on others' comments to develop collective thinking. Sitting in a circle is used to signify that there is no individual leader in charge of the conversation but rather a collective body at work (Mirvis & Ayas, 2003). This timeless format is often used in corporate "town meetings," leaderless group sessions, and peer conversations so that difficult issues can be addressed without anyone pulling rank or cutting off conversation.

## Activities/Sequencing

Many activities can fill the days of a journey (see Table 29.1).

Table 29.1. Journey Design Template

|  | *Day One* | *Day Two* | *Day Three* | *Day Four* |
|---|---|---|---|---|
| Theme | Reconnect with self | Reconnect with others | Work together | Celebrate together |
| Addresses... | Self-insight | Empathy for others | Difficult issues | Renew purpose |
| Before Breakfast | Arrival or assembly | Meditation, Yoga, martial arts, dance, or exercise | Meditation, Yoga, martial arts, dance, or exercise | Free |
| Morning | Movement to site to connect with humanity: young people, locals, tribes, infirm or dis-advantaged | Travelling: get people out of comfort zone, connected to each other. Strips away coat of attitudes | Start work-ing together in groups of twelve to fifteen by addressing issues | Work together in subgroups on issue from different perspective. Share whole community |
| Afternoon | Exercise: Peo-ple look into their selves, origins, values, beliefs, aspira-tions: lifeline, letter to par-ents, etc. | Experiences keyed to purpose: On leadership, sustainability, community— whatever the intent of the journey | Bring together discussions from sub-groups through dialogue | Closing. Travel to place of celebra-tion. Allow people time to freshen up, prepare for celebration/ feast. |
| Evening | Dialogue: Con-front people on whether they want to be part of the journey, leadership is a choice | Dialogue: Confront key question to be addressed at the outbreak. How can journey experiences shape thinking? | Action com-mitments. Celebrate with hosts | Celebration |

Here are some simple elements that are worth remembering in their selection and placement:

- *Multi-level.* Activities on a learning journey are aimed variously at individual, group, and collective levels. Typically, the starting point is to have an individual experience or inquiry, then move into a group, then to the community as a whole. But throughout a day, this cycle repeats itself over and over. Sometimes the sequence starts with the whole community and closes with individual reflection. Key considerations for sequences concern the nature of the activity, its purpose (individual or shared learning), the need for quiet time, air time, a diversity of voices, and so on. There is not a lot of science to this. Sense and feel the moment. Is it time for individuals to reflect or for the community to challenge a subject or affirm a direction?

- *Multi-sensory.* Remember childhood exercises about using your senses—eyes, ears, nose, taste, and touch? Ideally, all these senses are engaged in a learning journey. It helps, too, to use multiple media and modes of learning—high tech/primitive, talk/quiet, day/night, and so forth. The mix awakens and engages more of the self. It also ensures that people who respond best to action get their time and that those who revel in silence get their time, too. Also, don't forget the sixth sense! Create space for new ideas and insights to emerge and come forth in a group or community.

- *Head/heart/body/soul.* A variant of this is to have activities that appeal, variously, to the head, heart, body, and soul. Hence, there are physical activities, the soul-searching questions, and reflection time. With reference to change management, this aims to affect both the "mindsets" and "heartsets" of people.

- *Role modeling.* Finally, pay attention to who is leading the gathering. As journey facilitators, my colleagues and I are seldom up on stage leading anything. That's the business leader's job. Make sure your consultants are "back stage," too. Furthermore, we insist that senior leaders participate in every activity, ideally first, to demonstrate their willingness to take a risk, do something "weird," or open themselves up. Tex Gunning, for instance, presented his personal story—warts and all—during a journey prior to asking his people to share their own stories. The broader point is that it is important that senior leaders participate actively and demonstrate their commitment to the aims and activities of a journey. Their role is to model leadership principles and speak candidly about their own journeys, values, trials, and aspirations.

# SUMMARY

There was no attempt in these cases to document systematically the impact of these multi-level consciousness-raising experiences on individual executive behavior in the short term, let alone the longer-term implications. Fortunately, there is theory and evidence that show how gains in self-awareness and EQ contribute to a capacity for transformational leadership (c.f., Huy, 1999) and, at least in the Unilever case, how a series of journeys reshaped several leaders' life journeys and the directions and achievements of the business (Mirvis & Gunning, 2006). Said one leader, reflecting on the impact of the journeys: "With the kind of community and mission-driven approach that we have in Unilever, it is possible for us to make a difference to our society and still be in business. And it is important for us to be in business because that is the only way we will continue to make a difference to society."

Interestingly, the idea of learning journeys is taking hold in and across companies for a variety of purposes. For instance, Peter Senge, Joe Jaworski, and Adam Kahane, through the Society for Organization Learning, have used them in their leadership development programs and in multi-company forums in which the aim is to raise consciousness about environmental sustainability (Senge, Smith, Kruschwitz, Laur, & Schley, 2008). Karen Ayas and a variety of consultants and trainers, having participated in the Unilever programs, have incorporated journey elements into the development programs of their clients. My studies have concerned how service learning experiences—ranging from one-month overseas assignments for managers at IBM to week-long engagements by business school students—also serve the purpose of personal and organizational transformation. Early evidence suggests that these experiences, too, can awaken people's spirits to new possibilities for themselves and their organizations.

# References

Bolman, L.G., & Deal, T.E. (1995). *Leading with soul: An uncommon journey of spirit.* San Francisco: Jossey-Bass.

Boyatzis, R., & McKee, A. (2005). *Resonant leadership.* Boston: Harvard Business School Press.

Earley, P.C., & Peterson, R.S. (2004). The elusive cultural chameleon: Cultural intelligence as a new approach to intercultural training for the global manager. *Academy of Management Learning & Education, 3*(1), 100–115.

Frost, P. (2003). *Toxic emotions at work: How compassionate managers handle pain and conflict.* Boston: Harvard Business School Press.

Goleman, D., Boyatzis, R., & McKee, A. (2002). *Primal leadership*. Boston: Harvard Business School Press.

Huy, Q. (1999). Emotional capability, emotional intelligence and radical change. *Academy of Management Review, 24*, 325.

Kolenko, T.A., Porter, G., Wheatley, W., & Colby, M. (1996). A critique of service-learning projects in management education: Pedagogical foundations, barriers, and guidelines. *Journal of Business Ethics, 15*, 133–142.

Mirvis, P.H. (1997). "Soul Work" in organizations. *Organization Science, 8*(2), 193–206.

Mirvis, P.H. (2002). Community building in business. *Reflections 3*, 45–51.

Mirvis, P.H. (2008). Executive development through consciousness raising experiences. *Academy of Management Learning & Education. 7*(2), 173–188.

Mirvis, P.H., & Ayas, K. (2003). Reflective dialogue, life stories, and leadership development. *Reflections, 4*, 39–48.

Mirvis, P.H., Ayas, K., & Roth, G. (2003). *To the desert and back: The story of one of the most dramatic business transformations on record*. San Francisco: Jossey-Bass.

Mirvis, P.H., & Gunning, W.L. (2006). Creating a community of leaders. *Organizational Dynamics, 35*(1), 69–82.

Quinn, R.E. (1996). *Deep change: Discovering the leader within*. San Francisco: Jossey-Bass.

Schön, D. (1983*). The reflective practitioner*. New York: Basic Books.

Senge, P.M., Smith, B., Kruschwitz, N., Laur, J., & Schley, S. (2008). *The necessary revolution: How individuals and organizations are working together to create a sustainable world*. New York: Random House.

Tichy, N.M., Brimm, M.I., Charan, R., & Takeuchi, H. (1992). Leadership development as a lever for global transformation. In V. Pucik, N.M. Tichy, & C.K. Barnett (Eds.), *Globalizing management*. Hoboken, NJ: John Wiley & Sons.

Waddock, S. (2002). *Leading corporate citizens: Visions, values, and value added*. New York: McGraw-Hill.

Weick, K.E. (1995). *Sensemaking in organizations*. Thousand Oaks, CA: Sage.

Wuthnow, R. (1991). *Acts of compassion: Caring for others and helping ourselves*. Princeton, NJ: Princeton University Press.

# CHAPTER THIRTY

# The Personhood of the OD Practitioner*

### Saul Eisen

In this chapter I will share a perspective about the use of self as an instrument of OD practice. It is based on my belief that, to do our work well, we must not only be knowledgeable and skilled professionals, but also self-aware as human beings. The material in this chapter encourages you to observe your strengths and limitations, consider the emotions and biases that you may sometimes hide from yourself, and learn from noticing the feelings that arise as you work.

As many of us were, you were probably drawn to the practice of OD because you care about people and want to contribute what you can. You realize that you may not be able to change the world, but you wanted to find a profession through which you might do some good. You sense that our lives are entwined with other people's lives, with the organizations in which we work, and with the larger society around us. You probably recognize that improvement for individuals requires improving the systems of which they are part, that persons and organizations can grow, and that you can facilitate such growth. You are motivated by the sincere desire to help others.

Sometimes, though, the work may not go as expected. In the heat of an interaction, you might feel a growing frustration, even annoyance, and you

---

*This chapter is based on the work of Bob Tannenbaum, my friend and mentor, and one of the originators of the field of OD. It is abridged and updated from a chapter with a similar title, published in the second edition of this book, and largely written by him.

may become reactive in ways you later recognize as inappropriate. Your work in these situations may not be as effective as you intended, and you may even lose some colleagues, employees, or clients.

These experiences are common, in the sense that they often occur as part of difficult and important work. The key is to recognize them as clues—as valuable data about what may be an opportunity for growth, for yourself as an OD practitioner. This may also provide crucial perspective on the intrinsic issues and covert dynamics of your client organization. But if you are not open to this possible gift—and the work it requires of you—the opportunity for insightful understanding and effective intervention may be lost.

# THE SELF AS AN INSTRUMENT IN CHANGE

Most OD practitioners focus much of their learning efforts on expanding their conceptual knowledge and technical expertise. Doing so is certainly essential, and there is so much to become aware of, to learn, and to integrate. As you have learned in this book, there is an ever-growing body of strategies and intervention methods of which one must become aware. What is frequently under-emphasized in the profession (although it is often given lip service) is the personhood of the practitioner as a key variable in achieving professional effectiveness in practice.

Head-level learning is not enough. As an OD practitioner, you become the implementer of all of your learning as you try to facilitate desired change within a client system. The phrases "use of self" and "self as instrument," long used in some change professions, reflect the importance of the *being* of the practitioner in achieving effectiveness in the change process. As you interact with each client system, you must engage your awareness of self as well as all your integrated knowledge relevant to your task. Both are critical to your effectiveness in practice. If you primarily bring with you cognitive knowledge, or primarily your sense of self, you will be limited as a practitioner. You will be imbalanced and not whole. This balance has clear relevance to your professional role, but it also has relevance to your very being.

Emerging from this full and balanced use of cognitive and feeling functions, there are three elements that must interact appropriately in your consulting process: awareness, perception, and behavior (see Figure 30.1). To select the most appropriate change intervention, you must have the capacity to perceive accurately and fully what is going on in the client's world. And your ability to perceive and understand your client's behavior and experience is partly based on your access to your inner awareness and experience, including your feelings.

Conversely, when your inner world is blocked or unavailable to you, or when aspects of your inner self are at odds with each other (especially if this struggle is out of awareness), it becomes much more difficult to perceive interaction

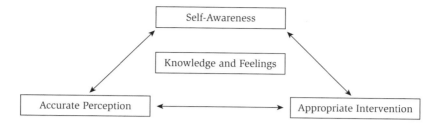

**Figure 30.1.** A Model of Self-As-Instrument

events accurately, and your intervention choices become more limited, inappropriate, or ineffective. You are then forced to rely on formulaic approaches, concepts, and techniques. At best, you are a good technician, with little responsiveness to the complex unfolding interpersonal, group, and organization dynamics in the client situation.

Having worked for many years as an educator and mentor to new OD practitioners, I have also collaborated with other practitioners on large projects that required a team of consultants. Over time, I have become aware of a number of personal and often unresolved problems that can haunt practitioners. No consultant is confronted by all of these issues, but all have struggled with at least some. Most of them are related to their awareness of feelings—their own and others'—and their attitudes about their relevance to the work at hand.

# FEELINGS: A CONTEXT

Having feelings is a basic aspect of being alive; feelings give color and dimension to our thoughts and actions. Without them, our experiencing of the world would be without flavor. But feelings can be powerful, exciting, or disturbing, and most people experience some problems with them. Starting in childhood, we develop the ability to ignore difficult feelings, and even to forget that we are ignoring them. We may be sad but are unaware of that sadness. Or even though we are aware of a feeling, we may be unable or unwilling to share our experiencing of it with others. For example, we may feel demeaned and be aware of it, but we put on a mask to hide the feeling from others. When we do, we are not of one piece; we do not experience ourselves as whole.

No person fully knows himself or herself, although individuals differ as to the extent and depth of their not knowing. OD practitioners and their clients are no exception. Consider this in the classic Johari Window (Luft, 1984). See Figure 30.2. As consultants, for example, we may be called on to give clients useful feedback—information about their behavior that may not be known to them, but it is known to their associates and us. We may similarly give feedback to a team or

| | Known to Self | Unknown to Self |
|---|---|---|
| Known to Others | Quadrant 1<br>**PUBLIC/OPEN** | Quadrant 2<br>**BLIND** |
| Unknown to Others | Quadrant 3<br>**PRIVATE/HIDDEN** | Quadrant 4<br>**BURIED/UNDISCOVERED** |

**Figure 30.2.** The Johari Window

larger unit based on information we have gathered about them and their impact on others. We may simply make information public that team members tend to exchange privately, but not in a public forum where it can be worked on. In this sense, we help clients to move relevant information from their private selves into their public selves. We similarly help them to remove blind spots about their behavior and its impact on others—either in terms of interpersonal and inter-group relationships or in terms of functional, task-related impacts. Once this kind of information enters the shared public environment, clients are empowered to do more effective problem solving or work redesign to improve their own work situations.

This describes our work with clients' Johari selves. But in order for you as an OD practitioner to help clients with this work, your own Johari selves become involved. If your clients have dysfunctional patterns of behavior, they are likely to affect you as much as others in the organization. Your decision to communicate your observations to them requires that you share material from your *private self*—not only what you observe in their interactions, but sometimes also how your client's behavior affects you. Such interventions can feel risky to you. What is more, if you don't have a clear awareness of your inner reactions, because the experience is not in your *private* but your *buried* self, then the choice is not even available to you. What you do know is that something is eating at you; you don't like it, you don't understand it, and you don't know what to do about it. This can only make you less effective as an OD practitioner and less whole as a person. It can sometimes put you at risk of reacting inappropriately to a client's behavior—creating possible harm to the client, the relationship, and yourself.

In using your self as an instrument of change, it is thus important that you recognize that the instrument has its limitations and needs periodic adjustment and calibration. Elements unknown to your self can strongly influence your view of data, decisions taken, the nature of your motivations, your actions, and more—with "the right hand not knowing what the left hand is doing." In such circumstances, you are at the mercy of your not knowing, of your being unaware.

As an OD practitioner, your *private self* is a repository for elements that you choose to hide from others. Your motivations for hiding may be many, for example, guilt, shame, embarrassment, and desire for privacy. You may hide elements that are irrelevant to the consultation. But when you hide relevant elements—particularly when you do so to protect yourself—you clearly are meeting your needs and not those of the client. Furthermore, working with clients effectively requires being aware of subtle, minimal cues; drawing inferences; and doing sensitive hunching. The less you are plagued by inner unresolved issues, the more attention you can give to the process of better understanding and working with your client. This is not a one-time clearing out process, but part of the ongoing work of being an OD practitioner—and a person.

## PERSONAL GROWTH AND PRACTITIONER EFFECTIVENESS

The experience of becoming a more aware, better-integrated human being can be an exhilarating and, fulfilling one, and it can also lead to increasing satisfaction and effectiveness in your professional work. But it can also require hard work from you, a willingness to attend to the challenges and opportunities for learning about yourself, and, occasionally, a degree of personal courage. This is a continuing task, and an important part of one's professional responsibility. In her conference presentation for the OD Network, for example, Mee-Yan Cheung-Judge stated that this work "necessitates a high degree of self-knowledge and personal development that must engage OD practitioners throughout their professional lives" (2001, p. 11).

Here are some dimensions of personal learning, and their relevance to your work as an OD practitioner:

- *The self as a laboratory for learning.* Change is a pervasive process in our lives. By paying close attention to your personal experiencing at such times, you can much better understand such change factors as readiness for change, resistance (feelings of threat, fear, anger, helplessness), boundary permeability (both to the inside and to the outside of a system), what can help a system to be open and receptive, and so forth. If you have experienced and understood it yourself, you will better understand it when you encounter it in other individuals, as well as in organizations.

- *Impact on others.* Knowing yourself reasonably well and being more whole, you will generate fewer confused reactions from others. You will perceive what is "out there" more accurately and will be able to take action more appropriately.

- *Being trustworthy.* If you are open, consistent with values, caring, not defensive, and not hurtful, others will tend to have confidence in you and trust who you are and what you say and do.

- *Understanding and accepting others.* Being able to discern, to accept, and to value individual differences and having the acuity to understand individuals in depth in spite of their masks—these and related talents stem from your clarity about yourself and your consequent ability to not be threatened by others.

- *Being positively motivated.* Persons who are emotionally torn inside must turn much of their attention inward in an attempt to deny, control, or mediate between the conflicting struggles inside. Not having this need, a relatively emotionally mature individual is typically energetic and joyous, with enthusiasm, and often with creativity and vision. This does not mean that you never have mixed feelings about certain situations; on the contrary, you understand mixed feelings as normal to human experience and are comfortable with holding such dualities while moving ahead with your work.

- *Ability to move into depth.* If I cannot accept my inadequacies, can I help others accept theirs? If I cannot express my feelings, can I help others comfortably to express theirs? If I avoid conflict, how can I coach others to facilitate conflict resolution? Your own work with these issues provides the foundation and empathy needed for guiding others, especially through difficult change and learning.

- *Loving others.* Genuinely caring for others—not through a facade or an act, but honestly with the heart—is a human quality that is often found missing in action. Many books and articles speak of the desirability of the practitioner, leader, teacher, or parent showing compassion, caring, or love to others. Carl Rogers called this *unconditional positive regard* (1961). It is not always mentioned, however, that the most important route to being able to love others is to first accept and love one's self—not to enhance one's ego, but rather as part of a process of becoming a whole human being. If this is rooted in a sense of wholeness and of self-worth, then you can naturally, genuinely, and deeply experience and express unconditional regard for others. You experience them as a part of yourself.

# THE ART OF THE OD PRACTITIONER

Acquiring relevant knowledge and skills, gaining hands-on experience, concerning yourself with professional and personal values, and involving yourself in personal learning processes are necessary for your development as a professional practitioner, but they are not sufficient. Beyond these lies an area about which we have little understanding; to a considerable extent it is shrouded in mystery. What has made possible the accomplishments of people such as Michael Jordan, Yo-Yo Ma, and Oprah Winfrey, as well as our most admired and valued colleagues in OD? In our professional field, if we try to understand what has made our "stars" into masterful professionals, we encounter more differences than similarities among them—differences in education, training, skills, personalities, areas of specialty, professional and life experiences, and more.

None of these professionals is just a sum of the parts; each is much more than genes inherited, things learned, skills developed, values embedded, or experiences lived. Something more involves the integration of those parts into a systemic wholeness. How this occurs is what is so little understood; here lies the mystery, the wonderment.

When we observe these professionals early in their careers, we often see at first technicians with a bag of tricks: "a technique I read about," "a method I saw demonstrated," "a successful procedure presented at a conference," or "a strategy Joe told me worked well for him." Some OD practitioners do not progress very far beyond this point. On occasion, they encounter a challenging problem with which they really don't know how to deal. Faced with the anxiety that accompanies this "not knowing," they reach for an intervention in their bag of tricks that, when made, has more to do with quieting their personal anxiety than with the here-and-now needs of the client. The intervention is primarily from the head; it is calculated, mechanical, and out of sync with the larger context. It doesn't flow. In contrast, think of Michael Jordan dribbling down the court, putting opponents off balance, sensing the positions and movements of all players, looking one way and moving in another, eyeing the basket, and using his total body—with grace and beauty—to propel the ball toward the basket. And it falls cleanly through the hoop.

If we observe them at work, we see many of our top OD practitioners effortlessly flowing in an unfolding process with their clients. They are one piece with their well-integrated knowledge-skills-values-techniques-methods-experience-sense of self. They would probably have difficulty telling us why they made a given intervention at the time that they did, and in the way that they did. They might say, "It just felt right; I trusted my gut, my intuition." Their clients, after a day's work, might say: "We made such good progress today. But we don't really know what made that possible. Our consultant certainly didn't say or do very much; it was like magic!"

It certainly isn't magic; it just seems that way. It is really art. Although there is a simplicity and apparent effortlessness in their interventions, it is often hard work. At their best, these practitioners are artists. They certainly are not perfect in any respect, and they have their lows as well as their highs. But they do have high batting averages. They have a professional wisdom—an ability to stay aware of the big picture patterns in a situation at the same time as they focus on the minute details of an interaction as it unfolds. They are not all feeling, but they are appropriately sensitive. And no matter how competent they are seen and experienced by peers, they do continue to monitor themselves, and they continue to seek new learning.

Being an artist in this work means not just being a sum of your parts, but something much more than that. Your being and its expression in action reflect this little-understood process of integration into an effectively functioning professional and person. As you move toward such integration, such wholeness, you are indeed moving toward artistry.

# References

Cheung-Judge, M. (2001). The self as an instrument: A cornerstone for the future of OD. *OD Practitioner, 33*(3), 11–16.

Luft, J. (1984). *Group processes: An introduction to group dynamics* (3rd ed.). Palo Alto, CA: Mayfield.

Rogers, C. (1961). *On becoming a person.* Boston, MA: Houghton Mifflin.

CHAPTER THIRTY-ONE

# The Organizational Fitness Process

*A System-Wide Alignment*

Michael Beer

"We have great strategy but cannot implement it." These were the words of Ray Gilmartin in 1990 shortly after he became CEO of Becton Dickinson (BD), a global medical technology company (Beer & Williamson, 1991). Implementing management's strategic intent is a challenge for most companies. Too often a business fails not because of a flawed strategy but because the *organization and management system*—organization design, strategic management system, human resource system, culture and leadership—does not "fit" (align with) the strategic tasks or key success factors of the organization (see Figure 31.1). Becton Dickinson's global strategy—to grow sales of products developed by the U.S. divisions in Europe, Latin America, and Asia—was impeded by lack of coordination between U.S. division and regional profit centers. It was inadequate because BD's corporate organizational system was not aligned with the strategy and therefore did not induce needed coordination. Alignment with business unit strategy was also a problem in BD's ten divisions.

Put simply, the total system of organizing and managing at the corporate and business unit level was ineffective and required change if investment analysts who rated BD a "hold" were going to revise their recommendations to "buy." Perhaps even more important, the causes of poor alignment were not clearly known or understood by senior teams at the corporate and business unit levels. Similarly, reservations some key people had about BD's strategy were not known to senior management because top management had not enabled truth to speak to power—lower levels that had reservations about the strategy and organizational barriers to

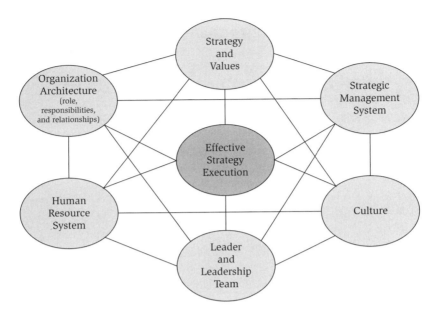

**Figure 31.1.** The Organizational Fitness Model

implementation were unable to speak truthfully about them. The Strategic Fitness Process discussed in this chapter has been designed to deal with these frequent causes of business failure. It has been designed to improve "fit" (organizational alignment with strategy and values) and "fitness" (the capacity of the organization to learn and respond to ever-changing circumstances).

## SILENT BARRIERS TO STRATEGY IMPLEMENTATION

What prevents organizations from aligning their organization with strategy? In the last twenty years, Russell Eisenstat and I have asked dozens of senior teams at the corporate, business unit, and operating level to appoint task forces of managers one to two levels below them. These task forces interviewed one hundred key people across all major parts of the organizations (functional departments, regions, and businesses, depending on the scale and scope of the organization) and asked them whether a strategic statement drafted by their senior team made sense and what organizational strengths and barriers would help or hinder strategy implementation. An analysis of what these task forces found revealed the six barriers listed below (Beer & Eisenstat, 2000):

1. Conflicting priorities, unclear strategy and/or unclear values;

2. An ineffective senior team;

3. Top-down or laissez-faire leadership;

4. Poor horizontal coordination and communication;

5. Inadequate leadership development and paucity of down-the-line leaders; and

6. Poor vertical communication.

We call these barriers "silent killers." Silent because, although known to key employees and discussed in private with trusted friends, senior teams had never acknowledged the barriers openly or met to develop a change plan to overcome them. The lack of public discussion of the barriers is a manifestation of a pervasive phenomenon in organizations, one that academics call *"organizational silence"* (Argyris & Schön, 1996; Morrison & Milliken, 2000; Senge, 1990) Open discussions between lower managers who experience these barriers and senior teams who might enable the organization to overcome these barriers do not occur.

We used the term "killers" for these six barriers because, like cholesterol and hypertension, the silent barriers are *symptoms of an ineffective organization that cause organizational failures to implement its strategy and perform.* These silent killers erode the capacity of organizations to survive long before they are actually discovered.

The six silent killers presented themselves as a cluster in virtually all of the companies we studied. Their causal relationship is circular and mutually reinforcing, and they are self-sealing. That is, once they are in place, their very nature and their relationships to each other prevent senior teams from learning and changing. All but exceptional leaders open to learning and armed with the method discussed in this chapter are able to confront them and transform them into organizational strengths. That is why we call them a syndrome (see Figure 31.2).

*The first three barriers*—conflicting priorities and unclear strategy and values; an ineffective senior team; and top-down or laissez-faire leadership—make it difficult for the organization to develop a *high quality direction*. It is not surprising that top-down or laissez-faire leaders are unable to create an effective senior team. Both styles prevent the engagement and constructive conflict essential for an effective senior team. Without the whole team working together to shape a direction, it is not surprising that the direction is unclear and that there are conflicting priorities. Lack of debate in such a team is also likely to undermine the substantive quality of the direction. And lack of agreement about strategy, priorities, and values in turn undermines cohesion in the top team. It is also true that an ineffective senior team can cause leaders who are conflict-averse to become directive or laissez faire.

The barriers of *poor coordination* and *inadequate leadership development* and insufficient effective down-the-line leaders with a general management

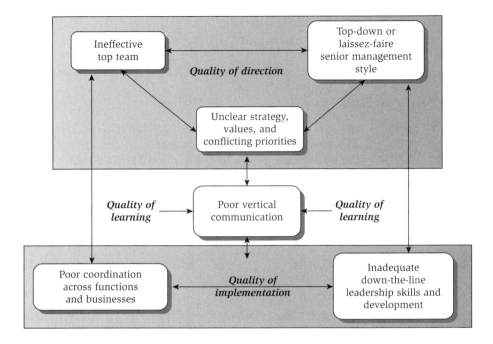

**Figure 31.2.** The Silent Killer Syndrome

perspective are a function of ineffective leadership at the top. Together these two barriers sharply reduce the capability of the organization to implement the organization's direction. An ineffective leader and leadership team are also unable to develop an organization capable of *high quality implementation*. An ineffective senior team causes poor coordination by not speaking with one voice to lower levels and marching to different priorities. They are also unlikely to have confronted the question of how to organize to enable coordination. Discussions of roles, responsibilities, and relationships needed to implement strategy and the structure and systems required to enable them inherently threaten established roles and are likely to be resisted by an ineffective senior team. An ineffective senior team is also unable to develop leaders who can lead cross-functional teams or other activities required to implement strategy and enforce common values. That is because they do not agree on values and on what constitutes good management, and they do not review high-potential managers and enable cross-functional and business career paths, as described earlier.

*Poor* or *closed vertical communication*, the sixth barrier, undermines quality of learning by the organization, a function that is essential for sustained alignment and performance in a constantly changing world. Without an honest two-way conversation between the senior team and key people at lower levels, the senior team is unable to learn about flaws in the direction they developed or about ineffectiveness in the organization and in their leadership that blocks commitment and performance. Consequently, the top team cannot change its role or behavior or consider making changes in how the business is organized and managed. The *capacity of the organization to learn* and *change* is undermined, and high performance cannot be sustained. This conclusion is illustrated powerfully by the dramatic and rapid changes in leadership and organization effectiveness that occur when truth is enabled to speak to power.

# THE STRATEGIC FITNESS PROCESS

The strategic fitness process (SFP) is a structured process that fosters an honest, collective (organization-wide), and public conversation about the effectiveness of the organization (Beer & Eisenstat, 2004). That conversation enables the senior team to conduct a diagnosis of the structural, cultural, and leadership factors that are causing ineffectiveness and enables them to change how the enterprise is organized and managed.

SFP is designed to enable an honest conversation between the senior team and approximately one hundred key people in the organization through a Fitness Task Force of eight key people who are one to two levels below the senior team. Senior teams are instructed to select outstanding performers they and others trust and whom they will believe when they report findings from their interviews of the one hundred. SFP moves through a series of steps shown in Figure 31.3. The process can be implemented in about six to eight weeks (elapsed time).

The process begins with a discussion between the consultant and the CEO or business unit leader about the performance and organizational challenge he or she faces. The process cannot and should not be launched unless the leader is motivated to employ SFP by a desire to close his or her organization's strategically critical performance gap. Unless the senior executive can identify real performance reasons for launching the process, SFP becomes a human resource program in search of a problem, rather than a powerful tool for leading strategic change. Of course, initial discussions should make it clear that SFP will reveal silent barriers to leadership and organizational effectiveness they will have to confront and deal with. We typically present to leadership teams the silent killers listed earlier and the dynamics of an ineffective organization shown in Figure 31.2.

Once a good contract has been developed with the CEO or business unit leader, a meeting with the senior team is necessary. The senior executive presents the reasons he or she would like to employ SFP to gain commitment. This meeting is essential to gain "buy in."

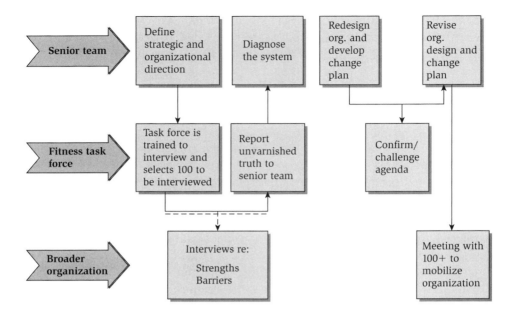

**Figure 31.3.** The Strategic Fitness Process (SFP)

The key motivating event is a *three-day "fitness meeting"* in which Steps 5 and 6 are implemented. The meeting begins with task force feedback from the interviews using the fishbowl method (see Figure 31.4). With the senior team in an outer inverted "U" and the task force seated in the middle, the latter discusses themes they developed the previous day. This discussion reveals the inner workings of the organization in a very graphic manner, in the language of the organization and with numerous illustrations.

The fishbowl conversation is enormously rich and motivates senior teams to act. SFP has proven to be extremely robust and has revealed silent killers that exist. Senior teams realize quickly that if they do not respond, they will severely erode their credibility and legitimacy as leaders. This is because the task force conveys the experience and positive and negative emotions of the people they have interviewed, something that the hierarchy normally prevents them from learning. This may be the first time senior teams come in touch with the whole truth. Previously, they have heard about specific issues. SFP enables them to "see" the total system.

The second day of the fitness meeting is devoted to a diagnosis of the organization—a discussion aimed at identifying how various elements in the system are causing the pattern of organizational behavior reported by the task force. With the aid of the organizational fitness model, task forces discuss the role of various aspects of the system—strategy, organization structure, business

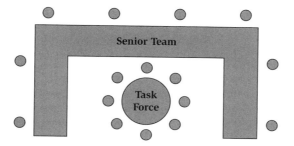

**Figure 31.4.** The Fishbowl: Building the Mandate for Change

processes, human resource policies and practices, culture, and their own leadership—in shaping the behavior and performance of the organization. On the third day, plans for change responsive to the diagnosis are developed.

It is important to understand that the process does not end with the fitness meeting. Step 7, the task force critique of the senior team's action plan, is essential. In some cases, senior teams have learned that their change plan is lacking and is not responsive to the task forces issues or is in some way deficient. This step solidifies a partnership between the senior team and task force members. Using the same method, a day-long meeting is held with the one hundred key people who were interviewed. Here the senior team shares what was heard, presents its action plan, and enables further dialogue and feedback—solidifying their partnership with key people.

In effect, SFP promotes *advocacy* of a direction (strategy and values) by the senior team through an employee task force that communicates a statement of direction to key people they interview and *inquiry* as the task force learns about and feeds back to the top team strengths and barriers that are perceived to help and hinder execution of the direction (Figure 31.5). That cycle is repeated again when the senior team advocates a plan for change to the task force and inquires into the efficacy of the change plan by asking the task force for a critique.

Not shown in Figure 31.5 is the step in which the consultants interview the senior team and feed this data back to the senior team after the task force has finished its feedback. We have found that this feedback is anticlimactic because, substantively, there is very little difference between what task forces report to the senior team and what senior team members, interviewed individually, tell the consultants. One of the major contributions of SFP is that it creates a mandate for change. Speaking openly, honestly, collectively, and publicly creates energy and begins a process of building a community of purpose.

The steps outlined in Figure 31.3 appear simple. In fact, they represent years of experience and adaptation intended to create a robust and replicable process.

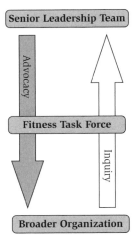

**Figure 31.5.** The Strategic Fitness Process: Iterative Advocacy and Inquiry

A detailed manual has been developed by TruePoint (www.truepoint.com) that gives the purpose of each segment of the process, a timeline for each segment, and detailed instructions for consultants.

# A CASE EXAMPLE

SFP has been employed in more than two hundred organizational units in over forty corporations in the United States, Europe, Latin America, India, Japan, and Canada at the corporate, business unit, and operating unit levels. It has been employed by organizations in multiple industries, such as pharmaceuticals, high technology, services (hotel and restaurants), healthcare, and communications. SFP has helped organizations cope with a wide array of substantive business and organizational problems. In most instances, SFP has led to several of the substantive changes listed below because of the system's nature of organizations: problems and solutions are interconnected and SFP's power is in helping senior teams see the connections and find solutions that solve several problems at once.

*Some Business Challenges That Have Been Addressed by SFP*

- Reexamination of strategy and the alignment of the organization
- New leaders taking charge
- Major organizational redesign to improve coordination and/or divisional decentralization

- Operational improvement
- Integrating two or more units resulting from a merger or acquisition
- Improvement of key functions such as quality, HR, or IT
- Response to a competitor's challenge with more rapid product development
- Moving from a top-down to a high-involvement culture
- Continuous strategic management and organizational learning
- Improving service delivery

Consider the Santa Rosa Systems Division of Hewlett-Packard (SRSD) (Beer & Rogers, 1997). As a newly formed business unit in HP's test and measurement sector, SRSD was formed to help HP enter the emerging telecommunication systems business in 1992. By 1994 the division was failing to meet its objectives for revenue and profit growth. The following were perceptions of problems within SRSD: "We have two competing strategies battling each other for the same resources. The resulting factions around these two strategies are tearing the organization apart; the members of the top team operate within their own functional silos. They are like a group of fiefdoms that refuse to cooperate for fear they will lose power; there is a cold war going on between R&D and the customer systems department; SRSD is still not sure what kind of business it wants to be" (Beer & Rogers, 1997, p. 1).

Having discussed and described these problems as *reporters* in the fishbowl for some five hours, the task force asked to speak for themselves. They told the senior team that they had to respond to these problems quickly if they wanted to save SRSD from failure. When the task force left, the senior team spent two hours discussing their internal team problems. They were given an overnight assignment to diagnose the root causes of the problems they had heard.

With the help of the consultants, who acted as both facilitators and expert resources on matters of strategy management, organization design, and leadership, the second and third day of the fitness meeting was spent in diagnosis and action planning and resulted in a comprehensive and systemic change plan. To improve coordination, SRSD's senior team decided to reorganize as a matrix organization, a radical departure from its functional organization. To enable the new matrix to function effectively, the senior team refined its role, agreed to decision rights of functional and business managers, agreed on ground rules for their behavior and decision making, and decided how each key side of the matrix would be measured. Each person on the senior team met individually with the division general manager in the week that followed to discuss his or her role in the new organization. Following a spirited critique of their plan for change by the task force, the senior team communicated its plan to the organization and began to implement it.

Three months after SRSD began the SFP process, they were operating in a matrix. In the next five years, SRSD employed SFP once a year as an integral part of its strategic management and planning process. The results were dramatic. Revenues grew by 250 percent, and profits improved six-fold. In the second year, the task force reported that morale and commitment were up significantly and that the leadership team was now seen in a much more positive light. The executive vice president of the test and measurement business commented about the dramatic changes he saw in SRSD.

> "They have done a terrific job after a year or so of struggling to figure out what the business was and how to get it rolling.... Today, I see them as one of our star divisions. In results, they have exceeded...expectations [not only] in terms of level of business and the speed with which they have made progress in achieving business results, but also in the magnitude of the turnaround. Today SRSD represents best practice in a lot of areas.... They have really turned around weaknesses into strengths. This was a marvelous success. They now have the infrastructure and skills to grow. Compared to other divisions, it's probably the most dramatic improvement." (Beer & Rogers, 1997, B3, p. 2)

A rigorous analysis of twelve applications of SFP at the corporate and business unit level shows that in all but two cases SFP led to positive results, although in each case the changes were different and fit the problems experienced. In two cases, changes were made but were not sustained because the leader did not learn, change, and follow up. Illustrative examples are shown in Figure 31.6.

| | | |
|---|---|---|
| Becton Dickinson | 1990–2006 | • From hold to buy<br>• Dramatic change in performance and commitment |
| Hewlett – Packard Div. | 1994–1999 | • Profit increase by 6x<br>• From worst-performing division to top-performing division |
| Merck – Latin America | 1996–2003 | • Transformation in business organization, processes, and culture across 10 countries<br>• 20% compounded annual growth |
| Mattel – Canada | 1998–2003 | • From poor to outstanding coordination across functions<br>• From least profitable international unit to most profitable |
| Comcast New England | 2003–2007 | • From centralised bureaucratic to low employee and customer commitment<br>• Improved performance, and employee and customer commitment |

**Figure 31.6.** Examples of SFP Fundamental Changes

# SUMMARY

For nearly twenty years, the strategic fitness process (SFP) has proven to be a powerful leadership platform that enables senior teams to develop a more effective, high-commitment, and high-performance organization. Its success is dependent, however, on several preconditions. First, the senior leadership team must have a business reason for entering into the process. They must be able to define a gap in effectiveness and/or performance they want to close. That gap can be because of a crisis or because the senior team wants to raise the bar of leadership and organizational effectiveness. Second, leaders must ultimately be willing to learn and, if necessary, change their leadership behavior and policies.

SFP is meant to be more than a one-off intervention. Its effects have been most profound when applied in multiple organizational subunits of the company and repeated as a core strategic organizational learning process. That is what happened at Becton Dickinson. Over the years, SFP was implemented more than once at the corporate level, in business units, country organizations, and key functions. It played an important role in the corporation's transformation and excellent performance. Ed Ludwig, its current CEO, has employed it as his corporate leadership and learning platform.

The SFP falls into the genre of large-group interventions that have been part of the OD intervention repertoire for at least two decades. It differs in important ways, however. It explicitly focuses on business strategy and performance gaps, requires a more rigorous analysis of the system, requires the senior team to perform a systemic diagnosis and plan for change, and can and has been integrated into the strategic management process of the business.

## References

Argyris, C., & Schön, D.A. (1996). *Organizational learning II: Theory, method and practice,* Reading, MA: Addison-Wesley.

Beer, M., & Eisenstat, R. (2000). The silent killers of strategy implementation and learning. *Sloan Management Review.*

Beer, M., & Eisenstat, R. (2004, November). How to have an honest conversation about your strategy. *Harvard Business Review.*

Beer, M., & Rogers, G. (1997). *Hewlett-Packard's Santa Rosa Systems Division (A) (A1) (A2) (A4) (B3).* Boston: Harvard Business School Press.

Beer, M., & Williamson, A.D. (1991). *Becton Dickinson (A).* Boston: Harvard Business School Press.

Morrison, E.W., & Milliken, F.J. (2000). Organizational silence: A barrier to change and development in a pluralistic world. *Academy of Management Review, 25*(4), 706–725.

Senge, P.M. (1990). *The fifth discipline: The art and practice of learning organizations.* New York: Doubleday.

# CHAPTER THIRTY-TWO

# Context Blindness

*What We Don't See* Will *Hurt Us*

Barry Oshry

One of the paradoxes of our human condition is that we are systems creatures—much of our lives is spent as components of larger systems—as members within the family, work group, organization, neighborhood, sports team, political party, faith group, nation, and more. On the other side, we are blind to how the structures and processes of these systems affect our everyday lives—our experiences of ourselves and others, our frustrations and satisfactions, and our effectiveness. Our orientation tends to be personal; we see people and not the contexts in which we and they operate. That blindness to context is costly in terms of stress, relationship breakdowns, and diminished organizational effectiveness, all of which can be avoided or reversed with system sight.

This chapter describes two forms of context blindness: *blindness to the contexts others are working in* and *blindness to our own contexts*. The costs of context blindness are examined, along with the productive possibilities of system sight. The challenge for the OD practitioner is to help our clients see, understand, and master the systemic contexts in which they and others are living. OD practitioners themselves must be sensitive to systemic contexts, too.

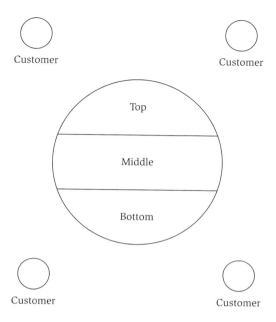

**Figure 32.1.** Structure of the Organizational Simulation

# FROM SYSTEM BLINDNESS TO SYSTEM SIGHT

Back in the 1980s, I had been experimenting with a variety of organizational simulations as part of management education programs; the model I used most frequently had an organization composed of Tops, Middles, and Bottoms interacting with Customers and potential Customers (see Figure 32.1). In these exercises, people were randomly assigned to their positions. *This random assignment is a key point.*

As part of each exercise, we would ask people to describe what life was like for them in their parts of the system—what issues they were dealing with, what feelings they had—and to describe how they saw other parts of the system.

At the time I was less focused on theory development than on creating engaging interactive experiences. What struck me as fascinating was the regularity with which people described themselves and others based not on who they were as personalities, but on the positions they occupied. There were unique and regular patterns of Top, Middle, Bottom, and Customer experiences. Whoever entered those worlds was likely to experience some variation of these patterns. I was wowed by this revelation.

One day, while strolling along Boston's Newbury Street, I ran into a colleague and shared my excitement over this discovery. "Barry," he said, "you have just discovered sociology." O.K., so I wasn't the first, yet it still felt like a fresh discovery with powerful implications.

# CONTEXT: THE MISSING INGREDIENT

Clearly, context was shaping people's experiences of themselves and others, yet context was invisible. People tended to be blind to the contexts others were operating from. As a consequence, they misunderstood others, had little empathy for them, made up often-incorrect stories about others' motivations, judged them, resisted them, or reacted against them.

People also tended to be blind to their own context and how it was shaping *their* experiences. For example, they were blind to how they were reflexively reacting to their own Top, Middle, Bottom, and Customer contexts in ways that caused stress, soured their relationships with others, and diminished their organizational effectiveness. People were seeing people, not context. This blindness was costly.

# THE CHALLENGE FOR THE OD PRACTITIONER

The challenge is to be able to see, understand, and master the systemic contexts in which we and others operate. Immediately, there is a problem. We do not see context; all we see are people. So we become fascinated with people, understanding them, analyzing them, assuming that if only we understood them better we would know how to interact with them. Unfortunately, in system life, this is not the case. To be personally effective, we need to understand and master the systemic contexts we move in and out of. To interact effectively with others, we need to understand and take into account the systemic contexts in which they are living. Let's observe the trials of Dora and Sam as they struggle to do well but are undone by their blindness to system context.

## I. Where in the World Is Dora?

Dora has had a tough day. Things didn't go well in the team meeting she was leading. She had a lot of complaints from members. Then she needed to pass down an unpopular initiative coming from above, which she knew was going to stir up trouble—and it did. Next, she learned that her project proposal was denied. Finally, the data analysis she was promised for today didn't come—*next week, we promise.*

In the course of this difficult day, Dora has passed through four distinct contexts, and Dora, being blind to context, has reflexively reacted in ways that

# CHAPTER THIRTY-THREE

# Transforming the HR-OD Audit by Using Whole Systems

T.V. Rao

The human resource development (HRD) audit follows all the traditional principles of OD: using diagnosis (consultant-driven as well as organization-focused), done by trained behavioral science specialists, and using participative values. The HRD audit has been extensively used in the last decade, and research evidence is being built to prove its effectiveness as a planned change tool. This chapter presents the methodology of the HRD audit and shows how the large scale interactive process (LSIP) can be used to conduct the audit. The LSIP workshop brings the whole system under one roof, diagnoses various HRD systems, and suggests remedies for enhancing HRD systems and their impact. This chapter illustrates this with a case study.

## WHAT IS THE HRD AUDIT?

In today's world, "people" or employees can give a profound competitive advantage to a company. To get the best from HR, there should be a comprehensive audit and good alignment of the function, its strategies, structure, systems, and styles, with business and its goals (financial, customer, and other parameters). It should be aligned both with short-term goals and long-term strategies. Besides this alignment, the skills and styles of HR staff, the line managers, and the top management should synergize with the HR goals and strategies. HRD audits attempt to identify the future HRD needs of an organization to improve the systems and processes.

In the last three decades, a large number of corporations have established HRD departments, introduced new systems of HRD, and made structural changes in terms of differentiating the HRD function and integrating it within the HR function. A good number of CEOs saw a hope in HRD for solving many of their problems. HR systems are people-intensive and require a lot of managerial time. There are examples of corporations in which HRD has taken a driver's seat and has given a lot of benefits. There are also examples of firms in which HRD did not have the desired impact (Mungale & Bhatiani, 2003). To maximize the impact of HRD on business accomplishments, the HRD audit came into existence.

# METHODOLOGY FOR THE HRD AUDIT

A team of professionally trained auditors visits the corporation and, using a variety of methodologies, assesses the appropriateness and adequacy of the various HRD systems, strategies, structures, competencies, culture, processes, and impact. A number of methods are used by consultants for auditing HRD. Some of these are described in detail elsewhere (see Rao, 1999). These include:

- *Individual interviews*. The auditors normally make it a point to interview the top-level management, union leaders, strategic leaders, and senior managers individually. Such interviews are a must for capturing their thinking about the future plans and opportunities available for the company.

- *Group interviews*. Group interviews are conducted normally for groups of four to eight individuals. It is preferable to have employees drawn from the same or similar levels, as in some cultures junior employees may not freely express their views in the presence of their seniors. However, it is quite common to give cross-functional representation of employees in the same group.

- *Questionnaire method*. Specialized HRD audit questionnaires are available (Rao, 1999; Rao, 2008). The utility of the questionnaire is that it helps in benchmarking.

- *Observation*. The auditors physically visit the workplace, including the plant, the machinery, the canteen, the toilets, the training rooms, the hostels, the hospital, the school, the living colony, and other physical facilities. These visits and observations are meant to assess the extent to which a congenial and supportive human-welfare-oriented climate exists in the company.

- *Analysis of secondary data*. Analysis of secondary data can give a lot of insight into the HRD assets and liabilities of the company. For example, in a company that had about fifty HRD people, only two were found to have the required technical training in the HRD area. Analysis of age profiles, training attended, minutes of the meetings held, and the like help in determining the assets and liabilities.

- *Analysis of reports, records, manuals, and other published literature.* Published literature of the company, including annual reports, brochures, training calendars, personnel manual, and various bulletins issued from time to time, are likely to help immensely in assessing the strengths and weaknesses of HRD.

The audit starts with a briefing by the CEO and the chief of HRD, who may set an agenda and focal areas of evaluation. The interview with top management starts with finding details of the future plans of the organization and using them as a basis for outlining the competency requirements of the organization. The current competencies, structures, and HRD systems are assessed in terms of their capability to prepare the organization for the future. Suggestions are made to improve for achieving the future business goals and plans. The HRD audit is contextual and uses the available knowledge of the potential of the HRD systems in helping the corporation achieve its goals (Rao, 1999).

The HRD audit seeks answers to issues like the following:

1. Where does the company plan to be five to ten years from the time of the audit, three years from now, and one year from now?

2. What is the current skill base of HRD staff in relation to role requirements?

3. What are the HRD subsystems available to help the organization build a competency base for the present, immediate future, and long term?

4. What is the current level of effectiveness of these systems in developing people and ensuring that human competencies are available at adequate levels?

5. Is the HRD structure that exists adequate enough to manage the human resources in the company?

6. Are the top management and senior manager styles of managing people in tune with a learning culture?

Suggestions are made on the basis of answers to questions above about the future strategies required by the company, the structure the company needs to have for developing new competencies, the systems that need to be strengthened, and what is needed, particularly with regard to the styles of the top management.

# HRD AUDIT AS AN OD INTERVENTION

In Pareek and Rao's (1998) model of an HRD department, the objective of such a department was to facilitate learning and change in the organization. An HRD department must have learning specialists who facilitate change process. In the Pareek and Rao model, OD was conceived as one of the main tasks of the HRD department. It was suggested that OD functions be institutionalized through HRD departments. In fact, today most change interventions have been and are being made by HRD departments (as differentiated from personnel departments). Many HRD managers in India do undertake a number of OD interventions, such as introducing performance management systems, conducting training, career planning, and succession management.

A great deal of work has been done in India using the HRD audit as an OD intervention. This is a unique feature of Indian organizations (Jomon, 1998; Rao, 2008). The author's experience in initiating OD with the aid of HRD audits has shown very positive results. A number of change activities have been initiated after these audits. For a review of this work, see this book's website.

# HRD AUDIT CASE STUDY

A power generation company with 1,200 employees (of whom three hundred were supervisory and managerial staff) conducted an audit that was limited to the assessment of HRD systems for the supervisory staff, including junior managers and executives to the general managers in charge of the unit. Two hundred supervisory staff took the audit.

The methodology required the large group to be divided into mixed groups by designation, age, and function. Each grouping had employees belonging to different age groups, functions, and levels. There were six to seven participants around each table. During the day they were taken through a series of diagnostic exercises using the following questions, among others:

- What are three good things in your performance appraisal system?
- What is one thing you would like to change in your performance appraisal system?
- How would you critically evaluate the job rotation in your company?
- What are three strengths in your training policies and practices?
- What is one thing you would like to see happen in training to make it more effective?
- What three adjectives describe the promotion policies as they exist in your company?

- What things are done well by your HRD department?
- What one thing would you like the HRD department to start doing?
- What one thing would you like the HRD department to stop doing?
- What new competencies would you like to see in the HRD staff?
- What three adjectives describe the culture of your organization?
- What would you like to see happen in the organization to develop people's competencies?
- Which of the HRD systems are facilitating the organization to build its intellectual capital or to manage talent?
- What systems should be modified for meeting the future needs of the company?

All items discussed were based on results of the audit process. Some items dealt with the competencies or development needs (long term and short term) of the organization, such as performance appraisal, manpower planning, recruitment, job rotation, training, promotion polices, career paths, and career planning, among others. Some items dealt with the competencies of HRD staff, learning attitude of line managers, credibility and image of the HRD department, HRD culture and values, impact and integration of HRD systems with organizational goals, and more.

The audit was also used to reinforce the purpose of various systems and practices in use. For example, a short lecture was given on the current training policy and practice. This was followed by a series of questions to be answered by the teams.

The results were compiled by a group of research assistants and fed into the computer, after which the analysis was fed back to the group. By the end of the day, the group knew the results of the audit and the recommendations the consultants were going to give to the top management.

Some topics were not amenable to be assessed during the workshop. For example, the competency levels of the HRD members could not be assessed, but their credibility and impact could be. The workshop was followed up by the audit team meeting with the HRD staff to supplement the audit data with their observations and secondary data analysis.

# SUMMARY

In the HRD audit example discussed above, the process was done with quality and provided good results. The audit process was fast; the entire audit was completed in a matter of four days—one day for planning the LSIP, one day for the LSIP-based audit, and two days for observation, administration of questionnaires to ascertain the knowledge levels of HRD staff, and secondary data analysis. Afterward, some of the top management team members participating were more motivated to improve the state of affairs. The audit results were available to the whole system that participated, so there was a great sense of ownership of the data on the part of the employees.

Because the consultants conducted the HRD audit using participative methods, they were able to diagnose problems and start the change process immediately. Thus, the HRD audit itself had become an OD intervention. Using this method requires a good understanding of HRD, people, and processes and excellent change management skills. If used as an OD intervention, the HRD audit has a high potential for management accepting and acting on the recommendations from the audit.

# References

Jomon, M.G. (1998). The effectiveness of HRD audit as an OD intervention. Unpublished doctoral dissertation, Academy of Human Resources Development–XLRI Fellow Program in HRD, XLRI, Jamshedpur.

Mungale, S., & Bhatiani, S. (2003, November). An evaluative study of the HRD function through HRD audit. Paper presented at the 4th Conference of Young Professionals of the National HRD Network, Delhi Chapter.

Pareek, U., & Rao, T.V. (1998). *Pioneering human resources development: The L&T system*. Ahmedabad: Academy of Human Resources Development. (Publication of the original consultancy reports, 1975 and 1977).

Rao, T.V. (1999). *HRD audit: Evaluating the human resources function for business improvement*. New Delhi: Response Books, Sage India.

Rao, T.V. (2008). *The HRD scorecard 2500*. New Delhi: Response Books Sage India.

*Ongoing presence:* Most results are gradual and the real impact is in their annualized savings. Thus, there is a need to be continually present. Give more "face time" to the client, which is sometimes difficult for externals when they work with penny-pinching clients.

*Real-time laboratory:* As a company employee, you get to try things with real company toys and customers. You can "put your money where your mouth is." For example, it's relatively easy to have the call center make a small change in its response technique for a day or to survey clients on how they are receiving an earlier change in contact routes.

*Historical and institutional memory:* You can appreciate company icons and precedent, and also avoid reinventing the wheel. In Hewlett-Packard, for example, it was historically more credible to have known "Dave and Bill," as they were fondly called, and then next best to understand "The HP Way." (In fact, new hires were given a book about it.) But if you don't understand the nature and structures of meetings, for example, and whether they can be used for confrontation or just validation, you're at an immediate disadvantage.

*Personal relationships:* Internally, you are able to nurture key connections with both formal and informal leaders and change agents who can immensely help your cause and give you guidance. You can also develop mentors who can advise you on how to circumvent resistance or overcome inertia.

*Content knowledge:* The more you understand the jargon, the interrelation-ships, and the interstitial nature of the company, the more effective you will be at instituting change and improvement. It doesn't hurt to know that a manager is obfuscating when he says, "We can't change the delivery of an XR-40 Gatchet Drive because customers request them too randomly."

*Connecting relationships for synergy:* The internal practitioner can readily understand how to create critical mass, where to begin pilots, how to rally the least resources to get the greatest return (ROI), and so forth. These often hidden connections and combinations would be lost on an outsider.

*Track record:* Assuming successful projects and engagements, one's track record and momentum create high degrees of credibility. However, this isn't always the case, and it can lead to ineffectiveness if credibility is lost or diminished.

## THE DISADVANTAGES OF THE INTERNAL OD PROFESSIONAL

This section presents the disadvantages faced by internal OD professionals:

*Poor credibility*: Too often OD is seen, along with HR and training, as areas in which people are placed who simply can't do anything else. The individuals are too academic, too theory-oriented, and too connected with the latest fad of the month.

*Insulation*: There is a tendency not to get out too often. In the best of all possible worlds, OD people should be spending considerable time (and even rotating assignments) in line areas, understanding what the woop and warf of the business are on an everyday basis. While working with Tastemaker, a world-class flavoring company, the CEO had placed his top OD person in charge of the Mexican operation, stating that, "He needs P&L responsibility if he is to understand our business and have credibility with peers."

*Vender fixation*: There are too many training companies selling too many training programs that are never measured for efficacy. From role plays and simulations to assessments and classroom training, the nearly $80 billion a year spent on this stuff (according to the American Society for Training and Development) is rarely measured. In fact, a 2008 article in *Training* magazine suggested that training really needn't be measured at all! (As it is, four simplistic measures cited by Don Kirkpatrick at the University of Michigan decades ago are as close as we get.)

*No clout*: It's tough to find three top executives in OD, HR, or training who were promoted to CEO of a Fortune 100 company in the last decade. That's because it's virtually never done (although actuaries, sales people, general counsels, manufacturing heads, and others are routinely promoted to the top job).

## THE KEYS TO THE KINGDOM

So if any of that is remotely true, what is an internal OD practitioner to do? Fortunately, there's a lot you can do, because you can build on the advantages and circumvent the disadvantages.

### Internal Practice Keys

1. **Build enduring, trusting relationships with senior people**. You have the ability to work directly with senior executives and not go through chains of command. Make the most of that. Learn to talk as a business person, become strategic in your thinking, and become comfortable in the presence of these people. *Suggestion: Take business etiquette lessons so that you dress properly on all occasions and know what fork to use at dinner. You need to be seen as a peer.*

2. **Focus on being a generalist, not a specialist.** External consultants can get away with specialization (although even they limit themselves in

this manner), but you can't afford to do that as an internal practitioner. You need to be the same as an aspiring actor who can also sing, dance, and tell jokes in order to ensure the widest possible casting call. *Suggestion: Don't become enamored with a "school" or "methodology." Try to become adept at many different approaches and pursuits.*

3. **Demonstrate a unique, specialized existence.** In some cases you may not wish to align yourself with HR or training. HR has outsourced the transactional work, and is left challenged by the transformational. OD practitioners should be the experts in transformational work, which is not in (nor should be in) the realm of HR. You cannot be everything to everyone. You are the leading change management specialists, for example (since the "change agent" had better be the leadership).

4. **Focus on the strategic, not the tactical.** Immerse yourself in the corporate strategy, vision, and mission and ensure that your proactive counsel is always in line with furthering progress toward those goals. Everyone around you will be thinking tactically and operationally. Your job is seeing the larger picture—the preventive actions, not the remedial; the innovative, not the quick fixes.

5. **Boldly partner where no partner has gone before.** Counter-intuitively, perhaps, the OD experts should determine when outside help is needed, be it for expertise, credibility, objectivity, best practices, or whatever. Don't allow external consultants to be foisted on you, but don't reject help either. The best position is to request it when the organization is most helped by it. "If we need them, why do we need you?" should be answered with, "Because you need someone to tell you when you need them."

## SO DO WE BUILD IT OR BUY IT?

This last point leads us to the ubiquitous question: Should we create it or obtain it? That question, again in keeping with point 5 above, should be within the purview of the OD professionals. Here are some logical areas of "traditional" internal OD responsibility. That is, an investment in OD by the organization should logically provide such interventions as the following: succession planning, career development, synthesis of succession and career planning, and much more.

Here are the logical areas for which outside help is sometimes needed, either in conjunction with internal OD or as an independent intervention:

• Strategy formulation;

- Executive assessments and audits;
- Merger and acquisitions, including divestitures;
- Major cultural mergers;
- Change management on an organization-wide basis;
- Creation and integration of relevant global best practices;
- Business scenario enactments, simulations, and assessment work;
- Executive level facilitation, coaching, and conflict resolution; and
- Organization-wide quality interventions.

Organizational leadership must make decisions about how much of the first list is to be built, but also understand that virtually all of the second list must be bought for objectivity and world-class considerations.

Marilyn Martiny, formerly of Hewlett-Packard, and Art Strohmer, formerly of Merck, were two of the finest OD practitioners I've ever met. Both were adept at bringing in outside resources when they felt it was in the best interests of the organization, without hesitancy and without ego problems.

"Otherwise," noted Marilyn, "we get stuck trying to breathe our own exhaust."

To be the most effective business partner, OD professionals should position themselves as a business partner of the senior executives. Think of yourself as an internal "trusted advisor." This requires credibility, presence, and sheer courage. But it will provide you with:

- Access to and participation in strategic discussions;
- The opportunity to influence key business priorities;
- The insights needed to align change management with strategic goals;
- A dual coaching and interventionist role;
- Access (even if only perceived) to the clout of the senior team; and
- A fast track to garnering support for key change initiatives.

Try to formalize this in the organizational reporting relationships. OD professionals should report to senior line authorities, no less than financial or legal people often do. Since all organizations are systems that are interdependent, it's important not to become someone's factotum or blind advocate. It's imperative to see the entire organization, the interrelationships, and the interstitial connections.

Thus, the very nature and strategy of the OD function, if it is separate, must be in tune and aligned with the organizational strategy. This is why the function and the practitioners must be insulated from HR and training. Clear clients must be established, be they operating units or actual members of the leadership team. Ideally, the reporting relationship should follow suit.

Resources must be provided for OD in terms of professional development, hiring external assistance, hiring internal assistance, proactive interventions, and so forth. OD cannot solely be at the mercy of others' budgets.

# GENERATING VALUE IN A PROFOUND MANNER

Here is one of the most profound roles the OD professional can play in establishing his or her expertise and value: make implicit knowledge explicit and explicit knowledge implicit. Outside resources can't possibly do this as effectively as internal OD experts.

By this I mean that the knowledge that key, effective employees keep in their heads for quick use, often idiosyncratically, must be placed into shared formats. So a top manufacturing person who knows that certain key customers are happy when they can influence minor designs during production, and involves them in that manner, must be able (and encouraged) to provide that information to others, including peers and superiors.

Conversely, procedures for travel agents that are hidden in a thick manual or intricate electronic database that are needed daily must be reframed so that people can quickly remember them (or be provided job aids for that purpose).

Too many times, people know important things that they assume others do, or they laboriously have to find important things they should really have in their heads. Only internal OD people can exploit these opportunities. An example of this occurred with Atlantic Electric many years ago. This is the utility that services Atlantic City and all of the casinos therein. There was not a strong internal OD function, which is not unusual for a utility, so I was asked to help with some developmental work. While I was there, senior management told me in passing about an early retirement package that tangentially touched on my project. At that point I made a lucky and important guess about some implicit knowledge.

"Have you tested who will accept this?" I asked.

"No, but we have a very solid estimate that about 27 percent of the eligible workforce will accept, and we need 25 percent, so we're quite well positioned."

"But what about the types of jobs being lost, and types of expertise?" I persisted.

"No problem," I was told, "it will be across-the-board."

I insisted that we run a test, and the executive vice president finally agreed just to get me out of his office. What we found is that 100 percent—that's right, *all*—of the linemen who could manually fix downed rigging would accept the package. Every single person (and they were all over fifty) who could re-rig a downed line in an ice storm (very common in the winter) would be gone, and this was a skill, in light of modern technology, that was not being taught to younger people.

Those are the kinds of situations in which consultants are golden, but internal people should be able to immediately see the problem. The senior linemen knew what would happen, but they assumed it was common knowledge. The senior management didn't have a clue, and assumed someone would have pointed it out. There were no channels for this that naturally developed. Excellent OD skills are needed. They ought to be resident, not borrowed, in these kinds of cases.

OD work will vary with the maturity of the company and its sophistication. OD efforts might differ in their ways and means based on organizational "life cycle." External OD consultants see an individual as the client, but internal people often view the organization as an entity, as the client, so that the life cycle of the organization is far more important to them.

# CREATING AN INTERNAL BRAND

A brand is a representation of uniform quality. It is as useful internally as externally, particularly so for staff functions such as OD. There are function brands (OD department) and individual brands (June Hudson, OD expert). Both brands are important, but particularly the latter. It requires building a reputation of excellence and relevance, no less so than manufacturing, finance, or sales. Here are the keys to effective brand creation for OD in both dimensions:

1. Meet regularly with key stakeholders to assist in defining needs (not merely reacting to them) and suggesting interventions.

2. Create both established and customized services. The former may be succession planning or career development help; the latter may be tailored assistance with product commercialization.

3. Create a departmental mission that encourages line clients to call on you. "Helping employees realize unseen potential" is a silly, faddish mission. "Assisting individual performers to accelerate progress toward corporate strategic goals" is much more enticing for potential "customers."

4. Create metaphors and names for processes and interventions that call attention to OD. "The Mentor Network" is far better than "We help establish mentoring relationships."

5. Facilitate key meetings. This places you not only in the framework of the strategic *content*, but also enables you to influence the strategic *process*.

6. Maintain rigorous communications with those you help in any way. Create mailing lists, newsletters, job aids, and so forth. As people are

promoted and transferred, you should be able to continue working with them in more important areas.

7. Try to create a presence in the hiring and selection process, so that high achievers and fast-track leaders get to know you early in their careers.

8. Use initiatives, such as "internal best practices" (which are woefully overlooked), to provide proactive help to existing operations that may not realize they can improve still more.

9. Work on current "hot issues" from a different (even contrarian) perspective. For example, if a senior leader must make some tough decisions about reductions in force, the obvious intervention is to suggest how best to do it. But an equally important and mostly over-looked need is to provide counseling and support for the leader in a time of such tough decisions and probably adverse reactions.

10. Author internally. Create articles, columns, tips, and so forth for the intranet, company newsletters, industry publications, and so forth. "You're never a hero in your home town," but you get to be a hero when the home town people suddenly realize you've been quoted in another town!

# THE TALENT BANK

What competencies are required to pull this off successfully? I would suggest that one needs skills, knowledge, and certain behavioral dispositions. The first two are "trainable"; the last is only modifiable. (You can teach someone the beer business and even corporate history and cultural realities, but you can't "teach" him enthusiasm.) The talent required is somewhat different from that of external consultants, because there is actually less freedom to fail (see the pros and cons at the beginning of this chapter).

Underpinning all of this is the particular tightrope that is held taut or becomes slack due to corporate politics (often worse in non-profits, education, and government, of course), turf battles, individual egos, economic blues, competitive surprises, and so forth. At the worst, an external consultant can "fire" the client (most of us who are successful have done so at several junctures in our careers). External OD people can tell a manager to "back off" or mediate a feud, or simply call on the engagement "buyer" to use some clout to sort things out.

Internal people have no such luxury or latitude. They must use their wits and wherewithal, and walk carefully to avoid land mines. I believe that is not a skill or knowledge, but a talent that is tough to teach!

# SUMMARY: A CAREER IN INTERNAL OD

Are you up to the considerable job here? You won't make as much as successful external people (emphasis on "successful"), but you can have much more impact on a longer term. Will you be the "content" expert, the "process" expert, or both? The former must stay within an industry (or even function); the latter has somewhat of a free rein, since processes are transferable.

My observation, over two decades, is that you are best off internally if you love methodology, are comfortable with interventions requiring political finesse, and *do not like to market or sell*. Although marketing is required internally, as indicated above, it is far less severe than doing so on the basis of earning money as an external consultant. I've tried to indicate above the similarities and differences in the positions. Here are the major benefits of internal OD as a profession:

- Create and sustain measurable change over long periods of time;
- Enjoy secure internal branding and a captive prospect base;
- Utilize a "laboratory" for learning, growth, and experimentation;
- Significantly help those around you to improve personally and organizationally;
- Work with thought leaders and business innovators daily and closely;
- Be an integral part of the strategic process;
- Leverage abilities by becoming a manager of other OD professionals;
- Create internal best practices;
- Become the ultimate team player; and
- Get broad exposure to many parts of the business and many people in the business.

Look to your heart and head and decide whether you are going to be the hidden talent that drives organizations forward. This is not a role for those seeking the limelight, but it is one for those whose gratification comes in results.

# CHAPTER THIRTY-SIX

# Estimating OD Success Rates at the National Level

### Robert T. Golembiewski

This chapter seeks to distinguish two relatively distinct emphases in estimating success rates in OD applications, roughly corresponding to two time periods—from the earliest period through the 1980s, and then following the 1980s. The emphasis will be broadly territorial, emphasizing applications in Western democracies, Korea, and India. (See Table 36.1.)

Much energy has gone into differentiating organization development (OD) or organization development and change (ODC) from other approaches to planned change, but those differences in definition will not be of concern here. The focus here is on the efficacy of a rather elaborate technology for change that seeks to increase the degree of responsible freedom available to those touched by an organization. In most cases, the interventions are labeled OD or ODC. Minor

**Table 36.1. Selective Features of Collections of Evaluations of OD Applications, Through 1985[†]**

| Estimates of Number of Applications | Average Success | Number of Hits Per Collection |
|---|---|---|
| 16 | 59 | Approximately 57 percent of comparisons are "hits" |

[†]Summarized from Golembiewski, 2003, pp. 23–27.

[§]Eleven of these sixteen collections use evaluative terms such as "effectiveness," "improvement," positive change," "major changes in expected direction," and so on, with raw average here indicating changes in expected directions.

references are also made to work here conventionally labeled as "quality of working life"(QWL). OD and QWL do not differ in essence, but the latter generally focuses on workaday and often-unionized levels of organizations (for example, see Skelley, 1989) while OD and ODC can focus on managers and executives.

# MAJOR FEATURES OF FOUNDATION LITERATURE THROUGH 1980s

This chapter recognizes two features of what will be called the "foundation literature" in its review of analyses of success rates in OD applications, roughly dated from the early studies in the petroleum industry through the research of the 1980s. Two themes dominate in this survey of foundation work. First, attention goes to a brief summary of estimates of success; second, leading factors obfuscating interpretation of those earlier studies of success.

## Success Rates in the Foundation Literature

Those seeking guidance about whether OD applications are worth the costs are buffeted by conflicting forces. The small number of evaluative studies encouraged moderated enthusiasm, with success estimates suggesting that more than 55 percent approximated a reasonable estimate of achieving intended effects as consequences of OD applications. A detailed view of the explicit success-oriented estimates in the foundation literature leaves no doubt about this summary (Golembiewski, 2003, pp. 1–97). The common assessment of OD applications tended toward a somber tone. One might expect such a view from those with no particular zest for OD. Curiously, however, a similar tone existed among many supporters of OD. The twice-yearly meetings of the OD Network were perhaps the most common locus of moderated enthusiasm.

Why might such an appraisal exist about foundation research? No one can tell for certain. The approach here reflects problems in the foundation in surveys of applications taking an explicit view of success. OD optimists emphasize the financial bottom line. On the other hand, those pessimistic about OD might oppositely see the foundation success rates as proving that OD was recalcitrant, perhaps impossible, as pessimists had claimed all along.

Let us move toward greater detail on the two central themes. Features of OD, ODC, in (a minor chord) to QWL are conveniently available at other places and will not further concern this analysis. The turfs of special interest are given rough texture by Table 36.1. In short, Table 36.1 tells us two things about foundational OD literature. First, many OD applications have long existed and are sufficient for authors to group them in evaluative survey collections. Despite the variability of "success" measures, the overall results also suggest that OD could generate intended effects in proportions of cases and in expected directions.

Given the short timeline of OD applications and the agreed response difficulties of targeted changes, many observers might have been enthusiastic. But the results of applications reflected in Table 36.1 did not exert much influence. The traditional work did not carry the day. Although much work existed, few ODers seemed motivated to search for the early evaluative literature. Although many evaluative OD studies did exist, that foundation literature was essentially a *terrain incognita*. Even many ODers gave too little attention to evaluations like those reflected in Table 36.1, largely because they were inactive in searching for relevant sources. Finally, even if ODers discovered evaluative studies like those referred to in Table 36.1, a substantial proportion of ODers seemed under-impressed by the literature—as imprecisely defining "success," as being methodologically deficient, and so on.

A review of the major methodological inadequacies of the traditional literature gives useful perspectives on the points above by way of beginning movement toward developments necessary to improve the maturing literature on OD success rates.

## Measurement Problems in Foundation Literature

The basic guesstimate of success rates in Table 36.1 deserves added perspective. Consider this selected list of difficulties in studies explicitly focusing on success in OD. Some major limitations of foundation success rate estimates in the foundation literature can be detailed with only sparse discussion. These limitations lead to or derive from concerns about success rates.

- Success rate estimates are assumed to rest on only a few applications, despite Table 36.1. "Success" was defined in highly subjective terms, and operational definitions covered a large and diverse range.

- The success literature contained few examples of panels of various approaches to change, which implied few comparative possibilities.

- OD applications seldom differentiated differences in organizational and broader cultural loci—hence the even pejorative view of OD as "North American change." This obviously conflicted estimates of success.

- The OD literature often sought creative, diverse designs for change; the foundation literature rather urges comparisons between designs, targets, or interventions related to specific target variables. This limited true comparisons. The reality is that OD change efforts can have both short-term and long-term impacts, just as training interventions can have short-term and far transfer of learning, and assessing the longer-term impacts can be quite difficult to pinpoint and measure.

- OD evaluative research gave little attention to specific operational and conceptual definitions of separate variables. In sharp contrast, small group analysis had long given intensive attention to cohesiveness and trust, among many other variables.

Such variables in rare cases are found in early OD but, with few exceptions (for example, see Gibb, 1978; Zand, 1977), few practitioners sought to provide rigor to their evaluations of OD effects by specifying discrete intervening variables. In sum, substantial pessimism existed about foundation OD research on success of applications.

# SUCCESS RATES IN MATURING OD

Given the shortfalls of the evaluative literature associated with the success of early OD applications, has it been possible to move beyond those unsatisfactory tethers like those above? Four major points will be required to suggest the how's and why's of progress that has been made. In sum, the following text should provide energy to adopt an optimistic view of maturing OD applications. Consider these questions:

- What changes have been made to enhance the usefulness of collections of OD applications in evaluative research on OD applications?

- What major improvements have been made, methodologically?

- What major improvements have been made in the choice of variables in comprehensive measures of the effects of OD application?

- How does the maturing literature permit dealing more satisfactorily with the success rates of OD applications?

## Size of Collections

Simply, the number of applications in each survey population has been enlarged. As Table 36.1 indicates, the average collection of early research contains fifty-nine applications. In contrast, Table 36.2 reflects a sharp increase in collection size, from fifty-seven applications to 574. For details, see Golembiewski (2003, pp. 1–95).

Noteworthy enhancements in research derive from a first major factor. Thus the larger size of collections permits more confident and detailed subclassification. For example, collections may be (1) classified by geographic locus and (2) differentiated by kind of OD intervention(s).

These geographic distributions of collectivities of their sizes proved surprising, but their test posed no great problems. More than two decades' worth of research in journals were searched for evaluative studies, dissertations were reviewed, and consultants were contacted. There simply were more cases in more loci than many observers anticipated. One only had to probe.

Table 36.2. Geographic Loci of Mature OD Applications, in Percent

| Categories of Success | U.S.[†] | Worksites[§] | Applications[*] |
|---|---|---|---|
| I. Highly positive and intended effects | 40% | 23% | 28% |
| II. Definite balance of positive and intended effects | 46% | 67% | 57% |
| III. No appreciable effects, or balance of intended and contrary effects | 5.6% | 14% | 4% |
| IV. Contrary effects, and especially those applications with a small proportion of estimates in a contrary direction that attain statistical significance | 8% | 4.5% | 4% |
| No Data | — | 9% | 4% |

[†]Proehl, 1980.
[§]Lee, Choi, & Park, 2002, p. 41; Golembiewski, 2003, p. 226.; Yoon, 2006.
[*]Jadav & Golembiewski, 2005

The raw changes suggested in Table 36.2 enriched analyses. Not only were geographic breakouts possible but, as later points suggest, various other comparisons were possible. These helped make practice more sensitive. Basically, raw sample sizes and geographic diffusion permitted more confidence in making comparisons. Table 36.2 clearly does not support usages like "North American OD." Additionally, researchers often note that cross-cultural research often emphasizes differences in culture more than similarities.

## Methodological Enhancements

To illustrate only the larger collections made it possible to develop breakouts in OD applications. Exhibit 36.1 summarizes the kinds of OD interventions in the

### Exhibit 36.1. Kinds of OD Designs

#### Character of Interventions

   I. Process Analysis for Individuals and Groups
  II. Skill Building
 III. Diagnosis, Both Individual and Organizational
 IV. Coaching/Consulting
  V. Team Building
 VI. Inter-Team Building
VII. Techno-Structural
VIII. System Building

maturing literature. Details are omitted here but can be conveniently consulted (Golembiewski, 2003, pp. 22–24).

Such breakouts were more risky in Table 36.1, obviously, and the practical costs involved were substantial. For example, comparing success rates versus all or many classes of interventions would have great practical potential. In Table 36.1, less cross-classification is safe, even when it is attempted.

## Maturing Research on OD Success Rates

Let us summarize the points above. Directly, have the three classes of effort devoted to improving on success rates proved useful so far? No doubt much remains undone, but is the research glass more full than it was? The readers will make personal judgments, but several points encourage the author to view progress optimistically.

1. *The broad dissemination and incidences of OD research constituted a major finding.* Here, three geographic areas get primary attention—North America, South Korea, and India. To give magnitude to the present conclusion, the three collections in Table 36.2 achieve the substantial success ratings. Specifically, all three collectivities achieve substantial success—defined as 86, 90, and 85 percent, respectively, the sums of categories I plus II in the three collections of cases. More preliminary work of a similar kind considers several other geographic collections of OD applications—Italy, Arabic-speaking countries, and Poland, among others. Second, consider the effects of augmented panels of process and outcome variables. To complement as well as exploit the use of the larger number and collectivities in Table 36.2, each OD application was coded for all of the relevant 306 variables differentiated by Porras and Berg (1979). Each study was coded by three experienced observers on the possible descriptors in applications (Porras & Berg, 1979). This feature permitted the coding of each application as a "hit" or a "miss" on a comprehensive batch of variables developed by the Porras and Berg catalog. The OD enhancement takes advantage of all comparisons permitted by the large number of studies of OD applications.

The larger panel of variables is intended to contribute to more reliable and probably valid rating of the success rate of OD applications. In cases of all ties, the rating used was the lowest of all those in contention. Exhibit 36.2 is concerned with operational definition help to establish the central points at direct issue here and provides detail about some major results of the maturing concern with measures of success. As an aid to understanding Table 36.2, Exhibit 36.2 provides detail about the maturing operational definition of a "success." In the maturing version of success rates, estimates are provided in Tables 36.1 and 36.2.

To add to the sense of Exhibit 36.2, each variable in OD applications is rated by multiple observers—usually three professionals, but only two on occasion.

Proehl, C.W., Jr. (1980). Planned organizational change. Unpublished doctoral dissertation, Department of Public Administration, University of Georgia.

Skelley, B.D. (1989). Workplace democracy and OD. *Public Administration Quarterly, 13*, 176–195.

Yoon, T. (2006). New trends of OD applications in Korea. Unpublished seminar paper, Department of Public Administration, University of Georgia, Athens, Georgia.

Zand, D. (1977). Trust and managerial problem-solving. *Administrative Science Quarterly, 12*, 229–239.

# THIRTY-SEVEN

# Four Risk Factors of the Unexamined Life

*BE-KNOW-DO*

Peter Koestenbaum

O rganization development (OD) is *process*, philosophy is *content*. OD asks the hard questions, is an active listener, provides empathy and compassion, and challenges people without alienating them. Philosophy gives you a comprehensive theory of the person. Through an OD-philosophy partnership, great organizations can be built. Given this premise, what follows for the OD practitioners? In terms of the U.S. Army's classic "BE-KNOW-DO" formulation (competent, confident, and agile), what lies ahead for them?

*BE* is to ask who you are and how you present yourself to the world. *KNOW* consists of basic skills you can add to your toolbox. *DO* is made up of impactful messages you can teach and market. Think of all three as your key responsibilities, and structure them not as an OD practitioner but as one who also awakens and mobilizes the philosopher within.

## THE OVERALL RISK

The greatest risk you will ever face is to lead an unexamined life, for, as we all know, "the unexamined life is not worth living." We learn through tested Socratic dialogues. We ask the questions for others to answer. That is how they learn. That is how integrity, substance, and character are fashioned. The final secret of leadership success is to come with a beginner's mind and not as knower but as learner.

The philosophic practice of leadership is encapsulated in the T. O. T. A. L. formula, "to lead is to 'teach others the teaching of authentic leadership.'" Leadership—practical, results-oriented, bottom-line effective leadership—is to assume the role of education, which makes leadership dialogues the heart of organizational communication.

# THE MARKET'S BOTTOM LINE: THE BUSINESS CASE

One measures the market value of a company and the effectiveness of an organization by the quality of BE-KNOW-DO leadership conversations that management is able to stimulate and sustain in hallways and boardrooms and transmit to clients. This is an inviolable principle of the philosophy-OD alliance. Here is where business and philosophy intersect, crafting new elements and generating new organisms.

The global history of philosophy has done precisely that, giving us, over millennia, the tested risk factors to address to actualize the human potential.

# BE-KNOW-DO

No matter how powerful the technology and how inspired the strategy, results are in the hands of those who are, know, and do: people. For it is people and their commitments who bridge the gap between Know and Do, Concept and Customer, Thought and Finish, or, philosophically, Essence and Existence.

Below are four foundational risk factors to consider in presenting a new face to OD customers. *To be* means you have faced these major risk factors in your own life. *To know* means you see them as fundamental philosophic attitudes in terms of which to address the world. *To do* means these ideas can be translated by you into the vernacular and the stories of your clients' worlds.

You may in your inward truth speak the language of a well-established philosophy of life, but, externally, in the jargon of your customer, you use the language and the symbols that will establish between and among you the trust and emotional safety that can contribute critical additional credibility to you as a professional.

## Risk Factor One: Do You Reflect as a Philosopher?

Have you activated the philosopher in you? The philosopher in you reflects. You activate the philosopher in you to the degree that not only do you roll up your sleeves and fully *engage*, but that you also step back and authentically *reflect* on who you are, how you know, and what you do—alone and when in relationships. Reflection can become your new and higher mode of being. Earlier, in Chapter Six, a leadership self-assessment process is suggested.

To engage is to watch a play and be in a state known as "Flow," in which you are pleasantly lost in the experience. You laugh, cry, are riveted to the stage; share feelings, hopes, and anxieties with the actors; and, in general, lose yourself in the activity. That is what it means to be engaged. That is also the good worker and valued employee.

The philosopher in you now reflects. You disengage, think about what it all means, how it is connected to history. You now establish a different relationship to your public, reading your next-day column in *The London Times*, analyzing wisely the experience of attending this new play in Piccadilly. As a philosophic OD practitioner, you are put in touch with the deepest ways possible to reflect on the human condition and on the mystery of relationships among people when they engage in passionately doing their business—in health or under pathology, in greed or under high ethics.

Furthermore, you transform yourself by valuing not only the *hope* that reflection can bring but, perhaps even more importantly, the *pain*, the *guilt*, and the *anxiety* that the act of reflection, true reflection, can threaten to arouse.

## Risk Factor Two: Do You Claim the Power of Your Free Will and of Your Freedom?

The free will in you is decisive. Leaders today are coping with unprecedented demands for increased personal responsibility and individual accountability, especially at the organization's top. Profound reflection reveals the core truth of the freedom and free will that dwell miraculously in our hearts. No matter what we have done, we could always have done it differently. That revelation can be a shock, but also a relief. We invert our lives and dwell in that region, the depth of free will, as if it were a new country, a fresh landscape, the stunning discovery of an unexplored continent.

Choosing responsibility, choosing consequences, and choosing accountability as a way of being is what we then challenge others to do, and which in turn we must accept from them when they challenge us. This lies at the core of the leadership organization. This is what we know and what we do as a philosophic OD practitioner. For an organization has no alternative but to hold within a critical mass of free and self-made individuals.

Leading is helping others experience the multifaceted phenomenon of free will, being a freedom, claiming one's freedom and free will. This is who we are, is what we know and what we do. This is how we speak about the world, and these are the messages we deliver. Such is the alpha and the omega of leadership. Messaging is transforming. Speech is action. Know this and practice this, and the leadership job is done. Ignore this, don't practice it, and there is then no leadership in the organization. Nor is there then, in reality, any organization in existence in the first place.

## Risk Factor Three: Do You Choose to Adapt to and to Master Ambiguity?

"Give up certainty and surrender to ambiguity." For it appears that Job One is to adjust to the uncertainties of the world. We see that in the pervasiveness of negotiations, democracy, dialogue, diversity, team building, alignment, competition, interdependence, and diplomacy as an alternative to war, as the critical success factors in managing life as it is. As Darwin so famously is thought to have put it, it is not the strong, nor even the intelligent, who survive, but the adaptable ones. Biology is the history of survival through adaptive behaviors.

This is who you are. This is what you know. This is what you do, in that you set up organizations that reflect it. Your everyday speech reflects the power of adaptation to ambiguity and change.

A big question emerges: Does this presumptive relativism endanger your ethics? Thomas Jefferson said that in matters of style he was like flowing water. But in matters of principle he stood like a rock. Are not ethical claims realities to which all of us need to adapt? Is not adjustment to ethics what makes societies work?

Adaptation was originally automatic: molecular mutations, the survival of the fittest, and mechanical laws. Today, with educated persons, evolution is deliberately chosen.

Facing ambiguities is exemplified by the polarities of central office versus regional vice presidencies and the complexities of heavily matrixed organizations, both requiring us to cope with severe conflicts and paradoxes. Carl Gustav Jung put it thus: "All the greatest and most important problems in life are fundamentally insoluble."

## Risk Factor Four: Do You Take Charge of Your Role in Co-Building Yourself and Others?

"If no one is in charge, it's your fault." And "If we do not take charge of our own lives, someone else will." Thoughts worth pondering. And this, as leader, is what you teach.

Free will enables us to construct worlds, in the sense of worldviews, belief and value systems, and constructions of reality. The world in which we live is laboriously constructed as the perceptual and cognitive apparatus of the child grows and develops. The perceived structure of the world is then massively influenced by how the child is socialized and educated.

In addition to our personal and lifelong contributions, our world is brought into being by the changes that occur in it, changes that accelerate as we speak. The result is a mixture of our involvement—plus discovering the external facts, the data the world sends to us, the changes that we make as cultures and as individuals, changes made by science and technology, and change caused by political action and by wars. What puts it all together in one comprehensive mix is of course the adaptation of which living beings—especially humans— are capable.

## MANAGE THE OVERALL RISK OF YOUR LEADERSHIP ANXIETY

We add to the four themes of BE-KNOW-DO the risk-factor questions to who I am, what I know, and what I do—that is, we add to *philosophic reflection, free will, adaptation to ambiguity*, and to *the construction of our own world*—the pervasive undercurrent of anxiety in the modern age.

Serious negative states of mind—*anxiety, guilt, anger, resistance, denial, frustration*, and *threats*—are released, and this is normal when we deal with change issues, when we feel compelled to shift patterns, habits, and mental and business models.

These negative states of mind are what is changing in today's environment. And this, as philosophical OD coaches to leaders, you accept and you master change, and you teach to accept and to master change. Human nature is well equipped to deal with philosophy, freedom, and adaptation to ambiguity—and more building. That is the good news.

*This is what the leader understands, what the leader lives, and what the leader teaches. Leaders lead by passing on these attitudes of how they show up, by their presence, and in their behavior. That is how authentic leadership is carried out.*

*Ask yourself, what are you building? To be a leader is to be a master builder. You are that builder, you know how to do it, that is, how to build, and you can teach others how building is done. Your gift is your personal involvement, your engagement in building a life. To the degree that you can teach similar engagement through their work to others, you are an effective leader. To the extent that you are but posturing, you are still not there, disengaged, and of course it shows, and then others will not follow.*

We are all in the same situation. We all need to reflect on the quality of our engagement. Then we connect, we re-engage, at that higher level of mutual reflection on our successful or deficient engagement at work. Thus we grow in who we are, what we know, and how we do it—and the organization prospers.

*Just remember one thing. You may think that all the words above apply to you. These were but a preparatory step. The apotheosis is that every word, every punctuation mark, and any intonation you give your words is meant to be placed in service of your customers. It is your customers who mirror and witness your credibility, your worth, your substance, and your character. Such is the philosophic OD practitioner's ethics and the philosophic OD practitioner's business.*

# CHAPTER THIRTY-EIGHT

# Whole System Transformation

*Becoming Dramatically Different*

Jennifer Todd, John Parker, and Arielle Sullivan

*"Whole system transformation fosters deep change. It requires personal change.
It requires courage to take an organization through this type of change.
The impacts are tremendous as well as the capability for change in the
organization. The employee engagement that results is an unbelievable
thing to see. It is worth it! It is hard work! It's emotional! It's draining!
And yes very rewarding!!"*
John Parker, Sponsor

This chapter presents the philosophy and principles of whole system trans-formation (WST), a robust methodology resulting in an organization-wide paradigm shift. This chapter also describes a case study of a 5,800 employee division of a Fortune 100 financial services company that moved every organization metric in a positive direction, enhanced cost-effectiveness substantially by saving millions of dollars, and increased customer service at unbelievable rates.

WST engages all facets of an organization to accomplish accelerated and sustainable positive change. In the last edition of *Practicing OD*, David Brad-ford wrote in the Foreword about his concern regarding what he perceived as a diminishing role of OD. He believes few are actually doing true OD because they work piecemeal rather than with a whole system, and they lack a sophis-ticated, integrated theory of change. His concerns are addressed when practi-tioners apply the methodology of behavioral-science-based WST. The focus is on the "whole" of the organization, although individuals and groups within it transform as part of the process. Like caterpillar to butterfly, transformation is a metamorphosis as the whole works in unison from the inside out to create itself anew.

In this case, nearly one-half billion customer transactions moved from 77 percent to 84 percent satisfaction over a seven-month time span. This type of change effort, or variations of enterprise-wide change, is now needed by most organizations to respond to the ever-upcoming chaotic and surprising milieu. Our research tells us that an organization performs better when the entire system—the "whole" all its interdependent parts—engages in the process of continuous change and emerges to work in harmony together.

# CASE PROFILE: WST IN A DIVISION OF A FORTUNE 100 CES GROUP

## The Background

The case involves this Fortune 100 company's customer and enterprise services (CES) group. This group includes 5,800 employees and covers most of the company's call centers and back-office functions that deliver crucial services to customers and internal business units. It works with more than 220 million customer interactions each year.

The customer and internal business clients were asking the CES group to change. Customer loyalty and satisfaction had been stagnant at best, and feedback suggested they needed great improvements in sales/service and product support. The business clients were asking for CES to reduce costs significantly and support them in meeting their business goals. It was clear their customers and internal clients had become very dissatisfied with the status quo.

The challenges CES faced had largely to do with the culture and structures that had been put in place two decades previous, as an internally focused, shared-service organization. The division was sub-optimized into eighteen locations across the country. Locations were acting as "kingdom and queendoms with no cooperation between them" (Parker, personal conversation). Managing change was managing it away and not "rocking the boat." The desired goal was to become a more innovative, cost-effective, value-added service provider as perceived by customers.

The focus of transformation was to engage employees at all levels, shift their mindsets and behaviors to make the customers their priority, become inclusive, and develop the people in meaningful ways. The intent was also to address the changes needed in the processes, structures, and relationships in and across the organization. The Star Model (Galbraith, 2002) guided the overall effort to align all the dimensions of the CES organization to the new vision and purpose of "thrilling our customers."

## Collectively Creating a Paradigm Shift

WST leads to dramatic differences—not just incremental *change*, but true *transformation*. Characteristics of organization transformation by definition suggest radical changes in how organizational members perceive, think, behave, and manage themselves (Cumming & Worley, 2005).

In our case, the mantra became "getting different." The leadership sponsor wanted the journey to create a deep paradigm shift—a breakthrough. This breakthrough meant a personal transformation for every person in the whole system and a collective shift in mindset across the division.

> *"We cannot get different results without getting different ourselves. It's not a 'feel good' and it is not like any other conversation we have had. It is not business as usual; it's about getting different."*
>
> John Parker

This mantra translated into our WST model in important ways, one of which included adapting a foundation from the classic Beckhard transformation DVF formula—a fundamental theory for creating a collective paradigm shift (Dannemiller, 2000). The internal change agents revised the founder's formula for this project based on Beckhard's original work. The original formula:

Dissatisfactions (D) × Vision (V) × First Actions (FA) > Resistance to Change was revised by the internal change agents to be:

Dissatisfactions (D) × Aspirations (A) × First Actions (FA) × Belief (B) × Others (O) = Transformational Breakthrough (TB).

This formula describes the conditions necessary for a paradigm shift.

- "D" means allowing participants to voice *dissatisfactions* with the current state. Contrary to traditional OD approaches, this formula pulls from the Gestalt theory of resistance, based on the paradoxical theory of change, a concept originated by Arnold Beisser (1970) and then adapted by Fritz Perls' Gestalt approach to change. The paradoxical theory is based on the belief that change rests on the full acceptance of status quo and assumes that resistance is expected, healthy, and must be supported in the process. The Gestalt theory is covered in Chapter Thirty-Four.

- "A" stands for engaging with *aspirations* of the future. The word "vision" was changed to aspiration to fit the organization's desire to become the butterfly, an organization that is dramatically different, created from within.

- "FA" represents the need for *first actions*, as in the original formula. Actions were focused on getting the commitment from everyone in the organization and the momentum to make a difference.

- "B" stands for a shift in *beliefs*. It represented the shift in beliefs collectively to being dramatically different.

- "O" describes the *inclusion and engagement of others*. This reinforced the inclusive culture they desired, as described later in the chapter.

The formula asserts that, when applied, a collective paradigm shift occurs that is greater than any change resistance. Research suggests it is impossible for an organization to return to its old ways of being once it has achieved the break-through (Dannemiller, 2000). Once the shift occurs, organization members see themselves and the company differently. New mindsets are uncovered, individually and collectively, as if a veil has been lifted, the blinders are off, and new things are seen that have always been in front of them. This breakthrough in mindset gives the organization the ability to shift its attitude and behaviors to align with a desired future instead of repeating unproductive patterns of the past.

# LAUNCHES OF TRANSFORMATION

The process for CES had four launches: pre-launch; Launch 1 (alignment of the core leadership team that sets direction for the organization), Launch 2 (20 percent of the organization participating in four large group interactive events or waves); and Launch 3 (evaluation and sustainability planning for the ongoing change) (see Figure 38.1). This section describes the launches and the transformation process.

## Pre-Launch

During the pre-launch phase, attention is paid to establishing relationships, understanding the business, and completing a preliminary scan to scope out the work. An elaborate contract is written that has enough specificity that people

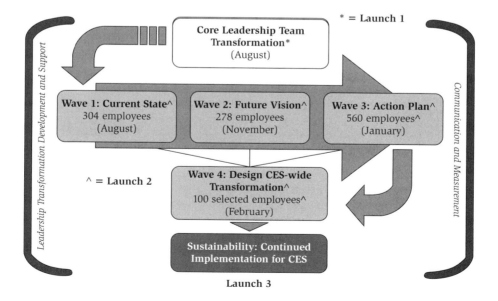

**Figure 38.1.** Whole System Transformation

know what they need to do, yet enough flexibility to support the constant and organic changes that occur. An essential step is the work with the executive sponsor to ensure he or she is truly ready to support the process of including and empowering employees to create the change. This is a critical element to assess in advance of undertaking this kind of effort.

> *"You have to be willing to let your employees engage and allow them to bring all of their voices to the table—all the 'goods' and all the 'bads' must be heard. A leader needs to be open and honest with how the organization is going to run and how he will lead it. The vulnerability required on my part was probably the biggest learning that I got out of the process."*
>
> John Parker

## Launch 1: Aligning the Core Leadership Team

As mentioned, in a successful whole system journey, a key ingredient is the active role and professional transformation of the executive leader. Of subsequent importance is the quality of the relationship between a top executive and his or her team. Next is the transformation of the leadership team itself as it relates to the larger organization. Repeatedly, we heard that the modeling of transformation by the leadership team was paramount in inspiring the remainder of the organization.

The team members decided to name themselves the "Core Leadership Team" (CLT) because they did not want to convey the notion of seniority in terms of privilege, level, or rank. They wanted to send the message to all employees that they can make an important contribution. They referred to this notion as "no stripes." Coming from a command-and-control environment since the company started seventy-five years earlier, the "no stripes" concept signified the shift to an inclusive culture of sharing power and valuing contributions from employees as equals, rather than the belief that only those in leadership positions (stripes) have power, voice, and value to add.

> *"I let go of everything I had ever been taught and practiced as a leader and engaged with my people in a completely different leadership mindset."*
>
> John Parker

**Launch 1 Process.** The following phases in the Launch 1 process were used:

1. *Initial meeting with executive sponsor*: Includes trust-building, reviewing historical data and strategies, exploring aspirations, and planning for working with their team and internal change agents.

2. *Preparation with core team*: Focuses on understanding the team's role and the process, invites commitment, and solicits input for interview questions in three key areas: What needs to change for each leader?

What must change for the team to be more effective? What changes must the team lead in the larger organization?

3. *Real-time data gathering and residential offsite planning*: Involves interviewing all members anonymously based on questions from the team and preparation of a feedback report for the sponsor and team. This serves as the basis of the design for the offsite session.

4. *Form a planning team*: Includes external and internal consultants and members of the leadership team to plan the session. The charge is to create a compelling purpose and a detailed script for a two-and-a-half-day residential session based on the breakthrough formula. Preparation and coaching of the leaders and internal consultants to own and facilitate the meeting were also paramount.

**Launch 1 Results.** The Launch 1 team alignment had the purpose of CLT speaking as "one voice."

Going into the session, the team members had spent years being competitive, lacked trust in one another, and didn't have a commitment to a collective vision. At the end of the session, the team had alignment around the changes needed and a shift from a shared service mindset to focus on process and effectiveness. One of the key objectives of this phase is team ownership and accountability for the future, not dictated by the leader, but through self-realization. There was a critical moment in the session when, after continued questioning of the sponsor about how to operate, the whole team stood up, walked over to the easel pad, and, without the sponsor, designed the service delivery model of the future. John Parker, the sponsor, said with a wink and look of pride, "Our work is done; we've accomplished our goal here." The team took full ownership of the model and of operating as a true team.

The team left the session with a common purpose, guiding principles, operating norms, and a new paradigm about their value to the corporation. At the end, they reported feeling a deep sense of pride, excitement, and focus like nothing they had ever experienced before. Before they left, using the concept of the microcosm (using representative views across the organization), a leadership group was defined, the "Operating Team," which included different views and levels that would be responsible for execution of the strategy.

The impact of the session was also realized during the large-group events later in the process. The openness and vulnerability of the CLT made a significant ripple effect across the organization. They spoke openly and publicly of the team's fears and perceptions and owned a part in creating the barriers of the past. They listened to the organization; critical feedback was acknowledged and, perhaps for the first time in years, employees at all levels felt heard; and employees had shared trust and renewed commitment in the leadership and the company.

## Launch 2: Convening Four Large-Group Interactive Waves

In this phase, the transformation work simultaneously supported an organization-wide inclusion effort that began several months prior. The inclusion intervention defined and brought to life twelve behaviors that defined the desired culture. Leadership determined inclusion and transformation needed to be integrated.

Through the integration, the efforts reinforced each other as participants received education on and lived the experience of inclusion while understanding how these behaviors connected to and resulted in hard-core business results. Modeling the inclusion behaviors in the waves supported participants in being "BIG," bringing democracy and all voices to the table (Katz & Miller, 2008). The messages about the importance of honoring people's differences and creating a safe environment for voices to be heard were called out publicly, whether they were happening or not, to reinforce the culture. Bringing the two together was a unique element that provided a business case for the behavior change and a deep understanding and clear connection of "how" (inclusion behaviors) with the "what" (CES desired business results).

**Key Principles of WST.** The ten key principles of WST were used:

1. Leaders must first model transformative mindsets and behaviors as individuals and leadership teams.

2. A compelling purpose drives everything, including conversations, relationships, actions, and events.

3. The entire effort is about the people and the business results "getting different."

4. Inclusion in behavior and attitude leverages different views so that each person contributes and is valued in the process.

5. Outcomes are a result of trusting the process of self-realization to self-actualization.

6. The wisdom is in the system; through using microcosms and collaborative interaction, the system listens and learns from itself in real time.

7. Robust tools, activities, and processes are utilized to maintain focused energy.

8. Conversations are multi-directional; truth-telling is elicited in a safe way so all contribute to the learning and change.

9. Valid current data is a key influence, bringing new awareness and direction to the system.

10. Freely choosing positive and shared aspirations with deep meaning leads to committed and aligned action.

**Design Team Role and Process.** The design team is intended to be a micro-cosm of the different locations, levels, roles, functions, and cultural or racial backgrounds that are represented in the organization. Microcosms guide the consultant group on what needs to happen and how to design it within the organization culture (Eggers, Kazmierski, & McNally, 2000). The design team creates a compelling purpose and script for the large group events. Creation of a compelling purpose statement drives the design that follows. It answers the question: What will be different in our world because of having had this meet-ing? (Dannemiller Tyson Associates, 2000a).

The design process is a parallel process or mirror image of what happens in the large meetings. "Studies of parallel process...show that what happens in one system has an impact on another. [As such] parallel process may be seen as the playing-out of experiences that are unresolved and out-of-awareness" (Davies, 1997, p. 114). Knowing this, parallel process becomes an awareness tool for diagnosing dynamics in the organization (Stevenson, 2002). This allows the consultants to build issues that arise on the team into the design, knowing they will show up in the system on a grander scale in the large-group sessions. Using the diverge/converge model, small groups diverge into deep conversations, shar-ing diversity of thought, and then they converge back out into the large group to build a common picture of the whole system (Lawrence & Lorsch, 1969).

Principles of whole system change are taught and traditional team building occurs during the design process. The group functions as a temporary project team with a critical and time-pressured task of creating the purpose, design, and script for the event. The brainstorming and alignment process typically gener-ates chaos and conflict as the group strives to produce a unique and impactful design. The consulting group was coined with the motto "trust the process," which made its way into ground rules of how to operate and was included in all orientations to the process. Meg Wheatley's (2005) emergent theory of change is paramount. Trusting the process means flowing with the emergence of con-stant change, knowing that the wisdom in the group will take us exactly where we need to go. The consultants need to be competent as "process consultants," guiding the group through task completion, as well as the developmental process, without being the "experts" giving the answers (Schein, 1988).

The design team produces a script in great detail of all that is to happen during the session. The longest script for the wave event was a fifty-four-page document that underwent twenty-seven revisions. It outlined the purpose, timing, activities, presenters, handouts, logistics, production, and anything pertinent to flawless exe-cution. The design team plays a key role, presenting different segments and paying attention to real-time feedback during and after the event. Each day they review every feedback form and discuss what's working and not working and assess the group's energy. Then the design was changed during the evening hours to support the feedback and to ensure the group purpose and objectives were met.

Immediately after every wave, a closure event was held with the consultants, design team, and CLT to discuss learning, acknowledge what had been accomplished, and bring closure to the group. As glasses clinked, stories were shared, and deep emotions surfaced as the design team members put their heart and soul into the event. Leadership was awestruck with the faith, hope, and trust the employees expressed.

**Event Logistics and Production.** In the 1950s, Dick Beckhard led the design of the first known OD large group in a three-day, five-thousand-member White House conference to develop nation-wide policies for children. He said, "Logistics are formidable. They are more important than they initially seem" (Beckhard, 1997, p. 23). Our experience suggests that participants allow one obvious logistical mistake, but the second one begins to erode the process. Convening a logistics team early in the process is important to create a detailed plan that meets the design criteria. Being proactive and paying close attention to all details of the space, materials, food, room setup, equipment, supplies, and timing can literally make or break the whole event. Logistics teams are under a great deal of pressure as they must pull everything together and adapt to the "emergent design" as it unfolds. It's important that the consultants support the team and work closely with the logistics leader.

Clearly, logistics is only one of the many facets of the event that the consultant must be closely attuned with. Kathie Dannemiller (2000) highlights the different roles to be played by the consultant when producing an event. As the consultant is managing these many roles, he or she is simultaneously building the competencies in the internal consultants who shadow and learn the process (see Figure 38.2).

**Magic of the "Waves": Large-Group Interactive Events.** In the wave itself, people sit at "max-mix" tables. Max mix is the maximum mixture of the widest possible representation of the different parts of the organization; essentially the table is a microcosm of the whole. As mentioned earlier, the design follows

| Relationship Building | Coordinating with Logistics and Production | Facilitating Design and Small Groups |
|---|---|---|
| Designing Ahead and in the Moment | Keeping the Consulting Team Whole | Coaching Leaders and Presenters |
| Gathering and Interpreting Data | Balancing Stakeholder Needs | Leading from the Front of the Room and Behind the Scenes |

Adapted from K. Dannemiller (2000b), *Whole-Scale Change Toolkit.*

**Figure 38.2.** The Roles Consultants Balance

the diverge/converge model of having tables work and discuss critical organizational issues (diverge), and then the whole room shares the results of the conversations (converge) to create a shared system view.

The sessions are always two and a half days over a three-day period to allow enough time to apply the breakthrough formula ($D \times A \times FA \times B \times O = TB$) for the collective paradigm shift to occur. The first day of the session involves context setting, group connections, and a sharing of the dissatisfactions or the current state of what is. The second day is a meaningful connection to the aspiration and what is possible. The third day generates confidence and enthusiasm as actions are generated at the individual, group, and organization levels. The design focuses on multiple levels of system in the transformation—individual, group, subgroup, and enterprise-wide. Blending whole system principles with the focus of the Gestalt level of system narrows the objective of each intervention to ultimately contribute to moving the "whole system" by the end of the third day. A key distinction of the waves is the depth of personal transformation at an individual level that is built into each day of the design. Our experience and the wisdom from the founders inform us that this shift is necessary for groups and the whole.

> "In the waves, people made personal and deep connection to the change we were talking about. We heard people talking about how to resolve barriers. We heard personal stories, innovative solutions, and generated commitment. We shared deeply among over five hundred people in one room. There were people crying. There were people laughing. There were people cheering. All of it was very surprising."
> John Parker

It's expected that the resistance is lower each day and the commitment grows higher. As the commitment gets higher, the emotions are released; by the third day of the wave, people were up giving standing ovations, dancing, singing, with tears of pride and joy flowing. Many proclaimed loudly and publicly to seas of people that they were "unleashed!"

## Launch 3: Evaluation and Sustainability

This section describes Launch 3: evaluation of the large group interactive events and the elements of sustainability planning.

As part of the evaluation of each large group interactive event, we always asked: "Did we fulfill our purpose and meet our original objectives?" We collected both quantitative and qualitative measures to assess what changes or shifts were made on business metrics and behaviors related to employee engagement and inclusion.

> "Before we even got home from the sessions, there were emails flying around, blog sites, and inspiring quotes being shared. People went back to their offices

*and put up poster boards and held their own focus groups. People of all levels went out to speak and talk about what was done. It had an impact on the way that we did our work. Instantly, we started to see change in the attitudes of our employees and that affected our customers. The results told us we were 'unleashing the magic!' as Kathie Dannemiller would say."*
John Parker

The immediate impact of the waves was astonishing and visible, through conversations, emails, and meetings. Employees at all levels were on fire! The actions and long-term impact began to take hold as many changes were made at the group, division, and whole system level. For example, business processes that had been "broken" for years were changed, the performance management process was updated, consistent performance standards were created for every employee, and a 360-degree view inclusion assessment was birthed, designed, and implemented by inspired employees.

The output of the last wave was an organization-wide action plan called "Six Bold Steps" (see Figure 38.3). This served as the beginning of the sustainability plan for measurement of business metrics and behaviors and the strategy for continuous assessment, planning, and engagement across CES.

**Figure 38.3.** Six Bold Steps

**Sustainability Planning.** This consulting team had three macro purposes for sustainability: (1) transform the CLT that results in lasting change in leadership, (2) create transformative waves that result in engagement and a sustainability plan for the organization, and (3) transfer the capability of ongoing transformation to the internal consulting team.

For the continuing transformation of the CLT, sessions were held six months and fourteen months after launch to assess and focus the team's development and create an organization strategy for the next two years.

For the rest of the organization, an elaborate ongoing measurement process, structure, and planning process were established to ensure long-term sustainability. The initial plan was developed by the participants of the last wave and then influenced by the CLT, operating, and transformation teams to ensure there was an inclusive view of the plan. In addition, based on the feedback gathered after the waves, the internal consulting team felt strongly that the remainder of CES employees (80 percent did not attend a wave, about 4,670 employees) needed a "transformation experience" to connect with the desired future state, feel included, and become engaged in the change. A series of one-day sessions was designed and executed in a cost-effective way across the country over a period of four months to provide this experience and connect all employees to the common purpose.

A permanent transformation team of internal change agents was established from the beginning to plan, monitor, and re-plan the entire effort long term. They learned by doing, working hand-in-hand with the external consultants and assimilating the competencies so that sustainable structures, processes, and experiences continue to evolve, ensuring long-term positive change. Throughout the process, special attention was paid to developing the internal consultants and transferring knowledge at each launch.

## SOLID BUSINESS RESULTS: EVIDENCE OF CHANGE

Following the transformation launches, evidence in the measurements was seen immediately. The post-surveys and various indices were at the highest level in the broader corporation, much higher than ever in the past. The post-call evaluation survey results, a survey that the customers take when they phone a call center, started to immediately improve. Years had gone by with absolutely no movement, and for seven months in a row, continuous improvement was shown, moving from 77 percent to 84 percent satisfaction.

Half-way through the year, there was concern about meeting sales goals, but after the waves, the numbers rose and CES eventually exceeded their sales goals by year-end. The organization experienced a positive change in the management of expenses. Without asking or giving direction, CES came in millions of dollars under plan, while investing more in advertising and providing resources back to the company.

A survey was conducted at intervals to measure the inclusion behaviors; focus groups were conducted with 10 percent of the population; and leadership "knee-to-knee" sessions were held to have intimate conversations to assess behavior change across the organization. These assessments, along with the yearly employee opinion survey, indicated collective behavioral change in this division with a strong seventy-five-year-old culture. The employee survey had the highest level of participation than ever before at 96 percent. Questions related to leadership scored an 89 percent favorable response, and employee engagement scored at 85 percent.

Employee engagement and learning significantly increased. Employees at all levels were leading activities as never before, with inspired enthusiasm and vigor—everything from department meetings, kick-off sessions, action planning teams, inclusion conversations, and business process changes across the organization. The masses were engaged in learning that their voices count, what they do every day counts, and their contributions are important to achieving CES's business goals.

The CES transformation proved that, by systemically engaging the whole organization in the change process, significant shifts are possible in business results, leadership, and the culture of a large, long-standing Fortune 100 corporation. As we revel when we see a new butterfly before us, so does one as he or she witnesses the tangible results and "magic" of a whole organization transformed.

# References

Beckhard, R. (1997). *Agent of change: My life, my practice*. San Francisco: Jossey-Bass.

Beisser, A.R. (1970). The paradoxical theory of change (pp. 77–80). In J. Fagen & I.L. Shepard (Eds.), *Gestalt therapy now*. Palo Alto, CA: Science and Behavior Books.

Cummings, T.G., & Worley, C.G. (2005). *Organization development and change* (8th ed.). Cincinnati, OH: South-Western.

Dannemiller, K. (2000). Values of whole system change. *Consulting today*. Hudson, NY: High Meadow Resources.

Dannemiller Tyson Associates, Inc. (2000a). *Whole-scale change: Unleashing magic in organization*. San Francisco: Berrett-Koehler.

Dannemiller Tyson Associates, Inc. (2000b). *Whole-scale change toolkit*. Ann Arbor, MI: Dannemiller Tyson Associates.

Davies, R. (1997). Parallel processes in organizational consulting. *British Gestalt Journal, 6*(2), 114–117.

Eggers, M., Kazmierski, S., & McNally, J. (2000). Unleashing the magic in healthcare. *British OD Practitioner, 32*.

Galbraith, J. (2002). Organizing to deliver solutions. *Organization Dynamics, 31*(2), 194–207.

Katz, J., & Miller, F. (2008). *Be big: Step up. Step out. Be bold.* San Francisco: Berrett-Koehler.

Lawrence, P., & Lorsch, J. (1969). *Developing organizations: Diagnosis and action.* London: Addison-Wesley.

Schein, E. (1988). *Process consultation: Its role in organization development* (Vol. 1) (2nd ed.). Boston, MA: Addison-Wesley.

Stevenson, H. (July, 2002). Parallel processes in organizational situations. Paper presented at Gestalt Institute of Cleveland.

Wheatley, M.J. (2005). *Finding our way: Leadership for an uncertain time.* San Francisco: Berrett-Koehler.

# CHAPTER THIRTY-NINE

# The Keys to Building a Transformative OD Practice

*An Interview with Edie Seashore*

Gina Lavery and Tracey Wik

Edie Whitfield Seashore is one of the pioneers in the field of organization development (OD). Edie spoke with us about her experience building a transformative practice that spans five decades.

From her college days at Antioch and her early work at the National Training Laboratories (NTL), to running NTL during its turbulent times in the 1970s, Edie's impact on the field has been far-reaching and memorable. During this interview Edie shares some compelling stories and key ideas that illustrate how she built her transformative consulting practice.

---

### Q. What is a transformative practice and its key elements?

The transformative part is to create something that isn't actually there at the time that makes a big difference. You have to shift your whole belief system or get into a new mindset that helps shift your practice.

My practice has shifted from groups to organizations that included issues of racism, sexism, inclusion, and use of self. With each shift, my practice was transformed. I was dealing with major themes in our society, and along the way I had to get rid of some of my old belief systems.

### Q. What is the animating philosophy of your consulting practice?

My animating philosophy is that people are very valuable. My practice is built on a belief in people working together and empowering themselves to be the best they can be. Then somehow I can be a catalyst in that process either by teaching, working professionally with people, or with the work I've done in organizations.

### Q. What is your passion? How has it evolved?

I'm passionate about people following their passion and not thinking that society has made better choices for them. People should choose work around things they are passionate about. I was often invited by colleagues who were excited about something because I wasn't hard to excite about ideas. I was turned on by good ideas and also began to add to and enhance them. As a result, my early work was about collaborating with people who were excited and interested about something—people who could tap into my energy, curiosity, and interest.

The latest transformation in my practice has been around the notions of triple impact and use of self. My passion now is to help leaders learn about themselves to be more effective. Then to help them understand how they use themselves to help their teams be more effective, which will then make improvements at the organizational level. My work is teaching leaders and colleagues to pass these concepts along. Getting the notion in their thinking has been difficult. It is not so much about systems but how to use yourself in a system.

### Q. What actions can OD practitioners take to stay current and to transform their practices?

OD practitioners can stay up-to-date by collecting sound and current data. We can go after information rather than working from a set of assumptions. Often we get off-target for the simple reason we don't have any current data. We're acting out of what we think we know, particularly those of us who think we are very smart.

### Q. How has your consulting practice evolved over the last fifty years?

The key thing that transformed my practice was keeping current with major societal trends and realizing, at each step of the way, how little I knew. I found myself in the middle of these trends and often at the right place at the right time. When I arrived at Antioch College, the veterans were returning on the GI bill, and I had some of the most exciting years in my life.

As I was beginning my career, two major social movements were occurring in this country: the Civil Rights Movement and the Women's Movement. I was able to help organizations during the Civil Rights Movement bring in people of color. I was able to achieve the same goals during the Women's Movement by helping institutions change from being male-dominated to include women and by helping organizations actively recruit women and to value their contributions. Transforming once exclusionary organizations into inclusive, multi-cultural, multi-ethnic organizations changed them and changed me.

During this period, I mentored colleagues who had values similar to mine regarding diversity and who themselves represented a wide ethnic and racial diversity. Going from working largely with white males to working with people of color and a different sexual orientation was a large leap for me. It forever transformed the way I lived in the world. I became the only white woman working in a black consulting firm and the straight woman in a gay and lesbian consulting firm. It enhanced my practice in ways nothing else could.

**Q. We had many discussions about technology and eventually landed on the term connectivity to describe this technological aspect of our work. For you, how does the concept of connectivity relate to the practice of OD?**

I think the only way anybody changes anything in the system is to get the right people connected to each other. With connectivity, things happen. When people get a critical mass of connectivity, they can bring about the change they want. I think it's essential. But I don't think it's obvious—people may not realize this. That's why we ask people to draw their system's map and then we ask where in their system people need to support one another.

Technology allows us to connect in ways we never thought possible and allows us to reach people anywhere, any time.

**Q. What led you to the field of OD?**

When I started my career, OD didn't exist.

I went to Antioch College because of an interesting educational experience I had in my youth. My progressive education at a John Dewey School from kindergarten through ninth grade was all about relationships, which made a big difference. I sent the word out into the universe that I needed a college that was co-ed and community-based, and that's how I ended up at Antioch.

During my junior year, I met Doug McGregor, the new president of Antioch, and hearing him speak was my first transformative experience. He talked about something that none of us knew anything about, and that was the whole notion of process. We had tasks. We did something, but we were unaware something else was going on in a group that was making a difference. This concept was so transformative that it changed my world. Doug sent me to NTL, where I was trained to work with process in groups.

**Q. What was it like as a woman at NTL?**

The first time they put me with the T-group, I gave my opening spiel, and then from across the room a man sitting literally opposite me said, "And what are your credentials for running this session?" I don't think they'd ever asked that question of a man and, in fact, this was just the question that everybody was so scared of being asked.

So I looked at him for a moment and I said, "Well, I'm here to facilitate your learning. If I can do that in the next three weeks, my credentials won't matter. And if I haven't done that, my credentials wouldn't have mattered." There was a dead silence and then we went to work. Incidentally, nobody ever asked me that question again.

THE KEYS TO BUILDING A TRANSFORMATIVE OD PRACTICE **611**

**Q. In many ways you appear to have been in the right place at the right time. Please share a transformative experience in your career.**

While I was at Antioch, I was working with the United Press in Washington. The head of the press corps got me into a press conference at the White House. The only piece of advice he had for me was to stay in the back of the room, keep absolutely still, and not move at all after he closed the conference with the words, "Thank you, Mr. President." In those days the press was dependent on the telephones to get their word in, and there were only so many telephones, so they were all going to rush out of the room to get to the telephones, and I'd be trampled.

So after he said, "Thank you, Mr. President," I stood very still as I was told to, and they all rushed out of the room. After coming to the realization that there were only two of us left in the room, the president and me, I walked across the room and introduced myself to President Harry S. Truman. I had a very nice talk with him about Antioch College before the Secret Service moved in and asked me to leave.

When I walked back in to the press room, they were all sitting in this big typing bank typing like crazy, reporting on what the president had just said. The head of the press corps said, "Edie, I'm sorry, I had to leave to get to the typewriter myself, so I wasn't able to introduce you to the president."

I said, "Oh, don't worry about it; I met him." The entire room stopped typing, and they just looked at me. No one in that room except my escort had ever met the president. As a result of that experience, I could do anything I wanted to do for the United Press and they opened any door I wanted.

**Q. What was the most difficult challenge you've ever faced as a practitioner, and how did you resolve it?**

One of the greatest challenges is when I go into a setting where I can see the wisdom of some things that could happen differently. I have to remember to be a consultant who is helping others to have that happen, rather than trying to make it happen for them. I have actually been excused from a couple of organizations in which I became more popular and more effective than the CEO who was my client. I wasn't clued in enough to myself and what was going on to recognize that was a lethal thing to be doing. I guess one of my biggest challenges is to stay in the consulting role.

**Q. What is the importance of building a support system as an OD practitioner?**

To build a transformative practice, you must have an up-to-date support system of people whom you can call upon. Two categories of people should make up your support system. One category is what I call "Blankets." The other I call "Sandpaper."

"Blankets" in our support system are those people who are nurturing. They help us to stay in touch with our strengths and help keep us empowered so that we can think and perform at our very best.

"Sandpaper" are people in our support system who challenge us to grow and change. They help us not to get stuck in out-of-date belief systems about ourselves and they encourage us to make choices that keep us in a continually transformational practice.

- Be curious;
- Follow unique trends in society;
- Seize opportunities and be in the right place at the right time;
- Work and learn with fascinating, interesting thought leaders; and
- Rearrange the furniture.

Edie's contributions to the field of OD come from a passion for her work and connections to family and community. She has benefited in every aspect of her life from the people with whom she interacted, both professionally in her practice and personally. Her practice and the clients she serves have also benefited from these interactions. Edie's choices, combined with her strong sense of purpose, determination, and belief in her value, allowed her to contribute substantially to the field of OD. Edie's life and beliefs leave an inspiring legacy—and for that we are forever grateful.

For an expanded version of this interview, please see this book's website.

PART FIVE

# THE FUTURE OF ORGANIZATION DEVELOPMENT

# CHAPTER FORTY

# Dialogic OD

*Turning Away from Diagnosis*

Gervase R. Bushe

The central point of this chapter is that some OD practices have moved away from the "scientism" or "modernist" mindset of the founders of the field and are taking us in new directions. Practitioners of these new forms don't do much in the way of "objective" data collection and diagnosis. What is emerging is more in line with interpretive, social constructionist, and other post-modern philosophies. However, much of this shift in practice is not being written about, and when it is, there isn't much awareness or discussion of how fundamentally different some of the assumptions behind what Bob Marshak and I have labeled "Dialogic OD" are from conventional, "Diagnostic OD" (Bushe & Marshak, 2009).

My intent in this chapter is to bring to our collective awareness this important evolutionary shift in OD practice so that we can think about it, talk about it, study it, and, we hope, become more effective at what we do. I'll identify what is common about these newer practices and point out how they violate key tenets of traditional OD practice. I will argue that they are OD, because they adhere to the basic values of OD. I think these new, dialogical OD practices are emerging because they are more successful at promoting transformational change in contemporary organizations and conclude with some thoughts on why that may be.

# KEY ASPECTS OF OD BEING VIOLATED BY NEW PRACTICES

OD emerged in the 1950s from attempts to apply the social and behavioral sciences to issues of leadership, teamwork, and change, so it's not surprising that at its core OD assumes there is something real and tangible about organizations that needs to be studied before prescriptions for change are made. In every contemporary OD textbook, and in many of the models in this book, practitioners are advised that a *diagnosis* needs to be made before any action is taken.

In some very successful OD practices, things are being decided and done well before any diagnosis is made, and in some cases there really isn't a diagnosis called for. In this book, one example is Mirvis's "learning journeys." A set of activities is designed without any "diagnosis" used to stimulate personal and group reflection. No "data" are collected or analyzed; rather, people reflect on their subjective experiences. Another example is Appreciative Inquiry. One of the core principles of AI, the simultaneity principle, posits that change happens the moment the practitioner engages with the system and that fateful decisions and choices are made up-front, before any "data" are collected. This doesn't mean that the practitioner isn't observing things going on and making decisions based on those observations, but it does mean that nothing "scientific" is going on.

While most of these newer processes talk about a phase of "inquiry," there are no attempts to structure data collection in ways that are "objective" or would meet any test in Nadler's (1977) classic OD text on the topic. Some people describe the "discovery" stage in AI as though it were a data-collection stage resulting in a diagnosis, but research shows that such approaches to AI don't result in transformational change. Instead, transformation requires the emergence of new ideas, particularly generative metaphors, during the AI process, and taking a data collection and diagnosis approach to the *discovery* phase of AI can work against that (Bushe & Kassam, 2005; Cooperrider & Srivastva, 1987).

The idea of diagnosis is based in a biological metaphor that is central to what we normally describe as OD, that is being violated by these newer practices, even by some who still use the biological metaphor. One of the big ideas that supported the early emergence of OD was that organizations are better thought of as open systems than closed systems, more like a live being than a machine (Lawrence & Lorsch, 1967). This approach resulted in much better methods of organizing, managing, and changing organizations, but it has run into some pretty severe limitations. The implication is that, if we could just understand all the interdependencies of all the processes and the varying impacts and co-evolutionary results of the environments we operate in, then we ought to be able to prescribe the right organization design, or leadership style, or change process.

Such a point of view makes the idea of diagnosis and prescription sensible and invites us, like the medical profession, to keep studying organizations to figure out the best way to diagnose, intervene, and manage their "health." But there are at least two problems with this point of view. First, when you fix a biological organism, it stays healthy until something else changes. But as Karl Marx pointed out long ago, any solution to the problems of human organization contains within it a new set of problems. Second, experience in the field vividly demonstrates that if organization B (operating with the same structure in the same environment) tries to copy a successful innovation from organization A, it almost never has the same result. In fact, attempts to transfer transformational changes between sub-units of the *same* organization rarely succeed.

In most cases when OD practitioners have dispensed with diagnosis, it's because they aren't looking at organizations primarily as open systems, but as interpretive, discursive, or meaning-making systems (Bushe, 2009; Marshak & Grant, 2008). From this point of view, the reason an innovation works differently in organizations A and B is that people make different meanings of the innovation in those different organizations. As a result, practitioners of organizational transformation have turned away from treating organizations as if they were biological systems in their change methods, even if they still talk like they are.

If you look at Chapter Seventeen by Axelrod, Cady, and Holman, you will see, in miniature, how this transition is playing out in the field. They use the language of systems to describe their process, but they don't really treat organizations as a living organism to be studied. Like most of these newer change processes, they are interested in "inquiry"—but that isn't really so much a research process as "asking questions that focus our attention toward deeply felt, collective aspirations, creating hospitable conditions that invite the diversity of the system to step in and take initiative." Their model is more interested in seeing what emerges than in studying "what is" in order to prescribe "what ought to happen."

## SIMILARITIES IN NEW FORMS OF OD THAT MAKE IT DIFFERENT FROM CLASSICAL OD

Perhaps the most important similarity in these new OD practices is that they assume organizations are socially co-constructed realities and, because of this, that there is nothing inherently real about how we organize, no ultimate truth about organizations to be discovered, and no model of the right way to organize independent of the people who make up any particular organization (Bushe & Marshak, 2008). There may be models of social process and organization dynamics that practitioners find useful, but as Kenneth Gergen (1978, 1997) has forcefully argued, most if not all of those are culturally specific—they are more descriptions of how things work inside a particular culture than transcendent truths about human organizations. What if we took seriously the idea that the only limitations to how we organize are our imagination and collective agreements about what is expected and possible? Newer forms of OD seem to take that idea seriously.

What these new forms of OD have in common is a search for ways to promote dialogue and conversation more effectively and a basic assumption that it is by changing the conversations that normally take place in organizations that organizations are ultimately transformed. Dialogical forms of OD are more focused on when, where, and how to promote the kinds of conversations they prescribe than on diagnosing the system against some kind of ideal model. When they engage in some form of inquiry as part of the change process, the inquiry's purpose is to surface, legitimate, and/or learn from the variety of "realities" that co-exist in the system. All these approaches assume that there isn't one "truth" to how things are but a variety of "truths." If we begin with the assumption that each human being creates his or her experience, then it follows that there will be multiple, competing, contradictory experiences in most groups of people. From this point of view, "diagnosis" is rejected because it tends to privilege one set of experiences over another. In Dialogic OD the purpose of an inquiry is not to decide what the right way to describe the system is or ought to be, but to bring to awareness people's own experience and all the different experiences contained in the system.

The when, where, and how to hold these conversations is less about diagnosis and more about creating the enabling conditions for successful conversations to take place. One of the biggest differentiators of these newer practices is how they think about and go about creating these enabling conditions. "Open Space," for example, could be described as a set of enabling conditions for innovative ideas and motivations to find kindred others. Axelrod's process of "collaborative loops" sets the enabling conditions as having a workshop with dissimilar teams that work together to create their own change processes following a prescribed sequence of activities. They have a set of prescriptions for increasing "engagement," which they view as central to their change process (Axelrod & Axelrod, 2000). The "technology of participation" from the Institute of Cultural Affairs attempts to replicate their model of human consciousness in creating focused conversations among groups of people. A specific sequence, led by a facilitator, is used to create consensual decisions (Oyler & Harper, 2007). By contrast, World Café's enabling conditions eschew the use of a facilitator, arguing that attempting to facilitate Café conversations reduces the quality of the conversations. Instead they use the image of a host and "etiquette" and prescribe a number of other unique enabling conditions, such as the creation of hospitable space and tables covered in blank paper with colored crayons for doodling (Brown & Issacs, 2005).

Two further similarities in many of these new forms of OD are a focus on exploring common aspirations and the design of preferred futures as key outcomes of the change process. An assumption of Dialogical OD is that creating new images, stories, texts, narratives, and other socially constructed realities will impact on how people think and make sense of things—and that, in turn, will impact how they act. Look, for example, at Stavros and Saint's SOAR framework or Amodeo and Cox's "systemic sustainability" model. As Amodeo and Cox put it, "There must be conscious intent to engage the whole system in dialogue and synergistic relationships in such a way that mental models are surfaced; new knowledge, structures, processes, practices, and stories are collaboratively created and shared; and diverse stakeholder voices and perspectives are heard."

This is a more profound difference from the classical form of OD than might at first appear. Conventional change processes try to change what people do based on new thinking done *by someone else*. In dialogical approaches, the focus is on eliciting new thinking in the targets of change themselves— new thinking that is not prescribed by some expert or action research team, but that emerges individually and collectively from going through the change process itself.

# WHY IT'S STILL OD

Even though some newer forms of OD are discarding data collection and diagnosis, I would argue they are still OD because they adhere to key values of OD. First, they are highly inclusive and participative—in many cases more so than the traditional OD approach of creating small representative groups to work on behalf of the whole. Many of the newer approaches advocate involving every stakeholder in the change process. Second, they tend to emphasize processes of inquiry that result in the free and informed choice of participants. They may even work harder than previous forms of OD at attempting to create what Habermas (1984) called "the ideal speech situation"—a situation in which people feel free from any social constraint to think and talk and act.

Third, in these newer forms of OD, the role of the practitioner is the same: to guide the process and to stay out of the content. Just as set out by the founders of OD, the practitioner is not an expert in what the organization should do but an expert in how to help the organization figure that out for itself. This leads to the fourth similarity, the focus on the practitioner as someone whose job is to ultimately enable or "develop" the system. The images of development in these newer approaches still look the same as the humanistic images of development that are implicit in OD.

# WHY OD IS CHANGING

Dialogic OD has emerged more from practice than theory—and theory needs to catch up. If practice is changing, it's changing because, in some cases, it's more effective to do things this way. I want to conclude with some ideas about why that might be. It might be that conventional action research processes have become too much a part of what normally happens in contemporary organizations to be transformational. It might be that "scientific" approaches to human systems only work in fairly homogeneous cultures. As our organizations become composed of ever more diverse people, the assumption that there is some social reality "out there" to be studied and understood becomes less tenable. It might be that in a world of persistent continuous change, the episodic change processes inherent in a diagnosis-treatment model are less effective, or that they take too long to get to a prescription, and the system has already changed too much for it to be valid. It may be that we live in a time when more organizational leaders are looking for something other than incremental, controlled change processes, and they recognize that planned transformation requires a much less controlled, emergent process.

For whatever reason, it seems an inescapable observation that a bifurcation in OD practice has taken place, and we therefore need more and better thinking about differences and similarities in the theory and practices of Dialogic and Diagnostic OD. For example, when is each kind most appropriate? What professional competencies are similar and different? Can they be combined in an intervention? These are just some of the questions we have to answer.

## References

Axelrod, R., & Axelrod, E. (2000). *The conference model.* San Francisco: Berrett-Koehler.

Brown, J., & Issacs, D. (Eds.) (2005). *The world café: Shaping our futures through conversations that matter.* San Francisco: Berrett-Koehler.

Bushe, G.R. (2009). *Clear leadership: Sustaining real partnership and collaboration at work* (2nd ed.). Palo Alto, CA: Davies-Black.

Bushe, G.R., & Kassam, A. (2005). When is appreciative inquiry transformational? A meta-case analysis. *Journal of Applied Behavioral Science, 41*(2), 161–181.

Bushe, G.R., & Marshak, R.J. (2009). Revisioning organization development: Diagnostic and dialogic premises and patterns of practice. *Journal of Applied Behavioral Science, 45*(3), in press.

Bushe, G.R., & Marshak, R.J. (2008). The post-modern turn in OD: From diagnosis to meaning making. *Organization Development Practitioner* (special issue on organization development for the 21st century). *40*(4), 10–12.

Cooperrider, D.L, & Srivastva, S. (1987). Appreciative inquiry in organizational life. In R.W. Woodman & W.A. Pasmore (Eds.), *Research in organizational change and development, Vol. 1* (pp. 129–169). Stamford, CT: JAI Press.

Gergen, K. (1978). Toward generative theory. *Journal of Personality and Social Psychology, 36*, 1344–1360.

Gergen, K.J. (1997). *Realities and relationships*. Cambridge, MA: Harvard University Press.

Habermas, J. (1984). *The theory of communicative action, Vol. 1*. Boston: Beacon.

Lawrence, P.R., & Lorsch, J.W. (1967). *Organization and environment*. Cambridge, MA: Harvard University Press.

Marshak, R.J., & Grant, D. (2008) Organizational discourse and new organization development practices. *British Journal of Management, 19*, S7–S19.

Nadler, D.A. (1977). *Feedback and organization development: Using data based methods*. Reading, MA: Addison-Wesley.

Oyler, M., & Harper, G. (2007). The technology of participation. In P. Holman, T. Devane, & S. Cady (Eds.), *The change handbook* (pp. 149–161). San Francisco: Berrett-Koehler.

# CHAPTER FORTY-ONE

# Valuable Insights on OD from the Contributors

D.D. Warrick

This chapter is based on the results of a survey completed by forty contributors to *Practicing Organization Development* (3rd ed.). Those who completed the survey represent an excellent cross-section of professionals involved in the field of OD. Included, for example, are founding pioneers, the authors of best-selling OD books, originators of key OD concepts, many of the researchers in OD, highly regarded practitioners, and those who are relatively new to the field.

This has been one of the most intriguing and enlightening OD projects I have been involved in. I hope that you will also find the results of the survey interesting and useful. Since the early days of OD, there have always been those who have predicted the demise of OD and questioned its usefulness. Yet OD is now practiced around the globe and has emerged as the principal field that deals specifically with change and transformation. Still, confusion exists about the field and there is concern about how OD is practiced by many who have little understanding of OD fundamentals. *With this is mind, the purpose of the survey was to collect valuable information that would bring some clarity to a number of the key issues OD practitioners, researchers, educators, and present and potential users struggle with.* The chapter is arranged so that the survey results are summarized in the exhibits with comments about the results included below them.

# HOW RELEVANT IS OD FOR TODAY'S ORGANIZATIONS?

There is little question of the relevancy of OD for today's organizations of any type or size all over the world. Organization members are searching for ways to thrive, survive, and adapt in an environment of dynamic, non-stop, unpredictable change. As shown in Exhibit 41.1, fully 93 percent of the respondents felt that OD was either very relevant (75 percent) or relevant (18 percent) for organizations. In many ways, OD has the opportunity to be the field for the times, as it addresses many of the critical issues that organizations are dealing with in these challenging times.

For the remaining 7 percent of the respondents and those who believe in the relevancy of OD, there was general agreement that OD is relevant, but there are concerns about the field. These concerns are (1) the way OD is being practiced by many who have little understanding of the fundamentals of OD; (2) the cost-driven and highly competitive environment that makes leaders reluctant to commit resources to OD efforts; (3) the unstable and constantly changing environment that makes it difficult to sustain OD efforts; and (4) the difficulty in the field of communicating to leaders what OD is and its value to organizations. These are legitimate concerns that should be addressed by OD practitioners. Surely we can apply our craft to finding imaginative solutions to these challenges.

## Exhibit 41.1. How Relevant Is OD for Today's Organizations?

**Survey Results**

| | |
|---|---|
| Very relevant | 75 percent |
| Somewhat relevant | 18 percent |
| Somewhat irrelevant | 0 percent |
| Very irrelevant | 5 percent |
| Other | 2 percent |

**Summary of Major Themes**

**Very Relevant**

- In times of dynamic change, fierce competition, and a global perspective, OD is extremely important as it is the principal discipline that deals specifically with organization health, effectiveness, change, and transformation.
- The ability of an organization to effectively manage change and make changes in today's chaotic global economy will be a major key to the success, growth, and sustainability of the organization, and OD is the major discipline that studies and develops expertise in managing change.
- OD is the primary field that focuses on building humane, high-performing organizations capable of competing in rapidly changing times while creating a quality work environment that brings out the best in people.
- OD is the most complete discipline organizations have at their disposal to help them develop, improve, and change. It is such an important discipline for the times

*(Continued)*

**Exhibit 41.1. How Relevant Is OD for Today's Organizations?** (*continued*)

that the fundamentals should be taught to leaders, managers, and key people throughout the organization.

- As the world accelerates into more uncharted territory, people and organizations need a collaborative approach such as OD to address the many issues facing organizations and nations.
- The ability of organizations to engage all of their stakeholders in creating innovative solutions to the challenges of today and tomorrow will differentiate and ultimately define their success, and OD offers unique expertise in facilitating these types of activities.

**Somewhat Relevant**
- OD is very relevant, but the relevance is often minimized by leaders who don't understand the value of OD and practitioners who aren't well trained in OD.
- The preoccupation of organizations with short-term, bottom-line results often makes OD efforts a low priority.
- Leaders seldom understand the importance of organization health in building successful organizations, and OD practitioners aren't very effective at communicating the well-documented payoffs of organization health or the human and organizational costs of being unhealthy.

**Very Irrelevant**
- The constantly changing environment of organizations should make OD more relevant, but it often creates an unstable environment that discourages starting or sustaining changes.
- Most of today's organizations are so cost and bottom-line driven that they aren't willing to allocate resources for internal or external OD efforts.

**Other**
- OD properly practiced is very relevant, but the way it is practiced by many who are not well trained in OD gives the field a bad name.

# HOW BRIGHT IS THE FUTURE OF OD?

The respondents were optimistic about the future of OD, and 88 percent rated the future as very bright or somewhat bright. Exhibit 41.2 lists many reasons for the optimism. Topping the list is "OD is spreading worldwide, with growing numbers of practitioners, conferences, and contributors to OD literature coming from all parts of the globe."

It is, however, noteworthy that only 53 percent of the respondents rated the future very bright and that 12 percent rated the future not very bright or definitely not very bright. Many of the same concerns expressed are listed under the relevance of OD. Other concerns primarily had to do with the lack of cohesiveness of thinking in the field. Edgar Schein said, "It seems to me that more and more organizations are doing something that is labeled OD so the practice seems to be alive and well." However, he also commented on the lack of coherent theory and practice in the field.

OD appears to have survived past criticisms and confusion over what OD is and how it is practiced and will likely continue to do so in the future. *However, this should not be an excuse for not trying to add clarity to the theory and practice of OD and to doing a better job of communicating and promoting the value of OD.* One of the respondents pointed out that almost everyone in an organization has at least some degree of understanding of what HR is, but few have any idea what OD is. Another respondent pointed out the unifying and edifying influence that the Society for Human Resource Management (SHRM) has on the field of HR, while OD has no similar voice of the same magnitude. A counterargument was also made, however, that HR is also struggling to reinvent itself so it can be more relevant for today's times and that few long-standing fields such as psychology and sociology are marked by united thinking on theories and practices.

### Exhibit 41.2. How Bright Is the Future of OD?

**Survey Results**

| | |
|---|---|
| Very Bright | 53 percent |
| Somewhat Bright | 35 percent |
| Not Very Bright | 10 percent |
| Definitely Not Very Bright | 2 percent |

*Summary of Major Themes*

**Very Bright**

- OD is spreading worldwide with growing numbers of practitioners, conferences, and contributors to OD literature coming from all parts of the globe.
- Dynamic change and the need to build organizations that can succeed in a rapidly changing environment should make OD increasingly needed.
- Successfully managing change is now a vital competency needed by organizations, and OD is the major source of knowledge and practice on managing change, especially large scale change.
- As business strategies and organizations become more complex, OD becomes increasingly important as a way to assist business leaders in building sophisticated organizations able to execute global and multi-dimensional strategies.
- OD practitioners can play a very important and valuable role in helping organizations succeed, manage change, and utilize and unleash talent in organizations.
- The values, concepts, tools, and research contributions of OD are needed now more than ever before and will become increasingly needed in the future.
- There is a constantly growing body of knowledge about OD available, and OD has become a standard in most organization behavior and management textbooks.
- OD master's and Ph.D. programs are available in several countries.
- The opportunities for those who can integrate theory, scholarship, and practice and clearly communicate what OD is and how to utilize it are great.
- Leaders of the future will need OD or at least OD principles as a core competency.
- It may not always be called OD, but the principles of OD will definitely be used in the future to improve organizations and manage change.

*(Continued)*

**Exhibit 41.2. How Bright Is the Future of OD?** (*continued*)

**Somewhat Bright**
- Organizations are under significant financial pressure and, while they need OD, they may not seek OD.
- The future will be brighter if OD can develop more methods and practices for the times and do a better job of communicating the value and payoffs of OD.
- The future of OD can be brighter if OD research and literature can do a better job of addressing today's issues in organizations and providing data that support the value and benefits of OD to organizations.
- We seem to be drifting toward a marketing-oriented, consultant-based, tips-and-techniques approach to OD, instead of the solid, research-and-principles-based approach OD was founded on.
- OD is often relegated to a secondary role in HR rather than having a place in top-level decision making.

**Not Very Bright**
- Many who practice OD are not well educated and trained in OD and, while they may be well intended, they create doubts about the value of OD.
- OD has not learned how to communicate and demonstrate the value of OD to the bottom line.
- OD principles and practices are being increasingly utilized and practiced by other disciplines, leaders, and organizations, but seldom under the name of OD.

**Definitely Not Very Bright**
- OD has not developed a coordinated and understood body of knowledge, so there is not a unified perception of what OD is.

# WHAT IS THE PURPOSE OF OD?

This question provided many valuable insights about OD that could indeed add more clarity to the field. Richard Beckhard (1969, p. 9), in one of the earliest definitions of OD, defined OD as:

> "An effort (1) planned, (2) organization-wide, and (3) managed from the top, to (4) increase organizational effectiveness and health through, (5) planned interventions in the organization's processes using behavioral science knowledge."

You could, of course, take issue with some parts of Beckhard's definition. However, the purpose of OD is made clear: *to increase organizational effectiveness and health.* Organizational effectiveness typically focuses on improving an organization's performance, results, operational capabilities, and ability to achieve the desired goals. Organizational health typically focuses on improving the leadership, quality of work life, teamwork, culture, processes, and ability to manage and adapt to change in an organization. Research on best-run and most successful organizations consistently shows that they focus on both the effectiveness and health of the organization, and that focusing on one without the other will eventually have consequences to the organization. This is particularly true of organizations today that are preoccupied with performance while neglecting building a healthy organization that brings out the best in leaders, employees, teams, and the organization and that can attract, motivate, and retain the best talent available. Other definitions have also included some version of *developing self-renewing capabilities* (building self-renewing learning organizations) to the purpose of OD.

There were, of course, a variety of perspectives on the purpose of OD expressed by the respondents, but the clear theme was to improve the *effectiveness, health, and self-renewing capabilities* of organizations. In evaluating the responses in Exhibit 41.3, you will see these themes expressed in different but consistent ways, which suggests that there may be more agreement among experts in the field of OD on the purpose of OD than previously thought.

#### Exhibit 41.3. What Do You Consider to Be the Purpose of OD?

*Summary of Major Themes*

- To help develop organizations and manage change in ways that will improve the effectiveness and health of individuals, groups, and whole organizations.
- To improve the performance of organizations and work lives of individuals.
- To help organizations: (1) perform effectively; (2) create a work environment that brings out the best in individuals, teams, and the organization; (3) increase the capacity and opportunities for learning, developing, and adapting; and (4) develop skills in managing change.
- To help build healthy, high-performing, self-renewing organizations that are skilled at managing change.
- To develop healthy, effective organizations.
- A process of planned interventions utilizing behavioral science principles to change a system and improve its effectiveness in such a way that the organization and its members learn and develop.
- Developing organizations to improve their performance, cultures, quality of work life, and ability to manage change.
- A process that involves stakeholders in creating organizations that achieve their mission and unleash human potential.
- To help organizations become successful, adaptable, and sustainable in the environments in which they function.
- To engage organizations in maximizing the potential of organizations, groups, and individuals.

## WHAT ARE THE MOST IMPORTANT CONTRIBUTIONS OF OD?

I found this part of the survey to be inspiring! Exhibit 41.4 lists fifteen major contributions that were identified by the respondents. No doubt many more could be added, but the list shows that OD has had a major impact in many ways on organizations and on the education of leaders, change agents (specialists in OD), and change champions (people who want to learn how to champion change). Certainly OD is the primary source for knowing how to build healthy, high-performing organizations and manage change. It also made popular such concepts as action research; systems thinking applied to organizations; the importance of process and content; interventions and techniques for improving individual, team, and organization performance; and for other concepts such as Appreciative Inquiry, sociotechnical systems, organization transformation, trans-organization development, large scale change, large group methods, T-groups, and many others now being used in organizations.

### Exhibit 41.4. What Do You Consider to Be the Most Important Contributions of OD?

***Summary of Major Themes***
- Developing a body of knowledge, processes, techniques, and research for improving organization effectiveness and health and understanding and managing change.
- Focusing attention on the importance of the human side of organizations and that organizations must emphasize organization health as much as organization performance to achieve the best results.
- Using systems thinking and theory to understand, develop, and change organizations.
- The action research approach to identifying and approaching organization issues, development, and change.
- Providing planned change models, methods, and processes.
- Developing techniques and interventions for improving the effectiveness of individuals, groups, and organizations.
- Introducing the concept of diagnosis for organizational purposes and using the results to discover reality and plan and implement change.
- Providing methods and research that emphasize the value of collaboration and participation.
- The focus on *process* (how you do things) being as important as *content* (what you do).
- The T-group model and other methods for helping people develop greater self-awareness and a better understanding of the dynamics of groups.
- Integrating and utilizing behavioral science knowledge to improve organizations.
- Introducing concepts such as appreciative inquiry, sociotechnical systems, large scale change, large group methods, organization transformation, transorganizational development, and other techniques for improving organizations.
- Providing research, literature, and results that emphasize that humanistic values can have powerful bottom-line results.
- Championing the importance of creating self-renewing and self-sustaining learning organizations that are capable of learning and adapting to change.
- Creating a field that is now being used worldwide to address organizational and global issues.

# WHAT ARE THE MAJOR MISTAKES MADE BY OD PRACTITIONERS?

The list of major mistakes made by OD practitioners shown in Exhibit 41.5 is another valuable contribution made by the respondents. Many OD practitioners wish they would have had access to a list like this as they were practicing OD and had to learn the hard way about what to do and what not to do. Topping the list is being well educated and trained in OD, and ending the list is continued personal and professional growth and development and staying up-to-date with the latest OD thinking and practices. It is what we teach and encourage, but don't always practice.

### Exhibit 41.5. What Are the Major Mistakes Made by OD Practitioners?

**Summary of Major Themes**

- Lack of education and training in OD, resulting in flawed strategies, interventions, and approaches to change.
- Lack of diagnostic skills and tools, which can result in treating symptoms rather than the real issues.
- Designing interventions that are not sufficiently grounded in OD theory or that are designed to fit what the practitioner knows, has learned to do, or is passionate about, rather than what the client needs.
- Lack of knowledge of organization dynamics, business, systems thinking, and what it takes for organizations to succeed.
- Not fully understanding the critical role of leaders in the change process and of the importance of keeping them actively engaged and involved.
- An inability to clearly and convincingly communicate to leaders the advantages of OD.
- Trying to create change without the necessary change structure (sponsorship, clear roles and goals, skilled change agents, change champions, and change team, depending on what is needed and what is available, and so forth).
- Not integrating interventions enough into an organization's mission, strategy, and operational issues.
- Lack of an action- and results-oriented approach that focuses on both organization health and effectiveness and measurable outcomes.
- Failing to help design, communicate, and implement interventions that are clearly understood.
- Designing interventions that are too complex and time-consuming and losing the commitment and interest of clients.
- Applying OD without an understanding of the history, dynamics, and culture of the organization or country in which OD is being used.
- For outsiders failing to build the necessary relationships and partnerships with HR, OD departments, and key leaders and players.
- Working alone without the perspectives of others may limit what you see and do that would be helpful to clients.
- Too much attention to process and not enough attention to results.
- Lack of understanding of how to apply current technology to OD.

# CHAPTER FORTY-TWO

# The Shifting Field of OD Practice

Jane Magruder Watkins

If we are living in a so-called post-modern era in which everything we believed about how human systems "work" seems to be turned upside down, what are OD consultants supposed to do now? How do we work in this environment? Is everything that we have known and practiced now "out-of-date?"

Well, not very out-of-date! The good news is that the OD required in this emerging era is deeply rooted in the early experiences, theories, and practices developed by the founders of the field. In the 1940s, Kurt Lewin and fellow behavioral scientists were musing about democracy, autocracy, and leadership in human systems. They pondered group phenomena such as the persecution of European Jews and racism in America. They experimented with groups and theorized about group processes. They began to make observations and to articulate new ideas about how groups develop and function. From their early experiments in the late 1940s, through the establishment of The National Training Laboratory and its work in the 1950s, the field of OD grew and began to flourish.

Over time, traditional OD became grounded in Kurt Lewin's "action research" cycle. Broadly, the process for an OD intervention was a variation of Gather Data; Analyze the Data; Make a Plan; Implement the Plan; and Evaluate. As practiced, the process usually includes an external OD consultant gathering information (data) from the people within an organization in order to analyze the data, identify the problems, and feed it back to the leadership team. Because of this feedback, the consultant often facilitates a group in the organization to plan for and to implement solutions for the identified "problems."

Arphorn Chuaprapaisilp warns OD consultants about reducing Lewin's Action Research Cycle to a rote process. He writes, "One of the legacies Kurt Lewin left us is the 'action research spiral'—and with it there is the danger that action research becomes little more than a procedure. The notion of a spiral may be a useful teaching device—but it is all too easy to slip into using it as *the* template for practice" (1997, p. 248).

That observation was prophetic, describing a dilemma for OD consultants today. The spiral, for many practitioners, *has* become the template for practice. The traditional cycle of the OD process, implemented in traditional ways and focused on looking backward to what is not working, is not adequate to keep up with the increasing rate of change.

By seeking information about what is not working, two things result. First, it leads people in the organization to focus on failures, problems, and troubling feelings about their work—a process that can lead to low energy and discontent. Second, because the consultant, interpreting the data, is from outside the system, there is little ownership of, and often resistance to, the messages the consultant delivers. Neither of these outcomes energizes the system to focus on strengths and successes that hold the lessons for creating a strong future. What, then, might OD consultants be doing in this emerging reality?

## THE SHIFTING ROLES OF ORGANIZATION DEVELOPMENT (OD) CONSULTANTS

It is generally accepted that the idea of an outsider "consulting" to an organization began with Frederick Winslow Taylor (1856–1915), an American mechanical engineer who sought to improve industrial efficiency. He is regarded as the father of scientific management and was one of the first *management consultants*. This early model of consulting was primarily one of an "expert" who came into the organization to "tell" and "fix." Such expert consultants are still needed today for tasks that require expertise in computers, accounting systems, retirement plans, and so forth. They provide skills the system needs to address a problem that is linear and mechanistic in nature.

The work of Lewin and his associates in the field of behavioral science led to consultants being called to help an organization address a particular "behavior" problem among the staff such as conflict, leadership, or team building. The notion that "outsiders" could come into organizations as *process consultants* and work to help the system become more functional was a step beyond the more traditional and mechanist model of "expert" consultants who came in to tell and direct.

Influenced by innovation in the field of OD over the last four decades and by the rapid acceleration of the rate of change in the world today, as mentioned in many chapters of this book, OD consultants are moving into new roles. Traditionally, we have understood that OD consultants are behavioral scientists who are well versed in how people behave; how groups form and function; and how human beings learn to change in order to create more effective and thriving systems. Good consultants also know a great deal about their own behavior as individuals, as consultants, and as a participant in groups. OD consultants often work with small groups and with separate parts of a larger system. Their task is to support people to work together more effectively and in ways that support the organization and help it to thrive.

The post-modern era calls for a process that is more complex and compelling—the engagement of *all* the people in an organization in identifying what is needed and in creating new ways forward. Such organization-wide engagement creates a continuous and cyclical process that is essential in a world of uncertainty and rapid change. What the organization does in a single engagement with the consultant must be facilitated in such a way that the organization creates and owns the process itself and takes responsibility for creating the way forward.

OD consultants are also discovering that when working in this reality, they are most successful when they function as *educators* and *facilitators*. Their job is to equip clients with knowledge and skills that enable them to create high-performing, agile, and successful human systems. This type of consulting is OD at its best for today's realities.

Most importantly, we are beginning to understand that human systems are highly interconnected wholes requiring larger and more complex processes. To understand what "whole systems" means, we turn not only to behavioral scientists, but also to physicists and their quantum theories. Dozens of books today reflect this connection between what we once called "pure science" and the field of "behavioral science." Thus, Albert Einstein's musings on human systems become relevant to our work (www.brainyquote.com):

- It has become appallingly obvious that our technology has exceeded our humanity.
- We cannot solve our problems with the same thinking we used when we created them.
- We shall require a substantially new manner of thinking if mankind is to survive.

# COMPETENCIES NEEDED IN OD CONSULTING TODAY

In a world where, according to Einstein, "our technology has exceeded our humanity," it is the job of OD consultants to help human beings in organizations "acquire a new manner of thinking." If OD consultants heed the warnings of Einstein, there are important competencies that must be added to the traditional human relations skills of well-trained OD practitioners. These competencies include:

1. To have a deep understanding of the phenomena of wholeness—the intimate connectedness of every part of the organization. Consultants need the ability to examine and challenge their own assumptions about their work and how human systems really function. They must, themselves, shift from traditional beliefs in dichotomous reality and the idea that we can study "parts" of a system, to an understanding of the concept of "whole systems," interconnected in complex ways that make it impossible to change one part of the system without affecting the whole.

2. To know how to transfer that knowledge of wholeness to the clients so that they understand the impact of their individual actions on the whole and, further, to understand that an intervention in any one part of the organization will ripple out to affect all other parts. This understanding on the part of those in the organization will lead to greater collaboration and stronger commitment to one another as they observe and learn from the impact of their own behavior on multiple parts of the organization.

3. To know how to enable people within the system to develop the skills needed to help their own organizations become high-performing, interconnected systems and to empower the people in the system to create ways of working creatively and effectively in an environment of continuous and accelerating change. It is essential that the people within the organization feel ownership for the process of managing continuous change. The consultant's task is to empower the system to know itself and to trust that by seeking to identify the strengths and the positive core of their enterprise, they will collectively imagine and then create their best possible future.

4. To have the capacity to engage multiple ideas and possibilities without judging, and the ability to facilitate the development of that capacity in those with whom they work.

5. To step aside as clients develop the understanding, skills, and abilities to function creatively and independent of outside guidance. Ideally, the

OD consultant facilitates the process so the role of consultant is almost invisible.

6. To understand and act congruently with the values and beliefs reflected in the theory and practice of OD. From its inception, OD has focused on helping consultants understand themselves and the impact of their behavior on the groups with whom they consult. It is from the consultants' "way of being" that client systems are able to observe, learn from, and eventually emulate the behavior of the consultant through an experiential learning process. Master OD consultants are the embodiment of the kind of behavior needed to facilitate and empower the people of an organization to become successful change agents within their own systems.

With these competencies, OD consultants can move easily into complex and daunting situations comfortable in the knowledge that within any system there resides all of the knowledge and expertise needed to create a successful enterprise.

The consultant's mantra in this new era is, "It's not about me; it's about all the people in the organization!"

# Reference

Chuaprapaisilp, A. (1997). Action research: Improving learning from experience in nurse education in Thailand. In R. McTaggart (Ed.), *Participatory action research: International contexts, and consequences*. New York: SUNY Press.

GUEST ESSAY

# Soular Power

*Angé Wayne*

There is a power that lies within the soul. It is a hidden tool that most of us do not recognize. It is the driving force behind ALL we do. When our souls are empowered, we can achieve greatness beyond our conditioned limitations. When our souls are disempowered, the losses are greater than we could ever imagine. Our lives, companies, communities, and economies suffer as we continue a journey down a "mind made" pathway, perceived as our current reality that we believe cannot change.

Organisation transformation cannot succeed as a complete solution without having a clear vision and purpose for every person involved. Pure intellectualisation of the process will not result in lasting, meaningful change. Organisation development (OD) will only continue to shift mindsets throughout any system when there is a heart and mind connection. This connection is called "Soular Power"—the energy source of life.

So why is it that some of us are sometimes so short of energy? How can we consistently create, apply, and develop effective transformation methodologies in our teams and their own complex structures? It starts with identifying and defining a vision, which will provide the driving purpose for change. Our passion and our purpose play the most important part in transformation and all the parts of the whole we would like to see change. The answer is staying self-empowered. This means not asking or expecting the "outside" or "them" to keep us motivated, but rather to find a place where we are on auto-pilot, soul-driven—where our energy drives those around us to achieve more in every possible way.

Have you experienced this energy form wherein we actually do what we love? Notice how we consistently stay in a place of unlimited creativity and drive—where our creative powers keep us working for days on end, never tiring? Where does this come from and *how* can we stay tapped into this as long as possible? This powerful resource that drives us as human beings comes from our souls.

How can we creatively work with soular power to change ourselves and those around us for the better? It is my opinion that soular power comes from pure love. Love is the conduit and energy is the carrier of this "living electricity." Love keeps us inspired, purpose-driven, and clear on our path of joyous desire. To experience *all* of life as it was meant to be experienced through the process of grateful learning and appreciation, we need to feel a certain way. We need to stay empowered to remain on this pathway to consistency instead of succumbing to the distractions of emotional sabotage.

Soular power is contained energy, with unconditional love as the spell-breaker or spell-maker to keep this creative vehicle—the human being—balanced, focused, and joyous. Our souls are here to experience through the eyes of higher purpose or the arms of God reaching out to create and experience Himself. Soul is here assisting us, opening more doors to an abundant and divine existence, or heaven on earth! All we have to do is understand—understand that when we allow the soul direct connection to that of which greatness itself wants to experience, we then allow ourselves to be—to be all we can be.

How can we become something greater or start to believe in our own greatness if we can't even begin to learn how to love ourselves? To allow growth we must learn to love our "selves," the part we dislike about ourselves the most. It is this part that incurs conditioning. It is the mind's illusion that we have a separate part to our entire existence, thus preventing the soul connection. The mind, self, or ego where our belief systems lie blocks our own ability to grow. Only when empowered by the soul and not the mind can change start happening. Loving our "selves" is not taught publicly. We have to literally seek out teachers to train us in our simple truths, yet to be acknowledged as purpose. We are trained or conditioned to love others instead of trained to start changing our current belief systems about how we feel about our "selves."

## SHIFTING THE FOCUS ON FEAR

To change your organisation, its behaviour, and your own reality, there needs to be a shift in focus—to focus on a "love" for doing something, instead of being focused on fear. We need to face our fears. As the frequency of negative incidents and news escalates in the world today, there is a drive toward creating an experience of the opposite—a society free of these fears. People are increasingly finding that their lives remain shallow and quite lonely in the materialistic world and so imagine a society in which people connect at a deeper level.

People are yearning to live fearlessly, to be happy, and to have a purpose. To create organisation transformation and personal development, we must choose change, reconnect with our hearts, and empower our souls.

# ABOUT THE EDITORS

**W**illiam J. Rothwell, Ph.D., SPHR (wjr9@psu.edu), is professor of workforce education and development in the Department of Learning and Performance Systems at Pennsylvania State University and leads a graduate emphasis in workplace learning and performance. He is also president of Rothwell & Associates, Inc. (see www.rothwell-associates.com), a full-service private HR consulting firm. Before entering academe in 1993, Rothwell had twenty years of experience as a practitioner, serving first as training director for the Illinois Office of Auditor General and later as assistant vice president and management development director for The Franklin Life Insurance Company, at that time a wholly owned subsidiary of a *Fortune* 50 multinational company.

Best known for his extensive and high-profile work in succession planning and management (see *Effective Succession Planning*, 3rd ed., 2005), Rothwell has authored, co-authored, edited, or co-edited over three hundred books, book chapters, and articles—including sixty-four books. His most recent publications include *Basics of Adult Learning* (2008) for ASTD Press; *Cases in Government Succession Planning: Action-Oriented Strategies for Public-Sector Human Capital Management, Workforce Planning, Succession Planning, and Talent Management* (2008), with J. Alexander and M. Bernhard for Human Resource Development Press; *Mastering the Instructional Design Process: A Systematic Approach*, 4th ed. (2008), with H. Kazanas for Pfeiffer; *Working Longer: New Strategies for Managing, Training, and Retaining Older Employees* (2008) with H. Sterns, D. Spokus, and J. Reaser for AMACOM; *Cases in Linking Workforce Development* to *Economic Development: Community College Partnering for Training, Individual Career Planning, and Community and Economic Development* (2008) with P. Gerity as editors for the American Association of Community Colleges; and *Human Resource Transformation: Demonstrating Strategic Leadership in the Face of Future Trends* (2008) with R. Prescott and M. Taylor for Davies-Black Publishing, a division of Consulting Psychologists Press.

Rothwell completed a B.A. in English at Illinois State University, an M.A. (and all courses for the doctorate) in English at the University of Illinois at Urbana-Champaign, an M.B.A. at the University of Illinois at Springfield, and a Ph.D. with a specialization in employee training at the University of Illinois at Urbana-Champaign.

Jacqueline M. Stavros, DM (jstavros@comcast.net), possesses twenty years of strategic planning, marketing, international, and organization development and change experience. Stavros is an associate professor for the College of Management, Lawrence Technological University, where she teaches and integrates strengths-based practices such as Appreciative Inquiry and sustainable development concepts in leading organizational change, strategic management, organization development, and leadership.

She has worked and traveled to over a dozen countries in Asia, Europe, and North America. Clients have included ACCI Business System, BAE Systems, Fasteners, Inc., General Motors of Mexico, Jefferson Wells, NASA, Tendercare, United Way, Girl Scouts USA, gedas International, Orbseal Technologies, and several Tier 1 and Tier 2 automotive suppliers, nonprofit organizations, and higher-education institutions.

She has co-authored and edited many books, book chapters, and articles. Books include: *Dynamic Relationships: Unleashing the Power of Appreciative Inquiry in Daily Living* (with Cheri Torres) and *The First Appreciative Inquiry Handbook: For Leaders of Change* (with David Cooperrider and Diana Whitney, 2003 and 2008). She completed three new book chapters on SOAR™, with the most recent for *Innovative Approaches to Global Sustainability* on "SOAR from the Mediocrity of Status Quo to the Heights of Sustainable Development" and "SOAR: A New Approach to Strategic Thinking and Planning" in *The Change Handbook*. She is working on the third edition of *Practicing Organization Development: A Guide for Leading Change* and *Thin Book of SOAR: Creating Strengths-Based Strategy*.

She earned a doctorate in management at Case Western Reserve University. She earned an MBA from Michigan State University and a BA from Wayne State University. Stavros is an associate for the Taos Institute and editor for Taos Institute Publishing. She is a board member of the Positive ChangCore, a virtual global organization that focuses on strengths-based approaches to learning in primary education (Pk–12th grade). She is a member of the Academy of Management the Organization Development Network, and the Organization Development Institute.

**R**oland Sullivan (r@rolandsullivan.com) has been a full-time professional organization change and development pioneer since the mid-1960s. He has been a change artist for change agents in nearly one thousand systems from fourteen countries and virtually every major industry. He coined the phrase "Whole System Transformation" to represent his passion for the development of personal consciousness, excellent team performance, and large interactive summits—all in the context of leading continuous comprehensive organization or trans-organization change. By having taught OD in eight universities and co-editing with Quade and Rothwell Pfeiffer's *Practicing Organization Development* and AI or Positive Change series, he evidences his commitment to propagating the OD profession.

NTL, Loyola University of Chicago, and Pepperdine University contributed significantly to his formal learning. His learning edge these days is around the integration of appreciative inquiry into traditional leading OD. Sullivan's website is www.rolandsullivan.com.

**A**rielle Threlkeld-Sullivan (arielle-threlkeld-sullivan@uiowa.edu) is finishing her bachelor's degree at the University of Iowa–College of Liberal Arts and Sciences. She has worked as an executive assistant for Best Practice Institute. Her position as co-editor for the third edition of *Practicing Organizational Development* is her first professional editing job. She views this experience as an opportunity to grow and learn more about the intriguing world of organization development. In 2008, she was also appointed the "go green" chair to build environmental awareness for her sorority, Gamma Phi Beta. Her major is business studies, with a minor in Spanish. She has earned both an International Business Certificate and an Entrepreneurship Certificate.

# About the Contributors

**B**illie T. Alban, M.F.A. (albanb@aol.com), is president of Alban & Williams, Ltd. Billie teaches in executive development programs at Columbia and other universities. Her consulting has focused on organization change. Billyie speaks fluent Spanish and has consulted in Latin America, Europe, the UK, and New Zealand. She has served on the board of the Organization Development Network and the board of advisors of the Yale University Divinity School. Her writing includes many articles and two books with Barbara Bunker: *Large Group Intervention* and *The Handbook of Large Group Methods* (Jossey-Bass, 1997 and 2006). Her most recent book with Loren Mead, *Creating the Future Together* (Alban Institute, 2008), is the application of large group methods to faith-based communities.

**M**ona A. Amodeo, Ph.D. (mona@idgroup.us), helps organizations create success within the context of social and environmental responsibility. Mona is a seasoned coach, facilitator, and strategist. She is the founder and president of Idgroup, a consulting and creative firm based in Pensacola, Florida, as well as the creator of Branding from the Core®. This process engages organizations and individuals in discovering, communicating, and living authentic brand stories that create unparalleled customer experiences, energized employee engagement, and strong marketplace recognition. Through her partnership in Branch Creek Collaborative, she facilitates the exploration of sustainability as a core value. Mona also leads seminars and conducts one-on-one and small group coaching programs to educate others about her approach to branding through The Branding from the Core® Network.

Julie Auger (Julie@stevecady.com) received a bachelor of science degree in environmental science and biology with an emphasis on ecology from Florida International University. This perspective is an advantage as she makes connections between the natural entangled networks of relationships and human systems. After thirteen years with the U.S. Fish & Wildlife Service and Forest Service, she began working in the field of large scale system change. As managing partner of Steve Cady & Associates Inc., Julie balances her time between business operations, research projects, facilitation, and consultation for large complex system change and other collaborative design projects. Julie was on the core design team for 2008 Nexus for Change Conference. She is currently pursuing a doctorate degree in OD.

Emily Axelrod, M.A. (Emily@axelrodgroup.com), is co-founder and principal in The Axelrod Group, Inc., created with her husband. For over twenty years, Emily has been a consultant to Fortune 500 companies, educational institutions, government agencies, healthcare organizations, and nonprofits. She uses strategic visioning, work redesign, and team development processes to help these groups build more sustainable, dignified enterprises. Her recent clients include Fraser Health Authority, Barrington School District 220, ThyssenKrupp, and Berrett-Koehler Publishers. Emily is speaker and coach, focusing on employee engagement and whole systems learning. She has presented to a variety of organizations, including the American Management Association and the London Strategic Planning Society. Emily co-authored *You Don't Have to Do It Alone* and *The Conference Model* and is a contributing author to *The Change Handbook* and *The Flawless Consulting Field Book*. Emily holds two master's degrees: from the University of North Carolina in education and from Loyola University in social work.

Michael Beer, Ph.D. (mbeer@hbs.edu), is Cahners-Rabb Professor of Business Administration, Emeritus, at the Harvard Business School and chairman and co-founder of TruePoint and TruePoint Center for High Commitment and Performance. Michael is a world-renowned researcher and practitioner in organization effectiveness, organization change, and human resource management. He has authored many articles and authored or co-authored nine books, among them *Managing Human Assets* and *The Critical Path to Corporate Renewal*, which received the Johnson Smith & Knisely award for the best book in executive leadership in 1990. His forthcoming book from Jossey-Bass is *High Commitment, High Performance: How to Build a Resilient Organization for Sustained Advantage*. Michael has consulted with dozens of

Fortune 500 companies, served on the editorial board of numerous professional journals, and on the board of governors of the Academy of Management.

**D**avid S. Bright, Ph.D. (david.bright@wright.edu), is an assistant professor in the Department of Management and International Business, Raj Soin College of Business Wright State University in Dayton, Ohio. His research interests center on positive organizational scholarship, organization development and change, appreciative inquiry, and virtue-based organizing. David continually strives for a deeper understanding of the key factors and conditions required for positive organizing. He uses this evolving knowledge in his research, consulting, and teaching practice. David has successfully consulted with a wide variety of corporate, government, and education organizations. In 2005, he received a Ph.D. in organizational behavior from the Weatherhead School of Management at Case Western Reserve University.

**L**ynnea Brinkerhoff (lynneabrink@gmail.com) is vice president of Flath & Associates, a full-service OD/HRD consulting firm. She is co-founder of the Center for Leadership and Innovation at the University of New Haven, where she is also adjunct professor of organization development and change. Lynnea is author of numerous articles and offers keynote addresses on the subject of building horizontal organizations to create an engaged, emotionally mature workforce. Her passion is in applying multi-stakeholder, large-scale events to resolve social ills. She cultivates this approach with a village in Kenya, Africa. As an ordained interfaith minister, her focus is on "tending to the heart as well as the chart" of an organization, employing innovative techniques along with a wit and wisdom that assists others to personalize and make sense of change. Lynnea has a B.A. in international business from Simmons College and an M.A. and an M.S.O.D. from Pepperdine University.

**W**. Warner Burke (wwb3@columbia.edu) is the Edward Lee Thorndike Professor of Psychology and Education, coordinator of the graduate programs in social-organizational psychology, and chair of the Department of Organization and Leadership at Teachers College, Columbia University, since 1979. He has consulted with a variety of organizations including corporate, nonprofits, educational institutions, and federal government agencies. Warner teaches leadership and organization change. In 2007–2009, he has served as visiting professor of leadership and public policy at Ohio University. Warner also co-directs the Eisenhower Leadership Development Program at the United States Military Academy, West Point. Warner's publications include sixteen books and over two hundred articles and book chapters. He holds an M.A. in organizational psychology from Teachers College, Columbia University. Warner

association of management scholars in the world. He has authored over seventy articles and twenty-two books and is listed in *American Men and Women of Science* and *Who's Who in America*. Thomas received B.S. and M.B.A. degrees from Cornell University and a Ph.D. in business administration from the University of California in Los Angeles.

**J**effrey H. Dyer, Ph.D. (jdyer@byu.edu), is the Horace Beesley Professor of Strategy at the Marriott School, Brigham Young University, where he is chair of the Department of Organizational Leadership and Strategy. Before coming to BYU, Jeff was a professor at the Wharton School, University of Pennsylvania, where he maintains an adjunct position. His experience includes five years as a consultant and manager for Bain Company, where he consulted with a diverse set of clients. Jeff teaches regularly in executive programs in strategy and strategic alliances at the Wharton School, Northwestern's Kellogg School, and UCLA. He also publishes in top journals such as the *Academy of Management Review*, the *Academy of Management Journal*, and the *Harvard Business Review*. He received his Ph.D. in management strategy from UCLA's Anderson Graduate School of Management. His Oxford University Press book, *Collaborative Advantage*, won the Shingo Prize Research Award for Excellence in Manufacturing.

**W**. Gibb Dyer, Ph.D. (W_dyer@byu.edu), is the O. Leslie Stone Professor of Entrepreneurship and the academic director of the Center for Economic Self-Reliance in the Marriott School of Management at Brigham Young University. Before coming to BYU, he was on the faculty at the University of New Hampshire, served as a visiting professor at IESE in Barcelona, Spain, and was recently a visiting scholar at the University of Bath in the U.K. Gibb received his B.S. and M.B.A. degrees from Brigham Young University and his Ph.D. in management philosophy from the Massachusetts Institute of Technology. In 2007, he was given the faculty teaching award from Brigham Young University's division of continuing education. In 2008, he was given the outstanding faculty award from the Marriott School of Management.

**T**erri Egan, Ph.D. (Terri.Egan@pepperdine.edu), is an associate professor of applied behavioral science at Pepperdine University and the co-founder of the consulting firm Lahl and Egan, LLC (www.lahlandegan.com). A nationally recognized educator, consultant, and researcher, Terri brings a holistic approach to teaching and consulting, grounded in an unwavering commitment to the evolution of human consciousness and social change. As a core faculty member in Pepperdine University's master's of science in organization development (M.S.O.D.) program, she teaches courses that facilitate the personal and group transformation required to successfully lead change.

Saul Eisen, Ph.D. (saul.eisen@sonoma.edu), is a founder of the master's program in OD at Sonoma State University. His international consulting practice integrates strategic planning, whole system redesign, and organization development. Saul works in partnership with clients to develop empowered individuals, high-performing teams, competitive organizations, and thriving communities. His work has been widely published in professional journals and books about organization development, and he is a frequent presenter at regional and national conferences. His current research is on the development of future-responsive strategies for managing and consulting effectively in our fast-changing world. Saul holds an M.B.A. from UCLA and a Ph.D. in organizational behavior from Case Western Reserve University. Saul is the 2006 recipient of the OD Network's Lifetime Achievement Award. He speaks fluent Spanish and likes to write and mentor new consultants.

Glenda H. Eoyang, Ph.D. (geoyang@hsdinstitute.org), is a pioneer in the field of human systems dynamics. Glenda applies principles of self-organizing systems to help people thrive in unpredictable environments. Since 1988, she has provided training, consulting, coaching, research, evaluation, and facilitation support to organizations in the public and private sectors. Glenda is an associate of the Center for Evaluation, Planning, and Assessment at Queens University in Kingston, Ontario, Canada; scientific advisor to the Plexus Institute; member of the Circle of Scholars of The Union Institute and University; and founding executive director of the Human Systems Dynamics Institute. Her published works include numerous scholarly and practical books and articles, including *Coping with Chaos: Seven Simple Tools* (Lagumo, 1996) and *Facilitating Organization Change: Lessons from Complexity Science* with Ed Olson (Pfeiffer, 2003).

Ann E. Feyerherm, Ph.D. (Ann.Feyerherm@pepperdine.edu), is director of the M.S. in Organization Development Program at Pepperdine University. Before earning her Ph.D. at the University of Southern California, Ann spent eleven years as a manager of organization development at Procter & Gamble, where she was involved in employee relations, organization design, and corporate downsizing. She has consulted with many organizations, including Healthways, Honeywell, Frito-Lay, and Boeing, on improving multifunctional teams, creating learning organizations, leadership development, and managing change. Ann conducts research on the role of leadership in multi-organization systems dealing with environmental issues and in increasing human capacity through strength-based approaches. Ann also currently serves on the Academy of Management Organization Development and Change Division Executive Board and on the JABS editorial board. Her work has been published in the *Leadership Quarterly, JABS, The Graziadio Business Report*, and several book chapters.

**R**ick Flath (rcflath@gmail.com) has served on several regional boards of directors, including the Board of Governors at the University of New Haven in Connecticut. In 1989 he started Flath & Associates Consulting, Inc., as a full-service human resource and organizational consulting company with offices in New Haven, Connecticut, and Warwick, Rhode Island. Areas of expertise include compensation design and performance management, employee relations, organizational change, and team development. He has authored or contributed to over one hundred human resource articles and co-authored *How to Develop an Effective Compensation Program* and *Supervisory Skills for Today's Workforce*. Rick has a B.A. in philosophy from Gettysburg College and an M.A. in industrial psychology and organization development from the University of New Haven. Rick was also recognized as the Connecticut Business Person of the Year by the Small Business Administration.

**M**arguerite Foxon, Ph.D. (margfoxon@yahoo.com), is a highly respected performance improvement specialist with twenty-five years' experience designing and delivering leadership development programs, managing small- and large-scale evaluations, and training practitioners in all facets of training. She teaches master classes around the world on evaluation strategy and advanced evaluation to develop in-house evaluation skills for organizations. Previously employed by major international companies in Australia and North America, she established her consulting practice in evaluation and performance improvement in 2006. Her clients include a number of global companies. She was a director with the International Board of Standards for Training, Performance and Instruction for nine years. Her latest book is *Evaluator Competencies: Standards for the Practice of Evaluation in Organizations* (2008).

**E**ric Gaynor-Butterfield, R.O.D.P. (odicoaching@dilhard.com.ar), is president of Organization Development International, a leading consulting-tutoring firm in Latin America specializing in intra and entrepreneurial tutorship, with special focus in creating entrepreneurs and creating enterprises. Eric edits the leading web page in OD in Spanish in the world (www.theodinstitute.org). He has delivered more than thirty years of consulting and training to leading firms and leaders in Latin America. Eric is a board member of the Organization Development Institute (1999 to date). He is working on his dissertation at Michigan State University. He is a research fellow at Inter-American Foundation and a visiting professor at Tufts University. Eric's non-profit interests are in the area of community development and family sustainability. His most recent book is *El Empresario: Creador de Riqueza Genuina* (The Entrepreneur: Creator of Genuine Wealth).

William Gellermann, Ph.D. (gmann@earthlink.net), is a consultant in management, organization, and human systems development. He has consulted with a wide variety of organizations in public and private sectors. William coordinated a ten-year process for clarifying the values and ethics of OD/HSD professionals (described in *Values and Ethics in Organization and Human Systems Development: Responding to Dilemmas in Professional Life* (Jossey-Bass, 1990). He is currently co-chair of the Communications Coordination Committee for the United Nations and is an ECOSOC representative to the UN. William received his Ph.D. in 1964 from UCLA in business administration. He received B.A. and M.B.A. degrees from the University of Washington and was a CPA for five years in New York and Detroit.

Robert T. Golembiewski, Ph.D. (rtgolem@arches.uga.edu), is retired from The University of Georgia, Athens, and holds the title of distinguished research professor, emeritus. He is the author and editor of over seventy books and one thousand journal articles that appear in several bodies of literature—in public administration and business, in several of the social and behavioral sciences, in various sources of opinion and commentary, as well as research that appears in foreign languages.

Royce Holladay (rholladay@hsdinstitute.org) is a consultant, writer, poet, and artist. Royce is also a change agent who is committed to bringing about organization and societal change by focusing on how groups can build their adaptive capacities to address issues of justice, diversity, and inclusion, peace, and personal fulfillment of individuals. Royce's practice is built on the foundations of human systems dynamics, a field of research and practice that emerges at the intersection of complexity and social sciences. A prolific writer, Royce uses language, images, and physical engagement to convey complex ideas in simple, applicable terms.

Peggy Holman (peggy@opencirclecompany.com) convenes and hosts conversations that matter by inviting the diverse people of a system to tackle what is most important to them. By growing their capacity to bring forth the human spirit for the individual and collective good, Peggy has been honored to witness organizations and communities unleash energy and wisdom to move their dreams to action. The vastly expanded second edition of *The Change Handbook* (Berrett-Koehler, 2007), co-edited with Tom Devane and Steven Cady, has been warmly received for aiding people in amplifying resilience, agility, collaboration, and aliveness in their organizations and communities. Peggy has worked with a Swiss-based pharmaceutical company, a Columbian social service organization, the Israeli Ministry of Education, and U.S. journalists. Her current inquiry is into how we scale the gifts that the art and practice of process bring to shifting our collective capacity for living well together.

**D**avid W. Jamieson, Ph.D. (davd.jamieson@pepperdine.edu), is president of the Jamieson Consulting Group, Inc., and an adjunct professor and practicum director in the Master of Science in Organization Development Program at AU/NTL. He has thirty-eight years of experience consulting on leadership, change, strategy, design, and human resource issues. He is a past national president of the American Society for Training and Development and past chair of the Management Consultation Division and Practice Theme Committee of the Academy of Management. Dave is co-author of *Managing Workforce 2000: Gaining the Diversity Advantage* and co-author of *The Complete Guide to Facilitation: Enabling Groups to Succeed* and *The Facilitator's Fieldbook* (2nd ed.). He serves as editor of *Practicing OD*, Reflections on Experience Section of the *Journal of Management Inquiry*, and serves on the editorial boards for the *Journal of Organization Change Management* and *The Organization Development Practitioner*.

**A**my Kates (akates@downeykates.com) is principal partner with Downey Kates Associates, an organization design and development consulting firm in New York City. She works with leaders of global companies to make sound decisions about their organizations. In addition to consulting, Amy teaches organization design in an executive M.B.A. program in Denmark and through USC and Cornell University. Amy is a co-author with Jay Galbraith of the book *Designing Your Organization: Using the Star Model to Solve Five Critical Design Challenges* (Jossey-Bass, 2007) and *Designing Dynamic Organizations: A Hands-On Guide for Leaders at All Levels* (AMACOM, 2002). Amy is also an editor of the journal *People & Strategy*. Her article, "(Re) Designing the HR Organization," was awarded the 2007 HRPS Walker Prize.

**J**udith H. Katz (judithkatz@kjcg.com) brings more than thirty years of experience to her consulting work in strategic culture change. Judith has consulted with many organizations, including Allstate, Cisco Systems, Dun and Bradstreet, E. I. du Pont de Nemours and Company, Eileen Fisher, Singapore Telecommunications Ltd., Toyota Motor Sales, and United Airlines. In 1985, she joined The Kaleel Jamison Consulting Group, Inc., and currently serves as executive vice president. She is the co-author with Frederick A. Miller of *Be BIG: Step Up, Step Out, Be Bold* (Berrett-Koehler, 2008) and *The Inclusion Breakthrough: Unleashing the Real Power of Diversity* (Berrett-Koehler, 2002). Judith is also co-editor of *The Promise of Diversity* (Irwin/NTL, 1994) and the author of *White Awareness: Handbook for Anti-Racism Training* (University of Oklahoma Press, 1978, 2003). In 2007, she was recognized for her work by *Profiles in Diversity Journal*, which named her one of forty Pioneers of Diversity.

**P**eter Koestenbaum, Ph.D. (peter@koestenbaum.com), was born in Germany, raised in Venezuela, and studied at Stanford, Berkeley, Harvard, and Boston University. He was a professor at San José State University for thirty-four years. He is a leadership consultant specializing in the use of philosophic concepts and the history of ideas to support companies in doing better bottom-line business. Peter has developed the concepts of Philosophy-in-Business, or PiB®, and the Leadership Diamond®, which endeavor to compress the history of philosophy, as a compendium of how the mind works, into twelve succinct propositions that are then biased toward organizational and business applications. He has spent a third of a century working in over forty countries helping companies install Diamond leadership conversations to strengthen their enterprises in four areas in particular: wisdom coaching, grand strategy, marketing and project management. Peter has a Ph.D. in philosophy.

**G**ina Lavery, M.S.O.D. (gina@ginalavery.com), has been creating environments that unleash the human spirit and produce breakthrough results for over two decades. She brings a broad, real-world perspective to her clients as a result of being a line leader with a Fortune 100 health care giant and being a global citizen through travel, study, and work in over thirty-five countries. Her focus on continuous discovery, learning, and exploration allows her to guide leaders to discover what is possible in their own organizations, to transform cultures, and to ultimately produce breakthroughs in employee motivation, engagement, accountability, and effectiveness. Gina writes and speaks on the topics of engagement, transformation, innovation, and work/life integration and is a contributing author to the bestselling book *Awakening the Workplace*. She is a creative catalyst for what's possible at work. Gina holds a master's degree in OD from Pepperdine University.

**M**itchell Lee Marks, Ph.D. (MitchLM@aol.com), is faculty at the College of Business at San Francisco State University and president of the consulting firm JoiningForces.org. He advises executives on managing major transitions, building team effectiveness, and developing organizational cultures to achieve desired financial and strategic objectives. He works with organizations ranging from small high-tech start-ups to massive global conglomerates to plan, implement, and recover from transitions. Mitchell is the author of five books and numerous articles on organizational change and development, including *Charging Back Up the Hill: Workplace Recovery After Mergers, Acquisitions, and Downsizings* and (with Philip Mirvis) *Joining Forces: Making One Plus One Equal Three in Mergers, Acquisitions, and Alliances*. Reports of his work have been featured in publications such as *The Wall Street Journal, Fortune, U.S. News, World Report, BusinessWeek, The New York Times, Financial Times*, and *Sports Illustrated*. Mitchell holds a Ph.D. in organizational psychology from the University of Michigan.

S. **Alan McCord**, Ph.D. (amccord@ltu.edu), serves as executive director of LTU Online and professor in the College of Management at Lawrence Technological University. He teaches in the doctor of management in information technology and doctor of business administration programs. He also leads development of Lawrence Tech's online degree programs. Prior to coming to LTU, Alan served in senior IT roles at the University of Michigan and at Eastern Michigan University. He is active in the Higher Learning Commission, the Sloan Consortium, and EDUCAUSE. Alan has authored many articles and book chapters on IT infrastructure, IT outsourcing, virtual work technologies, and plagiarism in online learning environments. He has consulted for several businesses and higher-education institutions and has served on nonprofit boards and advisory groups for broadband and wireless initiatives. Alan holds a B.A. from the University of Michigan and an M.A. and Ph.D. from Wayne State University.

F**rederick A. Miller** (familler@kjcg.com) is the CEO of The Kaleel Jamison Consulting Group, Inc. In his more than thirty years of experience, he has developed and implemented strategies that increase engagement, team and individual performance, and culture alignment with organizations' marketplace needs. He is the co-author with Judith H. Katz of *Be BIG: Step Up, Step Out, Be Bold* (Berrett-Koehler, 2008) and *The Inclusion Breakthrough: Unleashing the Real Power of Diversity* (Berrett-Koehler, 2002). He is managing editor of *The Promise of Diversity* (Irwin/NTL, 1994). Frederick was recognized for his work when he was named one of forty Pioneers of Diversity by *Profiles in Diversity Journal* (August/September 2007). He was also noted as one of the forerunners of corporate change in *The Age of Heretics* (Currency Doubleday, 1996). In 2007, he was honored with the Lifetime Achievement Award from the Organization Development Network.

P**hilip H. Mirvis**, Ph.D. (Pmirv@aol.com), is an organizational psychologist and senior research fellow at the Boston College Center for Corporate Citizenship. His studies and practice concern large-scale organizational change, the character of the workforce and workplace, and the role of business in society. Philip is a research fellow of the Work/Family Roundtable, a board member of the Foundation for Community Encouragement, and a trustee of the Society for Organization Learning. He has taught at Boston University, Jiao Tong University, Shanghai, China, and the London Business School. An advisor to businesses in the United States, Europe, Asia, and Australia, he has authored ten books on his studies, including *The Cynical Americans; Building the Competitive Workforce, Joining Forces,* and *To the Desert and Back*. His most recent is *Beyond Good Company: Next Generation Corporate Citizenship*. Philip has a B.A. from Yale University and a Ph.D. in organizational psychology from the University of Michigan.

Malaysia and for Ministries of Health and Development in Brunei Darussalam. She has done OD projects in Indonesia, Thailand, and the Philippines. Perla is the first recipient of the Richard Beckard Outstanding Organization Development Award given in 2002, 17th World Congress, Santiago, Chile. Perla holds a B.S.E. in elementary education from Silliman University, Philippines; a master's in science education from the University of Hawaii, and a Ph.D. in organization development and planning from Southeast Asia Interdisciplinary Development Institute, Philippines.

**J**ennifer Todd (jtodd@breakthroughpartner.com), founder and CEO of Breakthrough Partners Inc., is an executive coach and consultant. Her specialty is helping leaders transform their organizations through clarifying their visions, working collaboratively, and cultivating the culture needed for achieving tangible business results. Jennifer is experienced in the areas of leadership and team development, cultural change, change management, strategy execution, and whole system transformation. Her clients in the recent years include corporations, consulting firms, and law firms. Prior to establishing her business in 2004, Jennifer worked for Allstate Insurance, Arthur Andersen, and AON Consulting. Jennifer holds a M.S.O.D. from Pepperdine University. She also holds a B.A. in psychology from Michigan State University. Jennifer is Gestalt trained as an effective intervener and teaches coaching classes at the Gestalt Institute of Cleveland. She owns a Best Year Yet franchise and is certified in MBTI and other leadership tools.

**A**nn M. Van Eron, MCC, Ph.D. (avaneron@potentials.com), is principal of Potentials, an international coaching and organization development consulting firm. She has over twenty years of experience coaching leaders and teams all over the world. Her clients include Fortune 100 corporations, nongovernmental organizations, healthcare agencies, non-profit, and privately held companies. Ann provides leadership development and teaches executives how to be effective in coaching their teams. She assists organizations in creating cultures of respect and open communication that facilitate achieving goals. She supports people in having meaningful conversations for results using her unique and proven "OASIS" process. She is a faculty member at the International Gestalt Coaching Program and is one of the first certified as a master coach by the International Coach Federation. Ann earned her M.A. and Ph.D. from Columbia University. Ann is committed to making a difference and assisting people in fulfilling their potential and enjoying life.

**D**.D. Warrick, Ph.D. (DDWarrick@aol.com), is a professor of management and organization change at the University of Colorado at Colorado Springs. He is also the president of the Warrick Agency Training and Development Company and has been a consultant and trainer for many Fortune

500 companies, international companies, mid-size companies, public agencies, and universities. Don is the author or co-author of five books and numerous articles. He is President's Teaching Scholar at the University of Colorado and has received many outstanding teaching awards, including the Chancellor's Award. Don has also received numerous awards for his contributions to the field of OD, including a number of commendations from the Academy of Management, being named the David Bradford/McGraw-Hill Outstanding Educator of the Year, and receiving the Outstanding Organization Development Practitioner of the Year and Outstanding Human Resource Professional of the Year awards. He received his B.B.A. and M.B.A. degrees from the University of Oklahoma and Ph.D. from the University of Southern California.

**J**ane Magruder Watkins (jane@appreciativeinquiryunlimited.com) is principal of Appreciative Inquiry Unlimited and has been an OD consultant and trainer since the 1960s. She joined NTL in 1984 and served as chair of the NTL Board. She has worked from the perspective of appreciative inquiry (AI) since the mid-1980s and created the first AI workshop for OD Consultants at NTL in 1995. She instituted an NTL/Case Western University sponsored AI certificate program in 2005 and serves as the steward of NTL's AI Community of Practice. She is co-author of *Appreciative Inquiry: Change at the Speed of Imagination*. Jane has worked in seventy-five countries at all organization levels across all types of systems—corporate, government, and not-for-profit. She has an M.A. in English literature, an MSOD from AU/NTL, and postgraduate work at Cambridge University. She teaches in Pepperdine's MSOD and Ed.D. programs; Seattle University's OSR; and at Roffey Park Business School in the UK.

**A**ngé Wayne (ange@angelchange.com) is speaker, executive coach, and change strategist who shares with the world the simplicity behind self-motivated success. Moving to Australia in 1998, Angé had established three highly successful companies. In 2005, Angé knew there was more purpose to life than just financial success and sold these companies to really focus on following her passion—changing mindsets globally. The ANGEL Brand was born in 2006, with Angé stimulating companies around the globe to change productivity and multiply their bottom line by applying "soular power." Angé found an opportunity to move into a digital marketing space and, together with her inspirational coaching and dynamic seminars, the ANGEL brand continues to soar skyward.

**A**lan Weiss (www.summitconsulting.com) is one of the rare people who can say he is a consultant, speaker, and author, and mean it. His work has taken him to fifty-one countries and forty-nine states. The *New York Post* has called him "one of the most highly respected independent consultants

# NAME INDEX